CW01373954

PUBLICATIONS OF THE ISRAEL ACADEMY
OF SCIENCES AND HUMANITIES

SECTION OF HUMANITIES

GUIDE TO
HEBREW MANUSCRIPT COLLECTIONS

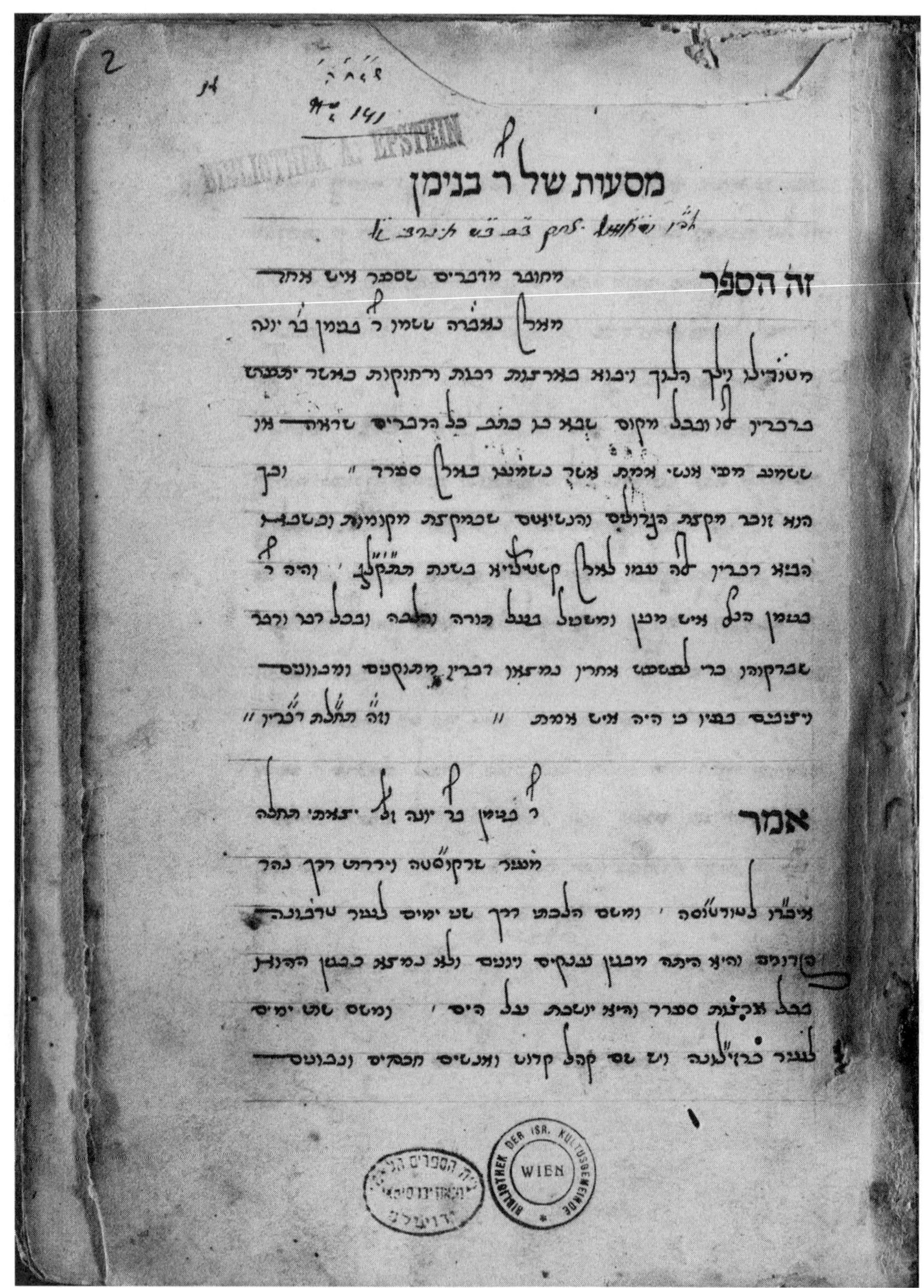

מסעות של ר׳ בנימן

זה הספר

אמר

Jerusalem, NLI, MS Heb. 8° 267, fol. 1r

Title page of the *Book of Travels* by Benjamin of Tudela, showing the Hebrew signature of its late nineteenth-century owner, Solomon J. H. Halberstamm (שזח"ה), and the stamps of subsequent owners: Abraham Epstein, the Israelitische-theologische Lehranstalt in Vienna and finally Vienna's Israelitische Kultusgemeinde, whose library was plundered by the Nazis during World War II. Rescue efforts after the war brought the manuscript into the possession of the Jewish National and University Library (now the National Library of Israel) in Jerusalem.

GUIDE TO
HEBREW MANUSCRIPT COLLECTIONS

Second, revised edition

by

BENJAMIN RICHLER

JERUSALEM 2014

THE ISRAEL ACADEMY OF SCIENCES AND HUMANITIES

Copy Editor: Deborah Greniman
Production: Yehuda Greenbaum

Cover illustration:
"Catalan Mahzor" (thirteenth century)
National Library of Israel, MS Heb. 8° 6537, fol. 4v.
Reproduced by permission of the National Library of Israel.

ISBN 978–965–208–185–8

Typesetting: Mostoslavsky Veronika
Printed in Israel at the Old City Press, Jerusalem

In memory of my beloved parents
Joseph V. and Sarah R. Richler

CONTENTS

Preface ix
Preface to the First Edition ix

Introduction 1

List of Abbreviations 5

THE GUIDE 11
Hebrew Entries: Abbreviations, Names, Cognomens and Titles 235

APPENDIXES 237
Appendix I: Present/Last-Known Locations or Call-Numbers of Manuscripts in Collections Treated in the *Guide* 239
1. MSS Asher 239
2. MSS Benzian 240
3. MSS Berenstein 241
4. MSS Biema 242
5. MSS Breslau 243
6. MSS Carmoly 248
7. MSS Coronel 252
8. MSS da Costa 255
9. MSS Cracovia 256
10. MSS in Florence (Italy), Biblioteca Medicea Laurenziana 256
11. MSS Gagin (Gaguine) 257
12. MSS Geiger 257
13. MSS Ghirondi 258
14. MSS Goldsmid 260
15. MSS Listed in *Hapalit* 261
16. MSS Heidenheim 261
17. MSS Henriques de Castro 262
18. MSS Fischl Hirsch 262
19. MSS Jacobson 264
20. MSS Jessurun Cardozo 264
21. MSS Jacob Wolf de Jonge 265
22. MSS Kennicott and de Rossi 265
23. MSS Lehren 282
24. MSS de Lima 283
25. MSS Loewe 283
26. MSS London, Beth Din and Beth Hamidrash Library 284
27. MSS Lotze 284
28. MSS Luzzatto 285
29. MSS Merzbacher 287

30. MSS Montefiore 291
31. MSS Paris, Collège de Clermont 294
32. MSS Pinsker 294
33. MSS Porges 295
34. MSS Barend Rubens 295
35. MSS Sassoon 295
36. MSS Schocken 301
37. MSS Schulting 302
38. MSS Listed in *Cat. Schwarz*, Austria, and *Cat. Schwarz–Loewinger–Róth* 303
39. MSS Sussex 307
40. MSS from Tunis 307
41. MSS in Turin, Biblioteca Nazionale Universitaria 308
42. MSS Wagenaar 310
43. MSS Wijnkoop 310

Appendix II: List of Collections Microfilmed for the Institute of Microfilmed Hebrew Manuscripts (IMHM) 311

INDEXES 347
Index of Individual Manuscripts Mentioned in the *Guide* 349
Index of Names of Libraries, Persons and Places 387

PREFACE

A new edition of the *Guide* has been a desideratum for several years. Even though less than twenty years have passed since the publication of the first edition, many of the entries need to be updated or corrected. During this short span of time several new catalogues of important collections have been published, hundreds of manuscripts (MSS) have changed ownership as private and public collections have been sold, and previously unknown MSS have been discovered. Thousands of MSS from Eastern Europe that were made accessible to researchers shortly before the first edition was published have now been catalogued, enabling the identification of MSS hitherto considered lost. Advances in technology have made it possible to trace the present locations of additional 'lost' MSS: The now-computerized catalogues of the Institute of Microfilmed Hebrew Manuscripts and other libraries enable complex searches, while the plethora of resources on the Internet and the ubiquity of electronic mail have facilitated the search for information. About twenty percent of the entries in the first edition have been corrected or revised, and new entries and appendixes have been added.

I wish to extend my gratitude to all those who helped me in the preparation of the first edition of this *Guide*; most of them have continued to contribute valuable information that has been incorporated in the entries in this edition. My sincere thanks to Prof. Yohanan Friedmann, former Chairperson of the Publications Committee of the Israel Academy of Sciences and Humanities, and to the Academy's Publications Department: to its Director, Tali Amir, to Deborah Greniman, Senior Editor of English-Language Publications, who went over the manuscript, corrected many errors, and prepared the book for publication, and to Yehuda Greenbaum, who oversaw its production. Thanks also to Evelyn Katrak, who again contributed a round of proofreading, and to Esther Rosenfeld, who expertly read the proofs.

B. R.

PREFACE TO THE FIRST EDITION

This *Guide* began as an offshoot of my work at the Institute of Microfilmed Hebrew Manuscripts in the Jewish National and University Library. Over the years I amassed information concerning Hebrew manuscript collections and their histories and began to arrange my findings on index cards. In 1973 I was awarded part of the grant offered by the Ruth Cahan-Ever scholarship for Librarianship and Bibliographic Research by the Israel Ministry of Education and Culture for a projected guide to Hebrew manuscript collections. Over the years I continued to revise and enlarge the *Guide*. One of its versions served as a thesis presented to the Graduate Library School of the Hebrew University in partial fulfillment of the requirements for the Master of Library Sciences degree.

At one time I submitted an earlier version of the *Guide* to Ktav Publishers, but I later withdrew it. For their remarks and corrections, which have certainly improved this book in many respects, I would like to thank Dr. Herbert Zafren of Ktav and especially Mr. Myron Weinstein, lately retired from the Library of Congress Hebraic Section and one of the most erudite bibliographers I have ever had the pleasure of meeting.

I also wish to extend my gratitude to all those who helped me over the years by providing me with information or by reading and correcting my typescripts. Prof. Malachi Beit-Arié, while still Director of the Institute of Microfilmed Hebrew Manuscripts, encouraged me to complete the project and offered many helpful suggestions and corrections. Prof. Yaakov Sussman and Dr. Mordecai Glatzer read the typescript and added valuable observations. My associates at the Institute, Prof. I. Ta-Shema, Drs. Nahum Weissenstern, Avraham David and T. Y. Langermann, Mrs. Rachel Nissan and Yael Okun were all of constant assistance. Yehoshua Mondshein of the Manuscripts Department in the Library brought to my attention much information concerning the provenance of manuscripts and many interesting booklists he discovered in the course of his work. I am also grateful to the Graduate Library School for allowing me free access to its personal computers in order to transcribe my typescript onto diskettes.

My heartfelt thanks to the Publications Department of the Israel Academy of Sciences and Humanities and especially to Mr. Shmuel Reem, who prepared the book for publication, to Mrs. Evelyn Katrak, who edited the manuscript, to Mr. Zion Busharia, who was responsible for the computer typesetting, and to Ms. Zofia Lasman, who supervised the final stages of the production process.

I could not have completed this work without the constant support of my wife, Carmelit, who bore with me while I laboured over this project through most of our married life, and of my children, Rivka, Yuval and Yael, who grew up constantly aware that their father was apt to be occupied with what they must have regarded as the Sisyphean task of revising yet another proof. I only regret that my parents, who probably looked forward to the publication of this book more than anyone else, passed away before it was completed.

As this Guide was being set, political upheavels were taking place in eastern Europe; empires and countries were splintered into many parts, cities adopted new or former names, and the official names of libraries were changed. Unfortunately, technical difficulties made it impossible to incorporate more than a few of these changes into the text. The majority are noted in the Addenda et Corrigenda at the end of the Guide.

B. R.

INTRODUCTION

The study of classical and mediaeval Hebrew texts has always been based, at least in part, on the perusal and study of Hebrew manuscripts (MSS). Ever since the emergence of the Wissenschaft des Judenthums some 150 years ago, no research on such texts could be considered complete without the use of these MSS. A scholar surveying the literature accumulated during the past century and a half in most fields of Hebraic studies will come across numerous references to MSS. Yet, should he attempt to trace and then consult all the MSS referred to, he is liable to encounter a number of obstacles. During the past 150 years many of the most important collections of Hebrew MSS have changed owners or been dispersed. Large and famous private libraries, rich in treasures of Judaica, have been sold at public auction after their owners had experienced financial difficulties or passed away. Although some of the MSS sold at auction have been purchased by other private collectors, there has been a marked tendency over the past century for MSS to find their way into public or institutional libraries. For any given MS, however, reaching an institutional library has not necessarily meant the end of its wanderings. During wars, especially during World War II, many MSS in libraries were destroyed or looted, or they disappeared – making it difficult for the scholar to retrace MSS referred to in publications that appeared 100, 50 or even 35 years earlier.

Other factors have contributed to this difficulty. Collections of MSS that have remained in the same library for centuries have had their numbers changed, and the scholar who remains unaware of this fact is unable to find the MS he is seeking. Scholars have often been careless in referring to MSS; in addition to the seemingly unavoidable typographical errors that appear in citations of MS call-numbers, scholars often refer to MSS by catalogue numbers (which can cause confusion when a collection has been described in more than one catalogue) or by arbitrarily abridged numbers (e.g., 'Oxford 599' instead of 'MS Mich. 599'; 'MS Oxford 599' may also be taken to indicate '*Cat. Neubauer* 599'). Scholars have also been known to assign a MS the name of the collection's cataloguer ('MS Neubauer' instead of 'MS Oxford, Bodleian Library') or a cognomen that is generally accepted (e.g., 'Go1den Haggada', 'Kaufmann Mishna MS') or one that was merely coined by the author for his particular publication.

As a result of all these factors, the novice encountering his first references to Hebrew MSS may be tempted to raise his hands in surrender and devote himself to some less esoteric field of study; and even the expert has often had to accept defeat in his attempts to trace the particular MS he has been searching for. The need for a guide to Hebrew MS collections has been felt for many years. While surveys of Hebrew MS holdings have appeared, and many of them contain valuable information concerning former provenances, no systematic attempt has been made within the past fifty years to trace the wanderings of MSS and to locate their present whereabouts.

Leopold Zunz provided his readers with a list of collections of Hebrew MSS and printed works in Jewish hands (*Zur Geschichte und Literatur*, Berlin 1845, pp. 230–249), which today raises more questions about the present locations of the books than it answers. In his *Vorlesungen über die Kunde hebräischer Handschriften, deren Sammlungen und Verzeichnisse*, Leipzig 1897, pp. 57–90 (Hebrew, pp. 76–115), Moritz Steinschneider, the master Jewish bibliographer, presented an exhaustive survey of MS collections that was up to date in 1897. The fruits of his research, which included the cataloguing of close to a dozen major MS collections, contain invaluable information concerning the migrations of MSS; but no work of this kind can remain totally valid a century after its publication. During the twentieth century a number of attempts have been made to bring Steinschneider's bibliographies of Hebrew MSS up to date; and while some information concerning changes in ownership may be found in these works, none of them attempts to duplicate or complete Steinschneider's work in this field. The research staff of the Commission on European Jewish Cultural Reconstruction, under the chairmanship of Salo Baron, compiled a 'List of Cultural Treasures' known to have existed in Europe before the Nazi occupation. The list, published as a supplement to *Jewish Social Studies*, VIII (1946) and X (1948), often includes details concerning the provenance of MSS and lists some collections that were confiscated by the Nazis for their (anti-Semitic) research institutes; but it leaves many questions unanswered.

More recently, a number of works have appeared that provide, sometimes incidentally, new information about Hebrew MS collections. In the posthumous publication of Aron Freimann's index cards of Hebrew works in manuscript (*Union Catalog of Hebrew Manuscripts and Their Location*, Vols. I–II, New York 1964–1973), the current whereabouts of many MSS listed in catalogues of private collections and booksellers' catalogues are indicated. Freimann worked in or visited many of the important libraries in Europe and was acquainted with the collection of the Jewish Theological Seminary of America (JTSA) in New York, which acquired thousands of MSS from collections that were dispersed towards the end of the nineteenth century and during the first half of the twentieth. His index cards, however, were never properly prepared for publication, and his indications and notes are not always clear or complete, so that some of the information obtained from the cards may be misleading. Freimann uses the equal sign, for example, both as a symbol to precede each notation of a new MS and in its more customary function as a symbol indicating that a particular MS is now in a particular collection (e.g., 'MS Adler = JTS', meaning that the Adler MS is now in the JTSA library). Another work, J. D. Pearson, *Oriental Manuscripts in Europe and North America*, Zug 1971, pp. 1–74, provides a survey of the major collections of Hebrew MSS in Europe and North America; in addition to the lists of printed and unpublished catalogues, it contains short histories of the large collections of MSS, which include much information concerning the provenance and acquisition of various private collections – in part derived from previously unpublished sources. Readers searching for information about particular collections are advised to consult the index of former owners on pp. 483–492.

In the four decades that I worked in the Institute of Microfilmed Hebrew Manuscripts (IMHM) in the Jewish National and University Library (now called the National Library of Israel) in Jerusalem, I was asked to locate MSS mentioned in various publications and catalogues. Experience, the most efficient teacher, has provided me with a wealth of information concerning MS collections and made me aware of the need to organize this information and systematically seek out further details. The results of my labours are presented in this volume.

The purpose of this *Guide* is to enable the reader – novice and expert alike – to locate the MSS referred to in the scholarly literature and to provide him or her with the basic bibliographical information concerning those MSS. The *Guide* is intended to serve first and foremost as a practical tool. It is not intended to be a complete bibliography of writings on or catalogues of Hebrew MSS; nor does it pretend to present an exhaustive study of the histories of collections of Hebrew MSS. The criterion that has guided the selection of material is a purely practical one: Will the information provide a clue as to the present location or past ownership of a MS or collection of MSS? In compiling this *Guide*, I have asked myself that question hundreds of times, and I can only hope that if I am guilty of not following my criterion, my sin is one of commission – the inclusion of irrelevant information – rather than one of omission – the exclusion of relevant facts.

Entries are listed in alphabetical order. The following information may be found in the *Guide*:

1. *Libraries*. Libraries are listed if they possess major collections of Hebrew MSS; if, though they possess small collections or even a single Hebrew MS, their MSS are referred to in scholarly literature; or if catalogues or descriptions of the MSS are available. The names of public or institutional libraries are usually listed according to the name of the city in which the library is found. City names are usually written according to their English spelling. Named libraries, such as the Bodleian, are cross-referenced, but not those bearing general names (National Library, Public Library, etc.). Private collections are listed according to the name of the owner. The entries for major collections include a very brief history of the collection, the number of MSS in the library, titles of the main catalogues of Hebrew MSS and a short description of the principal catalogue or catalogues. While catalogue descriptions include a list of the palaeographical and codicological information provided and of the indexes, special emphasis is placed on the numbers – catalogue numbers, call-numbers (signatures), previous call-numbers – to enable the reader to understand the many notations and numbers that frequently appear in catalogues, and to help him or her decipher a reference to a MS that seems obscure when an antiquated call-number or catalogue number has been used to indicate it. The entries list concordances to old numbers, call-numbers and catalogue numbers; and in collections where such concordances are wanting, they are provided in the Appendixes to this *Guide*.

2. *Collections*. Collections of MSS in private or public libraries that have been dispersed or have changed ownership over the years are listed, and whenever possible the present locations of the MSS are indicated. Thus, entries for the D. Oppenheim and H. J. Michael collections indicate that the MSS have passed into the possession of the Bodleian Library in Oxford, and the entry for the Halberstamm collection indicates that the MSS were partly in the Montefiore library and partly in the JTSA library. Information on the present locations of individual MSS, where available, is given in the relevant entries in Appendix I and cross referenced from the entries for these collections in the *Guide*.

3. *Booksellers' and auction catalogues*. Booksellers' and auction catalogues are noted in the entry for the previous owner or bookseller whose MSS are listed in the catalogue. Thus, a Sotheby's auction catalogue of MSS from the Sassoon collection appears under Sassoon, not Sotheby. However, if a bookseller's catalogue includes MSS from various or unnamed sources, it appears in the entry for the bookseller.

Whenever possible, information concerning the present location of the MSS is given. In some cases the collections described in these catalogues were acquired en bloc by libraries or collectors. In other cases the MSS were dispersed among a large number of collectors and libraries. Locating the MSS described in these catalogues has posed a number of problems. Some of the catalogues list no more than the book titles; others provide scant additional information. Only a few catalogues provide full bibliographical information – including detailed contents, number of pages, dates, colophons, owners, and even quotations from the works in the MSS.

In determining the present location of MSS listed in booksellers' catalogues, I have compared the descriptions of the MSS (whenever they were sufficiently detailed) with descriptions in catalogues of MSS in other public or private collections or with the catalogue of the IMHM; and I have used external evidence testifying to the acquisition of particular collections by particular libraries – such as notations concerning provenances in printed catalogues and information provided by Steinschneider in his *Vorlesungen*, by Freimann in his *Union Catalogue*, and by other bibliographical works. In some cases the *Guide* provides detailed information about the present location of a large number of MSS in booksellers' and auction catalogues; in others it provides only the most general information – such as the names of the libraries that purchased MSS from the catalogues. In general, I have systematically listed the present location of MSS in booksellers' and auction catalogues only in those cases where it has been possible to identify a relatively large proportion of the MSS. This information appears in the relevant entries in Appendix I and is cross referenced from the entries for the relevant collections in the *Guide*.

4. *Compilers of catalogues*. The names of compilers of major catalogues are listed among the entries.

5. *Names*. In the case of geographical names in Latin and other languages that are appreciably different from the common English forms, short entries indicate their English equivalents.

6. *Cognomens*. Names or cognomens given to MSS (e.g., 'Golden Haggada', 'Kaufmann Mishna MS') and their correct call-numbers are included among the entries.

7. *Hebrew references*. A list of Hebrew abbreviations, names, cognomens and titles, with cross-references to the relevant English entries, appears on pp. 235–236.

Cross-references are preceded by asterisks.

LIST OF ABBREVIATIONS

I. *Libraries and Institutions*

Amsterdam, UB = Amsterdam, Universiteitsbibliotheek
Berlin, SB = Berlin, Staatsbibliothek
Cambridge, UL = Cambridge University Library
Cincinnati, HUC = Cincinnati, Hebrew Union College
Hamburg, SUB = Hamburg, Staats- und Universitätsbibliothek
JCF = Judaica Conservancy Foundation
Jerusalem, IMHM = Jerusalem, Institute of Microfilmed Hebrew Manuscripts
Jerusalem, JNUL = Jerusalem, Jewish National and University Library (now NLI)
Jerusalem, NLI = Jerusalem, National Library of Israel
London, BL = London, British Library
Moscow, RSL = Moscow, Russian State Library (Rossiiskaia Gosudarstvennaia Biblioteka)
Moscow, RSMA = Moscow, Russian State Military Archives (Rossiiskii Gosudarstvennyi Voennyi Arkhiv)
Munich, BSB = Munich, Bayerische Staatsbibliothek
New York, JTSA = New York, Jewish Theological Seminary of America
New York, NYPL = New York, New York Public Library
Paris, AIU = Paris, Alliance Israélite Universelle
Paris, BnF = Paris, Bibliothèque nationale de France
Philadelphia, CAJS = Philadelphia (Pa.), University of Pennsylvania, Herbert D. Katz Center for Advanced Judaic Studies
Vienna, ÖNB = Vienna, Österreichische Nationalbibliothek
Warsaw, ŻIH = Warsaw, Jewish Historical Institute (Żydowski Instytut Historyczny)

II. *Bibliographical Abbreviations*

Baron = *Tentative List of Jewish Cultural Treasures in Axis-Occupied Countries*, by the research staff of the Commission on European Jewish Cultural Reconstruction ... affiliated with the Conference on Jewish Relations. Supplement to *Jewish Social Studies*, VIII/1 (1946), with 'Introductory Statement' signed by Salo W. Baron. Addenda and corrigenda: Supplement to *Jewish Social Studies*, X (1948). http://www.lootedart.com/index.php?r=MFEU4S32631.

Brann, *Geschichte* = M. Brann, *Geschichte des jüdisch-theologischen Seminars (Fränckel'sche Stiftung) in Breslau: Festschrift zum fünfzigjährigen Jubiläum der Anstalt*, Breslau [1904].

Cassuto, *Palatina* = U. Cassuto, *I manoscritti Palatini Ebraici della Biblioteca Apostolica Vaticana e la loro storia*, Vatican 1935.

Cat. Allony–Kupfer, II = רשימת תצלומי כתבי־היד העבריים במכון, חלק ב: נ׳ אלוני וא׳ קופפר, כה״י בספריות בלגיה, דנמרק, הולנד, ספרד ושווייצריה, ירושלים תשכ״ד (*List of Photocopies in the Institute*, Part II: N. Allony and E. [F.] Kupfer, *Hebrew Manuscripts in the Libraries* *of Belgium, Denmark, the Netherlands, Spain and Switzerland*, Jerusalem 1964). For a description of the catalogue see *Jerusalem, IMHM.

Cat. Allony–Loewinger, I = רשימת תצלומי כתבי־היד העבריים במכון, חלק א: נ׳ אלוני וד״ש לוינגר, כה״י בספריות אוסטריה וגרמניה, ירושלים תשי״ז (*List of Photocopies in the Institute*, Part I: N. Allony and D. S. Loewinger, *Hebrew Manuscripts in the Libraries of Austria and Germany*, Jerusalem 1957). For a description of the catalogue see *Jerusalem, IMHM.

Cat. Allony–Loewinger, III = רשימת תצלומי כתבי־היד העבריים במכון, חלק ג: כתבי־היד שבספריית הוואטיקאן, ירושלים תשכ״ח (*List of Photocopies in the Institute*, Part III: N. Allony and D. S. Loewinger, *Hebrew Manuscripts in the Vatican*, Jerusalem 1968). For a description of the catalogue see: *Jerusalem, IMHM, and *Vatican.

Cat. Bernheimer, Modena = C. Bernheimer, *Catalogo dei manoscritti orientali della Biblioteca Estense [Modena]*, Rome 1960.

Cat. de Rossi = G. B. de Rossi, *Manuscripti Codices Hebraici Biblioth. I. B. De-Rossi accurate ab eodem descripti et illustrati*, Parma 1803.

Cat. Delitzsch = 'Codices hebraici', described by F. Delitzsch with notes by L. Zunz, in A. G. R. Naumann (ed.), *Catalogus Librorum Manuscriptorum qui in Bibliotheca Senatoria Civitatis Lipsiensis Asservantur*, Grimma 1838, pp. 271–311, 314–328.

Cat. Halper = B. Halper, *Descriptive Catalogue of Genizah Fragments in Philadelphia*, Philadelphia 1924.

Cat. Kaufmann = M. Weisz, *Katalog der hebräischen Handschriften und Bücher in der Bibliothek des Professors Dr. David Kaufmann*, Frankfurt a/M 1906.

Cat. Loewinger–Weinryb = D. S. Loewinger and B. D. Weinryb, *Catalogue of the Hebrew Manuscripts in the Library of the Jüdisch-theologisches Seminar in Breslau*, Wiesbaden 1964.

Cat. Luzzatto = A. Luzzatto, *Hebraica Ambrosiana*, I: *Catalogue of Undescribed Hebrew Manuscripts in the Ambrosiana Library [Milan]*; II: L. Mortara Ottolenghi, *Description of Decorated and Illuminated Hebrew Manuscripts in the Ambrosiana Library*, Milan 1972.

Cat. Margoliouth = G. Margoliouth, *Catalogue of the Hebrew and Samaritan Manuscripts in the British Museum*, I–III, London 1899–1915.

Cat. Margoliouth–Leveen, IV = G. Margoliouth, *Catalogue of the Hebrew and Samaritan Manuscripts in the British Museum*, IV: J. Leveen, *Introduction, Indexes, Brief Descriptions of Accessions and Addenda and Corrigenda*, London 1935.

Cat. Montefiore = H. Hirschfeld, *Descriptive Catalogue of the Hebrew Manuscripts in the Montefiore Library*, London 1904.

Cat. Neubauer = A. Neubauer, *Catalogue of the Hebrew Manuscripts in the Bodleian Library and in the College Libraries of Oxford, Including MSS in Other Languages Which Are Written with Hebrew Characters, or Relating to the Hebrew Language or Literature; and a Few Samaritan MSS*, Oxford 1886 (reprinted 2004).

Cat. Neubauer, Addenda = *Supplement of Addenda and Corrigenda to Vol. I (A. Neubauer's Catalogue)*, compiled under the direction of M. Beit-Arié, edited by R. A. May, Oxford 1994.

Cat. Neubauer–Cowley, II = A. Neubauer and A. E. Cowley, *Catalogue of the Hebrew Manuscripts in the Bodleian Library*, II, Oxford 1906 (reprinted 2004).

Cat. Peyron = B. Peyron, *Codices Hebraici Manu Exarati Regiae Bibliothecae quae in Taurinensi Athenaeo Asservatur*, Rome–Turin–Florence 1880.

Cat. Richler, Parma = B. Richler (ed.), *Hebrew Manuscripts in the Biblioteca Palatina in Parma*, with palaeographical and codicological descriptions by M. Beit-Arié, Jerusalem 2001.

Cat. Richler, Vatican = B. Richler (ed.), *Hebrew Manuscripts in the Vatican Library: Catalogue*, compiled by the staff of the Institute of Microfilmed Hebrew Manuscripts in the Jewish National and University Library, Jerusalem, with palaeographical and codicological descriptions by Malachi Beit-Arié in collaboration with Nurit Pasternak, Vatican 2008 (Studi e Testi, 438), http://nli.org.il/imhm/vaticanhebmss.pdf.

Cat. Sassoon = D. S. Sassoon, *Ohel Dawid* (אהל דוד)*: Descriptive Catalogue of the Hebrew and Samaritan Manuscripts in the Sassoon Library, London*, I–II, London 1932.

Cat. Scholem = כתבי־היד העבריים הנמצאים בבית הספרים הלאומי והאוניברסיטאי בירושלם, א: קבלה, תיארם וחקרם גרשם שלום בהשתתפות יששכר יואל, ירושלם תר״ץ (*Catalogus Codicum Cabbalisticorum Hebraicorum quot Conservantur in Bibliotheca Hierosolymitana quae est Judaeorum Populi et Universitatis Hebraicae*, digessit G. Scholem adiuvante B. Joel, Jerusalem 1930).

Cat. Schwarz, Austria = A. Z. Schwarz, *Die hebräischen Handschriften in Österreich (ausserhalb der Nationalbibliothek in Wien)*, I: *Bibel–Kabbala*, Leipzig 1931.

Cat. Schwarz, Vienna = A. Z. Schwarz, *Die hebräischen Handschriften der Nationalbibliothek in Wien*, Leipzig 1925.

Cat. Schwarz–Loewinger–Róth = A. Z. Schwarz, D. S. Loewinger and E. Róth, *Die hebräischen Handschriften in Österreich (ausserhalb der Nationalbibliothek in Wien*), II, New York 1973 (= American Academy for Jewish Research, Texts and Studies, IV: *Hebrew Manuscripts in Austria*). Part IIA is by Schwarz and Part IIB by Loewinger and Róth.

Cat. Steinschneider, Berlin = M. Steinschneider, *Verzeichnis der hebräischen Handschriften*, I–II, Berlin 1878–1897.

Cat. Steinschneider, Hamburg = M. Steinschneider, *Catalog der hebräischen Handschriften in der Stadtbibliothek zu Hamburg und der sich anschliessenden in anderen Sprachen*, Hamburg 1878.

Cat. Steinschneider, Leiden = M. Steinschneider, *Catalogus Codicum Hebraeorum Bibliothecae Academiae Lugdono-Batavae*, Leiden 1858.

Cat. Striedl–Róth = H. Striedl (ed.), *Hebräische Handschriften*, ... described by Ernst Róth, II, Wiesbaden 1965 (Verzeichnis der orientalischen Handschriften in Deutschland, VI, 2).

Cataloghi dei Codici Orientali di Alcune Biblioteche d'Italia, I–VII, Florence 1878–[1904].

Catalogue général = *Catalogue général des manuscrits des Bibliothèques publiques des départments*, Paris 1885–.

de Rossi, *ext.* = G. B. de Rossi, *Variae lectiones veteris Testamenti* ... I, pp. cxxvi–cxxxv: 'Ms. codices exteri', Parma 1784.

del Barco, *Catálogo ... Madrid* = F. J. del Barco del Barco, *Catálogo de manuscritos Hebreos de la comunidad de Madrid*, I–III, Madrid 2003–2006.

EJ = *Encyclopedia Judaica*, Jerusalem 1972.

Freimann, 'Mitteilungen' = A. Freimann, 'Mitteilungen über den literarischen Nachlass von Autore, die über Juden und Judentum geschrieben haben', *ZfHB*, XXI (1918).

Freimann, *Scribes* = A. Freimann, 'Jewish Scribes in Medieval Italy', in *Alexander Marx Jubilee Volume*, New York 1950, pp. 231–342.

Freimann, *Union Catalog* = A. Freimann, *Union Catalog of Hebrew Manuscripts and Their Location*, I, New York 1973; II, New York 1964.

Fumagalli = P. F. Fumagalli, 'Fondi di manoscritti ebraici in Italia – Cenni storici e catalogo dei Cataloghi', Ph.D. Dissertation, Università Cattolica del S. Cuore, Milan 1975–1976.

Fumagalli, 'Emilia-Romagna' = P. F. Fumagalli, 'La formazione dei fondi ebraici nelle biblioteche dell'Emilia-Romagna', in F. Parente (ed.), *Atti del terzo convegno [dell'Associazione Italiana per lo Studio del Giudaismo] tenuto a Idice, Bologna ... 1982*, Rome 1985, pp. 85–102.

HB = *Hebräische Bibliographie* (המזכיר), I–XXI, Berlin 1858–1882.

HÜ = M. Steinschneider, *Die hebräischen Übersetzungen des Mittelalters und die Juden als Dolmetscher*, Berlin 1893.

HUCA = *Hebrew Union College Annual.*

Jerusalem Collections = *Hebrew Illuminated Manuscripts from Jerusalem Collections* (כתבי־יד עבריים מצויירים מאוספים בירושלים) [Jerusalem 1967] (Israel Museum Cat. no. 40). In English and Hebrew.

JJLG = *Jahrbuch der jüdisch-literarischen Gesellschaft*, I–XXII, Frankfurt a/M 1903–1931/32. http://www.compactmemory.de/.

JQR = *Jewish Quarterly Review.*

JJS = *Journal of Jewish Studies.*

Kennicott = B. Kennicott, *Dissertatio Generalis in Vetus Testamentum Hebraicum*, Oxford 1780 (published together with Kennicott's *Vetus Testamentum Hebraicum*).

KS = *Kiryat Sefer: Bibliographical Quarterly of the Jewish National and University Library* (קרית ספר: רבעון לביבליוגרפיה – כלי מבטאו של בית הספרים הלאמי והאוניברסיטאי בירושלים), Jerusalem.

Loewinger, *Report* = D. S. Loewinger, 'Report on the Hebrew MSS in Hungary, with Special Regard to the Fragments of the Cairo Genizah', in *Actes du XXIe Congrès International des Orientalistes, Paris, 23–31 July 1948*, Paris 1949, pp. 117–123; reprinted in idem and S. Scheiber (eds.), *Genizah Publications in Memory of Prof. Dr. David Kaufmann*, Budapest 1949, pp. v–xii.

Marx, *Bibl. Studies* = A. Marx, *Bibliographical Studies and Notes on Rare Books and Manuscripts in the Library of the Jewish Theological Seminary of America*, New York 1977.

Marx, 'Polemical MSS' = A. Marx, 'The Polemical Manuscripts in the Library of the Jewish Theological Seminary of America', in *Studies in Jewish Bibliography and Related Subjects in Memory of Abraham Solomon Freidus*, New York 1929, pp. 247–278.

Marx, *Proceedings* = A. Marx, 'A New Collection of Manuscripts', in *Proceedings of the American Academy for Jewish Research*, IV (1932/3), pp. 135–167; reprinted in Marx, *Bibl. Studies*, pp. 411–443.

MGWJ = *Monatsschrift für Geschichte und Wissenschaft des Judentums*, I–LXXXIII, Dresden–Leipzig–Breslau 1851–1939. http://www.compactmemory.de/.

MWJ = *Magazin für die Wissenschaft des Judentums*, I–XX, Berlin 1878–1893. Hebrew section: אוצר טוב. http://www.compactmemory.de/.

Narkiss = B. Narkiss, *Hebrew Illuminated Manuscripts*, Jerusalem 1969.

Narkiss, *Span. & Port.* = B. Narkiss, *Hebrew Illuminated Manuscripts in the British Isles*, I: *The Spanish and Portuguese Manuscripts*, Jerusalem–London 1982.

Oko = A. S. Oko, 'Jewish Book Collections in the United States', *American Jewish Yearbook*, XLV (1943), pp. 67–96.

Pearson = J. D. Pearson, *Oriental Manuscripts in Europe and North America: A Survey*, Zug 1971 (pp. 1–74: Hebrew MSS).

Rab., *Lit. Treas.* = H. M. Rabinowicz, *The Jewish Literary Treasures of England and America*, New York 1962.

Rab., *Treas. Jud.* = H. M. Rabinowicz, *Treasures of Judaica*, South Brunswick, NJ, 1971.

Register = *Register of the Jewish Theological Seminary of America*, New York 5665–(1904–). The section 'The Library', containing descriptions of MSS acquired by the Seminary during the years 1916–1973, was reprinted together with an index as A. Marx, *Bibliographical Studies and Notes on Rare Books and Manuscripts in the Library of the Jewish Theological Seminary of America*, New York 1977, pp. 1–366.

Reif, *Cat. Cambridge* = S. C. Reif, *Hebrew Manuscripts at Cambridge University Library: A Description and Introduction*, Cambridge 1997.

Reif, *Jewish Archive* = S. C. Reif, *A Jewish Archive from Old Cairo: The History of Cambridge University's Genizah Collection*, Richmond, Surrey, 2000.

REJ = *Revue des études juives*.

Ruysschaert, 'Les manuscrits Vaticans' = J. Ruysschaert, 'Les manuscrits hébraïques Vaticans: corrections et additions à la liste de 1968', *Miscellanea Bibliothecae Apostolicae Vaticanae*, III (1989), pp. 357–360.

Sadek = V. Sadek, 'Aus der Handschriftensammlung des staatlichen jüdischen Museums in Prag', *Judaica Bohemiae*, V (1969), pp. 144–151.

Shunami = S. Shunami, *Bibliography of Jewish Bibliographies*, 2nd enlarged edition, Jerusalem 1965. Supplement: Jerusalem 1975.

Sonne, *Relazione* = I. Sonne, *Relazione sui tesori bibliografici della comunità israelitiche d'Italia* [1935–1937] (typewritten copy in Jerusalem, NLI [R 50 B 954]).

Starkova, 'Les plus anciens mss.' = C. B. Starkova, 'Les plus anciens manuscrits de la Bible dans la collection de l'Institut des Etudes Orientales de l'Academie des Sciences de l'URSS', in *La Paleographie hébraïque médiévale*, Paris 1974, pp. 37–41.

Steinschneider, *Vorlesungen* = M. Steinschneider, *Vorlesungen über die Kunde hebräischer Handschriften, deren Sammlungen und Verzeichnisse* ..., Leipzig 1897. Hebrew edition: הרצאות על כתבי־יד עבריים, ירושלים תשכ״ה.

Striedl, *Geschichte* = H. Striedl, 'Geschichte der Hebraica-Sammlung der Bayerischen Staatsbibliothek', in *Orientalisches aus Münchener Bibliotheken und Sammlung*, ed. H. Franke, Wiesbaden [1957], pp. 1–37.

Swarzenski and Schilling, *Die illuminierten Handschriften* = G. Swarzenski and R. Schilling, *Die illuminierten Handschriften und Einzelminiaturen des Mittelalters und der Renaissance in Frankfurter Besitz*, Frankfurt a/M 1929.

Tamani, *Grimani* = G. Tamani, 'Codici ebraici Pico Grimani nella Biblioteca Arcivescovile di Udine', *Annali di Ca'Foscari*, X, no. 3, Oriental Series 2 (1971), pp. 1–25.

Tamani, *Padova* = G. Tamani, 'Manoscritti ebraici esistenti a Padova nei secoli scorsi', *Annali di Ca'Foscari*, XIII (1974).

Tamani, *Piacenza* = G. Tamani, 'Manoscritti e incunaboli ebraici nella Biblioteca Comunale di Piacenza', *Archivio Storico per le province Parmensi*, 4th Series, XXI (1969), pp. 131–141.

Tamani, *Rovigo* = G. Tamani, 'Manoscritti e incunaboli ebraica nella biblioteca dell'Accademia dei Concordi di Rovigo', *Annali dell'Istituto Orientale di Napoli*, XXXIII (1973), pp. 207–231.

Tamani, *Venezia* = G. Tamani, 'Catalogo dei manoscritti ebraici della Biblioteca Marciana di Venezia', *La Bibliofilia*, LXXIV (1972), pp. 239–301.

Tamani, *Verona* = G. Tamani, 'Manoscritti ebraici nella Biblioteca Comunale di Verona', *Rivista degli Studi Orientali*, XLV (1970), pp. 217–243.

TB = Babylonian Talmud.

ZDMG = Zeitschrift der deutschen morgenländischen Gesellschaft.

ZfHB = Zeitschrift für hebräische Bibliographie, I–XXIII, Berlin 1896–1911, 1913–1921.

ק״ס = קרית ספר: לביבליוגרפיה – כלי מבטאו של בית הספרים הלאמי והאוניברסיטאי בירושלים.

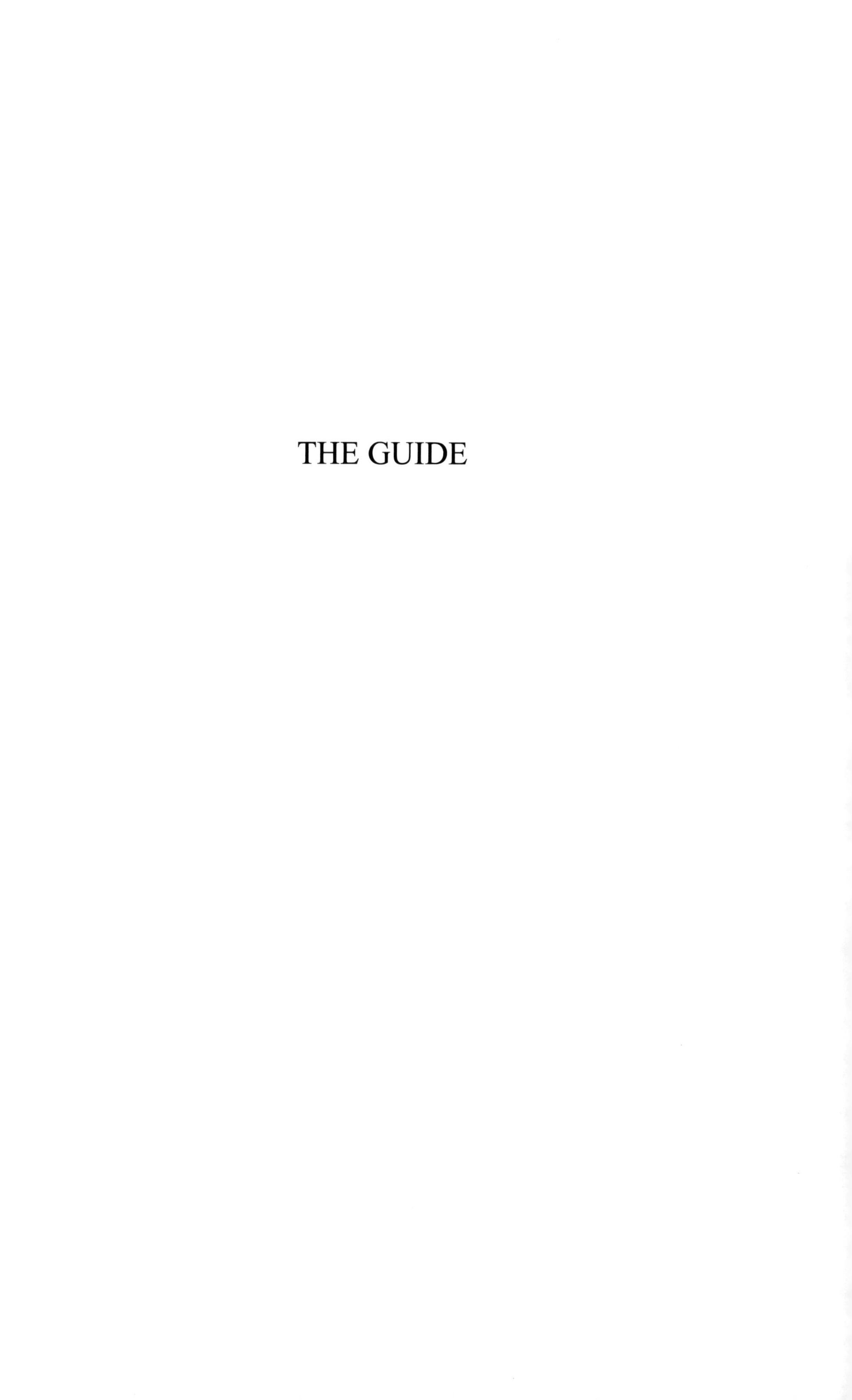

THE GUIDE

A

(1) *Amsterdam; (2) Angelica (see *Rome, Biblioteca Angelica).

Aberdeen (Scotland), University of Aberdeen, King's College Library and Historic Collections

In addition to the *Aberdeen Bible, the library holds an eighteenth-century MS of Joseph Fanso's *Asire hatikva*, copied from the printed edition, in the Biesenthal collection deposited in the Historic Collections on permanent loan from Christ's College, Aberdeen, in 1968. It was acquired about 1872 by Professor William Robertson Smith for what was at that time the Free Church College in Aberdeen from Dr. J. H. Biesenthal (1804–1886), a converted Polish Jew, then serving amongst the Jews of Leipzig as a missionary with the London Society for Promoting Christianity.

Aberdeen Bible

Name given to *Aberdeen, University, King's College Library, MS 23, an illuminated Bible dated 1494.

C. Roth, *The Aberdeen Codex of the Hebrew Bible*, Edinburgh 1958.

Aberdonia

Latin name for Aberdeen.

Aboab, Samuel

Hamburg, Germany, 1610 – Venice, Italy, 1694

The MS of *Sefer Zera' anashim* (ספר זרע אנשים), a collection of responsa once in the possession of Aboab, was formerly in *Livorno, Talmud Tora library, and is now *Jerusalem, NLI, Heb. 8° 2001.

מ׳ בניהו, רבי חיים יוסף דוד אזולאי, ירושלים תשי״ט, עמ׳ רלז.

Abrahams, Israel

England: London, 1858 – Cambridge, 1925; scholar

About fifteen of Abrahams's MSS were transferred in 1961 from the Library of the Faculty of Oriental Studies in Cambridge to the *Cambridge, University Library, where they bear the call-number MS Or. 2116. The fragment published by Abrahams in 'The lost "confession" of Samuel', *HUCA*, I (1924), pp. 377–384, is now *Cincinnati, HUC, MS 403.

Adler, Cyrus

USA, 1863–1940; scholar

Adler presented the *Geniza fragments in his possession to Dropsie College (now *Philadelphia, CAJS), where he taught.

Rab., *Lit. Treas*., p. 136.

Adler, Elkan Nathan

London, 1861–1946; bibliophile

Adler amassed a collection of over 4,000 Hebrew MSS. According to his *Catalogue of Hebrew Manuscripts in the Collection of Elkan Nathan Adler*, Cambridge 1921, 'Most were collected on travels or from travellers, generally travelling booksellers such as Jacob *Lipschütz, Jerocham Fischl *Hirsch, David *Fränkel and [Ephraim] *Deinard' (p. v). He collected MSS on trips to Egypt, Palestine, Corfu, Damascus, Morocco, Algiers, Tunis, Tripoli, Persia, Aleppo, Constantinople, the Balkans, North America, Russia, India and Aden. In 1923 he sold his collection to *New York, JTSA (H. Dicker, *Of Learning and Libraries*, New York 1988, pp. 34–36). The MSS that he acquired afterwards (the Second Adler Collection, including the Adler–Stroock Collection of *Geniza fragments) were purchased for the library by Alan *Stroock from Adler's estate after his death in 1946 but were partially destroyed in the fire that broke out in the library in 1966. Over 4,200 MSS are very briefly described in the 1921 *Catalogue*. The catalogue was compiled for the most part by Arthur Marmorstein (information from G. Scholem). It is arranged by subject, and some MSS containing various works are described partly in one section and partly in another. Several MSS were given identical numbers, and since there is no concordance to the numbers this oversight was not noticed. About half the MSS in the catalogue were described in the section 'Miscellaneous'. The letter 'V' suffixed to some of the numbers indicates that the MS was written on vellum or parchment. There is no indication of the number of pages in the MS or the type of script or date. Indexes: subjects, names and places. The MSS that Adler acquired in Persia, Bukhara and Samarkand were previously described in his book *The Persian Jews: Their Books and Ritual*, Oxford [1898]. MSS acquired in Persia were given numbers with the prefix 'T' (= Teheran), and those acquired in Bukhara and Samarkand the prefix 'B'. Thirteen MSS acquired by Adler in *Aleppo were described by himself, 'Aleppo', in M. Brann and F. Rosenthal (eds.), *Gedenkbuch zur Erinnerung an David Kaufmann*, Breslau 1900, pp. 134–136. Adler described 72 MSS of Karaitica in *JQR*, XII (1900), pp. 674–686, in greater detail than in his *Catalogue*. The numbers he assigned to the Karaitica MSS (201–272) do not correspond to those in the *Catalogue*. MS ENA 1595, a Samaritan text, is now in the collection of Dr. Michael Krupp in Jerusalem.

GENIZA Most of the 35,000 leaves of Geniza material in his collection were gathered by Adler in 1896, when he was allowed to fill up a sack with fragments during a visit of three or four hours to the Cairo *Geniza. In 1897 and again in 1907 Adler purchased from *Oxford, Bodleian Library, about 6,000 leaves from the Cairo Geniza that the Bodleian librarians considered 'waste'. Adler divided his collection of fragments into two parts: (1) bound volumes, mostly biblical, which were not separated from the other codices; (2) miscellaneous fragments, which were not arranged in any particular order and included fragments not deriving from the Cairo Geniza. There is also a 'new series' of Adler Geniza material, i.e., fragments that were not assigned catalogue numbers in Adler's original collection and now bear the preface 'NS'. Among the Adler MSS acquired after his death were a number of additional Geniza fragments. Several of Adler's Geniza fragments are kept outside the 'Geniza Collection' and were included among the rabbinical or biblical material catalogued, respectively, by Rabbi Judah Brumer and by Moses Lutzki (see *New York, JTSA). The halakhic and midrashic fragments from the Adler collection were described by Neil Danzig, *A Catalogue of Fragments of Halakhah and Midrash from the Cairo Geniza in the Elkan Nathan Adler Collection of the Library of the Jewish Theological Seminary of America*, New York–Jerusalem 1997 (קטלוג של שרידי הלכה ומדרש מגניזת־קאהיר באוסף א״נ אדלר שבספריית בית המדרש לרבנים באמריקה). Two unpublished fragments deriving from Adler's collection were recently acquired from a private collector and are now in *Jerusalem, NLI, MSS Heb. 4° 577.7/8. A fragment belonging to Adler that was published by S. Fraenkel, 'Geniza-Fragment', in D. Günzburg and I. Markon (eds.), *Festschrift zu Ehren des Dr. A. Harkavy* ..., St. Petersburg 1908, pp. 91–94, is now *New York, Yeshiva University, MS Lewin 76. Some *Geniza fragments belonging to Adler's half-brother, Marcus Nathan Adler, were acquired by Joseph *Halpern and purchased by the British Museum (now *London, British Library) in 1958 (MS Or. 12186; see D. Rowland Smith, in idem and S. P. Salinger [eds.], *Hebrew Studies*, London 1991, p. 23).

Adler, Nathan b. Simeon

Frankfurt a/M, Germany, 1741–1800; rabbi

Eighteen MSS from his estate were in the library of Mayer Selig *Goldschmidt and were acquired by *Jerusalem, Hekhal Shelomo Museum (י״ל ביאלר, מן הגנזים, א [תשכ״ז], עמ' 3). One MS, *Mordekhai gadol* (מרדכי גדול), from which Sulzbach published fragments in *JJLG*, III (1905) and V (1907), is in *New York, JTSA, R673 (ביאלר, שם, עמ' 34, הערה 21). In 1990 the Goldschmidt collection was deposited in *Jerusalem, JNUL (now NLI).

Aegidius da Viterbo

See *Egidio da Viterbo.

a. f.

*Ancien fonds.

Aghib

Livorno, Italy, eighteenth cent.

The MS belonging to Aghib described in de Rossi, *ext.*, no. 22, is now *New Haven, Yale University, Beinecke Library, MS Heb. 409.

Agnon, Samuel Joseph

Buczacz, Ukraine, 1888 – Jerusalem, 1970; author

Agnon's archives and MSS owned by him are now in *Jerusalem, NLI. Early drafts of five stories by Agnon are in the collection of David Sofer in London.

Aguilar

London, eighteenth cent.

The MS in the possession of the Aguilar family described by *Kennicott, no. 290, is now *Oxford, Bodleian Library, MS Kennicott 7 (*Cat. Neubauer*, 2331).

Aguilar, Moses Raphael

Netherlands, d. 1679; rabbi

Aguilar's MSS were listed in the catalogue of his collection (רשימת ספרי הר' משה רפאל די אגוילאר הספרדי, אמסטרדם ת״ם). I could find no extant copy of the catalogue. A handwritten catalogue of Aguilar's library, including printed books and some MSS, is found in *Oxford, Bodleian Library, MS Opp. Add. 4° 151, ff. 75–79. Johann Christoph *Wolf quotes MSS from the catalogue in his *Bibliotheca Hebraea*, III, pp. 428, 674 and passim. One MS, a collection of medical works, is now *Leeuwarden (Netherlands), TRESOAR, the Friesland Historical and Literary Centre, MS B. A. Fr. 23 (*HB*, XVII [1877], p. 57).

AIU

Alliance Israélite Universelle. See *Paris, AIU.

A-K

Allony–Kupfer. See *Jerusalem, IMHM.

A-L

Allony–Loewinger. See *Jerusalem, IMHM.

Alcalá de Henares (Spain), Collegio de San Ildefonso

The MSS in this library, some of them used in preparing the Complutensian Polyglot Bible printed in 1522, were removed to *Madrid, Biblioteca de la Universidad.

Aleppo (Syria)

The most famous MS originating in Aleppo is undoubtedly the Aleppo Codex or *Keter Aram Sova* (כתר ארם צובה), one of the earliest Bible codices, with vocalization and masora attributed to Aaron Ben Asher. It is now *Jerusalem, Ben-Zvi Institute, MS 1, preserved in the Israel Museum in Jerusalem. This MS and others were described by Elkan Nathan *Adler, who visited Aleppo at the end of the nineteenth century ('Aleppo', in M. Brann and F. Rosenthal [eds.], *Gedenkbuch zur Erinnerung an David Kaufmann*, Breslau 1900, pp. 134–136). The Pentateuch dated 1341 that Adler described is now MS 2 in the Ben-Zvi Institute. The MS of *Sefer hapeli'a*

(ספר הפליאה) dated 1497 was acquired by Victor *Klagsbald. Adler listed thirteen MSS that he acquired with the call-numbers he assigned, though a few of the numbers do not correspond to those in his *Catalogue of Hebrew Manuscripts*, Cambridge 1921. At the end of his edition of *Targum Megilat Ester*, published in Aleppo (תרגום מגלת אסתר ללשון ערבי מאת... יוסף אלשמסא, ארם צובה תרס"א), Shabbetai Hamway (Beyda) listed 28 MSS in his possession that he offered for sale. Several of the MSS in the list seem to be in *New York, JTSA; no. 1 may be MS 8313; nos. 7 and 17 may be in MS 2269; no. 18 is certainly MS 2945 and no. 20 is probably MS L959. Abraham *Harkavy described seven MSS he saw in Aleppo in his publication *Ḥadashim gam yeshanim* (חדשים גם ישנים, ו [תרנ"ה], עמ' 6–8).

On the Aleppo Codex, see the facsimile edition, Jerusalem 1976; the entire volume of *Textus*, I (1960); י' ייבין, כתר ארם צובה, ירושלים תשכ"ט; א' שמוש, הכתר: סיפורו של כתר ארם־צובה, ירושלים תשמ"ז; מ' גלצר, 'מלאכת הספר של כתר ארם צובה והשלכותיה', ספונות, יט (תשמ"ט), עמ' 167–276; י' עופר, 'כתר ארם צובה לאור רשימותיו של מ"ד קאסוטו', שם, עמ' 277–344; י' פנקובר, נוסח התורה בכתר ארם־צובה, רמת־גן תשנ"ג; M. Friedman, *The Aleppo Codex*, Chapel Hill 2012. On the Pentateuch, see Y. Ben-Zvi, 'The Codex of Ben Asher', *Textus*, I (1960), p. 16.

Alessandria (Italy), Comunità ebraica

Two Hebrew MSS formerly in the possession of the Jewish community in *Asti and later in the library of the community in Alessandria are now in the library of the Research Center for Italian Jewish Studies in Jerusalem, MSS 30 and 43. Sonne, *Relazione*, recorded 21 other documents in the library and mentioned a number of copies of occasional prayers, but did not list them.

All.

See *Paris, AIU.

Alliance Israélite Universelle

See *Paris, AIU.

Allony, Nehemia

Warsaw, 1906 – Jerusalem, 1983; scholar

Allony was the first director of *Jerusalem, IMHM. He co-edited all three volumes of the Institute's publication *List of Photocopies in the Institute* (= *Cat. Allony–Kupfer*, II, and *Cat. Allony–Loewinger*, I and III). Allony's collection of over 300 MSS was purchased in 1992 by *Jerusalem, JNUL (now NLI). His memoirs of his first years as director of the IMHM and his expeditions in search of manuscripts were published posthumously by his wife Edith (כתב־יד של משה רבנו, ירושלים 1992).

Allony–Kupfer

See *Jerusalem, IMHM.

Allony–Loewinger

See *Jerusalem, IMHM.

Alm.

*Almanzi.

Almanzi, Giuseppe

Italy; Padua, 1801 – Trieste, 1860; author

In 1816, Almanzi's father purchased for him part of the library of Hayyim *Azulai, including several MSS. Samuel D. Luzzatto described 331 of Almanzi's MSS, in French, with notes by M. Steinschneider, *HB*, IV–V (1861–1863). In 1864 a brief Hebrew abridgement of this catalogue was published (יד יוסף, פאדובה תרכ"ד). The collection was sold in 1865 by the booksellers A. *Asher & Co. to the British Museum (now *London, British Library). A concordance to the numbers in the Almanzi collection and those in *Cat. Margoliouth* is found in *Cat. Margoliouth–Leveen*, IV, pp. 171–174.

Rab., *Lit. Treas.*, p. 25; Steinschneider, *Vorlesungen*, p. 59 (Hebrew, p. 78).

Altdorf (Germany), Universitätsbibliothek

The university, which closed in 1809, had twelve Hebrew MSS in its library. They were removed to *Erlangen, Universitätsbibliothek, in 1818.

Cat. Striedl–Róth, p. xvii.

Alter, Abraham Mordecai

Gora Kalwaria, Poland, 1866 – Jerusalem, 1948; Gur Rebbe

Alter founded a bookstore, the Alter Hebrew Book Co., in New York, which he operated by proxy. In the 1901 catalogue of his collection (רשימת הספרים [?]), published in Warsaw, 231 MSS are listed. In a handwritten list dated 1913, about 320 MSS, including most of those in the 1901 catalogue, are described in greater detail in 311 entries. A copy of the 1913 list was acquired by Gershom *Scholem in 1938 and is now in the Archives Department of *Jerusalem, NLI. In a catalogue published in 1925 (רשימות הספרים מאוצר הספרים, א–ב, ניו יורק תרפ״ה), 308 MSS are listed, including most of the MSS in the 1913 list, but in far less detail and in a slightly different order. When the store was closed, some of the unsold MSS were given to a number of the Rebbe's hasidim. Most of the MSS in the private library of the Rebbe were lost in the Holocaust. A small number are in the possession of some of R. Abraham Mordecai's relatives in Jerusalem (see צ״י אברמוביץ, ׳האדמו״ר מגור, ביבליוגרף מובהק׳, תגים, א [תשכ״ט], עמ׳ 96). Some of the MSS listed in the catalogues were sold to *New York, JTSA, among them nos. 21, 29, 68, 95, 107 (=109), 108, 160, 170, 173, 183, 206, 224, 251, 253, 256, 261, 282, 285, 295 and 300 in the 1925 catalogue (according to A. *Marx's notations in a copy of the catalogue in *Jerusalem, NLI). MS Alter 279 (in the 1913 list = 282 in the 1925 catalogue), described by Scholem in *Studies in Memory of Asher Gulak and Samuel Klein*, Jerusalem 1942, p. 204, is now JTSA, MS 2194. The MS from which *Tosfot Harosh* on TB *Gitin* was edited (חידושי תוספות הרא״ש על מסכת גיטין, ורשה תרפ״ז) is now JTSA, MS R736.

Amarillo, Saul

Turkey, early twentieth cent.; rabbi

The MSS and documents of the Dönmeh sect in Salonika that survived the fire of 1917 were given to Rabbi Saul Amarillo when the members of the sect left Greece for Turkey in 1925. Rabbi Amarillo's son Abraham presented the material to *Jerusalem, Ben-Zvi Institute, in 1960.

G. Scholem, *Sabbatai Sevi*, Princeton 1973, p. xiii.

Ambr.

Ambrosiana. See *Milan, Biblioteca Ambrosiana.

Ambrosian Bible

Name given to *Milan, Biblioteca Ambrosiana, Cod. B 32 inf., a twelfth-century illuminated Ashkenazic Bible.

Narkiss, p. 90.

Amram, David Werner

Philadelphia, USA, 1866–1939; jurist and scholar

Amram was in possession of a collection of *Geniza fragments. He presented 30 fragments to the University of Pennsylvania Library in Philadelphia. Most of the remaining fragments were given to Dropsie College (now *Philadelphia, CAJS). Ephraim Lederer presented to Dropsie College seven fragments given to him by Amram (*Cat. Halper*, p. 10). Amram also gave six fragments to the *Philadelphia, YMHA. All of Amram's fragments are described in *Cat. Halper* and almost all of them, including most of those formerly in the University of Pennsylvania and YMHA libraries, are now in the library of CAJS. One of the fragments presented to the University of Pennsylvania (*Cat. Halper*, no. 338) is now in the Speer Library of the Princeton

Theological Seminary, in Princeton, N.J. (P. C. Hammond, 'A divorce document from the Cairo Geniza', *JQR*, LII [1961/2], pp. 131–153). Another fragment (*Cat. Halper*, no. 97) is missing, though photostat copies are available at CAJS.

Amst.
Amsterdam.

Amstelodamum
Latin name for Amsterdam.

Amsterdam (Netherlands), Ashkenazic Rabbinical Seminary
The MS of liturgical poems described by G. Polak in *Hakarmel* (הכרמל, ב [תרכ"ב], עמ' 294–293), is now *Cincinnati, HUC, MS Acc. 83. See also *Great Maḥzor of Amsterdam.

Amsterdam (Netherlands), Koninklijke Nederlandse Akademie van Wetenschappen
In 1837 the Academy bought six MSS in Hebrew or on Hebrew subjects from Johannes *Willmet. The MSS are now on permanent loan in *Leiden, Universiteitsbibliotheek. They were first described in H. E. Weijers & P. de Jong, *Catalogus Codicum Orientalium Bibliothecae Academiae* ..., Leiden 1862, pp. 1–8, and recently, in more detail and with the present call-numbers, in A. van der Heide, *Hebrew Manuscripts of Leiden University Library*, Leiden 1977, pp. 100–113, and by J. J. Witkam, *Inventory of the Oriental Manuscripts of the Royal Netherlands Academy of Arts and Sciences in Amsterdam* (Leiden 2006; http://www.islamicmanuscripts.info/inventories/amsterdam/inventory-academy-collection.pdf).

Amsterdam (Netherlands), Portugees Israëlitisch Seminarium Ets Haim – Livraria Montezinos
The library was founded in 1616 as part of the educational foundation Talmud Tora, renamed Ets Haim in 1637. In 1889, David *Montezinos presented his library including 98 MSS to the above, and its name was changed to Ets Haim Library – Livraria Montezinos. Prior to 1954 no inventory of the MSS was made; it is possible that some were lost during World War II when the Nazis confiscated the library. In 1954 the MSS were separated from the printed books and given call-numbers. Today there are close to 450 MSS in the library, mostly works of Sephardi authors and almost half of them in Spanish, Portuguese, Dutch and French. In October 1978 the MSS were sent to *Jerusalem, JNUL (now NLI), for an exhibition, and they remained there on standing loan until 2000, when they were returned to Amsterdam.

CATALOGUES AND CALL-NUMBERS *Cat. Allony–Kupfer*, II, lists 159 Hebrew MSS (pp. 62–75) and 135 MSS in other languages (pp. 189–198). Preceding each entry is the catalogue serial number. The old (1954) call-numbers, which have since been changed, are given in parentheses and are followed by another catalogue serial number with the prefix מ. The numbers at the left of each entry with the prefix ס are the microfilm numbers in the *Jerusalem, IMHM. The MSS were given new call-numbers when they were described for the new catalogue: L. *Fuks and R. G. Fuks-Mansfeld, *Catalogue of the MSS of Ets Haim / Livraria Montezinos Sephardic Community of Amsterdam*, Leiden 1975 (Hebrew and Judaic Manuscripts in Amsterdam Public Collections, II). In this catalogue 405 MSS in Hebrew and other languages are described in 458 entries, arranged according to subject. Collectanea including texts on various subjects are described in multiple entries according to their respectve subjects. A few MSS were described twice in different entries. Preceding each entry is a serial number followed by the present call-number (with the prefix 'HS EH'). There is no mention of the old call-numbers or of the Allony–Kupfer numbers; the Allony–Kupfer catalogue is not mentioned at all in the Fuks catalogue, nor is there any concordance to the call-numbers. Palaeographical and codicological information: date, material, language, size, number of leaves, lines per page, type of writing, catchwords, decorations and description of binding. Indexes: subject, names in Latin characters, names in Hebrew characters, titles in Latin characters and titles in Hebrew characters.

Amsterdam, UB
*Amsterdam, Universiteitsbibliotheek.

Amsterdam (Netherlands), Universiteitsbibliotheek, Bibliotheca Rosenthaliana
The library was founded when the collection of Leser Rosenthal was presented to the Universiteitsbibliotheek by his son George in 1880. In the first catalogue of the library, M. Roest, *Catalog der Hebraica und Judaica aus der L. Rosenthal'schen Bibliothek*, I–II, Amsterdam 1875, only 32 MSS are listed (II, pp. 1167–1171). After 1875 new acquisitions were made, and today the library owns over 850 Judaic MSS (about 175 of them single leaves and broadsheets) in Hebrew and other languages.
CATALOGUES AND CALL-NUMBERS *Cat. Allony–Kupfer*, II, lists 304 MSS (pp. 42–61, 134). Descriptions of a few of the MSS were printed twice in separate entries, so the total number of MSS described is about 300. Preceding each entry is the catalogue number. The old call-numbers, which have since been changed, are given in parentheses and are followed by another serial number with the prefix מ. The numbers at the left of each entry with the prefix ס are the microfilm numbers in the *Jerusalem, IMHM. Seven hundred MSS are described in L. *Fuks and R. G. Fuks-Mansfeld, *Catalogue of the Manuscripts of the Bibliotheca Rosenthaliana, University Library of Amsterdam*, Leiden 1973 (Hebrew and Judaic Manuscripts in Amsterdam Public Collections, I). The MSS are arranged according to subject. Preceding each entry is the catalogue serial number (with the prefix 'Hs. Ros.' or 'PL'). There is no mention of the old call-numbers or of the Allony–Kupfer numbers; *Cat. Allony–Kupfer* is not mentioned at all in the Fuks catalogue. Palaeographical and codicological information: date, writing material, language, size, number of leaves, lines per page, type of writing, catchwords, decorations and description of binding. Indexes: subjects, names in Latin characters, names in Hebrew characters, titles in Latin and Hebrew characters. E. G. L. Schrijver described 40 more Rosenthaliana MSS and one MS from the old University collection in 'An inventory of undescribed Hebrew manuscripts in the Bibliotheca Rosenthaliana', *Studia Rosenthaliana*, XX (1986), pp. 164–173; and M. H. Mirande de Boer described 51 more Portuguese and Spanish MSS, 'An inventory of undescribed Portuguese and Spanish manuscripts in the Bibliotheca Rosenthaliana', *ibid.*, pp. 176–190. A concordance to the call-numbers, the Allony–Kupfer numbers and the catalogue numbers in the Fuks catalogue and its supplements was provided by E. G. Schrijver, *ibid.*, pp. 191–199. Schrijver also described in greater detail 30 'previously undescribed manuscripts' in 'A specimen of a supplementary catalogue of Hebrew manuscripts in the Bibliotheca Rosenthaliana', in his *Towards a Supplementary Catalogue of Hebrew Manuscripts in the Bibliotheca Rosenthaliana*, Amsterdam 1993, pp. 57–123.

Amsterdam Maḥzor
See *Great Maḥzor of Amsterdam and see also *Esslingen Maḥzor.

Ancien fonds
Term for the old collection of *Paris, Bibliothèque nationale de France, numbering 516 Hebrew MSS that were listed in the 1739 catalogue of Oriental books and MSS (the ancien fonds). A concordance to the ancien fonds numbers and the present call-numbers, which was not given in the 1866 catalogue, was published by M. Steinschneider in *ZfHB*, VI (1902), pp. 150–152, 191.

Ancona (Italy)
A number of MSS and collections are referred to as 'MS Ancona' or 'Cod. Ancona'. MSS listed in *Catalogue d'une collection anconienne dont la plus grande partie dérive de la bibliothèque appartenant aux célèbres C. J. D. Azulai et son fils Rafaël, rabbin à Ancone, arrangée et mise en vente par Samuel Schönblum*, Lemberg [1872] (see *Azulai; *Schönblum), and the collection of Hayyim *Rosenberg, rabbi of Ancona, which included many MSS formerly in the possession of Hayyim J. D. *Azulai, are sometimes referred to as such. The commentary of Judah b. Nathan to Tractate *Nazir*, printed in the Romm edition of the Talmud (Vilna 1884) from a MS in an Ancona library, is now *Cambridge, UL, MS Or. 803. See also *Ancona, Comunità ebraica, and *Ancona, Yeshivat Shenot Eliyahu.

Ancona (Italy), Comunità ebraica
Thirty-seven MSS are listed in Sonne, *Relazione*. Thirty-four MSS have been microfilmed for the *Jerusalem, IMHM. Some of the MSS in this collection may have belonged to Hayyim J. D. *Azulai and his son Raphael Isaiah, rabbi of Ancona.

Ancona (Italy), Yeshivat Shenot Eliyahu
Asher b. Jehiel's Tosafot to Tractates *Nazir* and *Yevamot* were printed in the Romm edition of the Talmud (Vilna 1880–1886) from a MS of Hayyim J. D. *Azulai that was found in the Yeshiva and reached the publishers through Isaac *Hirschenson (אחרית דבר at the end of the Romm edition, p. 5). This MS is now *Jerusalem, NLI, Heb. 8° 2078.

Angelica
See *Rome, Biblioteca Angelica.

Ansbach (Germany), Staatliche Bibliothek
Formerly Regierungsbibliothek. The *Jerusalem, IMHM has microfilms of two Hebrew MSS and one fragment from a binding.

Anslo, Gerbrandt
Amsterdam, Netherlands, d. 1643; Orientalist
Most of Anslo's library was purchased by *Utrecht, Rijksuniversiteit. Many of his MSS, including a few in Hebrew, were acquired by Thomas Gale, who presented them to *Cambridge, Trinity College. Twelve MSS bought from Anslo's collection, possibly part of the bequest of Edmund Castell (1606–1685), are now in *Cambridge, University Library. Other MSS from Anslo's collection are now *Amsterdam, Ets Haim, HS EH 47 A 19, and *Leiden, Universiteitsbibliotheek, Cod. Or. 2066.

Antonin
Andrei Ivanovich Kapustin, Russia, 1817 – Jerusalem, 1894; Russian archimandrite
Antonin resided in Jerusalem from 1865 until his death. On one of his trips to Cairo he acquired 1,189 *Geniza fragments, which later passed into the possession of St. Petersburg, Publichnaia Biblioteka (now *St. Petersburg, NLR). A brief list of these fragments was published by A. I. Katsh, 'The Antonin Genizah in the Saltikov-Schedrin Public Library in

Leningrad', in *Leo Jung Jubilee Volume*, New York 1962, pp. 115–131.

Aptowitzer, Victor

Ternopil, Ukraine, 1871 – Jerusalem, 1942; scholar

The MS of *Midrash ḥakhamim* (מדרש חכמים) once owned by Aptowitzer is now *New York, JTSA, MS R2170.

Arch. Seld.

See *Selden, John.

Argentoratum

Latin name for Strasbourg.

Arias Montano, Benito

Spain, 1527–1598; Bible scholar

Thirty-one MSS formerly in his possession are now in *San Lorenzo del Escorial, Real Biblioteca.

G. de Andres, 'Historia de las procedencias de los codices de la réal Biblioteca de el Escorial', *Sefarad*, XXX (1970), pp. 27–30.

Arras (France), Bibliothèque municipale

The old collection of the library, including the Hebrew MSS, was based on the books found in the scriptorium of the Abbey of St. Vaast, founded in the seventh century. The Hebrew MSS are described in *Catalogue général*, IV (1872), p. 10, no. 4 (a maḥzor erroneously described as a Bible, now numbered 560), and pp. 383–384, no. 969 (a Talmud MS now numbered 889). These two MSS were also described by A. Guesnon in *Talmud et Machzor: Notice sur deux manuscrits hébreux de la bibliothèque d'Arras*, Paris 1904. Three other MSS presented to the library by the French historian Victor Advielle (1833–1903) in 1898 and described in *Catalogue général*, XL (1902), pp. 410–411, nos. 1103–1104 (two grammatical works by Christian Hebraists) and 1105 (on laws of *sheḥita*), were destroyed together with most of the other books when the library was demolished by fire following a bombardment in 1915, during World War I.

Arsenal

See *Paris, Bibliothèque de l'Arsenal.

Arundel, Thomas Howard, second Earl of

England, 1585–1646

Arundel bought some of his MSS through Sir Thomas Roe, British ambassador in Constantinople from 1626 to 1628 (A. Esdaile, *The British Museum Library*, London 1948, pp. 254–256). His collection passed into the possession of the Royal Society in London and was bought by the British Museum (now *London, British Library) in 1831 (*Cat. Margoliouth–Leveen*, IV, p. vi). A list of the seven Arundel MSS and their numbers in the Margoliouth catalogue is found in *ibid.*, p. 163.

AS

T–S Additional Series. See *Cambridge, University Library.

Asch, Sholem

Kutno, Poland, 1880 – London, 1957; Yiddish author

Through Louis M. Rabinowitz the library of Asch, including some 30 MSS, was acquired by *New Haven, Yale University, Beinecke Library. These MSS are described in L. Nemoy, *Catalogue of Hebrew and Yiddish Manuscripts and Books from the Library of Sholem Asch Presented to Yale University by Louis M. Rabinowitz*, New Haven 1945. One MS, a Passover haggada copied by David Leipnik in 1733, is now *New York, JTSA, MS 4452a. After his death the MSS that remained in Asch's possession were sold by his daughter to *London, Valmadonna Trust Library (library custodian: J. V. Lunzer, London). Some of the MSS were sold by the Trust to various collectors.

Ashburnham, Bertram, Fourth Earl of

England, 1797–1878; bibliophile

Ashburnham bought books from the collections of Guglielmo Libri, Jacques-Marie Barrois and *Stowe. His collection was offered for sale in 1883, after his death, and parts were purchased by various libraries. Five Hebrew MSS were among the 29 Oriental MSS purchased in 1884 by *Florence, Biblioteca Medicea Laurenziana (MSS Ashb. 928, 944, 1093, 1432 and 1797). Also in 1883, the British Museum (now *London, British Library) bought the Stowe collection, including its one Hebrew MS, an early starr (שטר; *Cat. Margoliouth*, no. 1206), from Bertram, the fifth Earl of Ashburnham. Some of Ashburnham's other MSS, not originating in these collections and called the Appendix MSS, were bought by Henry Yates Thompson in 1897. MS Appendix 231, a Hebrew MS, is now Princeton University Library, MS Garrett 26 (see *Thompson, Henry Yates).

A. Esdaile, *The British Museum Library*, London 1948, pp. 257–258.

Asher, Adolf & Co.

Booksellers in Berlin

Twenty-two MSS described by M. *Steinschneider were listed in Asher & Co.'s Catalogue no. 86 (1868). Many of the seventeen MSS described by Steinschneider under the heading 'Verkäufliche Handschriften' in various numbers of *HB*, VI–X (1863–1870), a periodical published at the time by Asher, were also sold by the firm. For the present whereabouts of the MSS see Appendix I, no. 1. Asher sold many other MSS to *Oxford, Bodleian Library, in 1854–1855 and 1873, among them MSS Opp. Add. 2° 5, 18 and 23; and Opp. Add. 4° 13, 38 and 114–115. The *Almanzi collection was sold by Asher to the British Museum (now *London, British Library) in 1865.

D. Paisey, 'Adolphus Asher (1800–1853): Berlin bookseller, Anglophile, and friend to Panizzi', *British Library Journal*, XXIII (1997), pp. 131–153.

Asher, Asher

Scotland–England, 1837–1889; physician

Asher's library was acquired by *London, Beth Din and Beth Hamidrash Library.

Rab., *Lit. Treas.*, p. 59.

Ashkenazi, Eliezer

Tunis, Tunisia, nineteenth cent.; bookseller

Ashkenazi sold MSS to many libraries in the nineteenth century. *Steinschneider possessed lists of MSS offered for sale by Ashkenazi (now in *New York, JTSA, MS 2863, fols. 41–57). L. Dukes briefly described fifteen MSS offered for sale by Ashkenazi in *Literaturblatt des Orients*, X (1849), pp. 369–370. *Oxford, Bodleian Library, MSS Opp. Add. 2° 14 and 21 and Opp. Add. 4° 28–36, 39, 42 and 44, were purchased from Ashkenazi in 1856–1858.

Steinschneider, *Vorlesungen*, p. 67 (Hebrew, p. 87).

Ashkenazi, Isaac Raphael

See *Tedeschi, Isaac Raphael.

Ashkenazi Haggada

See *Joel b. Simeon Haggada.

As. Mus.

Asiatic Museum. See *St. Petersburg, Institute of Oriental Manuscripts.

Assaf, Simha

Luban, Belarus, 1889 – Jerusalem, 1953; scholar

Assaf presented some of his MSS, and sold others, to *Jerusalem, JNUL (now NLI). Photocopies of MSS he used in his studies were presented to the JNUL and to *Jerusalem, Schocken Institute.

Assem.

*Assemani.

Assemani, Joseph Simon and Stephanus Evodius

Syria, 1687 – Rome, 1768; Syria, 1707 – Rome, 1782

The Assemanis, uncle and nephew, members of a Maronite family from Mount Lebanon, Syria, compiled a catalogue of the Hebrew MSS in the *Vatican, Biblioteca Apostolica, *Bibliothecae Apostolicae Vaticanae Codicum Manuscriptorum Catalogus, Recensuerunt Steph. Evodius Assemani et Jos. Sim. Assemani*, I: *Codices Ebraicos et Samaritanos*, Rome 1756 (facsimile reprint, Paris 1926). According to Steinschneider (*Vorlesungen*, p. 71; Hebrew, p. 93), quoting a handwritten remark by P. J. Bruns, the true author of the catalogue was G. Antonio Costanzi. S. E. Assemani's descriptions of ten Hebrew MSS in *Florence, Biblioteca Medicea Laurenziana, were appended to the 1757 catalogue of Greek and Hebrew MSS in that library.

Asti (Italy), Comunità ebraica

The two MSS in the possession of the community as recorded by Sonne, *Relazione*, were transferred to the community library in *Alessandria and are now in the Research Center for Italian Jewish Studies in Jerusalem, MSS 30 and 43.

Auerbach, Benjamin Hirsch

Germany, 1808–1872; rabbi

The MS of *Sefer ha'eshkol* (ספר האשכול) which was in Auerbach's possession and served as the basis for his edition (Halberstadt 1868) and the edition by S. and H. Albeck (Jerusalem 1935–1938) was deposited by the Auerbach family in the *Jerusalem, JNUL (now NLI, Heb. 4° 1159).

Augsburg (Germany), Staats- und Stadtbibliothek

Nine fragments taken from bindings are described in *Cat. Striedl–Róth*, pp. 1–4. Two additional fragments of two leaves each, from Alfasi's digest of Tractate *Megila* (removed from the binding of a book with the call-number 4° Ink. 256) and from Tosafot on TB *Nida* 12–15 (removed from the binding of Cod. fol. 68), were photocopied for the *Jerusalem, IMHM.

Augusta Vindelicorum

Latin name for Augsburg.

Augustus Frederick, Prince

See *Sussex, Duke of.

Avida (Zlotnick), Yehuda Leib

Plock, Poland, 1887 – Jerusalem, 1962; rabbi and writer

Many of Avida's MSS are now in *Ramat Gan, Bar-Ilan University Library. On the MS of Geonic responsa called 'MS Avida', see *Vivanti, David Abraham.

Avignon (France), Bibliothèque municipale

Also known as Bibliothèque municipale Livrée Ceccano, as it is housed in the Ceccano palace. Formerly, the library and the Calvet Museum (Bibliothèque et Musée Calvet) were parts of a single institution. In 1984 they were separated into two independent entities. Six Hebrew MSS, mostly Esther scrolls, are described in *Catalogue général*, XXVII (1894), nos. 5, 7 and 8; XXVIII (1895), nos. 1928 and 2336; and XXIX (1897), no. 3856.

Ayuso Marazuela, Teófilo

Valverde, Spain, 1906 – Zaragoza (Saragossa), Spain, 1962; biblical scholar

A fragment of TB *Nedarim* owned by Ayuso in Saragossa is now *Madrid, Consejo Superior de Investigaciones Científicas, Instituto de Filología, MS CVI–M/106.

Azulai, Hayyim Joseph David

Jerusalem, 1724 – Livorno, Italy, 1806; scholar and bibliographer

Azulai's library apparently passed into the possession of his son Raphael Isaiah Azulai, rabbi of Ancona. In 1816 Raphael sold part of the library, including some MSS, to the father of Giuseppe *Almanzi, who purchased it for Giuseppe, as noted by M. Benayahu (מ׳ בניהו, רבי חיים יוסף דוד אזולאי, ירושלים תשי״ט, עמ׳ פד). After Raphael Azulai's death, part of the collection came into the possession of H. J. D. Azulai's grandson Nissim Zerahiah ben Abraham Azulai. Many of the MSS that had belonged to Raphael Azulai were sold to Rabbi Abraham David *Vivanti and to Samuel *Schönblum. Some of the MSS seem to have been acquired by *Ancona, Comunità ebraica. MSS from the Vivanti collection were acquired by Rabbi Hayyim *Rosenberg of Ancona. Rosenberg described 40 MSS of Azulai's works in his possession (ח׳ רוזנברג, ׳חבורי רב חיד״א וכתביו שלא ראו עדיין אור הדפוס׳, ק״ס, ה [תרפ״ט], עמ׳ 142–162, 255–262, 388–395). These MSS are now in *New York, JTSA. The MSS remaining in Rosenberg's collection, including many formerly in Azulai's library, were acquired by *Los Angeles, University of California Library. Schönblum published a *Catalogue d'une collection anconienne dont la plus grande partie dérive de la bibliothèque appartenant aux célèbres C. J. D. Azulai et son fils Rafaël rabbin à Ancone*, Lemberg [1872], which lists 56 MSS. These MSS were sold to various libraries throughout the world (see Schönblum). Many of H. J. D. Azulai's MSS came into the possession of Judah Zerahiah Azulai. At the end of *Ḥidushe Haran 'al Massekhet Rosh hashana* (חדושי הר״ן על מסכת ראש השנה, ירושלים תרל״א) is a list of 40 titles comprising around 30 MSS bought from his estate. All or most of these MSS were sold to the book dealer Jacob Saphir, who sold most of them to the *Cambridge, University Library, *Oxford, Bodleian Library, and *Frankfurt a/M, Stadtbibliothek (now Universitätsbibliothek; see below). On Judah Zerahiah see the article by J. M. Toledano (י״מ טולידאנו, ׳תעודות לתולדות ר׳ יהודה זרחיה אזולאי׳, ירושלים: רבעון לחקר ירושלים ותולדותיה, ג [תשי״א], עמ׳ קלח–קמ). Judah Zerahiah's grandson, Abraham Azulai-Mandelbaum, presented 40 MSS to *Jerusalem, JNUL (now NLI; *KS*, II [1925/6], p. 232). Previously he had printed on a single sheet a list of 56[?] MSS in his possession (רשימת הספרים מכתבי ידות ... אשר לי בירושה מאבי ז׳ הר׳ חיים יוסף אזולאי, יפו חש״ד). On the bibliographical sources concerning this sheet, its date and the number of MSS it included, see S. Z. Havlin, 'Concerning one manuscript that was split in two' (ש״ז הבלין, ׳על כתב־יד אחד שנחלק׳, עלי ספר, א [תשל״ה], עמ׳ 84, הערה 12). *Jerusalem, Ben-Zvi Institute, MS 1805, includes a handwritten list of 49 of these MSS. Further details concerning the whereabouts of Azulai's MSS may be found in Benayahu's book.

MSS listed at the end of *Ḥidushe Haran* are now in the libraries listed below:

*Cambridge, University Library, MSS Add. 1169, 1170, 1178–1180, 1180.1, 1181, 1183, 1185.1, 1186, 1187, 1189, 1191; *Oxford, Bodleian Library, MSS Opp. Add. 4° 129, 130, 132, 133, 134; Opp. Add. 2° 48–50, 53; *Frankfurt a/M, Goethe Universität, Universitätsbibliothek, MSS qu. 2, oct. 3, oct. 69; *Moscow, RSL, MSS Günzburg 949 and 1133[?]; *London, BL, Or. 2822–2823.

Azulai, Judah Zerahiah
See *Azulai, Hayyim

Azulai, Nissim Zerahiah
See *Azulai, Hayyim.

Azulai, Raphael
See *Azulai, Hayyim.

B

B

(1) Berlin; (2) Bologna; (3) Breslau.

Bacher, Wilhelm

Liptó-Szent-Miklós, Hungary, 1850 – Budapest, Hungary, 1913; Semitic scholar

The Mishna MS in Bacher's possession mentioned in *ZDMG*, XLIV (1890), p. 394, is now *New York, JTSA, MS R222.

Badhab, Isaac Michael

Jerusalem, 1859–1947; rabbi

Badhab collected MSS, especially MSS found in Jerusalem, and published two catalogues of his MSS: *Pardes haTora vehaḥokhma* (פרד״ס התורה והחכמה ... רשימה ע״ס א״ב מכתבי ידות עתיקים האצורים באוצרות ציון ובגנזי ירושלם ומהם כמוסות תחת ידי, ירושלם תרנ״ח), comprising 265 entries, and *Kuntres Pardes haTora vehaḥokhma* (קונטריס פרד״ס התורה והחכמה ... ירושלים תרס״ד), comprising 307 entries. Most were sold to various collectors and libraries; others were lost or stolen. After Badhab's death, 285 of the most important MSS were acquired by *Jerusalem, JNUL (now NLI). Several other MSS are found in the collection of Meir *Benayahu in Jerusalem. A handwritten catalogue of the MSS acquired by the JNUL, prepared by Benayahu in 1947, is found in the NLI. It was published by Badhab's grandson Joseph Levy in his *R. Isaac Badhab (1859–1947): His Life's Work and Environs*, Jerusalem 1977 (ר׳ יצחק בדאהב, תר״ך–תש״ז: מפעל חייו ושכונתו), pp. 40–57.

מ׳ בניהו, ׳רבי יצחק בדאהב׳, ירושלים: רבעון לחקר ירושלים ותולדותיה, א (תש״ח), עמ׳ נח–ס.

Badische Landesbibliothek

See *Karlsruhe, Badische Landesbibliothek.

Baer, Seligmann Isaac

Mosbach, Germany, 1825 – Biebrich, Germany, 1897; scholar

Some of Wolf *Heidenheim's MSS passed into Baer's possession (*EJ*, IV, p. 80). Seventy-two MSS of Baer's are listed in *Katalog über den literarischen Nachlass des am 27 Februar 1897 verstorbenen S. Baer zu Biebrich a. Rhein*, Biebrich a/R [1897?]. Most of the collection was acquired by Baron David *Günzburg and is now in the *Moscow, RSL (Shunami, no. 220). Many of the MSS numbered 1340–1511 in the Günzburg collection derive from Baer's library.

Balliol College

See *Oxford, College Libraries.

Bamberg (Germany), Staatsbibliothek

Four MSS are described in *Cat. Striedl–Róth*, pp. 5–7. These MSS and two additional Esther scrolls are listed in *Cat. Allony–Loewinger*, I, p. 37.

Bamberger, Moses Loeb

Wiesenbronn, Germany, 1838 – Bad Kissingen, Germany, 1899; rabbi

Bamberger's MS, a Pentateuch dated 1189 including the Aramaic Targum of Onkelos, was used by A. *Berliner in his edition of Targum Onkelos and by A. Merx in his *Chrestomathia Targumica*, Berlin 1888. It was MS *Sassoon 282 and is now MS *London, Valmadonna Trust Library 1.

Bamberger and Wahrmann

Booksellers in Jerusalem

The firm sold MSS to several libraries, among them *Jerusalem, JNUL (now NLI), which purchased the collection of M. *Chamizer and other MSS. In 1963, after the firm went out of business, the remaining MSS, including a number from the *Berlin, Akademie für die Wissenschaft des Judentums and *Gaster collections, were sold to *Los Angeles, University of California Library (I. S. Brisman, 'The Jewish Studies collection at UCLA', *Jewish Book Annual*, XXVII [1969], pp. 45–46). One MS, *Sefer hadinim* (ספר הדינים), quoted as no. 144 by S. Lieberman, *Tosefet rishonim* (תוספת ראשונים, ב, ירושלים תרצ"ח), p. 122, is now *Jerusalem, Schocken Institute, MS 19520.

Bank, A. M.

Russia, c. 1900; collector

Bank sold the library of Leon Mandelstamm, which included several MSS, to the *New York Public Library in 1897.

Jewish Encylopedia, III, p. 311.

Barb. Or.

See *Barberini.

Barberini, Biblioteca

The library of the Barberini family was founded by Francesco Barberini (1597–1679). In 1902 the library was acquired by the *Vatican. The Hebrew MSS in the Barberini collection are listed in *Cat. Allony–Loewinger*, III, nos. 724–736, and in *Cat. Richler*, Vatican, pp. 507–515.

Barberini Triglot

Name given to MS *Vatican, Barb. Or. 1, a Samaritan Pentateuch with Aramaic and Arabic translations. A facsimile edition was published in Holon, 1966–1970.

Barcelona (Spain), Biblioteca de Cataluña

Formerly Biblioteca Central de la Diputación Provincial de Barcelona, in 1981 it became the National Library of Catalonia. Two Hebrew MSS (nos. 254 and 1664) are listed in *Cat. Allony–Kupfer*, II, nos. 1160–1161. MS 254, a collection of fragments and documents, is described in greater detail by D. Romano, 'Documentos hebreos del siglo XIV, de Cataluña y Mallorca', *Sefarad*, XXXIV (1974), pp. 289–312, and parts were discussed or published in other publications. The library also has a fragment from a medieval Tora scroll (MS 2595) described by Fernando Díaz Esteban and Amadeu-J. Soberanas, 'Fragmento de rollo litúrgico del Pentateuco en Barcelona', *Anuario de Filología, Universidad de Barcelona*, VII (1981), pp. 221–235, and a fourteenth-century ledger (see Codex *Soberanas).

Barcelona Haggada

Name given to *London, BL, MS Add. 14761 (*Cat. Margoliouth*, no. 605), an illuminated haggada of the fourteenth century. A facsimile edition was published in London, 1992.

Narkiss, p. 64.

Bardach, Julius (Jehudah)

See *Pinsker, Simha.

Bargès, Jean-Joseph-Léandre

Auriol, France, 1810–1896; abbé and Orientalist

In 1896, *Oxford, Bodleian Library, purchased from the catalogue of Bargès's library three Hebrew MSS, nos. 630, 633 and 640, now bearing the shelf-marks MSS Heb. f. 55, e. 64 and e. 65. Three other MSS, two of them nineteenth-century copies of MSS in *Paris, Bibliothèque nationale de France, are now in the Bibliothèque diocésaine – Centre Le Mistral in Marseille.

Bartolocci, Giulio

Celleno, Italy, 1613 – Rome, 1687; bibliographer

Bartolocci served as *scriptor hebraicus* in the library of the *Vatican and compiled catalogues (unpublished) of the Hebrew MSS in the library. He described many of the library's MSS in his five-volume work *Bibliotheca Magna Rabbinica*, Rome 1675–1694. The last two volumes were completed by his disciple Carlo Giuseppi Imbonati.

Basel (Switzerland), Öffentliche Bibliothek der Universität Basel

Seventeen MSS were described by M. Schwab in *REJ*, V (1882), pp. 250–257. Forty MSS are listed in *Cat. Allony–Kupfer*, II, pp. 126–128. Call-numbers are given in parentheses. The numbers 1520–1563 and 40–1מ are catalogue serial numbers. The numbers at the left of each entry with the prefix ס are the microfilm numbers at the *Jerusalem, IMHM. Fifty-two MSS were described in greater detail in a typewritten catalogue by J. Prijs, edited by Bernhard and David Prijs, *Die hebräischen Handschriften: Katalog auf Grund der Beschreibungen von Joseph Prijs*, Basel 1994. In that catalogue, the descriptions of the Buxtorf family papers (nos. 53–82) are by S. G. Burnett.

Bashuysen, Heinrich Jacob van

Hanau, Germany, 1679–1750; Christian Hebraist

A MS of his described by Johann Christoph *Wolf, *Bibliotheca Hebraea*, II, p. 301, is now *Parma, Biblioteca Palatina, MS Parm. 2948.

Cat. de Rossi 674; *Cat. Richler*, Parma, 147.

BAV

Biblioteca Apostolica Vaticana. See *Vatican.

Bayerische Staatsbibliothek

See *Munich, Bayerische Staatsbibliothek.

Bedell, William, Bishop of Kilmore and Ardagh

See *Bishop Bedell Bible.

Beer, Bernhard

Dresden, Germany, 1801–1861; scholar and bibliophile

Beer's widow presented 36 MSS to *Breslau, Jüdisch-theologisches Seminar. Eleven of these MSS were described in G. Wolf, *Catalog der Bibliothek des sel. Herrn Bernhard Beer in Dresden*, Berlin 1863, pp. xxxviii–xl, 1.

Cat. Loewinger–Weinryb, p. vii.

Belgrado, Yom Tov

Finale Emilia, Italy, eighteenth cent.

Belgrado's MS, described in de Rossi, *ext.*, no. 88, is now probably *Vienna, ÖNB, Cod. Hebr. 167 (*Cat. Schwarz*, Vienna, no. 3). Another MS from his collection is now in *Ramat Gan, Bar-Ilan University Library, MS 181.

Benaim, Joseph

Fez, Morocco, 1882–1961; rabbi

*New York, JTSA, acquired 150 MSS from Benaim's collection. In the fire that broke out in the JTSA library in 1966, 45 of the MSS were almost completely destroyed and most of the others were damaged. *A Reel Guide to the Benaim Collection of Hebrew and Judeo-Arabic Manuscripts*, [Ann Arbor], University Microfilms [1969?], briefly described 112 MSS. Sixty other MSS were purchased from Benaim's son by A. Elbaz, now in Montreal.

Benamozegh, Elijah

Livorno, Italy, 1822–1900; rabbi

The Harry *Hirsch collection, which is mostly derived from the Benamozegh collection, was sold to *New York, JTSA (Marx, 'Polemical MSS', p. 277). Hayyim Vital's *Sefer haḥezyonot* (ספר החזיונות), Jerusalem 1954, was published from an autograph MS formerly in Benamozegh's possession, later purchased from Nissim Shamama in Livorno by Rabbi Shabbetai Toaff and sold by his son and grandson, Rabbi E. and Prof. A. Toaff, to a dealer. The present whereabouts of the

MS are unknown. A new edition based on a photograph of the same MS was published by M. M. Faerstein (Jerusalem 2005).

Ben Asher Codex

Name given to a MS of the Latter Prophets with a colophon stating that it was written by Moses ben Asher in Tiberias in 895, formerly kept in the Karaite Synagogue in Cairo. According to M. Glatzer (מ׳ גלצר, ׳מלאכת הספר של כתר ארם צובה והשלכותיה׳, ספונות, יט [תשמ״ט], עמ׳ 250–259), the colophon is not original and the Codex was copied at the end of the tenth century or the beginning of the eleventh.

Benayahu, Meir

Jerusalem, 1926–2009; scholar

Benayahu owned a collection of over 1,500 MSS, mostly of Near-Eastern or Italian origin.

Bencini, Francesco Domenico

Italy, 1664–1744; scholar

Bencini, director of the Royal Library in Turin (now *Turin, Biblioteca Nazionale Universitaria) from 1729 to 1732, compiled an index of MSS in the library. A concordance to the numbers in his index and those in Bernardino *Peyron's catalogue is found in *Cat. Peyron*, pp. xli–xlvi.

Benguiat, Ephraim

Smyrna, Turkey – USA, 1918; businessman and collector

Benguiat's MSS, some of which were described by C. Adler and I. M. Casanowicz in *Descriptive Catalogue of a Collection of Objects of Jewish Ceremonial, Deposited in the U.S. National Museum by Hadji Ephraim Benguiat*, Washington, D.C., 1901, were acquired by *New York, JTSA.

EJ, XII, p. 544.

Bennett, Solomon Yom Tov

Polotzk, Belarus, 1761 – London, 1838; engraver and writer

A collection of MSS and documents formerly in Bennett's possession was acquired by Jews' College, London (now *London School of Jewish Studies), in 1952.

Pearson, p. 53.

Bension, Ariel

Baghdad, Iraq, 1881 – Paris, 1932

Bension's collection of MSS was bought by the University of Alberta in Edmonton and is described by S. I. Aranov in *A Descriptive Catalogue of the Bension Collection of Sephardic Manuscripts and Texts*, Edmonton 1979.

Benz.

*Benzian.

Benzian, Julius

Berlin, nineteenth cent; publisher and bookseller

Fifty-five MSS offered for sale were described by M. Steinschneider in *Catalogue d'une précieuse collection hébraïque de manuscrits, incunables et de livres rares et importants en vente chez Julius Benzian*, Berlin 1869. Twenty-nine additional MSS (nos. 56–84) were described by Steinschneider in *HB*, IX (1869), pp. 29–30, 60–62, 94, 117. Five Yiddish MSS numbered Benzian A–E, corresponding to nos. 80–84 in the catalogue, were described in greater detail by Steinschneider in *Serapaeum*, XXX (1869), pp. 130–138, 149–150. For the present whereabouts of these MSS, see Appendix I, no. 2. Other MSS were described in Benzian's auction catalogue *Verzeichniss der von mehreren gelehrten hinterlassenen Bibliotheken, enthaltend werthvolle Werke und Handschriften ...*, Berlin 1870. I could not find a copy of this catalogue. One MS, which may have been no. 4 in that catalogue (cf. Freimann, *Union Catalogue*, no. 2187), is now *Jerusalem, NLI, Heb. 4° 1038.

Berend Salomon, Isaac Seligmann Cohn

Hamburg, Germany, eighteenth century

The collection of David *Oppenheim was in the possession of his relative Berend Salomon at the end of the eighteenth century. He compiled a catalogue of the collection (רשימה תמה ... מן קבוצת ספרים ... מוהר"ר דוד אופנהיים ... המבורג תקמ"ב) based on a similar unpublished catalogue by Israel Breslau.

Berenstein, Issachar Baer

Netherlands, 1808–1893; rabbi

Twenty-five MSS are listed in the *Auctions-Catalogue* of his collection (בינה לעתים, Amsterdam 1907, nos. 1766, 2153–2177). At one time the MS of Maimonides' responsa, now *Copenhagen, Kongelige Bibliothek, MS Sim. Jud.-Arab. 1, was in Berenstein's possession (*HB*, VIII [1865], p. 39). The present locations of MSS from Berenstein's collection are listed in Appendix I, no. 3.

Berkeley (California), Magnes Collection of Jewish Art and Life at the Bancroft Library

Formerly the Judah L. Magnes Museum. In 2010, the Judah L. Magnes Museum, formerly housed in private premises in Berkeley, was transferred to the University of California's Bancroft Library and renamed the Magnes Collection of Jewish Art and Life. It holds about 45 Hebrew MSS, mostly Karaite, and over 125 *ketubot*.

Berl.

*Berlin, Staatsbibliothek zu Berlin – Preussischer Kulturbesitz.

Berlin, Akademie für die Wissenschaft des Judentums

The Akademie, founded in 1919, ceased to function in 1934. The library was moved to a synagogue, and Samuel Wahrmann was able to remove the books from the synagogue before it was demolished and bring them to Jerusalem. His firm, *Bamberger and Wahrmann, sold the library, including several MSS, to *Los Angeles, University of California Library, and they now form part of the Theodore E. Cummings collection. Some other MSS from the Akademie are in *Jerusalem, Schocken Institute.

Berlin, Deutsche Staatsbibliothek

See *Berlin, Staatsbibliothek zu Berlin – Preussischer Kulturbesitz.

Berlin, Hochschule für die Wissenschaft des Judentums

The Hochschule – downgraded by the Nazis to Lehranstalt – acquired Abraham *Geiger's collection of MSS. Fifteen were briefly described in *HB*, XVII (1877), pp. 11–12. In 1936, under the Nazi regime, the MSS were given for safekeeping to Alexander Guttmann, a professor at the Hochschule, who was about to emigrate to the United States. In 1984, Guttmann offered all the MSS listed in *HB*, with the exception of no. 3 (ספר בשמים ראש) and no. 8 (חזוק אמונה), together with a few other MSS from the Hochschule not listed in *HB*, for sale at an auction at Sotheby's in New York. The MSS are described in Sotheby's catalogue *Highly Important Hebrew Printed Books and Manuscripts*, New York 1984. After it became known that the MSS were originally the property of the Hochschule, the State of New York disputed the sale. A settlement reached by the parties resulted in the formation of the Judaica Conservancy Foundation, a joint undertaking of Jewish institutions of higher learning in the United States, England and Israel. Twenty-two lots, including nineteen MSS sold at the auction, were recalled and given to the Foundation, which deposited them in the libraries of some of its members. It also authorized the proceeds of the sale of two of the MSS, the *Prague Bible and the *Catalan Maḥzor, to be awarded to Guttmann in consideration of his role in saving the MSS. The present whereabouts of the MSS are listed in Appendix I, no. 12. Another MS, *Sukat shalom* (סכת שלם) by M. S. Landsberg, neither listed in *HB* nor included in the auction sale, is now *Jerusalem, NLI, Heb. 8° 2429.

H. C. Zafren, 'From Hochschule to Judaica Conservancy Foundation: The Guttmann affair', *Jewish Book Annual*, XLVII (1989), pp. 6–26.

Berlin, Jüdische Gemeinde

The MSS formerly in the library of the Jewish community in Berlin were confiscated by the Nazis during World War II and are now found in a number of libraries, including *Jerusalem, NLI (which now houses the Wolf Haggada; see *Wolf, Albert), *Warsaw, ŻIH, *Moscow, RSL, and *Tel Aviv, Rambam Library. The Orleans siddur is now in a private collection in Switzerland. The copy of David Oppenheimer's *Nish'al David* (נשאל דוד) that probably belonged to the Gemeinde, referred to by A. Elboim in *Hama'ayan*, XXXV, 2 (1995), p. 13, is now MS 1 in the Rambam Library (א' אלבוים, 'מהדורה גנוזה של שו"ת נשאל דוד', המעין, לה, 2 [תשנ"ה], עמ' 13). The liturgical Geniza fragments described by J. Schirmann, 'Die poetischen Genizafragmente in der juedischen Gemeindebibliothek', *MGWJ*, LXXVI (1932), pp. 339–354, are now in *Cincinnati, HUC. A few other *Geniza fragments were recently acquired by the Tel Aviv University Library. Photocopies of a number of MSS and Geniza fragments from the Berlin collection are held by *Jerusalem, Schocken Institute.

Berlin, Königliche Bibliothek

See *Berlin, Staatsbibliothek zu Berlin – Preussischer Kulturbesitz.

Berlin, M.

Newport, England(?); nineteenth cent.

The MS described in *Magazin für die Wissenschaft des Judentums*, XIII (1886), p. 264, is now *London, BL, MS Or. 10012 (*Gaster collection, 571).

Berlin, Naphtali Zevi Judah

Mir, Belarus, 1817 – Warsaw, Poland, 1893; rabbi and scholar

Berlin's MS of *She'iltot* (שאלתות) passed into the possession of his son Meir Bar-Ilan, who gave it to Saul Lieberman. The MS is now *New York, JTSA, MS R657.

ש' מירסקי, שאלתות, ירושלים תש"ך, מבוא, עמ' 33.

Berlin, Preussische Staatsbibliothek

See *Berlin, Staatsbibliothek zu Berlin – Preussischer Kulturbesitz.

Berlin, SB

*Berlin, Staatsbibliothek zu Berlin – Preussischer Kulturbesitz.

Berlin, Staatsbibliothek zu Berlin – Preussischer Kulturbesitz

Formerly known as the Preussische Staatsbibliothek or Königliche Bibliothek. After World War II the collections of the Preussische Staatsbibliothek were divided between the Kulturbesitz, located in new facilities in West Berlin, and the Deutsche Staatsbibliothek, in the old building in East Berlin. On the eve of World War II, the library's Hebrew MSS had been hidden away. After the war, almost all of them were discovered in the Universitätsbibliothek in Tübingen and in the Westdeutsche Bibliothek in Marburg (in *Cat. Allony–Loewinger*, I, these collections are referred to as 'Berlin–Tübingen' and 'Berlin–Marburg'). Later, they were returned to the library in West Berlin. On January 1, 1992, after the unification of East and West Germany, the two libraries were reunited and the library was named Staatsbibliothek zu Berlin – Preussischer Kulturbesitz. All the Hebrew MSS that were formerly in East Berlin (see below) are now preserved with the other Hebrew MSS in the new building in West Berlin.

The library's collection numbers over 500 Hebrew and Samaritan MSS, of which 124 were described by M. Steinschneider in *Cat. Steinschneider*, Berlin, I (1878). Twenty years later, 135 additional MSS, including those that came to the library from *Erfurt in 1880, were described in *Cat. Steinschneider*, Berlin, II (1897). The catalogue is arranged by subject. At the head of each entry the catalogue serial number is listed (Vol. II begins with no. 125), followed by the call-number in parentheses. Palaeographical and codicological information: writing material (parchment MSS are noted; when no mention of material is made, the MS is paper), type of script, and date and number of folios. Provenances and the immediate source from which the MS was acquired are noted as well. Indexes (at the end of each volume; the one at the end of Vol. II covers both volumes): authors, scribes, owners, titles and places. The indexes refer to the call-numbers of the MSS. A concordance to the call-numbers and the catalogue numbers is found in Vol. II, p. 172. Artur Spanier compiled handwritten descriptions of MSS acquired after the publication of *Cat. Steinschneider*, Berlin, II, up to ca. 1928. *Cat. Allony–Loewinger*, I, pp. 22–36, lists 250 Hebrew and Samaritan MSS acquired after 1897.

In *Cat. Allony–Loewinger*, I, the call-numbers are written at the end of each entry in parentheses. The other numbers at the head and end of each entry are serial numbers of the catalogue. The numbers to the left of each entry with the prefixes פ, ס or צ refer to the photocopy serial numbers in the *Jerusalem, IMHM. The four MSS in Spanier's handwritten list (*Cat. Allony–Loewinger*, I, p. 36) that the authors believed were lost (*ibid.*, p. 22) have since been found and have been microfilmed for the IMHM. The following MSS were formerly in the Deutsche Staatsbibliothek in East Berlin (*Cat. Steinschneider*, Berlin, numbers in parentheses): Or. 2° 133–134 (81–82), Or. 2° 380–381 (20), Or. 2° 1210–1211 (125), Or. 2° 1215–1218 (133–136), Or. 2° 3360, Or. 4° 828 (199), Or. 4° 830 (152). Four biblical fragments from the Deutsche Staatsbibliothek were described in *Cat. Striedl–Róth*, p. 8; none of these fragments could be found when the two branches of the library were reunited (e-communication from Dr. H-O. Feistel, November 2006).

A. Spanier, 'Über Umfang und Herkunft der Sammlung hebräischer Handschriften in der kurfürstlichen Bibliothek zu Berlin', in G. Abb (ed.), *Von Büchern und Bibliotheken: Festschrift für Ernst Kuhnert*, Berlin 1928, pp. 245–253.

Berliner, Abraham

Obersitzko, Poland, 1833 – Berlin, 1915; scholar

During his lifetime Berliner sold a number of MSS to various collectors – among them, Solomon *Halberstamm (according to a copy of Halberstamm's *Catalog hebräischer Handschriften* [קהלת שלמה, וינה תר״ן] found in *Jerusalem, NLI, with handwritten notes on the sources of his MSS) and Abraham *Epstein (*Cat. Schwarz*, Austria, no. 28). A medical miscellany belonging to Berliner and described by M. Steinschneider in *MWJ*, XII (1885), pp. 182–214, is now *Moscow, RSL, Günzburg 1481. Two of Berliner's MSS are now in the *Berlin, Staatsbibliothek (Or. 8° 257 and 8° 518, nos. 80 and 222 in *Cat. Steinschneider*, Berlin). One MS is in *New York, JTSA (MS L263), and another in *Budapest, Hungarian Academy of Sciences (MS Kaufmann 523). The commentary on prayers by Eliezer b. Nathan that Berliner recorded in his notes to S. Hurwitz's edition of *Maḥzor Vitry* (Nuremberg 1923, p. 184) is now in the Manfred *Lehmann collection (מ״ר ליהמן, ׳מחזור כתב־יד ליהמן והתשב״ץ שבתוכו׳, קבץ על יד, ס״ח יא [תשמ״ה], עמ׳ 179–212). After his death, Berliner's library was divided among H. Brody, Aron Freimann and Alexander *Marx (Freimann, 'Mitteilungen', p. 84).

Bernays, Jacob

Hamburg, Germany, 1824 – Bonn, Germany, 1881; philologist

Nine of his MSS were in *Breslau, Jüdisch-theologisches Seminar. A list of the MSS is found in Brann, *Geschichte*, pp. 124–126. A MS in *Jerusalem, NLI (Heb. 8° 382), was copied for Bernays by S. Frennsdorf (י׳ יואל, רשימת כתבי־היד העבריים הנמצאים בבית הספרים הלאומי והאוניברסיטאי בירושלם, ירושלים תרצ״ד, מס׳ 549).

Bern (Switzerland), Burgerbibliothek

O. Franz-Klauser described thirty MSS in 'Die hebräischen Handschriften der Burgerbibliothek Bern' in *Judaica: Beiträge zum Verstehen des Judentums*, LV (1999), pp. 247–271. The catalogue includes a brief description of the contents, palaeographical and codicological details and information concerning provenance. Twenty-five MSS are listed in *Cat. Allony–Kupfer*, II, pp. 128–130. The call-numbers are listed in parentheses at the end of each entry. The numbers 1564–1588 and those with the prefix מ are serial numbers of the catalogue. The numbers to the left of the entries with the prefix ס are the serial numbers of the microfilms in the *Jerusalem, IMHM. Five Esther scrolls described in the Franz-Klauser catalogue were not listed in *Cat. Allony–Kupfer*.

Bernheimer, Carlo

Livorno, Italy, 1877–1966

Bernheimer compiled catalogues of the MS collections of *Livorno, Talmud Tora, *Milan, Biblioteca Ambrosiana and *Modena, Biblioteca Estense (= *Cat. Bernheimer*, Modena), and wrote a work on Hebrew palaeography, *Paleografia ebraica*, Florence 1924.

Bernkastel-Kues (Germany), St. Nikolaus Hospital

The MSS of Cardinal Nicolaus von *Cusa are now in this library. Five MSS are described in Jakob Marx, *Verzeichnis der Handschriften-Sammlung des Hospitals zu Cues*, Trier 1905, and in *Cat. Allony–Loewinger*, I, p. 56.

Bernstein, Simon

Latvia, 1884 – USA, 1962; journalist and scholar

Bernstein presented a number of MSS to *New York, JTSA, including two maḥzorim. One of them, an incomplete Catalonian maḥzor, was purchased from Isaiah Sonne and is now MS 4418. Bernstein published a description of the MS in 1935, when it was still in Sonne's possession (׳שלשה פיוטים בלתי־נודעים של שלמה בן־גבירול׳, ספר השנה ליהודי אמריקה, ב [תרצ״ה], עמ׳ 197–217).

Register, 5697, p. 55; *ibid.*, 5700, p. 74 (Marx, *Bibl. Studies*, pp. 267, 292).

Berolinum

Latin name for Berlin.

Besançon (France), Bibliothèque municipale

A Hebrew Bible in two volumes formerly in the St. Vincent Abbey was described in *Catalogue général*, XXXII (1900), nos. 1–2, and by M. Schwab, 'Une Bible manuscrit de la bibliothèque de Besançon', *REJ*, XLII (1901), pp. 111–118.

Beth Hamidrash

See *London, Beth Din and Beth Hamidrash Library.

Bibas, Judah

Gibraltar, 1780 – Hebron, 1852; rabbi of Corfu

Bibas brought his library, including over 1,500 MSS and rare books, to Hebron, where it was ravaged during the 1929 riots. A list of books published from MSS owned by Bibas was published by Y. R. Malachi (see below). The MS from which Coronel published geonic responsa (תשובות הגאונים, וינה תרל״א) is now *Moscow, RSL, Günzburg 456. Another MS from Bibas's library is *Washington, D.C., Library of Congress, MS Hebr. 18.

י"ר מלאכי, 'מכתבי־היד שבספרית הרב יהודה בן שמואל ביבאס', אוצר יהודי ספרד, ב (תשי"ט), עמ' 116; מ' בניהו, 'ידיעות חדשות על רבי יהודה ביבאס', שם, ג (תש"ך), עמ' 102.

Bibliotheca Regis M. Brittaniae

King's Library. See *King's MS.

Bibl. Monast. Scotus

*Vienna, Unsere Liebe Frau zu den Schotten.

Bicart-Sée, Edmond M.

Colmar, France, 1865–1937

An illuminated late fifteenth- or early sixteenth-century Italian maḥzor that belonged to Bicart-Sée was sold at auction by Christie's in Paris on May 11, 2012 (Sale 3504, lot 62) to David Jeselsohn of Zurich. Two facsimile pages were reproduced in E. Adler, *Jewish Travellers*, London 1930, plates I and IV.

Bick, Abraham

Mogilew, Ukraine, 1835 – Pressburg (Bratislava), Slovakia, 1902, publisher and bookseller

The 23 MSS listed in Bick's catalogue (רשימת הספרים הנמצאים אתי, עתיקים וחדשים, פרעסבורג תרנ"ז) are now found in several libraries throughout the world. A number are in *Budapest, Jewish Theological Seminary, and several were bought by Solomon *Halberstamm. Bick sold MSS before printing the aforementioned catalogue. On the cover of one of the books he printed (ברכה משולשת, פרעסבורג תר"ן), Bick notes that he had printed a list of books and MSS that he had brought back from a trip to the Orient in 1888. According to *Cat. Neubauer–Cowley*, II, p. xiii, one MS (Heb. d. 17) was purchased by *Oxford, Bodleian Library, from Bick. Another MS, Heb. c. 22, was sold to the Bodleian by Solomon *Buber, who had purchased it from Bick; see Buber's edition of *Midrash agada* (מדרש אגדה על חמשה חומשי תורה, וינה תרנ"ד, עמ' [ה]). Buber mentions that Bick also offered him a copy of Hananel Sikili's *Torat haminḥa* (תורת המנחה), now *New York, JTSA, MS R1224.

Biema, Naphtali Hirz van

Amsterdam, Netherlands, 1836–1901

Van Biema's collection derives from that of Hirschl *Lehren. Forty-eight MSS are listed in the catalogue of his estate, *Catalog der reichhaltigen Sammlung hebräischer u. jüdischer Bücher, Handschriften, Portraits, etc., nachgelassen von N. H. van Biema in Amsterdam beschrieben von Sigmund Seeligmann ...*, Amsterdam 1904, nos. 3579–3626. Two MSS bound with printed volumes are listed in nos. 2416 and 2495 respectively. For the present whereabouts of the MSS see Appendix I, no. 4.

Bird's Head Haggada

Name given to *Jerusalem, Israel Museum, MS 180/57, an illuminated haggada in which human figures are drawn with birds' heads.

Narkiss, p. 96; facsimile edition, Jerusalem 1967.

Birmingham (England), Selly Oak Colleges

See *Birmingham, University of Birmingham.

Birmingham (England), University of Birmingham

M. H. Gottstein, 'Hebrew fragments in the Mingana Collection', *JJS*, V (1954), pp. 172–176, contains 18 entries describing *Geniza fragments from 25 MSS, totaling 134 leaves, in the *Mingana collection (no. 18 includes fragments from eight different MSS), along with descriptions of 22 fragments, totaling 64 leaves, in the *Mittwoch collection. Until 1999, the fragments from both collections were deposited in the library of the Selly Oak Colleges. In 1999 most of the Selly Oak Colleges merged with the University of Birmingham, which took over the management of the Mingana and Mittwoch collections. After the merger, two additional Hebrew manuscripts formerly belonging to E. *Grünhut were found in the J. Rendel *Harris collection: a copy of *Midrash Shir hashirim* (מדרש שיר השירים) from the Cairo *Geniza, dated 1147 and published by Grünhut, and a Yemenite manuscript including laws of ritual slaughter.

Birnbaum, Eduard

Cracow, Poland, 1855 – Koenigsberg, formerly Germany, 1920; cantor and musicologist

Birnbaum's library, including a number of MSS and musical scores, was acquired by *Cincinnati, HUC.

Oko, pp. 77–78.

Bisc.

*Biscioni.

Biscioni, Antonio Maria

Florence, Italy, 1674–1756; scholar and librarian

Biscioni compiled a catalogue of the Hebrew MSS in *Florence, Biblioteca Medicea Laurenziana.

Bishop Bedell Bible

Name given to Emmanuel College, Cambridge, MS 1.1.5–1.1.7, an illuminated Bible once in the possession of William Bedell, Bishop of Kilmore and Ardagh (1571–1642).

Narkiss, p. 132.

Bisl.

*Bislisches.

Bislisches, Mordecai (Marcus) and Ephraim

Brody, Ukraine, nineteenth cent.; booksellers

The brothers Bislisches offered for sale 45 MSS listed in *Wissenschaftliche Zeitschrift für jüdische Theologie*, III (1837), pp. 282–286, sometimes referred to as 'MSS Brody'. It is difficult to trace the present whereabouts of most of these MSS. No. 1 may be *Cincinnati, HUC, MS 480; no. 2 was *London, Montefiore, MS 484; no. 6 is now bound in two volumes in *Berlin, SB, Cods. Or. 2° 1387–1388; no. 14 may be *New York, JTSA, MS L825; no. 20 may be *Moscow, Günzburg, MS 233; no. 21 is *Oxford, Bodleian Library, MS Opp. Add. 4° 194; and no. 28 is *Vienna, ÖNB, Cod. Hebr. 106. In 1846, Mordecai Bislisches and Salomon *Stern purchased a collection of 111 MSS, most of them formerly in the possession of Moses *Foa, and sold it to Princess Maria Luisa of Austria, who purchased it on behalf of *Parma, Biblioteca Palatina. In 1850, L. Zunz published in **Hapalit* descriptions of 80 MSS, most or all of which belonged to M. Bislisches. Sixty-seven of these MSS were purchased by *Oxford, Bodleian Library, and the rest by various collectors. A list of the MSS purchased by the Bodleian and their numbers in *Cat. Neubauer* is found on pp. xxiv–xxv of the catalogue. For the whereabouts of the other MSS, see *Hapalit*.

Steinschneider, *Vorlesungen*, pp. 67, 75, 79 (Hebrew, pp. 88, 98, 102).

Bl.

*Berlin, Staatsbibliothek zu Berlin – Preussischer Kulturbesitz.

BL

*London, British Library.

Black, William Mead

London, 1808–1872; Christian clergyman

Black called the library housed in his church in Mill Yard, Whitechapel, London, *Ginze milyard* (גנזי מיליארד). Most of the MSS in his collection were acquired by *Cambridge, Trinity College Library (Rab., *Treas. Jud.*, p. 182). A number of MSS are now in *Manchester, John Rylands University Library (MSS Rylands 29, 30, 32), including the MS published by H. Edelmann in *Dibrey Hephez* (דברי חפץ), London 1853, pp. 15–18; in *Cambridge, University Library (MSS Add. 1019–1021, 1494, 1562–1568); and in *New York, JTSA (MSS 1646, 1730, 1966, 2383, 2604, L883, R282, R520, R1521). At least two MSS are in *London, British Library (MS Or. 4598 described in *Cat. Margoliouth*, no. 1011, and MS Or. 10197, formerly Gaster 998); a few are found in Emory University in Atlanta, Georgia; one is in the *Sassoon collection (no. 493); and another is in *Jerusalem, NLI (Heb. 8° 5354). The MS from 'Milliard' described by Neubauer, *JQR*, VI (1893/4), p. 401, is now JTSA, MS R1521.

Blau, Ludwig Lajos

Budapest, Hungary, 1861–1936; scholar

Seventy-seven of Blau's MSS, which in his time were deposited in *Budapest, Jewish Theological Seminary, were described by D. S. Loewinger (ד״ש לוינגר, 'קובץ כ״י של יהודה אריה בלוי', הצופה לחכמת ישראל, יג [תרפ״ט], עמ' 185–203). Many of these MSS originally belonged to Vivante *Viterbo. About 60 of them were acquired between 1960 and 1962 by *Jerusalem, JNUL (now NLI). The *Geniza fragments in the Blau collection are now in *Cincinnati, HUC, MSS 1085–1088 (J. Mann, *Texts and Studies*, I, Cincinnati 1931, p. 568). A few fragments remain in *Budapest, Jewish Theological Seminary. The fragments from *Tosfot haRosh* on TB *Ketubot* published by Blau in *Festschrift zu Ehren des Dr. A. Harkavy aus Anlass seines am 20 November 1905 vollendeten siebzigsten Lebensjahres*, Peterburg 1909, Hebrew section, pp. 357–367, are now in *Jerusalem, NLI, Heb. 8° 3791.

Bloch, Moses

Gailingen, Germany, 1805 – Buchau, Germany, 1841; rabbi

Bloch's MS of Rashi, described in *Wissenschaftliche Zeitschrift für jüdische Theologie*, IV (1839), pp. 138–140, passed into the possession of Rabbi Guldenstein (S. L. Heilberg, נטעי נעמנים: *Sammlung aus alten schätzbaren Manuscripten*, Breslau 1847, pp. 40–43) and was later acquired by Abraham *Geiger, who bequeathed his MSS to *Berlin, Hochschule für die Wissenschaft des Judentums. It is no. 10 on the list of the Geiger MSS in *HB*, XVII (1877). It is now deposited in *Cincinnati, HUC (MS JCF 1).

Bloch, Philipp

Tworog, Poland, 1841 – Berlin, 1923; rabbi

The MS of *Sefer Shevut Yehuda* by Judah Mehler Reutlingen owned and described by Bloch, 'Ein vielbegehrter Rabbiner des Rheingaues, Juda Mehler Reutlingen', in *Festschrift zum siebzigsten Geburtstag Martin Philippsons*, Leipzig 1916, pp. 114–134, is now *Jerusalem, Schocken Institute, MS 70057.

B. M.

British Museum. See *London, British Library.

Bodl. Or.

One of the call-numbers of MSS in *Oxford, Bodleian Library. This call-number was given to MSS taken from small collections or purchased before 1852. A list of the MSS bearing this call-number and their numbers in *Cat. Neubauer* is found on pp. xxv, xxx–xxxii of the catalogue. Additions are found in *Cat. Neubauer–Cowley*, II, p. 541. Some of the MSS formerly bearing the call-number 'Bodl. Or.' have been returned to their original collections and now bear different call-numbers. A list of these MSS is found in *Cat. Neubauer–Cowley*, II, p. 540.

Bodleian Library
See *Oxford, Bodleian Library.

Boesky, Ivan and Selma
Ivan Boesky: Detroit, 1937; businessman
Boesky accumulated a collection of 74 Hebrew MSS and deposited them in *New York, JTSA. In 2004, the MSS were returned to the Silberstein-Boesky Family Foundation and were sold at auction at Sotheby's in New York on December 2, 2004. The MSS were described in Sotheby's catalogue *Fine Books and Manuscripts Including Americana and Judaica*, New York 2004. The JTSA Library purchased lot nos. 33, 38, 40, 54, 69 and 79. The purchaser of lot 37, a *Diwan* by Samuel Hanagid, indicated his desire 'to loan the MS to JTSA on a long-term basis'.

Bol.
Bologna.

Bologna (Italy), Archivio del Dipartimento di Astronomia dell'Università di Bologna
See *Bologna (Italy), Archivio di Stato.

Bologna (Italy), Archivio di Stato
Leaves and fragments of 642 Hebrew MSS that had been used as wrappers or bindings for files of notarial records in the archive were described by M. Perani and S. Campanini in *I frammenti ebraici di Bologna: Archivio di Stato e collezioni minori*, Florence 1997. The catalogue is arranged by subject. Each entry bears a catalogue number with a prefix indicating the subject, and the call-numbers of the leaves or fragments are provided in square brackets. The descriptions include detailed codicological and palaeographical information and the title and date of the file from which the leaves were removed. Similarly described on pp. 137–144 are fragments in the minor collections in Bologna, including Archivio Generale Arcivescovile di Bologna (7 items), Civico Museo Bibliografico Musicale di Bologna (5 items), Archivio Parrocchiale di S. Martino in Bologna (1 item), Biblioteca della Camera di Commercio di Bologna (1 item), Archivio del Dipartimento di Astronomia dell'Università di Bologna (1 item), a private collection (1 item) and the Biblioteca Universitaria (9 items). The catalogue includes facsimiles of 200 pages. Indexes: Authors, titles, scribes, dates of archival records, archival sources, names of notaries, etc., and a concordance of call-numbers. After the publication of the catalogue, nine additional fragments were located in the Archivio di Stato, two in the Biblioteca del Seminario Arcivescovile, 16 in the Biblioteca Universitaria and two in the Archivio Provincale dei Padri Cappuccini di Bologna.

Bologna (Italy), Archivio Generale Arcivescovile di Bologna
See *Bologna, Archivio di Stato.

Bologna (Italy), Archivio Parrocchiale di S. Martino in Bologna
See *Bologna, Archivio di Stato.

Bologna (Italy), Biblioteca Universitaria
The Hebrew MSS in this library derive from the collections of L. F. *Marsili donated in 1712, Cardinal G. *Mezzofanti acquired in 1857 and the convents of San Salvatore and San Domenico. The collection includes 37 volumes of Hebrew MSS, 28 of which are described in L. Modona, *Catalogo dei Codici Ebraici della Biblioteca della R. Università di Bologna*, Florence 1889, pp. 323–372 (*Cataloghi*, IV, Part 1). At the head of each entry is the catalogue serial number, followed by the call-number in square brackets. Palaeographical and codicological information: writing material, size, number of leaves,

number of lines per page, type of writing and date. A single set of indexes to the MSS in all the libraries described in the six preceding volumes of the *Cataloghi* was published separately on pp. 675–698 in Vol. VII (1904). The MSS are indexed by titles, authors, scribes, owners, etc., place names, and censors.
Five additional MSS were described by I. Ventura Folli, 'Fondi ebraici della Biblioteca Universitaria di Bologna', in F. Parente (ed.), *Atti del terzo convegno [dell'Associazione Italiana per lo Studio del Giudaismo] tenuto a Idice, Bologna ... 1982*, Rome 1985, pp. 81–83. The article also includes a bibliography of handwritten catalogues in the library, including Hebrew MSS and articles on the MSS. Thirty-seven MSS were described in a new, more detailed catalogue prepared by G. Corazzol and M. Perani, *Catalogo dei manoscritti ebraici della Biblioteca Universitaria di Bologna*, in *In BUB, Ricerche e cataloghi sui Fondi della Biblioteca Universitaria di Bologna*, V, Argelato 2013. Nine of the 25 fragments partially removed from bindings were described by M. Perani and S. Campanini, *I frammenti ebraici di Bologna: Archivio di Stato e collezioni minori*, Florence 1997 (see *Bologna, Archivio di Stato).
Fumagalli, 'Emilia-Romagna', pp. 92–96.

Bologna (Italy), Camera di Commercio di Bologna
See *Bologna, Archivio di Stato.

Bologna (Italy), Civico Museo Bibliografico Musicale di Bologna
See *Bologna, Archivio di Stato.

Bologna (Italy), Monast. S. Michele in Bosco
The MS from this library described in de Rossi, *ext.*, no. 101, is now Monte Oliveto Maggiore, Biblioteca Capitolare, Cod. 37 A 2.

Manoscritti biblici Ebraici decorati ..., Milan 1966, pp. 86–87.

Bologna Haggada
Name given to an illuminated haggada found partly in a prayerbook (*Bologna, Biblioteca Universitaria MS 2559) and partly in *Modena, Biblioteca Estense, MS α K. 1.22.

Bonfil, Jacob
Livorno, eighteenth cent.
Bonfil's MS, described by *Kennicott, no. 25, is now *Cambridge, Trinity College, MS F. 12. 70–71.

Bonn (Germany), Universitäts- und Landesbibliothek
J. Gildemeister, *Catalogus Librorum Manuscriptorum Orientalium in Bibliotheca Academica Bonnensii*, Bonn 1864–1876, pp. 100–107, described nine Hebrew MSS (nos. So 34–42), including a Bible in three volumes (So 34–36), a copy of Job and Daniel (So 37), an Esther scroll (So 38), three fragments (So 39) and three other MSS (So 40–42). MSS So 34–38 were destroyed in World War II. After the publication of the catalogue three Hebrew fragments, two biblical (So 120 and 243) and one liturgical (So 183), and a Tora scroll (So 284) were acquired. One MS and two fragments were described in *Cat. Allony–Loewinger*, I. *Cat. Striedl–Róth*, pp. 9–11, described MSS So 39–42. All 13 MSS were listed in F.-J. Huschens, *Die orientalischen Handschriften der Universitäts- und Landesbibliothek Bonn*, Bonn 2000.

Bononia
Latin name for Bologna.

Borg. Ebr.
See *Borgiana.

Borgiana
A collection of MSS assembled by Stefano Borgia (1731–1804). The biblical MSS (in all languages) in the collection were housed in the Museo Borgiano di Propaganda Fide in Rome and were acquired by the *Vatican library in 1902. A list of the Hebrew MSS in this collection is found in *Cat. Allony–Loewinger*, III, nos. 737–755. Two additional MSS are listed in Ruysschaert, 'Les manuscrits Vaticans', p. 359. All 21 MSS (Borg. ebr. 1–21) are described in *Cat. Richler*, Vatican, pp. 516–526. The present whereabouts of the MSS from the Propaganda Fide listed by *Kennicott, nos. 472–474, and *De Rossi, *ext.*, nos. 85–97, are not known.

Boston (Mass.), Boston Medical Library
The library owns 30 Hebrew MSS, acquired from 1930 on by the Godfrey M. Hyams Trust for the purchase of rare medical Judaica in honor of Solomon M. Hyams. These are housed in the Center for the History of Medicine (formerly the Department of Rare Books and Special Collections) in the Francis A. Countway Library, in which the collections and administration of the Boston Medical Library and the Harvard Medical School Library have been combined since 1965, though each of the two original institutions continues to collect and retain ownership of its holdings. Seven of the MSS were described in J. F. Ballard, *A Catalogue of the Medical and Renaissance MSS and Incunabula in the Boston Medical Library*, Boston 1944. A handwritten catalogue by M. Glatzer is in *Jerusalem, IMHM.

Boston (Mass.), Francis A. Countway Library of Medicine
See *Boston, Boston Medical Library.

Boutelje, Israel Eliazer
Amsterdam, Netherlands, 1860 – Sobibor, Poland, 1943
Eleven Hebrew MSS are listed in the sales catalogue of International Antiquariaat, *Catalogue d'une collection importante formant la bibliothèque de ... J. E. Boutelje d'Amsterdam*, I: Hebraica, Amsterdam 1922, p. 55, nos. 914–924.

BPU
*Geneva, Bibliothèque publique et universitaire.

Braginsky, René
Zurich, Switzerland, b. 1949; businessman and collector
Over the past three decades Braginsky has been collecting Judaica. His collection includes over a hundred MSS, many of them illuminated, including *ketubot* and Esther scrolls. In 2009–2011 an exhibition of 103 selected items was displayed in Amsterdam, New York and Jerusalem. E. M. Cohen, S. L. Mintz and E. G. L. Schrijver edited the exhibition catalogue, *A Journey through Jewish Worlds*, Amsterdam 2009.

Braunschweig (Germany), Landesmuseum für Geschichte und Volkstum
Three MSS are described in *Cat. Striedl–Róth*, pp. 12–14.

Brecher, Gideon
Prossnitz, Moravia, 1797–1873; scholar
The MS formerly belonging to Brecher and described by M. Steinschneider, 'Ueber talmudische Realindices ... nebst Beschreibung einer bisher unbekannten Handschrift im Besitze des Herrn. G. Brecher in Prossnitz', in *Serapaeum*, VI (1845), pp. 297–300, is now *Berlin, SB, Cod. Or. 2° 702 (*Cat. Steinschneider*, Berlin, no. 33).

Breit, Chaim
Nineteenth cent.; bookseller
Thirty-two of Breit's MSS are described in

HB, X (1870), p. 142. No. 1 on the list is now *New York, JTSA, MS 2612; no. 10 is possibly *Moscow, RSL, Евр. 16; no. 15 is *Hamburg, SUB, Cod. Levy 66; no. 16 is *Hamburg, SUB, Cod. Levy 68; no. 18 may have been the MS belonging to Solomon *Halberstamm, part of which is extant in *Jerusalem, NLI, Heb. 8° 5728; and no. 29 is MS Tel Aviv, Nehorai 5 (י׳ פנקובר, נוסח התורה בכתר ארם־צובה: עדות חדשה, רמת־גן תשנ״ג, עמ׳ 91–92, הערה 41). The present whereabouts of the other MSS on the list are not known.

Breslau (Poland), Gymnasialische Bibliothek zu Maria Magdalena

The library, including four Hebrew MSS, was transferred to *Breslau, Stadtbibliothek.

Breslau (Poland), Jüdisch-theologisches Seminar

The basis of the MS collection of the Seminary is the collection of 69 MSS acquired in 1854 from the library of Leon *Saraval. About a decade later, 36 MSS from the library of Bernhard *Beer were presented to the Seminar. Other MSS were acquired over the years, including about ten MSS donated by Raphael *Kirchheim. At the outbreak of World War II there were 405 MSS in the collection; five MSS were missing: MS Saraval 66 and MSS nos. 18, 50, 51 and 55. The last three are now in the collection of the *Lehmann family in Silver Spring, Md. (nos. 87–91). In September 1939, the Nazis confiscated the library and deposited it in the central library (Zentralbibliothek) of the Reichssicherheitshauptamt in Berlin. When Berlin was bombed by the Allied air forces in August 1943, most of the books were removed to several locations in Silesia. In May 1944, these archives were transferred to a remote castle in Wölfelsdorf (Wilkanów), and in the summer of 1945 all the documents discovered there by the Red Army were shipped to Moscow and assigned to the Osobyi (Special) Archives (now *Moscow, RSMA). In 1948, about 200 MSS, including at least 39 from the Breslau Seminary, were transferred from the Special Archives to the Lenin State Library (now *Moscow, RSL). Many other Breslau MSS disappeared, but about 75 were found after the war in the cellars of the Gestapo in Glatz (now Kłodzko, Poland) and transferred to *Warsaw, ŻIH. M. Garel, 'Manuscrits hébreaux en Pologne', *Revue d'histoire des textes*, V [1975], pp. 365–367, lists 23 MSS that were brought to Warsaw. Thirty-four more manuscripts and six incunabula found in the Czech town of Trutnov were stored in the library of the Charles (Karlova) University in the National Library of the Czech Republic in Prague (Narodni Knihovna České Republiky). In 2004, the MSS that had been in Prague, together with the incunabula from the same collection, were returned to the Jewish community in Wrocław and are now stored in the *Wrocław, Biblioteka Uniwersytecka we Wrocławiu. A few other MSS from the Breslau Seminary were later acquired by *Jerusalem, JNUL (now NLI), *New York, JTSA, and perhaps other libraries or collectors. Most of the MSS in Warsaw and Moscow are late (eighteenth and nineteenth cent.), but many of those that reached Jerusalem and New York date from the Middle Ages.

The first report of the existence of the MSS in Prague was made by Gerard Weil of the Centre d'Analyse et de Traitement Automatique de la Bible (CATAB) in Lyon. In 'Sur une bibliothèque systématiquement pillée par les Nazis: le catalogue des manuscrits et incunables retrouvés de la Bibliothek des Jüdisch-Theologischen Seminars in Breslau', in *Hommage à Georges Vajda*, Louvain 1980, pp. 579–604, Weil relates the history of the Breslau collection and the story of his discovery of the additional MSS, and provides a list of all the Breslau MSS then known to exist. For a list of the present whereabouts of the Breslau MSS, see Appendix I, no. 5.

N. Cieślińska-Lobkowicz, 'Raub und Rückführung der Leon Vita Saraval Sammlung der Bibliothek des Jüdisch-Theologischen Seminars in Breslau in das Reichssicherheitshauptamt, Berlin', in R. Dehnel (ed.), *Jüdischer Buchbesitz als Raubgut* (Zweites Hannoversches Symposium), Frankfurt a/M 2006, pp. 366–378.

CATALOGUES Catalogues of the *Beer and *Saraval collections were published before they were acquired by the Seminary. The Beer catalogue, however, listed only 11 of the 36 MSS presented to the Seminary. In 1870, the Seminary published a catalogue compiled by B. Zuckermann, *Katalog der Seminar-Bibliothek*, Breslau 1870 (reprinted from *Jahresbericht des Jüd.-theol. Seminars Fraenckel'scher Stiftung*), listing 116 MSS in alphabetical order. A second edition was published in 1876, but despite its title, *Catalogus Bibliothecae Seminarii Jud.-theol. Vratislaviensis: continens CXC Codicum Mss. Hebr. Rarissimorum et CCLXIII bibliorum editionum descriptionem, Edition secunda* (*Catalog der Bibliothek des Breslauer jüdisch-theologischen Seminars von 190 seltenen hebraeischen Handschriften und 263 verschiedenen Ausgaben der Bibel und ihre Theile* ..., 2nd ed., Breslau 1876), only the same 116 MSS were described. During the 1930s, D. S. Loewinger and B. D. Weinryb prepared a catalogue of 364 MSS. Their unpublished manuscript survived the war, and they published it in 1965: *Catalogue of the Hebrew Manuscripts in the Library of the Jüdisch-theologisches Seminar in Breslau*, Wiesbaden 1965. Some additional MSS (nos. 365–405), which came into the possession of the library after the authors had left Breslau, were only briefly described on the basis of information obtained from various sources. The catalogue is written in German, but the foreword, which includes a brief outline of the history of the library and the story of the catalogue, is in English. The catalogue is arranged according to subject. Each entry is preceded by a catalogue serial number. Call-numbers are listed at the end of each entry. Palaeographical and codicological information: writing material, number of leaves, size, number of lines per page and type of script. Colophons and owners' entries are copied. Indexes: authors, titles, scribes, owners and geographical names. There are concordances to the numbers in the Saraval collection and the numbers in the Zuckermann catalogue. The catalogue numbers of the MSS described in the Zuckermann catalogue are identical with the call-numbers. In 2003, a *Catalogue of Manuscripts and Archival Materials of Juedisch-Theologisches Seminar in Breslau Held in Russian Depositories* was published by the Research Project on Art and Archives Inc. (USA) and the Ministry of Culture of the Russian Federation in Moscow, in which the 39 items held in Moscow, *Russian State Military Archives, and in *Moscow, RSL, were described briefly in Russian and English.

Brann, *Geschichte*.

Breslau (Poland), Staats- und Universitätsbibliothek

See *Wrocław, Biblioteka Uniwersytecka we Wrocławiu.

Breslau (Poland), Stadtbibliothek

In 1945 the library was transferred to *Wrocław (Breslau), Biblioteka Uniwersytecka we Wrocławiu.

Brit. Mus., British Museum

See *London, British Library.

British Museum Miscellany

Name given to *London, BL, MS Add. 11639 (*Cat. Margoliouth*, no. 1056), an illuminated miscellany.

Narkiss, p. 86.

Brl.
*Berlin, Staatsbibliothek zu Berlin – Preussischer Kulturbesitz.

Br. Mus.
British Museum. See *London, British Library.

Brody
See *Bislisches.

Brookline (Mass.), Hebrew College
Formerly Hebrew Teachers College. See *Newton Center (Mass.), Hebrew College.

Brotherton Library
Brotherton Library, Leeds University. See *Roth, Cecil.

Brussels
The anonymous (*ungenannter*) collector from Brussels mentioned by L. Zunz, *Zur Geschichte und Literatur*, Berlin 1845, p. 244, is Eliakim *Carmoly (Steinschneider, *Vorlesungen*, p. 59 [Hebrew, p. 79]).

Brussels, Bibliothèque royale (Koninklijke Bibliotheek van België)
Seven Hebrew MSS are listed in J. Van den Gheyn, *Catalogue des manuscrits de la Bibliothèque Royale de Belgique*, I, Brussels 1901: nos. 80–83, 217, 875 and 884. Sixteen MSS and fragments are listed in *Cat. Allony–Kupfer*, II, pp. 16–17. The call-numbers are listed at the end of the entries in parentheses and the Van den Gheyn catalogue numbers are added whenever they are relevant. The numbers 1–16 and 16–1מ are serial numbers of the catalogue. The number at the left of each entry with the prefix ס is the microfilm number at the *Jerusalem, IMHM. Four new acquisitions, IV 213, IV 526, IV 9444 (section 8) and IV 1170, were not listed in either of the catalogues. The call-numbers of MSS acquired before 1870 bear no prefix, those acquired between 1870 and 1950 bear the prefix II, and medieval and Oriental MSS acquired after 1950 bear the prefix IV.

Bry, Michel de
Paris, 1932–; art dealer
The illuminated psalter formerly in de Bry's possession was acquired by Jacob Michael of New York and sold at Sotheby's auction in 1981 to Michael J. Floersheim of Zurich (1938–1992).
G. Sed-Rajna, 'Le Psautier De Bry, manuscrit enluminé', *REJ*, CXXIV (1965), pp. 375–388.

BSB
Munich, Bayerische Staatsbibliothek

Buber, Solomon
Lemberg (Lviv), Ukraine, 1827–1906; scholar
The MS of *Midrash Lekaḥ tov* that Buber used in his edition (מדרש לקח טוב, ווילנא תרמ״ד), called MS Jerusalem, is now *Oxford, Bodleian Library, MS Heb. d. 53 (Cat. 2636). The MS used in his edition of *Midrash agada* (מדרש אגדה, וינה תרנ״ד) is now *Oxford, Bodleian Library, MS Heb. c. 22 (Cat. 2641).

Buchanan, Claudius
Cambuslang, Scotland, 1766 – Cheshunt, England, 1815
Scottish-born Christian minister who served as a chaplain in India from 1796–1808. In 1809 Buchanan presented about 100 Hebrew MSS that he had acquired in India to *Cambridge, University Library. S. Schechter described 23 of these MSS in *JQR*, VI (1893/4), pp. 136–145.
Rab., *Lit. Treas.*, p. 48; C. Buchanan, *Christian Researches*, Cambridge 1811, pp. 312ff; Reif, *Cat. Cambridge*, pp. 20–21.

Budapest (Hungary), Magyar Nemzeti Múzeum (Hungarian National Museum)
See *Budapest, Orsźagos Széchényi Könyvtár (National Szechenyi Library).

Budapest (Hungary), Magyar Tudományos Akadémia, Könyvtár (Hungarian Academy of Sciences Library)
The library's collection of Hebrew MSS is based on the library of David *Kaufmann, which was presented to the Academy by Kaufmann's widow. The Kaufmann collection includes 591 MSS and about 650 *Geniza fragments. The MSS are described in Weisz, *Cat. Kaufmann* (1906). The call-numbers in the Academy library consist of the catalogue numbers preceded by the prefix 'A'. The descriptions of the MSS are generally brief, with the exception of the responsa MSS and some others, which are described in great detail. Palaeographical and codicological information: size (2°, 4°, 8°), writing material, type of script, number of pages and date (of dated MSS only). Colophons are copied. Indexes: author and title. G. Jare added bibliographical notes on the catalogue in *Rivista Israelitica*, III (1906), pp. 76–78. The Academy published a *Microcard Catalogue of the Rare Hebrew Codices, Manuscripts and Ancient Prints in the Kaufmann Collection Reproduced on Microcards*, Budapest 1959, in which a selection of MSS offered for sale on microfiche are briefly described.

GENIZA According to the printed catalogues, the collection included 544 Geniza fragments in three boxes (nos. 592–594 in the catalogues); but according to Loewinger, *Report*, p. ix, the fragments numbered about 700. Forty fragments, mainly magical texts, on loan to Prof. Goldziher were lost during World War II (*ibid.*). The surviving fragments number approximately 650. According to *Cat. Kaufmann*, no. 592 included fragments in Judaeo-Arabic, and nos. 593–594, fragments in Hebrew. According to S. Widder, the fragments were stored in the three boxes in no particular order. He rearranged the Hebrew fragments and divided them into two groups: no. 593 – liturgical and secular poetry, and no. 594 – other Hebrew fragments. He published a catalogue of the poetry and liturgical fragments (ש׳ וידר, ׳רשימת הפיוטים והשירים בין כתבי הגניזה בספרית דוד קויפמאן שבאקדמיה המדעית ההונגארית בבודאפשט׳, in S. Scheiber [ed.], *Semitic Studies in Memory of Immanuel Löw*, Budapest 1947, Hebrew section, pp. 15–113) and assigned the fragments new numbers. M. Zulay added notes and additions (גנזי קויפמן, בודפשט תש״ט, עמ׳ 93–107); and S. Scheiber published poems newly discovered among the fragments (׳קרובות לחול׳, תרביץ, כב [תשי״א], עמ׳ 167–173). O. Komlós published a list of Targum fragments (י׳ קומלוש, ׳רשימת התרגומים של גנזי קויפמן׳, סיני, לא [תשי״ב], עמ׳ 237–240). Later, all the fragments were given new numbers. Both Widder's numbers (1–131) and the new numbers (43–182) are marked on the poetry fragments, the lower one in each case being Widder's.

S. Scheiber, 'The Kaufmann Genizah: Its importance for the world of scholarship', in E. Apor (ed.), *Jubilee Volume of the Oriental Collection*, Budapest 1978, pp. 175–188; *David Kaufmann Memorial Volume*, Budapest 2002; Bezalel Narkiss and Gabrielle Sed-Rajna, *Index of Jewish Art: Iconographical Index of Hebrew Illuminated Manuscripts*, IV: *Illustrated Manuscripts of the Kaufmann Collection at the Library of the Hungarian Academy of Sciences*, Jerusalem–Paris–Budapest 1988.

Budapest (Hungary), Orsźagos Magyar Zsidó Múzeum (Jewish Museum)
Over 20 illuminated MSS were described by S. Scheiber in I. Benoschofsky and S. Scheiber, *A Budapesti Zsidó Múzeum*, Budapest 1987, pp. 184–219. According to Scheiber, 'The fate of Jewish libraries and Jewish books in Hungary under Nazi occupation' (א׳ שייבר, ׳גורל ספריות וספרים יהודיים בהונגריה בזמן הכיבוש הנאצי׳, יד לקורא, א [תש״ז], עמ׳ 251), most of

the MSS in the Museum before World War II were destroyed or looted during the war.

Budapest (Hungary), Országos Rabbiképző – Zsidó Egyetem Könyvtár (Jewish Theological Seminary – University of Jewish Studies)

The library formerly possessed over 300 MSS, but today the collection numbers less than 250. Recently, many MSS from the library have been offered for sale anonymously at various auctions and other venues. Ten MSS were described by D. S. Loewinger ('כתבי־יד שבספרית בית המדרש לרבנים בבודפשט', *Magyar Zsidó Szemle*, LVII [1940], Hebrew section, pp. 28–51). E. Róth described a number of Talmud Geniza fragments formerly in the library (אנ"צ רות, 'כתבי־יד לתלמוד בבלי בהונגריה', ק"ס, לא [תשט"ז], עמ' 474–472).

Budapest (Hungary), Orsźagos Széchényi Könyvtár (National Szechenyi Library)

The library was founded in 1802, and from 1808 to 1949 the Magyar Nemzeti Múzeum (Hungarian National Museum) was part of the same institution. In 1949, the National Library was separated from the Museum, and in 1985 it was moved to separate quarters in the Buda Castle Palace. The library has 21 Hebrew MSS and scrolls; twelve of the MSS were described by S. Kohn, 'Die hebräischen Handschriften des ungarischen Nationalmuseums zu Budapest', *MWJ*, IV (1876), pp. 76–104. MSS Fol. Hebr. 1, 4, 5, 6 and Qu. Hebr. 3 and 4 were purchased from the Hungarian collector Miklós (Nikolaus) *Jankovich (1773–1846) in the 1830s (L. Mravic, *The Hungarian Quarterly*, XLIV, no. 169, 2003).

Busani, Shelomo

Sanaa, Yemen – Tel Aviv, first half of the twentieth century

*New York, JTSA, acquired Busani's MSS, including his MS of the commentary on the Mishna by Nathan Av Hayeshiva (MS R1492).

Marx, *Proceedings*, p. 136; ש' אסף, 'פירוש ששה סדרי משנה לרבינו נתן אב הישיבה', ק"ס, י (תרצ"ג–תרצ"ד), עמ' 381.

Butler Library

See *New York, Columbia University.

C

C

(1) Cambridge; (2) Cincinnati.

Cabilda Toledano

See *Toledo, Archivo y Biblioteca Capitulares.

Caen (France), Bibliothèque municipale

Two MSS written by Christian Hebraists are described in *Catalogue général*, XIV (1890), nos. 185 and 199. One of these was also described by M. Schwab, 'Manuscrits hébreux en France', *REJ*, LX (1910), pp. 98–105. A third MS, an eighteenth-century maḥzor, has been microfilmed for the *Jerusalem, IMHM.

Cagliari, Biblioteca Universitaria

Two Hebrew MSS from the private collection of Giovanni Spano (1803–1878), have recently been discovered in the library.

M. Perani, 'Giovanni Spano e gli ebrei in Sardegna: I manoscritti ebraici della Biblioteca Universitaria di Cagliari', in *Gli ebrei in Sardegna nel contesto Mediterraneo: La riflessione storiografica da Giovanni Spano ad oggi* (Proceedings of the Congress of Cagliari, 17–20 November 2008), Florence 2009.

Cahen, [Samuel]
France, 1796–1862; Hebraist
MS Cahen, a collection of Karaite works mentioned by S. Munk in *Mélanges de philosophie juive et arabe*, Paris 1859, p. 476, is now *Paris, BnF, MS héb. 670.
HÜ, p. 452, no. 580.

Cairo
See (1) *Geniza; (2) *Mosseri, Jacques Nissim.

Cairo Codex
See *Ben Asher Codex.

Cairo, RaDBaZ (רדב"ז) Synagogue
The MS formerly in this synagogue, described by R. J. H. Gottheil, 'Some Hebrew Mss. in Cairo', *JQR*, XVII (1904/5), pp. 618–619, no. 2, is now *Jerusalem, NLI, Heb. 4° 1112.

Caluso
See *Valperga di Caluso, Tommaso.

Camb.
Cambridge.

Cambrai (France), Bibliothèque municipale
One Hebrew MS, a prayerbook, is listed in *Catalogue général*, XVII (1891), no. 946, and is more fully described by M. Schwab, 'Un Rituel hébreu manuscrit à Cambrai', *REJ*, XXV (1892), pp. 250–254.

Cambridge (England), College Libraries
Sizeable collections of Hebrew MSS in Cambridge colleges outside the University Library are found only in *Cambridge, Trinity College, *Cambridge, Girton College, and *Cambridge, Westminster College (mainly *Geniza fragments, jointly purchased in 2013 by *Cambridge University Library, and *Oxford, Bodleian Library). Small collections are found in the following colleges: *Cambridge, St. John's College (7 MSS), Emmanuel (1 MS), Gonville and Caius (2 MSS), Christ College (1 MS) and Pembroke (1 MS). The Hebrew MSS are listed in M. R. James's catalogues of these libraries.
נ' אלוני, 'גניזה וכתבי־יד עבריים בספריות קמברידג'', ארשת, ג (תשכ"א), עמ' 395–407; Pearson, pp. 58–59.

Cambridge (England), Girton College
A collection of MSS, mostly Samaritan, was bequeathed to the library by Mary E. I. *Frere. About fifty MSS were described by H. Loewe, *Catalogue of the Printed Books and of the Semitic and Jewish Mss. in the Mary Frere Hebrew Library at Girton College, Cambridge*, Cambridge [1916].
Rab., *Treas. Jud.*, pp. 173–175; נ' אלוני, 'גניזה וכתבי־יד עבריים בספריות קמברידג'', ארשת, ג (תשכ"א), עמ' 396–398.

Cambridge, Lewis–Gibson
See *Lewis–Gibson.

Cambridge Medical Miscellany
Name given to *Cambridge, UL, MS Dd.10.68, an illuminated medical MS written in Italy in the fifteenth century.
Narkiss, p. 142.

Cambridge (England), St. John's College
The Library has seven Hebrew MSS. Four Hebrew MSS were described by M. Cowie, *A Descriptive Catalogue of the Manuscripts and Scarce Books in the Library of St. John's College, Cambridge*, Cambridge 1843, pp. 1 and 89.

Cambridge (England), Trinity College
Trinity College was founded in 1546 when two older institutions merged. A large part of the old collection of MSS belonged to Gerbrandt *Anslo of Amsterdam and was acquired by Dr. Thomas *Gale (1635–1702),

who presented it, in 1679, to Trinity College. Thomas Hyde, to whom the MSS were submitted, compiled a brief list of the MSS, which is still preserved in the Trinity College Library. Thirty MSS from the old collection, including six in English and Latin and four Samaritan MSS, were described by W. A. Wright and S. M. Schiller-Szinessy in their appendix to the catalogue edited by E. H. Palmer, *A Descriptive Catalogue of the Arabic, Persian and Turkish Manuscripts in the Library of Trinity College, Cambridge ... with an Appendix Containing a Catalogue of the Hebrew and Samaritan MSS. in the Same Library*, Cambridge 1870, pp. 209–235. In this catalogue, the call-numbers are printed at the head of each entry. H. Loewe, *Catalogue of the Manuscripts in the Hebrew Character Collected and Bequeathed to Trinity College Library by the Late William Aldis Wright*, Cambridge 1926, describes 158 additional MSS (and one printed book) bequeathed to the library by W. A. *Wright. Most of the MSS in the Wright collection came from the libraries of Christian *Ginsburg and William Mead *Black. The catalogue is arranged by subject. Preceding each entry is the catalogue serial number. Call-numbers are not listed in the catalogue. Palaeographical and codicological information: writing material, size, number of leaves, date and type of script. Owners' and censors' entries are copied. Indexes: authors and translators, titles (in Latin transliteration or English translation), titles in Hebrew, scribes, owners, etc., place names in English and Hebrew, dated MSS, watermarks, censors, languages and general subject indexes in Hebrew and English. The English language indexes should be consulted first, as they are more complete than the Hebrew ones.

נ' אלוני, 'גניזה וכתבי־יד עבריים בספריות קמברידג'', ארשת, ג (תשכ"א), עמ' 400–401; Rab., *Treas. Jud.*, pp. 180–187.

Cambridge, UL
*Cambridge (England), University Library.

Cambridge (England), University Library
More than a thousand Hebrew MSS and almost 140,000 *Geniza fragments are found in the Cambridge University Library. With the exception of the Taylor–Schechter Geniza collection (see 'Geniza' in this entry, below), the library acquired its MSS individually or in small collections over a long span of time. It was never enriched by gift or purchase of a large collection of MSS such as the *Oppenheim or *Michael collections, which doubled the number of Hebrew MSS in *Oxford, Bodleian Library, upon their acquisition in the early nineteenth century. A small number of MSS may have reached Cambridge before the emergence of the University Library early in the fifteenth century. A considerable number came from the collections of Christian Hebraists such as Thomas von *Erpe and Claudius *Buchanan; others were acquired between the seventeenth and nineteenth centuries. In the nineteenth century a large number of MSS were purchased from Jewish booksellers such as Hirsch *Lipschütz and Samuel *Schönblum. Many of these MSS derive from the libraries of Jewish scholars (Marco *Mortara, Samuel *Luzzatto, etc.). For further details concerning provenances, see the Index, s.v. Cambridge, University Library.
CALL-NUMBERS In the eighteenth century the Cambridge MSS were all given new call-numbers. These new numbers were assigned to the MSS without any meaningful method or system and without regard to language, size or subject. The 'new' call-numbers bear the prefixes 'Dd.', 'Ee.', etc., up to 'Oo.', but these tell us nothing about the MSS except that they were already in the library in the eighteenth century. In the nineteenth century MSS were given call-numbers with the prefix 'Add.' (Additional), which were assigned

in sequence. Thus MSS acquired earlier bear lower numbers than those acquired later. All Hebrew MSS acquired after 1903 were assigned call-numbers bearing the prefix 'Or.' (Oriental), which were also assigned in sequence, and today the call-numbers of all new Hebrew MSS receive this prefix.

CATALOGUES The first catalogue to appear in print is S. M. Schiller-Szinessy, *Catalogue of the Hebrew Manuscripts Preserved in the University Library*, Cambridge 1876 (reprint: Kessinger Publishing, 2004), comprising Section 1, 'The Holy Scriptures', and Section 2, 'Commentaries on the Bible'. A Hebrew title-page bears the title בניות ברמה. Seventy-two biblical MSS, including commentaries on the Bible, are described in the catalogue. The MSS are described in great detail, with copious notes on the contents, and comparisons with other MSS in Cambridge and other libraries. Each entry is preceded by the catalogue serial number. Call-numbers ('library marks') are listed in square brackets at the end of the entries.

Palaeographical and codicological information: writing material, size (in inches), number of leaves, number of leaves in each quire, number of lines per page, type of script and date. All colophons as well as owners' and censors' entries are copied, and there are notes concerning provenance. There are no concordances to call-numbers; these were reserved for the continuation of the catalogue, which never appeared. Schiller-Szinessy prepared an additional volume of the catalogue, a description of the talmudic MSS, of which 26 sheets (nos. 73–98) were printed but never published. Schiller-Szinessy left in manuscript very detailed descriptions of 495 more MSS. Herbert Loewe described MSS on cards during the first two decades of the twentieth century, and James Pearson and Raphael Loewe continued his work; by 1956 a typewritten version, *Handlist of Hebrew and Samaritan Manuscripts in the Library of the University of Cambridge*, was completed. Between 1965 and 1973, J. Leveen prepared a handwritten catalogue of the entire collection of Hebrew (and some Judaic) MSS, with the exception of the Taylor–Schechter collection.

Making use of all the previous cataloguing efforts, and with the assistance of scholars in Cambridge and Israel and the cooperation of the *Jerusalem, IMHM, and the *Hebrew Palaeography Project, Stefan C. Reif prepared a new printed catalogue, *Hebrew Manuscripts at Cambridge University Library* (= Reif, *Cat. Cambridge*, 1997). The catalogue has 1066 entries, including brief listings of Samaritana (nos. 980–999) and 'Other material relating to Hebraica and Judaica' (nos. 1000–1066), but it does not include *Geniza fragments from the Taylor–Schechter collections. The descriptions of the MSS are preceded on pp. 1–35 by the editor's essay, 'Hebrew and Hebraists at Cambridge: An historical introduction'. The catalogue is arranged by subject matter, with divisions into 23 main sections and numerous subsections. Each description is headed by the Cambridge University Library class-mark in bold print. A catalogue serial number, preceded by 'SCR', is printed at the end of each entry together with the numbers in Schiller-Szinessy's unpublished descriptions (SSN), catalogues (SS1 and SS2), and the unpublished *Handlist* (HL). The physical description preceding the description of the contents includes details about the material, size, number of folios or pages, number of columns if greater than one, number of lines, condition, script and date (determined with the assistance of Edna Engel of the *Hebrew Palaeography Project), and bindings of the MS. Languages, when Hebrew is not exclusively employed, are listed, as are indications of illuminations and autographs. The names of scribes, owners and censors are provided, as are details concerning provenance and date of acquisition. Bibliographical notes relating directly to the manuscripts are often included. Indexes: titles, biblical and talmudic sources and prayers; names of authors and translators, owners, scribes and censors; general index; list of dated MSS; and tables or concordances to class-marks. The catalogue includes 32 black-and-white plates.

For catalogues of the Geniza collection see below.

GENIZA Cambridge University Library owns a number of collections of fragments originating in the Cairo *Geniza. G. Chester presented to the library a number of fragments he had purchased in Cairo in the early 1890s. During the years 1893–1896 about 100 fragments were purchased from Solomon *Wertheimer. All these fragments were placed in the Additional collection (MSS Add. 3335–3388). The University collection (MSS Or. 1080–1081) consists of about 1,000 fragments purchased from Samuel *Raffalovich. This collection is stored in 34 binders, each designated by a numeral or letter (e.g, Or. 1080, 1; Or. 1080 A). There are also a few Geniza fragments in the Israel *Abrahams collection. The largest and most important collection of Geniza fragments in the library is the Taylor–Schechter collection (abbreviation: T–S). Much has already been written about this collection (see below and see also *Geniza). In December 1896, with the support of Charles *Taylor of Cambridge, Solomon *Schechter undertook an expedition to Cairo. He extracted from the geniza, or depository, of the so-called Ben Ezra Synagogue (and possibly from elsewhere as well) thousands of fragments of ancient Hebrew MSS. After the arrival of the collection in Cambridge, some 1,900 'important' fragments were placed between glass – the so-called 'glass' fragments – and about 27,000 other fragments were either mounted on paper and bound into volumes or placed in folders and stored in boxes. All these fragments form the 'Old Series' (T–S). Over 40,000 fragments considered to be of lesser importance, sorted in crates and made available only in the 1950s, are called the New Series (class-mark T–S NS). The 68,000 fragments remaining after the classification of the New Series was completed were classified and restored in the 1970s and designated the Additional Series (T–S AS). In 2013, the library, jointly with *Oxford, Bodleian Library, purchased the *Cambridge, Westminster College collection of Geniza fragments.

CALL-NUMBERS (CLASS-MARKS) OF THE TAYLOR–SCHECHTER COLLECTION Fragments from a single MS bound or gathered together are generally designated by a single class-mark. Fragments under glass were given class-marks consisting of two components: a number designating the fragment size (in inches) and a serial number assigned to fragments from the same MS (e.g., T–S 12.25, T–S 32.1). Fragments in bound volumes bear class-marks consisting of four components: a number designating the size of the fragments (in inches); a capital letter designating subject matter (A = Bible, B = Translations, C = Midrash and biblical commentaries, D = Massora, E = Mishna, F = Talmud, G = Responsa, H = Poetry, J = Documents and history, K = Miscellaneous); the box number; and an individual fragment number. A lower-case 'a' added to the capital letter signifies Arabic or Judaeo-Arabic texts. For example, 'T–S 6 Ja 1.2' refers to the second fragment in Vol. I of the bound volumes of fragments of documentary material in Arabic up to six inches in size. Fragments in boxes bear class-marks consisting of a capital letter (subject); the box number; and a fragment number (e.g., T–S E 4.1). In addition to the general subject classification (A, B, C, etc.), there is a secondary classification system for the boxes, with each box containing specific subject matter. For example, the box marked 'E 1' contains mostly vocalized Mishna fragments; box E 2 contains unvocalized Mishna fragments, and so forth. The Old Series also includes Arabic boxes containing fragments in Arabic and Judaeo-Arabic, arranged in 54 boxes according to subject matter, and 36 Miscellaneous Boxes (T–S Misc.), containing mainly biblical, talmudic and printed fragments. T–S Misc. 35–36 are also called T–S Loan (see *Loan). The fragments in the New Series (T–S NS) are stored in 342 boxes arranged according to subject, and those in the Additional Series, mostly small and minuscule fragments, in 225 boxes. In 1973, S. C. Reif, director of the Taylor–Schechter Genizah Research Unit, published a brief *Guide to the Taylor–Schechter Genizah Collection* (mostly reproduced on the collection's web page: http://www.lib.cam.ac.uk/Taylor-Schechter/guide.html), presenting a historical survey of the collection and an explanation of the class-marks, including a list of the subject classifications of the boxes, bound volumes, Arabic boxes and the New Series.

There is no complete catalogue of the Cambridge Geniza collections. Parts of the collections are described in S.C. Reif (ed.), *Cambridge University Library Genizah Series*, Cambridge 1978–2006, as follows:

No. 1: S. C. Reif, *The Cambridge Genizah Collections: Their Contents and Significance* (2002).

No. 2: *Hebrew Bible Manuscripts in the Cambridge Genizah Collections*, Part I: M.C. Davis, *Taylor–Schechter Old Series and Other Genizah Collections in the Cambridge University Library*, incorporating material compiled by H. Knopf (1978); Part 2: M. C. Davis, *Taylor–Schechter New Series and Westminster College Cambridge Collection* (1980); Part 3: M. C. Davis and Ben Outhwaite, *Taylor–Schechter Additional Series 1–31* (2003); and Part 4: eidem, *Taylor–Schechter Additional Series 32–255*, with Addenda to previous volumes (2003).

No. 3: Simon Hopkins, *A Miscellany of Literary Pieces from the Cambridge Genizah Collections* (1978), including facsimiles and descriptions of the MSS in box T–S A45, transcriptions, and English translation of selected texts.

No. 4: S. Morag, *Vocalised Talmudic Manuscripts in the Cambridge Genizah Collections*, I: *Taylor–Schechter Old Series* (1988).

No. 5: Robert Brody and Ernest J. Wiesenberg, *Post-Talmudic Rabbinic Manuscripts in the Cambridge Genizah Collections*, I: *Taylor–Schechter New Series* (1998).

No. 6: Stefan C. Reif et al., *Published Material from Cambridge Geniza Collections: A Bibliography 1896–1980* (1989), listing publications of Cambridge Geniza fragments in books and journals.

No. 7: Joseph Yahalom, *Palestinian Vocalised Piyyut Manuscripts in the Cambridge Genizah Collections* (1997).

No. 8: Michael L. Klein, *Targumic Manuscripts in the Cambridge Genizah Collections* (1992).

No. 9: G. Khan, *Karaite Bible Manuscripts from the Cairo Genizah* (1990).

No. 10: idem, *Arabic Legal and Administrative Documents in the Cambridge Genizah Collections* (1993), including transcriptions and English translations of the 159 documents.

No. 11: Haskell D. Isaacs and Colin F. Baker, *Medical and Para-Medical Manuscripts in the Cambridge Genizah Collections* (1994).

No. 12: C. F. Baker and Meira R. P. Polliack, *Arabic and Judaeo-Arabic Manuscripts in the Cambridge Genizah Collections: Arabic Old Series (T–S Ar.1a–54)* (2001).

No. 13: Rebecca J. E. Jefferson and Erica C. D. Hunter, *Published Material from the Cambridge Genizah Collections: A Bibliography 1980–1997* (2004).

No. 14: Avihai Shivtiel and Friederich Niessen, *Arabic and Judaeo-Arabic Manuscripts in the Cambridge Genizah Collections* (2006).

Most of the catalogues include brief descriptions of the texts and codicological details (material, size, physical state), but no conjectures regarding type of script or date, except for nos. 9, 10 and 12, which do identify the scripts. The descriptions of the vocalized talmudic MSS in no. 4, the Palestinian vocalized *piyyut* MSS in no. 7, and the Karaite Bible MSS in no. 9 are more detailed.

In addition to the published catalogues, a handwritten *Class Catalogue* of fragments under glass and bound volumes, compiled by E. J. Wormann at the turn of the twentieth century, is available to readers at the library. It includes very brief descriptions of the fragments and a partial bibliography of the published fragments. Catalogues of the *piyyut* and poetry fragments and of the Mishna and Talmud fragments are being prepared in cooperation with the Israel Academy of Sciences and Humanities. The *Friedberg Geniza Project is also preparing an on-line comprehensive catalogue of all the texts and is providing digital images of all the fragments.

נ' אלוני, 'גניזה וכתבי־יד עבריים בספריות קמברידג'', ארשת, ג (תשכ"א), עמ' 423–408; Rab., *Lit. Treas.*, pp. 38–51; S. C. Reif, *Guide to the Taylor–Schechter Genizah Collection*, Cambridge 1973; idem, 'Hebrew collections in Cambridge University Library', in D. Rowland Smith and S. P. Salinger (eds.), *Hebrew Studies*, London 1991, pp. 26–34; idem, *Jewish Archive*.

Cambridge (England), Westminster College

The college possessed a collection of over 2,000 *Geniza fragments presented by the *Lewis–Gibson sisters, now bound in fifteen volumes. When the College realized that it could no longer preserve the collection, it was offered for sale to *Cambridge, UL, and in 2013 the Cambridge, University Library, and *Oxford, Bodleian Library decided to purchase the collection jointly and rename it the Lewis–Gibson Collection. Forty of the most important fragments are kept under glass. The biblical fragments were described by M. C. Davis, *Taylor–Schechter New Series and Westminster College Cambridge Collection*, Cambridge 1980, pp. 373–414. Other fragments were described in some of the other volumes of the *Cambridge University Library Genizah Series*. A new catalogue of the entire collection was prepared in Hebrew by Elazar Hurvitz, *Catalogue of the Cairo Geniza Fragments in the Westminster College Library, Cambridge* (קטלוג קטעי גניזת קאהיר בספריית ווסטמינסטר קולג', קיימברידג'), I–II, New York 2006, released in 2009. Volume I is *A Historical Introduction to the Antiquity and Discovery of the Geniza from Cairo*. The fragments are described in volume II. A third volume, including copies of selected texts from the collection, is in preparation. The descriptions include title, author, description of the text with incipits and explicits, number of folios, material, number of lines and size. No attempt was made to date the fragments or to identify the type of script. There are indexes to Bible passages and different types of Bibles, etc.; Talmud, midrash and *halakha*; works in Judaeo-Arabic; *piyyut* and liturgy; documents and letters (including place names); varia (including languages, etc.); and names of authors, poets and persons mentioned. A Hebrew MS and a Samaritan MS presented to the library in 1899 by the Lewis–Gibson sisters were sold at Sotheby's in London and listed in the auction catalogue *Western Manuscripts and Miniatures, London, Friday, June 29, 2007*, nos. 31 and 32. Cambridge, University Library, and Oxford, Bodleian, are planning eventually to split the collection between the two libraries.

נ' אלוני, 'גניזה וכתבי־יד עבריים בספריות קמברידג'', ארשת, ג (תשכ"א), עמ' 400–398; Rab., *Treas. Jud.*, pp. 188–194.

Cambridge (Mass.), Harvard University

The Harvard College Library possesses 118 Hebrew MSS, as well as about 400 notebooks of nineteenth- and twentieth-century Yiddish plays and literature, songs, and correspondence and manuscript material in the archives of Yiddish scholars. Twenty-three MSS came with the Ephraim *Deinard collection, which was acquired in 1930, and 30 came with the Felix *Friedmann collection, acquired in 1951. Other MSS derive from the collections of the *Vienna, Israelitisch-theologische Lehranstalt (3 MSS), Adolf *Jellinek (2 MSS), Osias *Schorr (2 MSS), and Eliakim *Carmoly (1 MS). MSS 1–107 are briefly described in M. Glatzer, *Hebrew Manuscripts in the Houghton Library of the Harvard College Library: A Catalogue*, ed. Charles Berlin and Rodney Gove Dennis, Cambridge 1975. Palaeographical and codicological information: writing material, date, type of script, number of leaves or pages, size and provenance. Indexes: subject, titles, authors, owners, scribes, persons mentioned, languages, dated MSS and selected geographical names.

Rab., *Lit. Treas.*, pp. 137–140; C. Berlin, *Harvard Judaica: A History and Description of the Judaica Collection in the Harvard College Library*, Cambridge, Mass. 2004.

Campori, Giuseppe

Modena, Italy, 1821–1887; art historian

Campori bequeathed his library to *Modena, Biblioteca Estense. Six Hebrew MSS were listed in the catalogue of his collection, L. Lodi, *Catalogo dei Codici e degli Autografi Posseduti dal Marchese Giuseppe Campori*, Modena 1875. In the *Appendici* compiled by R. Vandini (Modena 1886–1894) another 15 MSS are listed. Only 19 Hebrew MSS from the Campori collection, however, were listed in *Cat. Bernheimer*, Modena. It is possible that the two missing MSS are in the Biblioteca Comunale in Modena or that they are bound together with other MSS.

Fumagalli, p. 63; *Cat. Bernheimer*, Modena, p. xiii.

Can. Misc.

See *Canonici, Matteo Luigi.

Can. Or.

See *Canonici, Matteo Luigi.

Canonic.

See *Canonici, Matteo Luigi.

Canonici, Matteo Luigi

Venice, 1727–1805; Jesuit scholar

Canonici's collections, including 110 Hebrew MSS, passed to his brother Giuseppe, and on his death in 1807 to Giovanni Perissinotti and Girolamo Cardina, who divided them. To the former fell the MSS, then about 3,550 in number, and, after many attempts by him to sell them, the *Oxford, Bodleian Library, purchased the greater part in 1817. MSS from Canonici's collection bear call-numbers with the prefixes 'Can. Or.' and 'Can. Misc.'. A list of these MSS and their numbers in *Cat. Neubauer* is found on pp. xxiv–xxv of the catalogue.

Rab., *Lit. Treas.*, p. 32; Tamani, *Venezia*, p. 250.

Cantabrigia

Latin name for Cambridge.

Cape Town, National Library of South Africa

Two Hebrew Bibles from Spain are included in the Sir George Grey collection, presented in 1861 to the South African Library (incorporated in 1999 into the National Library of South Africa). These MSS were described in Carol Steyn, *The Medieval and Renaissance Manuscripts in the Grey Collection of the National Library of South Africa, Cape Town*, II, Salzburg 2002, MSS 6.b.i and 48.b.2, and previously by P. E. Westra, *The Medieval and Renaissance Manuscripts in the Grey Collection: A Preliminary Catalogue*, Cape Town 1984. One of the MSS, 48.b.2, had been in the possession of Guglielmo Libri and was sold by Sotheby and Wilkinson in 1849, shortly after Libri arrived in England.

Carmoly, Eliakim [Goschel Baer]

Sulz, France, 1802 – Frankfurt a/M, Germany, 1875; scholar

Carmoly owned several hundred MSS during his lifetime; 285 of them are listed in the catalogue of his estate, *Catalog der reichhaltigen Sammlung hebräischer und jüdischer Bücher und Handschriften aus dem Nachlass des Seel. Herrn Dr. G. B. Carmoly*, Frankfurt a/M 1875. The catalogue numbers are not identical with the numbers quoted by Carmoly in his writings. The MSS are now found in various libraries. At least fifty MSS were purchased by Abraham *Merzbacher (and are now in *Frankfurt a/M, Goethe Universität, Universitätsbibliothek) and many of the remainder by Baron David *Günzburg, *Cambridge, University Library, and others. For the present locations of most of the MSS in the 1875 catalogue, see Appendix I, no. 6. A number of MSS of Carmoly's own writings, mainly biographical, are in *New York, JTSA. Carmoly's MSS of *Eldad Hadani* and of the travels of Petahiah of Regensburg, from which he published editions, are now in *Strasbourg, Bibliothèque nationale et universitaire, MSS 3981 and 3982; and his MS described by R. Kirchheim, 'Über einige seltene Schriften in der Bibliothek des Herrn Dr. Carmoly', *MGWJ*, IV (1855), pp. 104–108, is now *London, BL, Or. 1389.

Carpentras (France), Bibliothèque Inguimbertine

The library owns thirty Hebrew MSS. Five Hebrew MSS are described in *Catalogue général*, XXXIV (1901), nos. 4, 5, 48, 349 and 1008. Eleven additional MSS are described in the *Supplements* to the *Catalogue général*, LVIII (1971), nos. 2250, 2252, 2254, 2608–2612, 2626, 2627, 2636. In 1963, the library of a local Jewish family, including six Hebrew MSS, was donated to the Bibliothèque Inguimbertine. In 2006 the library acquired a seventeenth-century *ketuba*.

Cas., Casanatense

Casanatense. See *Rome, Biblioteca Casanatense.

Casanatense Haggada

Name given to *Rome, Biblioteca Casanatense, Cod. 2761, an illuminated haggada.

Cassuto, Alfonso

Hamburg, Germany, 1910 – Lisbon, Portugal, 1999

The Cassuto collection, which included over sixty MSS in Hebrew, Spanish and Portuguese, was founded by Jehuda de Mordechai Cassuto (Amsterdam, 1808 – Hamburg, 1893). His great-grandson, Alfonso, sold part of the collection to *Amsterdam, Universiteitsbibliotheek, in 1975. Fifty-eight MSS in Portuguese and Spanish acquired by that library were described by Margreet H. Mirande-de Boer, 'An inventory of undescribed Portuguese and Spanish manuscripts in the Bibliotheca Rosenthaliana', *Studia Rosenthaliana*, XX (1986), pp. 176–190. Other parts of the collection were offered for sale by Kestenbaum and Company in New York in 2011 and were described in the auction catalogues *Catalogue of Fine Judaica* ... February 24th, 2011, and June 23rd, 2011.

A. Offenberg, 'The Cassuto Collection', *Studia Rosenthaliana*, XXXIV (2000), pp. 93–94.

Cassuto, Umberto

Florence, Italy, 1883 – Jerusalem, 1951; rabbi and scholar

Cassuto compiled a catalogue of the *Vatican MSS (Cods. ebr. 1–115), *Bibliothecae Apostolicae Vaticanae Codices Manuscripti*

Recensiti, Codices Vaticani Hebraici, Codices 1–115, Vatican 1956; studies on the history of the collection (See *Vatican); and notices on MSS in *Florence, Biblioteca Nazionale Centrale.

Castelbolognesi, Gustavo

Milan, Italy, nineteenth–twentieth cent.; rabbi

Castelbolognesi's MS of Solomon b. Hayatom's commentary to TB *Mo'ed katan*, from which H. P. Chajes published his edition (Berlin 1910), was purchased by Elkan Nathan *Adler and is now *New York, JTSA, MS R840 (ENA 2553).

Castro, Henriques de David

See *Henriques de Castro, David.

de Castro Pentateuch

See *Henriques de Castro, David.

Cat.

Catalogue. References in this *Guide* are alphabetized according to the following word.

Catalan Maḥzor

Name given to a fourteenth-century Spanish maḥzor decorated with micrographic panels, formerly in the *Berlin, Hochschule für die Wissenschaft des Judentums. It was described in Sotheby's catalogue *Highly Important Hebrew Printed Books and Manuscripts*, New York 1984, no. 47, and is now *Jerusalem, NLI, Heb. 8° 6527.

Books from Sefarad, Jerusalem 1992, pp. 60–67.

Cento (Italy)

The MS belonging to the Levi family in Cento described by de Rossi, *ext.*, no. 83, is now Genoa, Biblioteca Universitaria, MS D. IX. 31.

Cervera Bible

Name given to Lisbon, Biblioteca Nacional, MS 72, a fourteenth-century illuminated Bible written in Cervera, Spain, 1299/1300.

Narkiss, p. 52.

Cesena (Italy), Biblioteca Malatestiana

Seven MSS were described by A. Luzzatto in 'I manoscritti ebraici della Biblioteca Malatestiana di Cesena', *La Bibliofilia*, LXX (1968), pp. 197–216.

Fumagalli, 'Emilia-Romagna', pp. 98–99.

Chamizer, Moritz (Mordecai)

Leipzig, Germany – Haifa, Israel, nineteenth–twentieth cent.

His library was sold to the booksellers *Bamberger and Wahrmann. 226 marriage contracts were acquired from his estate by *Jerusalem, JNUL (now NLI), in 1945, and 37 MSS from his collection were acquired from Bamberger and Wahrmann by the JNUL in 1959 (MSS Heb. 4° 934–941; 8° 3302–3330).

א"מ הברמן, אנשי ספר ואנשי מעשה, ירושלים תשל"ד, עמ' 83.

Chantilly (France), Musée Condé

Two Hebrew MSS in this museum are described in *Catalogue général: Bibliothèques de l'Institut [de France] – Musée Condé*, Paris 1928, nos. 6 and 732.

Chantilly Haggada

Name given to *Chantilly, Musée Condé MS 732, an illuminated haggada.

B. Narkiss and G. Sed-Rajna, *Index of Jewish Art*, I, Jerusalem–Paris 1976.

Chapira, Bernard

Eliezer Dov Shapira, 1880–1967; scholar

During the years 1910–1912, Chapira, together with Jacques *Mosseri and others, gathered *Geniza fragments in Cairo. Some fragments ostensibly from his collection are now in the *Mosseri collection; others were sold to *Jerusalem, JNUL (now NLI), and are now numbered Heb. 4° 577.5. Chapira also described the first 56 MSS in the library of *Paris, AIU, in 'Les manuscrits de la Bibliothèque de l'Alliance Israélite', *REJ*, CV (1939), pp. 53–79.

Chazanowicz, Joseph

Bialystok, 1844–1919; physician and collector

Chazanowicz sent over 20,000 books, including some MSS, to the Midrash Abarbanel library in Jerusalem, which added the words 'Ginzei Yosef' to its name in recognition of his contribution. The library was later incorporated into *Jerusalem, NLI.

Cheb (Czech Republic)

See *Eger.

Cheltenham

See *Phillipps, Thomas.

Chester Beatty Library

See *Dublin, Chester Beatty Library.

Codex Chethamensis

Name given to an early Tora scroll in *Manchester, Chetham's Library, described by C. G. K. Gillespie, 'Codex Chethamensis: A description of the Hebrew roll of the Pentateuch', in *Transactions of the Lancashire and Cheshire Antiquarian Society*, II, 1884, published separately as *Codex Chethamensis*, London 1885.

Chicago (Ill.), Spertus College, Asher Library

In 1967, Maurice Spertus donated a collection of 95 Yemenite MSS in Hebrew and Judaeo-Arabic to the college that bears his name. The MSS were described by N. Golb, *Spertus College of Judaica Yemenite Manuscripts: An Illustrated Catalogue*, Chicago 1972. The catalogue is arranged by subject. Palaeographical and codicological information: number of folios and size; occasional identifications of type of script and date. Indexes: titles, authors, scribes, geographical names, personal names, dated texts. On pp. 36–109 are facsimiles of pages from each of the manuscripts. The library owns at least four additional MSS not described in the Golb catalogue. The entire collection has been catalogued and can be found online by doing a search for 'YEMEN' under the field 'Collection' in the catalogue at http://helen.spertus.edu.

Chigiana, Biblioteca

The library of the Chigi family was founded in the seventeenth century by Fabio Chigi, who later became Pope Alessandro VI. The library was purchased by the Italian government in 1918 and in 1922 was acquired by the *Vatican Library. The collection includes one Hebrew MS, Chigiana R VI 37, a Bible (*Cat. Allony–Loewinger*, III, no. 795; *Cat. Richler*, Vatican, pp. 526–527).

Christ Church College

See *Oxford, Christ Church College.

Chufut-Kale MSS

MSS found in the library of Abraham *Firkovich in Chufut-Kale (Tschufut-Kale), Crimea. H. L. Strack and A. *Harkavy made a list of the MSS after Firkovich's death. The MSS were purchased by the Imperial Public Library in St. Petersburg (now *St. Petersburg, NLR) in 1876 and form part of the Second Firkovich Collection. The dated biblical MSS were described by Strack in *Zeitschrift für die gesammte Lutheranische Theologie und Kirche*, XXXVI (1875), pp. 585–624.

Churchill, Sidney John Alexander

England, 1862–1921; orientalist

Eight Judaeo-Persian MSS were purchased from Churchill in the late nineteenth century by the British Museum (now *London, British Library).

Cat. Margoliouth–Leveen, IV, p. ix.

Chwolson, Daniel

Vilna, Lithuania, 1819 – St. Petersburg, Russia, 1911; orientalist

Chwolson described his collection of twenty MSS, eleven of them modern copies of MSS in other libraries, in a supplement appended to some copies of his *Catalog der hebräischen Bücher in der Bibliothek des Professors D. Chwolson*, Vilna 1897, pp. 156–157 (רשימת ספרי ישראל הנמצאים באוצר הספרים אשר להפרופיסור דניאל חוואלזאן). The MSS are now in *St. Petersburg, Oriental Institute.

Cincinnati (Ohio), Hebrew Union College (HUC)

The library possesses over 1,000 Hebrew MSS, including a number of *Geniza fragments from the collection of Ludwig *Blau and some purchased by Jacob Mann in 1924 (J. Mann, 'Obadye Prosélyte Normand … et sa meguilla', *REJ*, LXXXIX [1930], pp. 246–247). The liturgical Geniza fragments from the *Berlin, Jüdische Gemeinde, described by J. Schirmann, 'Die poetischen Geniza-fragmente in der juedischen Gemeinde-bibliothek', *MGWJ*, XXVI (1932), pp. 339–354, are now in the HUC library. The MSS come from various sources, among them David *Fränkel, Samuel *Margulies and others. There is no printed catalogue of the entire collection of MSS. The only published lists of MSS are E. Spicehandler, 'A Descriptive List of the Judeo-Persian Manuscripts at the Klau Library of the Hebrew Union College', *Studies in Bibliography and Booklore*, VIII (1966/68), pp. 114–136; a brief description of 49 Samaritan MSS in *A. B.: The Samaritan News*, no. 287, November 1, 1981; and a detailed description of 61 Samaritan MSS in B. Tsedaka, אוסף כתבי היד השומרונים בספריית קלאו, היברו יוניון קולג' (Cincinnati 2011).

Rab., *Lit. Treas.*, pp. 119–131; Oko, pp. 73–87.

Cincinnati Haggada, First

Name given to *Cincinnati, HUC, MS 444, an illuminated haggada written by Meir b. Israel Yaffe in the fifteenth century. Online: www.cn.huc.edu/libraries/haggadahs/1stcinc/index.html.

F. Landsberger, 'The Cincinnati Haggadah and its decoration', *HUCA*, XV (1940), pp. 529–558; Narkiss, p. 130.

Cincinnati Haggada, Second

See *Van Geldern Haggada.

Clarke, Adam

England, ca. 1762–1832; theologian and biblical scholar

Clarke purchased ten Hebrew MSS, mainly biblical codices and scrolls, at the auction sale of the library of the heirs of Rev. Johannes van der Hagen in Utrecht in 1823. Van der Hagen had purchased the MSS in 1726 at the sale of the property of the deceased Cornelius *Schulting, a Reformed Church minister from Amsterdam. The MSS were described in Johann Christoph *Wolf's *Bibliotheca Hebraea*, IV, Hamburg 1733, pp. 79–84. See Clarke's report of the sale in his commentary on Isaiah lxvi in his edition of the Bible, London 1810–1825. A similar report precedes the description of the MSS in J. B. B. Clarke, *A Historical and Descriptive Catalogue of the European and Asiatic Manuscripts in the Library of the Late Adam Clarke*, London 1835, pp. 105–117. Most of the biblical MSS are now in *London, British Library, and are listed in *Cat. Margoliouth–Leveen*, IV, p. 15. One MS is in *New York, JTSA (Shunami, no. 3120).

Clermont, Collège de
See *Paris, Collège de Clermont.

Cobern, Camden McCormack
Uniontown, Pa., 1855 – Battle Creek, Mich., 1920; theologian
Cobern's *Geniza fragments and papyri, probably acquired on one of his frequent trips to Egypt during the 1890s, were purchased from his widow in 1920 by Dropsie College (now *Philadelphia, CAJS).
Rab., *Lit. Treas.*, p. 136.

Coblenz (or Koblenz, Germany), Landeshauptarchiv
Fragments from eight MSS are described in *Cat. Striedl–Róth*, pp. 171–174.

Coburg Pentateuch
Name given to *London, BL, MS Add. 19776 (*Cat. Margoliouth*, no. 80), an illuminated Pentateuch written in Coburg in 1396.
Narkiss, p. 114; J. Erdmann, 'Der Coburg-Pentateuch', *Jahrbuch der Coburger Landesstiftung*, XXV (1980), pp. 85–110.

Cochran, John
London, nineteenth century; bookseller
A Hebrew MS, no. 325 in Cochran's *A Catalogue of Manuscripts* ..., 1829, was in the *Phillipps collection (no. 6349) and was sold at Sotheby's auction in London on November 30, 1976.

Codex
References in this *Guide* are alphabetized according to the following word (e.g., 'Codex Chetamensis' appears between 'Chester' and 'Chicago').

Cohen, Abraham
London, nineteenth cent.
Cohen's MS of *Pesikta rabati* (פסיקתא רבתי), described in *Bet haTalmud* (בית התלמוד, ה [תרמ"ד], עמ' 2–4), is now *Philadelphia, CAJS (formerly Dropsie College), RAR MS 26.
N. J. Cohen, 'The London manuscript of Midrash Pesiqta Rabbati: A key text-witness comes to light', *JQR*, LXXIII (1983), pp. 209–237.

Cohen, Isaac Seligmann
See *Berend Salomon, Isaac Seligmann Cohn.

Cohen, Lipmann
Hanover, Germany, eighteenth cent.
Father-in-law of David *Oppenheim. For fear of the censor, Oppenheim did not bring his library with him to Prague but left it in the custody of his father-in-law in Hanover.
Jewish Encyclopedia, III, p. 311.

Cohen, Salomon Samuelzoon
Thirty-two MSS are listed in the sale catalogue of Cohen's collection (... רשימה מספרים הנמכרים בראטרדם, יום ב' לחדש אב תקמ"ו).

Cohn, Abraham
Posnan, Poland, nineteenth cent.
Twelve of Cohn's MSS were purchased by *Breslau, Jüdisch-theologisches Seminar.
Brann, *Geschichte*, p. 80.

Cohn, Isaac Seligmann
See *Berend Salomon, Isaac Seligmann Cohn.

Coimbra Bible
Name given to an illuminated Bible found in the Biblioteca Geral de Universidade de Coimbra in Coimbra (Portugal).
J. Mendes dos Remédios, *Uma Biblia Hebraica de Biblioteca da Universidade de Coimbra*, Coimbra 1903.

Colbert, Jean Baptiste
Reims, France, 1619 – Paris, 1683
Colbert's Oriental MSS, including 171 Hebrew MSS, purchased by his agents in Aleppo and Constantinople, Jean Michel Vansleb and

Joseph Besson, were bought from his estate by the Royal Library in Paris (now *Paris, Bibliothèque nationale de France). In 1668, while officiating as Minister of Finance, Colbert, ordered the *Paris, Bibliothèque Mazarine to transfer MSS, including 102 Hebrew MSS, to the Royal Library, in exchange for duplicates.

י' הקר, 'שליחו של לואי ה־14 בלבאנט ותרבותם של יהודי האימפריה העות'מאנית בדיווח משנת 1675', ציון, נב (תשמ"ז), עמ' 25–44.

Coll. Neophyt.
See *Rome, Pia Casa dei Neofiti.

Coll. Ss. Trinity
See *Cambridge, Trinity College.

Collegio Emmanuel
Emmanuel College, Cambridge. See *Cambridge, College Libraries.

Collegio Neophyti
See *Rome, Pia Casa dei Neofiti.

Collegio Romano
See *Rome, Collegio Romano.

Cologne (Germany), Collegii Societatis Jesu Colonia
The MS described by *Kennicott, no. 158, is now *Paris, BnF, MS héb. 1–3.

Cologne (Germany), Historisches Archiv der Stadt
Eighteen fragments were described by L. Duenner, 'Die hebräischen Handschrift-Fragmente in Archiv der Stadt Cöln', *ZfHB*, VIII (1904), pp. 84–90, 113–117. These fragments and four additional ones were described in *Cat. Allony–Loewinger*, I, pp. 56–57. The call-numbers were not given in this catalogue. The building housing the Archiv collapsed in March, 2009. The fate of the Hebrew fragments remains undetermined.

Colon.
See *Cologne.

Colonia
Latin name for Cologne.

Columbia University
See *New York, Columbia University.

Columbina
Biblioteca Capitular Colombina, Seville.

Consistoire Israélite
See *Paris, Consistoire Israélite.

Copenhagen (Denmark), Kongelige Bibliothek
Founded in the seventeenth century, the library has an old collection of 46 Hebrew MSS, which were described in the catalogue *Codices hebraici et arabici Bibliothecae regiae Hafniensis jussu et auspiciis regiis enumerati et descripti*, Copenhagen 1851. Since 1851 the library has acquired many other MSS, including the collections of David *Simonsen in 1932 (134 MSS) and of Lazarus *Goldschmidt in 1949. According to Pearson, p. 8, the Goldschmidt collection includes 20 MSS and fragments; but according to *Cat. Allony–Kupfer*, II, p. 18, there are only 7 MSS in the collection, even though 15 MSS bearing call-numbers with the prefix 'Cod. Gold.[schmidt]' are listed in the catalogue. Altogether, 244 MSS from the Kongelige Bibliothek are listed in *Cat. Allony–Kupfer*, II, pp. 19–34. Call-numbers are listed in parentheses. 21–264 and מ225 – מ1 are serial numbers of the catalogue; the numbers with the prefixes ס and פ are the photocopy numbers of the *Jerusalem, IMHM. The MSS in the Simonsen collection have been digitized and can be accessed at www.kb.dk/manus/judsam/2009/maj/dsh/en.

Copenhagen (Denmark), Mosaiske Troessamfund (Jewish Community Library)

Seventy MSS are listed in *Cat. Allony–Kupfer*, II, pp. 34–38. The library was closed to the public in 1983. Most of the MSS were placed on deposit in the *Copenhagen, Kongelige Bibliothek. They include about thirty MSS not listed in *Cat. Allony–Kupfer*. The 2,000 printed books and a few MSS were purchased by Herman R. Samson, a native of Copenhagen, and in 2003 they were acquired by the Stanford (California) University Library, where they form the Samson/Copenhagen Judaica Collection. Only a few MSS and some handwritten ephemera and fragments are included in the Samson collection. Two of the MSS in Stanford were described in *Cat. Allony–Kupfer*, II, serial numbers 289, 298. Some other items were deposited in the Danish State Archives.

Corneliana, Biblioteca (Venice)

Library of the Venetian family Corner (Cornaro). It included MSS originally in the collection of Jacopo *Soranzo. *Kennicott describes four MSS from the Corneliana (nos. 564–567). Two were acquired by *Canonici and are now in *Oxford, Bodleian Library, and two are now in the de *Rossi collection in *Parma, Biblioteca Palatina.

Kennicott 564 = Oxford, Bodleian Library, MS Can. Or. 91 (*Cat. Neubauer* 22)
Kennicott 565 = Parm. 2207 (de Rossi 629)
Kennicott 566 = Parm. 2846 (de Rossi 735)
Kennicott 567 = Oxford, Bodleian Library, MS Can. Or. 62 (*Cat. Neubauer* 26)

Tamani, *Venezia*, p. 248.

Corner

See *Corneliana.

Coronel, Nahman Nathan

Amsterdam, Netherlands, 1810 – Jerusalem, 1890; scholar

Coronel was born in Amsterdam and late in life settled in Jerusalem. He collected a large number of MSS, many of them described in the prefaces to his books. He sold MSS to various collectors and libraries – among them Solomon *Halberstamm (80 MSS), *Vienna, Österreichische Nationalbibliothek (22 or 23 MSS; see *Cat. Schwarz*, Vienna, index of owners), *Cambridge, University Library, *Oxford, Bodleian Library (among them MSS Opp. Add. 4° 107–113), and the British Museum (now *London, British Library). In 1871, Coronel published in London a catalogue (רשימה מספרי כתיבת יד) in which 130 MSS were listed. Close to 100 of these MSS were acquired by Baron David *Günzburg and are now in *Moscow, RSL. For a list of the present locations of MSS from this catalogue, see Appendix I, no. 7. *Steinschneider had a handwritten list of 42 MSS belonging to Coronel (now *New York, JTSA, MS 2863). The work by Abraham b. Eliezer Halevi published from a MS of Coronel's in *Kerem chemed*, IX (1856), pp. 141–148, is now *New York, Columbia University Library, MS X893 H 13.

Steinschneider, *Vorlesungen*, p. 67 (Hebrew, p. 87).

Corpus Christi College

See *Oxford, College Libraries.

Corsiniana, Biblioteca

Formerly the library of the Corsini family. In 1883 it was acquired by the Accademia Nazionale dei Lincei in Rome.

Costa, Isaac da

Amsterdam, Netherlands, 1798–1860; poet and writer

Da Costa's printed books and MSS were listed in the auction-catalogue *Catalogue de la collection importante de livres et manuscrits hébreux, espagnols et portugais ... provenant de la Bibliothèque de feu Mr. Isaac da Costa à Amsterdam*, Amsterdam

1861. Twelve MSS, nos. 2100, 2253, 2254, 2261, 2266, 2270, 2271, 2288, 2563, 2599, 2769 and 2769*, are in Hebrew; nos. 2164, 2227, 2311, 2453, and 2595 are in Spanish; nos. 2468, 2472, 2476, 2521, 2582, 2635, 2719, and 2728 are in Portuguese, and no. 2591 is mainly in Portuguese; nos. 2312, 2325–2331, 2463–2464 and 2596 are in Spanish and Portuguese; no. 2458 is in Portuguese and Dutch; and nos. 2617–2622 are in Spanish and other languages. The present or last-known locations of some of the MSS are listed in Appendix I, no. 8.

Costa Athias, Solomon da

Amsterdam, Netherlands, 1690 – London, 1769

In 1759 Costa Athias presented three Bible MSS to the British Museum (now *London, British Library). The MSS were described by *Kennicott, nos. 124–126. Their call-numbers in the British Library are Add. 4707–4709. A Bible MS (Kennicott 128) was presented by Costa Athias to the Royal Society in London in 1766. The MS disappeared, was found in the India Office in 1921 by 'Mr. Adler' and was given on loan to the British Museum. Its present call-number in the British Library is Loan 1.

Rab., *Lit. Treas.*, p. 18.

Cotton, Robert Bruce

Huntingdonshire, England, 1571 – London, 1631; librarian

In 1702 Cotton's collection, including a Samaritan MS and three Hebrew charters, was acquired by the British Museum (now *London, British Library) from Cotton's grandson, John. The MSS are listed in *Cat. Margoliouth–Leveen*, IV, p. 162. Cotton lent a number of MSS to his friend John *Selden, and these are now in *Oxford, Bodleian Library (E. N. Adler, 'Hebrew treasures of England', *Transactions of the Jewish Historical Society of England*, VIII [1918], p. 9).

Cowley, Arthur Ernest

Forest Hill, England, 1864 – Oxford, England, 1931; orientalist

Cowley compiled most of the second volume of the catalogue of Hebrew MSS in *Oxford, Bodleian Library. *Geniza fragments formerly in his possession are now in the Bodleian.

Cracovia, Abraham Hayyim

Venice, late eighteenth cent.

Five of Cracovia's MSS are described by *Kennicott, nos. 571–575. The present locations of nos. 571–574 are listed in Appendix 1, no. 9; the whereabouts of no. 575 are unknown.

Tamani, *Venezia*, p. 249.

Cracow Bible (Regensburg Pentateuch)

Name given to *Jerusalem, Israel Museum, MS 180/52, an illuminated Pentateuch written in Bavaria, perhaps in Regensburg, around 1300. The MS, which formerly belonged to the Cracow Jewish community, was described by Z. Ameisenowa, *Biblja Hebrajska XIVgo wieku w Krakowie*, Cracow 1929. During World War II it was taken to the Historisches Museum in Hanau and later reached the Israel Museum.

Narkiss, p. 98; *Jerusalem Collections*, no. 4; *Cat. Striedl–Róth*, no. 195.

Cramer, Hermann

See *Jerusalem *Mishne Tora*.

Crawford, Alexander William, Earl of

England, 1812–1880

His library, which included 37 Hebrew MSS and 27 Samaritan MSS, was inherited by his son James Ludovic Lindsay (hence the name Bibliotheca Lindesiana), who sold it in 1901 to Mrs John Rylands. The collection is now in the *Manchester, John Rylands University Library. The two so-called 'Crawford Haggadas' are now MSS Rylands 6 and 7.

Rab., *Treas. Jud.*, pp. 154–156; Pearson, p. 59.

Crawley, George A.

Norwood, England, 1864 – London, 1926; architect

A Yemenite Pentateuch dated 1470, which was sold at Sotheby's sale of Crawley's library in 1927, was later MS *Sassoon 964. The MS was sold again at auction and is now *London, Valmadonna Trust Library, MS 11.

Cremona Maḥzor

Name given to *Turin, Biblioteca Nazionale Universitaria, MS A III 14, a maḥzor copied by *Joel b. Simeon in Cremona in 1452/3. According to M. Beit-Arié, 'Joel ben Simeon's manuscripts', *Journal of Jewish Art*, III–IV (1977), p. 25, the MS, damaged by fire in 1904, is in very poor condition.

J. Gutmann, 'Thirteen manuscripts in search of an author: Joel Ben Simeon, 15th century scribe-artist', *Studies in Bibliography and Booklore*, IX (1969–1971), p. 93.

Cremifansis

Latin name for Kremsmünster.

CUL

*Cambridge, University Library.

Codex Curtisianus

Name given to a MS of the Later Prophets and Hagiographa, formerly in the library of John C. Curtiss and presently *Cincinnati, HUC, MS 13. The first part of this MS, which was not in the Curtiss library, is *Cambridge, UL, MS Add. 468. Cincinnati, HUC, MS 601 (*Sod hashem* by David Lida), also derives from the Curtiss library. MS *Moscow, RSL, Günzburg 848, dated May 1868, contains descriptions of four Curtiss Bible MSS, the first of which is the Codex Curtisianus. The present whereabouts of the other three MSS are unknown.

Cusa, Cardinal Nicolaus von

Bernkastel-Kues, Germany, 1401 – Todi, Italy, 1464; jurist, philosopher, astronomer

His collection of MSS, including five in Hebrew, is in *Bernkastel-Kues Hospital library.

D

Dalla Volta, Samuel Vita

Mantua, eighteenth–nineteenth cent.; scholar

According to M. Steinschneider, *Catalogus Librorum Hebraeorum in Bibliotheca Bodleiana*, II, Berlin 1852–1860, no. 7353, Dalla Volta had a collection of 131 MSS. A number of MSS from his collection were acquired by *Cambridge, University Library (MSS Add. 383, 397, 403, 404, 636). S. M. Schiller-Szinessy, *Catalogue of the Hebrew Manuscripts Preserved in the University Library, Cambridge*, I, Cambridge 1876, p. 39, describes one MS (Add. 383,3) that once belonged to Dalla Volta and then passed into the possession of Marco *Mortara. Other MSS are now *Paris, AIU, MS H 47 A, *New York, JTSA, MSS 2098 and R718 and *Budapest, Hungarian Academy of Sciences, MS Kaufmann A 140. A number of Dalla Volta's own works in manuscript are now in the David *Kaufmann collection, much of which was acquired from Mortara. Samuel D. *Luzzatto purchased a twelfth- or thirteenth-century MS of philological works from Dalla Volta (now *London, BL, MS Add. 27214).

Damascus (Syria)

The Bible known as the Damascus Keter, formerly in the synagogue of Hushbasba Al'anabi, is now *Jerusalem, NLI, Heb. 4° 790. The last leaf of the MS with a carpet page was sold at an auction by Sotheby's in 1987 and is now in the Museo Sefardi in Toledo, Spain. The Damascus Pentateuch, formerly MS *Sassoon 507, was sold to *Jerusalem, JNUL (now NLI), at Sotheby's sale in Zurich in 1975 and now bears the call-number Heb. 4° 5702. A. Harkavy described thirteen MSS he saw in Damascus, including the *Farhi Bible (חדשים גם ישנים, ו [תרנ״ה], עמ׳ 5). A. Yellin described six Bibles (*ketarim*) found in synagogues and in private hands in Damascus (א׳ ילין, ׳על ה״כתרים״ בדמשק׳, מזרח ומערב, א [תר״ף], עמ׳ 117–127), including the Damascus Keter and another *keter* found in the synagogue of the Shama'a (now *Jerusalem, NLI, Heb. 4° 7205). The 'Damascusrolle', a Tora scroll from the Karaite community of Damascus, presented to the Imperial Public Library in St. Petersburg (now *St. Petersburg, NLR) by Abraham *Firkovich in 1862, was described in A. Harkavy and H. L. Strack, *Catalog der hebräischen Bibelhandschriften der Kaiserlichen öffentlichen Bibliothek in St. Petersburg*, St. Petersburg–Leipzig 1875, pp. 275–276, and is now St. Petersburg, NLR, MS Евр. II biblical MSS on leather 160.

Danon, Abraham

Adrianople, Turkey, 1857–1925; scholar

Danon presented MSS, including 48 in Hebrew, to *Paris, Institut national des langues et civilisations orientales. These MSS were described by S. Kerner, 'Les manuscrits hébreux du "Fonds Danon" de la Bibliothèque de l'Institut National des Langues et Civilisations Orientales', *Bulletin des Bibliothèques de France*, XXII (1977), pp. 449–460.

Darmstadt (Germany), Universitäts- und Landesbibliothek

Until 2004 it was called the Hessische Landes- und Hochschulbibliothek. Fifteen Hebrew MSS are described in *Cat. Striedl–Róth*, pp. 15–27.

Darmstadt Haggada

Name given to *Darmstadt, Universitäts- und Landesbibliothek, Cod. Or. 8, an illuminated fifteenth-century haggada. Facsimile editions of this MS appeared in Leipzig (1927) and Berlin (1971/2). Another illuminated fifteenth-century Darmstadt haggada is Cod. Or. 28. Cod. Or. 7, an illuminated haggada dated 1769, was published in a facsimile edition in 1989.

Davidson, Israel

Yonava, Lithuania, 1870 – New York, 1939; scholar

Davidson's MSS were given to *New York, JTSA, by his widow.

Register, 5701, p. 61 (Marx, *Bibl. Studies*, p. 312).

Deinard, Ephraim

Odessa, Ukraine and USA, 1846–1930; bookseller

Deinard sold many MSS to Judge Mayer *Sulzberger, who purchased MSS for his own collection and for the library of *New York, JTSA (Rab., *Lit. Treas.*, p. 66). Deinard compiled a catalogue of Sulzberger's private collection, which was later given to JTSA (אור מאיר, ניו יורק תרנ״ז). At the beginning of his book *Devir Efrayim* (דביר אפרים, סנט לואיס תרפ״ו), a description of his collection, Deinard relates how he sold books and manuscripts to various libraries in the United States, among them *Washington, D.C., Library of Congress, *New York, Public Library, JTSA, and *New York, Columbia University, to which he sold about 135 MSS some time between 1889 and 1891. Previously, Deinard had sold MSS to *Oxford, Bodleian Library (listed in *Cat. Neubauer–Cowley*, II, pp. xii–xvi). Among those he sold to Oxford in 1886 is a collection of colophon pages of biblical MSS (MS Heb. c.6, *Cat. Neubauer–Cowley*, II, 2616). The MSS, complete with colophons, from which these pages were torn out, had been described by Deinard himself in his report of a journey to Crimea (1878 משא קרים, ורשה). In 1930, 23 MSS from Deinard's collection were acquired by *Cambridge (Mass.), Harvard University (H. A. Wolfson, 'Hebrew Books in Harvard', *Harvard Alumni Bulletin*, April 29, 1932, p. 7). M. *Steinschneider possessed a handwritten catalogue of 145 MSS belonging to Deinard in 1877 (now JTSA, MS 2863).

Delitzsch, Franz

Germany, 1813–1890; Christian Hebraist

Delitzsch compiled a catalogue of the Hebrew MSS in *Leipzig, Stadtbibliothek (= *Cat. Delitzsch*).

Della Torre

See *Torre.

Della Vida

See *Vida.

Derbent Tora

Name given to a complete ancient Tora scroll with a forged epigraph recording the wanderings of Jews exiled from Samaria until their settlement in the Caucasus, acquired by Abraham *Firkovich in 1840 from the city of Derbent (or Derbend) in Dagestan. The MS was formerly in *Odessa, Society for History and Antiquities, and was described by E. M. Pinner in *Prospectus der der Odessaer Gesellschaft für Geschichte und Alterthümer gehörenden ältesten hebräischen und rabbinischen Manuscripte*, Odessa 1845, pp. 5–7. In 1863, the Imperial Public Library (now *St. Petersburg, NLR) acquired the Odessa Collections, including the Derbent Tora, which now bears the call-number Евр. I A.

T. Harviainen, 'The epigraph of the Derbent Torah and the Madjalis scroll discovered by Abraham Firkovich in 1840', *Studia Orientalia*, XCV (2003), pp. 55–77; D. Shapira, 'Remarks on Avraham Firkowicz and the Hebrew "Mejelis document"', *Acta Orientalia Academiae Scientiarum Hungaricae*, LIX (2006), pp. 131–180.

Derenbourg, Joseph Naphtali and Hartwig

Mainz, Germany, 1811 – Paris, 1895; Paris, 1844–1908

Documents, transcriptions from MSS and a few *Geniza fragments formerly in the possession of the Derenbourgs are now in *Paris, Institut de France, MSS 3371–3405. Joseph Derenbourg was one of the compilers of the 1866 catalogue of Hebrew MSS in *Paris, Bibliothèque nationale de France. Hartwig Derenbourg prepared the first published catalogue of Hebrew MSS in the British Museum (now *London, British Library).

de Rossi, G. B.

See *Rossi.

Deutsch, Simon

Nikolsburg (Mikulov, Czech Republic), 1822 – Vienna, 1877; scholar and revolutionary

Deutsch described the Hebrew MSS of the k. k. Hofbibliothek in Vienna (now *Vienna, Österreichische Nationalbibliothek) in 'Die hebräischen Manuskripte der k.k. Hofbibliothek zu Wien', *Österreichische Blättern für Litteratur und Kunst*, III (1847), and together with Albrecht *Krafft compiled a catalogue of the library's MSS in 1847.

Deutschen Morgenländische Gesellschaft

See *Halle, Bibliothek der Deutschen Morgenländischen Gesellschaft.

Dietrichstein, Prince

See *Nikolsburg.

Digby, Kenelm

Gayhurst, England, 1603 – London, 1665; diplomat and philosopher

Digby's collection was based on the library

bequeathed to him by his teacher at Oxford, the mathematician Thomas Allen. Digby presented the collection, including five Hebrew MSS, to *Oxford, Bodleian Library, in 1634. The MSS were placed in the *Laud collection, and they are so listed in *Cat. Neubauer*. Before the catalogue's second volume (*Cat. Neubauer–Cowley*, II) was published, the Digby MSS were restored to their original collection and given the call-numbers Digby Or. 32–36. A list of the MSS and their numbers in *Cat. Neubauer* is found in *Cat. Neubauer–Cowley*, II, p. 541.

Dijon (France), Archives départementales de la Côte-d'Or

Two fourteenth-century tradesman's notebooks were described by I. Loeb, 'Deux livres de commerce du commencement du XIVième siècle', *REJ*, VIII (1884), pp. 161–196, and IX (1884), pp. 21–50, 187–213.

D. K.

David *Kaufmann.

Dolni Kounice

See *Kounice.

Donaueschingen (Germany), Fürstlich Fürstenbergische Hofbibliothek

The library was dismantled and sold in 1999. The only Hebrew MS, a fragment numbered MS AI1, described in *Cat. Striedl–Róth*, p. 28, is now in the *Stuttgart, Württembergische Landesbibliothek.

Double Maḥzor

Name given to an illuminated Ashkenazic maḥzor, the first part of which is *Dresden, Sächsische Landesbibliothek, MS A 46a, and the second part is *Wrocław, Biblioteka Uniwersytecka we Wrocławiu, Cod. Or. I.1.

P. de Haas, 'Beschreibung der Breslauer deutschen Machsor-Handschriften', *Soncino Blätter*, II (1927), pp. 33–35.

D. R.

de *Rossi.

Dragon Haggada

Name given to *Hamburg, SUB, Cod. hebr. 155, an illuminated haggada written in France in the thirteenth century. A central motif of the illuminations is the dragon.

Narkiss, p. 84.

Draguignan (France), Médiathèque Communautaire

Formerly Bibliothèque municipale. One Hebrew MS was described in *Catalogue général*, XIV (1890), p. 407, no. 36.

Dresden (Germany), Bücherei der Israelitischen Religionsgemeinde, Wünsche Bibliothek

One MS from this library, an eighteenth-century copy of TB *Berakhot*, is now *Cincinnati, HUC, MS 696. In the Trofiana collection in *Moscow, RSL, is a folder labeled 'Dresden' that may include items from this library.

Dresden (Germany), Sächsische Landesbibliothek – Staats- und Universitätsbibliothek

Formerly Sächsische Landesbibliothek; renamed in 1996. Six Hebrew MSS were described by H. L. Fleischer in *Catalogus Codicum Manuscriptorum Orientalium Bibliothecae Regiae Dresdensis*, Leipzig 1831, nos. 138, 140, 384, 399, 442, 443. Two MSS (nos. 442, 443) were destroyed in World War II. The four remaining MSS, as well as an additional five MSS now found in the library, were described in *Cat. Striedl–Róth*, pp. 31–40.

Dresden Maḥzor

Name given to *Dresden, Sächsische Landesbibliothek – Staats- und Universitätsbibliothek, Cod. D. 22, a fourteenth-century Ashkenazic maḥzor.

Dropsie, Moses A.
Philadelphia, Pa., 1821–1905; philanthropist
Dropsie College (now *Philadelphia, CAJS) was named in honour of M. A. Dropsie. Mayer *Sulzberger presented a collection of MSS to *New York, JTSA, in 1908, in memory of Dropsie (information from M. Schmelzer).

Dropsie College
See *Philadelphia, CAJS.

Dublin (Ireland), Chester Beatty Library
The library holds the private collection of Sir Alfred Chester Beatty (1875–1968), left in trust for the public benefit. It includes four Hebrew MSS, a small number of Esther scrolls and mezuzot and three Samaritan MSS.

Dublin (Ireland), Marsh's Library
The library was built in 1701 by Archbishop Narcissus *Marsh. A number of Hebrew MSS are listed in N. J. D. White (ed.), *Catalogue of the Manuscripts Remaining in Marsh's Library, Dublin*, Dublin 1913. Some of them are late copies of the works of Christians. See 'Hebrew' in the index to the catalogue.

Dublin (Ireland), Trinity College Library
About 22 Hebrew MSS are listed in T. K. Abbott, *Catalogue of the Manuscripts in the Library of Trinity College, Dublin*, London 1900. The *Jerusalem, IMHM has microfilms of a few other MSS as well.

Dubno, Solomon
Dubno, Ukraine, 1738 – Amsterdam, Netherlands, 1813; scholar
Dubno himself compiled a handwritten catalogue of his library (*Amsterdam, UB, HS. Ros. 469), in which he listed only a few MSS, together with his printed books. A specimen of this catalogue was published by G. I. Polak in *Halikhot kedem* (הליכות קדם, אמסטרדם תר״ז). In the auction catalogue of his collection (רשימה מספרים ... הנמצאים בעזבון ... שלמה מדובנא ... אמסטרדם, תקע״ד), 106 MSS are listed in brief without any codicological information. According to A. Marx, *Studies in Jewish History and Booklore*, New York 1944, pp. 219–221, the author of this catalogue was J. Spiegelmann, who bought most of the MSS. Dubno's collection is now scattered among various libraries. An illuminated Bible MS copied in Prague in 1488, described in de Rossi, *ext.*, 51, used by Dubno in preparing his *Tikun soferim* (תיקון סופרים) and also used in preparing the Berlin 1783 edition of the Pentateuch, in which Dubno's *Tikun soferim* was reprinted, is now *New York, Yeshiva University, MS 1247 (see *Prague Bible). Another part of Dubno's legacy, including letters and writings of Moses Mendelssohn and Rabbi Zevi Hirsch Levin of Berlin, was acquired by Samuel *Fuenn of Vilna. Ephraim *Pinner, the source of this information, published excerpts from the correspondence between Mendelssohn and Levin in the untitled catalogue of his library (Berlin 1861–1870), pp. 51–58.

Dukas, Jules
Paris, 1828–1915
Dukas's MSS of sermons by Solomon Azubi, described in a series of articles in *REJ*, XI–XII (1895/6), are now *Paris, AIU, MS H 98 A.

Duke of Sussex
See *Sussex, Duke of (Prince Augustus Frederick).

Duke of Sussex Catalan Bible
Name given to *London, BL, MS Add. 15250 (*Cat. Margoliouth*, no. 53), an illuminated Bible written in Spain, probably in Catalonia, in the fourteenth century. Formerly in the possession of the Duke of *Sussex (Pettigrew catalogue, no. 2) and purchased by

the British Museum at the sale of his library in 1844 (lot 101).

Narkiss, *Span. & Port.*, no. 19.

Duke of Sussex Pentateuch

Name given to *London, BL, MS Add. 15282 (*Cat. Margoliouth*, no. 74), an illuminated Pentateuch written in South Germany about 1300, formerly in the collection of the Duke of *Sussex (Pettigrew catalogue, no. 3) and purchased by the British Museum at the sale of his library in 1844 (lot 313).

Narkiss, p. 104.

Duke of Sussex Portuguese Pentateuch

Name given to *London, BL, MS Add. 15283 (*Cat. Margoliouth*, no. 84), an illuminated Pentateuch written in Lisbon towards the end of the fifteenth century. Formerly in the possession of the Duke of *Sussex and purchased by the British Museum at the sale of his library in 1844 (lot 315).

Narkiss, *Span. & Port.*, no. 43.

Dusnus, Baruch Bendit

Netherlands, the Hague, 1811 – Leeuwarden, 1886; rabbi

Eight Hebrew MSS, including two Esther scrolls, are listed in the sales catalogue of his library, *Catalog der sehr werthvollen Sammlung ... grössentheils hinterlassen von ... B. Dusnus*, Amsterdam 1886, nos. 715–722. No. 719 on the list is now *New York, JTSA, R 1917.

Dyson Perrins

See *Perrins.

E

Eck, Oswald von

Germany, d. 1573; humanist

One of his MSS, an illuminated haggada, is in *Stuttgart, Württembergische Landesbibliothek (Cod. Or. 4° 1).

Ecole Rabbinique

*Paris, Séminaire Israélite de France.

Edelmann, Zvi Hirsch

Svisloch, Belarus, 1805 – Berlin, 1858; scholar

The MS of a commentary by Thomas Aquinas on Aristotle's *Metaphysics* belonging to Edelmann and described in *Kerem chemed* (כרם חמד), VIII (1854), pp. 110–111, later belonged to L. *Zunz and was *London, Montefiore, MS 296. Edelmann sold a number of MSS to *Oxford, Bodleian Library, between 1851 and 1854 (MSS Opp. Add. 2° 13, Opp. Add. 4° 3–4, 8, 45). A MS referred to by Edelmann in his edition of *Kaftor vaferaḥ* (כפתור ופרח, ברלין תרי"א), p. xxix, was *Jerusalem, Schocken Institute, MS 13160, until it was sold at Christie's in New York in 2005.

Codex Edinburgensis

Name given to *Edinburgh, National Library of Scotland MS 18.7.23, an Ashkenazic Bible.

Edinburgh (Scotland), National Library of Scotland

The Library has four Hebrew MSS in its collection.

Eger (now Cheb, Czech Republic)

The MS formerly found in Eger, from which A. Hübsch published a commentary on the Five Scrolls (Prague 1866), is now *Prague, National Library, MS XVIII F 6.

Egerton, Francis Henry

England, 1756 – Paris, 1829

Egerton bequeathed his collection of MSS to the British Museum (now *London, British Library) in 1829 and established a fund for the purchase of additional MSS. A list of the three Egerton Hebrew MSS is found in *Cat. Margoliouth–Leveen*, IV, p. 163.

Egidio da Viterbo

Viterbo, Italy, ca. 1469 – Rome, 1532; Italian humanist

Egidio studied Kabbala and in the course of his studies acquired a number of Hebrew MSS, some of which were copied expressly for him. A list of Latin and Hebrew books belonging to Egidio was published by C. Astruc and J. Monfrin, 'Livres latins et hébreux du Cardinal Gilles de Viterbe', *Bibliothèque d'Humanisme et Renaissance*, XXIII (1961), pp. 551–554. Egidio's MSS may be found today in several libraries: *Paris, BnF, MSS héb. 15, 98, 768, 927 and 981; *Munich, BSB, Cods. hebr. 74, 81, 96, 103, parts of 217–219 and possibly 285; *London, BL, MSS Harley 5707 and Add. 27199; *Rome, Biblioteca Casanatense, MS 2971; *Rome, Biblioteca Angelica, MSS Or. 45 and Or. 72, and *Vatican, Cod. Neof. 1, which was copied for Egidio.

Eilat MSS

Name given to a collection of over 400 MSS brought to Israel by immigrants from Yemen who arrived during the early years of the state. The MSS were collected in Eilat and later brought to *Jerusalem, JNUL (now NLI).

Elberg, Yehuda

Poland, 1912 – Montreal, Canada, 2003; Yiddish author

Elberg amassed a collection of over 300 MSS. Many of them were sold during his lifetime and after his death. A few were acquired from a bookdealer by *Vatican, Biblioteca Apostolica. Some are still in the possession of his heirs.

Em. Vit.

Rome, Biblioteca Vittorio Emanuele II. See *Rome, Biblioteca Nazionale Centrale di Roma.

Emmanuel College

Emmanuel College, Cambridge. See *Cambridge, College Libraries.

EMC

Enelow Memorial Collection. See *Enelow, Hyman George.

ENA

Elkan N. *Adler.

Enelow, Hyman George

Kovno, Lithuania, 1877 – New York, 1934; rabbi

In the early 1930s, with the help of Mrs. N. *Miller, *New York, JTSA acquired from the Viennese bookdealer Jacob Halpern a collection of over 1,100 MSS from the Orient and North Africa, many of them MSS collected by Rabbi Jacob Toledano. Some of the MSS in the collection were briefly described in Marx, *Proceedings*. After Enelow's death in 1934, this collection was named the Enelow Memorial Collection (EMC) (Rab., *Lit. Treas.*, p. 74). Enelow's private collection was presented to the JTSA library and was called the Hyman G. Enelow Collection (HGE). To the HGE collection were added MSS purchased from funds provided by the sale of duplicate copies of printed books from the collection (*Register*, 5699, pp. 69–72 [Marx, *Bibl. Studies*, pp. 273–276]).

Enelow Memorial Collection (EMC)

See *Enelow, Hyman George.

Epstein, Abraham

Staro-Konstantinov, Russia, 1841 – Vienna, 1918; scholar

Epstein's MSS were acquired by *Vienna, Israelitisch-theologische Lehranstalt, and passed, together with the entire MS collection of the Lehranstalt, into the possession of *Vienna, Israelitische Kultusgemeinde. Forty-nine MSS of Epstein's are described in *Cat. Schwarz*, Austria. A list of these MSS is found in *Cat. Schwarz–Loewinger–Róth*, p. 150. A photocopy of the MS of Yuspa Shammash's *Minhage Worms* (מנהגי וורמס), described by Epstein, 'Die Wormser Minhagbücher', in M. Brann and F. Rosenthal (eds.), *Gedenkbuch zur Erinnerung an David Kaufmann*, Breslau 1900, pp. 308–316, is now in *Jerusalem, Schocken Institute. The MS of *Sefer Hayashar* (ספר הישר) by Rabbenu Tam, from which Epstein published an edition, is now *Jerusalem, NLI, Heb. 4° 370. The MS of *She'iltot* (שאילתות) that he owned is now *Cincinnati, HUC, MS 136, and his MS of *Midrash ḥakhamim* (מדרש חכמים), formerly in the possession of V. *Aptowitzer, is now *New York, JTSA, MS R2170. A copy Epstein had made of the Prague MS of *Bereshit rabati* (בראשית רבתי) was presented by Aptowitzer to the Mekize Nirdamim Society and was published by H. Albeck (Jerusalem 1940). The MS is now JTSA, MS R2142.

Epstein, Gershon

Paris, early and mid-twentieth century

Epstein was the principal collector of MSS, printed books and documents in France and Germany for *New York, YIVO, after World War II. The Gershon Epstein Collection in YIVO contains mainly rabbinical and historical MSS. Epstein's personal library included a few dozen MSS, most of which were acquired by *Jerusalem, JNUL (now NLI).

Erfurt (Germany), Evangelisches Ministerium

In 1880, the MSS in the Ministry of Protestant Affairs, which was housed in the old Augustine Monastery in Erfurt, were removed to the *Berlin, Staatsbibliothek. The Hebrew MSS that came to the Staatsbibliothek are Cods. Or. 2° 1210–1224 and Or. 4° 685. From the end of World War II until 1992, most of these MSS were kept in the Deutsche Staatsbibliothek in the old building in East Berlin. In 1992 they were moved to the new building of the Staatsbibliothek, where all the other Hebrew MSS are preserved. One of the Erfurt MSS, Or. 2° 1220 (*Cat. Steinschneider*, Berlin, no. 159), is the so-called Erfurt MS of the Tosefta. The Bible MSS in large folio were used by J. H. Michaelis in his 1720 edition and by Baer in his critical edition (see his *Liber Duodecim Prophetarum*, Leipzig 1878, p. vi). They were described by J. J. Bellermann in *De Bibliothecis et Museis Erford*, 1800–1803; by Lagarde, *Symmicta*, I, Göttingen, 1877, pp. 130ff. (see *HB*, XIX, 1879, p. 28); and in the *Katalog der Ministerial-Bibliothek zu Erfurt*, 1876. Two other MSS from Erfurt that belonged to Bellermann, one of them from the Benedictine monastery, are now *Berlin, SB, Cods. Or. 8° 147 and 148.

Ergas, Emanuel

Livorno, Italy, eighteenth cent.

The MS formerly in Ergas's possession, described by de Rossi, *ext.*, 17, is now New York, Hispanic Society of America MS HC 371/169.

Erlangen (Germany), Jüdische Gemeinde

The maḥzor of the Jewish community of Erlangen is now in the *Erlangen, Universitätsbibliothek (MS 2601).

Erlangen (Germany), Universitätsbibliothek Erlangen-Nürnberg
Eight MSS, nine Tora and Esther scrolls, 44 fragments, mezuzot, etc., and two Latin MSS are described in *Cat. Striedl–Róth*, pp. 43–64. The call-numbers (with the prefix 'Ms.') are written at the head of each entry. Recently, a few Yiddish MSS were discovered in the *Wagenseil collection of the library.

Erlangen Haggada
Name given to *Erlangen, Universitätsbibliothek, MS 1262, an illuminated haggada dated 1747 (*Cat. Striedl–Róth*, no. 70).

Erna Michael Haggada
Name given to *Jerusalem, Israel Museum, MS 180/58, an illuminated haggada written in South Germany in the fifteenth century. The MS was presented to the Museum in 1966 by Jacob Michael in memory of his wife, Erna.

Narkiss, p. 116; B. Narkiss and G. Sed-Rajna, *Index of Jewish Art*, I, Jerusalem–Paris 1976.

Erpe (Erpenius), Thomas van
Netherlands, 1584–1624; orientalist
In 1632, the widow of George Villiers, the Duke of Buckingham, purchased the van Erpe collection, including more than ten Hebrew MSS, for *Cambridge, UL.

Rab., *Lit. Treas.*, p. 46. Reif, *Cat. Cambridge*, p. 8.

el-Escorial
See *San Lorenzo del Escorial.

Esslingen Maḥzor
Name given to *Amsterdam, UB, HS. Ros. 609, a maḥzor written in Esslingen, Germany, in 1290. The first part of the maḥzor is *New York, JTSA, MS 9344.

J. A. Brombacher, 'The Esslingen Mahzor', *Studia Rosenthaliana*, XVIII (1984), pp. 103–119; M. Beit-Arié, 'The Esslingen Mahzor: Some remarks', *ibid.*, XXII (1988), pp. 44–45; E. G. L. Schrijver, 'The colophon page of the Esslingen Mahzor', *ibid.*, XXI (1987), pp. 185–197; E. M. Cohen, 'The Esslingen Mahzor', *ibid.*, XXV (1991), pp. 55–82.

Ets Haim
See *Amsterdam, Ets Haim.

Eupatoria (Gozlow; Yevpatoria, Crimea)
Many MSS from the Karaite National Library in Eupatoria were destroyed by the Soviets in the late 1920s and early 1930s. Some were saved by I. J. Krackovskij of the *St. Petersburg, Institute of Oriental Manuscripts, and presented to the Institute (S. Szyszman, 'Une source auxiliare important pour les études qumrân: Les collections Firkowicz et Qumran', in M. Delcor, *Qumrân: Sa piété, sa théologie et son milieu* (Paris–Louvain 1978, p. 73), which presently has 413 MSS from Eupatoria (Starkova, 'Les plus anciens mss.', p. 37). At least two MSS (MSS 133, 162–163) are now in the so-called Schneerson Collection in *Moscow, RSL, fond 182, and it is possible that the four other Karaite MSS belonging to the Schneerson Collection (formerly numbered 128, 225, 240, 262) also belonged to the Karaite National Library. MSS belonging to the Semita Isaakovna Kushul Museum in Eupatoria, which may previously have belonged to the Karaite library, were purchased by *St. Petersburg, NLR (V. Lebedev, *Sovietish Heimland*, IX [1976], p. 168). The Karaites Samuel Ne'eman and Abraham Yafet of Eupatoria possessed collections of MSS in the nineteenth century, but only a few of those MSS can be located today. MSS belonging to Ne'eman are now in *St. Petersburg, Institute of Oriental Manuscripts, nos. B 244, B 314, B 416, C 134 and D 29.

'European Geniza'
Refers to leaves and fragments from Hebrew MSS in secondary use, mainly in bindings of MSS and printed books or as wrappers for notarial records in libraries and archives

in Europe. Most of the fragments are from parchment MSS dating from the thirteenth and fourteenth centuries, though some are from MSS dating back to the tenth and eleventh centuries. Most of the manuscript leaves discovered derive from archives and libraries in Italy (see *'Italian Geniza'), though sizeable numbers have been found in Germany, Austria and Spain and lesser numbers in other countries. A research group was set up in December 2007 by scholars in Europe working on this project. Their findings are being published in a new series called *Studies in the 'European Genizah' (SEG)*. The first volume is A. Lehnardt (ed.), *Genizat Germania: Hebrew and Aramaic Manuscript Fragments in Context*, Proceedings of the Conference held in Mainz in 2007, Leiden–Boston 2010; the second will be M. Perani (ed.), *The Italian 'Genizah': Death and Rebirth of Medieval Hebrew Manuscripts in Italy*.

F

F

(1) Florence; (2) Frankfurt.

Farhi Bible

Name given to MS *Sassoon 368, an illuminated Bible formerly in the possession of the Farhi family of Damascus.

Cat. Sassoon, pp. 6–14; Narkiss, p. 72.

Ferrara (Italy) Comunità ebraica

Nineteen MSS from the Talmud Tora collection are described in Sonne, *Relazione*. *Jerusalem, IMHM, lists 108 MSS, but several of the MSS described by Sonne have disappeared. It is possible that after World War II, MSS in small communities in the vicinity of Ferrara were transferred to the library. Most of the MSS that were in the library after the war were acquired by *London, Valmadonna Trust Library.

FGP

Friedberg Genizah Project; see *Friedberg, Albert Dov.

Fi.

(1) Firenze (see *Florence); (2) Jerocham Fischl *Hirsch.

Fidalgo, Benjamin Musaphia

Altona, Germany, 1711–1801

Thirteen MSS from Fidalgo's collection, most of them in Spanish and Portuguese, were acquired by *Hamburg, SUB, in 1859 (*Cat. Steinschneider*, Hamburg, p. v).

Firenze

See *Florence.

Firkovich, Abraham

Lutsk, Ukraine, 1786 – Chufut Kale, Crimea, 1874; Karaite scholar

Firkovich collected a large number of MSS on his trips to Palestine, Syria and Egypt, and on the archaeological expeditions in Crimea and the Caucasus that he initiated. The methods Firkovich used to acquire his MSS were not always ethical (see, for example, Kahle, *The Cairo Geniza*, Oxford 1959, p. 6). In his attempts to prove that the Karaites had settled in Crimea earlier than had been supposed and that their importance was far greater than had been acknowledged, Firkovich did not hesitate to forge and emend texts, colophons and inscriptions in many of his MSS. In 1845, Firkovich sold some 50 MSS to the *Odessa, Society for History and Antiquities, and he continued to sell MSS to the Society until 1852. These MSS were purchased in 1863 by the Imperial Public Library in St. Petersburg (now *St. Petersburg, NLR), where they became known as the Odessa collections. In 1862 Firkovich himself sold to the St. Petersburg library a large collection of MSS that he had assembled, and in 1876, two years after his death, a second collection was purchased by the same library. These are called the First and Second Firkovich Collections; the Odessa Collections are included in the First Firkovich Collection. Firkovich sold a few MSS to other collectors. One of these MSS is now *Oxford, Bodleian Library, MS Mich. 363, another is *St. Petersburg, Institute of Oriental Manuscripts, MS B 291, and a third is in the private collection of D. Sofer in London, MS 102. For a description of the Firkovich collections and bibliographical details, see *St. Petersburg, NLR.

Firmian, Carlo Giuseppe di
1716 – Milan, Italy, 1782
Three of Count Firmian's MSS, described by *Kennicott, nos. 417–419, are now *Parma, Biblioteca Palatina, MSS Parm. 2516 (de Rossi 940), Parm. 1834–1835 (de Rossi 941) and Parm. 1998–2000 (de Rossi 942).

First
References in this *Guide* are alphabetized according to the following word (e.g., for First Cincinnati Haggada, see *Cincinnati Haggada, First).

Fischl or Fischl-Hirsch
See *Hirsch, Jerocham Fischl.

Fishman, Judah Loeb
See *Maimon.

Fl. pl.
Florence, pluteo. See *Florence, Biblioteca Medicea Laurenziana.

F. L. D.
See *Lair-Dubreil.

Fleischer, Heinrich Lebrecht
Germany, 1801–1888
Fleischer compiled a catalogue of MSS in *Dresden, Sächsische Landesbibliothek – Staats- und Universitätsbibliothek.

Floersheim Haggada
Name given to an illuminated Ashkenazic haggada copied in 1502, formerly MS *Sassoon 511, purchased by the late Michael Floersheim of Zurich at the 1978 sale of MSS from the Sassoon collection in Zurich. The MS is presently in the possession of Alexander Floersheim of Zurich and Herzliya.

Floersheim Mishne Tora
See *Jerusalem *Mishne Tora*.

Florence (Italy), Bibliotheca Carmelitarum S. Pauli
The MS described by *Kennicott, nos. 520–521, was sold several times. From the mid-nineteenth century until 2002 it was in the library of the Marquess of Bath in Longleat, Warminster, England. It was sold at an auction at Christie's in London in June 2002 and is now MS 243 in the Braginsky Collection in Zurich.

Florence (Italy), Biblioteca Medicea Laurenziana
Originally the library of the Medici family, it was founded by Cosimo the Elder (1389–1464) and annexed to the Basilica of San Lorenzo, after whom it was named. Its main growth, however, took place during the time of Lorenzo (1449–1492). The library was opened to the public in 1571. About 130 Hebrew MSS from the Medici collection are described, along with other MSS, by A. M. Biscioni, in *Bibliothecae Mediceo-Laurentianae Catalogus ab Antonio Maria Biscionio*

et Basilicae S. Laurentii canonico digestus atque editus, complectens codices orientales omnes, et XXXIII priores codices Graecos Plutei IV, I: *Codices Orientalis Complectens*, Florence 1752, pp. 1–168. Most of the descriptions are based on an earlier handwritten catalogue by Montfaucon. Along with the MSS, a large number of early printed books (impr.) are also described. At the end is a set of indexes to the entire catalogue (not for MSS in each language separately): names, subjects, dates, printed works quoted in the entries, scribes, etc. The same descriptions later appeared in a small format, with only minor corrections but without the introduction and the indexes, in A. M. Biscioni, *Bibliothecae Ebraicae Graecae Florentinae sive Bibliothecae Mediceo-Laurentianae*, II, Florence 1757; this volume describes only the Hebrew MSS, and therefore the catalogue numbers are not always consecutive. Appended to this edition of the catalogue are the descriptions of ten MSS (nos. 528–537) described by S. E. *Assemani in his catalogue of the Oriental MSS in the library: *Bibliothecae Mediceae Laurentianae et Palatinae codicum mms Orientalium, Catalogus* (Florence 1742 [1743]). The MSS are listed in the catalogue according to their shelf-marks, which consist of the prefix Pluteo (or Plut.) – i.e., the number of the *pluteo* or 'bench' on which the books were arranged – and a serial number. The present call-numbers of the MSS described by Biscioni consist of the 'bench' number and the MS number on each shelf (e.g., MS Plut. II. 23 = MS no. 23 on bench II). The catalogue includes MSS Plut. I. 1–61 (pp. 3–159), Plut. II. 1–53 (pp. 160–345), Plut. III. 1–16 (pp. 346–387), Plut. IV. 24–57 (pp. 471–550), Plut. XXI. 32 (p. 550), Plut. XLIV. 1–22 (pp. 388–426) and Plut. LXXXVIII. 2–23 (pp. 427–470). In addition to the MSS described in Biscioni's catalogue, the library has acquired about 45 other MSS, which have not yet been described in print. These MSS bear the call-numbers 'Acq. e doni' (acquisitions and gifts), 'Conv. Sopr.' (= Conventi Soppressi, i.e., MSS confiscated from religious libraries after the Napoleonic edict of 1808), 'Gaddi' (MSS bought from the Gaddi family in 1755) and 'Or.' The MSS described in the appendix to the 1757 catalogue (see above) now bear new call-numbers; see Appendix 1, no. 10.

Steinschneider, *Vorlesungen*, p. 72 (Hebrew, p. 95).

Florence (Italy), Biblioteca Nazionale Centrale

The library was founded in 1861, with the merger of the *Magliabechiana and Palatina libraries. Fourteen MSS from the Magliabechiana collection – the private library of Antonio Magliabechi (or Magliabecchi), founded in 1714 and opened to the public in 1747 – were described by D. Castelli, 'Catalogo dei codici ebraici magliabechiani e riccardiani di Firenze', *Giornale della Società Asiatica Italiana*, XV–XVI (1902/3), pp. 169–174. Two of these MSS (III, 44,7 and III, 45,11) were also described by R. J. H. Gottheil, 'Bible MSS in Roman Synagogues', *ZfHB*, IX (1905), pp. 183–184. Continuing Castelli's catalogue, U. Cassuto described 21 additional MSS, 'Nuovi manoscritti ebraici della Biblioteca Nazionale di Firenze', in *Giornale della Società Asiatica Italiana*, XXI (1908/9), pp. 101–109, 309–311; XXII (1909), pp. 273–283. In both Castelli's and Cassuto's descriptions the call-numbers appear at the head of each entry in parentheses after the catalogue serial number. One additional MS (Nuovi acq. 209), a copy of the Mishna with Maimonides' commentary, was described by H. P. Chajes, 'Un MS. della Mishna', *Rivista Israelitica*, V (1908), pp. 75–77.

Florence (Italy), Biblioteca Riccardiana

Library of the Riccardi family, founded in the sixteenth century. Since 1813 the library has belonged to the state. Three Hebrew MSS are described by D. Castelli, 'Catalogo dei codici ebraici magliabechiani e riccardiani di Firenze', *Giornale della Società Asiatica Italiana*, XV–XVI (1902/3), pp. 174–175. The library has two additional Hebrew MSS, Ricc. 26 and Ricc. 98.

Florence (Italy), Collegio Rabbinico Italiano

See *Rome, Collegio Rabbinico Italiano.

Florence (Italy), Ohave Tora Brotherhood

Twenty-seven MSS from the library of the brotherhood are listed in Sonne, *Relazione*. The library was acquired by the Collegio Rabbinico Italiano in Florence (see *Rome, Collegio Rabbinico Italiano), now deposited in the Centro Bibliografico dell'Ebraismo Italiano in Rome. Not all the MSS listed by Sonne are in the Centro Bibliografico.

Florence (Italy), Strozzi

See *Strozzi.

Florence (Italy), Università degli Studi, Biblioteca della Facoltà di Lettere e Filosofia

Eight MSS were described by Kalman Friedmann, 'I manoscritti ebraici della R. Università di Firenze', *Giornale della Società Asiatica Italiana*, NS II, Fasc. III (1932), pp. 193–208. Call-numbers of the MSS are given at the head of each entry. Palaeographical and codicological descriptions are detailed.

Florentia

Latin name for Florence.

Foa, Moses Benjamin

Reggio nell'Emilia, Italy, 1729–1822; bibliophile and bookseller

Most of Foa's MSS were sold by Salomon *Stern in 1846 to Princess Maria Luisa of Austria, who purchased them for *Parma, Biblioteca Palatina. Foa himself sold ten MSS to *Modena, Biblioteca Estense. These MSS are listed in *Cat. Bernheimer*, Modena, pp. xii–xiii.

Steinschneider, *Vorlesungen*, p. 60 (Hebrew, p. 79).

Foa Bible

Name given to an illuminated Bible belonging to the *Foa family until the nineteenth century, now in the Bibliothèque de la Compagnie des Prêtres de Saint-Sulpice, Paris, MS 1933.

M. Garel, 'The Foa Bible', *Journal of Jewish Art*, VI (1979), pp. 78–85.

F. P.

Florence, pluteo. See *Florence, Biblioteca Medicea Laurenziana.

Franeker (Netherlands), Akademie

The MSS in this library were transferred to *Leeuwarden, Provinciale Bibliotheek van Friesland (now part of TRESOAR, the Friesland Historical and Literary Centre) in 1813, when Napoleon closed the library.

Cat. Allony–Kupfer, II, p. 42.

Fränkel, David

Sanok, Poland, 1876 – New York, 1948; bookseller

Fränkel was Lippa *Schwager's brother-in-law and for a number of years, from 1906 on, his partner. At various times his business was based in Husiatyn and in Vienna. He issued a large number of catalogues in hectograph, print and handwriting. Fränkel sold 600 MSS to *New York, Columbia University, in the period 1930–1932 (Rab., *Lit. Treas.*, p. 104), including the MSS listed in his *Zur Geschichte der Juden in Griechenland* (לקורות ישראל במלכות יון, וינה 1931), and many MSS to other libraries such as *New York, JTSA, *Cincinnati, HUC, *Oxford, Bodleian Library, and to private collectors, including Elkan Nathan *Adler. A MS of a commentary on the Pentateuch (פירוש רש״י עה״ת: מהדורא בתרא), described by Fränkel, *Journal of Jewish Bibliography*, II (1940), pp. 31–32, is now *New Haven, Yale University Library, MS Heb. 54 (see L. Nemoy, 'Hebrew and kindred manuscripts in the Yale University Library', *Journal of Jewish Bibliography*, III [1942], p. 44). See also *Schwager, Lippa.

Frankfurt Mishne Tora

Name given to an illuminated fifteenth-century *Mishne Tora* MS, formerly *Frankfurt a/M, Stadtbibliothek, Cod. Ausst. 6. The MS, given in lieu of reparations to a German-Jewish private collector in New York after World War II (see *Frankfurt a/M, Goethe Universität, Universitätsbibliothek), was purchased by Michael Steinhardt and lent to *Jerusalem, Israel Museum, in 2007. It was offered for sale by Sotheby's at an auction in New York on April 29, 2013 (*A Treasured Legacy: The Michael and Judy Steinhardt Judaica Collection*, lot 55), and was purchased jointly by the Israel Museum and the Metropolitan Museum of Art in New York.

Narkiss, p. 160.

Frankfurt a/M (Germany), Goethe Universität, Universitätsbibliothek Johann Christian Senckenberg

Formerly called the Stadt- und Universitätsbibliothek, the library was renamed in January 2005. The library has a collection of 339 Hebrew MSS, 148 of them from the Abraham *Merzbacher collection, purchased for the library by a committee of wealthy Jews after the death of Merzbacher's son and heir, Eugen, in 1903. The 156 Merzbacher MSS (of which only 148 remain in the library) had been described by R. N. Rabbinovicz in 1888 in the catalogue *Ohel Avraham* (אהל אברהם, מינכען תרמ״ח). After World War II the collection was considered lost for the most part, and an envoy sent by the *Jerusalem, IMHM was able to find only 39 MSS when he visited the library in 1952. These were listed in *Cat. Allony–Loewinger*, I, pp. 52–55. In the 1960s, most of the 'lost' MSS, with the exception of six MSS from the Merzbacher collection, were found by Ernst Loewy in a bunker on the site of a destroyed synagogue on Friedberger Anlage. However, 4,314 *Geniza fragments purchased for the library in 1899 by a consortium of individuals at the initiative of Rabbi Markus Horovitz of Frankfurt were lost when the library was bombed during the war. Photocopies of many of the poetry and *piyyut* fragments, made before the war, are found in *Jerusalem, Schocken Institute. Eight MSS, including two from the Merzbacher collection, which were exhibited in the 1920 exhibition (Ausstellung) in Frankfurt and described by E. Sarnow in *Katalog der ständigen Ausstellung: Handschriften, Einbände, Formschnitte und Kupferstiche des 15. Jahrhunderts, Druckwerke und Einblattdrucke des 15. bis 20. Jahrhunderts*, Frankfurt a/M 1920 (nos. 4–11) together with 80 uncatalogued MSS and a few printed books, were given in lieu of reparations to a German-Jewish private collector in New York (now deceased; see *Frankfurt *Mishne Tora*). Illuminated MSS were described in Swarzenski and Schilling, *Die illuminierten Handschriften*, nos. 48, 67, 215, 231, 232 and 234.

The entire collection of MSS remaining in the library was described in the catalogue by E. Róth and L. Prijs, *Hebräische Handschriften* [I] (Verzeichnis der orientalischen Handschriften in Deutschland, VI, la–c). MSS 8° 1–150 were described in Part la (Wiesbaden 1982), MSS 8° 151–275 in Part 1b (Stuttgart 1990), and the quarto and folio MSS in Part lc (Stuttgart 1993). The MSS are arranged according to call-numbers. At the head of each entry are the catalogue number and the call-number. Palaeographical and codicological information: number of leaves, writing material, detailed physical description of the MS (including size of MS, size of written area, number of lines per page, script, date, colophons, owners' entries, provenance, etc.). Indexes at the end of the third volume: names, titles in Hebrew and subjects.

R. Heuberger, *Bibliothek des Judentums; die Hebraica- und Judaica-Sammlung der Stadt- und Universitätsbibliothek Frankfurt am Main: Entstehung, Geschichte und heutige Aufgaben*, Frankfurt a/M 1996. On the exchange of 88 MSS in lieu of property, see pp. 120–131. On the discovery of the 'lost' MSS by E. Loewy, see pp. 136–138.

Frankfurt a/M (Germany), Museum jüdischer Altertümer

One MS from this library, an illuminated *Sefer mitsvot katan*, was in the possession of H. Eisemann of London.

Cat. Allony–Loewinger, I, p. 21.

Franklin, Arthur Ellis

London, 1857–1938; banker and art collector

Franklin's collection of Jewish ceremonial art, including a number of MSS, had been on loan to *London, Jewish Museum, since 1932. In 1967 the collection was purchased by the museum from Franklin's son.

E. D. Barnett (ed.), *Catalogue of the ... Collections of the Jewish Museum*, London 1974, pp. xi, xiv.

Frauberger, Heinrich

Germany, 1845–1920; art historian

Frauberger founded the Gesellschaft zur Erforschung jüdischer Kunstdenkmäler, whose collections formed the nucleus of the *Frankfurt a/M, Museum jüdischer Altertümer. Some of Frauberger's own illuminated Hebrew MSS were described in his *Verzierte hebräische Schrift und jüdischer Buchschmuck (Mitteilungen der Gesellschaft zur Erforschung jüdischer Kunstdenkmäler zu Frankfurt am Main)*, V–VI, Frankfurt a/M 1909. A number of his MSS were bought by Salli *Kirschstein and are now in *Cincinnati, HUC (Oko, p. 83). At least one MS was in the possession of Felix *Guggenheim of Los Angeles (F. Landsberger, 'The Washington Haggadah and its illuminator', *HUCA*, XXI [1948], p. 79), and in 1973 it was presented to *Jerusalem, JNUL (now *Jerusalem, NLI, Heb. 8° 5492). Johann *Krengel acquired *Geniza fragments through Frauberger.

Freer, Charles L.

See *Washington, D.C., Smithsonian Institution, Freer Gallery.

Freiburg im Breisgau (Germany), Universitätsbibliothek

One MS, three *megilot* and six fragments are described in *Cat. Striedl–Róth*, pp. 65–69.

Freimann, Jacob

Cracow, Poland, 1866 – Frankfurt a/M, Germany, 1937

About 30 of Freimann's MSS are in *Jerusalem, NLI.

Frensdorff, Solomon

Hamburg, Germany, 1803 – Hanover, Germany, 1880

Frensdorff wrote an unpublished catalogue of the Hebrew MSS in Hamburg, Stadtbibliothek (now *Hamburg, SUB).

Cat. Steinschneider, Hamburg, p. xi.

Frere, Mary Eliza Isabella

Gloucestershire, England, 1845 – Sussex, England, 1911; author and collector

Frere's MSS, mainly Samaritan, were bequeathed to *Cambridge, Girton College, in 1911.

Rab., *Treas. Jud.*, pp. 173–175; H. Loewe, *Catalogue of the Printed Books and of the Semitic and Jewish Mss. in the Mary Frere Hebrew Library at Girton College, Cambridge*, Cambridge [1916], pp. v–xii.

Friedberg, Albert Dov

Toronto, Canada

Friedberg donated a collection of over 100

Hebrew MSS and rare books, including 44 MSS, to *Toronto, University of Toronto, Thomas Fisher Rare Book Library in 1996. In 1998, he established the Friedberg Genizah Project to help complete the cataloguing of all the fragments and documents from the Cairo *Geniza deposited in various libraries, produce an on-line comprehensive catalogue of all the texts, provide digital images of all the fragments, transcribe as many texts as possible and promote research on the Cairo Geniza.

Friedberg (Germany), Stadtarchiv

Fragments of 171 MSS in the Stadtarchiv were described by A. Lehnardt, 'Die hebräischen Einbandfragmente in Friedberg', in *Wetterauer Geschichtsblätter*, LVIII (2010), pp. 265–313. Previously, fragments of 27 MSS were described in *Cat. Striedl–Róth*, pp. 70–82. The article by Lehnardt (pp. 139–350) includes an overview of the fragments found in the region of Friedberg and a history of its Jewish community, as well as descriptions of the two fragments found in the library of the Theologischen Seminars in Friedberg (pp. 212–214), the fragments of 28 MSS in *Darmstadt, Universitäts- und Landesbibliothek (pp. 215–228), and the fragments of 17 MSS in *Laubach, Graf zu Solms-Laubach'sches Archiv (pp. 228–238).

Friedenwald, Harry

Baltimore, Md., 1864–1950; ophthalmologist and historian of medicine

In his book *Jewish Luminaries in Medical History*, Baltimore 1946, Friedenwald's MSS are listed together with his printed books. His library, including the MSS, was acquired by *Jerusalem, JNUL (now NLI). One MS, a Yemenite haggada, not listed in his book, is now in *New York, JTSA (*Register*, 5685, pp. 125–126 [Marx, *Bibl. Studies*, pp. 38–39]).

Friedenwald, Herbert

Baltimore, Md., 1870–1944; scholar

Friedenwald's *Geniza fragments were presented to Dropsie College in Philadelphia (now *Philadelphia, CAJS).

Cat. Halper, p. 10.

Friedland, Moses Arye Leib

Dünaburg, Russia, 1826 – St. Petersburg, Russia, 1899

According to the title page of S. Wiener's catalogue of Friedland's collection (קהלת משה, פטרבורג תרנ"ג–[תרצ"ו]), printed books and MSS were to have been described. But the catalogue was not completed, so the MSS were not described. In the preface, Wiener wrote that Friedland's library included about 300 MSS, some of them from the library of Joseph *Massel of Viasin and others purchased from Raphael N. *Rabbinovicz, and that the collection was presented to the Asiatic Museum (now *St. Petersburg, Institute of Oriental Manuscripts).

א"י כ"ץ, 'משה אריה לייב פרידלנד וספרייתו', פרקים, ג, ניו יורק תשכ"ג, עמ' 169–191.

Friedman, Harry G.

USA, 1882–1965

Friedman purchased MSS for *New York, JTSA, and presented his own MSS to the library. Some of these are described in various volumes of the JTSA *Register*.

Friedman, Lee Max

Memphis, Tenn., 1871 – Boston, Mass., 1957; lawyer and collector

Friedman presented ten MSS to *Cambridge (Mass.), Harvard University, and purchased MSS for Harvard from the Felix *Friedmann collection.

Friedmann, Felix

Amsterdam–Vienna, early twentieth century; collector

Thirty of Friedmann's MSS were purchased

by Lee *Friedman for *Cambridge (Mass.), Harvard University (MSS Heb. 20, 35–39, 42–55, 57–66). Many of the MSS in his collection had previously been described by J. M. Hillesum, 'De Friedmann-bibliotheek te Amsterdam', *De Vrijdagavond*, III, Part 2, Nov. 1926, pp. 98–103.

Friedmann, Israel

1797 – Ruzhin, Ukraine, 1850; rabbi

The illuminated fifteenth-century Ashkenazic siddur formerly in Friedmann's possession is now *Jerusalem, Israel Museum, MS 180/53.

Jerusalem Collections, no. 10; I. Fishof, 'The origin of the *siddur* of the Rabbi of Ruzhin', *Jewish Art*, XII/XIII (1987), pp. 73–82.

Friedmann, Nahum Dov of Sadagora

Ruzhin, Ukraine, 1843 – Vienna, 1883

Seventy-seven MSS formerly in the possession of Rabbi Friedmann and 25 MSS from other owners were offered for sale in Vienna by Jacob *Halpern and are listed in the undated catalogue he compiled (רשימת כתבי יד [נומר 9] של בית עקד ספרים של הרב הצדיק המפורסם ר' נחום דוב פריעדמאן ז"ל מסאדאגורא ... עומדים למכירה ע"י *Jacob Halpern, Wien*, n.p., n.d.; hectograph). More than half of the MSS were eventually acquired by *Jerusalem, Mosad Harav Kook (nos. 6, 7, 13–16, 18, 19, 22, 23, 30, 31, 35–46, 48–51, 53, 55–59, 61–66, 70, 77–79, 83, 85). Ten of these (nos. 15, 18, 36, 38, 48, 49, 57, 58, 62, 65), which were copied for Friedmann during his lifetime, were described by N. Ben-Menahem (נ' בן מנחם, 'כתבי־יד מספרייתו של רבי נחום דובער פרידמאן', ארשת, א [תשי"ח], עמ' 396–413). Ben-Menahem did not know of the existence of the Halpern catalogue. Nos. 15 and 48 were later acquired by William *Gross (MSS 273 and 272). Nos. 2, 5, 27 were acquired by *Berlin, Staatsbibliothek, in 1926 (MSS Or. 8° 2414, 1558, and 2409). No. 24 is now *Jerusalem, NLI, Heb. 4° 6898 (formerly in the N. *Allony collection). Nos. 29 and 67 are *New York, JTSA, MSS 8558 and 9632. At the end of another undated catalogue of Halpern's (רשימת ספרים מעזבון ... ר' נחום דוב מסאדאגורא ומעזבון חכמים מפורסמים מארץ אשכנז), 40 MSS are listed, but there is no certainty that any of them belonged to Rabbi Friedmann. Many of them, perhaps most, are now in the *Enelow Memorial Collection in *New York, JTSA.

Friesland

See *Leeuwarden.

Fuenn, Samuel Joseph

Vilna, Lithuania, 1818–1890; author

One MS belonging to Fuenn and six MSS of his works are now in *Jerusalem, NLI. At least one MS of his was purchased by Moses *Friedland and is now *St. Petersburg, Institute of Oriental Manuscripts, MS B 512.

י' צינברג, תולדות ספרות ישראל, ב, תל־אביב 1960, עמ' 377; B. Purin, *Das Wiener Memorbuch der Fürther Klaus-Synagoge*, Fürth 1999.

Fugger, Ulrich

Germany, 1526–1584

Fugger was a convert from Catholicism to Protestantism who fled from his native Augsburg to Heidelberg for shelter. He collected hundreds of MSS, among them 177 Hebrew MSS, 72 of them originating in Candia (Heraklion, Crete). He purchased many MSS from Elia Capsali of Candia and 13 MSS from the library of G. *Manetti (1396–1459). In 1584 he bequeathed his library to the *Heidelberg, Biblioteca Palatina, which in turn was acquired by the *Vatican after being sacked by the Catholic League in 1622.

Cassuto, *Palatina*, pp. 17, 22–48; מ"ד קסוטו, 'תולדותיו של אוסף כתבי־יד עבריים', יד לקורא, א (תש"ז), עמ' 62.

Fuks, Leo (Lajb)

Kalisz, Poland, 1908 – Amsterdam, Netherlands, 1990

Fuks edited catalogues of the Hebrew and Judaica MSS in *Amsterdam, Rosenthaliana and *Amsterdam, Ets Haim. He donated MSS from his collection to *Amsterdam, Rosenthaliana, and his library, including some MSS, was bequeathed to the Provinciale Bibliotheek in Leeuwarden, now, *Leeuwarden, TRESOAR. The MS from which G. Scholem edited two letters from Eretz Israel in *Tarbiz*, XXV (1956), pp. 428–440, is now MS *Amsterdam, Rosenthaliana, Ros. 682.

A. K. Offenberg & E. G. L. Schrijver, 'Ex libris L. Fuks', *Studia Rosenthaliana*, XXIV (1990), pp. 204–206.

Fuld, Aaron

Frankfurt a/M, Germany, 1790–1847; communal leader

Fifteen MSS from Fuld's collection were given by his son Salomon to Frankfurt a/M, Stadtbibliothek (now *Frankfurt a/M, Goethe Universität, Universitätsbibliothek) in 1867.

Freimann, 'Mitteilungen', p. 84; R. Heuberger, *Bibliothek des Judentums: Die Hebraica- und Judaica-Sammlung der Stadt- und Universitätsbibliothek Frankfurt am Main: Entstehung, Geschichte und heutige Aufgaben*, Frankfurt a/M 1996, p. 16.

Fulda (Germany), Hochschul- und Landesbibliothek

The Hessische Landesbibliothek, established in 1776 with collections that were largely collected after the Thirty Years War, was integrated into the Hochschule library in 2001. Fourteen MSS and fragments from another eight MSS are described in *Cat. Striedl–Róth*, pp. 83–96. The MSS and most of the fragments are listed in *Cat. Allony–Loewinger*, I, pp. 51–52 (nos. 687–711). In *Cat. Allony–Loewinger* the call-numbers are listed in parentheses, but they are not complete because the prefixes 2°, 4° and 8° are missing, and the call-numbers of one MS, no. 687 (call-number 2° A 1), and the fragments are not given. The call-number of no. 696 should read: 8° A 10. Correct call-numbers are given in *Cat. Striedl–Róth.* The MSS, but not the fragments, were described by M. Weinberg, 'Die hebraeischen Handschriften der Landesbibliothek Fulda', *JJLG*, XX (1929), pp. 273–296.

Fürstlich Oettingen-Wallersteinsche Bibliothek

See *Harburg.

Fürth (Germany), Klaus (synagogue)

An illuminated *memorbuch* of the Klaus (synagogue) is now in the Jüdisches Museum Franken in Fürth, Inv. Nr. 2–98.

G

G

*Günzburg.

Gagin (Gaguine), Hayyim Abraham

Constantinople, Turkey, 1787 – Jerusalem, 1848; Chief Rabbi of Jeusalem

Gagin's library, which included books that belonged to his father-in-law, Abraham Shalom Mizrahi Sharabi, son of the kabbalist Shalom Sharabi, passed into the possession of his son Shalom and later into that of his grandson Isaac, who sold the collection. An undated broadsheet found in *Jerusalem, NLI, 93 L 11, lists 74 MS titles (nos. 17–19 are parts of a single MS) offered for sale by 'Rabbin Isaac H. Gaguine, Jerusalem'. According to the heading, the MSS were purchased by Isaac's forefather Sar Shalom [Sharabi?]

from Gedaliah Hayyun (d. 1777), founder of the kabbalistic Bet-El Yeshiva in Jerusalem, where Shalom Sharabi taught. The broadsheet is not dated, but it must have been printed between 1905 and 1919, as there is a reference to the Russo-Japanese War (1904–5), and one of the MSS was listed in a sales catalogue in 1919. One of the MSS, no. 51, was offered for sale in *Literarischer Palästina-Almanach* (לוח ארץ ישראל), IX (1903), p. 19, and four others (nos.17–19, 21, 22, 33) in *ibid.*, XII (1912), pp. 98–100.
For the locations of MSS listed in the broadsheet whose whereabouts may be established see Appendix I, no. 11.

Gale, Thomas
Scruton, England, ca. 1635 – York, England, 1702; classical scholar
Gale presented his MSS, many of them acquired from the orientalist Gerbrandt *Anslo from Amsterdam, to *Cambridge, Trinity College. The MSS were described by A. Wright and S. Schiller-Szinessy in an appendix to E. A. Palmer, *A Descriptive Catalogue of the Arabic, Persian and Turkish Manuscripts in the Library of Trinity College, Cambridge, ... with an Appendix Containing a Catalogue of the Hebrew and Samaritan MSS in the Same Library*, Cambridge 1870.

Gans, Mozes Heiman
Amsterdam, 1917–1987, author and collector
Fifty-two MSS and documents from Gans's collection are listed in *Cat. Allony–Kupfer*, II, nos. 819–871. A few of the MSS were sold; the rest remain in the possession of his son.

Gaon, Joshua Ibn, Bible
See *Joshua Ibn Gaon Bible.

Garrett, Robert
Baltimore, Md., 1875–1961; banker and collector
Garrett's collection is now in Princeton University Library. The Hebrew MS described by E. Panofsky, 'Giotto and Maimonides in Avignon: The story of an illuminated Hebrew manuscript', *Journal of the Walters Art Gallery*, IV (1941), pp. 27–44, is now Princeton University Library, MS Garrett 26.

Gaster, Moses
Bucharest, Rumania, 1856 – London, 1939; Sephardi Hakham and collector in England
Almost 1,200 Hebrew MSS and many *Geniza fragments from Gaster's collection were purchased in 1925 by the British Museum (now *London, British Library; see Rab., *Treas. Jud.*, p. 30). During World War II the MSS that remained in the collection were stored in cellars; some suffered damage from the damp, and a few were lost. In 1954 about 350 Hebrew MSS (177 original MSS and about 190 volumes of nineteenth-century copies of original Hebrew MSS), 10,000 Geniza fragments and 342 Samaritan MSS were sold to *Manchester, John Rylands University Library (*Bulletin of the John Rylands Library*, XXXVII [1954/5], pp. 2–6; Rab., *Treas. Jud.*, pp. 158–164). A few MSS were in the possession of the Jerusalem booksellers *Bamberger and Wahrmann, who had purchased the remainder of Gaster's library in 1957, after no suitable institution was found to accommodate them. In 1963 these MSS were sold by the firm to *Los Angeles, University of California Library. An illuminated MS written by Aaron Wolf Herlingen, MS Gaster 737, is now *Jerusalem, Israel Museum, MS 180/6. MS Gaster 15 is now *Budapest, Jewish Theological Seminary MS K 52, and MS Gaster 1366 is now MS K 117 in the same library. In addition to the MSS he acquired for his own collection, Gaster purchased MSS from Solomon *Halberstamm and Leopold *Zunz for the Montefiore library (see *London, Montefiore Collection) (Rab., *Lit. Treas.*, p. 54).
The only printed catalogue of any substantial part of the Gaster collection is E. Robertson,

Catalogue of the Samaritan MSS in the John Rylands Library, Manchester, II: *The Gaster MSS*, Manchester 1962. Photocopies of two unpublished lists of the Gaster MSS are available in the British Library and in *Jerusalem, IMHM: (1) *Handlist of Gaster Manuscripts held mostly in the British Library ... and in the John Rylands Library, Manchester*, prepared by Gaster himself, with annotations by M. Ettinghausen and some addenda by Gaster's son, V. I. Gaster, and with indications in the margins of the eventual disposition of the MSS; and (2) an incomplete list of the Gaster collection in the British Library, *Catalogue of Hebrew Manuscripts in the Gaster Collection, the British Library, London, reproduced from the manuscript and typescript blue-slips, prepared by Jacob Leveen, Joseph Rosenwasser and David Goldstein*. The IMHM prepared a typewritten list of the Gaster MSS in the British Library, and in addition to the numbers assigned by Gaster and the British Library call-numbers, an arbitrary serial number was added. For many years, only this arbitrary serial number appeared on the IMHM's catalogue cards. As a result, MSS were referred to by this number in many publications, and attempts by scholars to locate them have ended in utter confusion.

Gaster Bible

Name given to two MSS, *London, BL, MSS Or. 9879–9880 (formerly MSS *Gaster 150–151), fragments from illuminated ninth- and tenth-century Bible MSS. The MSS are called the First Gaster Bible (Or. 9879, Gaster 150) and the Second Gaster Bible (Or. 9880, Gaster 151). Both are described in M. Gaster, *Hebrew Illuminated Bibles of the IXth and Xth Centuries*, London 1901.

Gayangos, Pascual y Arce de

Spain, 1809–1897; orientalist

One MS from Gayangos's collection is in *Madrid, Biblioteca Nacional.

Pearson, p. 42.

Geiger, Abraham

Frankfurt a/M, Germany, 1810 – Berlin, 1874; Reform rabbi

Fifteen of Geiger's MSS were listed in *HB*, XVII (1877), pp. 11–12. They were acquired by *Berlin, Hochschule für die Wissenschaft des Judentums, and were taken to the U.S. in 1936 by Alexander Guttmann, a professor at the Hochschule. Thirteen of these and a few more of Geiger's MSS, also acquired by the Hochschule, were listed in Sotheby's catalogue *Highly Important Hebrew Printed Books and Manuscripts*, New York 1984, and were thereafter transferred to the auspices of the Judaica Conservancy Foundation; for details, see Berlin, Hochschule. Geiger's MS of a commentary by Thomas Aquinas on Aristotle's *Metaphysics*, listed in *HÜ*, p. 485, note 129, later belonged to Z. H. *Edelmann and L. *Zunz and was *London, Montefiore, MS 296. For the present locations of the MSS, see Appendix I, no. 12.

Steinschneider, *Vorlesungen*, p. 64 (Hebrew, p. 85).

Geldern

See *Van Geldern Haggada.

Geneva (Switzerland), Bibliothèque centrale juive

Ten MSS are described in *Cat. Allony–Kupfer*, II, nos. 1617–1625. No. 1622b is erroneously listed in the catalogue as the second work found in MS 1622, when in fact it is a separate MS on microfilm no. 10555 in the *Jerusalem, IMHM.

Geneva (Switzerland), Bibliothèque publique et universitaire

Twelve MSS were listed in J. Senebier, *Catalogue raisonné des manuscrits conservés dans la Bibliothèque de la Ville et République de Genève*, Geneva 1779, pp. 18–25. Fourteen MSS are listed in *Cat. Allony–Kupfer*, II, p. 131. In that list, there are several errors in the call-numbers, given in parentheses at the end of each entry and consisting of the prefix 'm.h.', a MS number and an inventory number. For example, the first call-number in the Allony–Kupfer catalogue should read 'm.h. 9; inv. 1901'. Nos. 1601 and 1602 are both parts of a single MS. The call-number of no. 1603 should read 'm.h. 1; inv. 887', that of no. 1609, 'm.h. 13; inv. 1906', and of those of nos. 1613–1614 (which also form one MS), 'm.h. 10; inv. 1902'. The call-numbers of nos. 1615 and 1616 are interchanged in the catalogue.

A collection of MSS that belonged to Sion *Segre Amar (1910–1993) is on deposit in the Comites Latentes (hidden friends), a private foundation founded by Segre Amar, which entrusted its collection to the Library's safe-keeping in 1977. Jules Nicole (1842–1921) presented the library with a small collection of 150 Geniza fragments together with a large collection of Greek papyri he had purchased in Egypt. These Geniza fragments were described by D. Rosenthal, אוסף הגניזה הקהירית בז׳נבה, *The Cairo Geniza Collection in Geneva*, Jerusalem 2010. The catalogue includes detailed descriptions in Hebrew, facsimiles of at least one page from each fragment, publications of selected texts, and essays by various authors on some of the texts.

Geniza

Term denoting a depository where Hebrew books and ritual objects no longer in use are stored. The most famous Geniza is the one found in the ancient synagogue in Fustat (Old Cairo), the synagogue of the Palestinians, also known as the Shamiyin, the Elijah, the Moses or the Ben Ezra Synagogue (see R. J. H. Gottheil and W. H. Worrell, *Fragments from the Cairo Genizah in the Freer Collection*, New York 1927, p. xi). In this Geniza over 200,000 pages and fragments from Hebrew books, letters and documents were found. The Cairo Geniza was visited by Simon van Geldern as early as 1750, but it was not until the middle of the nineteenth century that any of its treasures were taken out. In 1889 or 1890, when the synagogue building was being renovated after the roof collapsed and was torn down, the Geniza chamber and all the thousands of fragments it held came to light. Gottheil and Worrell, quoting an 'anonymous correspondent', wrote that for weeks the MSS were lying in the open courtyard and dealers could obtain bundles of leaves for nominal sums (*op. cit.*, p. xiii). These leaves were sold to tourists and libraries. Among those who acquired Geniza fragments during the early 1890s were Solomon *Wertheimer (who sold many fragments to the *Oxford, Bodleian Library, and the *Cambridge, University Library), Elkan Nathan *Adler, A. H. Sayce and G. Chester. The latter, in turn, sold to Oxford (see the letter sent by Sayce to Adler, published in a Hebrew translation: א״מ הברמן, הגניזה והגניזות, ירושלים 1971, עמ׳ 76–78). Earlier, in 1889, and again until 1895, the Bodleian purchased almost 5,000 leaves from close to 1,000 MSS from Count Riamo d'Hulst, an excavator for the Egypt Exploration Fund in Cairo; see R. J. W. Jefferson, 'A Genizah secret', *Journal of the History of Collections*, XXI (2009), pp. 125–142; and see idem, 'The Cairo Genizah unearthed', in S. Bhayro and B. Outhwaite (eds.), *Cambridge Genizah Studies*, I: *Proceedings of the First International Conference on Genizah Studies, Westminster College*, Cambridge 2007, pp. 171–200. In 1896, Solomon *Schechter went to Cairo and returned to England with all the fragments that remained in the chamber, over 140,000 in all, and presented them to the Cambridge library (for a detailed account of Schechter's mission to Cairo see N. Bentwich, *Solomon*

Schechter: A Biography, Philadelphia 1948, pp. 126–163). It should be noted that not all the so-called 'Geniza' fragments come from the Ben Ezra synagogue repository. A large number of fragments were excavated from the Basatin cemetery, east of Old Cairo. Most of the fragments in the *Mosseri collection were found in a systematic excavation of the cemetery in 1912 and 1913. Some of the overflow from the Geniza in the synagogue was buried in the courtyard near the synagogue. Sayce sold some fragments excavated from the courtyard to the Bodleian Library (see his letter to Adler quoted above). In the *Firkovich and Adler collections, and quite probably in others as well, are fragments that were found in cemeteries and genizas in other places (Damascus, Jerusalem, Crimea, etc.) as well as fragments found in bindings and elsewhere, and it is often difficult or impossible to distinguish the Cairo Geniza material from the other fragments.

Geniza fragments served as the raw material for a large number of scholarly works in various fields of study. Much of the work of such scholars as L. Ginzberg, J. Mann, S. Assaf and S. D. Goitein is based on this material.

While catalogues of Geniza materials held in a few individual libraries exist, there is no catalogue of all the Geniza fragments in print or on-line, nor even a complete bibliography of the Geniza. Perhaps the first attempt to publish a comprehensive bibliography of Geniza texts in a single field was that of Saul Shaked, *A Tentative Bibliography of Geniza Documents*, Paris–The Hague 1969, which lists all documentary material from the Geniza published until 1965. The Taylor–Schechter Genizah Research Unit at the Cambridge University Library has published a series of bibliographies and catalogues of parts of its collection (for a list of these publications see *Cambridge, University Library). In an attempt to remedy this situation, the Friedberg Genizah Project (FGP), conceived and initiated by Albert D. *Friedberg of Toronto, Canada, started to operate in 1999. The goal of the FGP is to produce an on-line union catalogue of all the Geniza texts, to digitize all the fragments and make them available to scholars on-line, to transcribe as many texts as possible and to promote research in the Cairo Geniza.

The history of the Cairo Geniza and its discovery is related in a number of publications, chiefly Reif, *Jewish Archive* (2000), A. Hoffman and P. Cole, *Sacred Trash*, New York 2011, and, in Hebrew, E. Hurvitz, *Catalogue of the Cairo Geniza Fragments in the Westminster College Library, Cambridge* (קטלוג קטעי גניזת קאהיר בספריית ווסטמינסטר קולג', קיימברידג'), I: *A Historical Introduction to the Antiquity and Discovery of the Geniza from Cairo*, New York 2006 (released in 2009). A more complete survey of the latest research in Geniza studies may be found in the second edition of *Encyclopaedia Judaica,* VII, Detroit 2007, pp. 460–483.

Substantial collections of Geniza fragments are found today in over 25 public and private libraries. The principal collections are listed below, in descending order of size. The number (or approximate number) of fragments in each collection is given in parentheses. The abbreviation 'Cat.' following some of the listings indicates that a catalogue exists for at least part of the collection. Details concerning these catalogues and the collections in general may be found in the respective main entries in this *Guide*.

Major Collections of Geniza Fragments

*Cambridge, University Library (140,000). Cat.

*New York, JTSA (24,000). Cat.

*Manchester, John Rylands University Library (10,000, mostly small scraps).

*St. Petersburg, NLR (1,200 in the *Antonin collection and many, perhaps, in the *Firkovich collection). Cat.

*Oxford, Bodleian Library (5,000). In *Cat. Neubauer–Cowley*, II, 2,675 fragments are described. The remaining fragments – mainly purchased from Joseph Offord, acquired in exchange for books from Christian *Ginsburg or presented by Arthur *Cowley – are briefly described in a typewritten list in the library.

*London, British Library (5,000). A few fragments are described in *Cat. Margoliouth.* Most of the fragments, with the exception of those from the *Gaster collection, are in MSS Or. 5556–5566. S. D. Goitein described 'Geniza Papers of a Documentary Character in the Gaster Collection of the British Museum', *JQR*, LI (1960/61), pp. 34–46. A typewritten list of the Geniza fragments in the British Museum collection exists in the library.

*Mosseri, Jacques N., and family collection (7,000). Cat. (Presently deposited in *Cambridge, University Library.)

*Paris, AIU (over 3,500). Cat.

*Cambridge, Westminster College (over 2,000; jointly purchased in 2013 by *Cambridge, University Library, and *Oxford, Bodleian Library). Cat.

*Strasbourg, Bibliothèque nationale et universitaire (1,000).

*Budapest, Hungarian Academy of Sciences (650). Cat.

*Philadelphia, CAJS (formerly Dropsie College) (over 450) and University Museum (21). Cat.

*Jerusalem, NLI (300). Cat.

Cairo, Museum of Islamic Art (260). About 260 fragments, mostly from very late MSS, recovered from the Mosseri cemetery in El-Basatin by a mission of Egyptian archaeologists, were described in Arabic in the catalogue *Guide to the Latest Geniza Documents Collection*, Cairo 1993, [compiled by H. M. El-Hawary] and edited by H. M. Rabie.

Cincinnati, HUC (250).

*Vienna, Österreichische Nationalbibliothek, Rainer Collection (186). Cat. The fragments seem to derive from the Geniza. See *Rainer.

*Geneva, Bibliothèque publique et universitaire (150). Cat.

*Washington, D.C., Smithsonian Institution, Freer Gallery (52). Cat.

*Birmingham, Selly Oak Colleges, *Mingana and *Mittwoch collections (47). Cat.

*Sassoon, Solomon [formerly] (30). MSS nos. 17–19, 187, 217–227, 521–532, 537, 566, 713. Cat. Most if not all of these are no longer in the Sassoon collection; for their present locations, see Appendix I, no. 35.

*Toronto, University of Toronto (19).

*Kiev, Vernadsky National Library,*Harkavy collection (dozens of fragments).

Collections of Geniza Fragments that Were Destroyed or Lost

*Frankfurt a/M, Stadt- und Universitätsbibliothek (now Goethe Universität, Universitätsbibliothek; 4,314 fragments). Photocopies of the liturgy and poetry fragments are in *Jerusalem, Schocken Institute.

*Berlin, Jüdische Gemeinde. Partly in *Cincinnati, HUC.

*Warsaw, Tłomackie Street Synagogue. Photostats of over 100 fragments are preserved in *Jerusalem, Schocken Institute.

Genoa (Italy), Biblioteca Civica Berio

The Hebrew Bible in this library (Cod. D IX 31) was described by A. Luzzatto, 'La Bibbia ebraica della Biblioteca "Berio" di Genova', *Miscellanea di Storia Ligure*, IV (1966), pp. 41–65. The decorations in the codex were described by L. Mortara Ottolenghi in *ibid.*, pp. 67–84.

Genoa (Italy), Biblioteca della Comunità ebraica

Eight MSS are listed in Sonne, *Relazione*. The MSS were taken by the Nazis during the war. *Cincinnati, HUC, MS 279, bears the stamp of the library but was not listed by Sonne.

Genova
See *Genoa.

Gerona (Spain), Arxiu Históric
More than 2,000 fragments dating from the second half of the thirteenth century, mainly from paper MSS – mostly of administrative documents, such as sale contracts, *ketubot*, and wills, as well as fragments from rabbinical literature – are found in the bindings of archival records in this archive.

M. Perani, 'The "Gerona Genizah": An overview and a *ketubah* of 1377', *Hispania Judaica Bulletin*, VII (2010), pp. 137–173.

Gh.
*Ghirondi, Mordecai Samuel.

Ghir.
*Ghirondi, Mordecai Samuel.

Ghirondi, Mordecai Samuel
Padua, Italy, 1799–1852; scholar
After Ghirondi's death his library remained closed for a number of years. It was then acquired by the bookseller Samuel *Schönblum, who printed a catalogue, *Catalogue de la bibliothèque de Mr. M. S. Girondi*, Lemberg 1870, in which 152 MSS were listed in alphabetical order of their titles. Some of the MSS were sold to the British Museum (now *London, British Library). In a hectograph publication of Moritz *Steinschneider's handwritten *Catalog hebräischer Handschriften, grössten Theils aus dem Nachlass des Rabb. M. S. Girondi*, Berlin 1872, 146 MSS offered for sale by Schönblum are described in greater detail in a different order. At the beginning of the catalogue is a concordance to the numbers in the earlier catalogue. The MSS were sold to various collectors and libraries. For the present locations of the MSS that can be traced, see Appendix I, no. 13.

Gianfilippi, Paolinio
Verona, Italy, d. 1827
Sixteen Hebrew MSS from Gianfilippi's collection are now in Verona, Biblioteca Civica.

Tamani, *Verona*, pp. 217–219.

Gibson, Margaret Dunlop
See *Lewis–Gibson.

Gieldzinski, Lesser
Danzig (formerly Germany, now Gdansk, Poland), 1830–1910; collector
Gieldzinski's collection of Jewish ceremonial art, including a small number of MSS, which he donated to the Jewish community in Danzig, was described in the catalogue *Sammlung jüdischer Kunstgegenstände der Synagogen-Gemeinde zu Danzig*, Danzig 1933. The collection (including the MSS?) was sent to *New York, JTSA, before the outbreak of World War II, with the stipulation that they would be returned to Danzig if the Jewish community survived. After the War, the collection remained in JTSA (*Treasures of the Jewish Museum*, New York 1986, pp. 10–11). Forty of the 52 Tora scrolls in the collection were destroyed in the fire that ravaged the JTSA Library in 1966 ('Report on the Library of the Jewish Theological Seminary of America, Jan. 1 – September 30, 1966' [mimeographed]).

Giessen (Germany), Universitätsbibliothek (Bibliothek der Justus-Liebeg Hochschule)
One Hebrew MS was described in *Cat. Striedl–Róth*, no. 153. The MS was also described in brief in *Cat. Allony–Loewinger*, I, no. 519.

Ginsburg, Christian David
Warsaw, Poland, 1831 – London, 1914; scholar
Several of Ginsburg's MSS were described by A. Neubauer, 'Kurze Notizen über Handschriften', *Israelietische Letterbode*, XI

(1885/6), pp. 157–165. Most of his MSS were acquired by W. A. *Wright, who left his collection to the *Cambridge, Trinity College Library. The MSS were described in H. Loewe, *Catalogue of the Manuscripts in the Hebrew Character Collected and Bequeathed to Trinity College Library by the Late William Aldis Wright*, Cambridge 1926. MS B.1 in the *Letterbode* list is now *New York, JTSA, MS L883 (formerly Adler 3860). Some of Ginsburg's MSS are in *London, British Library (MSS Or. 4220–4224). A number of *Geniza fragments belonging to Ginsburg were acquired from him in exchange for other books by *Oxford, Bodleian Library. In his book *Introduction to the Massoretico-Critical Edition of the Hebrew Bible*, London 1897, pp. 469–778, Ginsburg described 60 biblical MSS, 49 of them from the British Museum (now *London, British Library). A list of the London MSS described by Ginsburg is found in *Cat. Margoliouth–Leveen*, IV, p. 174.

Girton College

See *Cambridge, Girton College.

Glaser, Eduard

Deutsch-Rust, Bohemia, 1855 – Munich, Germany, 1908; orientalist

One of Glaser's MSS, acquired in Yemen and containing fragments of a Bible, was presented by Glaser's brother to *New York, JTSA (MS L510) (P. Kahle, *Die hebräischen Bibelhandschriften aus Babylonien*, Giessen 1928, p. 6). Three Yemenite MSS were purchased by Dropsie College (now *Philadelphia, CAJS) in 1923 (Pearson, p. 72). A MS of Joseph Halevy's journey in Yemen was bequeathed to the Österreichische Akademie der Wissenschaften in Vienna, as described in Goitein's edition of the text (ש' גויטין [עורך], מסעות חבשוש, תל־אביב 1939, מבוא, עמ' 13–12).

Glasgow (Scotland), University Library

The library has two medieval Hebrew MSS that came with the Hunterian collection in 1807. The collection was named after its original owner, Dr. William Hunter (1718–1783). There are also three nineteenth-century MSS in the library as well as four Esther scrolls and four Tora scrolls.

Glass

See *Cambridge, University Library, 'Geniza' section.

Cod. Gold.

See *Goldschmidt, Lazarus.

Golden Haggada

Name given to *London, BL, MS Add. 27120 (*Cat. Margoliouth*, no. 607), a fourteenth-century illuminated Spanish haggada. It appeared in a facsimile edition (London 1970). MS London, Or. 2884 (*Cat. Margoliouth*, no. 608), is very similar to the Golden Haggada in style and iconography and is called the 'sister' to the Golden Haggada.

Narkiss, pp. 56–58; Narkiss, *Span. & Port.*, nos. 11–12.

Goldenberg, Samuel Lob

See *Leonowitsch.

Goldschmidt, Lazarus

Plongian, Lithuania, 1871 – London, 1950; scholar

Seven MSS from Goldschmidt's collection were acquired by *Copenhagen, Kongelige Bibliothek. The MSS bear call-numbers with the prefix 'Cod. Gold.'

Cat. Allony–Kupfer, II, p. 18.

Goldschmidt, Mayer Selig (Manfred)

Frankfurt a/M, Germany, 1828–1896

Ninety-seven of Goldschmidt's MSS were presented to *Jerusalem, Hekhal Shelomo Museum, by Sir Isaac Wolfson in 1967.

Most were described in the catalogue of the Hekhal Shelomo MSS, *Min hagenazim* (מן הגנזים, א–ג, ירושלים תשכ"ז–תשל"ד). In 1990 the MSS were acquired by the Department of Antiquities and deposited in *Jerusalem, JNUL (now NLI). Three of Goldschmidt's MSS were described in Swarzenski and Schilling, *Die illuminierten Handschriften*, nos. 68, 69 and 233. No. 68, a Bible dated 1294, is now *New York, Public Library, Spencer Collection, MS 1 (see *Xanten Bible). No. 69 comprised five leaves from the *Nuremberg maḥzor, including one that was acquired by E. Bodenheimer of New York (see Narkiss, p. 110) and then by David Sofer in London; these are now rejoined to the maḥzor, which is owned by Dr. David and Jemima Jeselsohn of Zurich and deposited in *Jerusalem, Israel Museum. No. 233, a maḥzor, is now *New York, JTSA, MS 8641. Other Goldschmidt MSS are in *New York, JTSA (MSS 2661, 2872 and R673), and in the Schocken Institute. The siddur described by D. Kaufmann, 'Three centuries of the genealogy of the most eminent Anglo-Jewish-family before 1290', *JQR*, III (1891), pp. 555–566, was MS Schocken 19522 and was offered for sale at Christie's in New York (*Important Hebrew Manuscripts from the Salman Schocken Collection ... 15 November 2005*, no. 10). JTSA, MS 2833 includes a list, probably compiled by E. N. *Adler, of about 90 MSS and some printed books that belonged to Goldschmidt. A MS belonging to Angelo Piatelli of Jerusalem includes a catalogue compiled by Samuel b. Naphtali Bamberger of 105 MSS and one incunabulum that belonged to Goldschmidt.

Goldsmid, Julian

England, 1838–1896: politician

Twelve MSS from Goldsmid's collection were described in *Catalogue of the Anglo-Jewish Historical Exhibition ... 1887*, London 1888, nos. 775, 2070–2080. More than half of these MSS were purchased from the library of the Duke of *Sussex. The collection has been dispersed, and Goldsmid's MSS may be found in various libraries. For the present locations of some of the MSS see Appendix I, no. 14.

Gollancz, Hermann

Bremen, Germany, 1852 – London, 1930; English rabbi

The MS of Maimonides' *Guide of the Perplexed* in his possession from which Gollancz published poems in his edition of Joseph Kimchi's *Shekel hakodesh* (Oxford 1919) was sold at auction by Sotheby's in London, July 12, 1971, and is now MS H 001 in the Elias Nahmias collection in *Paris, AIU. The whereabouts of Gollancz's MS of *Mafteaḥ Shelomo* from which he published a facsimile edition (London 1914) are unknown to me.

Golnitzki, Heshil

Poland – Haifa, Israel, twentieth century

Golnitzki's MSS, described in his *Bemaḥzor hayamim* (במחזור הימים, חיפה תשכ"ג), were formerly in *Jerusalem, Hekhal Shelomo Museum.

Gorizia (Italy), Biblioteca della Comunità ebraica

The MS, formerly in the possession of the Gorizia Jewish community, which was described by *Kennicott, no. 585, is now *Oxford, Bodleian Library, MS Can. Or. 138 (*Cat. Neubauer*, 50). Four MSS that were in the library before World War II and were described by Sonne, *Relazione*, were looted by the Nazis and have disappeared.

Gotha (Germany), Universitäts- und Forschungsbibliothek Erfurt/Gotha

The library's name has changed several times. From its founding in 1647 until 1920 and from 1925 to 1945, when it was confiscated by the Red Army, it was called the Herzogliche Bibliothek. From 1920 to 1925 it was called the Landesbibliothek, and this was the name restored to it when it was returned to East Germany in 1956. Between 1969 and 1990 it was called the Forschungsbibliothek and in 1991 it was renamed the Forschungs- und Landesbibliothek. In 1999 it became part of Erfurt University. Fifteen Hebrew, Yiddish and Samaritan MSS were described by A. Merx in W. Pertsch, *Die orientalischen Handschriften der Herzoglichen Bibliothek zu Gotha*, Gotha 1893, nos. 20–32, 57–59. Two additional fragments are not listed in this catalogue.

Gottheil, Richard James Horatio

Manchester, England, 1862 – New York, 1931; orientalist

The MS of works by the historian Joseph b. Joshua Hakohen formerly in Gottheil's possession (*Proceedings of the American Jewish Historical Society*, II [1893], pp. 129–137) is now *New York, Columbia University, Butler Library, MS X893 K 82. Together with W. H. Worrell, Gottheil compiled the catalogue *Fragments from the Cairo Genizah in the Freer Collection [in Washington]*, New York 1927. Gottheil also described MSS he saw in Cairo ('Some Hebrew Mss. in Cairo', *JQR*, XVII [1905], pp. 609–652) and Rome ('Bible MSS in Roman Synagogues', *ZfHB*, IX [1905], pp. 177–184).

Göttingen (Germany), Niedersächsisiche Staats- und Universitätsbibliothek

Founded in 1734. Twenty-one MSS are listed in *Cat. Allony–Loewinger*, I, pp. 38–39. Two other MSS, as well as fragments from five MSS, are described in *Cat. Striedl–Róth*, pp. 98–101, which, however, omits the MSS described in *Cat. Allony–Loewinger*. The MSS had previously been described by I. Hannover in W. Meyer (ed.), *Die Handschriften in Göttingen* (Verzeichniss der Handschriften im Preussischen Staate, 1), Berlin 1893, I, pp. 383–386.

Gottweig (Austria), Stiftsbibliothek

One Hebrew MS in two volumes (numbered 1010–1011) was described in *Cat. Schwarz*, Austria, no. 2. Thirty-one fragments are described and displayed on the website of the Austrian Academy of Sciences at http://www.ksbm.oeaw.ac.at/hebraica.

Gozlow

See *Eupatoria.

Gradiscia

Latin name for Gorizia.

Graz (Austria), Steiermärkisches Landesarchiv

Fragments from six MSS were described in *Cat. Schwarz–Loewinger–Róth*, pp. 80–81. Fragments from four of these MSS were described in Hebrew in *Cat. Allony–Loewinger*, I, p. 18. Neither publication listed call-numbers. These fragments, with call-numbers, are described and displayed on the website of the Austrian Academy of Sciences at http://www.ksbm.oeaw.ac.at/hebraica.

Graz (Austria), Universitätsbibliothek

Fragments of 33 MSS removed from bindings were described in *Cat. Schwarz–Loewinger–Róth*, pp. 81–86. The call-numbers of two of the fragments listed in the 'Nachträge' on p. 86 could not be determined. Fragments from 16 of the 33 MSS were described in Hebrew in *Cat. Allony–Loewinger*, I, pp. 18–19. The call-numbers of most of the MSS are given in parentheses at the end of each entry. Fragments removed from 43 MSS and printed books are described and displayed on the website of the Austrian Academy of Sciences at http://www.ksbm.oeaw.ac.at/hebraica.

Graziano, Abraham Solomon Joseph

Mantua, Italy, d. 1685; rabbi and book collector

Close to 200 MSS from Graziano's library are

scattered in *Parma, Biblioteca Palatina, *Oxford, Bodleian Library, and other collections.

י׳ אוקון, ׳היחס שבין כתובי־יד לדפוסים בספרייתו של אי״ש ג״ר׳, אסופות, י (תשנ״ז), עמ׳ רסז–רפה. Tamani, *Grimani*; idem, 'I libri ebraici del cardinal Domenico Grimani', *Annali di Ca' Foscari*, vol. XXXIV, no. 3 (1995), pp. 5–52; A. van der Heide, *Hebrew Manuscripts of Leiden University Library*, Leiden 1977, pp. 6–7.

Great Maḥzor of Amsterdam

Name given to an early Ashkenazic maḥzor written in Cologne around the middle of the thirteenth century, belonging to the Jewish community in Amsterdam (Nederlands-Israelietische Hoofdsynagoge, Inv. no. 126), now deposited in the Joods Historisch Museum in Amsterdam.

N. Golb, 'In search of the original home of the great Mahazor of Amsterdam', *Studia Rosenthaliana*, X (1976), pp. 195–211; A. van der Heide & E. van Voolen (eds.), *The Amsterdam Mahzor*, Leiden 1989.

Greek Haggada

Name given to MS *Paris, BnF, héb. 1388, an illuminated haggada written in Candia (Heraklion, Crete) in 1583.

B. Narkiss and G. Sed-Rajna, *Index of Jewish Art*, I, Jerusalem–Paris 1976.

Grimani, Domenico

Venice, Italy, 1461 – ca. 1523; cardinal

Cardinal Grimani owned about 200 Hebrew MSS, including 107 from the library of *Pico della Mirandola, which he purchased. Most of the MSS were destroyed in 1687 by the fire that ravaged the church of San Antonio, where Grimani's collection had been stored. However, many of them had previously been removed surreptitiously by persons unknown or ceremoniously by royal ambassadors. Nine MSS thus acquired by G. G. Fugger are now in *Munich, Bayerische Staatsbibliothek, six are in *Udine, Biblioteca Arcivescovile, and two or three are in *Leiden, Universiteitsbibliotheek. According to Steinschneider, *Vorlesungen*, p. 68 (Hebrew, p. 89), there are MSS from Grimani's collection in *Oxford, Bodleian Library.

Groningen (Netherlands), Rijksuniversiteit

Three Hebrew biblical MSS are described by H. Brugmans in *Catalogus Codicum Manuscritorum Universitatis Groninganae Bibliothecae*, Groningen 1898, MSS 455–457. MSS 455 and 457 are also listed in *Cat. Allony–Kupfer*, II, nos. 883–884. MS 455 was described in greater detail by P. A. H. de Boer in 'Hebrew Biblical Manuscripts in the Netherlands', in M. Black and G. Fohrer (eds.), *In Memoriam Paul Kahle*, Berlin 1968, pp. 45–46. MS 456 is a scroll. MSS 459, 466 and 467 have Hebrew writing but were written by seventeenth-century Christian orientalists.

Gross, William L.

Minneapolis–Tel Aviv, 1939–; collector

In 2013, the private collection of William Gross of Tel Aviv included 285 codices and 50 scrolls. A few illuminated MSS were described in B. Narkiss et al., *Gross Family Collection*, Part 1, vol. II, Jerusalem 1985.

Grossman, Louis

Vienna, 1863 – Detroit, Mich., 1926; rabbi in USA

Grossman's MSS are now in *Cincinnati, HUC.

Oko, p. 81.

Grünhut, Lazarus (Eleazar)

Gerenda, Hungary, 1850 – Jerusalem, 1913

Grünhut's MS of responsa from Candia (Heraklion, Crete), described by himself in German, 'Handschriftliches von Moses ibn Al-aschkar und Levi ibn Chabib', *ZfHB*, X (1906), pp. 190–191, and in Hebrew (׳לתולדות הרב ר׳ משה ן׳ אלאשקר׳, העולם, א [תרס״ז], עמ׳ 76–77), is now *Washington,

D.C., Library of Congress, Hebr. MS 18. Two other MSS of his, *Midrash Shir hashirim*, which he published (מדרש שיר השירים, ירושלים תרנ״ז), and a treatise on ritual slaughter by Yahya al-Dahari, which he described ('Der südarabische Siddur', *MGWJ*, L [1906], pp. 87–88), were acquired by J. Rendell *Harris and are now found in the University of *Birmingham.

Guelf.
Guelferbytem. Latin name for Wolfenbüttel.

Guggenheim, Felix
Constance, Germany, 1904 – Los Angeles, Calif., 1979; literary agent
Guggenheim's maḥzor, dated 1480, formerly in the possession of Heinrich *Frauberger, was acquired by Salli *Kirschstein and was listed as no. 215 in the catalogue *Die Judaica-Sammlung S. Kirschstein, Berlin*, Munich 1932. Guggenheim presented it to *Jerusalem, JNUL (now *Jerusalem, NLI, Heb. 8° 5492). See F. Landsberger, 'The Washington Haggadah and its illuminator', *HUCA*, XXI (1948), p. 79.

Güldenstein (rabbi in Buchau)
See *Bloch, Moses.

Gunther, Charles F.
Germany, 1837 – Chicago, Ill., 1920; collector
MS no. 191 in the auction catalogue *Selections from the Charles F. Gunther Collection Sold by Order of the Chicago Historical Society*, New York 1925–1926, was bought by L. Bamberger and presented to *New York, JTSA (MS L315).

Register, 5687, p. 134 (Marx, *Bibl. Studies*, p. 69).

Günzburg family
The library of the Günzburg family was founded by Joseph Yozel Günzburg (Vitebsk, Russia, 1812 – Paris, 1878) and his sons Horace and Uri. Later, the library was in the possession of Baron David Günzburg (1857–1910) in Paris and from 1887 in St. Petersburg. The library, including over 1,900 MSS, was about to be purchased by *New York, JTSA, but the outbreak of World War I prevented the conclusion of the transaction (M. Stanislawski, 'An unperformed contract: The sale of Baron Günzburg's library to the Jewish Theological Seminary of America', *Transition and Change in Modern Jewish History*, Jerusalem 1987, pp. lxxiii–xciii). In 1917 the library was purchased by Russian Zionists from the widow of Baron David for the Jewish National Library in Jerusalem (now *Jerusalem, NLI); but before it could be shipped abroad it was confiscated by the new revolutionary government and presented to the Publichnaia Biblioteka in Moscow (now *Moscow, RSL) for safekeeping. On the unsuccessful negotiations for the return of the collection to the Jewish National Library, see M. Nadav, 'An account of the efforts made to acquire the Baron David Ginsburg collection for the Jewish National Library' ('לתולדות המאמצים לרכישת אוסף דוד גינצבורג'), in M. Nadav and J. Rothschild (eds.), *Essays and Studies in Librarianship Presented to Curt David Wormann on his Seventy-Fifth Birthday*, Jerusalem 1975, Hebrew section, pp. 81–95, and a sequel ('לתולדות המאמצים להבאת אוסף דוד גינצבורג אל בית הספרים הלאומי בירושלים') in *Jewish Studies* (מדעי היהדות), XXXV (1995), Hebrew section, pp. 69–81. There is no printed catalogue of the entire collection. For details of the handwritten catalogues, see *Moscow, RSL.

Gurland, Jonas
Kletsk, Belarus, 1843 – Odessa, Ukraine, 1890
Gurland described mathematical and astronomical MSS in the *Firkovich collection now in *St. Petersburg, NLR, in his

Kurze Beschreibung der mathematischen, astronomischen und astrologischen hebräischen Handschriften der Firkowitsch'schen Sammlung in der Kaiserlichen öffentlichen Bibliothek zu St. Petersburg, St. Petersburg 1886.

H

H

Hamburg.

Hafnia

Latin name for Copenhagen.

Hagen, Johannes van der

Leiden, 1665--Amsterdam, 1739; Reformed Church minister

Van der Hagen purchased the twenty MSS of the deceased Cornelius *Schulting in 1726. The MSS were described in Johann Christoph *Wolf's *Bibliotheca Hebraea*, IV, Hamburg 1733, pp. 79–84. Adam *Clarke purchased ten Hebrew MSS in Utrecht in 1823, at the auction sale by the heirs of van der Hagen. For the present whereabouts of the MSS, see *Clarke, Adam.

Hal. or Halb.

*Halberstamm.

Hala

Latin name for Halle.

Halberstamm, Solomon Joachim

Cracow, Poland, 1832 – Bielsko, Poland, 1900

From 1860 until his death Halberstamm was a merchant in Bielsko (Bielitz). Moses *Gaster purchased 411 of the MSS listed in the catalogue of Halberstamm's MSS, *Catalog hebräischer Handschriften* (קהלת שלמה, וינה תר"ן), for the *London, Montefiore Collection, where they constituted about 80 percent of the MSS in that library. *Cat. Montefiore* (1904), pp. ix–xi, contains a concordance to the numbers in the Halberstamm catalogue. Two hundred additional MSS that Halberstamm acquired later were purchased by Judge Mayer *Sulzberger for *New York, JTSA, after Halberstamm's death (Rab., *Lit. Treas.*, p. 65). Before his 1890 catalogue was published, Halberstamm had sold a number of MSS to Abraham *Epstein and others. Most of Epstein's MSS later reached the *Vienna, Israelitische Kultusgemeinde library. A list of the Halberstamm MSS in the Vienna collection is found in *Cat. Schwarz–Loewinger–Róth*, p. 150. The MS of Rabbenu Tam's *Sefer hayashar* (ספר הישר), from which the 1898 edition was prepared, is now *Jerusalem, NLI, Heb. 4° 370. Some of Halberstamm's MSS are now in various libraries, such as *Oxford, Bodleian (*Cat. Neubauer–Cowley*, 2651, 2696), *Cambridge, UL, MS Or. 786, and *Berlin, Staatsbibliothek (*Cat. Steinschneider*, Berlin, nos. 237, 247). In JTSA there are a number of handwritten catalogues of Halberstamm's MSS, some of them in his own hand. JTSA, MS 2816 lists 410 MSS. The numbers in the list generally correspond with those in the printed catalogue except for a few dozen MSS that were sold, mostly to Epstein, before the catalogue was published. Over 500 MSS are listed in MS 2823, and the names of the former owners and prices paid are also indicated. Nos. 485–507 are described by M. Brann and others in JTSA, MS 2846, and nos. 414–560 are also described by Brann in JTSA, MS 10713. A. Marx compiled a catalogue of nos. 412–562 from Halberstamm's notebooks for use in the JTSA library.

Halevy, Eliezer
See *Loewe, Louis.

Halevy, Hayyim Bekhor
Izmir, Turkey, nineteenth cent.
Halevy's MSS were acquired from his grandson by *Jerusalem, NLI (MSS Heb. 8° 3901–4000, 4° 1096–1109).

Halle (Germany), Bibliothek der Deutschen Morgenländischen Gesellschaft (DMG)
Since 1925, the library has been situated in *Halle, Universitäts- und Landesbibliothek. Twelve MSS, scrolls and fragments, many from the collection of Albert *Socin, were described in *Cat. Striedl–Róth*, pp. 104–110.

Halle (Germany), Universitäts- und Landesbibliothek
Nine MSS are described in *Cat. Striedl–Róth*, pp. 111–119. The *Jerusalem, IMHM has a microfilm of one additional MS, Yb.2° 7 (an abridgement of the *Mordekhai* [מרדכי]). *Halle, Bibliothek der Deutschen Morgenländischen Gesellschaft, with its collection of MSS, is also housed in the library.

Halper, Benzion
Zhosli, Lithuania, 1884 – Philadelphia, Pa., 1924; scholar
Halper compiled a *Descriptive Catalogue of Genizah Fragments in Philadelphia*, Philadelphia 1924. Most of the fragments described in the catalogue are now in *Philadelphia, CAJS (formerly Dropsie College).

Halpern, Jacob
Vienna, twentieth cent.; bookseller
Halpern sold to *New York, JTSA, the collection of 1,100 MSS now known as the *Enelow Memorial Collection. See also *Friedmann, Nahum Dov.

Halpern, Joseph
London, twentieth cent.
A collection of Geniza fragments belonging to Halpern, microfilmed for *Jerusalem, IMHM, in 1958, had formerly belonged to Marcus Nathan Adler and was acquired by the British Museum (now *London, BL, MS Or. 12186); see *Adler, Elkan Nathan.

Ham.
(1) Hamburg; (2) *Hamilton, William, Duke of.

Hamburg (Germany), Museum für Völkerkunde
Formerly Museum für Völkerkunde und Vorgeschichte. Ten Yemenite MSS are described in *Cat. Striedl–Róth*, nos. 185–194.

Hamburg (Germany), Staats- und Universitätsbibliothek (SUB)
Formerly the Stadbibliothek. The library's collection of Hebrew MSS is based on the collections of Christian Hebraists, mainly that of Johann Christoph *Wolf, who purchased the library of Zacharias von *Uffenbach, but also those of Christian *Unger and others. The Wolf collection was acquired for the library in 1749 by its librarian, Johann Christian Wolf (brother of Johann Christoph). Around 1840, Leopold Dukes compiled an unpublished catalogue of 328 MSS in the library. *Cat. Steinschneider*, Hamburg (1878), describes 354 MSS, including 15 not in Hebrew. The catalogue is arranged according to subject. Each entry is preceded by a serial number (in heavy type), the call-number (without the prefix 'Cod. hebr.', which should be added when the MS is quoted) and, in the case of MSS coming from the Uffenbach collection, the number in J. H. Mai, *Bibliotheca Uffenbachiana*, Halle 1720 (with the prefix 'Uff.').

Palaeographical and codicological information: writing material (for parchment MSS only), number of leaves, size, type of script and date. Colophons are copied. If the MS contains more than one work, the description is subdivided. Subdivision numbers are in small print and are followed by the folio number of the beginning of each work in regular print. A concordance to the Uffenbach numbers in the Mai catalogue and present call-numbers (not catalogue numbers!) is found on p. 200. On p. 201 is a concordance to the call-numbers (C) and the catalogue numbers (N). Indexes: authors, scribes, owners, titles and place names. In 1905, the Staatsbibliothek acquired 177 MSS from the collection of Heimann *Levy. Of the Levy MSS, 163 were described in the catalogue of his collection by S. Goldschmidt (מקדש מעט, המבורג תר״ס), and ten of the remaining 14 were listed in *Cat. Allony–Loewinger*, I, p. 40. All the MSS were described, in German, in E. Róth and H. Striedl, *Hebräische Handschriften*, III: *Die Handschriften der Sammlung H. B. Levy an der Staats- und Universitätsbibliothek Hamburg*, Wiesbaden 1984 (Verzeichnis der orientalischen Handschriften in Deutschland, VI, 3). The MSS are arranged according to subject. At the head of each entry are the catalogue number, the call-number (Cod. Levy) and the Hamburg accession number. Palaeographical and codicological information: number of leaves, writing material, detailed physical description of the MS (including ink, binding, illuminations, size of the MS, size of written area, number of lines per page, script, date, colophons, owners' entries, provenance, etc.). Indexes: authors, scribes, owners, titles in Hebrew, titles in Latin transliteration, titles of Spanish MSS, subjects, censors, place names, concordance to call-numbers and the catalogue numbers, dated MSS and plates. The present call-numbers consist of the prefix 'Cod. Levy' and the Goldschmidt catalogue number.

Hamburg (Germany), Stadtbibliothek
See *Hamburg, Staats- und Universitätsbibliothek.

Hamburg (Germany), SUB
*Hamburg, Staats- und Universitätsbibliothek.

Hamburg Halakha Miscellany
Name given to *Hamburg, SUB, Cod. hebr. 337 (*Cat. Steinschneider*, Hamburg, no. 353), an illuminated MS written in Padua in 1477.

Narkiss, p. 158.

Hamburger, Julius
Frankfurt, Germany, nineteenth century
The illuminated *Mishne Tora* he purchased at the sale of the collection of Marquis Carlo Trivulzio in Milan in 1880 is now *Jerusalem, NLI, Heb. 4° 1193 (see *Jerusalem *Mishne Tora*).

Narkiss, p. 134.

Hamilton, William, Duke of
London, 1767–1852
The Hamilton collection was formed by Alexander Douglas, 10th Duke of Hamilton, between the last decade of the eighteenth century, when he visited Italy, and his death in 1852. William, the 12th Duke of Hamilton, sold the library in 1882 to the Prussian government. Many of the MSS, including six Hebrew codices (Cods. Ham. 80, 81, 235, 288, 547, 687), were deposited in the *Berlin, Staatsbibliothek in 1919. Cod. Ham. 288, an illuminated Spanish maḥzor of the thirteenth century, is known as the Hamilton Siddur.

Hanau (Germany), Historisches Museum
See *Cracow Bible.

Hapalit
Leopold Zunz, in *Hapalit*, Berlin 1850 (יו״ט ליפמן צונץ, הפליט הבא להגיד ... פליטת סופרים

(וספרים ... ברלין תר״י), describes eighty MSS, most or all of which came from the collection of M. *Bislisches. Sixty-seven of these MSS were purchased by *Oxford, Bodleian Library, and received call-numbers with the prefix 'Mich. Add.', though they have nothing to do with the Michael collection. A list of the MSS and their numbers in *Cat. Neubauer* is found on pp. xxiv–xxv of the catalogue. For the present or last-known locations of some of the MSS listed in *Hapalit* and not purchased by the Bodleian see Appendix I, no. 15.

Harburg (Germany), Fürstlich Oettingen-Wallerstein'sche Bibliothek

Five MSS (in ten volumes) were described in *Cat. Striedl–Róth*, pp. 133–145. Three of the MSS were described in *Cat. Allony–Loewinger*, I, pp. 40–41, but the call-numbers were not listed. One MS was described by J. Perles, 'Eine hebräische Handschrift der Fürstlich Oettingen-Wallerstein'schen Bibliothek,' *MGWJ*, XXVII (1878), pp. 317–324.

Harkavy, Abraham Elijah

Novogrudok, Belarus, 1835 – St. Petersburg, Russia, 1919; scholar

Towards the end of his life, Harkavy sold his library, including its MSS and *Geniza fragments, for a nominal sum, to *St. Petersburg, Society for the Promotion of Culture (OPE), while retaining their use for the rest of his life. The MSS and Harkavy's papers are now in the *Kiev, Vernadsky National Library. A list of Harkavy's historical and liturgical MSS is found among the Simha *Assaf papers in *Jerusalem, NLI. Among David Maggid's papers in the *St. Petersburg, NLR, are a few Geniza fragments that seem to have belonged to Harkavy (information from B. Sheinin, formerly a librarian in the library). *Oxford, Bodleian Library, purchased two MSS from Harkavy (MSS e. 8 and e. 9, *Cat. Neubauer–Cowley*, II, nos. 2799–2800). The MSS from which Harkavy published his edition of geonic responsa (Berlin 1887) are now bound in one volume, St. Petersburg, NLR, MS Евр. II A 32.

צ' הרכבי, אישים ודמויות בחכמת ישראל באירופה המזרחית, [תל-אביב] תשי״ט, עמ' 130; V. Viknovich, *Sovietish Heimland*, III (1989), pp. 132–134; V. Gessen, 'The strange fate of the archives of the St Petersburg Jewish societies', *Soviet Jewish Affairs*, XXI, 2 (1991), p. 63.

Harley, Robert

London, 1661–1724

Harley's collection, including 99 Hebrew MSS and 17 Hebrew charters, was sold to the House of Commons in 1753 and is now in *London, British Library. A list of the MSS and their numbers in the catalogue is found in *Cat. Margoliouth–Leveen*, IV, pp. 162–163.

Harris, James Rendel

Plymouth, England, 1852 – Birmingham, England 1941; Bible scholar

Harris taught at a number of colleges, among them *Haverford College in Pennsylvania (1882–1892). In 1889 and 1890, while on leave from Haverford, he purchased MSS in the Middle East, among them 21 Hebrew codices that he donated to Haverford College. Later, he became Director of Studies at Woodbrooke College near Birmingham. Two MSS of his that formerly belonged to E. *Grünhut, a copy of *Midrash Shir hashirim* (מדרש שיר השירים) from the Cairo *Geniza dated 1147, published by *Grünhut, and a Yemenite manuscript including laws of ritual slaughter, are now in the J. Rendel Harris collection in the University of *Birmingham.

Harrison, Sigmund

Villanova, Pa., twentieth cent.

The Harrison Miscellany, an illuminated eighteenth-century MS formerly owned by Sigmund Harrison, was sold at Sotheby's auction in New York in 1983 and again at Christie's auction in 1998. It is now MS 67 in the *Braginsky Collection in Zurich. One of the manuscripts in Harrison's collection, a divorce bill (*get*) dated 748/9, was photographed in *EJ*, VI, p. 124. The *get*, considered by many scholars to be a forgery, was presented to Dropsie College (now *Philadelphia, CAJS) in the 1980s (see D. Goldenberg, 'Notes on the library of the Annenberg Research Institute', *JQR*, LXXXII, 1992, pp. 483–484).

Harvard University
See *Cambridge (Mass.), Harvard University.

Hassidah, Menahem Zev
Aleksandrow, Poland, 1888 – Jerusalem, 1965; editor
*Jerusalem, NLI, has four MSS formerly belonging to Hassidah, two of which had belonged to Isaac Michael *Badhab. Two of the MSS had been published by Hassidah in his journal *Hasegula*: Heb. 4° 962, a work by Moses Cordovero, formerly in the possession of Badhab, and Heb. 8° 1785, a few leaves from the novellae of the R. Yom Tov Ishbili (הריטב"א) on TB *Nida*.

Hatton, Christopher
England, c. 1605 – Kirby, England, 1670; British politician
Hatton's MSS were purchased in 1671, a year after his death, by *Oxford, Bodleian Library. The collection included three Hebrew MSS (Bodl. Or. 155, Hatton Or. 34–35).

Hauck, Cornelius J.
Cincinnati, Ohio, 1893–1967
Hauck acquired a collection of books, manuscripts and antiquities that was donated in 1966 to the Cincinnati Historical Society (now Cincinnati Museum Center). The collection was sold in June 2006 at Christie's New York auction sale. Six Hebrew MSS are listed in the sale catalogue *The History of the Book: The Hauck Collection*, lots 204, 205, 303, 424, 541 and 542. Lots 424 and 542 were bought by R. *Braginsky in Zurich.

Haverford (Pa.), Haverford College
Twenty-one of J. Rendel *Harris's MSS were described by R. W. Rogers, 'A catalogue of the manuscripts (chiefly Oriental) in the Library of Haverford College', *Haverford College Studies*, IV (1890), pp. 28–50.

Hb.
Hamburg.

Heb. Univ.
*Jerusalem, National Library of Israel (NLI); formerly *Jerusalem, Jewish National and University Library (JNUL).

Hebrew Palaeography Project (HPP)
Established in 1965 as a joint project of the Israel Academy of Sciences and Humanities and the Institut de Recherche et d'Histoire des Textes, under the auspices of the Centre National de la Recherche Scientifique in France. The HPP is studying all dated Hebrew MSS up to 1540, as well as undated but otherwise 'colophoned' or named medieval MSS, and collecting all pertinent palaeographical and codicological information, with the intention of analyzing the data and establishing a precise Hebrew palaeography. The information is stored in *SfarData*, a sophisticated quantitative database and retrieval system of the measurable codicological attributes. *SfarData* is now accessible on the Internet (http://sfardata.nli.org.il/sfardataweb/home.aspx). Descriptions of Hebrew MSS in collections in Israel and France have been published in C. Sirat and M. Beit-Arié, *Manuscrits médiévaux en caractères hébraïques portant des indications de date jusque'à 1540* (אוצר כתבי־יד עבריים מימי־הביניים בציוני תאריך עד שנת ה'ש), I–III, Jerusalem–Paris

1972–1986. Each volume of this publication consists of two parts, one of plates and one of descriptions in Hebrew and French. Indexes accompany each volume. Volume I (1972) contains descriptions of MSS of folio size; Volume II (1979) describes MSS of smaller format dating up to 1470; and Volume III (1986) describes MSS dated from 1471 to 1540. Another series in four volumes, M. Beit-Arié, C. Sirat and M. Glatzer, *Codices Hebraicis litteris exarati quo tempore scripti fuerint exhibentes*, Turnhout, 1997–2006, describes MSS dated until 1200 preserved in libraries throughout the world, with the exception of those previously described. In each volume MSS are arranged according to date and given numbers consisting of the volume number and a serial number (e.g., I, 23). The HPP also published *Specimens of Mediaeval Hebrew Scripts*, I: *Oriental and Yemenite Scripts*, compiled by M. Beit-Arié in collaboration with E. Engel and A. Yardeni (אסופות כתבים עבריים מימי־הביניים, א: כתב מזרחי וכתב תימני), Jerusalem 1987; and II: *Sefardic Script*, compiled by M. Beit-Arié and E. Engel (אסופות כתבים עבריים מימי־הביניים, ב: כתב ספרדי), Jerusalem 2002. Vol. III: *Ashkenazic Script* is in preparation.

Heid.
*Heidenheim.

Heidelberg (Germany), Biblioteca Palatina

The library held 288 Hebrew MSS, many of them from the Ulrich *Fugger collection. In 1622, Heidelberg was sacked by the Catholic League, and the books and manuscripts that were not destroyed or looted by private hands were presented to Pope Gregory XV and stored in the *Vatican Library.

Cassuto, *Palatina*, pp. 1–16; מ״ד קסוטו, ׳תולדותיו של אוסף כתבי־יד עבריים׳, יד לקורא, א (תש״ז), עמ׳ 62–65.

Heidelberg (Germany), Universitätsbibliothek

One MS, one letter and two collections of fragments (one of them from the library of Adalbert *Merx) were described in *Cat. Striedl–Róth*, pp. 146–150. In *Cat. Allony–Loewinger*, I, p. 41, only one of the fragment collections is listed. The call-numbers listed in parentheses in *Cat. Allony–Loewinger* have been changed; the new call-numbers are listed in *Cat. Striedl–Róth*. In addition, the library possesses 30 Hebrew and Aramaic papyrus fragments not described in the catalogues cited above.

Heidenheim, Moritz

Worms, Germany, 1824 – Zurich, Switzerland, 1898; convert to Christianity; clergyman

Heidenheim's collection of over 200 Hebrew MSS was purchased by the Jewish community in Zurich after his death and presented to *Zurich, Zentralbibliothek. MSS *Oxford, Bodleian Library, Opp. Add. 2° 32–34, Opp. Add. 4° 54, 59, 60, and probably also Opp. Add. 8° 9–13 were purchased from Heidenheim in 1863. One MS in *London, British Library (MS Add. 26,883, *Cat. Margoliouth*, no. 640), also comes from his library, as does *New York, JTSA, MS 2287.

O. Franz-Klauser, *Ein Leben zwischen Judentum und Christentum: Moritz Heidenheim (1824–1898)*, Zurich 2008.

Heidenheim, Wolf

Heidenheim, Germany, 1757 – Rödelheim, Germany, 1832; scholar

Seventy-two MSS are listed in the catalogue of Heidenheim's estate (רשימת הספרים אשר הניח אחריו ... וואלף היידנהיים), printed in Rödelheim in 1833. Close to half of the MSS in the catalogue were purchased by Heimann J. *Michael, whose collection is now in *Oxford, Bodleian Library. Heidenheim presented many of his MSS to Seligmann *Baer (*EJ*, IV, p. 80), and they are presently in *Moscow, RSL. For his work on Massora, Heidenheim used the Bible that later passed to M. S. *Goldschmidt, now *New York, Public Library, Spencer Collection, MS 1 (see *Xanten Bible). For a list of MSS used by Heidenheim in the preparation of his commentary on the liturgy, see L. Lewin, 'Materialien zu einer Biographie Wolf Heidenheims', *MGWJ*, XLV (1901), pp. 429–432; ד' גולדשמידט, מחזור לימים נוראים, א, ירושלים תש"ל, עמ' נ. For the present locations of some of the MSS in the 1833 catalogue, see Appendix I, no. 16.

Heiligenkreuz (Austria), Stiftsbibliothek

The Pentateuch formerly in the library (*Cat. Schwarz*, Austria, no. 3) is now *Copenhagen Kongelige Bibliothek, Cod. Hebr. 12.

Cat. Allony–Kupfer, II, p. 18.

Heilsbronn (Germany), Zisterzienserkloster

A number of fragments removed from the bindings of books in the library are now in *Erlangen, Universitätsbibliothek (*Cat. Striedl–Róth*, nos. 77, 83, 94).

Held, Hans Ludwig

Neuburg, Germany, 1885 – Munich, Germany, 1954; librarian

Seventeen MSS formerly in Held's private collection in Munich were destroyed by the Nazis.

Cat. Allony–Loewinger, I, p. 21.

Helmst.

*Helmstadium.

Helmstadium

Latin name for Helmstedt. The Hebrew MSS formerly in the Helmstedt University library, which was closed in 1809, are now in *Wolfenbüttel, Herzog August Bibliothek.

Henriques, Reginald Quixano

England, 1868–1913

A collection of *Geniza fragments acquired by Henriques, a merchant from Manchester who represented his firm in Cairo, was presented to *Cambridge, University Library, in 1898 and is now preserved in Box T–S NS 172.

Reif, *Jewish Archive*, pp. 89, 237.

Henriques de Castro, David

Amsterdam, 1826–1898

Eighteen Hebrew MSS are listed in the auction catalogue of his collection, *Catalogue de vente de la succession de feu M. D. Henriques de Castro*, Amsterdam 1899, nos. 474–491. The Pentateuch described in no. 474 is known as the De Castro Pentateuch and was later MS *Sassoon 506. It is presently *Jerusalem, Israel Museum, MS 180/94. A palaeographical description of the MS is found in *Manuscrits médiévaux en caractères hébraïques*, III, Jerusalem–Paris 1986, no. 101. For the present locations of some of the other MSS see Appendix I, no. 17.

Herzog August Bibliothek

See *Wolfenbüttel.

Heschel, Jakob

Austria, nineteenth–twentieth century

One MS owned by Heschel was described in *Cat. Schwarz*, Austria, no. 77. Its present whereabouts are unknown.

Hess, J.

Ellwangen, Germany, nineteenth cent.; bookseller

The MS of Hess's described in *HB*, V (1862), p. 148, is now *Berlin, SB, Cod. Or. 2° 2193 (*Cat. Steinschneider*, Berlin, no. 229).

Hessische Landesbibliothek

See *Darmstadt, Universitäts- und Landesbibliothek.

Hg.
Hamburg.

HGE
Hyman George *Enelow.

HGF
Harry G. *Friedman.

Hilleli Codex
Name given to a lost ancient Bible copied by Hillel b. Moses b. Hillel. A Pentateuch from a Bible copied in Toledo in 1241 and later collated with the Hilleli Codex has survived (*New York, JTSA, MS L44a) and was reproduced in facsimile (Jerusalem 1974).

Hinckelmann, Abraham
Döbeln, Germany, 1652 – Hamburg, Germany, 1695; Christian Hebraist
Ten Hebrew MSS listed in the catalogue of Hinckelmann's collection were acquired after his death by Joachim Morgenweg (d. 1730). They are now in *Hamburg, SUB (*Cat. Steinschneider*, Hamburg, p. ix), and are listed in the index of owners in *Cat. Steinschneider*, Hamburg.

Hirsch, Harry
Germany, 1859–1938; bookseller
Son of Jerocham Fischl *Hirsch. His collection of MSS, most of which came from the *Benamozegh collection, was presented to *New York, JTSA, by Mayer *Sulzberger (Marx, 'Polemical MSS', p. 277; information from M. Schmelzer, former librarian of JTSA). A list of Hirsch's MSS is found in JTSA, MS 2837.

Hirsch, Jerocham Fischl
Sometimes referred to as J. Fischl; bookseller, Berlin, d. 1899
Forty-nine MSS belonging to Fischl Hirsch that were offered for sale were described in detail by M. Steinschneider in *HB*, XI (1871), pp. 9–16, 37–46, 90–95, 119–133 (reprinted Berlin 1872), and 11 other MSS were described by Steinschneider in *HB*, XVII (1877), pp. 109–114. In the Hebrew section of *Catalog der von Herrn Fischl Hirsch nachgelassen Bücher und Handschriften*, Berlin 1899 (רשימה מספרים ... וכתבי יד ... אשר השאיר אחריו מוהר״ר פישל הירש ... ברלין תר״ס), 288 other MSS were catalogued by David Künstlinger. The MSS described in *HB* were purchased by various collectors and libraries, among them, *Oxford, Bodleian Library (see *Cat. Neubauer*, p. xxxii), Joseph *Günzburg and the British Museum (now *London, British Library). The present locations of most of these MSS are listed in Appendix I, no. 18. About 150 MSS were purchased from Hirsch in the 1870s by *Cambridge, University Library and are listed in the index of owners in Reif, *Cat. Cambridge*, p. 585. Other MSS formerly in the possession of Fischl Hirsch are now *Oxford, Bodleian Library, MSS Opp. Add. 2° 45–46, 51–53, 57, 64, Opp. Add. 4° 33–36, 39–42, 97, 116–123, 125–128, 137–140, 146, 160, 163–167, *Berlin, SB, Cods. Or. 4° 823 and 825, *Cambridge, UL, MS Add. 1751, and *Moscow, RSL, Günzburg 1658 and 1749. The MSS belonging to Hirsch described in *HB*, XIX (1879), p. 63, and XXI (1882), p. 98, are now *Moscow, RSL, Günzburg 921 and 1122. The MS described by [N. Brüll], 'Beiträge zur jüdischen Sagen- und Spruchkunde im Mittelalter', in *Jahrbücher für jüdische Geschichte und Literatur*, IX (1889), pp. 1–71, was purchased by L. P. Prins and presented by his grandson to the Beit Midrash Mizrachi for Teachers in Jerusalem (now the Lifshitz College of Education) and deposited in 1945 in *Jerusalem, JNUL (now NLI, Heb. 8° 3182); see *KS*, XI (1934/5), p. 498; *ibid.*, LI (1975/6), p. 492.

Hirschell, Solomon
London, 1761–1842; Chief Rabbi of England

Hirschell's library was acquired by *London, Beth Din and Beth Hamidrash Library.

Rab., *Lit. Treas.*, p. 57.

Hirschenson, Hayyim

Safed, 1857 – Hoboken, N.J., 1935; rabbi

Mikhel *Rabinowitz purchased MSS from Hirschenson (מ׳ רבינוביץ, ׳תשלום שיטת מהר״י בי רב׳, ספר היובל לד״ר בנימין מנשה לוין, ירושלים [ת״ש], עמ׳ קצז). Rabinowitz's MSS are now in *Jerusalem, NLI.

Hirschenson, Isaac

Pinsk, Belarus, 1845 – London, 1896; rabbi

In 1886, Hirschenson briefly listed 109 of his MSS in *Hatsvi* (הצבי, ב [תרמ״ו], הוספות למס׳ 31). Some of the MSS on the list are now in *Jerusalem, NLI; others are in *New York, JTSA; but most cannot be located. The MS from which Hirschenson published some of Solomon Bet-Halevi's letters in *Hamisdarona* (המסדרונה ב, תרמ״ז) is probably *Budapest, Hungarian Academy of Sciences, MS Kaufmann A 586.

Hirschf.

*Hirschfeld.

Hirschfeld, Hartwig

Thorn, Germany, 1854 – London, 1934; scholar

Hirschfeld compiled printed catalogues of the *London, Montefiore (= *Cat. Montefiore*), and Louis *Loewe collections of MSS and a handwritten catalogue of the MSS in Jews' College (see *London School of Jewish Studies).

'Dr. Hirschfeld's selections' of *Geniza fragments from the Taylor–Schechter collection in *Cambridge, University Library, many of which he published, are now numbered T–S Arabic 51–54. A few are incorporated into other parts of the collection.

Hispano-Moresque Haggada

Name given to *London, BL, MS Or. 2737 (*Cat. Margoliouth*, no. 609), an illuminated haggada.

Narkiss, *Span. & Port.*, no. 9.

Hoepli

Booksellers in Milan

The Hebrew MS described in Hoepli's catalogue no. 79, in the *Jewish Chronicle*, June 4, 1886, and elsewhere, a copy of Maimonides' *Mishne Tora* (supposedly an autograph!), is now *Jerusalem, NLI, Heb. 4° 1193 (See *Jerusalem *Mishne Tora*).

Hoerning, Reinhardt

Hoerning's brief handwritten descriptions of MSS in the British Museum (now *London, British Library) served as the basis for the list of British Museum MSS published by H. Derenbourg, 'Les manuscrits Judaïques entrés au British Museum de 1867 à 1890', *REJ*, XXIII (1891), pp. 99–116, 279–301, and for G. *Margoliouth's first catalogue in 1893. About half the descriptions in the first volume of Margoliouth's more detailed catalogue (1899) were originally written by Hoerning. He also described in great detail six Karaite MSS in his *Description and Collation of Six Karaite Manuscripts*, London 1899.

Holkham,

See *Leicester, Earl of.

Holub, David

Dub, Bohemia (now Czech Republic), nineteenth cent.; rabbi

The MS of Tosafot on TB *Shabat* belonging to a friend in Vienna that was described by Holub in *Literaturblatt des Orients*, XI (1850), pp. 556–558, is now *Moscow, RSL, Günzburg 636.

Hönisch, Rudolf
See *Porges, Nathan.

Horowitz, Hayyim M.
Pinsk, Belarus, 1855 – Frankfurt a/M, Germany, 1904; author and bookseller
Horowitz sold MSS to various libraries and collectors, among them S. J. *Halberstamm and Ephraim *Deinard (who sold the MSS he bought to *Washington, D.C., Library of Congress). One MS of his is in the *Oxford, Bodleian Library (*Cat. Neubauer*, 2589). On his copy of the Venice edition of *Pirke deRabi Eli'ezer* (פרקי דרבי אליעזר), Horowitz added many marginal notes, as he was preparing a critical edition of the work. Part of this copy is now in the *Tel Aviv, Rambam Library (no. 27), and part was in the possession of the publishing firm Makor, which published a facsimile edition of that part (Jerusalem 1972).

Horowitz, Joel b. Alexander Halevi
Stanislav, Ukraine, 1838 – Antwerp, Belgium, 1911
Horowitz's MS containing a commentary on TB *Ta'anit* and *Megila* referred to in *Hamelits* (המליץ), XXXIV, 1894, nos. 219 and 225, is now *New York, JTSA, MS R866.

Hottinger, Johann Heinrich
Zurich, Switzerland, 1620–1667; philologist
The medical MS Hottinger mentions in his *Bibliotheca Orientalis* is now *New York, JTSA, MS 2661.
Register, 5700, p. 66 (Marx, *Bibl. Studies*, p. 284).

Houghton Library
See *Cambridge (Mass.), Harvard University.

Howard, Thomas
See *Arundel.

Howitt, Arthur
1885 – Richmond, England, 1967; collector
A number of MSS and 27 Esther scrolls are listed in the auction catalogue of Howitt's collection of Jewish ceremonial art, *The Collection of Jewish Antiquities and Ritual Art Comprising Silver, Pewter ... Illuminated Manuscripts ... the Property of Councillor Arthur Howitt, Which Will Be Sold by Auction by Christie, Manson & Woods ... May 9, 1932*. One MS (no. 200) and three Esther scrolls were purchased by *London, Jewish Museum (E. D. Barnett [ed.], *Catalogue of the Permanent and Loan Collections of the Jewish Museum, London*, London 1974, pp. xiv–xv). One MS (no. 201) and 11 scrolls were purchased by *New York, JTSA (MSS Acc. 01260–01270, 01272).

HPP
*Hebrew Palaeography Project.

HU
Hebrew University. See *Jerusalem, NLI.

HUC
*Cincinnati, Hebrew Union College.

Hunt.
*Huntington.

Huntington, Robert
Deerhurst, England, 1637 – Dublin, Ireland, 1701; clergyman
While he was chaplain to the Levant Company of English merchants in Aleppo from 1671 to 1680, Huntington acquired about 200 Hebrew MSS. Some were donated to *Oxford, Bodleian Library in the years 1678, 1680 and 1683 and now bear call-numbers with the prefix 'Hunt. Don.'; others were purchased by the library in 1693 and bear call-numbers with the prefix 'Hunt.'. A concordance to the Huntington MSS and their catalogue numbers is found in *Cat. Neubauer*, pp. xxv, xxx and xxxi.

Hüpsch-Lontzen, Johann Wilhelm Carl Adolph von Honvlez-Ardenn, Baron von

Cologne, Germany, 1726–1805

The so-called *Darmstadt Haggada, an illuminated haggada that was formerly in Hüpsch's possession, was bequeathed together with his entire collection to the *Darmstadt, Universitäts- und Landesbibliothek, where it is now Cod. Or. 8.

Die Darmstädter Pessach-Haggadah, Leipzig 1927, Text volume, p. 45.

Hurwitz, M. Chaim.

nineteenth–early twentieth cent., rabbi in Amersfoort

Six MSS are listed in *Auctionscatalog* מקור חיים ... *aus dem Nachlass des Ehrw. Herrn M. Ch. Hurwitz ...*, Amsterdam 1907, p. 78. The entries for the MSS are not numbered. The fourth entry is now *New York, JTSA, MS L782 and the sixth is now *Amsterdam, UB, HS. Ros. 312.

Husiatyn

The booksellers *Schwager and *Fränkel from Husiatyn published a number of sales catalogues. The MSS listed in these catalogues are sometimes referred to as MSS Husiatyn. The catalogue in which the largest and most important collection of MSS was listed is *Katalog hebräischer Handschriften* (אוצר כלי חמדה), XI, Husiatyn 1906.

I

Ibn Gaon Bible

See (1) *Joshua Ibn Gaon Bible; (2) *Shem Tov Bible.

Ibn Merwas Bible

Name given to *London, BL, MS Or. 2201 (*Cat. Margoliouth*, no. 52), an illuminated Bible copied by Joseph b. Judah ibn Merwas.

Narkiss, *Span. & Port.*, no. 2.

IMHM

*Jerusalem, Institute of Microfilmed Hebrew Manuscripts.

INA

Leningrad, Institut Narodov Azii (now *St. Petersburg, Institute of Oriental Manuscripts).

Innsbruck (Austria), Universitätsbibliothek

One Hebrew MS (Cod. 291) in this library was described in *Cat. Schwarz*, Austria, no. 75. *Jerusalem, IMHM also has microfilms of Cods. 506, a sixteenth-century Hebrew–German–Latin dictionary and 1155, a fragment of a Tora scroll. Fragments from fifteen MSS and a printed book are described and displayed on the website of the Austrian Academy of Sciences at http://www.ksbm.oeaw.ac.at/hebraica.

Institut Narodov Azii

See *St. Petersburg, Institute of Oriental Manuscripts.

IOS

Leningrad/St. Petersburg, Institute of Oriental Studies (now *St. Petersburg, Institute of Oriental Manuscripts).

Israelitisch-theologische Lehranstalt

See *Vienna, Israelitisch-theologische Lehranstalt.

Istanbul (Turkey), Topkapu Serai

Hebrew MSS (nos. 53, 61, 69), fragments from Tora scrolls (nos. 128–135) and Samaritan MSS (nos. 101–112) were described by D. A. Deissmann in *Forschungen und Funds im Serai*, Berlin–Leipzig 1933.

'Italian Geniza'

This expression refers to folios or bifolia of Hebrew MSS, mostly large parchment volumes, in secondary use as covers or bindings for books or document files in libraries and archives in Italy. Most of the Hebrew fragments found were re-employed from the mid-sixteenth century until the mid-seventeenth century. In 1981, Prof. G. B. Sermoneta initiated a project to search systematically for Hebrew leaves in libraries and archives and to photograph and catalogue them.

For an overview of the Italian Geniza, see the introduction to M. Perani and E. Sagradini, *Frammenti ebraici negli Archivi di Cesena, Faenza, Forlì, Imola, Rimini e Spoleto* (Inventari dei manoscritti delle Biblioteche d'Italia, 114), Florence 2012. For a general catalogue of the talmudic and midrashic fragments see eidem, *Talmudic and Midrashic Fragments from the Italian Genizah: Reunification of the Manuscripts and Catalogue*, Florence 2004. For an updated report and new discoveries see M. Perani (ed.), *The Italian 'Genizah': A Treasury of Reused Medieval Hebrew Manuscripts* ('European Genizah': Texts and Studies, 3), Leiden–Boston 2013.

Catalogues of Hebrew fragments in the following institutions have been compiled:

Acqui, Biblioteca del Seminario Vescovile – M. Perani, 'Un frammento di un manoscritto ebraico medievale riusato come legatura scoperto presso la Biblioteca del Seminario Vescovile di Acqui', *Arte e carte nella diocesi di Acqui*, Turin 2006, pp. 96–109.

Alessandria, Biblioteca Civica e Archivio di Stato – M. Perani, 'Catalogo dei frammenti di manoscritti ebraici della Biblioteca Civica e dell'Archivio di Stato', in F. Quaglia, *I libri ebraici nei fondi storici della Biblioteca Civica di Alessandria*, Alessandria 2004, pp. 51–76.

Bazzano, Archivio Storico Comunale – M. Perani (ed.), 'I frammenti ebraici di Bazzano: Un piccolo tesoro nella "Genizah italiana"' (Atti del forum internazionale, Bazzano [Bologna], 25 Maggio 2000), *Materia giudaica*, VI/2 (2001), pp. 193–219; M. Perani, 'I frammenti di manoscritti ebraici riusati come legature nell'Archivio Storico di Bazzano', *Il tesoro dei Capitani: Documenti dall'Archivio dei Vicariati del Capitanato della Montagna di Bazzano*, Bazzano 2007, pp. 68–77.

Bologna, Archivio di Stato and smaller collections – M. Perani and S. Campanini, *I frammenti ebraici di Bologna: Archivio di Stato e collezioni minori*, Florence 1997.

Cento, Archivio Notarile e Archivio Comunale – M. Perani, 'Manoscritti e frammenti ebraici copiati o conservati a Cento e Pieve di Cento', in *Gli ebrei a Cento e Pieve di Cento fra Medioevo ed Età moderna*, Cento 1994, pp. 93–156. The fragments are described on pp. 104–129.

Cesena, Archivio di Stato e Archivio della Curia Vescovile – M. Perani and E. Sagradini, *Frammenti ebraici negli Archivi di Cesena, Faenza, Forlì, Imola, Rimini e Spoleto* (Inventari dei manoscritti delle Biblioteche d'Italia, 114), Florence 2012.

Città di Castello – M. Perani and M. Borchiellini, *Le Pergamene ebraiche di Città di Castello*, Città di Castello 2008.

Corinaldo, Archivio Storico Comunale – M. Perani, 'Frammenti di manoscritti ebraici medievali nell'Archivio Storico Comunale di Corinaldo (Ancona)', *Henoch*, XIV (1992), pp. 301–306.

Correggio, Archivio Storico Comunale – M. Perani and S. Campanini, *I frammenti ebraici di Modena, Archivio Capitolare: Archivio della Curia, e di Correggio, Archivio Storico Comunale*, Florence 1999.

Cremona, Archivio di Stato – P. F. Fumagalli and B. Richler, *Manoscritti e frammenti ebraici nell'Archivio di Stato di Cremona*, Rome 1995.

Faenza, Archivio di Stato – M. Perani, 'Frammenti di manoscritti ebraici nell'Archivio di Stato di Faenza', *Henoch*, XII (1990), pp. 227–229. See also Cesena.

Faenza, Biblioteca Comunale – see Cesena.

Florence, Archivio di Stato – U. Cassuto, 'Frammenti ebraici in archivi notarili', *Giornale della Società Asiatica Italiana*, XXVII (1915), pp. 147–157.

Florence, Università di Firenze (Facoltà di Lettere) – K. Friedmann, 'I manoscritti ebraici della R. Università di Firenze', *Giornale della Società Asiatica Italiana*, III (1932), pp. 193–208.

Forlì, Archivio di Stato – M. Perani with the cooperation of C. Santandrea and M. Muratori, *I frammenti ebraici di Forlì, Rimini e Spoleto*, Florence 2010. See also Cesena.

Gorizia, Biblioteca Statale Isontina – G. Tamani, 'Un frammento di un manoscritto ebraico nella Biblioteca Statale Isontina', *Studi Goriziani: Rivista della Biblioteca Statale Isontina di Gorizia*, LXXXV (1997), pp. 111–116.

Imola, Archivio della Curia Vescovile – see Cesena.

Imola, Archivio di Stato – M. Perani, 'Frammenti di manoscritti ebraici medievali negli Archivi di Stato di Imola e Ravenna', *La Bibliofilia*, XCIII (1991), pp. 1–20. See also Cesena.

Imola, Archivio Storico Comunale – see Cesena.

Imola, Sezione di Archivio di Stato – see Cesena.

Lodi, Archivio Storico – V. Frenkel, 'Frammenti ebraici nell'Archivio Storico del Comune di Lodi', in M. Perani (ed.), *La 'Genizah italiana'*, Bologna 1999, pp. 211–214.

Massa Carrara, Archivio di Stato – H. M. Sermoneta, 'I frammenti ebraici scoperti nell'Archivio di Pontremoli', in P. Radicchi, P. and I. Zolesi (eds.), *Codicum fragmenta: Sul ritrovamento di antiche pergamene negli Archivi di Stato di Massa e Pontremoli (sec. XII–XV)*, Pisa 1999, pp. 217–220.

Matera, Biblioteca Provinciale – M. Perani, 'I frammenti ebraici rinvenuti in legature della Biblioteca Provinciale Stigliani e del Seminario Arcivescovile di Matera', in *Sefer Yuḥasin, Anno XXVII*, 2011 (5771/72), pp. 31–51.

Matera, Seminario Arcivescovile – see previous entry.

Modena, Archivio Capitolare – M. Perani and S. Campanini, *I frammenti ebraici di Modena, Archivio Capitolare: Archivio della Curia, e di Correggio, Archivio Storico Comunale*, Florence 1999.

Modena, Archivio della Curia – see Correggio.

Modena, Archivio di Stato – M. Perani and L. Baraldi, *I frammenti ebraici Modena Archivio di Stato*, I, Florence 2012.

Modena, Archivio Storico Comunale – M. Perani and S. Campanini, *I frammenti ebraici di Modena: Archivio Storico Comunale*, Florence 1997.

Modena, Biblioteca Estense – M. Perani with the cooperation of E. Mongardi and E. Chwat, '385 Printed Books of the 15th–18th Centuries bound with 1,300 fragments of Medieval Hebrew Manuscripts in the Estense Library in Modena', in A. Lehnardt (ed.), *'Genizat Germania': Hebrew and Aramaic Fragments from German Archives and Libraries in their European Context*, Leiden–Boston 2009.

Montepulciano, Archivio Storico Comunale – M. Perani, 'La catalogazione dei manoscritti ebraici medievali riusati come legatura', in B. Cenni, C. M. F. Lalli and L. Magionami (eds.), *Zenit e Nadir: I manoscritti dell'area del Mediterraneo: La catalogazione come base della ricerca*, Montepulciano 2007, pp. 127–142.

Nonantola, Archivio Storico Comunale –

M. Perani, *Frammenti di manoscritti e libri ebraici a Nonantola*, Nonantola–Padua 1992; idem, 'Addenda e corrigenda a M. Perani, *Frammenti di manoscritti e libri ebraici a Nonantola*, Nonantola–Padova 1992', in E. Fregni and M. Perani (eds.), *Vita e cultura ebraica nello stato estense*, Nonantola–Bologna 1993, pp. 81–86.

Norcia, Archivio Storico Comunale – M. Perani, 'Il più antico frammento della "Genizah italiana": La Tosefta di Norcia (ca. 1000 e.v.): Rilievi codicologici e paleografici', in idem, *La Genizah italiana*, Bologna 1999, pp. 261–265.

Parma, Archivio di Stato – M. Perani, 'Frammenti di manoscritti ebraici nell'Archivio di Stato di Parma', *Henoch*, XI (1989), pp. 103–108.

Pergola, Archivio Storico Comunale – M. Perani, 'Scoperto nell'Archivio Storico Comunale di Pergola un importantissimo manoscritto ebraico', in *Pergola Racconta* (April 2006), p. 4.

Perugia, Università degli Studi, Biblioteca del Dottorato – M. Perani, 'I frammenti di manoscritti ebraici scoperti nelle legature di libri della Biblioteca del Dottorato dell'Università di Perugia', http://documentiebraici.unipg.it/index.php.

Pesaro, Archivio di Stato – H. M. Sermoneta and P. F. Fumagalli, *Manoscritti ebraici nell'Archivio di Stato di Pesaro*, Rome 2002.

Pescocostanzo – G. Sabatini, *Frammenti di antichi codici ebraici in pergamena conservati in Pescocostanzo*, Rome[?] 1927[?].

Pieve di Cento, Archivio Storico Comunale – M. Perani, 'Manoscritti ebraici medievali riutilizzati come copertine nell'Archivio Storico Comunale di Pieve di Cento', in *Gli ebrei a Pieve di Cento: Testimonianze e memorie storiche*, Pieve di Cento 1993, pp. 65–102. See also Cento.

Pontremoli, Archivio di Stato – see Massa Carrara.

Ravenna, Archivio Arcivescovile – M. Perani, 'Nuovi frammenti di manoscritti ebraici scoperti a Ravenna presso l'archivio Arcivescovile e la Biblioteca Classense', in idem (ed.), *L'interculturalità dell'ebraismo*, Ravenna 2004, pp. 147–151.

Ravenna, Archivio di Stato – 'Frammenti di manoscritti ebraici medievali negli Archivi di Stato di Imola e Ravenna', *La Bibliofilia*, 93 (1991), pp. 1–20.

Ravenna, Biblioteca Comunale Classense – see Ravenna, Archivio Arcivescovile.

Rieti, Archivio Notarile – U. Cassuto, 'Frammenti ebraici in archivi notarili', *Giornale della Società Asiatica Italiana*, XXVII (1915), pp. 147–157.

Rimini, Archivio di Stato, Biblioteca Civica 'Gambalunga' and Biblioteca del Seminario Vescovile – see Cesena and Forlì.

Rome, Archivio di Stato – N. Pavoncello, *Pergamene ebraiche nell'Archivio di Stato di Roma*, pubblicazione celebrativa in occasione del matrimonio di G. Nahum e D. Anticoli, Rome, 30 Tishrì 5750/29 ottobre 1989, pp. 1–6.

Sant'Agata Bolognese, Archivio della Partecipanza Agraria – 'Frammenti di manoscritti ebraici nell'Archivio della Partecipanza Agraria di Sant'Agata Bolognese appartenente all'antico territorio di Nonantola', *Quaderni della Bassa Modenese*, 4 (1990), pp. 39–46.

Spoleto, Archivio di Stato – see Cesena and Rimini.

Ithaca (N.Y.), Cornell University Library

The Library has 26 Hebrew MSS, 25 of them from the collection of the late Prof. Isaac *Rabinowitz, as well as seven Samaritan MSS. Four Samaritan and two Hebrew MSS from the old collection were described by Rabinowitz, 'Semitic manuscripts in the Library', *Cornell Alumni News*, LX (1957), pp. 281–282.

J

Jabetz, Sussmann and his son Abraham

Łomża, Poland, nineteenth cent.

The MSS Jabetz purchased in Jerusalem in 1861, listed in the approbation by Joseph Saul Natanson at the beginning of *Berakha meshuleshet* (ברכה משולשת, ורשה תרכ״ג), which he published, were later in the *Warsaw, Tłomackie Street Synagogue library. In 1892, M. Moscowski described them in *Hatsefira* (הצפירה, תרנ״ב, מס' 245). The library's entire collection was lost in World War II. One MS of novellae attributed to R. Nissim Gerondi, from which the Warsaw 1862 edition was published, is probably MS *St. Petersburg, Institute of Oriental Manuscripts, B 184.

ש״ז הבלין, 'על כתב-יד אחד שנחלק', עלי ספר, א (תשל״ה), עמ' 84; B. Richler, 'The lost manuscripts of the library for Jewish Studies in Warsaw', in I. Zwiep et al. (eds.), *Omnia in Eo: Studies on Jewish Books and Libraries in Honour of Adri Offenberg* [= *Studia Rosenthaliana,* 38/39], 2006, pp. 360–387.

Jablonski, Daniel Ernst

Nassenhuben, Germany, 1660 – Berlin, 1741; Hebraist

Jablonski's MS, described in Johann Christoph *Wolf, *Bibliotheca Hebraea*, III, pp. 14ff., is now *Berlin, SB, Cod. Or. 4° 290 (*Cat. Steinschneider*, Berlin, no. 45). MSS Berlin, Or. 4° 291–292 (*ibid.*, 46–47), are also from Jablonski's library and were purchased in 1842. His MS described by Wolf, *op. cit.*, II, p. 1293, no. 177, and IV, p. 486, is now *Leipzig, Universitätsbibliothek, Cod. B. H. 17 (*Cat. Delitzsch*, no. 38), and the one described in Vol. IV, pp. 484–485, is now *Rostock, Universitätsbibliothek, Or. 38.

Jacobsohn, Wilhelm & Co.

Bookdealers in Breslau

The MS described by M. Brann, 'Additions à l'autobiographie de Lipman Heller', *REJ*, XXI (1890), pp. 270–277, is now *New York, Columbia University, Gen. MS 153.

Jacobson, Meijer Levien

Amsterdam, 1782–1864

Seventeen of Jacobson's MSS are described in Part I of the auction catalogue *Me'ir 'enayim* (מאיר עינים הוא רשימת ספרים מאת מאיר ב' יאקב הלוי יאקאבסאן ...), with the added title: *Catalogus I van eene boekverzameling ... door ... Meijer Levien Jacobson*, Amsterdam 1864 (Part II lists the MSS of Meijer Barend *Rubens). For the present locations of some of the MSS see Appendix I, no. 19.

James, Montague Rhodes

Goodnestone, England, 1862 – Eton, 1936; scholar

James compiled catalogues of several of the college libraries within Cambridge University, of which Christ's College, Emmanuel College and St. John's College include Hebrew MSS. See *Cambridge, College Libraries.

Jankovich, Miklós (Nikolaus)

Hungary, 1773–1846; collector

In the 1830s he sold his collection, including a number of Hebrew MSS, to the Magyar Nemzeti Múzeum (Hungarian National Museum) in Budapest (L. Mravic, 'Plucked from the Abyss of Oblivion: The Collections of Miklós Jankovich, 1773–1846', *The Hungarian Quarterly*, XLIV, no. 169 [2003]). See *Budapest, National Szechenyi Library.

Jaré, Giuseppe

Mantua, Italy, 1840 – Ferrara, Italy, 1915; rabbi

Some of Jaré's MSS, mostly documents, were in *Ferrara, Comunità ebraica (Sonne, *Relazione*). Other MSS of his are dispersed among various libraries. Jaré purchased many MSS for David *Kaufmann.

Jellinek, Adolf
Moravia, c. 1820 – Vienna, 1893; scholar
Most of Jellinek's MSS were in the *Vienna, Israelitisch-theologische Lehranstalt, which library passed into the possession of *Vienna, Israelitische Kultusgemeinde. A list of 66 or 67 of Jellinek's MSS in that library is found in the index of owners in *Cat. Schwarz–Loewinger–Róth*, p. 150. Two of Jellinek's MSS not listed in the Vienna catalogue were acquired by *Cambridge (Mass.), Harvard University (MSS Heb. 58, 62). Another is in *Berlin, Staatsbibliothek (Cod. Or. 2° 1056, *Cat. Steinschneider*, Berlin, no. 111). The MS from which Jellinek published in the journal *Hakol* (הקול, שנה ו, ה שבט, תרמ״ה), is now *Jerusalem, NLI, Heb. 8° 2921. Jellinek's MS of a work by Sahl b. Bishr, described by M. Steinschneider in *HÜ*, p. 605, and in *Die arabische Literatur der Juden*, Frankfurt a/M 1902, p. 25, is now NLI, Heb. 8° 5563.

Jena (Germany), Thüringer Universitäts- und Landesbibliothek
Ten MSS are described in *Cat. Striedl–Róth*, pp. 151–162.

Jer.
Jerusalem.

Jerus.
Jerusalem.

Jerusalem
In general 'MS Jerusalem' refers to *Jerusalem, NLI. Some other collections of MSS in Jerusalem are listed in the entries that follow. A number of collections belonging to Sephardic Jews and Sephardic institutions in Jerusalem were described in an article by M. Benayahu (מ׳ בניהו, ׳אספי הספרים לבני העדה הספרדית בירושלים׳, יד לקורא, א [תש״ז], עמ׳ 243–247, 315–323). Most of the libraries in the Old City described by Benayahu were destroyed after the city fell in 1948.

Jerusalem, Ben-Zvi Institute
The Institute has a collection of over 3,000 MSS, mostly from Oriental countries, the most famous being the *Aleppo Codex. A handwritten list of the MSS, arranged according to country of origin, is available at the library. Several collections have been described: Yemenite MSS (י׳ טובי, כתבי־היד התימניים במכון בן־צבי, ירושלים תשמ״ב), Judaeo-Persian MSS (א׳ נצר, אוצר כתבי־היד של יהודי פרס במכון בן־צבי, ירושלים תשמ״ו) and rabbinic MSS from the Maghreb: (י׳ אביב״י, כתבי־היד של יהודי המגרב במכון בן־צבי, ירושלים תשנ״ג, כרך א: יצירה רבנית). M. Benayahu published a survey of the biblical MSS in the Institute in *Ha'universita* (האוניברסיטה, טו [תש״ל], עמ׳ 56–63).

Jerusalem, Bezalel National Art Museum
See *Jerusalem, Israel Museum.

Jerusalem, Central Rabbinical Library
See *Jerusalem, Hekhal Shelomo Museum.

Jerusalem, Hekhal Shelomo Museum
The museum of Hekhal Shelomo had a collection of several hundred MSS deriving from various sources. In 1967, Sir Isaac Wolfson presented it with his collection of manuscripts and rare prints, containing 97 MSS formerly belonging to Mayer Selig *Goldschmidt of Frankfurt. Seventy-five of the MSS were described in *Min hagenazim* (מן הגנזים, א–ג, ירושלים תשכ״ז–תשל״ד). In 1990 the 97 MSS of the Wolfson collection were acquired by the Department of Antiquities and deposited in *Jerusalem, JNUL (now NLI). Most of the other MSS were sold to dealers and other libraries in the late 1990s.

Jerusalem, Institute of Microfilmed Hebrew Manuscripts (IMHM)
Formerly called the Institute of Hebrew Manuscripts and later the Institute of Microfilms

of Hebrew Manuscripts, the Institute was founded in 1950 for the purpose of collecting microfilm copies of all the Hebrew MSS, or MSS written in Hebrew characters, in the world. From 1950 to 1963 the Institute, under its first director, Nehemiah *Allony, belonged to the Ministry of Education and Culture of the State of Israel; since 1963 it has been located in the *Jerusalem, National Library of Israel (formerly the Jewish National and University Library). To date, more than 80,000 Hebrew MSS from over 600 collections, and hundreds of thousands of *Geniza fragments, have been microfilmed for the IMHM. Most of the major collections in the world have been or are being microfilmed. In 1987 the card catalogue was closed and cataloguing was continued electronically using the ALEPH program. The entire card catalogue has been computerized, together with the catalogue of the Manuscript Department of the NLI (with which the IMHM was merged in 2007), and it can be consulted online at www.nli.org.il. Three catalogues listing parts of the holdings of the IMHM have appeared in the series *List of Photocopies in the Institute* (רשימת תצלומי כתבי־היד העבריים במכון), referred to herein as *Cat. Allony–Kupfer*, II, and *Cat. Allony–Loewinger*, I and III (see the List of Bibliograpical Abbreviations).

The catalogues generally do not include MSS adequately described in the more familiar printed catalogues of Hebrew MS collections (e.g., *Steinschneider's catalogues of the Hamburg, Munich and Berlin collections). However, the greater part of the Vatican collection, previously described in Latin in the 1756 *Assemani catalogue, was described again in Hebrew in *Cat. Allony–Loewinger*, III. In all three catalogues, MSS are described very briefly. Palaeographical and codicological information: total number of leaves in each MS (but no indication of folio numbers for separate parts of the MS), exact or approximate date, name of scribe, place of writing, illuminations and decorations. A serial number enumerating the entries in each catalogue appears to the right of each entry. Call-numbers are listed in parentheses towards the end of each entry and are followed by another number (preceded by the prefix מ) enumerating the MSS in each collection. This final number appears on the IMHM's early catalogue cards. The microfilm number at the IMHM is listed to the left of each entry, preceded by the prefix ס. Indexes: Part I has indexes to names (authors, scribes and names mentioned), titles, poems, place names and languages. Parts II and III have, in addition to the indexes in Part I, a separate index of scribes and indexes of dated MSS and subjects. Part III also has an index of illuminated MSS. Descriptions of interesting MSS and recent acquisitions were printed in *KS*, beginning with Vol. LVI (1981), and reprinted in *From the Collections of the Institute of Microfilmed Hebrew Manuscripts* (מגנזי המכון לתצלומי כתבי היד העבריים, ירושלים תשנ״ו). The staff of the IMHM prepared a number of catalogues of manuscript collections in cooperation with other libraries: *Cat. Neubauer, Addenda*; *Cat. Richler*, Parma; and *Cat. Richler*, Vatican (see the List of Bibliographical Abbreviations). A microfiche copy of all the catalogue cards and computer output up to the end of 1989 was published by Chadwyck-Healey, Paris 1989. The *User's Guide* accompanying the microfiche copy provides information about the IMHM, including a list of the microfilmed collections (1950–1987), and is available at the Institute. A newer version of this list, updated to 2012, appears herein, in Appendix II.

Jerusalem, Israel Museum

The Museum, incorporating the Bezalel National Art Museum, has a collection of about 100 Hebrew MSS, mainly illuminated or decorated. Seven MSS were described in *Jerusalem Collections* (1967). See also *Bird's Head Haggada, *Cracow Bible, *Erna Michael Haggada, *Frankfurt *Mishne Tora*, *Friedmann, Israel, *Henriques de Castro, *Nuremberg Haggada, and *Nuremberg Maḥzor.

Jerusalem, Jewish National and University Library (JNUL)

Former name of *Jerusalem, National Library of Israel. The library's name and legal status were changed in 2007.

Jerusalem, Mosad Harav Kook (Rabbi Kook Institute)

The library had a collection of over 1,400 MSS, many of them from the library of Rabbi J. L. *Maimon (Fishman). N. Ben-Menahem described ten MSS formerly in the possession of Rabbi Nahum Dov *Friedmann of Sadagora (נ' בן מנחם, 'כתבי־יד מספרייתו של רבי נחום דובער פרידמאן מסאדיגורה', ארשת, א [תשי"ח], עמ' 396–413), and 20 other MSS from the library's collection ('תיאורים של עשרים כתבי־יד [מגנזי מוסד הרב קוק]', שם, ב [תש"ך], עמ' 378–407). An unpublished catalogue of the entire collection is found in the library. Since the 1970s many of the MSS have been sold to collectors and dealers.

Jerusalem, National Library of Israel (NLI)

Formerly the Jewish National and University Library (JNUL). The NLI collection includes about 8,500 Hebrew MSS, 270 *Geniza fragments (ca. 700 leaves), over 1,000 marriage contracts, bills of divorce, etc., over 90 scrolls, 74 Samaritan MSS and about 600 archives. The MSS in the library derive from various sources. The collection includes many MSS from the Isaac Michael *Badhab, Hayyim Bekhor *Halevy and *Yahuda libraries, as well as MSS from a number of Jewish communal libraries in Italy (*Livorno, *Trieste and *Pitigliano). Until 1975 the call-numbers of the Hebrew MSS in the library consisted of the prefix 'Heb.', a prefix denoting size (8°, 4°, 2°) and a consecutive serial number for each of the two size divisions (e.g., MS 8° 123; MS 4° 123). In December 1975, when the collection numbered MSS Heb. 8° 1–5713 and 4° 1–1497, a new system of numbering the MSS was introduced, and since then all MSS regardless of size are given consecutive serial numbers beginning with 5714. Prefixes (8°, 4°, 24°, 38°, etc.) attached to the call-numbers of new acquisitions are used only to designate the locations of the MSS in the stacks.

CATALOGUES Almost all the Hebrew MSS in the NLI were described in card catalogues, some in detail and others in brief or temporary cards. A microfiche copy of the detailed cards was published by Chadwyck-Healey, Paris 1989. All the information on the cards has been computerized, together with the catalogue of the Institute of Microfilmed Hebrew Manuscripts, and can be consulted online at www.nli.org.il. About 1,200 MSS are described in Hebrew in several printed catalogues: 157 Kabbala MSS were described by G. Scholem and B. I. Joel, *Catalogus Codicum Cabbalisticorum Hebraicorum ...*, Jerusalem 1930 (כתבי־היד העבריים הנמצאים בבית הספרים הלאומי והאוניברסיטאי בירושלם, תיארם וחקרם גרשם שלום בהשתתפות יששכר יואל), and 648 further MSS were described by B. I. Joel in *Catalogue of Hebrew Manuscripts in the Jewish National and University Library, Jerusalem (except Cabbalah MSS)*, Jerusalem 1934 (רשימת כתבי־היד העבריים הנמצאים בבית הספרים הלאומי והאוניברסיטאי בירושלים [מלבד כתבי־יד בקבלה]). Another 29 MSS, acquired from the Romm publishing house, were described by Joel in *KS*, XIII (1936/7) (י' יואל, 'אוסף כתבי־יד מבית־דפוס ראם', ק"ס, יג [תרצ"ז], עמ' 513–523). During the years 1954–1959, 139 MSS, including nine non-Hebrew and seven Samaritan MSS, were acquired by the Ministry of Education and Culture of the

State of Israel and presented to the JNUL (now NLI). They were described in brief in *List of Manuscripts, Books, Documents and Art Objects Acquired in Europe after the Second World War by the Ministry of Education and Culture*, Jerusalem 1960 (רשימת כתבי־יד, ספרים, תעודות וחפצי אמנות שנרכשו באירופה אחרי מלחמת העולם השניה על ידי משרד החינוך והתרבות, ירושלים תש״ך). Among the MSS described are a few from the *Trieste, Talmud Tora library. The NLI call-numbers are listed in each entry. 285 MSS acquired from the estate of Isaac *Badhab were catalogued in brief by M. Benayahu in 1947. Benayahu's descriptions were published by Badhab's grandson Joseph Levy in *Isaac Badhab (1859–1947): His Life's Work and Environs*, Jerusalem 1977 (ר׳ יצחק בדאהב, תר״ך–תש״ז: מפעל חייו ושכונתו, ירושלים תש״ז), pp. 40–57. The dated Hebrew MSS written up to 1540 were included among those described in Hebrew and French in *Manuscrits médiévaux en caractères hébraïques* (אוצר כתבי־יד עבריים מימי־הביניים), Paris–Jerusalem 1972–1986. Twelve *Geniza fragments were described by A. Yellin (א׳ ילין, ׳אסף כתבי ה״גניזה״ אשר בבית עקד הספרים הלאמי בירושלים׳, ק״ס, ב [תרפ״ו], עמ׳ 292–297), and four fragments in Arabic by E. Ashtor (א׳ אשתור, ׳אסף כתבי ה״גניזה״ אשר בבית־הספרים הלאומי והאוניברסיטאי בירושלם׳, ק״ס, ז [ת״ש], עמ׳ 109–116).

Jerusalem, Schocken Institute

The private collection of Salman Schocken was transferred from Germany to Jerusalem in 1934. After Schocken's death in 1959, the Schocken Institute was founded, and his library, which included about 300 MSS, was housed in the Institute. Since 1961 the Institute has been associated with the Jewish Theological Seminary of America, but a small part of the manuscript collection remained the property of the Schocken family, including the First and Second *Nuremberg Haggadas and the *Nuremberg Maḥzor. Some of the MSS belonging to the Schocken family, including the second Nuremberg Haggada and the Nuremberg Maḥzor, have been sold. Some of the MSS were sold at the following auctions: *Important Judaica* (Sotheby's, Tel Aviv, December 9, 1999); *Judaica* (Sotheby's, Tel Aviv, October 30, 2002, no. 47); *Important Judaica* (Sotheby's, New York, March 18, 2004); *Important Hebrew Manuscripts from the Salman Schocken Collection* (Christie's, New York, November 15, 2005). For a list of the MSS that were sold and their present whereabouts, see Appendix I, no. 36. There is no printed catalogue of the collection.

Jerusalem Mishne Tora

Name given to *Jerusalem, NLI, Heb. 4° 1193, an illuminated copy of Maimonides' *Mishne Tora* written in Italy around 1400. The MS was purchased by Julius *Hamburger in 1880 from the Marquis Carlo Trivulzio. Hamburger published variant readings from this MS in *Abweichungen des gedruckten Textes der Jad Hachasaka ... von einer Handschrift ... aus der Sammlung des Marchese Carlo Trivulzio* ..., Frankfurt a/M 1889. At the beginning of the twentieth century the MS was in the possession of Hermann Cramer of Frankfurt. The MS was acquired by the *Jerusalem, JNUL (now NLI), from S. Floersheim in 1966.

Swarzenski and Schilling, *Die illuminierten Handschriften*, no. 109; *Jerusalem Collections*, no. 15; *Books from Sefarad*, Jerusalem 1992, no. 57.

Jessurun Cardozo, Jacob de Raphael

Amsterdam, Netherlands, 1792–1869; cantor of the Spanish and Portuguese synagogue

Twenty-one Hebrew MSS are described in the auction catalogue, *Catalog einer ... Sammlung hebräischer und jüdischer Bücher und Handschriften unter anderen sehr viele und höchst seltene Werke spanisch-jüdischer*

Autoren enthaltend sämmtlich nachgelassen von Jacob de Raphael Jessurun Cardozo ... Hirsch Isaacsohn und andern ..., Amsterdam 1870, nos. 930–950. Seventeen MSS in Spanish and Portuguese are described in nos. 1390–1406. For the present locations of some of the MSS see Appendix I, no. 20.

Jesus College

See *Oxford, College Libraries.

Jews' College

See *London School of Jewish Studies.

JMC

Jewish Museum Catalogue. Fifty-five illuminated Hebrew MSS from the library of *New York, JTSA, that were on exhibition in the Jewish Museum in New York were described in *Illuminated Hebrew Manuscripts from the Library of the Jewish Theological Seminary of America*, New York 1965.

JNUL

Jewish National and University Library (now *Jerusalem, NLI).

Joel b. Simeon

Southern Germany and northern Italy, fifteenth century, copyist

Joel illuminated the so-called *Joel b. Simeon Haggada, and he also copied the First and Second *New York Haggadas, the *Washington Haggada, the first *Nuremberg Haggada, the *Cremona Maḥzor, the so-called *Lady's Maḥzor, the *Moskowitz Maḥzor and the Dyson *Perrins Haggada. One of the two *Parma Haggadas and a haggada in *Stuttgart, Württembergische Landesbibliothek, Cod. Or. 4° 1, are also attributed to Joel.

M. Beit-Arié, 'Joel ben Simeon's manuscripts', *Journal of Jewish Art*, III (1977), pp. 25–39.

Joel b. Simeon Haggada

Also known as the London Haggada or the Ashkenazi Haggada. Name given to *London, BL, MS Add. 14762 (*Cat. Margoliouth*, no. 610), a fifteenth-century haggada illuminated by *Joel b. Simeon (facsimile edition: *The Ashkenazi Haggadah*, with an introduction by David Goldstein, London 1985). According to M. Glatzer, 'The Ashkenazic and Italian Haggadah and the *haggadot* of Joel b. Simeon', in Myron M. Weinstein (ed.), *Library of Congress Haggadah (1478)*, Washington, D.C., 1991, the copyist of the MS was Meir b. Israel Yaffe.

Narkiss, p. 124; M. Beit-Arié, 'Joel ben Simeon's manuscripts', *Journal of Jewish Art*, III (1977), pp. 25–39.

Joffe, Judah Achilles

Bakhmut, Russia, 1873 – New York, 1966; linguist

*New York, JTSA, acquired 25 MSS from Joffe in 1959 (*Register*, 5721, p. 118 [Marx, *Bibl. Studies*, p. 351]).

Jonge, Jacob Wolf de

Amsterdam, Netherlands, d. 1866?

Twelve Hebrew MSS, some from the estate of de Jonge and some from the estate of Naftali H. Rubens, were listed in *Catalog einer werthvollen Sammlung hebräischer und jüdischer Bücher, Handschriften, etc., ... aus den nachgelassenen Bibliotheken des Herrn Jacob Wolf de Jonge in Amsterdam und ... Naftali H. Rubens in Haag* ... Amsterdam (J. L. Joachimsthal) 1885, nos. 1472–1483. For the present locations of some of the MSS see Appendix I, no. 21.

Jonge, Wolf de

Amsterdam, Netherlands, d. before 1839

Sixty-five MSS are listed in the sales catalogue of his library (רשימה מן כמה ספרים ... עם כתבי יד ... מעזבון המנוח ... וואלף דע יונג זצ"ל אשר ימכר ... באמסטרדם, Amsterdam 1839). Due to the brevity of the descriptions and the lack of any physical descriptions, the present locations of most of the MSS cannot be determined. It is probable that no. 4 in the catalogue is MS 28 in the collection of S. Abrahams in Jerusalem; no. 12 is probably *Amsterdam, Ets Haim HS 47 B 4; no. 45 is probably *London Montefiore 42; no. 53 is probably *Amsterdam, Ets Haim HS 47 C 44; and no. 59 is probably *Cambridge, UL, MS Add. 1496.

Joshua Ibn Gaon Bible

Name given to *Paris, BnF, MS héb. 20, a Bible copied by Joshua ibn Gaon in 1300. Other Bibles copied by Joshua are the Second *Kennicott Bible, *Dublin, Trinity College, MS M. 2. 6, and *Oxford, Bodleian Library, MS Opp. Add. 4° 75.

Narkiss, *Span. & Port.*, nos. 4–5.

Jost, Isaac Marcus

Bernburg, Germany, 1793 – Frankfurt a/M, Germany, 1860; historian

Many of Jost's MSS are now in *Frankfurt a/M, Goethe Universität, Universitätsbibliothek. One of his MSS is *Amsterdam, UB, HS. Ros. 82.

JTSA (JTS)

*New York, Jewish Theological Seminary of America.

Judaica Conservancy Foundation

See *Berlin, Hochschule für die Wissenschaft des Judentums.

K

K...m

*Kirchheim, Raphael.

Kafiḥ, Yosef

Yemen, 1917 – Jerusalem, 2000; rabbi and scholar

R. Kafiḥ owned over 100 MSS, most of them Yemenite. There is no catalogue of the collection. Most of the MSS were microfilmed for the *Jerusalem, IMHM, where they were assigned call-numbers. After his death, most of R. Kafiḥ's MSS were sold.

Kahana, Abraham

Skomorochy, Ukraine, 1874 – Tel Aviv, 1946; scholar

Kahana's MSS and archives are now in *Jerusalem, NLI. The MS described in I. Davidson, *Thesaurus of Mediaeval Hebrew Poetry* (י' דודזון, אוצר השירה והפיוט, ד, נויארק תרצ"ג), p. 8, and referred to by J. Mann, *Texts and Studies*, II, Cincinnati 1935, p. 554, as MS Kahana I, is now NLI, Heb. 8° 5204. The MS referred to by Mann (*ibid.*) as MS Kahana II is now NLI, Heb. 8° 3795.

Kahn, Zadoc

Mommenheim, France, 1839 – Paris, 1905; Chief Rabbi of France

The collection of responsa described by M. G. Montefiore, 'Un recueil de consultations rabbiniques', *REJ*, X (1885), pp. 183–203, is now *New York, JTSA, MS R1355.

Kais. Bibl.

Kaiserliche Bibliothek. See *St. Petersburg, NLR.

Kanitz

See *Kounice.

Kaplan, Mitchell

1881–1944; Yiddish poet

Kaplan's MSS described in the catalogue he wrote, *Panorama of Ancient Letters*, New York 1942, pp. 229–262, are now in New York University, Bobst Library, Fales Collection.

Kapon, Judah

Russia, nineteenth–twentieth century

Eleven MSS acquired by Kapon from Karaites in Crimea were purchased in 1904 by the Oriental Institute (now *St. Petersburg, Institute of Oriental Manuscripts). The MSS were described by P. Kokowzow in Latin in *Bulletin de l'Académie Impériale des Sciences de St-Pétersbourg*, Ve Série, XXIII (1905), pp. 1–12.

Pearson, p. 48.

Kapustin, Antonin

See *Antonin.

Karassou-Bazar (Crimea, Ukraine), Synagogue

Seventy-nine MSS formerly in the synagogue are now in *St. Petersburg, Institute of Oriental Manuscripts. Among them is MS D 62, a Bible known as the Karassou-Bazar Codex.

Starkova, 'Les plus anciens mss.', p. 37.

Karay-Bitikili

Name for *Eupatoria.

Karlsruhe (Germany), Badische Landesbibliothek

Fourteen MSS, thirteen of them from the collection of Johann von *Reuchlin, were described by S. Landauer in *Die Handschriften der Grossherzoglich Badischen Hof- und Landesbibliothek in Karlsruhe*, II: Orientalische Handschriften, Karlsruhe 1892, pp. 1–28. Call-numbers are listed at the head of each entry. Thirteen MSS were described in *Cat. Allony–Loewinger*, I, pp. 57–58. One additional MS and four fragments are described in *Cat. Striedl–Róth*, pp. 163–165. The MSS from the Reuchlin collection were also described in W. Abel and R. Leicht, *Verzeichnis der Hebraica in der Bibliothek Johannes Reuchlins*, Ostfildern, Germany, 2005. MS Reuchlin 6, philological works by David and Moses Kimhi, and a collection of polemical works acquired in 1935 without a call-number, nos. 21 and 22 in the Abel-Leicht publication, were lost or destroyed in World War II. The MS acquired in 1935 was previously described by K. Preisendanz, 'Eine neue Handschrift aus Johann Reuchlins Bibliothek', in *Neue Heidelberger Jahrbücher* (1936), pp. 100–111. Codex Reuchlin 3, a MS of Prophets with Targum copied in 1105 and known as Codex Reuchlinianus, was reproduced in facsimile, *The Pre-Masoretic Bible*, Copenhagen 1956.

Karp, Abraham

Rochester, N.Y., 1921–2003

Karp's MSS were acquired mainly by *Philadelphia, CAJS and *New York, JTSA. Three MSS (MSS Karp 2, 8, 11) were acquired by the *New York Public Library (**P MSS Heb. 236, 238, 246).

Kasher, Menahem

Warsaw, Poland, 1895 – Jerusalem, 1983

Kasher's MS of *Midrash Ma'ayan ganim* (מדרש מעין גנים), quoted in his work *Tora shelema* (תורה שלמה), is now *New York, JTSA, MS R1687.

Kassel (Germany), Landesbibliothek und Murhardsche Bibliothek

Two MSS and fragments from six MSS are described in *Cat. Striedl–Róth*, pp. 166–169. One of these MSS and a Tora scroll are described in *Cat. Allony–Loewinger*, I, p. 56. The MSS in this library may be viewed online at http://orka.bibliothek.uni-kassel.de/viewer/browse/handschriften*/-/1/-/-/.

Katznellenbogen, Zevi Hirsch

Vilna, Lithuania, 1796–1868; author

Nine of Katznellenbogen's MSS were listed in *Literaturblatt des Orients*, VI (1845), p. 210. Nos. 3 and 6 on the list are MSS *Moscow, RSL, MSS Günzburg 1063 and 1421. Nos. 8 and 9 are *St. Petersburg, Institute of Oriental Manuscripts, MSS B 168 and B 457. The present location of the others is not known.

Kauffmann, J.

Booksellers in Frankfurt

Many MSS are listed in the catalogues of the J. Kauffmann firm, published in the years 1870–1935. The MSS were sold to various libraries, and many of them are now in *New York, JTSA. Several MSS purchased from the 1883 catalogue by *Oxford, Bodleian Library, are listed in *Cat. Neubauer*, p. xxxii, and *Cat. Neubauer–Cowley*, II, pp. xii–xvii.

Kaufmann, Aaron

Kaufmann's MSS passed into the possession of *St. Petersburg, Society for the Promotion of Culture among the Jews of Russia.

Kaufmann, David

Kojetein, Moravia, 1852 – Budapest, Hungary, 1899; scholar and bibliophile

Kaufmann left a collection of 591 MSS and about 600 *Geniza fragments. The collection included many MSS acquired from Marco *Mortara, 27 MSS bought from the *Trieste brothers and MSS acquired through Giuseppe *Jaré. After his death, Kaufmann's widow requested Max *Weisz to compile a catalogue of the collection (= *Cat. Kaufmann*, 1906), and then presented the collection to *Budapest, Hungarian Academy of Sciences. The Kaufmann Haggada is Budapest MS A 422, an illuminated fourteenth-century Spanish haggada, (facsimile edition, Budapest 1954; Narkiss, p. 70). The Kaufmann Mishna is MS A 50, an early complete MS of the Mishna (facsimile edition, The Hague 1930). The Kaufmann *Mishne Tora* is MS A 77, an illuminated copy of Maimonides' work written in Cologne in 1295/6 (partial facsimile edition, Budapest 1980; Narkiss, p. 100). The MS from which Kaufmann published the regulations of Yeshivat Shalom (האסיף, ג [תרמ"ז], עמ' 209–227) was not listed in the catalogue and is now *Jerusalem, NLI, Heb. 8° 4002.

David Kaufmann Memorial Volume, Budapest 2002; B. Narkiss and G. Sed-Rajna, *Index of Jewish Art: Iconographical Index of Hebrew Illuminated Manuscripts*, IV: *Illustrated Manuscripts of the Kaufmann Collection at the Library of the Hungarian Academy of Sciences*, Jerusalem–Paris–Budapest 1988.

Kennicott, Benjamin

Totnes, England, 1718–1783; Christian Bible scholar

In Kennicott's *Dissertatio Generalis in Vetus Testamentum Hebraicum*, Oxford 1780, which was printed at the end of his *Vetus Testamentum Hebraicum*, 694 Hebrew biblical MSS used in his apparatus are briefly described (see also de *Rossi). The present locations of most of these MSS are listed in Appendix I, no. 22. The MSS in Kennicott's own collection were in Radcliffe College, Oxford, and were transferred to *Oxford, Bodleian Library, in 1879. A list of the MSS, their old and new numbers and their numbers in *Cat. Neubauer* is found in the catalogue, p. xxv, and in *Cat. Neubauer–Cowley*, II, p. 540. A list of the British Museum MSS used by Kennicott is found in *Cat. Margoliouth–Leveen*, IV, p. 174. The First Kennicott Bible is a name given to Oxford, Bodleian Library, MS Kennicott 1 (*Cat. Neubauer*, 2322), an illuminated Bible written by Moses ibn Zabara in 1476 and illuminated by Joseph ibn Hayyim. A facsimile edition was published in London in 1985. The Second Kennicott Bible is Oxford MS Kennicott 2 (*Cat.*

Neubauer, 2323), a Bible written and illuminated by Joshua ibn Gaon at Soria (Spain) in 1306.

Narkiss, *Span. & Port.*, no. 3.

Keter Aram Sova
See *Aleppo.

Keter Damascus
See *Damascus.

Kiev (Ukraine), Vernadsky National Library
The library is affiliated with the National Academy of Sciences of Ukraine. Its Hebraica and Judaica holdings derive mainly from the collection of the *St. Petersburg, Society for the Promotion of Culture among the Jews of Russia (OPE), including the collection of Abraham *Harkavy and that of the *St. Petersburg, Jewish Historical Ethnographic Society, which were removed to the Institute for Jewish Proletarian Culture in Kiev when the OPE was closed in 1929. The Institute for Jewish Proletarian Culture was closed in 1936, to be succeeded by the Office (Kabinet) for the Study of Soviet Yiddish Literature, Language and Folklore, under the aegis of the Academy of Sciences of the Ukrainian SSR, as it was then called. During World War II, part of the collection was confiscated by the Nazis. In 1950, after the Kabinet was closed, most of the archives of the OPE and the Jewish Historical Ethnographic Society were moved to Leningrad (St. Petersburg), and the contents of the now defunct library were stored in caverns and catacombs in Kiev. In the late 1980s the material was rediscovered and removed to the Vernadsky Library.
The manuscript department of the Library now holds several thousand items, including autographs, archival material, Hebrew MSS, 109 *pinkasim* and *Geniza fragments. The cataloguing of the manuscripts has not been completed, and the number of pre-twentieth-century 'literary' MSS (other than documents, etc.) cannot be determined accurately, though it may be estimated at around 700.

Z. M. Baker, 'History of the Jewish Collections at the Vernadsky Library in Kiev', *Shofar*, X, no. 4 (1992), pp. 31–48; *Soviet Jewish Affairs*, XXI, no. 2 (1991).

King's College
King's College, Aberdeen University.

King's MS or King's Bible
Name given to *London, British Library, MS King's 1 (*Cat. Margoliouth*, no. 56), an illuminated Bible presented to the British Museum by King George IV in 1823.

Narkiss, *Span. & Port.*, no. 22.

Kirchheim, Raphael
Frankfurt a/M, Germany, 1804–1889; scholar
Kirchheim donated nine MSS to the library of *Breslau, Jüdisch-theologisches Seminar. The MS of Joseph Kara's commentary on the Prophets, known as 'MS Kirchheim', was MS no. 178 in the Seminary before World War II, but its present location is not known. The fragments of the Tosefta belonging to Kirchheim described by M. Zuckermandel, 'Erhaltene Trümmer eines dritten Toseftacodex', *Jüdisches Literaturblatt*, VII, nos. 20–21 (1878), are now *Jerusalem, Schocken Institute, MS 2041. Kirchheim's copy of *Midrash Tehilim* (Venice 1546), with manuscript notes, used by S. Buber in his edition, is now *Jerusalem, NLI, Heb. 4° 1404.

Kirschstein, Salli
1869 – Berlin, 1935; collector
A collection of Judaica, including a few MSS, was sold to *Cincinnati, HUC, in 1925. Another collection including over 100 of Kirschstein's MSS, some of which were purchased from H. *Frauberger, are listed

together with his ceremonial art objects in the sales catalogue *Die Judaica-Sammlung S. Kirschstein, Berlin*, Munich 1932, nos. 167–212 (scrolls) and 213–278 (mainly liturgical manuscripts, *ketubot* and other documents). No. 215 in the catalogue was formerly in the possession of Felix *Guggenheim, who presented it to *Jerusalem, JNUL (now NLI, Heb. 8° 5492). I have been unable to trace the present whereabouts of any of the other MSS in the catalogue.

Oko, pp. 82–84.

Klagsbald, Victor

Paris and Jerusalem, 1924–; collector

Fifty-seven MSS, mostly from the Abensour collection in Morocco, were described in Klagsbald's *Catalogue des Manuscrits Marocains de la Collection Klagsbald*, Paris 1980. His many other MSS were never catalogued in print.

Klau Library

*Cincinnati, HUC, Klau Library.

Kleerekoper, Joseph

Amsterdam, Netherlands, 1848–1912; cantor

Twenty Hebrew MSS from his collection are listed in the *Auctions-Catalog* (עדות ביהוסף), Amsterdam 1913, nos. 1530–1550. No. 1530 is probably *Cincinnati, HUC, MS Acc. 139. Nos. 1538, 1546, 1547 and 1550 are now in *Amsterdam, Rosenthaliana (Hss. Ros. 226, Ros. PL. C-22, Ros. PL C-20 and Ros. 465).

Klosterneuburg (Austria), Bibliothek des Augustiner-Chorherrenstifts

Fragments from ten MSS are described in *Cat. Schwarz–Loewinger–Róth*, pp. 86–88. More fragments have been uncovered, and close to 40 fragments are described and displayed on the website http://www.ksbm.oeaw.ac.at/hebraica. The MS mentioned in *Cat. Schwarz*, Vienna, Anhang B, no. 1 (p. 244), is no longer in the library.

Koblenz

See *Coblenz.

Kohut, George Alexander

Szekesfehervar, Hungary, 1874 – New York, 1933; scholar

Many of Kohut's MSS were presented to the Jewish Institute of Religion–Hebrew Union College in New York (Oko, p. 88). *New Haven, Yale University Library, also acquired some 30 Hebrew MSS from Kohut's collection (MSS Heb. 46–78). They were briefly described by L. Nemoy, 'Hebrew and kindred manuscripts in the Yale University Library', *Journal of Jewish Bibliography*, III (1942), pp. 44–47.

Köln

Cologne.

Königsberg, Stadtbibliothek

Königsberg formerly belonged to Germany but was annexed to Russia in 1945 and called Kaliningrad. The library was destroyed in World War II. In A. Seraphim, *Handschriften-Katalog der Stadtbibliothek Königsberg*, Königsberg 1909, one Hebrew MS (S 80 fol.) and one Yiddish MS formerly in the possession of Augustus *Pfeiffer (S 44 8°) are listed. The Hebrew MS, a Bible described by *Kennicott, no. 223, is now Princeton University Library, MS Scheide M 136. The Princeton MS has also been described by D. S. Berkowitz in *In Remembrance of Creation*, Waltham 1968, no. 16, without mention of its former provenance.

Kounice (Czech Republic), Hevra Kadisha

The MS of the regulations of the Hevra Kadisha described by H. Flesch, 'Aus jüdischen Handschriften in Mähren', *Jahrbuch der Gesellschaft für Geschichte der Juden in* *der Čechoslovakischen Republik*, II (1930), p. 289, is now *Prague, Jewish Museum, MS 98, and has been described again by V. Sadek, ‘From the MSS collections of the State Jewish Museum in Prague (illuminated mss.)’, *Judaica Bohemiae*, X (1974), pp. 109–110.

Krafft, Albrecht

1816 – Vienna, 1847; orientalist

Krafft wrote a catalogue of the MSS in the Royal Library of Vienna with S. *Deutsch. See *Vienna, Österreichische Nationalbibliothek.

Krems Ketuba

Name given to *Vienna, Österreichische Nationalbibliothek, Cod. Hebr. 218 (*Cat. Schwarz*, Vienna, 202), a marriage contract (*ketuba*) written in Krems in 1392.

Kremsmünster (Austria), Stiftsbibliothek

Fragments from 15 MSS are described in *Cat. Schwarz–Loewinger–Róth*, pp. 89–90. The call-numbers are not listed. The numbers at the head of each entry are catalogue numbers. More fragments have been uncovered, and over 30 fragments are described and displayed on the website http://www.ksbm.oeaw.ac.at/hebraica.

Krengel, Johann

Born 1872; rabbi

Through Heinrich *Frauberger, Krengel received 150 *Geniza fragments, some of which he described in ‘Einige Genisa-Fragmente’, in *Festschrift zu Israel Lewy's siebzigstem Geburstag*, Breslau 1911, pp. 36–46. They disappeared during World War II and were found in the 1970s in *New York, JTSA, in an old, worn leather briefcase, mixed up with Krengel's typewritten sermons in German. The collection is now called the *Krengel Genizah*.

M. Schmelzer, ‘One hundred years of Genizah discovery and research: The American share’, *Judaica Librarianship*, XI (2002/3), p. 58.

Kupfer, Ephraim (Franciszka)

Pozowice, Poland 1905 – Jerusalem, 1994; historian and talmudic scholar

Kupfer, who for many years was a cataloguer of Hebrew MSS at the *Warsaw, ŻIH, and at the *Jerusalem, IMHM, published many articles and monographs from and on Hebrew MSS. Together with S. Strelcyn he compiled an unpublished catalogue of the Hebrew MSS in the Warsaw Institute (in Polish); and together with N. Allony he compiled *Cat. Allony–Kupfer*, II, in which MSS from five European countries were described, and a brief catalogue of 64 MSS from *Milan, Biblioteca Ambrosiana (‘כתבי־יד עבריים נוספים באמברוזיאנה’, ארשת, ד [תשכ"ו], עמ' 234–270).

L

L

(1) Leiden; (2) Leipzig; (3) Leningrad; (4) *Loan; (5) London.

Lady's Maḥzor

Name given to *London, BL, MS Add. 26957 (*Cat. Margoliouth*, no. 615), a siddur written by *Joel b. Simeon in 1469 for Menahem b. Samuel and his daughter Maraviglia.

Lair-Dubreuil, Fernand

Paris; auctioneer

MS no. 25 in the auction catalogue *Collection de M. F. L[air]-D[ubreuil]: Manuscrits avec* *miniatures du IXe au XVe siècle*, Paris 1909, p. 30, became *Jerusalem, Schocken Institute, MS 13873. The MS was sold in 2005 to a private collector in Israel.

Landau, Emil Elias

Klasno-Wielitzka, Galicia, 1842 – Weilburg, Germany, 1924; rabbi

Landau's MS, mentioned in *Cat. Steinschneider*, Berlin, no. 191, and in *ZfHB*, I (1896/7), p. 178, was sold to the booksellers J. *Kauffmann Co. (Cat. XIV MS no. 40), from whom it was purchased by *Oxford, Bodleian Library, where its present call-number is MS Heb. e. 68 (*Cat. Neubauer–Cowley*, II, 2869).

Landauer, Samuel

Huerben, Germany, 1846 – Augsburg(?), Germany, 1937

Landauer wrote catalogues of Hebrew MSS in *Karlsruhe, Badische Landesbibliothek, and *Strasbourg, Bibliothèque nationale et universitaire.

Landi, Ferdinando

Italy, nineteenth cent.; marquis

Landi's collection, which included six Hebrew MSS, two of which were formerly in the collection of Giovanni de *Rossi, was presented to the *Piacenza, Biblioteca Comunale, in 1846.

Tamani, *Piacenza*, p. 137.

Landsberg, Mendel

Kremenetz, 1786–1866; collector

Two of Landsberg's MSS were purchased from Ephraim *Deinard by *Berlin, Staatsbibliothek (Cods. 2° 1387–1388, *Cat. Steinschneider*, Berlin, nos. 214–215). MSS *New York, Public Library, **P (MSS Heb. 100 and 124), *New York, Columbia University, X893 Ez 7 and L 97, and *New York, JTSA, MS 2858, also come from Landsberg's collection.

Lansdowne, Marquess of

See *Petty-Fitzmaurice, Sir William.

Lattes, Abraham

See *Lattes, Mosé.

Lattes, Mosé

Venice, Italy, 1846–1883; rabbi

At least 13 MSS belonging to Lattes and his father, Abraham, are in *Milan, Biblioteca Ambrosiana.

Cat. Luzzatto, p. 5

Laubach (Germany), Graf zu Solms-Laubach'sches Archiv

See *Friedberg, Stadtarchiv.

Laud, William

Reading, England, 1573 – London, 1645

Laud presented 44 Hebrew MSS to *Oxford, Bodleian Library, during the years 1635–1640. In *Cat. Neubauer* the call-numbers of the MSS from the Laud collection are printed without the prefix 'Or.', and they should be corrected to read 'Laud Or.'. In the same catalogue, p. xxx, is a list of the Laud MSS described in *Uri's catalogue. MSS nos. 154, 267, 268, 318 and 320 are included erroneously; they belong to the *Digby collection and have since been returned to their proper place. In *Cat. Neubauer–Cowley*, II, pp. 537–540, is a revised list of the MSS in Uri's catalogue, in which the correct numbers of the Laud MSS appear. The list is according to the Uri catalogue numbers, and the Laud MSS are listed together with MSS from other collections. A list of MSS from the Laud collection not described by Uri is found in *Cat. Neubauer*, p. xxv.

Laud Maḥzor

Name given to *Oxford, Bodleian Library, MS Laud Or. 321 (*Cat. Neubauer*, 2373), an illuminated Ashkenazic maḥzor.

Narkiss, p. 94.

Laurent. or Laurenziana
*Florence, Biblioteca Medicea Laurenziana.

Laur. Pl.
Laurenziana Pluteo. See *Florence, Biblioteca Medicea Laurenziana.

L-D
*Lair-Dubreuil.

Lebrecht, Fürchtegott
Memmelbach, Germany, 1800 – Berlin, 1876; scholar
According to Freimann, 'Mitteilungen', p. 84, Lebrecht's MSS came into the possession of the 'Veitel-Heine'schen Stiftung' [= Veitel-Heine Ephraim'schen Lehranstalt] in Berlin. Solomon *Halberstamm purchased a number of MSS from Lebrecht, and one of Lebrecht's MSS is in *Berlin, Staatsbibliothek (Cod. Or. 4° 553). Lebrecht listed all MSS of the Talmud known to him in his *Handschriften und erste Ausgaben des Babylonischen Talmud*, Berlin 1862.

Lee, John
England, 1779–1859; minister and educator
Lee's books were sold by Sotheby's in at least two auctions, in 1876 and 1888. One Hebrew MS is now *Cambridge, Trinity College, MS F. 12. 33.

Lee.
*Leeuwarden, Provinciale Bibliotheek van Friesland; see Leeuwarden, TRESOAR.

Leeds, Brotherton Library
See *Roth, Cecil.

Leeuwarden (Netherlands), TRESOAR, the Friesland Historical and Literary Centre
Formerly the Provinciale Bibliotheek van Friesland. In 2002, the Provincial Library and several other institutions merged to form TRESOAR. Most of the MSS in the library were brought from the library in Franeker in 1813, when Napoleon closed the University in Franeker. Six Hebrew MSS were briefly described in Latin by M. J. de Goeje in *Catalogus Codicum Orientalium Bibliothecae Academiae Lugduno-Batavae*, V, Leiden 1873, pp. 305–306. These MSS were later described by A. Neubauer in *Israelietische Letterbode*, II (1876/7), pp. 83–86, and in *Cat. Allony–Kupfer*, II, p. 80. In *Cat. Allony–Kupfer* the call-numbers are listed in parentheses at the end of each entry. L. *Fuks bequeathed his library to the Provinciale Bibliotheek, and it entered the library after his death in 1990. Fuks's collection included a few Hebrew MSS.

Leghorn
See *Livorno.

Le Havre (France), Bibliothèque municipale Armand Salacrou
Around 1800, Mr. Marx Cahen of Le Havre presented the library with a gift of 26 MSS. These MSS were listed in *Catalogue général*, II (1888), nos. 461–484, and described in greater detail by M. Schwab, 'Manuscrits hébreux de la Bibliothèque Municipale de Havre', *REJ*, LXVIII (1914), pp. 264–271.

Lehmann, Manfred R.
Stockholm, Sweden, 1922 – New York, 1997; businessman and scholar
Lehmann's collection included about 1,000 Hebrew MSS. Kabbala, Bible and *Mishne Tora* MSS were described in a series of catalogues in Hebrew collectively entitled *Ohel Hayim: Catalogue of Hebrew Manuscripts of the Manfred and Anne Lehmann Family* (אהל חיים: קטלוג כתבי־היד העבריים בספריית משפחת מנשה ושרה ליהמן). Volume I, *Kabbalistic Manuscripts*, prepared by Moshe Hallamish with the participation of Elazar Hurvitz, New York 1988 (כתבי־יד בקבלה, מתוארים בידי משה חלמיש, בהשתתפות אלעזר הורביץ, ניו יורק

תשמ״ח), describes 135 Kabbala MSS. Volume II (כתבי־היד של התנ״ך), *Biblical Manuscripts*, prepared by Israel Yeivin, New York 1990, describes about 20 biblical MSS and leaves from 200 others in 224 entries. Volume III, *Printed Books, Incunabula and Sixteenth-Century Books* (ספרים נדפסים, אינקונבלים וספרי המאה השש־עשרה), prepared by S. M. Iakerson, New York 1996, describes incunabula and early printed books. Volume IV, *Manuscripts of the Mishneh Torah by R. Moshe Ben Maimon: Maimonides: Sefer Zemanim, the Book of Seasons*, New York 1998, with variants from the manuscripts prepared and edited by the members of the Ariel Institute, Jerusalem (כתבי־היד של ספר ׳משנה תורה׳ לרבינו משה בן מימון/הרמב״ם: ספר זמנים), lists textual variants in *Sefer Zemanim* based on the MSS of the *Mishne Tora* in the Lehmann collection (pp. 1–459), describes in detail 119 fragments from all the Books (pp. 465–500) and lists in brief ten MSS of parts of the *Mishne Tora* (p. 501) and 24 MSS and fragments of works by Moses b. Maimon in the original Judaeo-Arabic (pp. 501–502). The descriptions of the Bible and Kabbala MSS include writing material, size, script, date, a facsimile of a page from each MS and multiple indexes. There are no facsimiles or indexes in Volume IV. Volume V, describing poetry and *piyyutim*, is in preparation.

After Manfred Lehmann's death in 1997, his library was placed in storage. When it was removed from storage to be sent to the Lehmann family in Silver Spring, Md., several crates were found to be missing. The missing books, including over 35 Kabbala MSS, most of the *Mishne Tora* fragments, a few other MSS and rare printed books have never been recovered.

Lehren, Hirschl

The Hague, Netherlands, 1784–1853; philanthropist

Lehren's collection forms the basis of the van *Biema collection.

Lehren, Jacob Meijer and Akiba

Amsterdam, Netherlands, 1793–1861; 1795–1876

Forty-one MSS that had belonged to the two brothers are listed in *Catalog der reichhaltigen Sammlung hebräischer und jüdischer Bücher, Handschriften*, שופרות, מגילות, ספרי תורה *u.s.w. nachgelassen von den ehrw. Herren Meijer Lehren, Akiba Lehren und Moses de Lima, welche am 13 Februar bis 2. März 1899, Abends von 6 Uhr ab durch J. L. Joachimsthal im Amsterdam ... öffentlich versteigert werden sollen*, Amsterdam [1898], nos. 3483–3506. MSS and scrolls from other sources were listed in the 'Nachtrag', nos. 4272–4287.

Moses Hayyim Luzzatto's *Ma'amar 'al haderasha* (מאמר על הדרשה) was printed from no. 3487, in *Kerem chemed* (כרם חמד), VI (1841). The MS was purchased in 1933 by Moritz *Stern and later acquired by *Cincinnati, HUC (I. Sonne, 'Some Luzzatto manuscripts', *Studies in Jewish Bibliography and Booklore*, II [1956], p. 158). *Fuks's catalogue of the MSS in *Amsterdam asserts that Ets Haim, no. 332, HS EH 47 C 48, is identical with no. 3487 in the Lehren catalogue; but the description of the Ets Haim MS is far from identical with the description of the Lehren MS. On the other hand, the HUC MS as described by Sonne (and examined by myself on microfilm in the *Jerusalem, IMHM), is undoubtedly the same as the Lehren MS. For the present or last-known locations of some of the MSS see Appendix I, no. 23.

L. Kruijer-Poesiat, 'The Lehren/De Lima sale', in A. K. Offenberg et al. (eds.), *Treasures of Jewish Booklore*, Amsterdam 1994, no. 48.

Leicester, Earl of

The Bible MS described by *Kennicott, no. 135, and by C. D. Ginsburg in *Introduction to the Massoretico-Critical Edition of the Hebrew Bible*, London 1897, no. 51, was in the possession of the present Earl of Leicester in his library at Holkham and was sold to

Martin Schøyen of Oslo. It is now MS 5070 in the *Schøyen Collection.

Leiden (Netherlands), Universiteitsbibliotheek

Formerly Bibliotheek der Rijksuniversiteit; renamed in 1998. The library's Hebrew MSS come mainly from the collections of Levinus *Warner and Joseph Justus *Scaliger, who lived in the sixteenth and seventeenth centuries. Most of the Warner MSS were first described in *Catalogus Bibl. Publ. Lugd. Batavae*, Leiden 1674 (the present MSS Warn. 1–64, but in a different order) and in *Catalogus Librorum tam impressorum quam manuscriptorum Bibliothecae Publicae Universitatis Lugduno-Batavae, cura & opera Wolferdi Senguerdii, ... Jacobi Gronovii ... & Johannis Heyman*, Leiden 1716 (nos. 1–63, in the present order). M. Steinschneider, in *Cat. Steinschneider*, Leiden (1858), described in Latin and at great length 77 Hebrew MSS from the Warner collection, many of them Karaite (nos. 57 and 61 are in Syriac and Armenian), 13 later acquisitions (nos. 80–94 with the exception of nos. 91–92, which are in Latin), 18 MSS from the Scaliger collection (nos. 17–18 are not in Hebrew) and two additional MSS at the end of the catalogue. Several other MSS were described in *Catalogus Codicum Orientalium Bibliothecae Academiae Lugduno–Batavae*, V, Leiden 1873, nos. 2341, 2361, 2606, 2808, 2809; and VI, Leiden 1877, no. 2836 = Warn. 99. Since the publication of *Cat. Steinschneider*, the library has acquired several additional MSS. Six MSS from *Amsterdam, Koninklijke Nederlandse Akademie van Wetenschappen, described by H. E. Weijers & P. de Jong in *Catalogus Codicum Orientalium Bibliothecae Academiae Regiae Scientiarium*, Leiden 1862, pp. 1–8, are now on permanent loan in the Leiden University library. Most of these later acquisitions were described by Albert van der Heide in *Hebrew Manuscripts of Leiden University Library*, Leiden 1977. The MSS in the Leiden library all bear two press-marks: a serial number (Or. ...), which should be used in references to the MSS, and a shelf-mark (Warn., Scal. Hebr.) indicating the bookcases where the MSS are stored.

In *Cat. Steinschneider*, the MSS are arranged according to their shelf-marks and no indication of their serial numbers is given. Palaeographical and codicological information: writing material, size, number of leaves, script and date. Long quotations from the beginning and end of most of the MSS are copied, as are colophons. At the end of the catalogue are additions and transcriptions from some of the MSS. Indexes: authors, titles, scribes and owners. In the indexes, the names of the Karaites are preceded by asterisks, and names of non-Jews are printed in cursive type. At the end are concordances to the Warner and Scaliger numbers in the 1674 and 1716 catalogues of the Leiden library. Van der Heide's catalogue includes a history of the collections of Hebrew MSS in the library. Supplementing *Cat. Steinschneider*, it supplies some additions and corrections, but mostly codicological information concerning foliation, quire composition, catchwords, watermarks, etc., and descriptions of all the MSS not described by Steinschneider. MSS are listed by their shelf-marks, and serial numbers, including those of the Warner and Scaliger collections, are listed in parentheses. Indexes: general (names, places, titles, etc.), poetry, press-marks and dated MSS.

All the Oriental MSS in the library were briefly described by Jan Just Witkam, *Inventory of the Oriental Manuscripts in Leiden University Library* (25 vols., Leiden 2006–2007; www.islamicmanuscripts.info/inventories/leiden/index.html). The *Inventory* is arranged by the serial numbers (Or.) and includes MSS acquired until 2002. The following Hebrew, Judaeo-Persian, Judaeo-Arabic and Yiddish MSS were acquired after

the publication of Van der Heide's catalogue: MSS Or. 14396–14403 (Brill's catalogue no. 485), 14655–14656 (fragments), 22306 (fragment), 22581 (amulets).
MS Or. 4720 (Scal. 3) is the only complete copy of the Jerusalem (Yerushalmi) Talmud, commonly referred to as 'MS Leiden'.

Leiding, Gilbert

Hamburg, Germany, eighteenth cent.

A MS of his described by Johann Christoph *Wolf, *Bibliotheca Hebraea*, III, p. 6, and IV (1733), p. 749, is now *Hamburg, SUB, Cod. hebr. 306.

Leipzig (Germany), Pauliner Bibliothek

The collection is now in the *Leipzig, Universitätsbibliothek.

Leipzig (Germany), Stadtbibliothek

Formerly Ratsbibliothek. The MSS formerly in this library are now in *Leipzig, Universitätsbibliothek.

Leipzig (Germany), Universitätsbibliothek

The collections of the Universitätsbibliothek and the former Stadtbibliothek of Leipzig are now both in the the Universitätsbibliothek. Twenty-one Hebrew and Samaritan MSS were described by K. Vollers in *Katalog der islamischen, christlich-orientalischen, jüdischen und samaritanischen Handschriften der Universitätsbibliothek zu Leipzig*, Leipzig 1906, pp. 433–442. N. Porges added notes and corrections in 'Die hebräischen Handschriften der Leipziger Universitäts-Bibliothek', *ZfHB*, XI (1907), pp. 13–22, 54–63, 81–86. The 43 MSS of the Stadtbibliothek were described in *Cat. Delitzsch* (1838). Three additional small MSS are described in *Cat. Striedl–Róth*, nos. 242–244.

A. David, 'Die hebräische Handschriftsammlung der Universitätsbibliothek Leipzig; Bibliotheca Albertina', in S. Wendehorst (ed.), *Bausteine einer jüdischen Geschichte der Universität Leipzig*, Leipzig 2006, pp. 305–319.

Leipzig Maḥzor

Name given to *Leipzig, Universitätsbibliothek, MS 1102, a fourteenth-century illuminated Ashkenazic maḥzor. A facsimile edition of this MS with an introduction was published (Vaduz 1964).

Leningrad

See *St. Petersburg.

Leningrad Bible, First

Name given to *St. Petersburg, NLR, MS Евр. II B 17, an illuminated fragment from a Pentateuch dated 929.

Narkiss, p. 42.

Leningrad Bible, Second

Name given to *St. Petersburg, NLR, MS Евр. I B 19A, a Bible dated 1008. In 1839, Abraham *Firkovich offered to sell the codex, together with other MSS, to *Odessa, Society for History and Antiquities, which eventually purchased it in 1845. The MS was described in the Appendix to E. M. Pinner, *Prospectus der der Odessaer Gesellschaft für Geschichte und Alterthümer gehörenden ältesten hebräischen und rabbinischen Manuscripte*, Odessa 1845. It was acquired with the Odessa collections by the Imperial Public Library in St. Petersburg (now *St. Petersburg, NLR) in 1863. A facsimile edition of this MS, the earliest extant complete dated Hebrew Bible, was published in Jerusalem in 1971. A new facsimile edition prepared from the original manuscript was also published as *The Leningrad Codex*, Grand Rapids 1998.

Leonowitsch, Abraham

Halicz, Poland, 1802–1851; Karaite leader

Leonowitsch gave six of his Karaite MSS to Samuel Loeb Goldenberg in order to have them published by the Viennese printer Anton *Schmid. Before the MSS could be published, Goldenberg ran into financial difficulties and took a loan from Schmid, leaving the MSS as security. After Goldenberg's death, Schmid presented the MSS to the Royal Library in Vienna (now *Vienna, Österreichische Nationalbibliothek). They are listed in *Cat. Schwarz*, Vienna, nos. 130–134.

S. Poznanski, 'Karäische Drucke und Druckereien', *ZfHB*, XXI (1918), p. 67.

Letchworth, D. S. Sassoon

See *Sassoon, Solomon David.

Letteris, Meir

Zolkiew, Ukraine, c. 1800 – Vienna, 1871

Letteris sold six or seven of his MSS to the Royal Library in Vienna (now *Vienna, Österreichische Nationalbibliothek). The MSS are listed in the index of owners in *Cat. Schwarz*, Vienna. One MS formerly belonging to Letteris is now *Cambridge (Mass.), Harvard University, MS Heb. 55.

Leveen, Jacob

Jerusalem, 1891 – London, 1980

Leveen compiled *Cat. Margoliouth–Leveen*, IV – Part IV of the catalogue of Hebrew MSS in the British Museum (now *London, British Library). He also compiled a catalogue (unpublished) of MSS in *Cambridge, University Library.

Reif, *Cat. Cambridge*, p. 34.

Levertoff, Paul P.

Orsha, Belarus, 1878 – London, 1954; apostate and theologian

Five Hebrew MSS are listed in the catalogue Levertoff compiled of the collection of an anonymous collector, *Notes upon an Important Collection of Hebraica*, London 1924. The collection was sold by Walpole Galleries a year after the publication of the catalogue. Three of the MSS are now in *New York, JTSA: no. 1 = MS R1610; no. 2 = MS 2926; and no. 31 = MS 8249. According to Freimann, *Union Catalogue*, no. 41, MS no. 26 in the Levertoff catalogue is now in *New York, Public Library, but there is no record of this MS in the library. For further details and corrections to the catalogue, see the report by A. Marx ('רשימה חדשה מספרים וכתבי יד', ק"ס, ב [תרפ"ו], עמ' 157–158).

Levi, Abraham Zevi (Cervum)

Italy, nineteenth century

According to *Almanzi, *Kerem chemed* (כרם חמד), III (1838), p. 127, Levi had a MS of Moses Hayyim Luzzatto's writings. Its present whereabouts are unknown. Levi's Bible MS, described by *Kennicott, no. 578, is now *Oxford, Bodleian Library, MS Opp. Add. 4° 26 (*Cat. Neubauer*, 30). Another MS owned by Levi is now *New York, JTSA, MS 1618.

Levi, Israel

Paris, 1856–1939; Chief Rabbi of France

Fifteen of Levi's MSS were purchased for *New York, JTSA. Levi also had a number of *Geniza fragments (S. Shaked, *A Tentative Bibliography of Geniza Documents*, Paris–The Hague 1969, p. 239; H. Brody, 'Fragmente von Gabirols Dîwân', *MGWJ*, XXXIX, 1911, pp. 83–84). One of the two fragments listed by Shaked (no. *2, a letter to Egypt from Saadia Gaon) is now in the Goldsmith Museum of the Chizuk Amuno Congregation in Baltimore Md., but the present locations of the other fragments are not known.

Register, 5691, p. 157 (Marx, *Bibl. Studies*, p. 184).

Levi Nahum, Yehuda

San'a, Yemen, 1915 – Holon, Israel, 1998; collector

Levi Nahum established the Project for Exposure of Yemen's Treasures (מפעל לחשיפת גנזי תימן) around 1940. The dozens of MSS and over 20,000 fragments from MSS removed from bindings that were housed in Levi Nahum's home in Holon, Israel, were acquired by *Jerusalem, NLI, in 2012; see the project's website: http://nachum.genizah.org. Levi Nahum, with the assistance of Yosef Tobi, described several hundred MSS and fragments or gatherings of leaves, mainly from Yemenite MSS, in two volumes (ספר צהר לחשיפת גנזי תימן [מס' 1–469], תל־אביב תשמ"ו; ספר מכמנים מחשיפת גנזי תימן, תל־אביב תש"ן [מס' 470–586]). In each of the volumes some of the texts in the MSS are published or discussed. Some texts were published in other books by Levi Nahum (ספר חשיפת גנוזים מתימן, חולון תשל"א; מיצירות ספרותיות מתימן, חולון תשמ"א).

Levisson, G., and D. Proops

Booksellers

A number of MSS are listed in their sales catalogues and are now found in various libraries.

Levy, Hayyim Bekhor

See *Halevy.

Levy, Heimann Baruch

Hamburg, Germany, d. 1904; jurist

Levy's collection of 177 MSS was acquired by *Hamburg, SUB. S. Goldschmidt described 168 MSS in the catalogue of the collection published in Hamburg in 1900 (מקדש מעט, המבורג תר"ס). E. Róth and H. Striedl described 177 MSS in *Hebräische Handschriften*, III (*Die Handschriften der Sammlung H. B. Levy an der Staats- und Universitätsbibliothek Hamburg*), Wiesbaden 1984 (= Verzeichnis der orientalischen Handschriften in Deutschland, VI, 3).

Lewenstein, Moses J.

Paramaribo, Surinam, 1830–1864; Chief Rabbi of Surinam

Lewenstein's library (including MSS?) was one of those listed in M. Roest's sales catalogue, *Bet hasefer* (בית הספר), Amsterdam 1868. All the books in the catalogue were purchased by Temple Emanu-El in New York and presented to *New York, Columbia University Library.

Lewin, Benjamin Manasseh

Gorodets, Russia, 1879 – Jerusalem, 1944; scholar

A MS of geonic responsa from which the collection *Ḥemda genuza* (חמדה גנוזה) was probably published, formerly in the possession of D. Simonsen, was acquired by B. M. *Lewin and was in *Ramat Gan, Bar-Ilan University Library, according to Y. Alfasi (י' אלפסי, 'כתב־יד חדש של תשובות הגאונים', ארשת, ד [תשכ"ו], עמ' 175–179); but it has since disappeared. A MS formerly owned by Lewin of Nathan b. Jehiel's *Sefer 'Arukh* (ספר ערוך) is now *Cincinnati, HUC, MS 2032, and one of *Iggeret Rav Sherira Gaon* (אגרת ר' שרירא גאון) is *Jerusalem, NLI, Heb. 8° 7039 (formerly Nehemiah *Allony 110). The fragments of an index of Geonic responsa published from Lewin's MS in *Ginze kedem* (גנזי קדם, א [תרפ"ב], עמ' 7–8) are now *Ramat Gan, Bar-Ilan University Library, MS 626.

Lewin, Louis

Znin, Poland, 1868 – Bene Berak, Israel, 1941; rabbi and historian

Lewin's collection of several hundred rabbinic MSS is now in *New York, Yeshiva University Library, and was described in Y. Avivi, *Rabbinic Manuscripts, Mendel Gottesman Library, Yeshiva University*, New York 1998. Lewin also collected historical records relating to the Jews in Poland, Germany and the Czech Republic, including original documents, manuscripts and copies he made of documents in various archives. These are now stored in some 400 boxes in the Yeshiva University Library. Fourteen more boxes of historical material are stored in *Cincinnati, HUC, MSS Acc. 1982–1985.

EJ, XI, p. 173; M. R. Schiffman, 'Sources for Central and Eastern European Jewish history: The Louis Lewin Collection at Yeshiva University', *Judaica Librarianship*, XI (2002/3), pp. 7–11.

Lewinson, Jehiel Judah

Vilna, nineteenth century

A *Geniza fragment containing 27 leaves of the Arabic text of Bahya's *Kitāb al-Hidāya ilā Farā'id al-Qulūb* that was in his possession is now *New York, JTSA, MS 2240.

Register, 5691, p. 165 (Marx, *Bibl. Studies*, p. 192).

Lewis, Agnes Smith

See *Lewis–Gibson.

Lewis, John Frederick

Philadelphia, Pa., 1860–1932; philanthropist and collector

Lewis's collection, including six Hebrew MSS, is now in the Free Library of Philadelphia and has been described by M. A. Simsar in *Oriental Manuscripts of the John Frederick Lewis Collection in the Free Library of Philadelphia*, Philadelphia 1937.

Lewis–Gibson

Twin scholarly sisters, Agnes Smith Lewis (1843–1926) and Margaret Dunlop Gibson (1843–1920), purchased *Geniza fragments in 1896. The fragments were all presented to *Cambridge, Westminster College, with the exception of a few leaves from the Hebrew original of *Ben Sira*, which were presented to *Cambridge, University Library in 1926 (now MS Or. 1102). The fragments in Westminister College were purchased jointly in 2013 by Cambridge, University Library, and *Oxford, Bodleian Library.

Rab., *Treas. Jud.*, pp. 188–194; Reif, *Jewish Archive*, pp. 64–69, 75–85.

Lewisohn, Adolph

Germany, 1849 – New York, 1938; businessman and philanthropist

A number of MSS and scrolls, some of them decorated, were listed in Lewisohn's *Catalog of the Private Library of Mr. Adolph Lewisohn*, New York 1923, and in the sales catalogue of the collection, *Library of the Late Adolph Lewisohn*, New York 1940. Two scrolls and a Kabbala MS from the collection are now in *New York, JTSA. A Provençal rite maḥzor for Yom Kippur (no. 172 in the catalogue) is now *Jerusalem, Schocken Institute, MS 15987.

Register, 5700, p. 63; *ibid.*, 5701, p. 48 (Marx, *Bibl. Studies*, p. 299).

Leyden

See *Leiden.

Li.

Livorno, Talmud Tora.

Library of Congress Haggada

See *Washington Haggada.

Liburna

Latin name for Livorno (Leghorn).

Lieberman, Saul

Motol, Belarus, 1898 – New York, 1983; scholar

Lieberman presented many MSS to *New York, JTSA. His MS of novellae by R. Yom Tov b. Avraham Asevilli, described in *KS*, XIII (1936/7), p. 112, is now MS R1515 in JTSA.

Lilienthal, Max

Munich, Germany, 1815 – Cincinnati, Ohio, 1882; rabbi

Lilienthal described the Hebrew MSS in *Munich, Bayerische Staatsbibliothek, in a series of articles in *Allgemeine Zeitung des Judenthums: Literarisches und homiletisches Beiblatt*, 1838–1839.

Lillieblad, Gustaf Peringer von
see *Peringer, Gustaf.

Lima, Moses Hartog de
Amsterdam, Netherlands, 1819–1897; banker
Fourteen Hebrew MSS and nine scrolls and other objects that had belonged to de Lima are listed in *Catalog der reichhaltigen Sammlung hebräischer und jüdischer Bücher, Handschriften ... u.s.w. nachgelassen von ... Meijer Lehren, Akiba Lehren und Moses de Lima* ... Amsterdam [1898], nos. 4184–4206, 4272–4274, 4275–4286 (scrolls). For the present locations of some of the MSS see Appendix I, no. 24.

Lincoln College
See *Oxford, College Libraries.

Lindsay, James Ludovic
See *Crawford.

Linz (Austria) Oberösterreichische Landesbibliothek
Formerly Bundesstaatliche Studienbibliothek. Fragments from seven MSS were described by V. Kurrein, 'Die hebräischen Handschriftenfragmente in Linz', *Jüdisches Archiv*, I (1928), Part 4/5, and 'Neue Fragmentfunde in der Linzer Studienbibliothek', *ibid.*, 11/12, and again in *Cat. Schwarz–Loewinger–Róth*, pp. 91–92. Call-numbers are listed at the end of each entry in the catalogue.

Lipmann Cohen
See *Cohen, Lipmann.

Lippert [J. F.]
Halle, Germany, nineteenth cent.; bookseller
Four MSS are listed in Lippert's auction catalogue, Berlin 1845 (רשימת ספרים אשר ימכרו באוקציאן ע״י האדון ליפפערט בהאללע בערלין, אדר שני תר״ה). Nos. 2 and 4 in the catalogue are now *Berlin, SB, Cods. Or. 2° 383 (*Cat. Steinschneider*, Berlin, no. 21) and Or. 4° 308 (*ibid.*, no. 49). No. 3 is now *Paris, BnF, MS héb. 1468 (formerly MS *Sassoon 601).

Lips.
Lipsia. Latin name for Leipzig.

Lipschütz, Hirsch
Cracow, Poland, nineteenth cent; bookseller
*Steinschneider possessed a handwritten list of MSS offered for sale by Lipschütz, including MSS from the collection of Marco *Mortara (*HÜ*, p. 1073). Lipschütz sold MSS to many libraries, including over 100 to *Cambridge, University Library (MSS Add. 445–450, 464–560), and many to *Oxford, Bodleian Library (MSS Opp. Add. 2° 41 and 44 and Opp. Add. 4° 69, 70, 75–78). Solomon *Halberstamm and *Vienna, Österreichische Nationalbibliothek also purchased MSS from him.

Lipschütz, Jacob
Twentieth cent.; rabbi
Lipschütz's MS, described by S. Assaf (ש' אסף, 'רשימת ספרים מראשית המאה הט״ו', ק״ס, כד [תש״ח], עמ' 249–248), was acquired by Abraham *Yahuda in 1945, and is now *Jerusalem, NLI, Yah. Ms. Heb. 3.

Lisbon Bible
Name given to *London, BL, MS Or. 2626–2628 (*Cat. Margoliouth*, no. 62), an illuminated Bible written in Lisbon in 1482. A facsimile edition of the Pentateuch with an introduction by G. Sed-Rajna was published in Tel Aviv in 1988.

Narkiss, p. 80; Narkiss, *Span. & Port.*, no. 42; G. Sed-Rajna, *Manuscrits hébreux de Lisbonne*, Paris

1970, no. 2; T. Metzger, *Les manuscrits hébreux copiés et décorés à Lisbonne dans les dernières décennies du XVe siècle*, Paris 1973, no. 2.

Liv.
Livorno.

Livorno, Aghib
See *Aghib.

Livorno (Leghorn, Italy), Talmud Tora
The library's collection included 161 MSS. Of these, 53 were acquired by *Jerusalem, JNUL (now NLI; see below). The other MSS, except for a few that disappeared, remain in the library in Livorno. Carlo *Bernheimer wrote a short history of the collection and briefly described 25 MSS, listed by their old numbers, in 'La Bibliothèque du Talmud Tora de Livourne', *REJ*, LXV (1913), pp. 301–308. Later, Bernheimer described 130 MSS in his *Catalogue des manuscrits et livres rares hébraïques de la Bibliothèque du Talmud Tora de Livourne*, Livorno [1915], pp. 2–63 (nos. 1–118); 64–74 (notes and additions to the preceding entries, including descriptions of nos. 119–126 on pp. 71–74); and 187–192 (nos. 127–130, from the Castelnuovo and Perera collections). Next to the catalogue number, which also serves as the call-number, the name of the former collection is recorded. The collections are: TT (Talmud Tora), the earliest collection; Msl. (Monselles), MSS from the collection of R. H. Monselles, which were acquired in 1806, perhaps the rarest and most important MSS in the library; and Mnd. (Mondolfi), MSS acquired from Ismael *Mondolfi in 1909. Palaeographical and codicological information: type of script, size, writing material and sometimes the estimated date. No folio numbers are given in the descriptions, but a list of the MSS and the number of leaves in each MS is found on pp. 74–78. Indexes: authors and translators; titles; scribes, censors and owners; places. The MSS acquired by *Jerusalem, NLI, are nos. 1–5, 9–12, 14, 16, 18–29, 35, 37, 39, 43–47, 50, 54, 59, 61, 64, 65, 68, 76, 79, 81–83, 85, 87, 88, 92–95, 96[?], 99, 110. Sixty-three MSS that remain in the library were described by M. Perani, *I manoscritti della biblioteca del Talmud Toràh di Livorno*, Livorno 1997. The catalogue is arranged by subject and the entries are numbered 1–60 (three MSS added to the catalogue after it was set in print were numbered 8 bis, 35 bis and 51 bis). Palaeographical and codicological information: writing material, size, type of script, date, folio numbers and size of written space. There are indexes of authors, titles, translators, commissioners, scribes, owners, censors, names and places. The indexes are in Latin letters (including transliterations of Hebrew titles) and, except for the index of censors, are repeated in Hebrew. There are concordances to the Bernheimer numbers and their counterparts in this catalogue, and to the numbers in *Jerusalem, IMHM.

Loan
*Geniza fragments from the Taylor–Schechter collection in *Cambridge, University Library, that were loaned to Solomon *Schechter when he left Cambridge for America in 1902, were called the Loan Collection. Schechter had selected the fragments himself and had hoped to publish them. After his death it was decided that the faculty of the Jewish Theological Seminary (see *New York, JTSA) should publish these fragments in a series of volumes, arranged according to subject matter. Three volumes were eventually published as *Genizah Studies in Memory of Doctor Solomon Schechter (Ginze Schechter)*, I–III, New York 1928/9, and they include Geniza material from other collections as well. Volume I, edited by Israel Davidson, includes liturgical poetry; Volumes II–III, edited by Louis Ginzberg,

were devoted to midrash and Geonica. The Loan fragments were later returned to Cambridge and were assigned the call-marks 'TS Misc. 35' (formerly Loan 1–108) and 'TS Misc. 36' (Loan 109–209). All the fragments labeled 'T–S' in *Genizah Studies* come from the Loan collection and today bear the same numbers (e.g., T–S 87 in *Genizah Studies* is Loan 87 or T–S Misc. 35.87).

Loewe, Herbert Martin James

London, 1882–1940

Loewe, the grandson of Louis *Loewe, was curator of Oriental Literature in the *Cambridge, University Library from 1909 to 1911. He compiled catalogues of the Hebrew MSS in *Cambridge, Girton College, and *Cambridge, Trinity College. He also compiled an unpublished handlist of Hebrew MSS in the University Library.

Reif, *Cat. Cambridge*, pp. 33–34.

Loewe, Louis

Eliezer Halevy, Zuelz, Germany, 1809 – Ramsgate, England, 1888; orientalist and secretary to Moses Montefiore

Loewe collected the MSS forming the old stock of the Montefiore collection before the acquisition of the *Halberstamm and *Zunz MSS. Twenty-two of Loewe's own MSS were described by H. Hirschfeld, 'Die Handschriften Dr. L. Loewe's', *MGWJ*, XXXVIII (1894), pp. 360–366, 404–414. This description also appeared in *A Descriptive Catalogue of a Portion of the Library of the Late Louis Loewe with a Portrait, a Short Biography and Some Rough Bibliographical Notices, by James H. Loewe, to Which Is Added a Reprint of the Paper Contributed to the Breslauer Monatsschrift (Vol. 38) by Hartwig Hirschfeld Describing the Manuscripts Collected by Loewe, at Present in the Possession of His Widow*, London 1895.

MSS IV–VII were purchased by JTSA from V. Kurrein (*Register*, 5682, p. 31 [Marx, *Bibl. Studies*, p. 24]). According to *Cat. Schwarz*, Vienna, no. 192 (*Vienna, ÖNB, Cod. Hebr. 157), may also have come from Loewe's library. For the present locations of some of the MSS listed in the *Descriptive Catalogue* see Appendix I, no. 25.

Loewinger, David Samuel

Debrecen, Hungary, 1904 – Jerusalem, 1981

Loewinger compiled catalogues of the MSS in *Breslau, Jüdisch-theologisches Seminar, *Budapest, Jewish Theological Seminary, and part of the collection of Ludwig *Blau. Together with E. Róth, Loewinger completed the catalogue of Hebrew MSS in Austria begun by Arthur *Schwarz (= *Cat. Schwarz–Loewinger–Róth*), and together with N. Allony he compiled lists of the Hebrew MSS on microfilm in *Jerusalem, IMHM, from libraries in Austria and Germany (= *Cat. Allony–Loewinger*, I) and from the *Vatican library (= *Cat. Allony–Loewinger*, III).

London, Aguilar

See *Aguilar.

London, Beth Din and Beth Hamidrash Library

After the death of Rabbi Solomon Hirschell in 1842, 148 MSS were purchased from his estate for the Beth Din library. These MSS are described in A. Neubauer, *Catalogue of the Hebrew Manuscripts in the Jews' College, London* (בית המדרש דק״ק אשכנזים בלונדון), Oxford 1886. The name of Jews' College (now *London School of Jewish Studies) appeared on the title page by mistake, and this has caused no little confusion in references to the library's MSS in scholarly literature. The catalogue is very similar in layout to Neubauer's catalogue of the Hebrew MSS in *Oxford, Bodleian Library. MSS are arranged according to subject. The catalogue number at the head of each entry is also the call-number of the MS. Palaeographical and codicological information: writing material, number of leaves and type of script. No estimate of date is given for MSS without colophons. Indexes: authors, translators, family names, titles, scribes, owners, witnesses, censors and places. In addition to the MSS in Neubauer's catalogue, the library acquired another 15 MSS. The *Jerusalem, IMHM has microfilm copies of the library's MSS, including nos. 127 and 144, which, according to Pearson, p. 54, were missing from the library. In 1999, almost all the MSS described in the Neubauer catalogue and a few incunabula and other early printed books were sold at Christie's auction house in New York. The MSS were described in the auction catalogue, *Important Hebrew Manuscripts and Printed Books from the Library of the London Beth Din, Sold ... Wednesday, 23 June 1999*. The descriptions of the MSS are arranged in alphabetical order of the authors' names or the titles of anonymous works. A concordance to the numbers in Neubauer's catalogue is found on pp. 238–239. For the present locations of the MSS that can be traced, see Appendix I, no. 26.

Rab., *Lit. Treas.*, pp. 56–59.

London, Bibliot. Archiep. Lambeth
*London, Lambeth Palace.

London, Bibl. Eccl. Westmonaster
Westminster Abbey, London.

London, BL
*London, British Library.

London, British and Foreign Bible Society
See *Swindon, Bible Society.

London, British Library
Formerly British Museum Library. In 1972 the British Museum Library and several other British libraries were merged, and the British Library was formed. The Hebrew MSS are now housed in the Department of Asia, Pacific and Africa Collections. The nucleus of the Hebrew MS collection in the library was derived from the *Cotton, *Sloane, *Royal, Solomon da *Costa Athias and *Harley collections. The Harley collection, acquired in 1753, was the largest and included 99 Hebrew MSS and 17 Hebrew charters. In 1840 there were 200 Hebrew MSS in the British Museum. In 1865 the *Almanzi collection of 332 MSS, some of them from the library of H. J. D. *Azulai, was acquired. Between 1877 and 1882 about 300 MSS, including 145 Karaite MSS and a large number of Yemenite ones, were purchased from the bookseller Moses *Shapira. Since 1882 the library has acquired about 350 MSS, in addition to almost 1,200 MSS in the Moses *Gaster collection, acquired in 1925. Today the library holds over 2,500 Hebrew MSS, including the Gaster collection. For details concerning individual collections in the British Library and their catalogues, see the entries for each collection.

CATALOGUES In 1850, Leopold Dukes described about 300 MSS in an unpublished handwritten catalogue kept in the British Library. R. *Hoerning described new acquisitions in a handwritten list, also kept in the library. From this list and others H. Derenbourg published, in French, descriptions of the MSS acquired during the years 1867–1890, 'Les manuscrits Judaïques entrés au British Museum de 1867 à 1890', *REJ*, XXIII (1891), pp. 99–116, 279–301. His descriptions are arranged according to the year of acquisition. At the end are indexes to subjects and names. In 1893 the British Museum published G. Margoliouth's first catalogue, *Descriptive List of the Hebrew and Samaritan MSS in the British Museum*, London 1893, based on Hoerning's descriptions but also including MSS from the old collections and recent acquisitions, as well as 63 Samaritan

MSS. The catalogue is arranged according to subject, and in each subject MSS are arranged according to their call-numbers. The main catalogue of Hebrew MSS in the British Library is *Cat. Margoliouth* (1899–1915). In its three volumes, Margoliouth described 1,206 Hebrew MSS. Contrary to what is stated in its title, the catalogue does not describe any Samaritan MSS. About half of the 340 descriptions in the first volume were first written by R. Hoerning. The fourth volume (*Cat. Margoliouth–Leveen*, IV), published in 1935, includes indexes prepared by J. *Leveen and a Supplementary List providing brief descriptions of 89 MSS and volumes of *Geniza fragments omitted from the first three volumes or acquired during the years 1915–1935 – except for the Gaster collection, which is not listed at all. The catalogue is arranged according to subject. At the head of each entry the catalogue number is printed in bold type (nos. 1–1206), and immediately preceding the description the call-number is printed in smaller letters. The descriptions of the MSS are generally quite detailed and include lengthy transcriptions from the texts, especially from the beginning and end of rare or unknown works. Colophons and owners' entries are also transcribed. At the beginning of each entry the following palaeographical and codicological information is provided: writing material, size (in inches), number of lines per page, number of quires and their composition, catchwords, type of script and date. The MSS described in volume IV, pp. 151–161, are arranged according to their call-numbers, and their descriptions are very brief. The volumes of Geniza fragments are listed but not described in detail. Indexes (in Vol. IV): I: Index of persons; boldface letters following the name indicate whether the names are those of censors (C), persons mentioned or quoted (M), liturgical writers (L), scribes (S), etc. II: Titles. III: Subjects. IV: Geographical place names. V: Additions to the previous indexes and corrections. VI: Concordances to call-numbers, *Almanzi catalogue numbers, MSS listed in Christian *Ginsburg's *Introduction to the Massoretico-Critical Edition of the Hebrew Bible*, London 1897, and MSS described by *Kennicott. On pp. 175–181 are lists of dated MSS, illuminated MSS and autographs. At the end of the volume are addenda and corrigenda for all four volumes of the catalogue. Corrections to the descriptions of Kabbala MSS are found in G. Scholem, *Einige kabbalistische Handschriften im Britischen Museum*, Jerusalem 1932, a pre-publication of the article of the same title in *Festschrift f. Aron Freimann*, Berlin 1935, pp. 51–69. Twenty Karaite biblical MSS were briefly listed, and six of them exhaustively described, in R. Hoerning, *British Museum Karaite MSS: Descriptions and Collations of Six Karaite Manuscripts of Portions of the Hebrew Bible in Arabic Characters*, London 1889. The Judaeo-Persian MSS in the library, including those in the Gaster collection, were described by J. Rosenwasser, 'Judeo-Persian manuscripts in the British Museum', in G. M. Meredith-Owens, *Handlist of Persian Manuscripts, 1895–1966*, London 1968, pp. 38–44. A. D. Crown described 178 Samaritan MSS in *A Catalogue of the Samaritan Manuscripts in the British Library*, London 1998. Photocopies of an incomplete list of the Gaster collection, *Catalogue of Hebrew Manuscripts in the Gaster Collection, the British Library, London, reproduced from the manuscript and typescript blue-slips, prepared by Jacob Leveen, Joseph Rosenwasser and David Goldstein* (1996), including a short preface, are available in the British Library and in *Jerusalem, IMHM.

CALL-NUMBERS MSS belonging to the major collections in the library bear the call-numbers of these collections (e.g., MS Sloane 237, MS Harl. 5701). Until 1867 the other MSS were placed in the Additional

Collection and assigned call-numbers with the prefix 'Add.'. In 1867 the Department of Oriental MSS was opened and all the Oriental MSS were transferred to the new department. From that time on all new Hebrew MS acquisitions were assigned call-numbers with the prefix 'Or.'.

Rab., *Lit. Treas.*, pp. 17–26; Rab., *Treas. Jud.*, pp. 15–62.

London, British Museum Library

See *London, British Library. The library was part of the British Museum until 1973. After the passing of the British Library Act of 1972, it became a separate entity called the British Library and is no longer housed in the British Museum.

London Haggada

See *Joel b. Simeon.

London, Jewish Museum

Twenty-seven MSS belonging to the Museum or on loan were described by A. Schischa in R. D. Barnett (ed.), *Catalogue of the Permanent and Loan Collections of the Jewish Museum, London*, London 1974, pp. 116–128.

London, Jews' College

See *London, School of Jewish Studies.

London, Lambeth Palace

The library of Lambeth Palace, the historic library of the archbishops of Canterbury, was founded in 1610. Its collection includes two Hebrew MSS, a copy of Psalms with Latin glosses and an illuminated Esther scroll.

London, Montefiore Collection

Until 1898 the library of Sir Moses Montefiore was housed in Montefiore College at Ramsgate, the site of Montefiore's home. In 1898 most of the MSS were transferred to Jews' College, London (now *London School of Jewish Studies), where they remained on permanent deposit until 2001, when they were returned to the trustees, the Montefiore Endowment Committee of the Spanish and Portuguese Congregation in London. In 2004, most of the MSS, with the exception of the 'Montefioriana' items and about a hundred others, were sold at Sotheby's auction house in New York.

The Montefiore collection of MSS consisted of the old stock of MSS collected by L. *Loewe during Montefiore's lifetime (less than 100 MSS), 412 MSS from the collection of Solomon *Halberstamm (described in his *Catalog hebräischer Handschriften* [קהלת שלמה, וינה תר״ן]) and 27 MSS from the collection of Leopold *Zunz purchased for Montefiore College by Moses *Gaster, and a number of later purchases and MSS associated with the public activities of Montefiore. *Cat. Montefiore* (1904) describes 580 MSS. The catalogue is arranged according to subject. Preceding each entry is the catalogue number, which also serves as the call-number. At the end of each entry, in square brackets, is the old MS number. Old numbers with the prefix 'H' are the MS numbers in Halberstamm's catalogue. On pp. ix–xi of the catalogue is a concordance to the old numbers. Palaeographical and codicological information: type of script, size (2°, 4°, 8°) and number of leaves. In general no estimated date is given for undated MSS. Indexes: authors and translators, titles, writers, owners and censors. The entire collection of MSS was reproduced on microfiche in 1995 by Emmett Publishers. The MSS offered for sale in 2004 were described in the auction catalogue *Important Hebrew Manuscripts from the Montefiore Endowment, New York, October 27 & 28, 2004*. The descriptions of the MSS in the catalogue generally follow the order of *Cat. Montefiore*.

For the present location of the MSS that can be traced, see Appendix I, no. 30.

London, Royal Society

The *Arundel collection in *London, British Library, was purchased from the Royal Society in 1831 (*Cat. Margoliouth–Leveen*, IV, p. vi). See *Costa Athias, Solomon da, for the Bible MS presented by him to the Royal Society in 1766.

London School of Jewish Studies

Formerly Jews' College. Three collections are referred to, sometimes erroneously, as 'Jews' College': (1) the *Montefiore Collection, which was on permanent deposit in Jews' College until 2001; (2) The collection of the *London, Beth Din and Beth Hamidrash Library, owing to the erroneous English title page of Neubauer's 1886 catalogue of this collection (*Catalogue of the Hebrew Manuscripts in the Jews' College, London*); and (3) the collection of 90 MSS in the library of Jews' College, now the London School of Jewish Studies. There is no printed catalogue of the latter collection, but a handwritten catalogue by H. *Hirschfeld exists in the library. Ten MSS in the Asher I. *Myers collection are listed in the College's eightieth *Annual Report*, 1936. Seven MSS from the library were offered for sale by Kestenbaum and Company in New York on December 17, 2002, and were described in the auction catalogue *Magnificent Hebrew Manuscripts, Incunabula and Other Valuable Hebrew Printed Books*. Of these, five MSS were sold: MSS 7 (now in a private collection in Switzerland), 14, and 32, and Asher Myers 9 and 10.

R. P. Lehmann, *Jews' College Library: A History*, London 1967.

London, Soc. Reg.

*London, Royal Society.

London, University College

See *Mocatta Library.

London, Valmadonna Trust Library (library custodian: J. V. Lunzer)

291 MSS were described in B. Richler (ed.), *The Hebrew Manuscripts in the Valmadonna Trust Library*, Jerusalem 1998. Most of the MSS derive from sources in Italy, many from the Jewish community of *Ferrara. Some were purchased at the sales of the *Sassoon collection. Most of the MSS date from the seventeenth to the nineteenth centuries but about a dozen date from the eleventh to the fifteenth centuries. The catalogue is in Hebrew and English in facing columns and arranged according to subject. Palaeographical and codicological information: number of leaves, writing material, size (2°, 4°, 8°), place, date and type of script. Indexes: persons, titles, place names (all in both English and Hebrew), poems (in Hebrew) and subjects (in Hebrew). The collection was put up for sale early in 2009 by Sotheby's, with the proviso that it be sold as a whole and not broken up, but it has not been sold and remains in storage at Sotheby's in New York.

London, Wellcome Institute

The Library of the Wellcome Institute was established by Sir Henry Wellcome (1853–1936). The library includes 36 Hebrew MSS in section A, including two *ketubot* and a few amulets; and fragments from 58 Tora and Esther scrolls. The Hebrew collection was described and catalogued by N. Allan, 'Catalogue of Hebrew manuscripts in the Wellcome Institute, London', *Journal of Semitic Studies*, XXVII (1982), pp. 193–220.

N. Allan, 'Some Wellcome Hebraica considered', in D. Rowland Smith and S. P. Salinger (eds.), *Hebrew Studies*, London 1991, pp. 13–19.

Los Angeles, University of California Library

The library holds over 300 Hebrew MSS. In 1963 it acquired the MSS remaining in the stock of the booksellers *Bamberger and Wahrmann in Jerusalem. Some of these MSS were originally in the Moses *Gaster collection. The MSS acquired in Jerusalem are now in the Theodore E. Cummings collection in the library. In 1962 the library also acquired most of the Hayyim *Rosenberg collection. There is no printed catalogue of the library's Hebrew MSS collection. The MSS in the Rosenberg collection bear call-numbers with the prefix 779; those of the Cummings collection bear the prefix 828; and those in the N. Feldman collection bear the prefix 960.

Lotze, Hermann

Bautzen, Germany, 1817 – Leipzig, 1881; philosopher

Lotze's MSS are listed in the catalogue of his library, *Verzeichniss der von ... Hermann Lotze, Privatgelehrten zu Leipzig, hinterlassen ... Bibliothek*, Leipzig 1876, nos. 1662–1780. According to M. Steinschneider, *HB*, XVI (1876), pp. 84–85, some of the books were purchased by Baron David *Günzburg through the bookseller Jerocham Fischl *Hirsch. For the present locations of some of Lotze's MSS see Appendix I, no. 27.

Louvain (Belgium), Jesuiten Collegium

In 1798, Napoleon transferred the MSS from this college to *Paris, Bibliothèque nationale de France. In 1815 they were returned to Belgium and placed in *Brussels, Bibliothèque royale, where they are found today.

Cat. Allony–Kupfer, II, p. 16.

Louvain (Belgium), Université Catholique

The university was founded in 1425. Most of the ancient books and manuscripts were lost when the library was burned in World War I and again in World War II. In 1968, the university split into two separate institutions, the French speaking Université Catholique and the Flemish-speaking Katholieke Universiteit. There are two eighteenth-century Hebrew MSS in the Université Catholique and ten in the Katholieke Universiteit.

Lovania

Latin name for Louvain.

Lovenstein, M. J.

See *Lewenstein.

Löw, Immanuel

Szeged, Hungary, 1854 – Budapest, Hungary, 1944; rabbi and scholar

Löw presented many of his MSS and those of his father, Leopold, to *Vienna, Jüdisches Museum. They are described in *Cat. Schwarz*, Austria, nos. 150, 187, 205, 260 and 292. A MS of Abraham Zacuto's *Tashlum he'arukh* (תשלום הערוך) acquired by L. Löw (*Ben-Chananja*, VIII [1865], p. 840, n. 4) was later acquired by Abraham *Geiger and is now *Jerusalem, NLI, Heb. 8° 6424. The MS of *'Olat re'iya* (עולת ראיה) by Loeb Stasow belonging to Löw, described in *Ben-Chananja*, I (1858), p. 19, was listed in the 1890 catalogue of the bookdealer J. Kauffmann, no. 1268, and is now MS no. 253 in *Budapest, Jewish Theological Seminary. Two other MSS in *Jerusalem, NLI, MSS Heb. 8° 959 and 8° 3141, also belonged to the Löw family.

Löw, Leopold

See *Löw, Immanuel.

Lowe MS

Name sometimes given to *Cambridge, UL, MS Add. 470.1, a Mishna MS published by W. H. Lowe under the title *The Mishnah on which the Palestinian Talmud Rests*, Cambridge 1883. Today, scholars doubt if the MS represents the Palestinian Talmud Mishna.

Löwen

Louvain.

Lp.
Leipzig.

Lpz.
Leipzig.

Lublin (Poland)
The fragment of a prayerbook found in the Solomon Luria synagogue in Lublin and described by S. B. Nisenbaum, 'Un manuscrit de la *Gueniza* de Lublin', *REJ*, L (1905), pp. 84–89, is now *New York, JTSA, MS 3881.

Lugduno-Batavae
Latin name for Leiden.

Luncz, Abraham Moses
Kovno, Lithuania, 1854 – Jerusalem, 1918
In the section called *Zimrat ha'arets* (זמרת הארץ) in *Literarischer Palästina-Almanach* (לוח ארץ ישראל), the yearbook he edited from 1894 to 1913 (5654–5673), Luncz often listed MSS found in the Holy Land. Among these were a number belonging to Isaac Gagin (yearbook for 5672; see *Gagin, Hayyim Abraham) and some described by Samuel *Raffalovich. Of the MSS listed in the 5656 yearbook, *Piske R. Isaiah di Trani* (פסקי רי״ד) is now *London, BL, MS Or. 5024 (*Cat. Margoliouth*, no. 523), and *Sefer Ḥem'at haḥemda* (ספר חמאת החמדה), which was later described again by Solomon *Wertheimer (גנזי ירושלים, ג [תרס״ב]), is now MS *Musayof 58 (=*Ramat Gan, Bar-Ilan University Library, MS 1007). The MS of *Sefer Mesharim* (ספר מישרים) described in the 5659 yearbook is now *New York, JTSA, MS R671. The MS of *Me'arat sede hamakhpela* (מערת שדי המכפלה) described in the 5668 yearbook is now JTSA, MS 2187. The MS of *Sefat emet* (שפת אמת), actually *Leshon limudim* (לשון לימודים) by David ibn Yahya, described in the 5663 yearbook, pp. 119–120, is now JTSA, MS 2891. A Yiddish MS belonging to Luncz himself is now *Jerusalem, NLI, Heb. 8° 4294. The collection of letters by Yedidya Abulafia that was edited by Luncz (ירושלים, ד [תרנ״ב], עמ׳ 112–102) is now *Paris, AIU, MS 246.

Lund (Sweden), Universitetsbibliothek
Seven Hebrew MSS were described by C. J. Tornberg, *Codices Orientales Bibliothecae Regiae Universitatis Lundensis*, Lund 1850. N. Allony listed ten MSS (נ׳ אלוני, ׳כתבי יד עבריים בשבדיה׳, יד לקורא, טז [תשל״ז], עמ׳ 101–100), and described five of them in greater detail (׳חמישה כתבי יד עבריים בספריית לונד [שבדיה]׳, עלי ספר, ד [תשל״ז], עמ׳ 19–5).

Luzzatto, Samuel David
Trieste, Italy, 1800 – Padua, Italy, 1865; scholar
Luzzatto owned a collection of over 100 Hebrew MSS. In his works he often referred to his MSS and described some of them (for a list of sources in which Luzzatto described his MSS, see Steinschneider, *Vorlesungen*, p. 59 [Hebrew, p. 78]). In one of his letters to Osias *Schorr in 1846 he enclosed a list of 111 MSS (ש״ד לוצאטו, אגרות שד״ל, ז, קראקא [תרנ״א], עמ׳ 1003–1000). A list of 99 of Luzzatto's MSS compiled in 1868 is found in the *Steinschneider collection in *New York, JTSA, MS 2863, fols. 22–25. After his death 121 MSS were described by Luzzatto's son Joseph, in *Catalogue de la bibliothèque de litterature hébraïque et orientale de feu Samuel David Luzzatto rédigé par son fils Joseph*, Padua 1868. The numbers given to the MSS in Luzzatto's letter to Schorr are different from those in the 1868 catalogue. Luzzatto's MSS are now to be found in a number of libraries, among them *Paris, AIU (53 MSS), *Oxford, Bodleian (see *Cat. Neubauer*, p. xxxii), *London, British Library, and *Berlin, Staatsbibliothek; and some were in the *London, Montefiore Collection. Joseph Luzzatto sold at least three MSS to David *Kaufmann (*Cat. Kaufmann*, nos. 18, 369, 379). For the present location of many of the MSS in the 1868 catalogue, see Appendix I, no. 28.

Lyell, James P. R.
England, 1871–1948; collector
One hundred MSS from the Lyell collection, including seven in Hebrew, were bequeathed to *Oxford, Bodleian Library, and were described in *Catalogue of the Collection of Medieval Manuscripts Bequeathed to the Bodleian Library by James P. R. Lyell*, Oxford 1971. The MS described by C. Roth, 'Eastertide stoning of the Jews', *JQR*, XXXV (1944/5), pp. 367–370, is now MS Lyell 97 in the Bodleian Library.

Lyon (France), Bibliothèque municipale
Nine MSS, several comprising more than one volume, were described in *Catalogue général*, XXX (1900), nos. 3–15. Two fragments found in the bindings of MSS 479 and 1235 are listed in the same catalogue and were later described in greater detail by M. Schwab, 'Manuscrits hébreux en France', *REJ*, LX (1910), pp. 98–99.

M

M
(1) Milan; (2) Moscow; (3) Munich.

Madjalis Scroll
Name given to a scroll acquired by Abraham *Firkovich from the Jewish community in the village of Madjalis (Mangelis) or Mejelis in Dagestan. The scroll, a copy made in 1513 of the epigraph in the *Derbent Tora (q.v.), was in the Odessa Collections (see *Odessa, Society for History and Antiquities) and is now *St. Petersburg, NLR, MS Евр. I C 10 (formerly Nova seria 91).

Madrid (Spain)
Del Barco, *Catálogo ... Madrid*, I–III (2003–2006), describes 201 Hebrew MSS in libraries in Madrid. Vol. I (nos. 1–64) includes biblical texts and commentaries and philological MSS from the libraries of *San Lorenzo del Escorial; *Madrid, Biblioteca de la Universidad Complutense; and *Madrid, Biblioteca del Palacio Real. Vol. II (nos. 65–124) includes Hebrew MSS in all subjects from the libraries of *Madrid, Biblioteca Nacional; the Archivo Histórico Nacional and Museo Lázaro Galdiano (1 MS); and the biblical and philological MSS in *Madrid, Real Academia de la Historia. Vol. III (nos. 125–201) includes all subjects except for Bible and philology from the libraries of the Escorial; the Universidad Complutense; the Consejo Superior de Investigaciones Científicas, Instituto de Filología; and the Real Academia de la Historia.
Each volume is arranged by subject. The descriptions include title, author, date, codicological information, language, type of script, place of copying, name of scribe and colophons, description of the text, physical description of the manuscript, illuminations, and bibliographies, with provenance and call-numbers at the end of each entry. Each volume includes indexes of MSS by library call-number and by names in Latin letters and in Hebrew. There is no index of titles. At the end of Vol. III is an index of library call-numbers in all three volumes.
In addition to the descriptions of the MSS, the volumes include introductory essays by various authors and historical surveys of the libraries and their Hebrew collections.

Madrid (Spain), Biblioteca Nacional de España
In 1868, there were only four Hebrew MSS in the library (MSS 5468, 5474, 7542 and 4188;

the latter two were copied by Alfonso de Zamora in the sixteenth cent.). That year, during the short-lived first Spanish republic, MSS and rare books from various provincial libraries were transferred to the National Library in accordance with the law nationalizing cultural treasures. Over 40 Hebrew MSS reached the library in this manner, among them about 20 MSS from *Toledo, Archivo y Biblioteca Capitulares, which formerly belonged to Cardinal *Zelada. Other MSS came from the San Martin monastery in Madrid. Thirty-two MSS (nos. 5454–5485), including one Latin MS, were described by M. Gaspar Remiro, 'Los manuscritos rabínicos de la Biblioteca Nacional de Madrid', *Boletín de la Real Academia de la Historia*, V (1918), pp. 601–617; VI (1919), pp. 43–53; 221–234; 354–371; 552–567; VII (1920), pp. 343–355; 472–481; VIII (1921), pp. 40–57; 337–348; IX (1922), pp. 345–358; XI (1923), pp. 266–274. Gaspar Remiro's descriptions contain detailed palaeographical and codicological information. J. Millás Vallicrosa, 'Nuevas aportaciones para el estudio de los manuscritos hebraicos de la Biblioteca Nacional de Madrid', *Sefarad*, III (1943), pp. 289–327, provided additions to the descriptions and described four additional MSS, including one not in Hebrew. One additional MS, a Bible, was described in detail by F. Cantera Burgos, 'Nueva serie de manuscritos hebreos en Madrid', *ibid.*, XVIII (1958), pp. 220–228. Thirty-three MSS were listed in *Cat. Allony–Kupfer*, II, pp. 84–86. Four MSS were not described, either because they were not written in Hebrew characters or because no microfilm copy was available at the *Jerusalem, IMHM. In *Cat. Allony–Kupfer* the library's call-numbers are written in parentheses at the end of the entries. All the other numbers are catalogue serial numbers or the microfilm numbers of the IMHM. Forty-eight MSS were described by Carlos del Valle Rodriguez in *Catálogo descriptivo de los manuscritos Hebreos de la Biblioteca Nacional*, Madrid 1986. Forty-six MSS were described in del Barco, *Catálogo ... Madrid*, II (see *Madrid). Del Barco purposely omitted two eighteenth-century MSS describing the La Blanca synagogue in Toledo (nos. 45–46 in del Valle's catalogue). Six Hebrew biblical MSS from the Zelada collection were also described at the end of K. Reinhardt and R. González, *Catálogo de códices bíblicos de la Catedral de Toledo*, Madrid 1990, nos. *5–*7, *17, *19 and *20. On the history of the Hebrew manuscript collection see the introduction to del Valle's catalogue, and M. T. Ortega Monasterio, 'Las Bibliotecas y sus manuscritos hebreos', in del Barco, *Catálogo ... Madrid*, II, pp. 19–43.

Madrid (Spain), Biblioteca del Palacio Real de Madrid

A complete Bible in 16 very small volumes (MSS II/3231–3246) copied in Toledo in 1487 was acquired in Livorno in 1817 for the library of the Palacio Real. The MS was described in del Barco, *Catálogo ... Madrid*, I, no. 3. On the library and the acquisition of the MS see M. T. Ortega Monasterio, 'Las Bibliotecas y sus manuscritos hebreos', in *ibid.*, pp. 18–25.

Madrid (Spain), Biblioteca de la Universidad Complutense

The 21 Hebrew MSS in the library are held in the Biblioteca Histórica Marqués de Valdecilla. With the exception of two MSS, the collection was acquired from the library of *Alcalá de Henares, Collegio de San Ildefonso, in the first half of the nineteenth century. Originally, the MSS were in the possession of Alfonso de Zamora, a convert to Christianity who lived in the first half of the sixteenth century. The MSS were described by J. Villa-Amil y Castro, *Catálogo de los manuscritos existentes en la Biblioteca del Noviciado de la Universidad Central*, I: Códices, Madrid 1878. Seventeen MSS were described by J. Llamas in *Sefarad*, V (1945), pp. 261–284. The whereabouts of four MSS were unknown at the time Llamas wrote his descriptions, but they were later found and included among the 21 MSS listed in *Cat. Allony–Kupfer*, II, pp. 86–87. The numbers 21–1מ are the Villa-Amil numbers which now form the call-numbers of the MSS. In this catalogue the old call-numbers of the MSS were listed at the end of each entry in parentheses. In both catalogues there are a number of errors in the listings of the call-numbers. In the Llamas catalogue MS 118-Z-29 should read 118-Z-28, 118-Z-30 should read 118-Z-29, and 118-Z-28 should read 118-Z-30. In *Cat. Allony–Kupfer* the call-number of no. 1059 should read 116-Z-40. Today, the MSS bear the call-numbers of the Villa-Amil catalogue (Villa-Amil 1–21). The MSS were catalogued again in del Barco, *Catálogo ... Madrid.* On the history of the Hebrew manuscripts in the library sec M Sánchez Mariana, 'Los manuscritos hebreos en la Universidad Complutense', in F. Cortés Cortés et al. (eds.), *Raíces hebreas en Extremadura ... actas [de las] Jornadas Extremeñas de Estudios Judaicos, Hervás ... 1995*, Badajoz 1996, I, pp. 33–48; and M. T. Ortega Monasterio, in del Barco, *Catálogo ... Madrid*, I, pp. 25–33.

Madrid (Spain), Consejo Superior de Investigaciones Científicas, Instituto de Filología

Includes the MSS that were in the Instituto Arias Montana that became part of the Instituto de Filología in 1985. Del Barco, *Catálogo ... Madrid*, III, describes five MSS, one fragment from a Talmud MS, three Esther scrolls, seven *ketubot* and four amulets. A list of the call-numbers of the MSS and their catalogue numbers is found on pp. 262–263 of the catalogue. One of the MSS (no. 175 in the catalogue) was previously described in *Cat. Allony–Kupfer*, II, no. 1085, and by F. Cantera Burgos, 'Nueva serie de manuscritos hebreos de Madrid', *Sefarad*, XIX (1959), pp. 42–47.

Madrid (Spain), Real Academia de la Historia

The Academy was established in 1738. Most of the Hebrew MSS came from Jesuit libraries that were confiscated in 1767 and placed in the library of the Cortes that was closed in 1838. Fourteen MSS, of which eight are in Hebrew, were described by F. Cantera Burgos, 'Nueva serie de manuscritos hebreos en Madrid', *Sefarad*, XVIII (1958), pp. 229–240, and *ibid.*, XIX (1959), pp. 3–35. The eight Hebrew MSS were also described in *Cat. Allony–Kupfer*, II, p. 88. The Biblical and philological MSS in the library were described in Spanish in del Barco, *Catálogo ... Madrid*, Vol. II, and the non-biblical and non-philological MSS were described in Vol. III. The history of the collection by M. T. Ortega Monasterio is included in Vol. II, pp. 43–54.

Magl.

*Magliabechiana.

Magliabechiana

Name of a collection in *Florence, Biblioteca Nazionale Centrale, named after Antonio Magliabechi (1633–1714), a collector of books and the librarian of the Palatine library in Florence, which today is part of the Biblioteca Nazionale Centrale.

Maḥzor Cremona

See *Cremona Maḥzor.

Maḥzor Lipsiae

See *Leipzig Maḥzor.

Maḥzor Pesaro

See *Pesaro Maḥzor.

Mai, Angelo

Schilpario, Italy, 1782 – Albano, Italy, 1854; cardinal

Mai described 78 MSS in the *Vatican library (Cods. ebr. 454–531) that were not previously described in *Assemani's catalogue, in 'Appendix ad Catalogum codicum hebraicorum Bibliothecae Vaticanae', in his *Scriptorum Veterum Nova Collectio e Vaticania Codicibus*, IV, Rome 1831, pp. 83–93.

Mai, Johann Heinrich, the younger

Durlach, Germany, 1688 – Giessen, Germany, 1732

Mai compiled a catalogue of the *Uffenbach collection (*Bibliotheca Uffenbachiana*, Halle 1720), now in *Hamburg, SUB.

Maihingen (Germany), Fürstlich Oettingen-Wallerstein'sche Bibliothek

See *Harburg.

Mailand

German name for Milan.

Maimon (Fishman), Judah Loeb

Marculesti, Romania, 1875 – Jerusalem, 1962; rabbi

Most of Maimon's MSS were in *Jerusalem, Mosad Harav Kook. Two Yemenite MSS of the Talmud are now in Yad Harav Herzog Library in Jerusalem.

Mainz (Germany), Akademie der Wissenschaften und der Literatur

Ten MSS and fragments from eight MSS described in *Cat. Striedl–Róth*, pp. 178–189, were acquired in 1966 by *Munich, Bayerische Staatsbibliothek (Cods. hebr. 452–465).

Mainz (Germany), Jesuitenkolleg

The MS formerly in the library and described by *Kennicott, no. 375, is now *Mainz, Stadtbibliothek, Hs. 378 (= *Cat. Striedl–Róth*, no. 291).

Mainz (Germany), Jüdische Gemeinde

Thirty-one MSS were described in *Cat. Striedl–Róth*, nos. 260–290. These MSS are deposited on loan at the Seminar für Judaistik in the Johannes Gutenberg-Universität in Mainz. Two fragments supposedly from this library, described in *Cat. Allony–Loewinger*, I, nos. 578–579, do not belong to the Jüdische Gemeinde. The MS of the Nuremberg Memorbuch formerly in the possession of the Orthodox community of Mainz is now in a private collection in Israel.

Mainz (Germany), Wissenschaftliche Stadtbibliothek

Two MSS are described in *Cat. Striedl–Róth*, nos. 291–292. Several fragments from Hebrew MSS were recently found in bindings.

Malatestiana, Biblioteca

See *Cesena.

Manchester (England), Chetham's Library

An early Tora scroll in the library was described by C. G. K. Gillespie, 'Codex Chethamensis: A description of the Hebrew roll of the Pentateuch', *Transactions of the Lancashire and Cheshire Antiquarian Society*, II (1884), and separately as *Codex Chethamensis*, London 1885. M. Wallenstein described six Geniza fragments, four of them biblical, in 'Fragments in the Chetham's Library, Manchester', *Bulletin of the John Rylands Library*, L (1967), pp. 159–177. The MSS were presented to the library in 1892 by George Ellis of London.

Manchester (England), John Rylands University Library

Formerly John Rylands Library. The library's collection includes 37 Hebrew MSS and 27 Samaritan MSS purchased in 1901 from the Earl of *Crawford, as well as 342

Samaritan MSS, over 350 Hebrew MSS (177 original MSS and about 190 volumes containing nineteenth-century copies of original Hebrew MSS) and over 10,000 *Geniza fragments (most of them minute) purchased from the M. *Gaster collection in 1954; and a few other Hebrew and Samaritan MSS deriving from other sources. There is no catalogue of the Hebrew MSS. The Samaritan MSS from the Crawford collection are described by E. Robertson in *Catalogue of the Samaritan Manuscripts in the John Rylands Library, Manchester*, I, Manchester 1938. Those from the Gaster collection and later acquisitions are described in Vol. II, Manchester 1962.

Bulletin of the John Rylands Library, XXXVII (1954/5), pp. 2–6; F. Taylor, 'The Oriental manuscript collections in the John Rylands Library', *ibid.*, LIV (1971–2), pp. 449–478; Pearson, p. 59.

Manetti, Giannozzo

Florence, Italy, 1396–1459; humanist

Thirteen of Manetti's MSS are now in the *Vatican library. They were originally in the *Fugger library, were later acquired by *Heidelberg, Biblioteca Palatina, and reached the Vatican in 1622.

Cassuto, *Palatina*, pp. 44–47; מ״ד קסוטו, ׳תולדותיו של אוסף כתבי־יד עבריים׳, יד לקורא, א (תש״ז), עמ׳ 62; Tamani, *Grimani*, p. 10, note 8.

Mans, Le (France), Bibliothèque municipale

The *Jerusalem, IMHM has microfilms of two Hebrew MSS from this library: a Bible described in *Catalogue général*, XX (1893), p. 10, no. 162, and a work by Moses Narboni (MS 191 A).

Mantua (Italy), Comunità ebraica

There are 161 Hebrew MSS in the library (MS 6 has been missing since 1899). The first collection of Hebrew MSS to be acquired by the library came from Raphael Emmanuel Meldola in 1767. Nine MSS from the library's collection were described by M. Mortara in a series of articles in *HB*, I–IV (1858–1861), but Mortara's descriptions were discontinued after a fire in the library in 1861 in which many of the MSS suffered water damage (*HB*, V [1862], p. 71). Later, Mortara described 84 MSS in his *Catalogo dei Manoscritti Ebraici della Comunità Israelitica di Mantova*, Livorno 1878. 49 of these MSS are also described in Sonne, *Relazione*. G. Busi described 81 kabbalistic MSS and the kabbalistic works in eight additional MSS in *Catalogue of the Kabbalistic Manuscripts in the Library of the Jewish Community of Mantua*, Fiesole 2001, and G. Tamani described 80 MSS in *Catalogo dei manoscritti filosofici, giuridici e scientifici nella Biblioteca della Comunità ebraica di Mantova*, Fiesole 2003. Since 1931 the MSS have been kept in the Biblioteca Teresiana (formerly the Biblioteca Comunale) of Mantua.

Mantua (Italy), Biblioteca Teresiana

Formerly Biblioteca Comunale. See *Mantua, Comunità ebraica.

Maraviglia Siddur

See *Lady's Maḥzor.

Marburg (Germany)

See also *Berlin, Staatsbibliothek zu Berlin – Preussischer Kulturbesitz.

Marburg (Germany), Hessisches Staatsarchiv

One MS and fragments taken from bindings are described in *Cat. Striedl–Róth*, pp. 216–226. Most of the fragments, but not the MS, were described in *Cat. Allony–Loewinger*, I, pp. 44–46, without call-numbers being listed.

Marciana

See *Venice, Marciana.

Mareschall
See *Marshall.

Margaliot, Mordecai
Warsaw, Poland, 1909 – New York, 1968; scholar
One collection of Margaliot's MSS was presented to *Ramat Gan, Bar-Ilan University Library. Some of the MSS from his second collection were in the possession of his widow, others have been sold to various collections and institutions. His collection of geonic responsa was sold to M. R. *Lehmann. The Sabbatean MS from Persia belonging to Margaliot, described by M. Benayahu (מ׳ בניהו, ׳פיוטים ותעודות על השבתאות בכתב־יד מפרס׳, ספונות ג–ד [תש״ך], עמ׳ 15–20), is now *Cincinnati, HUC, MS 2001.

Margol.
*Margoliouth; *Cat. Margoliouth.*

Margolinsky, Julius
1895 – Copenhagen, Denmark, 1978; librarian,
Eight MSS from Margolinsky's collection are described in *Cat. Allony–Kupfer*, II, pp. 39–40. Most of these MSS as well as a few additional ones were presented by his estate to *Jerusalem, JNUL (now NLI).

Margoliouth, George
England, 1853–1952; scholar
Margoliouth compiled two catalogues of the Hebrew MSS in the British Museum. For details see *London, British Library.

Margulies, Samuel Hirsch
Galicia, 1858 – Florence, Italy, 1922; Chief Rabbi of Florence
Most of his MSS were acquired by *Cincinnati, HUC (Oko, p. 81). A collection of letters described by the owner in *Rivista Israelitica*, III (1906), p. 105, n. 2, and elsewhere, was purchased by Alexander *Marx and is now *New York, JTSA, MS 3830. At least one MS is in *Rome, Collegio Rabbinico Italiano (MS 135).

Marseilles (France), Bibliothèque municipale
A Bible, known as the *Marseilles Bible*, in three volumes, is described in *Catalogue général*, XV (1892), p. 436, no. 1626.

Marsh, Narcissus
Hannington, England, 1638 – Dublin, Ireland, 1713; Archbishop of Armagh
Marsh collected books in Arabic and other Oriental languages, including rabbinic literature in Hebrew. He bequeathed his library, including 35 Hebrew MSS, to *Oxford, Bodleian Library. A small number of Hebrew MSS are found in *Dublin, Marsh's Library, which the Archbishop helped establish. In his catalogue, Neubauer confused the Marsh MSS with those from the Thomas *Marshall collection in the Bodleian. A list of the Marsh MSS is found in *Cat. Neubauer*, pp. xxx and xxv.

Marshall (Mareschall), Thomas
England, 1621–1685
Marshall bequeathed his MSS, including twenty Hebrew MSS, to *Oxford, Bodleian Library. He had acquired many of his MSS from Robert *Huntington, Bishop of Aleppo. In *Cat. Neubauer*, I, MSS from the Narcissus *Marsh collection are erroneously listed as bearing call-numbers with the prefix 'Marsh.', which seems to be an abbreviation of Marshall. The correct prefix for those MSS is 'Marsh', without a period. The Marshall MSS had been dispersed and given call-numbers with the prefixes 'Bodl. Or.' and 'sub. Fen.', and that is how they appear in *Cat. Neubauer*. After the catalogue was published, the Marshall collection was reconstituted and the MSS returned to it, and

today they bear call-numbers with the prefix 'Marshall (Or.)'. Neubauer's error was pointed out in *Cat. Neubauer–Cowley*, II, pp. 536–541, which includes (on p. 541) a list of the Hebrew MSS in the Marshall collection and their current numbers.

Marsili, Luigi Ferdinando

Bologna, Italy, 1658–1730; naturalist

The nucleus of the *Bologna, Biblioteca Universitaria, was a gift from Count Marsili in 1712. Some sources quote the number of Hebrew MSS in the collection as 70, but it seems that figure includes printed books as well as MSS. In fact, there is only one Hebrew MS (3574H) in the Bologna library that can be identified as originating in the Marsili collection.

Fumagalli, 'Emilia-Romagna', pp. 93–94.

Marti, Karl

Basel, Switzerland, 1855 – Berne, Switzerland, 1925; Bible scholar

Biblical fragments formerly in Marti's possession are now *Jerusalem, NLI, Heb. 4° 1192.

Marx, Alexander

Eberfeld, Germany, 1878 – New York, 1953

Marx was librarian at *New York, JTSA, from 1903 to 1953. He described MSS acquired by the Seminary in various issues of the JTSA *Register*. He also published a survey of some of the *Enelow Memorial Collection MSS, before the collection was named after Enelow (Marx, *Proceedings*), and described 72 polemical MSS (Marx, 'Polemical MSS'). All these descriptions were republished, with an introduction by M. Schmelzer and an index by J. Brumer, under the title *Bibliographical Studies and Notes on Rare Books and Manuscripts in the Library of the Jewish Theological Seminary of America*, New York 1977 (= Marx, *Bibl. Studies*). Marx also compiled a handwritten catalogue of several hundred MSS in the JTSA library. The MSS described in this catalogue once bore call-numbers with the prefix 'JTS'. Marx's own MSS are now in the JTSA library.

Masal, Joseph of Viazona

See *Massel.

Massel, Joseph, of Viasin

Vilna, nineteenth cent.

Massel's library, which included several hundred MSS, was acquired in part by Moses *Friedland (S. Wiener, introduction to the catalogue of Friedland's collection קהלת משה, p. ii, and *Bibliographie der Oster-Haggadah*, St. Petersburg 1902, pp. iv–v), whose library was presented to the Asiatic Museum in St. Petersburg (now *St. Petersburg, Institute of Oriental Manuscripts). One of Massel's MSS is *New York, JTSA, Rab. 192 (*Register*, 5699, p. 72 [Marx, *Bibl. Studies*, p. 276]), and two are in the Sassoon collection (nos. 1281–1282). The MS of *Yalkut hamekhiri* (ילקוט המכירי) from which S. Buber published his edition is now *London, BL, MS Or. 9960 (formerly Gaster 100). A MS of *Sefer mezukak* (ספר מזקק) by Omar b. Muhammad is probably now *Jerusalem, NLI, Heb. 8° 3167 (see *HÜ*, p. 577).

ש"י פין, קריה נאמנה, וילנה תר"ך, עמ' 304–306.

Mayence

See *Mainz.

Mazarin, Jules

See *Paris, Bibliothèque Mazarine.

MC

Mosseri Collection or Mosseri-Chapira. The Jacques Nissim *Mosseri collection of *Geniza fragments is often referred to as MC.

Med. or Mediceo
Medicea Laurenziana. See *Florence, Biblioteca Medicea Laurenziana.

Medina, Henrique
Amsterdam, Netherlands, eighteenth cent.
Medina's MS, described by *Kennicott, no. 642, is now Lisbon, Biblioteca Nacional MS 72.

Mediolanum
Latin name for Milan.

Meerman, Gerard
Delft, Netherlands, 1722 – Aachen, Germany, 1771; Dutch jurist and bibliophile
The most important part of the collection of MSS belonging to Meerman and his son Johan M. Meerman (1753–1815) came from the Jesuit Collège de Clermont (see *Paris, Collège de Clermont) following the ban on the Jesuit order in 1762. Gerard Meerman purchased more than 850 manuscripts *en bloc* in Paris in 1764, including six Hebrew MSS. It had been intended that Meerman's library should remain in the house bequeathed by his son to the city of The Hague, but the books and manuscripts were put up for auction in Amsterdam in 1824. Part of the collection was purchased by Baron Westreen van Tielland and presented to what is now the Museum Meerman–Westreenianum in The Hague, but that part included no Hebrew MSS. A substantial part was bought by Thomas *Phillipps, whose collection was dispersed in a number of sales. The German government bought most of the Meerman collection from the Phillipps library in 1887. Cod. Meerman Or. 5 is now *London, BL, MS Add. 19943 (*Cat. Margoliouth*, no. 1035); Cod. Or. 11 is now *New York, JTSA, MS 8225 (formerly Duke of *Sussex 6); Cod. Or. 12 is now *Berlin, SB, Cod. Phillipps 1392; and Cod. Or. 23 is now *Amsterdam, Ets Haim, HS EH 47 D 20. Berlin, SB, Cod. Ham. 80 (formerly Duke of Sussex 1) also comes from the Meerman collection.

Meiningen (Germany), Landesbibliothek
The MS formerly belonging to this library, described by F. Delitzsch, 'Ueber eine Handschrift des hebräischen Psalmen-Commentars von David Kimchi', *Serapaeum*, XX (1859), pp. 369–372, was in the library of Sholem *Asch and is now *London, Valmadonna Trust Library, MS 4.

Melbourne (Australia), State Library of Victoria
Until 1960 the library was called the Public Library of Victoria. There are seven Hebrew MSS in the library.

Melk (Austria), Stiftsbibliothek
Fragments from 15 MSS are described in *Cat. Schwarz–Loewinger–Róth*, pp. 92–94. Call-numbers are listed at the end of each entry. The fragments had previously been described in Hebrew in *Cat. Allony–Loewinger*, I, pp. 19–20, but the call-numbers were not listed. Fragments removed from 40 MSS and printed books are described and displayed on the website http://www.ksbm.oeaw.ac.at/hebraica.

Melun (France), Bibliothèque municipale
One Hebrew MS was described by M. Schwab, 'Un manuscript hébreu de la Bibliothèque de Melun', *REJ*, XIII (1886), pp. 296–300.

Memmingen (Germany), Stadtbibliothek
Two MSS are described in *Cat. Striedl–Róth*, nos. 322–323. These, as well as a Hebrew-Latin dictionary and grammar, are listed in *Cat. Allony–Loewinger*, I, nos. 659–661.

Merton College
See *Oxford, College Libraries.

Merwas Bible
See *Ibn Merwas Bible.

Merx, Adalbert
Bleicherode, Germany, 1838 – Heidelberg, Germany, 1909; orientalist
Three ancient documents formerly in Merx's possession and published in his *Documents de Paléographie hébraïque et arabe*, Leiden 1894, were presented in 1905 to *Heidelberg, Universitätsbibliothek, and are now MSS Heid. or. 78–80. Merx described the Hebrew MSS in *Gotha, Universitätsbibliothek, in the catalogue edited by W. Pertsch.

Merz.
*Merzbacher, Abraham.

Merzbacher, Abraham
Baiersdorf, Germany, 1812 – Munich, Germany, 1885; banker and bibliophile
The 1888 catalogue of Merzbacher's library compiled by R. N. Rabbinovicz (אהל אברהם: רשימת הספרים אשר אסף וקבץ ... מו״ה אברהם מערצבאכער, הוצאתיה ... לאור רפאל נטע ראבינאוויץ ... מינכען תרמ״ח) lists 156 MSS. These were purchased after the death of Merzbacher's son Eugen, in 1903, by a committee of wealthy Jews and presented to the Frankfurt a/M, Stadt- und Universitätsbibliothek. All the MSS, except for two that were exchanged for confiscated property after World War II (see *Frankfurt a/M, Goethe Universität, Universitätsbibliothek) and six others that may have been lost in the War, are in the Frankfurt library. For a list of the Merzbacher MSS and their present call-numbers in Frankfurt, see Appendix I, no. 29. Four MSS not listed in the 1888 catalogue remained in the possession of the Merzbacher family and were eventually acquired by *New York, JTSA: MSS 8252 and R1621 and a MS of *Tikune shabat* bound with MS 4432.

Meyers, Asher I.
See *Myers.

Mezzofanti, Giuseppe Caspar
Bologna, Italy, 1774 – Rome, 1849; cardinal
Mezzofanti's collection, which included two Hebrew MSS was acquired by Pope Pius XI in 1857 and presented to the *Bologna, Biblioteca Universitaria. The call-numbers of the MSS are 3574L and 4100.
Fumagalli, 'Emilia-Romagna', p. 94.

M. F. L. D.
See *Lair-Dubreuil.

Mich.
See *Michael, Heimann Joseph.

Mich. Add.
Michaelianorum Additamenta. According to E. N. Adler, 'Hebrew treasures of England', *Transactions of the Jewish Historical Society of England*, VIII [1918], pp. 5–6, the 69 MSS in *Oxford, Bodleian Library, bearing call-numbers with the prefix 'Mich. Add.' came from the Heimann Joseph *Michael collection. In fact, they have nothing to do with the Michael collection. MSS Mich. Add. nos. 1–65, described in **Hapalit*, came from the collection of M. *Bislisches. Nos. 1–57 (= 59 MSS, including 1b and 2b) were purchased from the Bislisches brothers in 1850, while nos. 58–65 were bought later from another or other dealers. Nos. 66–68 were bought from the same dealers but did not come from the Bislisches collection. No. 69 was bought from Moritz *Steinschneider in 1855 and placed in the Mich. Add. section by pure caprice. A list of the MSS in the Mich. Add. collection and their numbers in *Cat. Neubauer* is found in the catalogue, pp. xxiv–xxv.

Michael, Erna, Haggada
See *Erna Michael Haggada.

Michael, Heimann Joseph
Hamburg, Germany, 1792–1846; bibliophile
In the catalogue of Michael's library (אוצרות חיים : רשימת ספרי המנוח מהור״ר חיים בן כהה״ר יוסף מיכל הנכתבים והנדפסים ... עם הערות מאת ... משה שטיינשניידער ופתיחה בל״א מאת ... ד״ר צונץ, המבורג תר״ח), 860 MSS are listed. The bookseller Asher offered the MSS for sale to the British Museum, but the Museum library purchased only the printed books. The MSS were purchased in 1848 by *Oxford, Bodleian Library. The 860 MSS are now bound in 629 volumes, and they received new numbers, with the prefix 'MS Mich.', after they reached the Bodleian. In *Cat. Neubauer* the new numbers are listed at the end of each entry and are followed by the old numbers in parentheses, with the prefix 'ol.' (Latin: *olim*, 'formerly'). A concordance to the old numbers in the 1848 Michael catalogue and the new numbers, as well as the Neubauer catalogue numbers, is found in *Cat. Neubauer*, pp. xix–xxiii. A concordance to the new numbers and the catalogue numbers is found in *Cat. Neubauer, Addenda*, pp. xi–xv.

Michaelides, George
Cairo, Egypt, d. 1973; antiquities collector and dealer
In 1979, the Oriental Department of the British Museum (now *London, British Library), acquired Oriental MSS from the Michaelides collection, among them three Hebrew MSS (Or. 13887–89). MS Or. 13888 is a collection of over 30 *Geniza fragments.

Mikulov
See *Nikolsburg.

Milan (Italy), Biblioteca Ambrosiana
The library possesses about 200 Hebrew MSS, a large number of which came from the library of Cardinal Federico Borromeo, who founded the Ambrosiana in 1609. In the catalogue, *Codices Hebraici Bybliothecae Ambrosianae*, Florence 1933, 122 MSS were described in Latin by Carlo *Bernheimer. At the head of each entry is the catalogue number. Call-numbers of the library are listed in parentheses at the beginning of each entry. For most of the works described in the catalogue, folio numbers are given for the beginning and end of each work, designated by the Latin abbreviations *inc.* (*incipit*, meaning 'beginning') and *desi.* (*desinit*, meaning 'end'). Usually, a few lines from the beginning and end of each text are transcribed in the catalogue. Palaeographical and codicological information: writing material, number of leaves, size, number of lines per page, quire composition, type of script, date, names of scribes, owners, censors, etc. Colophons and owners' entries are transcribed in full. At the end of the catalogue are additional notes and transcriptions. Indexes: authors, scribes, owners and witnesses, censors, titles and geographical place names. Following the index is a concordance to the call-numbers and catalogue numbers. Gershom Scholem published some notes and corrections to the entries on Kabbala MSS in Bernheimer's catalogue in *KS*, XI (1934/5), pp. 184–190. No. 61 in Bernheimer's catalogue is Vatican, Cod. ebr. 288. The MS had been taken from the Vatican library, apparently by Napoleon's troops, and was later returned not to the Vatican but to the Ambrosiana. In 1953, the Ambrosiana library returned the MS to the Vatican. In 1966, N. Allony and E. Kupfer published a brief Hebrew catalogue of 64 Hebrew MSS from the Ambrosiana ('כתבי־יד עבריים נוספים באמברוזיאנה', ארשת, ד [תשכ״ו], עמ' 234–270). Of the 64 MSS, six had previously been described by Bernheimer (Allony–Kupfer, nos. 29, 44, 63, 16, 32, 43 = Bernheimer, nos. 84, 109, 112, 114, 118, 119), but 58 others had escaped his attention. The descriptions of

Allony and Kupfer were based on the microfilm copies at the *Jerusalem, IMHM. At the head of each entry the catalogue number, library call-number, former call-number (in parentheses) and IMHM microfilm number are listed. *Incipits* of most of the works in the MSS are copied. But only the total number of folios in each MS is given; and for MSS including more than one work, no indication is provided of the number of folios in each work. Palaeographical and codicological information: writing material, number of leaves, size, type of script and date. Gemma Villa described the illuminated Hebrew codices in the Ambrosiana in M. L. Gengaro et al., *Codici Decorati e Miniati dell'Ambrosiana Ebraici e Greci* (Milan [1958?]), pp. 1–62. The 58 MSS first described by Allony and Kupfer as well as an additional 17 MSS not previously described in any catalogue are described in English in *Cat. Luzzatto* (1972). Included among them are MSS from the Lattes collection (at least 13) and the Caprotti collection of Yemenite MSS (6). The catalogue is preceded by introductions in English, Hebrew and Italian, in which the history of the Hebrew MS collections in the library is related. At the head of each entry the catalogue number is listed in bold type, followed by the call-number. As in the Bernheimer catalogue, the beginnings and endings of the works in the MSS are transcribed and folio numbers for each work are listed. Palaeographical and codicological information is the same as in the Allony–Kupfer catalogue. L. Mortara Ottolenghi's descriptions of the decorated and illuminated MSS are found on pp. 113–144. Indexes: titles, illuminated and decorated MSS, authors, scribes, owners, censors, other names, scribes and owners of decorated MSS, place names, and concordances to present and former call-numbers and catalogue numbers. Since the publication of the 1972 catalogue a few additional Hebrew MSS have been found in the Ambrosiana library.

Milan (Italy), Biblioteca Nazionale Braidense

The library was opened to the public in 1786. The major part of the Hebrew collection, including ten MSS, was donated by the brothers Alessandro and Elia Lattes in the nineteenth century.

Milan (Italy), Biblioteca Reina

*London, BL, MS Add. 11639 (*Cat. Margoliouth*, no. 1056), was purchased from the Reina library in 1839.

Milan (Italy), Firmian

See *Firmian.

Miller, Linda R.

Mrs. Nathan J., USA, 1877–1936

With Mrs. Miller's financial help, *New York, JTSA, purchased a collection of 1,100 MSS from the bookseller Jacob Halpern in the early 1930s. This collection is now known as the *Enelow Memorial Collection (EMC).

Mill Yard (Milliard)

See *Black.

Mingana, Alphonse

Sharansh, Iraq, 1878 – Birmingham, England, 1937; orientalist

Twenty-five *Geniza fragments from Mingana's collection were in *Birmingham, Selly Oak Colleges, which has merged with the University of Birmingham. They were described in 18 entries by M. H. Gottstein, 'Hebrew fragments in the Mingana Collection', *JJS*, V (1954), pp. 172–174.

Miroslav (Czech Republic; German: Misslitz), Jewish Community

The prayerbook dated 1814 described by H. Flesch, 'Aus jüdischen Handschriften in Mähren', *Jahrbuch der Gesellschaft für*

Geschichte der Juden in der Čechoslovakischen Republik, II (1930), p. 289, is now *Prague, Jewish Museum, MS 1.

V. Sadek, 'From the MSS collections of the State Jewish Museum in Prague (illuminated mss.)', *Judaica Bohemia*, X (1974), p. 109.

Misc.

T–S Misc. See *Cambridge, University Library, 'Geniza' section.

Misslitz

See *Miroslav.

Mittwoch, Eugen

Schrimm, Germany, 1876 – London, 1942; orientalist

In *ZDMG*, LVII (1902), p. 61, Mittwoch stated that he had purchased forty Geniza fragments. Twenty-two *Geniza fragments that E. Mittwoch purchased in 1899 were in *Birmingham, Selly Oak Colleges, which has merged with the University of Birmingham, and were described by M. H. Gottstein, 'Hebrew fragments in the Mingana Collection', *JJS*, V (1954), pp. 172, 174–176.

Mitzri (Mitschri), Abraham

Nineteenth cent.; Karaite

Several of Mitzri's MSS were listed in S. Pinsker's *Likute kadmoniyot* (ש' פינסקר, לקוטי קדמוניות, וינה תר"ך). Some, or all of these MSS are now in *St. Petersburg, Institute of Oriental Manuscripts.

Mocatta Library

Frederic David Mocatta (London, 1828–1905), an Anglo-Jewish philanthropist, bequeathed his library to the Jewish Historical Society of England, which deposited it in University College, London, in 1905. The collection includes about a dozen Hebrew MSS. The Mocatta Haggada is a name given to Mocatta Library, MS 1, an illuminated thirteenth-century Spanish haggada. In addition to the Mocatta MSS, the University College Library holds two additional Hebrew MSS.

Rab., *Treas. Jud.*, pp. 69–87; Narkiss, *Span. & Port.*, no. 10.

Modena (Italy), Biblioteca Estense Universitaria

The library has close to seventy Hebrew MSS. The first five came with a collection of Oriental MSS from the library of Alberto Pio di Carpi, a nephew of *Pico della Mirandola, after his death in 1573. In the second half of the eighteenth century the library purchased ten MSS from Moses Benjamin *Foa. Others entered the library in the eighteenth and nineteenth centuries (see the historical introduction by P. Puliatti in *Cat. Bernheimer*, Modena, pp. vii–xiii). Thirty-three MSS from the Oriental collection were described by S. Jona in *Catalog der ebräischen Handschriften der kgl. Bibliothek in Modena*, von S. Jona aus dem Italienischen ins Deutsche übertragen und mit Anmerkungen versehen von Dr. M. Grunwald, Belovar (Bjelovar) 1883 (offprint from *Jüdisches Centralblatt*). The numbers in this catalogue are the Oriental collection numbers. The manuscript of the original Italian catalogue is now in *Jerusalem, NLI. The Hebrew MSS in the *Campori collection were first described in the catalogues of the Campori collection by L. Lodi and R. Vandini (Modena 1875–1894). Forty-six Hebrew MSS from the Oriental collection, two *ketubot* and 21 MSS from that collection were described in *Cat. Bernheimer*, Modena. Each entry has the catalogue number listed above it in boldface and is preceded by the present call-number. Palaeographical and codicological information: writing material, number of leaves and size; occasionally, type of script and date. The beginnings and endings of all works are copied and their folio numbers listed. At the end of the catalogue are concordances to all the old and new numbers and an index of names. Eight additional

MSS from the Campori collection and a few leaves and fragments in the Estense library were not described.

Recently, about 1,300 fragments of medieval Hebrew MSS on parchment (mainly entire folios and bifolios), reused as wrappers in the bindings of 385 printed books, were discovered in this library; see M. Perani with E. Mongardi and E. Chwat, '385 printed books of the 15th–18th centuries bound with 1,300 fragments of medieval Hebrew manuscripts in the Estense Library in Modena', in A. Lehnardt (ed.), *'Genizat Germania': Hebrew and Aramaic Fragments from German Archives and Libraries in Their European Context*, Leiden–Boston 2010.

Moguntia

Latin name for Mainz.

Mon.

*Monaco [= Munich].

Monaco

Latin name for Munich.

Monast. Scotus

See *Vienna, Unsere Liebe Frau zu den Schotten.

Mondolfi, Ismael Eliezer

Italy, nineteenth century

Mondolfi's collection, including eight Hebrew MSS, was presented by his son Rodolfo to *Livorno, Talmud Tora, in 1909; see C. Bernheimer, *Catalogue des manuscrits et livres rares hébraïques de la Bibliothèque du Talmud Tora de Livourne*, Livorno 1915, p. v.

Montague, Ed.

Eighteenth century.

Montague's MS, described by *Kennicott, no. 136, is now *Oxford, Bodleian Library, MS Kennicott 3 (*Cat. Neubauer*, no. 2325).

Montefiore, Elia

Florence, Italy, nineteenth cent.

Thirty MSS from his library are listed in Sonne, *Relazione*. The library was acquired by the Collegio Rabbinico Italiano in Florence (see Rome, Collegio Rabbinico Italiano), now deposited in the Centro Bibliografico dell'Ebraismo Italiano in Rome. Not all the MSS listed by Sonne are in the Centro Bibliografico. MS 1 in Sonne's list is now in the private collection of Mr. F. Greenwood in Toronto (formerly of London).

Montefiore, Moses

See *London, Montefiore Collection.

Montpellier (France), Bibliothèque universitaire

The two Hebrew MSS are listed in *Catalogue général*, I (1849), pp. 342–344 and 402–403, Nos. 148 and 286.

Montezinos, David

Amsterdam, Netherlands, 1828–1916; librarian of *Amsterdam, Portugees ... Ets Haim – Livraria Montezinos

In 1889 Montezinos presented his private collection, including 98 MSS, to the Ets Haim Library, and in return the name of the library was changed to Ets Haim – Livraria Montezinos. The MS of responsa by Meir b. Barukh of Rothenburg published by M. Bloch, Berlin 1891, is now *Toronto, University of Toronto, MS Friedberg 3-012.

Montserrat (Spain), Abadia de Santa María

In the library of this ancient monastery are over 80 Hebrew MSS, including 20 marriage contracts, amulets, etc. Most of the MSS are eighteenth- and nineteenth-century codices collected by Bonaventura Ubach (1879–1960), one of the monks, who acquired most of them on his journeys to Italy, mainly between 1913 and 1924, and others in Palestine and Jordan. Eighty-six MSS were briefly described by N. Allony and A. M. Figueras, 'Manuscritos hebraicos de la Biblioteca de Montserrat', *Sefarad*, XIX (1959), pp. 241–272. In this catalogue the MSS are arranged by subject. At the head of each entry the catalogue number is listed, followed by the call-number in parentheses. Palaeographical and codicological information: date, writing material, size and type of script. In *Cat. Allony–Kupfer*, II, pp. 100–104 and 135, 92 MSS are described in no apparent order, with call-numbers listed in parentheses at the end of each entry. Eighty-three MSS are described by F. J. del Barco del Barco in *Catálogo de Manuscritos Hebreos de Montserrat*, Barcelona 2008, which is arranged by call-numbers. The descriptions include title, author, date, codicological information, language, type of script, place of copying, name of scribe, colophons, description of the text, physical description of the manuscript, illuminations, bibliographies, provenance and call-numbers. The discrepancy between the numbers of MSS listed in 1964 in *Cat. Allony–Kupfer*, II, and in 2008 in the del Barco catalogue is due to the theft of 5 MSS in 1996 (MSS Or. 45, 51, 56, 59 and 60), the disappearance of several others, the acquistion of new MSS and the recent removal of several fragments from bindings.

Morbio, Carlo

Novara, Italy, 1811 – Milan, Italy, 1881; historian

An illuminated haggada in the collection of Carlo Morbio listed in the sales catalogue of the collection (Leipzig 1889) as no. 1195 was purchased by Albert *Wolf. It was later in the *Berlin, Jüdische Gemeinde, and then in the *Warsaw, ŻIH, MS 242. For its present location, see *Wolf, Albert.

M. Garel, 'The rediscovery of the Wolf Haggadah', *Journal of Jewish Art*, II (1975), pp. 22–27.

Morgenweg, Joachim

See *Hinckelmann, Abraham.

Morpurgo, Abraham b. Joseph

Trieste, Italy, eighteenth cent.

The MS described in *Kennicott, no. 586, was later in the collection of the Duke of *Sussex and then came into the possession of Julian *Goldsmid (*Catalogue of the Anglo-Jewish Exhibition*, London 1887, no. 2070). It is now MS Nicholson 33 in the Fisher Library in the University of *Sydney, Australia.

Morpurgo family

According to Pearson, p. 33, seven MSS were in the possession of the Morpurgo family in 1933, and some of them were presented to the Biblioteca di Storia della Medicina in Padua. However, no MSS are listed in the catalogue of the collection, *Raccolta Morpurgo ... Catalogo Generale*, Padua 1924; and according to Tamani, *Padova*, p. 4, there are no Hebrew MSS in that library. The *Pesaro Maḥzor, which belonged to a member of the Morpurgo family in Ancona and was described in de Rossi, *ext.*, no. 15, was MS *Sassoon 23 and is now owned by the Safra family in São Paolo.

Mortara, Marco

Viadana, Italy, 1815 – Mantua, Italy, 1894; rabbi

The bookseller Hirsch *Lipschütz bought MSS from Mortara and sold them to various libraries. *Cambridge, University Library, purchased many MSS from Mortara's collection through Lipschütz. M. *Steinschneider had a handwritten list in which over 50 of these MSS were included (*HÜ*, p. 1073; Steinschneider, *Vorlesungen*, p. 60 [Hebrew, p. 80]). In 1895, David *Kaufmann purchased a large number of MSS from the Mortara collection, some of which had previously been described by Mortara in the periodical *Mosé*, V–VI (*Cat. Kaufmann*, Foreword). MS no. 31 in *Mosé*, V, p. 337 is now *St. Petersburg,

Institute of Oriental Manuscripts, B381. Other MSS formerly belonging to Mortara are or were found in *Berlin, Staatsbibliothek (four MSS listed in the index of owners and Cod. 2° 1618); *Paris, AIU (MS H 80 A); *Vienna, Israelitische Kultusgemeinde (*Cat. Schwarz*, Austria, nos. 91 and 286; see Appendix I, no. 38), in the Abraham *Epstein and Adolf *Jellinek collections; *Oxford, Bodleian Library (MS Opp. Add. 4° 114); and *Hamburg, SUB (Cod. Levy 144). The last two MSS were formerly MSS *Asher 16–17 (*HB*, XVI [1876], pp. 127–128). The MS belonging to Mortara and described by him in *Ozar Nechmad* (אוצר נחמד), III (1860), p. 153, is now *Cambridge (Mass.), Harvard University, MS Heb. 62. Mortara also compiled a catalogue of the Hebrew MSS in *Mantua, Comunità ebraica.

Moscow, Rossiiskaia Gosudarstvennaia Biblioteka (Russian State Library, RSL)

Formerly Publichnaia Biblioteka; renamed Lenin State Library in 1925 and Russian State Library in 1992. The library now possesses the *Günzburg family collection, which it took over in 1917. For the background to its acquisition see *Günzburg. There is no published catalogue of the collection, but there exists a lithographic edition of a handwritten catalogue by Senior *Sachs describing in brief 830 MSS (בית יוסף הוא רשימה מכל הספרים היקרים כתבי יד הנמצאים באוצר נחמד של הרב הגביר המרומם והאדיר שר וגדול בישראל כש״ת מו״ה יוסף יוזל גינצבורג נ״י הי״ו ובניו הגבירים הרמים והנשאים היקרים ונחמדים כבוד הרב החכם השלם בכל מיני שלימות ומעלות ומדות תרומיות כש״ת מו״ה נפתלי הירץ נ״י הי״ו וכבוד אחיו המשכיל היקר והנכבד הנעים והנחמד לרב כש״ת הי״ו אוריה נ״י). A stencilled copy of this catalogue, written by a different hand and without the title-page, formerly in the possession of Aron Freimann of Frankfurt, is now MS Var. 378 in the National Library of Israel. An additional catalogue in a different handwriting describes MSS 831–1913. The second catalogue was compiled after Sachs's death in 1892, as it includes MSS purchased from the estate of Seligmann *Baer after 1897. It is possible that the catalogue was compiled by Samuel Wiener, who wrote to Solomon Buber in 1896 that he was spending several hours every day examining Günzburg's MSS (*Jerusalem, NLI, Archives 4° 1222/500). According to a letter sent by Solomon *Schechter to Alexander *Marx in 1911 (catalogued papers of Elkan Nathan *Adler in the archives of *New York, JTSA), 2,330 Hebrew MSS were found in the library. However, it seems that no more than 1,913 MSS from the Günzburg collection are now found in the Russian State Library. The second catalogue has two sets of numbers, serial numbers 1–1080 and, in Hebrew letters, Günzburg nos. 831–1913. In his *Union Catalog*, Freimann refers to the first catalogue as GI and to the second as GII, and lists the serial numbers of GII. Copies of both catalogues are found in the *Jerusalem, IMHM. Sachs apparently planned to publish a catalogue of the collection and in 1866 published in Paris a booklet, without a title-page, describing at great length (48 pages) MSS Günzburg 1 and 2. In his *Catalogue of Hebrew Manuscripts Preserved in the USSR*, I, New York 1957, A. Katsh describes a number of Günzburg MSS acquired by him on microfilm.

In addition to the Günzburg collection, numerous Hebrew MSS are held in the Oriental and other collections of the Russian State Library. A collection of 275 ḥasidic MSS (mostly Ḥabad) was described by I. Medvedev in *Sovietish Heimland* (April 1989), pp. 132–134. These MSS are now stored in fond 182 and are often referred to as the Schneerson Collection or the Poliakov Collection. In fact, fond 182 includes many MSS that definitely do not derive from the library of Rabbi Joseph Isaac Schneerson. Recently, over 100 MSS were added to this fond; it now includes 458 MSS, and all the call-numbers have been changed (see Patricia Kennedy Grimsted, 'Chabad Sacred Texts, Russian-American Art Loans, and a Tall Ship Named "Hope": Beyond Cold War over a Restitution Claim?' forthcoming). The Trofiana collection includes about 300 MSS confiscated by the Nazis from Jewish libraries such as *Breslau, Jüdisch-theologisches Seminar; *Berlin, Jüdische Gemeinde; *Vienna, Israelitische Kultusgemeinde; *Dresden Israelitischen Religionsgemeinde; and Jewish libraries in Munich and Vilna, which were found during or after World War II (see *Moscow, RSMA). Most of the pre-sixteenth-century MSS that may have been in the library apparently are no longer there. Some of the Vilna MSS may have been returned to the national library in Vilna in 1995. A small collection of eleven *Geniza fragments, formerly in the library of the Imperial Theological Academy in Moscow, is preserved in the Manuscript Department of the RSL (MSS Or. F. 173.II, 118.1–11). These fragments were described in Yiddish by L. Vilsker, *Sovietish Heimland* (1984), no. 3, pp. 159–164, and again, in Hebrew, by E. Fleischer, *KS*, LIX (1984), pp. 609–624.

Moscow, Rossiiskii Gosudarstvennyi Voennyi Arkhiv (Russian State Military Archives, RGVA or RSMA)

The Archives were first established in 1920 as the Archives of the Red Army. Its status and name were changed several times until it received its present name in 1992. In 1999 it took over the holdings of the former Special Archive, which had been renamed the Center for the Preservation of Historico-Documentary Collections in 1992. The Special Archive was established in March 1946 to house archival materials of foreign origin that were captured by the Soviet Army at the end of World War II in Germany and Eastern Europe and brought back to Moscow, including many documents, books and manuscripts from Jewish libraries throughout Europe. These included MSS from *Breslau, Jüdisch-theologisches Seminar and *Vienna, Israelitische Kultusgemeinde that had been transferred in May 1944 to a remote castle in Wölfelsdorf (Wilkanów), and discovered there by the Red Army in the summer of 1945. Some of these MSS were transferred in 1948 to the Lenin State Library (now *Moscow, RSL). The Research Project on Art and Archives, Inc. (USA), and the Ministry of Culture of the Russian Federation in Moscow have published two catalogues describing briefly, in Russian and English, MSS and documents from two Jewish libraries found in the RSMA and the RSL. Thirty-nine MSS from *Breslau, Jüdisch-theologisches Seminar, 16 of them held in the RSMA, were described in *Catalogue of Manuscripts and Archival Materials of Juedisch-Theologisches Seminar in Breslau Held in Russian Depositories*, Moscow 2003; and 78 MSS from *Vienna, Israelitische Kultusgemeinde, 35 of them held in the RSMA, were described in *Rukopisi i arkhivnye dokumenty Evreĭskoĭ obshchiny goroda Veny v rossiiskikh sobraniiakh: Katalog / Manuscripts and Archival Documents of the Vienna Jewish Community Held in Russian Collections: Catalogue*, Moscow 2006.

P. K. Grimsted (ed.), *Archives of Russia*, Armonk, N.Y., 2000, pp. 220–230.

Moscow, RSL

Moscow, Rossiiskaia Gosudarstvennaia Biblioteka (Russian State Library).

Moskowitz Maḥzor

A fifteenth-century Ashkenazic-rite maḥzor copied and illuminated by *Joel b. Simeon, presented to the *Jerusalem, JNUL (now NLI), by Henry Moskowitz in 1970 (= NLI, Heb. 4° 1384). Shlomo Zucker published a study of the maḥzor in Hebrew and English (abridged): מחזור מוסקוביץ: מעשה ידיו של יואל בן שמעון, *The Moskowitz Mahzor of Joel ben Simeon*, Jerusalem 2005.

Mosseri, Jacques Nissim

Cairo, Egypt, 1884–1934; banker

During the years 1910–1912, Mosseri, Richard *Gottheil, Raymond Weill and Bernard *Chapira collected all the fragments that remained in the Shamiyin (Ezra) Synagogue *Geniza in Cairo and in the Basatin cemetery near Cairo. The fragments they collected, about 7,000 in number, were intended to form part of the collection of the library that was to be established in the Ismailia synagogue in Cairo (J. Mosseri, *Jewish Review*, IV [1913], pp. 208–216; י' מוצירי, מזרח ומערב, א [1919/1920], עמ' 27–31). Chapira compiled a catalogue of the fragments, but it was never published and has since disappeared. Mosseri eventually took the fragments out of Egypt, and from 1934 until 2006 they were in the possession of Mosseri's widow and sons in Paris. In his will Jacques Mosseri stipulated that the fragments be deposited in *Jerusalem, JNUL (now NLI), but for various reasons the family hesitated to deliver the collection to it. In 2006 the family agreed to deposit the fragments in *Cambridge, University Library, where they are being restored and preserved. Eventually, the collection will be deposited in the NLI.

The fragments are arranged in 17 groups according to subject. The principal groups are: A (= *actes*), documents; C (= *commentaires*), commentaries on the Bible and other works; L (= *lettres*), letters; P, Pi (= *poemes, piyyut*); T (= Talmud); and V (= *versions*), translations. Each fragment bore a number consisting of the group letter and a serial number (e.g., P 26, L 56). In some of the groups there were two series of fragments each bearing numbers beginning from 1, which may cause some confusion in references to fragments in these groups. In 1971 the collection was microfilmed in Paris by Dr. Israel Adler, then director of the JNUL, and the microfilms were deposited in the *Jerusalem, IMHM. The filming was done under conditions that required a new arrangement of the fragments. The collection was divided into ten groups numbered I–X (with some subgroups numbered Ia, IIa, etc.), adhering as far as possible to the original order of the fragments. Some of the fragments, mostly in group X, bore no previous call-numbers. A brief catalogue of the collection has been published by the IMHM: קטלוג של אוסף ז'אק מוצרי, ירושלים תש"ן. 'A Catalogue of the medical and para-medical manuscripts in the Mosseri Genizah Collection', by Efraim Lev, was published in *JJS*, LXII (2011), pp. 121–145. Seventy-five responsa fragments were described in greater detail, with facsimiles and transcriptions, in S. Glick, *Seride teshuvot: A Descriptive Catalogue of Responsa Fragments from the Jacques Mosseri Collection, Cambridge University Library* (Cambridge Genizah Studies Series, 3), Leiden 2012. In addition to the Geniza fragments, Mosseri also possessed a number of MSS that were previously in the Jewish Community library in Cairo, but most of them are no longer in the possession of his heirs and have disappeared.

Mostajef (Mostajub)

See *Musayof.

Moussaieff

See *Musayof.

Muller, Frederick

Amsterdam, Netherlands, nineteenth cent.; publisher and bookseller

In 1868, Temple Emanu-El in New York purchased from Muller 43 MSS listed in a catalogue (בית הספר, אמסטרדם 1868) and presented them to *New York, Columbia University.

München

Munich.

Munich

In general 'MS Munich' refers to a MS in *Munich, Bayerische Staatsbibliothek. Sometimes, however, the reference is to the collection of Abraham *Merzbacher of Munich. The oldest complete Talmud MS, known as 'MS Munich', is Munich, Bayerische Staatsbibliothek, Cod. hebr. 95. See *Pfersee.

Munich (Germany), Bayerisches Reichsarchiv

Four Hebrew MSS in the Reichsarchiv were acquired by *Munich, Bayerische Staatsbibliothek (Cods. hebr. 153, 393–395).

Striedl, *Geschichte*, p. 35.

Munich (Germany), Bayerische Staatsbibliothek (BSB)

Formerly Königliche Hof- und Staatsbibliothek. The library's collection numbers about 450 Hebrew MSS. The Hebrew collection was founded in the sixteenth century when the library of J. A. *Widmanstetter, which included about 125 Hebrew MSS, was acquired by the Munich library. Among the more recent acquisitions is the collection of 37 MSS from the library of Etienne *Quatremère, acquired in 1858. In 1909 the library acquired Cods. hebr. 421–428, including a few formerly in the library of Ottheinrich, prince elector of the Palatinate in the sixteenth century, from the Provenzialbibliothek in Neuburg an der Donau, where they were poorly conserved. The MSS in Munich were first described in print in a series of articles by Max Lilienthal in *Allgemeine Zeitung des Judenthums: Literarisches und homiletisches Beiblatt*, 1838–1839. M. Steinschneider described the collection in two catalogues, *Die hebräischen Handschriften der K. Hof- und Staatsbibliothek in Muenchen*, Munich 1875, and a revised and enlarged edition of the same title published in 1895. In both catalogues the MSS are arranged according to size, in three sections: 8°, 4°, 2°. In the first edition the following MSS were described: Cods. hebr. 1–151 (8°), 200–389 (4°) and 400–418 (2°). Nos. 152–199 and 390–399 were reserved for later acquisitions. In the second edition the following MSS were described: Cods. hebr. 1–154, 200–396, 400–418. Cod. hebr. 320 was bound with Cod. hebr. 327. Arabic MSS in Hebrew characters were listed but not described. One Judaeo-Arabic MS described by J. Aumer in *Die arabischen Handschriften der K. Hof- und Staatsbibliothek*, Munich 1866, no. 877, was not listed in Steinschneider's catalogue, nor were six Arabic MSS in Hebrew characters (Cods. arab. 816a–816f) described by Aumer in *Verzeichniss der orientalischen Handschriften der k. Hof- und Staatsbibliothek in München, mit Ausschluss der hebräischen, arabischen und persischen* (Catalogus codicum manu scriptorum Bibliothecae Regiae Monacensis), I, Part IV, Munich 1875, pp. 163–165, nos. 970–975. The catalogue number printed in bold type at the head of each entry in the Steinschneider catalogue together with the prefix 'Cod. hebr.' forms the present call-number (e.g., 'Cod. hebr. 327'). After the catalogue number, the number of leaves is listed, followed by the type of script and the date and number in the original collection whenever such a number exists. MSS containing more than one work are divided into subsections. The numbers of the subsections are printed in small type and are followed by the folio numbers in larger type. At the end of the catalogue are additional notes and transcriptions from several MSS. Indexes: authors, scribes, owners, titles and place names. Notes and corrections to the descriptions of the Kabbala MSS were published by G. Scholem ('הערות ותקונים לרשימת כתבי היד שבמינכן', ק"ס, א [תרפ"ה], עמ' 293–284). Thirty-three additional MSS and a number of fragments that were later added to Cods. hebr. 151, 153 and 356 were described in *Cat. Striedl–Róth*, pp. 230–308. The library continues to acquire Hebrew MSS, and since the publication of *Cat. Striedl–Róth* it has acquired Cods. hebr. 452–507, including the MSS formerly in the *Mainz, Akademie der Wissenschaften und der Literatur (Cods. hebr. 452–465).

Striedl, *Geschichte*.

Munich (Germany), Jüdische Gemeinde

About a dozen MSS from Jewish libraries in Munich, including some from the Cossmann Werner Bibliothek der Isr. Kultusgemeinde, are now in the Trofiana collection in *Moscow, RSL.

Munich (Germany), Königliche Hof- und Staatsbibliothek

Now called *Munich, Bayerische Staatsbibliothek.

Murphy Haggada

Name given to an illuminated fifteenth-century haggada formerly in the possession of Edmond de *Rothschild. Until 1941 the MS was in the possession of the Rothschild family. It was lost during World War II, but it was found by an American soldier towards the end of the war and was acquired by a Yale alumnus, Fred Towsley Murphy (hence its name), who bequeathed it in 1948 to *New Haven, Yale University Library. In 1980 it was identified as a Rothschild MS and returned to its legal owner, Mrs. James de Rothschild, who presented it in 1981 to the *Jerusalem, JNUL (now NLI), where it is MS Heb. 4° 6130. Three leaves were missing in the MS. Two of the leaves were sold at at the Ader auction house in Paris on 30 May 2007 and were eventually acquired by the NLI and inserted into the MS. Digital images of the MS may be accessed at http://jnul.huji.ac.il/dl/mss/heb6130/index_eng.html.

Musayof (Mostajef, Moussaieff, Mussajoff, Mostajub)

Shelomo Musayof came to Palestine from his native Bokhara in 1890. His collection of antiquities, coins, books, etc., included over 200 Hebrew MSS. Musayof died in 1921 and stipulated in his will that his library be kept in a yeshiva that would bear his name. In 1934, his sons deposited the collection for a period of five years in the *Jerusalem, JNUL (now NLI), where the MSS were given the numbers 1–226 (see *KS*, XI [1934/5], p. 406). They were later returned to Shelomo's son Rehavia Moussaieff. A list of the MSS was prepared by David Yehudayof in 1962, and they were renumbered 1–236, in a different order. The collection was then deposited in *Jerusalem, Mosad Harav Kook library, pending a legal decision concerning their ultimate placement. Following the decision, 224 MSS were microfilmed in 1969 for the *Jerusalem, IMHM, and they were then stored in the yeshiva named after Musayof, Yeshivat Shem, in the Bokharan quarter of Jerusalem. Several MSS were 'borrowed' or stolen from the Yeshiva. In the late 1980s Dr. Shelomo Moussaieff, a grandson of the original owner, removed the MSS from the yeshiva, acquired many of the missing MSS, and, in 2000, presented them to the *Ramat Gan, Bar-Ilan University Library. A number of MSS described by various scholars have disappeared. 228 MSS were described by Y. Avivi in 1992, in an edition limited to five copies (י׳ אביב״י, אוהל ש״ם: רשימת כתבי היד אשר באוסף ר׳ שלמה מוסאיוף, ירושלים תשנ״ב).

Mussajoff

See *Musayof.

Mutina

Latin name for Modena.

Muzari

See *Mosseri.

Myers, Asher Isaac

London, 1848–1902; journalist

Ten MSS formerly belonging to Myers were in the *London School of Jewish Studies (formerly Jews' College). They were listed in the College's *Eightieth Annual Report*, 1936. MSS 9 and 10 were sold at the Kestenbaum and Company auction in New York on December 17, 2002, and were described in the auction catalogue *Magnificent Hebrew Manuscripts, Incunabula and Other Valuable Hebrew Printed Books*. *Cambridge, University Library, purchased four MSS from Myers in 1896 (MSS Add. 3404–3407).

N

N

(1) *Cat. Neubauer*, see *Oxford, Bodleian; (2) *New York, JTSA.

Nahum, Yehuda Levi

See *Levi Nahum, Yehuda.

Nani, Jacopo

Venice, Italy, 1725–1797; collector

Nani's MSS, mostly Greek and Oriental, were kept in the Nani Museum created by his brother Bernardo. Over 1000 MSS of Nani's were acquired by *Venice, Biblioteca Marciana in 1797, but it is doubtful that any of them were in Hebrew. At least three of the Hebrew MSS described by de Rossi, *ext.*, nos. 46, 53–55 and 121, were acquired by Matteo *Canonici and are now in *Oxford, Bodleian Library (MSS Can. Or. 20, 49 and 53; see Appendix I, no. 22).

Naples (Italy), Biblioteca Nazionale Vittorio Emanuele III

Fourteen MSS from this library were described by A. Berliner, 'Hebräische Handschriften in Neapel', *MWJ*, XVI (1889), pp. 46–51; twelve were described by A. Monaco, 'Les mss. orientaux de la Bibliothèque de Naples', *Le Muséon*, I (1892), pp. 101–102; and fifteen were described by G. Moscati Steindler, 'I manoscritti ebraici della Biblioteca Nazionale di Napoli', *Annali dell'Istituto Orientale di Napoli*, XXXI (1971), pp. 313–340.

Naples (Italy), Collegio del Gesuiti

At least four MSS from this library are now in *Naples, Biblioteca Nazionale Vittorio Emanuele.

G. Moscati Steindler, 'I manoscritti ebraici della Biblioteca Nazionale di Napoli', *Annali dell'Istituto Orientale di Napoli*, XXXI (1971), p. 316.

Nash Papyrus

A second-century BCE papyrus containing the Ten Commandments and the Shema. The papyrus was bought by W. L. Nash in Egypt and is now *Cambridge, UL, MS Or. 233.

EJ, XII, p. 833.

Nauheim, Sigmund

Germany, 1879–1935; businessman and collector

Twenty-seven of Nauheim's MSS are now in *Jerusalem, NLI. An illuminated Esther scroll dated 1567 (or 1628, depending on how the acronym is deciphered) copied by Jacob b. Solomon Tsoref of Castelnuovo and described in Swarzenski and Schilling, *Die illuminierten Handschriften*, no. 238, is now MS Heb. 4° 197/20 in the NLI.

י׳ יואל, ׳אוסף מגלות אסתר׳, ק״ס, לב [תשי״ז], עמ׳ 238, מס׳ 19.

Neof. or Neofiti

See *Rome, Pia Casa dei Neofiti.

Neoph.

Ncophyti. See *Rome, Pia Casa dei Neofiti.

Neppi, Graziadio

Ferrara, Italy, 1759 – Cento, Italy, 1863; rabbi

Some of Neppi's writings, and apparently some MSS once in his possession, were in *Ferrara, Comunità ebraica.

Nessel, Daniel

Austria, seventeenth century.

Nessel wrote a catalogue of the MSS in the k. k. Hofbibliothek, Vienna (now *Vienna, Österreichische Nationalbibliothek) (1690).

Netter, Solomon

Vienna, d. 1879; publisher and bookseller

M. *Steinschneider possessed two lists of MSS belonging to Netter, one dated 1853 (51 MSS) and one from 1857 (18 MSS). Both lists are now *New York, JTSA, MS 2863. Netter sold his MSS to various libraries, among them to Baron David *Günzburg and to the British Museum (now *London, British Library). In 1854 he sold MSS to *Oxford, Bodleian Library (MSS Opp. Add. 2° 17, 19–20 and Opp. Add. 4° 21–24).

HB, XIX (1879), p. 136.

Neubauer, Adolf

Bittse, Hungary, 1831 – London, 1907

Neubauer compiled catalogues of the Hebrew MSS in *Oxford, Bodleian Library (= *Cat. Neubauer*), and *London, Beth Din and Beth Hamidrash Library, and described and wrote extensively about these as well as other MSS in various publications. A number of MSS from Neubauer's own collection are now in *London, British Library, MSS Or. 1041, 2451–2453 (*Cat. Margoliouth*, nos. 92, 160, 949, 100), and *Oxford, Bodleian Library, MSS Heb. d. 40 and Pers. e. 27 (*Cat. Neubauer–Cowley*, II, 2698, 2902, 2906).

Neuburg an der Donau (Germany), Provenzialbibliothek

See *Munich (Germany), Bayerische Staatsbibliothek.

New Haven (Conn.), Yale University

There are over 380 Hebrew MSS in the libraries of Yale University. Over 150 are in the Beinecke Rare Book and Manuscript Library. Seventy-eight of them were briefly described by L. Nemoy, 'Hebrew and kindred manuscripts in the Yale University Library', *Journal of Jewish Bibliography*, I (1939), pp. 107–111, and III (1942), pp. 44–47. Twenty-eight additional MSS, mostly marriage contracts and Esther scrolls, and ten MSS of Sholem Asch's works were described by Nemoy in *Catalogue of Hebrew and Yiddish Manuscripts and Books from the Library of Sholem Asch, Presented to Yale University by Louis M. Rabinowitz*, New Haven 1945, nos. 1–10, 109–136. In addition to the MSS in the Beinecke Library, MSS are also housed in the Manuscripts and Archives Department in the Sterling Memorial Library. MS 1824 includes 95 *pinkasim* of various Jewish communal organizations, mainly in Europe, with a few from the Middle East and the United States, acquired from Yeshayahu Vinograd and Moshe Rosenfeld in Jerusalem and Bery Gross in New York. These are described in J. Cohen, *Guide to the Jewish Communal Registers (Pinkese kehilah) Collection*, New Haven 2008 (http://drs.library.yale.edu:8083/fedora/get/mssa:ms.1824/PDF). MS 1825 is a collection of MSS and documents from North Africa, mainly from Morocco, acquired by the library in 2009. It includes 32 MSS.

New Norcia (Australia), Benedictine Abbey

A MS of the kabbalistic text *Shoshan sodot* (שושן סודות), presented to the Abbey in 1950 by a rabbi in nearby Perth, was returned to the Perth Jewish community thanks to the efforts of Rabbi M. J. Bernstein and presented to *Jerusalem, JNUL (now NLI) in 2003 (Heb. 4° 7538).

Newton Center (Mass.), Hebrew College

Formerly located in Brookline, Mass. The library had a collection of 70 Hebrew MSS, mostly dating to the eighteenth century or later. In 2008 most of the MSS and rare printed books were sold to the auctioneers Kestenbaum and Company. Fourteen MSS were described in Kestenbaum's catalogue *Fine Judaica: Printed Books, Manuscripts & Graphic Art to be Sold at Auction by Kestenbaum & Company on Thursday, September 18th, 2008*, lots 320–324, 331–335, 341, 343, 348, 349. Other MSS were listed in *Fine Judaica: Printed Books, Manuscripts & Graphic Art to be Sold at Auction by Kestenbaum & Company on April 2nd, 2009*, lots 256, 257, 264, 265, 273, 276–279, 283, and in *Fine Judaica: Printed Books, Manuscripts & Graphic Art to be Sold at Auction by Kestenbaum & Company on December 9, 2011*, lots 284, 293, 297, 300, 302, 308, 318 and 321. Some of the lots included multiple MSS. *Philadelphia, CAJS purchased a number of MSS at the 2011 sale (formerly Hebrew College, MSS nos. 27, 29, 34, 35, 39, 41, 42, 44, 45 and 49).

New York, Chassidei Chabad Ohel Yosef Yitzchak Lubavitch Library

The Lubavitch Library in Brooklyn, N.Y., houses several thousand MSS, the great majority of them writings and copies of writings by the Lubavitcher Rebbes. Few of the books in the libraries of the earliest Rebbes survived the two fires that ravaged the home of the founder of the dynasty, Rabbi Shneur Zalman of Lyady. The roots of the existing collection go back to the third generation of the dynasty in the mid-nineteenth century. Though substantial portions of the library were lost in fires and confiscated by the Soviet authorities in 1924, a considerable part survived in Poland until 1941, when it was shipped to New York. Many books and MSS that were confiscated or stolen by the Nazis were removed to *Moscow, RSL, and *Warsaw, ŻIH. In 1977, over 100 MSS were returned by the ŻIH to the library of the Rebbe in Brooklyn. In 1979 ten MSS that had been found after the War and sent to *Jerusalem, JNUL (now NLI), were returned to the Rebbe.

Though the vast majority of the MSS are writings of ḥasidic content, the library also includes MSS on Kabbala and other subjects. The Rebbe Shalom Dov Ber purchased 22 MSS from the booksellers Schwager & Fränkel, listed in their catalogue no. 11 (אוצר כלי חמדה), Husiatyn 1906, nos. 48, 80–89, 107, 117, 134, 143, 144, 150, 367–369, 384 and 446, of which 18 MSS (nos. 1972–1989 in the library) are still extant (S. D. Levine, *The Lubavitch Library* [see below], p. 47).

ש״ד לוין, ספריית ליובאוויטש, ברוקלין תשנ״ג.

New York, Columbia University, Butler Library

The library's Hebrew collection includes about 2,000 MSS bound in over 1,200 volumes. Most of the MSS are in Hebrew, but the collection also includes Judaica MSS in other languages (mainly Spanish, Dutch, Italian and French). Forty-three MSS purchased from the bookseller F. Muller were presented to the library in 1892 by Temple Emanu-El of New York. The MSS were previously listed in the catalogue *Bet hasefer* (בית הספר): *Catalog der reichhaltigen Sammlung hebräischer und jüdischer Bücher, Handschriften, Kupferstiche, Portraits, etc., nachgelassen von Giuseppe Almanzi in Padua, vom Rabbiner Jacob Emden in Altona, vom Oberrabbiner M. J. Lewenstein in Paramaribo und Anderen, redigirt von M. Roest*, Amsterdam 1868. At the beginning of his book *Devir Efrayim* (דביר אפרים), a description of his collection (St. Louis 1926), Ephraim

*Deinard relates how he convinced Prof. Richard *Gottheil to cultivate a Judaica collection at Columbia and sold about 135 MSS to a consortium that gave them to the library some time after 1888 and before 1892. During the years 1930–1932, Salo Baron purchased about 700 MSS for the library from the bookseller David *Fränkel, including those listed in his book *Zur Geschichte der Juden in Griechenland* (ד׳ פרנקל, לקורות ישראל במלכות יון, [וינה] 1931). There are also Hebrew MSS in the Smith/Plimpton Collections and in the General Manuscript Collection.

There is no published catalogue of the Columbia University MSS. A typewritten catalogue of 620 Hebrew MSS compiled by Isaac Mendelsohn (1898–1965) exists in the library (for a description of this catalogue, see Pearson, p. 67).

Rab., *Lit. Treas.*, pp. 103–105.

New York, General Theological Seminary

The Ashkenazic Bible dated 1264, formerly in the General Theological Seminary, was sold at an auction in 1980 to A. D. *Friedberg of Toronto and sold again to D. Sofer in 1995 (MS 1). An illuminated Esther scroll from the library was purchased by William *Gross of Tel Aviv (MS 194).

New York, Jewish Theological Seminary of America Library (JTSA or JTS)

The Jewish Theological Seminary owns what is perhaps the largest collection of Hebrew MSS in the world, about 11,000 MSS, in addition to 35,000 leaves from the *Geniza, archival records, marriage contracts, etc. The Seminary was founded in 1886, and the nucleus of the MS collection was acquired during the early years of the twentieth century. Some of the major collections of MSS in the JTSA library are listed below, according to size. Commonly used abbreviations are given in parentheses. Details concerning catalogues, dates of acquisition, former owners, etc., may be found in the respective entries for each collection. The number of MSS listed for each collection is in most cases an approximation.

Table 1
Major Collections of MSS in the
Library of the
Jewish Theological Seminary of America

Collection	*Number of MSS*
Elkan N. *Adler (ENA)	4,200
*Enelow Memorial Collection (EMC)	1,100
Mayer *Sulzberger (S., Sulz.)	500
Ephraim *Deinard (D.)	500
Solomon *Halberstamm (H., Halb.) (nos. Halb. 412–562)	150
Joseph *Benaim (originally 145)	112
Moritz *Steinschneider (ST)	30
Judah A. *Joffe	25

Other sizeable collections in the JTSA library are the Harry *Hirsch (H., Hi.) and the Hyman George *Enelow (HGE) collections.

CATALOGUES The library's MSS are listed together with the printed books in the library's online catalogue at http://alpha3.jtsa.edu. The only printed publication listing most of the Hebrew MSS in the JTSA library is *A Guide to the Hebrew Manuscript Collection of the Library of the Jewish Theological Seminary of America*, compiled by J. E. Rovner, Vols. I–V, New York 1991. Vols. I–III provide a brief description of some 10,000 items arranged according to the MS numbers. Vols. IV–V provide title, author, place, date and topic indexes. There are other catalogues and publications describing various parts of the JTSA collection. The Adler MSS were described very briefly in *Catalogue of Hebrew Manuscripts in the Collection of Elkan Nathan Adler*, Cambridge 1921. The halakhic and midrashic fragments from the Adler collection were described by Neil Danzig, *A Catalogue of Fragments of Halakhah and*

Midrash from the Cairo Geniza in the Elkan Nathan Adler Collection of the Library of the Jewish Theological Seminary of America, New York–Jerusalem 1997 (קטלוג של שרידי הלכה ומדרש מגניזת קאהיר באוסף א״נ אדלר שבספריית בית המדרש לרבנים באמריקה). A. Maman described the philological MSS and Geniza fragments in the JTSA library in *Otsrot Lashon: The Hebrew Philology Manuscripts and Genizah Fragments in the Library of the Jewish Theological Seminary of America* (אוצרות לשון: כתבי־היד וקטעי הגניזה בחכמת הלשון מאוסף בית המדרש לרבנים באמריקה, ניו יורק 2006). A survey by Alexander Marx of some of the Enelow Memorial Collection MSS was printed, before the collection was named after Enelow (Marx, *Proceedings*). Numerous MSS were described by Marx and others in various issues of the JTSA *Register*. Marx also described 72 polemical MSS (Marx, 'Polemical MSS'). Marx's descriptions were reprinted, with an introduction by M. Schmelzer and an index by J. Brumer, in Marx, *Bibl. Studies* (1977). Fifty-five illuminated MSS that were on exhibition in the Jewish Museum are described in *Illuminated Hebrew Manuscripts from the Library of the Jewish Theological Seminary of America*, New York 1965. Several other partial catalogues of JTSA MSS, mainly subject and exhibition catalogues, are listed by Pearson, pp. 69–70. In many of these lists the MSS are not identified by valid call-numbers. After the great majority of the JTSA MSS had been microfilmed by University Microfilms (now merged with ProQuest), a number of Reel Guides to certain subject collections were published in which the MSS are described with utmost brevity. Reel Guides have appeared for the biblical, liturgical, Benaim, philosophy, Kabbala, polemical, philological and poetry, belles lettres, history of sciences, Maimonides' *Mishne Tora* and Adler special collections. A number of handwritten and typewritten catalogues are available in the library. The 'JTS catalogue' compiled by A. Marx briefly describes MSS, mainly from the Halberstamm, Sulzberger and other early collections acquired before the ENA and EMC collections entered the library. The catalogue is arranged according to subject. MSS described in the catalogue formerly bore call-numbers with the prefix 'JTS' followed by the catalogue number. The Enelow Memorial Collection was described on cards by David *Fränkel. Over 1,050 biblical MSS were described on cards by M. Lutzki, and 2,600 rabbinic MSS were described by Judah Brumer. Microfiche editions of the unpublished *Lutzki Catalog of Biblical Manuscripts* and the *Brumer Catalog of Rabbinic Manuscripts* are available for purchase.

CALL-NUMBERS AND SIGNATURES Just as there exists no single published catalogue of the JTSA MSS, so until the 1970s there existed no uniform system of numbering for them. MSS in the Adler, Halberstamm and Steinschneider collections, for instance, bore their original collection numbers. Numbers were given to MSS in the major collections (e.g., MS EMC 252, MS Sulzberger 345), but MSS acquired individually often bore only an accession number (Acc.). Originally the accession numbers stamped on the first and last pages of each book were assigned both to printed books and to MSS without distinction. Later two sets of numbers were introduced, and those assigned to MSS were preceded by a zero (e.g., Acc. 012145). Very often MSS were given more than one number: an accession number, a collection number, a bookseller's catalogue number and/or a subject collection number. Abbreviations used to designate particular collections could also designate other MSS. For instance, 'S' could stand for Sulzberger or for MSS purchased from Lippa *Schwager; and 'S.2' could designate MSS purchased from Schwager's catalogue no. 2 and not necessarily MS Sulzberger 2. The result was that uninitiated scholars often referred to a JTSA MS by a variety of inaccurate designations that supplied only the slightest hint as to their location in the library's stacks. MSS were referred to by the volume number of the JTSA *Register* in which they were described or by a number without any prefix indicating the name of the collection to which it belonged. Years ago, the various collections (ENA, EMC, etc.) were dispersed and their MSS arranged according to subject. When the MSS were being prepared for microfilming, each MS was given a serial number, preceded by the prefix 'Mic.' The prefix 'Mic.' has been replaced by the prefix 'MS', and now the call-numbers of the JTSA MSS consist of the prefix 'MS' followed by serial numbers, with four major exceptions: (1) Biblical MSS are arranged according to the Lutzki catalogue numbers and bear the prefix 'L' (e.g., MS L2). (2) Rabbinical MSS up to MS R2602 bear call-numbers with the prefix 'R' and are arranged according to these numbers (e.g., MS R2). Although they also bear 'MS' numbers (as a secondary shelf-mark) the 'R' numbers are generally identical to the numbers in Brumer's catalogue (subsequently catalogued rabbinical MSS are assigned only a regular MS number, the 'R' number series having been closed). (3) The Benaim collection is arranged according to the Benaim numbers. (4) *Geniza fragments are arranged according to their ENA numbers in two size groups.

A. Marx, 'The Library', in C. Adler (ed.), *The Jewish Theological Seminary of America Semi-Centennial Volume*, New York 1939, pp. 87–120; N. M. Sarna, 'The Library of the Jewish Theological Seminary of America', *Jewish Book Annual*, XXI (1963/4), pp. 53–59; Rab., *Lit. Treas.*, pp. 63–82; Pearson, pp. 68–70; H. Dicker, *Of Learning and Libraries*, New York 1988.

New York, Public Library

The Dorot Jewish Division in the New York Public Library has approximately 250 Hebrew MSS, mostly early modern Italian and Yemenite. They include a collection of Hebrew MSS formerly held by the library's Manuscript Division, of which 38 (nos. 1–13, 101–125) were described by A. Freimann in a typewritten catalogue dated 1942, and 9 (nos. 126–134) were added afterwards. Three Esther scrolls and a Hebrew Bible dated 1294 (see *Xanten Bible), formerly in the possession of Mayer *Goldschmidt of Frankfurt, are in the Spencer Collection (MSS 1–4). Dozens of items have been bought at auction over the past decades, including several manuscripts from the *London, Montefiore Collection.

Three Aramaic amulets held by the library are described in Joseph Naveh and Shaul Shaked, *Magic Spells and Formulae*, Jerusalem 1993, pp. 91–101. Among the items transferred from the Manuscript Division to the Jewish Division in 2006 are one Tora scroll (and eleven leaves from five different scrolls), three Esther scrolls and one scroll of Ecclesiastes. All of these scrolls are late, from the eighteenth or nineteenth centuries. On the Chinese Tora scroll once held by the NYPL, see Michael Pollack, *The Torah Scrolls of the Chinese Jews*, Dallas 1975, p. 58 (updated version online at: http://www.smu.edu/bridwell/publications/chinesetorahscroll/torahscrollstitle.htm).

The Library also houses several hundred Yiddish plays and works of fiction in manuscript, as well as hundreds of archival documents, primarily the correspondence of Joseph Sossnitz, Abraham Baer Dubsewitz, Nehemiah Samuel Libowitz and the Jaffe family from Lithuania – all figures who immigrated to New York in the 1890s.

New York, Temple Emanu-El

In 1868 Temple Emanu-El purchased 43 MSS and 2,500 printed books from the Amsterdam bookseller F. Muller, and in 1892 the collection was presented to *New York, Columbia University.

Rab., *Lit. Treas.*, p. 103.

New York, Yeshiva University

The library of Yeshiva University has a collection of several hundred MSS, mostly works written in the eighteenth to twentieth centuries, and several hundred *pinkasim* of communities in Germany from the Louis *Lewin collection. Included in the collection are the MSS formerly in the possession of Berthold *Strauss. The manuscripts are described in the library's YULIS online catalog: http://yulib.mc.yu.edu:8000/cgi-bin/gw/yulis. Y. Avivi described 400 rabbinic MSS in the Rare Book Room Manuscript Collection in the catalogue *Rabbinic Manuscripts, Mendel Gottesman Library, Yeshiva University*, New York 1998. The catalogue is divided into three sections: (1): Early Manuscripts (pre-1600 authors); (2): Ashkenaz (post-1600 authors); and (3): Oriental Jewry. Each section is further divided into works on exegesis and rabbinics followed by works on ethics, philosophy and Kabbala. The MSS are described in Hebrew and again, in a separate section, in English (abridged). Codicological and palaeographical information: size, size of written area, leaves, number of lines, date and type of script. Indexes (in Hebrew only): Authors, titles, subjects, scribes, owners, names mentioned, titles mentioned, dates and places (with Latin letter equivalents). There are also concordances to the catalogue numbers and the library call-numbers as well as to numbers in other catalogues.

New York, YIVO (Yidisher Visnshaftlekher Institut / Institute for Jewish Research)

Founded at a conference in Berlin but headquartered in Vilna, the early YIVO also had branches in Berlin, Warsaw and New York City. During World War II the Nazis carried a portion of YIVO's archives from Vilna to Berlin, where the papers survived the war intact and eventually ended up in New York. These archives include manuscripts of writings by Jewish literary figures, scholars, playwrights, etc. The Rabbinical and Historical Manuscripts Collection (RG 128) includes over 400 manuscripts from 1567 to the 1930s. This collection is of mixed provenance. Part of it was deposited in the *Vilna, YIVO Archives before World War II. The rest of the collection was gathered in France and Germany after the war by Gershon *Epstein, a YIVO collector (see *Guide to the YIVO Archives*, New York 1998, no. 874). The Abraham Sutzkever–Szmerke Kaczerginski Collection (RG 223) includes, inter alia, historical and literary manuscripts that belonged to the YIVO Institute in Vilna and to the *Strashun Library before the war. The manuscripts were hidden and preserved by a group of ghetto inmates that included the Yiddish poets Abraham Sutzkever and Szmerke Kaczerginski (see *ibid.*, no. 1039). Towards the end of the War and up to 1946, Sutzkever and Kaczerginski surreptitiously sent shipments of MSS and documents to YIVO in New York. After the war the remaining books and archives were deposited in a newly established Jewish Museum in Vilna, but the museum was closed a few years later, and they were subsequently removed to the inner recesses of the Lithuanian National Book Chamber, where they were discovered in 1988 and 1993 and sent to YIVO in New York.

D. Fishman, *Embers Plucked from the Fire: The Rescue of Jewish Cultural Treasures in Vilna*, New York 1996.

New York Haggada, First

Name given to *New York, JTSA, MS 4481, an illuminated haggada written by *Joel b. Simeon in the fifteenth century.

New York Haggada, Second

Name given to *New York, JTSA, MS 8279, an illuminated haggada written by *Joel b. Simeon in 1454.

Narkiss, p. 124.

Nice (France)
The MSS from Nice described by M. Schwab, 'Manuscrits hébreux en France', *REJ*, LX (1910), pp. 100–103, nos. 1–8, are now *Paris, AIU, MSS 250–257. The present location of nos. 9–10 is not known.

Nicolaus von Cusa
See *Cusa.

Niederhoffen, Benjamin
Frankfurt a/M, Germany, nineteenth cent.
The siddur dated 1306 that was in Niederhoffen's possession and was described by S. *Baer in his siddur (סדר עבודת ישראל, רעדעלהיים תרכ"ח / Rödelheim 1868), p. v, and mentioned by several other scholars in the nineteenth century, was *Jerusalem, Schocken Institute, MS 13160 (see S. Emanuel, דרשה לפסח, Jerusalem 2006, p. 7, note 23). At least four other MSS of his are found in other libraries. A handwritten catalogue of his printed books in *Jerusalem, NLI, Heb. 8° 2401, includes, on f. 21v, a short description of one MS, a collectanea of various texts whose present whereabouts are unknown.

Niger, W.
Pseudonym of *Black, William Mead.

Nikolsburg (Mikulov, Czech Republic), Fürstlich Dietrichsteinsche Bibliothek
Nine Hebrew MSS from this library were described by A. Z. Schwarz, 'Nikolsburger hebräische Handschriften', in *Studies ... in Memory of Abraham Solomon Freidus*, New York 1929, pp. 170–181. After the library was dispersed in 1933, most of them were acquired by the *Boston Medical Library, now part of the Francis A. Countway Library of Medicine (J. F. Ballard, *Manuscripts and Incunabula in the Boston Medical Library*, Boston 1944, p. ix). No. 1 is *Oxford, Bodleian Library, MS Lyell Empt. 62. One MS not described by Schwarz is now *New York, JTSA, MS 2977.

Nîmes (France), Bibliothèque municipale
Fourteen of the sixteen Hebrew MSS in Nîmes were brought to the library in 1800 when it was opened from the Carthusian Convent in Villeneuve-les-Avignon (F. de Forbin, in A. Girard and D. Le Blevec [eds.], *Les Chartreux et l'Art XIVe–XVIIIe siècle*, Paris 1989, pp. 39–63). All the MSS were described by J. Simon in 'Les manuscrits hébreux de la bibliothèque de Nîmes', *REJ*, III (1881), pp. 225–237, and idem, 'Un nouveau manuscrit de la bibliothèque de Nîmes', *ibid.*, XX (1890), p. 147, and again, briefly, in *Catalogue général*, VII (1885), nos. 10–13, 17–20, 22–27, 43, 365.

Nogent-sur-Marne (France), Fondation Smith-Lesouëf
The library of August Lesouëf (1829–1906) and his sister Mme. Smith and her daughters were presented by the Fondation to *Paris, Bibliothèque nationale de France in 1913 and transferred to the Oriental Department in 1950. The collection includes two Hebrew MSS (nos. 250–251).

Norimberga
Latin name for Nuremberg.

Norsa Manuscript
An illuminated MS of Maimonides' *Guide of the Perplexed* copied in 1349; formerly in the possession of the Norsa family in Mantua, it is presently in a private collection.
T. Metzger, 'Le manuscript Norsa', in *Mitteilungen des Kunsthistorischen Instituts in Florenz*, 46/1 (2002), pp. 1–73.

Nuremberg (Germany)
A MS from Nuremberg described by *Kennicott, no. 201, is now *London, BL, MS Add. 21161 (*Cat. Margoliouth*, no. 116).

Nuremberg (Germany), Germanisches Nationalmuseum

Six Hebrew MSS are described in *Cat. Striedl–Róth*, pp. 313–316. Two illuminated haggadas formerly in the library, the so-called First and Second *Nuremberg Haggadas (nos. 2107b and 2121), were transferred in 1958 to *Jerusalem, Schocken Institute. They were recently sold (see *Nuremberg Haggada).

Nuremberg (Germany), Israelitische Kultusgemeinde

A maḥzor in the possession of the Jewish community of Nuremberg has been presented on permanent loan to *Erlangen, Universitätsbibliothek, and bears the number MS 2601 (Cat. *Striedl–Róth*, no. 67).

Nuremberg (Germany), Landeskirchliches Archiv der Evangelisch-Lutherischen Kirche in Bayern

Four MSS are described in *Cat. Striedl–Róth*, pp. 326–328. One of the MSS is listed in *Cat. Allony–Loewinger*, I, p. 50, without a call-number.

Nuremberg (Germany), Staatsarchiv

Three MSS and two fragments are described in *Cat. Striedl–Róth*, pp. 309–312. Fragments from seven other MSS formerly in *Pappenheim, Gräflich Pappenheim'sche Bibliothek, described in *Cat. Allony– Loewinger*, I, nos. 680–686, were transferred to the Staatsarchiv in 1965.

Nuremberg (Germany), Stadtbibliothek

A Bible in seven volumes and another eight MSS are described in *Cat. Striedl–Róth*, pp. 317–325, and in *Cat. Allony–Loewinger*, I, pp. 49–50. MS Cent. IV 100, the so-called *Nuremberg Maḥzor, was transferred to the *Jerusalem, Schocken Institute, in 1951.

Nuremberg Haggada, First

Name given to *Jerusalem, Schocken Institute, MS 24086, an illuminated haggada written by *Joel b. Simeon in the fifteenth century. The MS was formerly *Nuremberg, Germanisches Nationalmuseum, MS 2107b. In 1958 it was transferred to the Schocken Institute, though it remained the property of the Schocken family. In 2001 it was purchased by Mrs. Erica Jesselson at a Sotheby's auction and donated to *Jerusalem, Israel Museum.

Jerusalem Collections, no. 13.

Nuremberg Haggada, Second

Name given to *Jerusalem, Schocken Institute, MS 24087, an illuminated fifteenth-century Ashkenazic haggada. The MS was formerly *Nuremberg, Germanisches Nationalmuseum, MS 2121. In 1957 it was transferred to the Schocken Institute, though it remained the property of the Schocken family. It was sold to David Sofer of London and is now on deposit in *Jerusalem, NLI. A digitized version of the maḥzor is available on the NLI website: http://jnul.huji.ac.il/dl/mss-pr/mss_d_0076/open_eng.html.

Jerusalem Collections, no. 11; B. Narkiss and G. Sed-Rajna, *Index of Jewish Art: Iconographical Index of Hebrew Illuminated Manuscripts*, II: *The Ḥileq and Bileq Haggadah; The 2nd Nürnberg Haggadah; The Yahuda Haggadah*, Jerusalem–Paris 1981.

Nuremberg Maḥzor

Name given to an illuminated Ashkenazic maḥzor dated 1331. The MS, formerly *Nuremberg, Stadtbibliothek, MS Cent. IV 100, was acquired by Salman Schocken and transferred to *Jerusalem, Schocken Institute, in 1951, receiving the call-number MS 24100. Since the beginning of the nineteenth century, eleven decorated leaves were separated from the MS. Five of them were acquired by Mayer *Goldschmidt in Frankfurt and were described in Swarzenski and Schilling, *Die* *illuminierten Handschriften*, no. 69. One of these leaves was presented to Salman Schocken in 1937, and in 1938 he purchased another three of them. These four leaves (ff. 78, 120, 154, 364, according to the old foliation) were later reinserted into the maḥzor, as was another leaf that came into the possession of Ernst Bodenheimer of New York and was later acquired by David Sofer of London. The maḥzor, which belonged to members of the Schocken family and not to the Schocken Institute, was offered for sale at the auction of Judaica held at Sotheby's in Tel Aviv on October 30, 2002, and was no. 47 in the auction catalogue *Judaica*. In 2007, it was sold to Dr. David and Jemima Jeselsohn of Zurich and deposited in *Jerusalem, Israel Museum. A digitized version of the maḥzor is available at the *Jerusalem, NLI, website: http://jnul.huji.ac.il/dl/mss-pr/mahzor-nuremberg/open_eng.html.

B. Ziemlich, *Das Machsor Nürnberg*, Berlin 1886; Narkiss, p. 110; *Jerusalem Collections*, no. 6; C. Sirat and M. Beit-Arié, *Manuscrits médiévaux en caractères hébraïques*, I, Paris–Jerusalem 1972, no. 34.

Nuremberg Memorbuch
See *Mainz, Jüdische Gemeinde.

NY
New York.

NYS
*New York, Jewish Theological Seminary of America.

O

O
(1) *Oppenheim, David; (2) *Oxford, Bodleian Library.

O. A.
Opp. Add. See *Oppenheim, David.

Odessa (Ukraine), Odesskoe Obshchestvo Istorii i Drevnostei (Gesellschaft für Geschichte und Alterthümer or Society for History and Antiquities)
Abraham *Firkovich sold about 50 MSS to the Society in 1845 (the 'First Odessa Collection') and continued to sell MSS to it until 1852 (the 'Second Odessa Collection'). The MSS in the 'First Collection' were described by E. M. Pinner in *Prospectus der der Odessaer Gesellschaft für Geschichte und Alterthümer gehörenden ältesten hebräischen und rabbinischen Manuscripte*, Odessa 1845. In 1863, the Imperial Public Library in St. Petersburg (now *St. Petersburg, NLR) acquired the Odessa Collections, comprising about 95 MSS. Most of these MSS now bear call-numbers with the prefixes Евр. I A, Евр. I B, Евр. I C and Евр. I Библ. (nos. 147–170). Series Евр. I A includes 36 Tora scrolls (15 of which are described in Part A of the *Prospectus*). Series Евр. I B, nos. 1–20 (nos. 9, 12, 15, 16 and 18 are not in use), includes the biblical codices and one Karaite prayerbook (no. 20) from the First Odessa Collection (described in Part B of the *Prospectus*); no. 19A is the *Leningrad Bible, described in the Appendix to the *Prospectus*. Series Евр. I C includes 11 mostly talmudic and rabbinic MSS and one Karaite MS (nos. 1–9 are described in Part C of the *Prospectus*). Twenty-six biblical codices from the Second Odessa Collection bear the call-numbers Евр. I Библ. 147–153a, 154–157a and 158–170; of these, MSS 147, 149, 154, 158, 159 and 161 are missing.

O. Vasilyeva, 'The Firkovich Odessa Collection: The History of its acquisition and research, present condition and historical Value', *Studia Orientalia*, XCV (2003), pp. 45–53.

Ol.
Latin: *olim*, 'formerly'.

Olim Palatina
See *Heidelberg, Biblioteca Palatina.

Olomouc (Czech Republic; German: Olmütz), Vědecká Knihova (State Research Library)
One Hebrew MS, a collection of philological works on the Hebrew language by Sebastien Münster (Cod. 364), was described by A. Z. Schwarz, 'Eine Handschrift Sebastian Münsters', *Soncino-Blätter*, II (1927), pp. 55–58. Schwarz also described Cod. 27, 'Kod. 27 der Studienbibliothek in Olmütz', *ibid.*, III (1930), pp. 155–158. Two additional MSS are numbered 484 and 485. Four Hebrew fragments are found in bindings of other books in the library. Several other fragments are found in the Zemský Archiv in Olomouc.

ÖNB
*Vienna , Österreichische Nationalbibliothek.

Opp.
*Oppenheim, David.

Opp. Add.
See *Oppenheim, David.

Oppenheim (Oppenheimer), David
Worms, Germany, 1664 – Prague, 1736; rabbi in Nikolsburg and Prague
Oppenheim was a scholar and bibliophile whose library was perhaps the largest private Jewish collection in the eighteenth century. In addition to printed books the library contained over 750 Hebrew MSS. The Christian scholar Johann Christoph *Wolf obtained most of the material for his *Bibliotheca Hebraea* from the Oppenheim library. For fear of the censor, Oppenheim did not take his library with him to Prague but left it with his father-in-law Lipmann *Cohen in Hanover. After his death the library was inherited by his son Joseph, and it eventually passed into the possession of an Oppenheim relative, Isaac Seligmann Cohn *Berend Salomon of Hamburg. After being offered for sale several times, the collection was purchased in 1829 by *Oxford, Bodleian Library, where it is now. The MSS were described in a handwritten catalogue, formerly in the possession of Eliakim *Carmoly and now MS Oxford, Opp. Add. 4° 135 (*Cat. Neubauer*, 2418; a second copy written by the same scribe is MS *London, Montefiore, MS 516), and again in the catalogue compiled in 1782 by Isaac Seligmann *Berend Salomon (רשימה תמה ... מן קבוצת ספרים ...מוהר״ר דוד אופנהיים, המבורג תקמ״ב), based on a similar unpublished catalogue by Israel Breslau; and in Hebrew and Latin by Isaac Metz (קהלת דוד: רשימת אוצר הספרים המפואר, אצרו ואספו מוהר״ר דוד אפפענהיים אב״ד פראג אלפי ספרי בית ישראל הנחמדים מזהב ומפנינים בהם כמה מאות כתבי־יד יקרי ערך ... המבורג, נדפס באלטונא, תקפ״ו). The Oppenheim MSS are also included in *Cat. Neubauer*. In the Berend Salomon catalogue, the MSS, arranged in alphabetical order of their titles, are briefly described. The catalogue by Isaac Metz is divided into four sections according to the size of the MSS (folio, quarto, octavo and duodecimo). Each section is further divided according to subject, and in each subject MSS and printed books are described separately. There are four sets of numbers; thus, for example, printed Bibles in folio are numbered foll. 1–100, and Bible MSS in folio are numbered foll. 101–111. After their arrival in Oxford, the MSS were given new numbers, Opp. 1–780, without regard to size. In *Cat.*

Neubauer, both the new numbers and the old Metz catalogue numbers are listed at the end of each entry, with the old numbers, prefixed 'ol.' (Latin: *olim*, 'formerly'), in parentheses. A concordance to the *Cat. Neubauer* numbers, the new numbers and the Metz catalogue numbers is found on pp. xvi–xix. 273 additional MSS, purchased from various sources between 1844 and 1897, were added to the Oppenheim collection and bear the call-numbers Opp. Add. 4° 1–194 and Opp. Add. 8° 1–79. A list of these MSS and their numbers in *Cat. Neubauer* is found on pp. xxiii–xxiv of the catalogue.

Orat. or Oratoire
See *Paris, Oratoire.

Oriel College
See *Oxford, College Libraries.

Orléans (France), Médiathèque
Formerly Bibliothèque municipal. One Hebrew MS, a prayerbook, is listed in *Catalogue général*, XII (1889), no. 5. In addition the *Jerusalem, IMHM has microfilms of two biblical MSS from the library.

Osimo, Leone (Judah Arye)
Montagnana, Italy, 1841 – Padua, Italy, 1869; rabbi
Seven MSS of Osimo's were described in the catalogue of his collection (רשימת הספרים אשר הניח אחריו ... כמוהר״ר יהודה אריה אוזימו בק״ק פאדובה ..., Padua 1870). No. 6 in the catalogue was later *London, Montefiore, MS 297. A maḥzor that belonged to Osimo is now *Paris, AIU, MS H 23 A.

Ottoboniana
Collection belonging to the Ottoboni family, which passed into the possession of the *Vatican library in 1790 (*Encyclopedia Italiana*, XXV, p. 782). There is one Hebrew MS in the collection, Cod. Lat. 2911 (*Cat. Allony–Loewinger*, III, no. 794; *Cat. Richler*, Vatican, p. 564).

Oxford (England), Bodleian Library
The Bodleian Library's collection of Hebrew MSS and volumes of *Geniza fragments numbers about 3,150, including Samaritan MSS. It is made up, for the most part, of various collections that were presented to or purchased by the library. Among the collections making up the Bodleian's Hebrew MS holdings are those of Robert *Huntington, William *Laud, Thomas *Marshall, Edward *Pococke and John *Selden – all from the seventeenth century. Among the collections acquired in the nineteenth century are those of David *Oppenheim (780 MSS), Heimann Joseph *Michael (629), Matteo Luigi *Canonici (110), Benjamin *Kennicott (75), Isaac Samuel *Reggio (60) and Mordecai *Bislisches (ca. 67). In 2013, the library, jointly with *Cambridge, University Library, purchased the *Cambridge, Westminster College collection of Geniza fragments. For further information about these collections and others in the library, consult the entries for each collection. The MSS are kept in the Department of Oriental Collections.

CATALOGUES About 500 MSS were described by J. Uri in *Bibliothecae Bodleianae Codicum Manuscriptorum Orientalum*, I, Oxford 1787, pp. 1–98. Eight Samaritan MSS and 14 Arabic MSS in Hebrew characters were described by A. Nicoll in the second part of this catalogue (Oxford 1821), pp. 1–9. M. Steinschneider's *Conspectus Codd. MSS. Hebraeorum in Bibliotheca Bodleiana*, Berlin 1857, a brief list of the Bodleian's Hebrew MSS based on the descriptions of Uri and Nicoll, was printed at the end of the third volume of Steinschneider's catalogue of the printed Hebrew books in the Bodleian, *Catalogus Librorum Hebraeorum ...*, Berlin 1852–1860. There exist a number of printed catalogues to some of the collections in the Bodleian (Oppenheim, Michael, etc.); for details consult the entries for each collection. The most complete are *Cat. Neubauer* and *Cat. Neubauer–Cowley*, II (1886–1906). The first volume (*Cat. Neubauer*), containing entries 1–2602, was compiled by Neubauer. The second (*Cat. Neubauer–Cowley*, II), containing entries 2603–2918, was begun by Neubauer and completed by A. Cowley, who began working on the catalogue in 1896. Nos. 2603–2634 were written entirely by Neubauer and sent to the printer before Cowley began his work. Neubauer had collected material pertaining to nos. 2635–2813, and Cowley completed their descriptions. Nos. 2814–2918 were described entirely by Cowley.

Cat. Neubauer is arranged according to subject up to no. 2321, followed by descriptions of additional and omitted MSS (nos. 2322–2434), MSS found in *Oxford College libraries (nos. 2435–2458), MSS in Latin characters (nos. 2459–2482), recent acquisitions (nos. 2483–2524), omitted MSS (nos. 2525–2531), Samaritan MSS not described in previous catalogues (nos. 2532–2541), and, in cols. 1113–1132, further additions, including additional College MSS (nos. 2542–2602). Each entry is preceded by the catalogue number (1–2602). Call-numbers are listed at the end of each entry in square brackets. In parentheses, inside the brackets, is the number in Uri's catalogue or, for the Oppenheim and Michael MSS, the old catalogue number, preceded by 'ol.' (Latin: *olim*, 'formerly'). The MSS are generally described in brief. Poetry and liturgical MSS are described in much greater detail; in fact, the entire contents of many of these MSS are listed. Palaeographical and codicological information: type of script, exact dates, size (2°, 4°, 8°), writing material and number of leaves. At the end of the catalogue are additional descriptions of some of the MSS (cols. 1141–1148), and corrections and additions (cols. 1149–1164). Concordances to the numbers in various collections and previous catalogues may be found on pp. xii–xxxii; for details, see the entries for the individual collections, herein. Indexes (cols. 917–1112, with additions in cols. 1133–1140 and corrections in cols. 1165–1168): authors, translators, family names, titles, scribes, owners, witnesses, censors and geographical places. *Cat. Neubauer, Addenda* (1994) was prepared by the staff of the *Jerusalem, IMHM, in *Jerusalem, NLI. In addition to corrections and additions, it includes palaeographical descriptions of all the MSS, prepared by M. Beit-Arié; and indexes of censors, dated MSS, localized MSS and autographs.

Cat. Neubauer–Cowley, II, describes MSS acquired between 1886 and 1906. In all, 150 MSS and 166 volumes holding 2,675 Geniza fragments are described in this volume. Many of the Geniza fragments were bought from Solomon *Wertheimer; others were acquired from Count Riamo d'Hulst, an excavator for the Egypt Exploration Fund in Cairo, from G. Chester between 1889 and 1892, and from A. H. Sayce; see R. J. W. Jefferson, 'A Genizah secret', *Journal of the History of Collections*, XXI [2009], pp. 125–142, and idem, 'The Cairo Genizah unearthed', in S. Bhayro and B. Outhwaite (eds.), *Cambridge Genizah Studies*, I: *Proceedings of the First International Conference on Genizah Studies, Westminster College*, Cambridge 2007, pp. 171–200. Most of the MSS were purchased from booksellers. Like the first volume, this catalogue is arranged by subject. At the head of each entry, the catalogue number (2603–2918) is printed in bold type, followed by the call-number in parentheses. Call-numbers in the second volume generally bear the prefix 'MS Heb.'. Palaeographical and codicological information is the same as in *Cat. Neubauer*. The folios in the volumes of Geniza fragments are numbered consecutively in each volume. At the beginning of the volume (pp. xii–xvi) is a concordance to the call-numbers, including the provenance of each MS. Indexes: a single index in Latin letters lists together persons (authors, scribes, owners, etc.) and place names. Names of authors are written in capital letters, and the other names are distinguished by a series of symbols (C = Censor, S = Scribe, etc.), listed at the bottom of each page in the index. A second index in Hebrew lists names, titles and place names. A list of dated MSS is found on pp. vii–xi. Corrections are found at the end of the volume. In addition to the MSS listed in the Neubauer–Cowley catalogues, about 175 Hebrew MSS, including 200 Geniza fragments and 50 Samaritan MSS, are listed in typewritten catalogues in the library. F. Madan, *A Summary Catalogue of Western Manuscripts in the Bodleian Library at Oxford*, I–V, Oxford 1905, lists all the MSS acquired by the Bodleian in chronological order. As all the Hebrew MSS had previously been described in Neubauer's catalogue, Madan supplied only call-numbers, references to *Cat. Neubauer* and the subject or title. In volume V, MSS acquired from 1853 on, the Hebrew MSS are listed by year of purchase in the 'Miscellaneous' section under 'Oriental Manuscripts'. The listings include the names of the owners or dealers from whom the MSS were acquired.

CALL-NUMBERS Until 1886, when *Cat. Neubauer* was published, MSS were referred to by the call-numbers of their collections (e.g., 'MS Opp. 237'), with few exceptions. Many of the call-numbers assigned to MSS acquired between 1853 and 1897 bear the prefix Opp. Add. (e.g., 'MS Opp. Add. 2° 1'), though they have nothing to do with the *Oppenheim collection. Similarly, MSS purchased from the **Hapalit* catalogue were assigned call-numbers with the prefix Mich. Add., though they have nothing to with the Michael collection. Some call-numbers were changed after the publication of *Cat. Neubauer* in 1886, and others were printed incorrectly. A list of corrections is found in *Cat. Neubauer–Cowley*, II, pp. 536–541. For further details concerning call-numbers, consult the entries for each collection, herein. After 1897, new acquisitions, except those belonging to special collections, were assigned call-numbers combining a letter from 'a' to 'g', according to the size of the volume (the largest are marked 'a' and the smallest 'g'), and a serial number (e.g., 'MS Heb. c. 4').

Rab., *Lit. Treas.*, pp. 27–37; Pearson, pp. 55–56; R. Judd, 'Hebrew collections in Oxford', in D. Rowland Smith and S. P. Salinger (eds.), *Hebrew Studies*, London 1991, pp. 6–12.

Oxford (England), College Libraries

Most of the Hebrew MSS belonging to the College libraries in Oxford are kept in the *Oxford, Bodleian Library, and were described in *Cat. Neubauer*. Following is a list of the college libraries owning Hebrew MSS and the numbers of the entries in *Cat. Neubauer* in which they are described:

Balliol College: 2438, 2542.

Christ Church College: 2444–2448, 2450–2458.

Corpus Christi College: 2435, 2440. MS Corpus Christi 133 was not described by Neubauer (see *KS*, LVI [1981], p. 741).

Jesus College: 2436.

Keble College: Three Hebrew and eight Samaritan MSS. not in *Cat. Neubauer*.

Lincoln College: 2544–2545.

Merton College: 2443, 2449. Hebrew starrs were described by Neubauer in *JQR*, II (1904), pp. 527–530.

Oriel College: 2437.

Pusey House: 3 MSS, not in *Cat. Neubauer*.

Radcliffe College: Benjamin *Kennicott's MSS, formerly in Radcliffe College, were acquired by *Oxford, Bodleian Library, in 1879. A list of the MSS, their old and new numbers and their numbers in *Cat. Neubauer* is found in the catalogue, p. xxv, and in *Cat. Neubauer–Cowley*, II, p. 540.

St. John's College: 2439 (described by P. E. Pormann, in E. Savage-Smith, *A Descriptive Catalogue of Oriental Manuscripts at St John's College*, Oxford 2005, no. 35).

Worcester College: 2441–2442.

Oxonia
Latin name for Oxford.

Ozimo
See *Osimo.

P

P
(1) Paris; (2) Parma.

Padova
See Padua.

Padua (Italy), Biblioteca della Comunità ebraica
Five MSS and six illuminated *ketubot* are described by Sonne in *Relazione*, but they are no longer in the library (Fumagalli, p. 77). One of the MSS, no. III, is now *New York, Public Library, **P (MS Heb. 225). A second MS, not described by Sonne, is also in the Public Library, **P (MS Heb. 224). Two of the *ketubot* (nos. 1 and 3) are now in the Jewish Museum in New York (JM 68–60 and F3799); no. 2 was, in the collection of M. H. Gans of Amsterdam and is now in a private collection; no. 4 was sold at Sotheby's in New York (*Property from the Delmonico Collection ... December 17, 2008*, lot 202); and no. 6 is in the collection of *ketubot* in *New York, JTSA (Ket. 49). The *Pinkas* of the Padua community remains in the community's possession (ד' קרפי, פנקס ועד ק"ק פאדוואה של"ח–שס"ג, ירושלים תשל"ד, עמ' 50).

Padua (Italy), Convento dei Canonici Regolari Lateranensi di S. Giovanni di Verdara
The eight Hebrew MSS formerly in the library were confiscated in 1784 by *Venice, Biblioteca Marciana.

Tamani, *Venezia*, p. 253; Tamani, *Padova*, p. 8.

Padua (Italy), Convento di S. Giustina
The Hebrew MSS formerly in the library, including those described by *Kennicott (nos. 559–560), were confiscated by the French in 1797 and are now *Paris, BnF, MSS héb. 4 and 85.

Tamani, *Padova*, p. 3.

Padua (Italy), Istituto Convitto Rabbinico
See *Rome, Collegio Rabbinico Italiano.

Padua (Italy), Bibliotheca S. Johan in Virdario
See *Padua, Convento ... di S. Giovanni di Verdara.

Padua (Italy), Bibliotheca S. Justinae Patrum Benedict
See *Padua, Convento di S. Giustina.

Padua (Italy), Seminario Vescovile
Seven MSS were described by G. Tamani in *Annali di Ca' Foscari*, vol. IX, no. 3 (1970), pp. 1–12.

Palatina
See (1) *Heidelberg, Biblioteca Palatina; (2) *Parma, Biblioteca Palatina.

Palit
See **Hapalit*.

Pamplona (Spain), Biblioteca de la Catedral

Two Hebrew MSS were listed in the hand-list of MSS in the library published by A. S. Hunt, 'The library of the Cathedral of Pamplona', *Zentralblatt für Bibliothekwesen*, XIV (1897), no. 17 on p. 286 and no. 67 on p. 290. One of these MSS, a Bible, remains in the library, while the other, MS Estante 6,21, also described by F. Baer, *Die Juden im christlichen Spanien*, Berlin 1929, pp. xvi–xvii, is now *New York, JTSA, MS 2341. There are also a number of documents, etc., relating to the Jews, in Hebrew or Spanish, in the library and in the Archivo Real y General de Navarra.

Pappenheim (Germany), Gräflich Pappenheim'sche Bibliothek

The fragments described in *Cat. Allony–Loewinger*, I, nos. 680–686, were transferred to the *Nuremberg, Staatsarchiv, in 1965.

Paris, Alliance Israélite Universelle (AIU)

Before World War II, the library's collection numbered about 500 MSS, including over 100 not in Hebrew. Many of the MSS came from the collections of Samuel David *Luzzatto and S. Munk. A number of MSS were lost during the Nazi occupation of France, when the Nazis confiscated the library's books. Two MSS, nos. 71–72, are now in *New York, JTSA. The library's collection now includes over 3,500 *Geniza fragments deposited in it by the Consistoire Israélite in 1945.

M. Schwab, 'Les manuscrits et incunables hébreux de la Bibliothèque de l'Alliance israélite', *REJ*, XLIX (1904), pp. 74–88, 270–294, described 230 MSS. This catalogue is arranged according to titles, in alphabetical order. At the head of each entry is the call-number of the MS. Palaeographical and codicological information: size (2°, 4°, 8°), number of leaves and type of script. An index of names is provided on pp. 287–292. On pp. 292–294, Judaica MSS in languages other than Hebrew are described. MSS 1–56 were described at greater length by B. Chapira, 'Les manuscrits de la Bibliothèque de l'Alliance israélite', *REJ*, CV (1939), pp. 53–79. The Geniza fragments of the Consistoire were described by Schwab, 'Les manuscrits du Consistoire israélite de Paris provenant de la Gueniza du Caire', *REJ*, LXII (1911), pp. 107–119, 267–277; LXIII (1911), pp. 100–120, 276–296; and LXIV (1912), pp. 118–141. The fragments are listed according to subject. The Roman numerals I–X refer to major subjects, the letters A, B, C, etc., to subdivisions in each subject. At the beginning of the catalogue is an explanation of all the numerals and letters. About 100 fragments in Arabic characters were not described. In 1979, the first volume of a catalogue of the Alliance's MSS was published, *Catalogue des Manuscrits de la Bibliothèque*, I: *Manuscrits Judaica (non-hébraïques) N° 103 à 522*, with a historical introduction by Georges J. Weill, Paris 1979. Only non-Hebrew Judaica MSS are described, but the numbers of the Hebrew MSS in the library are listed. The catalogue also includes a list of missing MSS, from which the recently rediscovered nos. 89, 90, 101, 370 and 428 should be deleted. In *REJ*, X (1885), pp. 248–250, and XVI (1888), pp. 28–56, I. Loeb described four MSS of works by Joseph Hakohen that were to be acquired by the Alliance library. Two of the MSS are indeed in the Alliance, but two are not: The first, described in *REJ*, X, was eventually acquired by Moses *Gaster and is now *London, BL, MS Or. 10387; and the third, a collection of letters described by I. Loeb, 'Joseph Haccohen et les chroniqueurs juifs', *REJ*, XVI (1888), pp. 28–56 and 211–235, was loaned to David *Kaufmann shortly before he passed away. In a footnote to his article 'Lettres de Scheschet b. Isaac …', *REJ*, XXXIX (1899), p. 62, Kaufmann thanked the

Alliance for lending him the MS (I thank my colleague A. David for calling my attention to this reference). After Kaufmann's death the MS was presented, together with the other books in his collection, to the *Budapest, Hungarian Academy of Sciences, where it has remained (MS A 332). A new series of catalogues of the Hebrew MSS in libraries in France, *Manuscrits en caractères hébreux conservés dans les bibliothèques de France*, supervised by Colette Sirat and published by the Bibliothèque nationale de France and the Institut de Recherche et d'Histoire des Textes (CNRS), is in preparation, with two volumes published as of this writing. Volume II, Michele Dukan, *Fragments bibliques en hébreu provenant de guenizot*, Turnhout 2008, describes biblical fragments from the *Geniza, including some in the AIU. The text of each fragment is identified, full codicological and palaeographical descriptions are provided, and a high-quality facsimile of each fragment is included. (On Volume I, see *Paris, Bibliothèque nationale de France.)

Paris, Bibliothèque de l'Arsenal

Most of the Hebrew MSS in the library were transferred in 1860 to *Paris, Bibliothèque nationale de France. Today, only two Hebrew MSS (nos. 8863 and 8864) and one fragment (no. 449) remain in the library.

Paris, Bibliothèque imperiale

See *Paris, Bibliothèque nationale de France.

Paris, Bibliothèque Mazarine

Library of Cardinal Jules Mazarin (1602–1661). In 1668, the library was obliged by the Minister of Finance, Jean-Baptiste *Colbert, to transfer MSS, including 102 Hebrew MSS, to the Royal Library (now *Paris, Bibliothèque nationale de France) in exchange for duplicates. Only a few Hebrew MSS remain in the library. Five of them, bearing old call-numbers, were described by M. Schwab, 'Manuscrits hébreux de la bibliothèque Mazarine', *REJ*, XI (1885), pp. 158–159. In the section 'Manuscrits hébreux' in *Catalogue des manuscrits de la Bibliothèque Mazarine*, III, Paris 1890, seven MSS are listed, nos. 4472–4478 (the present call-numbers), including one containing Christian prayers (no. 4473) and one a printed text with Latin notes (no. 4475).

Paris, Bibliothèque nationale de France (BnF)

Formerly the Royal Library and, after the French Revolution, the Imperial Library. Until 1599, the old royal collection (ancien fonds) included no more than 30 Hebrew MSS. When the Royal Library was merged with the library of Catherine de Medici in 1599, the collection was enriched with about 20 additional Hebrew MSS, mostly acquired from *Egidio da Viterbo. In the seventeenth century the library acquired Hebrew MSS from Cardinal *Richelieu and others. In 1668 the library exchanged books with the Mazarin library (see *Paris, Bibliothèque Mazarine), thus adding 102 Hebrew MSS to its collection. An additional 127 Hebrew MSS in the Gilbert Gaulmin library were acquired a few years later. In 1732, with the purchase of the *Colbert collection, which included 171 Hebrew manuscripts, the number of Hebrew MSS, many of them originating in the Near East, rose to 645. After the French Revolution many libraries associated with the Catholic church were confiscated and deposited in the Imperial Library. Thus were acquired the Hebrew MSS of the libraries of *Paris, Oratoire (207 MSS, many from Constantinople), *Paris, Sorbonne (258 MSS from the Cardinal Richelieu collection) and *Paris, Bibliothèque St. Germain-des-Prés (34 MSS). In 1860, Hebrew MSS from *Paris, Ste. Geneviève and *Paris, Bibliothèque de l'Arsenal were deposited in the Bibliothèque nationale. Today the number of Hebrew MSS in the library is close to 1,550 (including over 60 Samaritan MSS).

A short history of the Hebrew MSS collection appears at the beginning of *Catalogues des manuscrits hébreux et samaritains de la Bibliothèque Imperiale*, Paris 1866, in which 1,313 Hebrew MSS and 11 Samaritan MSS are described. The catalogue was edited by H. Zotenberg, who used the unpublished partial catalogues of A. Franck, J. *Derenbourg and S. Munk. These catalogues and others are found in the library (MSS héb. 1295–1307). The 1866 catalogue is arranged according to subject. The catalogue numbers at the head of each entry also serve as the present call-numbers, with the addition of the prefix 'MS héb.'. Old numbers are listed in parentheses at the end of each entry. The number of leaves in each MS is not indicated, but in the descriptions of MSS including more than one work the folio number on which each work begins is given. Palaeographical and codicological information: writing material, size (small, medium or large) and date. Indexes: subjects, titles and authors. M. Steinschneider added indexes to scribes and other names, and concordances to the old numbers, in *ZfHB*, VI (1902), pp. 83–90, 108–112, 147–156, 191. Corrections and notes on the Kabbala MSS were printed by G. Scholem in *KS*, XXIV (1947/8), pp. 250–257. MSS 1314–1415 were described by M. Schwab, *REJ*, XXXVII (1898), pp. 127–136; LXI (1911), pp. 82–87; LXIV (1912), pp. 153–156, 280–281; and LXVI (1913), pp. 290–296. MSS 1457–1459 and some fragments were described by I. Adler, *REJ*, CXXI (1962), pp. 194–209. S. Munk described many of the Hebrew MSS in the Oratoire collection in 'Manuscrits hébreux de l'Oratoire à la Bibliothèque nationale de Paris', *ZfHB*, XI–XIV (1907–1910), and his catalogue was published as a separate publication under the same title (Frankfurt a/M 1911). Dated Hebrew MSS (until 1540) were described in *Manuscrits médiévaux en caractères hébraïques*, I–III, Paris–Jerusalem 1972–1986. Samaritan MSS were described by J.-P. Rothschild in *Catalogue des manuscrits samaritains*, Paris 1985. Philosophical, scientific, kabbalistic and some other MSS were described by Georges Vajda in a handwritten, unpublished catalogue preserved in the library, with a photocopy in the *Jerusalem, IMHM. A new series of catalogues of the Hebrew manuscripts in libraries in France, *Manuscrits en caractères hébreux conservés dans les bibliothèques de France*, supervised by Colette Sirat and published by the BnF and the Institut de Recherche et d'Histoire des Textes (CNRS), is in preparation, with five volumes published as of this writing: I: Philippe Bobichon, *Bibliothèque nationale de France: Hébreu 669 à 703, Manuscrits de théologie*, on the basis of notes by Georges Vajda, Turnhout 2008; III: S. Di Donato, *Bibliothèque nationale de France: Hébreu 214 à 259, Commentaires bibliques*, Turnhout 2011; IV: J. Del Barco, *Bibliothèque nationale de France: Hébreu 1 à 32, Manuscrits de la bible hèbraïque*, Turnhout 2011; V: Philippe Bobichon, *Bibliothèque Nationale de France: Hébreu 704 à 733, Manuscrits de théologie*, Turnhout 2013; and VI: Cristina Ciucu, *Bibliothèque Nationale de France: Hébreu 763 à 788, Manuscrits Cabalistiques*, Turnhout 2013. The entries are very detailed, more so than in any previous catalogue of Hebrew manuscripts. Each entry is preceded by a colour facsimile of an opening from the manuscript, reproduced on facing pages. The entries include: number of leaves, material, size, place, date, general physical description, author, title in French and Hebrew, followed by four units: I: a detailed codicological description, including material (paper and/or parchment), composition of quires, exact dimensions, pricking, ruling, script, ink and another original-size facsimile of a few lines of script; II: a more detailed description of the text, including incipits, excipits and bibliography; III: provenance and history of the MS, former class-marks, type of binding; IV: additional remarks. There is one alphabetical index of names, titles, places, etc., all in Latin letters. (For volume II, see *Paris, AIU.)

Paris, Bibliothecae Regiae
Latin name for the Imperial Library in Paris, now *Paris, Bibliothèque nationale de France.

Paris, Bibliothèque Ste. Geneviève
The Hebrew MSS in this library were transferred to *Paris, Bibliothèque nationale de France, in 1860.

Paris, Bibliothèque St. Germain-des-Prés
During the French Revolution the MSS in this library, including 34 in Hebrew, were transferred to the Imperial Library in Paris (now *Paris, Bibliothèque nationale de France). A concordance to the old numbers in the St. Germain library and the 1866 Bibliothèque nationale catalogue numbers, which are also the present call-numbers, was made by Steinschneider in *ZfHB*, VI (1902), p. 156.

Paris, Collège de Clermont (Collège Louis-le-Grand)
Twelve Hebrew MSS were listed in F. Clement, *Catalogus Manuscriptorum Codicum Collegii Claromontani*, Paris 1764, nos. I–IV and VI–XIII, and three in *Catalogus Manuscriptorum Codicum Bibliothecae Domus Professae Pariensis* (appended to the previous catalogue), nos. I–III. The MSS of Clermont College were sold when the college was suppressed, in the same year the catalogue appeared following the ban on the Jesuit order in 1762. Six of the MSS (nos. I, II, VI, VII, X and XIII) were acquired by Gerard *Meerman and passed on to his son Johan M. Meerman. The younger Meerman sold these MSS to Thomas *Phillipps, whose collection was later sold at a series of public auctions. Most of the information concerning the Clermont MSS was communicated by J.-P. Rothschild of Paris. For the present locations of some of the MSS see Appendix 1, no. 31.

H. Omont, 'Documents sur la vente des manuscrits du Collège de Clermont à Paris (1764)', *Bulletin de la Societé de l'histoire de Paris et de l'Ille-de-France*, XVIII (1891), pp. 7–15.

Paris, Consistoire israélite
The collection of the Consistoire, including over 3,500 *Geniza fragments, was deposited in *Paris, AIU in 1945.

Paris, École rabbinique
See *Paris, Séminaire israélite de France.

Paris, Institut de France
In *Catalogue général des manuscrits des bibliothèques publiques de France: Bibliothèque de l'Institut*, Paris 1928, one Hebrew MS is listed (no. 1766). Among the papers of Joseph and Hartwig *Derenbourg (nos. 3371–3405) are some copies of Hebrew MSS and a volume of 49 *Geniza fragments (no. 3381).

Paris, Institut national des langues et civilisations orientales
Forty-eight MSS bequeathed by Abraham *Danon were described by S. Kerner, 'Les manuscrits hébreux du "Fonds Danon" de la Bibliothèque de l'Institut National des Langues et Civilisations Orientales', *Bulletin des Bibliothèques de France*, XXII (1977), pp. 449–460.

Paris, Musée de Cluny
The items described in the privately printed catalogue of the collection of Isaac *Strauss by George Stenne (pseudonym of D. Schornstein), *Collection de M. Strauss: Description des objets d'art religieux hébraïques exposés*

dans les galeries du Trocadéro à l'exposition universelle de 1878, Poissy 1878, were purchased by Baron Nathaniel de *Rothschild and presented to the Musée de Cluny. The Strauss collection included a siddur (no. 70 in the catalogue, now Cl. 12290), two *ketubot* (nos. 74–75, now Cl. 12294–95), a wedding poem (no. 100, now Cl. 12311) and five Esther scrolls (nos. 76–80, now Cl. 12296a–e, and 149, now Cl. 12263). The museum's collection also includes seven additional Esther scrolls acquired from Isaac Camondo and others, and another siddur (Cl. 13995) presented to the museum by Rodolphe Kann. The two siddurs were described by M. Schwab, 'Manuscrits hébreux du Musée de Cluny', *REJ*, L (1905), pp. 136–139, and a number of illuminated Esther scrolls and marriage contracts were described in 'Documents hébreux du Musée de Cluny', *REJ*, LXI (1911), pp. 294–296. All these items were described by V. Klagsbald in *Catalogue raisonné de la collection juive du Musée de Cluny*, Paris 1981.

Paris, Oratoire

The library of the Oratoire includes 207 Hebrew MSS, some formerly in the possession of the Karaite scholar Caleb Afendopolo, who died in 1525 in Constantinople. Almost all the MSS came from the collection of Achille de Harlay de Sancy (1581–1646), former French ambassador in Constantinople, where about half the collection was purchased. The Oratoire was closed in 1791 during the French Revolution, and in 1796 the MSS were transferred to the Imperial Library (now *Paris, Bibliothèque nationale de France). Nos. 1–159 were described in a handwritten catalogue by S. Munk (BnF, MS héb 1298). All the MSS, together with the other Hebrew MSS in the Bibliothèque nationale, were described in *Catalogues des manuscrits hébreux et samaritains de la Bibliothèque imperiale*, Paris 1866 (see Paris, Bibliothèque nationale de France), and some were described separately, in greater detail, by S. Munk in a series of articles in *ZfHB*, XI–XIV (1907–1910; reprinted as *Manuscrits hébreux de l'Oratoire à la Bibliothèque nationale de Paris*, Frankfurt a/M 1911). A concordance to the Oratoire numbers and the 1866 Bibliothèque nationale catalogue numbers, which are also the present call-numbers, was made by M. Steinschneider in *ZfHB*, VI (1902), pp. 153, 191.

Pearson, p. 10; F. Richard, 'Achille de Harlay de Sancy et ses collections de manuscrits hébreux', *REJ*, CXLIX (1990), pp. 417–447.

Paris, Séminaire israélite de France (École rabbinique)

The library has a collection of 193 MSS, numbered 1–208, a few of them in French. Before World War II the library had 179 MSS (nos. 1–178, N.C. 1). A number of MSS were lost during the war; some have since been found, but at present 15 MSS are still missing: nos. 7, 76, 77, 111, 114, 125, 138–140, 154, 163, 165–167 and 173 (information from Gila Prebor). Meyer Abraham Halevy described 142 MSS in 'Catalogue des manuscrits de l'École Rabbinique de France', in *REJ*, LXXIX (1924), pp. 1–27, and added a supplement in *REJ*, LXXX (1925), pp. 81–87. This catalogue is arranged according to subject, and the catalogue numbers, written in Roman numerals, are identical with the present call-numbers. The MSS of the Séminaire that were removed for safekeeping in the 1990s to the library of the *Paris, AIU, have since been returned to the Séminaire.

Paris, Société des manuscrits des assureurs français

The society owns manuscripts produced in France or by French authors. It includes four Hebrew MSS formerly in the *Sassoon collection (nos. 280, 495, 683, 706). These MSS were described by M. Garel in the exhibit catalogue *Manuscrits du Moyen-Âge et manuscrits littéraires modernes*, Paris 2001.

Paris, Sorbonne

Before the French Revolution there were 258 Hebrew MSS in the Sorbonne library, all of them from the collection of Cardinal *Richelieu. During the Revolution most of the MSS were transferred to the Imperial Library (now *Paris, Bibliothèque nationale de France). Today the Sorbonne retains only three Hebrew MSS and a few fragments. A concordance of the Sorbonne numbers and the Bibliothèque nationale numbers was made by Steinschneider in *ZfHB*, VI (1902), pp. 154–155, 191.

Parma (Italy), Biblioteca Palatina

The great majority of the 1,591 Hebrew MSS in the Palatina library in Parma come from the collection of Giovanni de *Rossi, which was purchased for the library by Princess Maria Luisa of Austria in 1816 and numbers 1,432 MSS. Next in size is the collection of 111 MSS purchased by Maria Luisa for the library in 1846 from Salomon *Stern and Mordecai *Bislisches. In addition to these collections the library possesses about 50 other MSS acquired in the eighteenth and nineteenth centuries. All the MSS have been given new call-numbers in the library (MSS Parm. 1679–3356).

DE ROSSI COLLECTION In *Cat. de Rossi* (1803), de Rossi himself described most of his Hebrew MSS. The catalogue, which describes MSS nos. 1–1377, is written in Latin and is arranged according to the numbers de Rossi assigned to his MSS without regard to subject matter. At the end of the catalogue a number of MSS in other languages are described, ten of them written in Hebrew characters (Ital. 1, 2, 5, 6, 7, Hisp. 5, Jud.-Germ. 1–2, Pol. 1–2). Palaeographical and codicological information: writing material, type of script, size (8°, 4°, 2°) and date or estimated date. Corrections and notes on the catalogue were published by P. Perreau in *Bolletino Italiano degli Studi Orientale*, I (1876/7) and II (1877–82), and by L. Zunz, *Gesammelte Schriften*, III, Berlin 1876, pp. 5–13. A few corrections by H. M. *Horowitz were recorded by M. Higger (מ׳ היגר, ׳הנגלות והנסתרות׳, ספר היובל לכבוד ... אלכסנדר מארכס, ניו יורק תש״ג, עמ׳ 66–63). MSS nos. 1378–1432 were briefly described by de Rossi in his *Libri Stampati di Letteratura Sacra Ebraica ed Orientale della Biblioteca del Dottore G. B. de Rossi*, Parma 1812, pp. 79–82, and by P. Perreau in German, with notes by M. Steinschneider, in *HB*, X (1870), pp. 96–104, and XII (1872), pp. 31–37, 53–57, 104–120. Later, Perreau published his descriptions in Italian in *Cataloghi*, II (1880), pp. 111–152. In the entries for the De Rossi collection, the catalogue number appears at the head of each entry, followed in square brackets by the present call-number in the library and the number in the collection. There is no concordance to the various numbers in the catalogue. Palaeographical and codicological information: writing material, size, number of leaves, number of lines per page, type of script and date. A single set of indexes to the MSS in all the libraries described in the six preceding volumes of the *Cataloghi* was published separately on pp. 675–698 in Vol. VII (1904). The MSS are indexed by titles, authors, scribes, owners, etc., place names and censors.

STERN COLLECTION The greater part of this collection of 111 MSS, purchased in 1846 from S. G. Stern and M. Bislisches, derives from the collection of the bookseller Moses *Foa. The MSS in the collection were described by Stern himself in a handwritten list compiled in 1847, but this description was never published and remains in manuscript in the Parma library (MS Parm. 3558). Other handwritten catalogues of this collection are found in MSS *Warsaw, ŻIH, 311, and *New York, JTSA, MS 2809 (formerly in the *Halberstamm collection). The collection was first described in print by P. Perreau, 'Hebräische Handschriften in Parma', *HB*, VII (1864), pp. 66–68, 114–120, 134–136; and VIII (1865), pp. 26–30, 62–69, 95–103, 122–125, 146–150. The description is in German with notes by M. Steinschneider. This list is arranged according to subject, and MSS containing a number of works on different subjects are described in two or more entries, so that the total number of entries (121) is larger than the number of MSS (111). At the head of each entry the catalogue number is listed, followed by the Stern collection number in parentheses. Perreau published another catalogue of the collection in Italian in *Cataloghi*, II, pp. 153–194. In the entries for the Stern collection, which are arranged and numbered differently than in the German description, the catalogue number at the head of each entry is followed in square brackets by the Stern collection number and the present call-number in Parma.

Sixty-nine other MSS (including 17 Tora and Esther scrolls) were described by G. Tamani in 'I manoscritti ebraici della Biblioteca Palatina di Parma', *Studi sull'Oriente e la Bibbia*, Genoa 1967, pp. 201–226. Many of these MSS had previously been described in other publications. Tamani described (1) 32 MSS in the old collection of the Palatina Library, acquired during the years 1762–1769, of which 29 had previously been described by Perreau in *HB*, VII (1864), pp. 66–68, 114–118; (2) 19 MSS that belonged to Pietro Vitali, acquired in 1828, 7 of which had been described by Perreau in *Cataloghi*, II, pp. 195–196, nos. 1–3, 5–8; (3) 4 MSS in the Fondo Palatino; (4) 4 MSS in the Salomone Betesh-Levi collection; and (5) 10 MSS in various other collections. Tamani also described 50 medical MSS in the Parma library in 'Inventario dei manoscritti ebraici di argomento medico della biblioteca Palatina di Parma', *La Bibliofilia*, LXIX (1967), pp. 245–276; and 222 illuminated MSS in 'Elenco dei manoscritti ebraici miniati e decorati della "Palatina" di Parma', *ibid.*, LXX (1968), pp. 39–136.

Cat. Richler, Parma, a new catalogue with descriptions of all the MSS, compiled by the staff of the *Jerusalem, IMHM, was issued in 2001. The catalogue is arranged by subject and includes entries numbered 1–1591. It includes 'The history of the collection' by Giulano Tamani on pp. xix–xxvii. Palaeographical and codicological information: number of leaves, writing material, size, size of written area, place, date, type of writing, colophons, owners' entries and censors. Indexes: Persons, censors, subjects, place names, dated MSS, illuminated and decorated MSS, quoted MSS, concordances to Parma call-marks and previous catalogue numbers, Hebrew place names, titles (in Hebrew) and poems (in Hebrew).

Parma A

This is the name given to a Mishna MS in *Parma, Biblioteca Palatina, MS Parm. 3173 (de Rossi 138, *Cat. Richler*, Parma, 710). Parma B is Mishna MS Parm. 2596 (de Rossi 497, *Cat. Richler*, Parma, 711), and Parma C is MS Parm. 3174 (de Rossi 984, *Cat. Richler*, Parma, 713).

Parma Bible

Name given to *Parma, Biblioteca Palatina, MS Parm. 3286–3287 (de Rossi 440, *Cat. Richler*, Parma, 7), a fourteenth-century illuminated Bible written in Ashkenaz.

Narkiss, p. 112.

Parma Haggada

Name given to *Parma, Biblioteca Palatina, MS Parm. 2411 (de Rossi 1107, *Cat. Richler*, Parma, 1123), an illuminated Spanish haggada, and to MS Parm. 2998 (de Rossi 111, *Cat. Richler*, Parma, 1120), an illuminated haggada attributed to *Joel b. Simeon.

Pasini, Giuseppe

Padua, 1687 – Turin, 1770

Pasini compiled a catalogue of MSS in the Royal Library in Turin (now *Biblioteca Nazionale Universitaria). A concordance to the Pasini catalogue numbers and those of *Cat. Peyron*, as well as to the present call-numbers, is found on pp. xli–xlvi of *Cat. Peyron*.

Cat. Peyron, pp. xv–xix.

Patavium

Latin name for Padua.

Pb

Petersburg.

Peiresc, Nicolas-Claude Fabri de

1580–1637; French astronomer

Several Samaritan MSS owned by Peiresc are now in *Paris, Bibliothèque nationale de France (MSS sam. 1, 5, 8–11).

PER

Papyrus-Sammlung Erzherzog Rainer. See *Rainer.

Pérez Bayer, Francisco

Valencia, Spain, 1711–1794; Canon Treasurer of the Metropolitan Church of Toledo

*Kennicott listed six biblical MSS belonging to Bayer (Pérez Bayer) in nos. 293–298, but their present whereabouts are unknown. Pérez Bayer donated a Pentateuch with a Spanish translation, presented to him by *Tychsen, to the Royal Library in Madrid (now *Madrid, Biblioteca Nacional MS 5468).

Peringer, Gustaf

Strängäs, Sweden, 1651 – Stockholm, Sweden, 1710; from 1693, von Lillieblad; Swedish orientalist

Peringer's collection is now in the Universitetsbibliothek in *Lund.

Steinschneider, *Vorlesungen*, p. 81 (Hebrew, p. 105).

Perl, Joseph

Tarnopol, Ukraine, 1773–1839; writer

Perl's library was transferred after his death to the school in *Tarnopol that bore his name.

Perpignan Bible

Name given to *Paris, BnF, MS héb. 7, an illuminated Bible written in Perpignan in 1299.

Perr.

*Perreau, Pietro.

Perreau, Pietro

Piacenza, Italy, 1827 – Parma, Italy, 1911

Perreau compiled catalogues of the de *Rossi MSS in *Parma, Biblioteca Palatina, that had not been described in *Cat. de Rossi*, and of the MSS in the *Stern collection in Parma.

Perrins, Charles William Dyson

Claines, England, 1864 – Malvern, England, 1958; bibliophile

An illuminated haggada written by *Joel ben Simeon, formerly in the Dyson Perrins collection, is now Cod. Bodmer 81 in the Bibliotheca Bodmeriana of the Foundation Martin Bodmer in Cologny-Genève, Switzerland.

J. Gutmann, 'Thirteen manuscripts in search of an author: Joel Ben Simeon, 15th century scribe-artist', *Studies in Bibliography and Booklore*, IX (1969–1971), p. 93, n. 6.

Perr. Stern

Perreau–Stern. Refers to the catalogue compiled by Pietro *Perreau of the MSS from the *Stern collection in *Parma, Biblioteca Palatina.

Pesaro Maḥzor

Name given to MS *Sassoon 23, an illuminated maḥzor written in Pesaro in 1480 (= de Rossi, *ext.*, no. 15). The MS was purchased by the Safra family in São Paolo.

Narkiss, p. 146.

Petermann, Julius Heinrich

Glauchau, Germany, 1801 – Bad Nauheim, Germany, 1876; orientalist

A number of Samaritan MSS belonging to Petermann are now in *Berlin, Staatsbibliothek.

Petersburg

St. Petersburg.

Petrie, William Matthew Flinders

London, 1853 – Jerusalem, 1942

Five papyri were purchased from Petrie by the British Museum (now *London, British Library) in 1922 (MS Or. 9180).

Petropolitanus Codex

Petropolitanus is the Latin name for Petersburg (Leningrad). Codex Petropolitanus is the name given to *St. Petersburg, NLR MS Firkovich I Bibl. 3, a codex of the Later Prophets with Babylonian vocalization dated 916. A facsimile edition (reconstructed, not photographically reproduced) was published by H. L. Strack, *Prophetarum Posteriorum Codex Babylonicus Petropolitanus*, Petersburg 1876 (repr. New York 1971).

Pettigrew, Thomas Joseph

London, 1795–1861; antiquarian

Pettigrew compiled a catalogue of the books and MSS in the library of the Duke of *Sussex.

Petty-Fitzmaurice, Sir William

1st Marquess of Lansdowne; Dublin, Ireland, 1737 – London, 1805; Prime Minister of England

In 1807 the Marquess's collection, including one Hebrew MS and four charters, was purchased by the British Museum (now *London, British Library). A list of the MSS is found in *Cat. Margoliouth–Leveen*, IV, p. 163. See also *ibid.*, p. vi.

Peyron, Bernardino

Turin, Italy, 1828–1903; orientalist

Peyron compiled a catalogue (= *Cat. Peyron*) of the Hebrew MSS in *Turin, Biblioteca Nazionale Universitaria. Six of his own MSS are now in that library.

Pfeiffer, Augustus

Erlangen, Germany, 1748–1817; orientalist

A Yiddish MS of Pfeiffer's was formerly *Königsberg, Stadtbibliothek, MS S 44 8°.

Pfersee MS

Name given to *Munich, BSB, Cod. hebr. 95, the earliest complete MS of the Babylonian Talmud. The MS was formerly in the possession of the Ulma-Günzburg family in Pfersee. Another collection in Pfersee belonged to Low Simon *Ulman.

Pforzheimer, Carl H.

New York, 1879–1957; bibliophile

Pforzheimer presented two MSS to *New York, JTSA.

Register, 5700, p. 16 (Marx, *Bibl. Studies*, p. 294).

P. Heid.

Papyrus-Sammlung der Universitat *Heidelberg.

Philadelphia (Pa.), CAJS

See *Philadelphia, University of Pennsylvania, Herman D. Katz Center for Advanced Judaic Studies.

Philadelphia (Pa.), Dropsie College

See *Philadelphia, CAJS.

Philadelphia (Pa.), Free Library

Six Hebrew MSS were described by M. A. Simsar in *Oriental Manuscripts of the John Frederick Lewis Collection in the Free Library of Philadelphia*, Philadelphia 1937; see *Lewis, John Frederick.

Philadelphia (Pa.), University of Pennsylvania, Herbert D. Katz Center for Advanced Judaic Studies (CAJS); and University Museum

Formerly Dropsie College for Hebrew and Cognate Learning and, from 1986 to 1993, the Annenberg Research Institute. In 1993 the Institute merged with the School of Arts and Sciences of the University of Pennsylvania to form its Center for Judaic Studies. The Center was renamed the Center for Advanced Judaic Studies in 1998. The Dropsie College library's collection included 42 Hebrew MSS (recently renumbered HB 1–42), a number of scrolls, 45 Samaritan MSS and over 450 *Geniza fragments. Most of the MSS and fragments were donated by Mayer *Sulzberger and Cyrus *Adler. J. Reider compiled a catalogue of the library's MSS in 1933, but it has never been published. Most of the Geniza fragments are described in B. Halper, *Descriptive Catalogue of Genizah Fragments in Philadelphia*, Philadelphia 1924, nos. 1–487. Twenty-one fragments in the University Museum were described by S. D. Goitein, 'The Geniza collection of the University Museum of the University of Pennsylvania', *JQR*, XLIX (1958/9), pp. 35–52.

The Geniza fragments are accessible for viewing on the Center's website (http://sceti.library.upenn.edu/genizah/index.cfm). The fragments given the following numbers in Halper's catalogue are missing: 11, 13, 97 (photostat copies of this MS are found in CAJS), 203, 347, 449, 479, 482, 486. Halper no. 471 is now RAR MS 73 in CAJS, and no. 441 is RAR MS 47 (e-communication from CAJS). The library continues to add to its MSS collection and recently purchased a number of Hebrew MSS listed in *Fine Judaica: Printed Books, Manuscripts & Graphic Art to be Sold at Auction by Kestenbaum & Company on December 9, 2011*, lots 300, 302, 308 and 321 (formerly *Newton Center, Hebrew College, MSS nos. 27, 29, 34, 35, 39, 41, 42, 44, 45 and 49).

The Rare Book and Manuscript Library of the University includes some Hebrew MSS, mainly from the collection of Lawrence J. *Schoenberg.

Pearson, p. 72.

Philadelphia (Pa.), Young Men's Hebrew Association (YMHA)

David *Amram presented six *Geniza fragments to the YMHA library. They are now in *Philadelphia, CAJS.

Phillipps, Thomas

England, 1792–1872; collector

Phillipps owned a very large library on his estate in Cheltenham. He purchased the greater part of the Gerard *Meerman collection at auction. The Phillipps collection was sold in parts at auctions beginning in 1891, the final sale taking place in the early 1980s. The German government bought most of the Meerman collection, and one Hebrew MS (Phillipps 1392) was presented to the *Berlin, Staatsbibliothek. Another Hebrew MS was offered for sale at Sotheby's November 1966 auction.

Pia Casa dei Neofiti

See *Rome, Pia Casa dei Neofiti.

Piacenza (Italy), Biblioteca Comunale Passerini Landi

Five Hebrew MSS were described in Tamani, *Piacenza* (1969).

Piacenza (Italy), Bibliothecae Patrum Praedicatorum

The MS from this library described in de Rossi, *ext.*, no. 28, was later in the *Landi collection and is now *Piacenza, Biblioteca Comunale, MS Landi 181.

Pico della Mirandola, Giovanni

Mirandola, Italy, 1463 – Florence, Italy, 1494; Italian Renaissance humanist

Pico was interested in Kabbala and other Jewish studies, and he acquired about 100 Hebrew MSS. Two inventories of Pico's library were published, the earlier one by P. Kibre, *The Library of Pico della Mirandola*, New York 1936, pp. 37–48, and the later one by F. Calori Cesis, *Memorie Storiche della Città e dell'Antico Ducato della Mirandola*, XI (1897), pp. 31–76. J. Gaffarel described three Kabbala MSS used by Pico, at the end of Vol. I of Johann Christoph Wolf's *Biblioteca Hebraea*, Hamburg 1715. Cardinal *Grimani purchased a large number of Hebrew MSS from Pico's estate in 1498 (see his entry for the present locations of some of Grimani's MSS). A joint project by the Institut für Judaistik of the Freie Universität in Berlin and the Istituto Nazionale di Studi sul Rinascimento in Florence, 'The Kabbalistic Library of Giovanni Pico della Mirandola', edited by G. Busi, is publishing texts from Pico's library. To date, four volumes have appeared: *The Great Parchment*, Turin 2004; *The Book of Bahir*, Turin 2005; Menaḥem Recanati, *Commentary on the Daily Prayers*, Turin 2008; and Joseph Giqatilla, *The Book of Punctuation*, Turin 2010.

Pinner, Ephraim Moses

Pinne, Poland, c. 1800 – Berlin, 1880; scholar

Thirty-six MSS are listed in the catalogue of Pinner's library, Berlin 1861–1870, in Hebrew, with no title page. Six MSS whose present whereabouts are unknown are described on p. 1. Thirty other MSS (numbered 1–30) are described in the Appendix on pp. 51–73. MS no. 1 in the Appendix is now MS *Moscow, RSL, Günzburg 946. No. 7 seems to be MS *London, BL, Or. 12254 (*Gaster 1073), or the source from which the BL MS was copied. MSS from Pinner's estate were acquired by *Berlin, Staatsbibliothek (*Cat. Steinschneider*, Berlin, II, p. iii), including MSS Berlin, Cods. Or. 2° 1210–1224, 4° 678–700 and 8° 353–357. Nos. 17–30 in the Appendix – mainly broadsheets and individual leaves – are bound in Cod. Or. 2° 1267. A number of fragments are found in *Munich, BSB, Cod. hebr. 436. One MS is now *Manchester, John Rylands University Library, MS Gaster 59. Pinner compiled a catalogue of the MSS in *Odessa, Society for History and Antiquities.

Pinsker, Simha

Tarnow, Poland, 1801 – Odessa, Ukraine, 1864; scholar

Pinsker's MSS were described in the 1869 catalogue of his estate by J. Bardach (מזכיר לבני רש״ף, והוא רשימה מקבוצי וכתבי יד הנשארים מעזבון ... ר׳ שמחה פינסקער, מאת יהודה ברד״ח, וינה תרכ״ט). Nos. 1–15: complete MSS; nos. 16–20: fragments; nos. 21–54: transcriptions made by Pinsker from other MSS; nos. 55–103: Pinsker's writings. Most of Pinsker's MSS came into the possession of the *Vienna, Israelitisch-theologische Lehranstalt, and, together with the other MSS in the Lehranstalt, were acquired by the *Vienna, Israelitische Kultusgemeinde. Many of the MSS disappeared after Pinsker's death and never reached the Lehranstalt (*Cat. Schwarz*, Austria, foreword). Seven MSS are listed in *Cat. Schwarz*, Austria, and other MSS are found in various libraries. For the present or last-known locations of some the MSS see Appendix I, no. 32.

The MS of Bardach's catalogue is now in Harvard University (MS Heb. 52). In addition to the fragment from the Koran, a number of fragments from a Tora scroll are now in *Halle, Bibliothek der DMG (*Cat. Striedl–Róth*, nos. 165, 174).

Pisa (Italy), Biblioteca Universitaria

Four Hebrew MSS, five MSS of translations

of Hebrew texts into Latin and a Hebrew grammar in Latin are described by A. Vivian, 'I manoscritti ebraici della Biblioteca Universitaria di Pisa', *Egitto e Vicino Oriente*, II (1979), pp. 93–100.

Pitigliano (Italy), Comunità ebraica

Seven of the eleven MSS formerly in the library are now in *Jerusalem, NLI. In 1970, when the Jewish Community library was closed, the collection was removed to the local Biblioteca Comunale e Consiglio (Biblioteca Comunale Zuccarelli), which is no longer open to the public. According to G. Tamani, 'Collections in Europe', in D. Rowland Smith and S. P. Salinger (eds.), *Hebrew Studies*, London 1991, p. 53, there may be Hebrew MSS in the library.

Pius VI

1717–1799; Pope

A Bible in two volumes that had belonged to cardinal Carlo Camillo Massimo (1620–1677) was presented to Pope Pius VI by Francesco Camillo Massimo (1730–1801). In 1797 the MS was seized by the French forces from the Pope's residence in Rome and in 1798 it was deposited in the Bibliothèque imperiale (now *Paris, Bibliothèque nationale de France), where it was assigned the call-numbers MS héb 17–18.

De Rossi, *ext.*, p. cxxvi, no. 1; M. Garel, *D'une main forte*, Paris 1991, no. 117.

Placentia

Latin name for Piacenza.

Pn.

*Paris, Bibliothèque nationale de France.

Poc.

*Pococke.

Pococke, Edward

Oxford, England, 1604–1691

Pococke was a clergyman in Aleppo in the years 1630–1636. His collection of MSS, probably acquired in Aleppo and including close to 100 Hebrew MSS, is now in *Oxford, Bodleian Library. Lists of the MSS and their numbers in *Cat. Neubauer* are found on pp. xxv and xxxi of the catalogue.

Rab., *Lit. Treas.*, p. 31; L. Twells on the life of E. Pococke in a preface to *The Theological Works of Dr. Pocock*, London 1740; S. D. Sassoon in the introduction to Vol. I of the facsimile edition of Maimonides' *Commentary on the Mishna*, Copenhagen 1956, p. 48.

Polak, Felix

The Netherlands, nineteenth century

Five MSS, including two Esther scrolls, are listed in the sales catalogue *Verzeichnis von hebräischen und jüdischen Büchern, Handschriften, etc., aus der Bibliothek des Herrn Felix Polak*, The Hague 1886, nos. 1–5. No. 1 in the catalogue is now *Amsterdam, UB, HS. Ros. 72.

Pollak, Ludwig

See *Prato Haggada.

Pollak–Prato Haggada

See *Prato Haggada.

Pollard, John E. T.

Norwich, England, nineteenth–twentieth cent.; lawyer

The documents in Pollard's possession, which were described in I. Abrahams et al. (eds.), *Starrs and Jewish Charters Preserved in the British Museum*, II, London 1932, pp. 306 ff., were presented to *Cambridge, University Library, in 1945 and now bear the call-numbers Doc. 3780–3792.

Porges, Nathan

Prossnitz, Moravia, 1848 – Leipzig, Germany, 1924

Porges's library was acquired by a number of

booksellers, who offered his books for sale. MSS from Porges's library are included in the following catalogues: O. Harrasowitz, *Bibliotheca Judaica–Hebraica–Rabbinica Pinczower–Porges*, Leipzig 1931/2, nos. 5229–5302; R. Hönisch, *Bibliotheca Orientalis*, nos. 2–4, Leipzig [ca. 1920]; and the auction catalogue of the bookseller P. A. Hemerijck, Amsterdam 1935 (12 MSS, most of which were listed in the Harrasowitz catalogue). Many of the MSS in the Hönisch list are now in *New York, JTSA, and *Copenhagen, Kongelige Bibliothek.
The locations of most of the MSS in the Harrasowitz catalogue cannot be established; those whose locations are known are listed in Appendix I, no. 33.

Porto (Portugal), Biblioteca Pública Municipal

There are four Hebrew MSS in the library (MSS 14, 98, 105, 367) and fragments from a Bible (MS 475). The MSS came from the monastery of Santa Cruz in Coimbra after the monastery was closed in 1834.

Portuguese Bible

Name given to *Paris, BnF, MS héb.15, an illuminated Bible whose illuminations were executed partly in Lisbon at the end of the fifteenth century and partly in Florence at the beginning of the sixteenth century.

Narkiss, p. 156; G. Sed-Rajna, *Manuscrits hébreux de Lisbonne*, Paris 1970, pp. 58–63; M. Garel, *D'une main forte*, Paris 1991, no. 145.

Poznanski, Adolph and Samuel Abraham

Lubraniec, Poland, 1854 – Vienna, 1920; rabbinical scholar; Lubraniec, Poland, 1864 – Warsaw, Poland, 1921; rabbinical scholar)

Many of the MSS from Adolph Poznanski's legacy and some from his brother Samuel Abraham's legacy are now in *Jerusalem, NLI.

Prag, Isaac

Jerusalem, nineteenth cent.

Prag's large collection of MSS was dispersed after his death (א״ל פרומקין, תולדות חכמי ירושלם, א, ירושלים תרפ״ח–תר״ץ, עמ׳ 118). One MS, containing notes on a number of Talmudic tractates, is now *London, BL, MS Or. 5014 (*Cat. Margoliouth*, no. 421).

מ׳ בניהו, ׳אספי הספרים לבני העדה הספרדית בירושלים׳, יד לקורא, א [תש״ז], עמ׳ 319 ; א׳ שוחטמן, ׳״בנין שלמה״ ל״חכמת בצלאל״ [אשכנזי] לר׳ שלמה עדני׳, עלי ספר, ג (תשל״ז), עמ׳ 69.

Prague, Jüdische Gemeinde (Nábozenska Obec Zidovská Knihovna)

The library of the Jewish community in Prague was opened in 1874. The manuscript collection which numbered over 350 in 1939 is based on 33 MSS from the library of Salomon *Rapoport. The MSS, including those described by H. Brody, 'Die Handschriften der Prager Jüd. Gemeindebibliothek', *'Talmud-Thora': Bericht über das Schuljahr 1910/1911, 1913/1914: Religionsschule der isr. Kultusgemeine zu Prag*, II, 4–5 (Prague 1911–1914), are now mostly in *Prague, Jewish Museum (Sadek, p. 144). Some of the MSS disappeared during World War II.

Prague, Narodni Knihovna České Republiky (National Library of the Czech Republic)

The library has 17 Hebrew MSS. After World War II, 34 MSS from the *Breslau, Jüdisch-theologisches Seminar that had been seized and abandoned by the Nazis were preserved in the library. In 2005 they were returned to the Jewish community in Wrocław and deposited in *Wrocław, Biblioteka Uniwersytecka we Wrocławiu.

Prague, Židovské Muzeum v Praze (Jewish Museum)

The library has a collection of 400 MSS, including those formerly in *Prague, Jüdische

Gemeinde. Descriptions of the MSS in German, Czech, Russian or English have been published from time to time in the periodical *Judaica Bohemiae*, the first descriptions appearing in Vol. V (1969).

Prague Bible

Name given to an illuminated Bible copied in Prague in 1488. Described by de Rossi, *ext.*, 51, it was used by Solomon *Dubno in preparing his *Tikun soferim* (תיקון סופרים) and also used in preparing the Berlin 1783 edition of the Pentateuch, in which the *Tikun soferim* was reprinted. The MS later belonged to Abraham *Geiger and was listed in 'Geiger's Handschriften', *HB*, XVII (1877), p. 11, nos. 4–6. It was acquired by *Berlin, Hochschule für die Wissenschaft des Judentums (q.v.), brought to New York in 1936 by A. Guttmann, and listed in Sotheby's catalogue, *Highly Important Hebrew Printed Books and Manuscripts*, New York 1984, no. 39. It is now *New York, Yeshiva University, MS 1247. A digitized version is available on the library's website.

Prato Haggada

Name given to an illuminated fourteenth-century Spanish haggada, now *New York, JTSA, MS 9478. Before World War II the MS was in the possession of Dr. Ludwig Pollak, a native of Prague who lived in Rome. Before he perished in Auschwitz, Pollak had promised to give the MS to his friend Rabbi David Prato. In 1951, Pollak's sister-in-law presented the MS to Prato's son Dr. Jonathan Prato, who was in Rome on the way to his post at the Israeli embassy in Buenos Aires. In 1964 the MS was purchased for the JTSA library. A facsimile edition with essays and introductions was published in 2006.

Preussische Staatsbibliothek

See *Berlin, Staatsbibliothek zu Berlin – Preussischer Kulturbesitz.

Proceedings

Refers to Alexander *Marx, 'A New Collection of Manuscripts', *Proceedings of the American Academy of Jewish Research*, IV (1932/33), pp. 135–167, a survey of the collection donated to *New York, JTSA, later known as the *Enelow Memorial Collection. The library's call-numbers are not recorded in the publication. The article was republished in facsimile in Marx, *Bibl. Studies*, pp. 411–443. The facsimile edition includes an index.

Q

Quatremère, Etienne Marc

Paris, 1782–1857; orientalist

Quatremère's Hebrew MSS were acquired by *Munich, Bayerische Staatsbibliothek, in 1858.

Striedl, *Geschichte*, pp. 31 ff.

R

R

(1) de *Rossi; (2) Rome (also Vatican).

Rabb. or Rabbin.

*Rabbinovicz, Raphael Nathan.

Rabbinovicz, Raphael Nathan

Novo-Zhagory, Lithuania, 1835 – Kiev, Ukraine, 1888; scholar and bookseller

Hundreds of MSS are listed in the sales catalogues Rabbinovicz issued from 1880 to 1888. Many of the MSS were sold to Solomon *Halberstamm, David *Kaufmann, Baron David *Günzburg and M. A. L. *Friedland, and others were sold to various collectors and libraries. Rabbinovicz edited and published several texts, most notably the sixteen volumes of *Dikduke soferim* (דקדוקי סופרים, תרכ״ז–תרנ״ז) containing variant readings of the Babylonian Talmud based on *Munich, BSB, Cod. hebr. 95, and other MSS. He was aided in his scholarly work by Abraham *Merzbacher, who let Rabbinovicz use his library. Rabbinovicz purchased books and MSS for Merzbacher, and after Merzbacher's death he published a catalogue of the library (אהל אברהם, מינכן תרמ״ח), which included 156 MSS. The MS of responsa by Meir b. Baruch of Rothenburg from which Rabbinovicz published his edition (Lemberg 1860) was in *Kiev, Vernadsky National Library.

Rabinowitz, Isaac

Brooklyn, N.Y., 1909 – Ithaca, N.Y., 1988; professor

Rabinowitz left his collection of rare books, including 25 Hebrew MSS, to *Ithaca, Cornell University Library.

Rabinowitz, Mikhel

Mir, Belarus, 1879 – Jerusalem, 1948; bookdealer

Most of Rabinowitz's MSS were acquired after his death by *Jerusalem, JNUL (now NLI). One MS, a miscellany of kabbalistic texts, was formerly *Jerusalem, Schocken Institute, Kab. 101 (previously 15926).

Radcliv

See *Oxford, Radcliffe College.

Raffalovich (Raffaeli), Samuel

Jerusalem and London, 1866–1923; antiquarian

Raffalovich sold some MSS to *Cambridge, University Library, in 1897 (MSS Or. 549–558), and also some *Geniza fragments (many of the Or. 1080 fragments). He also sold a number of MSS to the British Museum, now *London, British Library, Or. 5429, 5435, 5469, 5470, 6357–6359 (*Cat. Margoliouth*, nos. 1114, 1116, 1119, 1120, 1147–1149). Some of his MSS are listed in the 'Zimrat ha'arets' (זמרת הארץ) section in the 1897–1900 issues of *Literarischer Palästina-Almanach* (לוח ארץ ישראל), the yearbook edited by Abraham *Luncz.

Rainer, Ferdinand Maria Johann Evangelist Franz Ignaz von Österreich

Milan, Italy, 1827 – Vienna, 1913; Archduke (Erzherzog)

The Rainer collection of fragments, mostly papyri found in excavations at Faiyum, Egypt, and acquired by Rainer in 1884, includes about 140 Hebrew fragments comprising about 370 leaves and 46 small fragments, mainly papyri. The greater part of the Hebrew fragments are on paper and parchment and seem to derive not from Faiyum but from a different source, perhaps from the Cairo *Geniza (D. H. Müller and D. Kaufmann, *Mittheilungen aus der Sammlung der Papyrus Erzherzog Rainer*, V,

Vienna 1892, p. 127). Rainer donated his collection to the Royal Court Library of Austria (now *Vienna, Österreichische Nationalbibliothek) in 1899. The Hebrew fragments were described in *Cat. Allony–Loewinger*, I, pp. 9–16, and in *Cat. Schwarz–Loewinger–Róth*, pp. 57–79.

Ramat Gan, Bar-Ilan University Library

The library holds over 1,200 MSS. 218 MSS derive from the *Musayof collection, which was acquired in 2000. Other MSS come from the *Avida and Mordecai *Margaliot collections. There is no printed catalogue of the MSS; most are described in the online catalogue: http://sifria.lnx.biu.ac.il.

Ramsgate (England), Judith Montefiore College

See *London, Montefiore Collection.

Rapoport, Salomon Jehuda Loeb

Lemberg (Lviv), Ukraine, 1790 – Prague, Czech Republic, 1867; rabbi and scholar

Thirty-three of Rapoport's MSS that were in the library of the Jewish community in Prague are now in *Prague, Jewish Museum (Sadek, p. 144, note 1). According to Baron, p. 46, some of his MSS were in the Jewish Community Library in Lvov.

Rappaport, Samuel

Twentieth century

Three of Rappaport's MSS are listed in *Cat. Schwarz*, Austria, nos. 162, 231, 232. Rappaport left Austria and emigrated to South Africa.

Cat. Schwarz–Loewinger–Róth, p. 112.

Rashba Bible

Name given to MS *Sassoon 16, an illuminated Bible written in 1383 for a grandson of R. Solomon b. Adret (known in Hebrew by his acronym, RaSHBA). The Bible now belongs to the Safra family in São Paulo.

Ravenna (Italy), Biblioteca Comunale Classense

The two Hebrew MSS in the library (cods. 27 and 69) came from the Camaldolese Monastery in Ravenna, which was suppressed in 1798. Recently, a few fragments were found in bindings in the library.

Fumagalli, 'Emilia-Romagna', p. 101; M. Perani, 'Nuovi frammenti di manoscritti ebraici scoperti a Ravenna presso l'archivio Arcivescovile e la Biblioteca Classense', in idem (ed.), *L'interculturalità dell'ebraismo*, Ravenna 2004, pp. 147–151.

Rawlinson, Richard

1690 – Oxford, 1755: collector

Among the MSS Rawlinson bequeathed to *Oxford, Bodleian Library, in 1735 are ten Hebrew MSS. A list of the MSS and their catalogue numbers is found in *Cat. Neubauer–Cowley*, II, p. 541.

Real Biblioteca de San Lorenzo de El Escorial

See *San Lorenzo del Escorial.

Reg.

*Register.

Regensburg (Germany), Dominican Monastery

One MS including two works, previously in the Regensburg Stadtbibliothek, is now in *Munich, BSB, Cod. hebr. 390–391.

Regensburg (Germany), Stadtarchiv

One Hebrew MS was described in *Cat. Striedl–Róth*, no. 529.

Regensburg Pentateuch

See *Cracow Bible.

Reggio, Isaac Samuel

Gorizia, Italy, 1784–1855; Italian scholar

Reggio sold 300 MSS to Osias *Schorr in Brody. In 1853, M. *Steinschneider selected 60 MSS for purchase by the *Oxford, Bodleian Library (Steinschneider, *Vorlesungen*, p. 59 [Hebrew p. 78]). A list of the MSS and their numbers in *Cat. Neubauer* is found on p. xxv of the catalogue. Four MSS from the Reggio collection bought from Schorr are now in *Berlin, Staatsbibliothek (see the index of owners in *Cat. Steinschneider*, Berlin), and one MS is listed in *Cat. Schwarz*, Austria, no. 237 (now *Jerusalem, NLI, Heb. 8° 2492). Other MSS belonging to Reggio are *New York, JTSA, MS 4599, *Budapest, Jewish Theological Seminary, MS K40; and *Prague, Jewish Museum, 229. A handwritten catalogue of Reggio's MSS selected for the Bodleian, compiled by Steinschneider, is JTSA, MS 2806, and another brief list of 204 MSS from his collection is JTSA, MS 2810 (formerly *Adler, 536).

Reggio Emilia (Italy), Biblioteca Panizzi

Formerly Biblioteca Comunale. Eight Hebrew MSS were described by G. Tamani, 'Manoscritti ebraici nella Biblioteca Comunale di Reggio Emilia', *Annali dell'Istituto Orientale di Napoli*, XXXI (1971), pp. 256–262. The library also has a Passover haggada (MS Vari. D. 118), not listed by Tamani.

Fumagalli, 'Emilia-Romagna', p. 98.

Reggio Emilia (Italy), Talmud Tora Library

The MS of *Maḥzor Vitry* that was formerly in the library, mentioned by A. Berliner in his *Likute betar likute* (ליקוטי בתר ליקוטי), appended to the Berlin 1894 edition of *Maḥzor Vitry* (p. 172), is now *New York, JTSA, MS 8334.

D. Goldschmidt, *REJ*, 125 (1966), pp. 63–75.

Regiomontum

Latin name for Königsberg.

Register

After 1917, selected recently acquired books and MSS were described in the annual *Register of the Jewish Theological Seminary of America* by Alexander *Marx and his successors as librarians in *New York, JTSA. The descriptions from 1917 to 1973 were republished in facsimile in A. Marx, *Bibl. Studies*, pp. 1–366. The facsimile edition includes an index; however the library's call-numbers are not listed.

Reifmann, Jacob

Lagow, Poland, 1818 – Szczebrszyn, Poland, 1895; scholar

A list of 12 MSS and fragments belonging to Reifmann was published in 'Literatur-Berichte', *Literaturblatt des Orients*, V (1844), pp. 481–482. MS no. 4 in the list was MS no. 59 in *Warsaw, Tłomackie Street Synagogue. The present locations of the other MSS are not known to me. Articles and autograph letters by Reifmann are found in the *Adler collection in *New York, JTSA; *Jerusalem, NLI; *Prague, Jewish Museum; and elsewhere.

Reina

See *Milan, Biblioteca Reina.

Reinach, Théodore

St.-Germain-en-Laye, France, 1860–1928; French archaeologist

The whereabouts of the six fragments from Reinach's collection published by M. Schwab, 'Textes Judéo–égyptiens du XIième siecle', *REJ*, LXX (1920), pp. 44–69, are unknown.

Reuchlin, Johann von

Pforzheim, Germany, 1455 – Liebenzell, Germany, 1522; Christian Hebraist

Thirteen Hebrew MSS from Reuchlin's

library are now in *Karlsruhe, Badische Landesbibliothek, and were described by S. Landauer and S. Baer (biblical MSS) in *Die Handschriften der grossherzoglich badischen Hof- und Landesbibliothek in Karlsruhe*, II: *Orientalische Handschriften*, Karlsruhe 1892, pp. 1–28. Other MSS of Reuchlin's are now in *London, British Library, Add. 11416 (*Cat. Margoliouth*, no. 740), in *Stuttgart, Württembergische Landesbibliothek (Cod. Or. fol. 2), and in *Munich, Bayerische Staatsbibliothek (Cod. hebr. 425). Karl Christ, *Die Bibliothek Reuchlins in Pforzheim* (52nd Supplement to *Zentralblatt für Bibliothekswesen*, Leipzig 1924), pp. 6–7, 36–51, lists 36 Hebrew printed books and MSS belonging to Reuchlin. Christ was able to account for 21 items, including the 13 Karlsruhe MSS. The MSS and printed books from the Reuchlin collection were also described in W. Abel and R. Leicht, *Verzeichnis der Hebraica in der Bibliothek Johannes Reuchlins*, Ostfildern 2005. In his studies of the Kabbala, Reuchlin made use of *New York, JTSA, MS 1887 (formerly Halberstamm 444), or a similar MS (G. Scholem in *EJ*, X, p. 646). The Reuchlin Bible is the name given to Karlsruhe, Cod. Reuchlin 1, an illuminated thirteenth-century Bible. Codex Reuchlinianus is Karlsruhe, Cod. Reuchlin 3, a MS of Prophets with Targum copied in 1105, reproduced in facsimile as *The Pre-Masoretic Bible*, Copenhagen 1956.

RGVA

Moscow, Rossiiskii Gosudarstvennyi Voennyi Arkhiv (Russian State Military Archives)

Rheno-Trajectina

Latin name for Utrecht.

Riccardiana

See *Florence, Biblioteca Riccardiana.

Richelieu, Armand du Plessis, duc de

Paris, 1585–1642; cardinal

256 Hebrew MSS from Richelieu's collection, formerly in the *Paris, Sorbonne library, were deposited in the Imperial Library (now *Paris, Bibliothèque nationale de France) after confiscation of the Sorbonne library following the French Revolution. A few other MSS from Richelieu's collection had been acquired in the seventeenth century by the Royal Library, predecessor of the Imperial Library.

L. V. Delisle, *Le cabinet des manuscrits de la Bibliothèque imperial*, Paris 1874, p. 207.

Rochester (N.Y.), Public Library

A Hebrew MS formerly in the library is now *New York, JTSA, MS 4328.

Register, 5731, p. 123 (Marx, *Bibl. Studies*, p. 363).

Roest, Meijer Marcus

Amsterdam, Netherlands, 1821–1890

Roest compiled a number of booksellers' and auction catalogues, among them *Bet hasefer* (בית הספר), Amsterdam 1868. Most of the MSS listed in this catalogue are now in *New York, Columbia University. No. 5128 is *Amsterdam, Ets Haim, HS EH 47 D 38; no. 5138 is Ets Haim, HS EH 47 C 44; and no. 5158 is *London, Montefiore, MS 20. Roest also compiled a catalogue of the L. Rosenthal collection, Amsterdam 1875 (the MSS listed in this catalogue are now in *Amsterdam, Universiteitsbibliotheek).

Rome

See also *Vatican.

Rome, Accademia Nazionale dei Lincei e Corsiniana

Four Hebrew MSS were described by G. Lacerenza, 'I manoscritti ebraici dell'Accademia Nazionale dei Lincei', *Materia Giudaica*, VIII/1 (2003), pp. 155–175.

Rome, Biblioteca Angelica

Fifty-four Hebrew MSS are described by A. di Capua in 'Catalogo dei codici ebraici della Biblioteca Angelica', *Cataloghi*, I, (1878), pp. 83–103. At the head of each entry is the catalogue number, followed by the old call-number in square brackets. Since the publication of the catalogue new call-numbers have been assigned to the MSS. Palaeographical and codicological information: writing material, size, number of leaves, number of lines per page, type of script and exact dates, where known. A single set of indexes to the MSS in all the libraries described in the six preceding volumes of the *Cataloghi* was published separately on pp. 675–698 in Vol. VII (1904). The MSS are indexed by titles, authors, scribes, owners, etc., place names, and censors.

The *Jerusalem, IMHM has microfilms of 58 MSS from the Angelica. According to Pearson, p. 35, there are 62 Hebrew MSS in the library.

Rome, Biblioteca di Casa Farnese

The collection, including nine Hebrew MSS, was transferred to *Naples, Biblioteca Nazionale.

G. Moscati Steindler, 'I manoscritti ebraici della Biblioteca Nazionale di Napoli', *Annali dell'Istituto Orientale di Napoli*, XXXI (1971), p. 315.

Rome, Biblioteca Casanatense

The Casanatense Library was founded by the Dominicans of the Monastery of Santa Maria sopra Minerva in Rome and opened to the general public at the behest of Cardinal Girolamo Casanate. The library opened on November 3, 1701, only one year after Cardinal Casanate's death. During the years 1743–1746 the library purchased MSS in Greek and Hebrew from the 'neofiti' (converts from Judaism), among them Giovanni Antonio Costanzi. In 1873, after the Italian government extended to Rome the law on the suppression of religious houses, the legal title of the Casanatense was forfeited to the state. Appeals to the courts were rejected, and the decision was made final in 1884. A total of 226 Hebrew and five Samaritan MSS were described by G. Sacerdote in 'Catalogo dei codici ebraici della Biblioteca Casanatense', *Cataloghi*, VI (1897), pp. 475–665. At the head of each entry appears the catalogue number, followed by the old and present call-numbers in square brackets. A concordance to the call-numbers is found on pp. 659–662 of the catalogue. Palaeographical and codicological information: writing material, size, number of leaves, number of lines per page, type of script and exact dates. A single set of indexes to the MSS in all the libraries described in the six preceding volumes of the *Cataloghi* was published separately on pp. 675–698 in Vol. VII (1904). The MSS are indexed by titles, authors, scribes, owners, etc., place names and censors.

Recently, a few additional Hebrew MSS were discovered in the library.

Rome, Biblioteca Chigiana

See *Chigiana.

Rome, Biblioteca Corsiniana

See *Corsiniana.

Rome, Biblioteca Maronitarum

The MS described by *Kennicott, no. 242, is now *Vatican, Cod. ebr. 482.

Rome, Biblioteca Nazionale Centrale di Roma

Formerly Biblioteca Nazionale Centrale 'Vittorio Emanuele II'. The collection of Hebrew MSS in this library is based on the collection formerly in the Collegio Romano in Rome (27 MSS). One MS comes from the Casa Professa della Compagna di Gesù in Rome. Twenty-eight Hebrew MSS are described by

A. di Capua, 'Catalogo dei codici ebraici della Biblioteca Vittorio Emanuele', *Cataloghi*, I (1878), pp. 39–53. At the head of each entry the catalogue number is printed, followed by the old call-number in square brackets. Since the catalogue was printed the MSS have been assigned new call-numbers. Palaeographical and codicological information: writing material, size, number of leaves, number of lines per page, type of script and exact dates, where known. A single set of indexes to the MSS in all the libraries described in the six preceding volumes of the *Cataloghi* was published separately on pp. 675–698 in Vol. VII (1904). The MSS are indexed by titles, authors, scribes, owners, etc., place names and censors. The *Jerusalem, IMHM has microfilms of six MSS in addition to those listed in the catalogue, three of them from the S. Maria della Scala collection.

Rome, Cardinal Zelada
See *Zelada.

Rome, Collegio Rabbinico Italiano
The Collegio, founded in 1829 in Padua as the Istituto Convitto Rabbinico, was transferred to Rome in 1882, and its name was changed to Collegio Rabbinico Italiano. In 1899 the Collegio moved to Florence; in 1934 it moved back to Rome, where it still continues to function. The collection of MSS, begun when the seminary was in Padua, moved to Rome, to Florence, where the libraries of Elia Montefiore and the Ohave Tora brotherhood were acquired, and then back to Rome, but a number of MSS disappeared over the years. Today the collection is housed in the Centro Bibliografico dell'Ebraismo Italiano belonging to the Union of Jewish Italian Communities in Rome, together with a MS formerly from the Jewish Community in Pitigliano and archives and *ketubot* from other Jewish communities (Siena, Pisa, Mantua). 277 MSS from the Collegio Rabbinico Italiano collection are described by R. Di Segni, *Catalogue of the Manuscripts of the Collegio Rabbinico Italiano, Rome, Italy*, special supplement to *'Alei sefer*, Ramat Gan–Rome 1990 (in Hebrew). In an Appendix to the *Catalogue*, Di Segni described the Pitigliano MS and listed the MSS from the other libraries. On a recent visit to the Centro Bibliografico, I was unable to find all the MSS listed in the Appendix.

Rome, Collegio Romano
The MSS formerly in the library are now in *Rome, Biblioteca Nazionale Centrale.
Pearson, p. 35.

Rome, Comunità ebraica
Fourteen Bible MSS were described by R. J. H. Gottheil in 'Bible MSS in the Roman Synagogues', *ZfHB*, IX (1905), pp. 177–184. Twenty-six other MSS were described by Sonne, *Relazione*. In 1943 the library was looted and confiscated by the Nazis, and its rare books, incunabula and most of its MSS were removed and never located. The ancient Bible MSS were hidden before the looting of the library, and, with the possible exception of no. X, all the Bible MSS in Gottheil's list, together with a few other documents and MSS, are still preserved in the Museo Ebraico di Roma in the Tempio Maggiore, the main synagogue. Of the MSS described by Sonne, *Relazione*, nos. 12 and 17 were acquired before the war by *New York, JTSA (MSS 2321 and 2325); all the others were confiscated in 1943 and are still missing.

D. Tedeschi, 'Research of the Roman Jewish Community's library looted in 1943', in R. Dehnel (ed.), *Jüdischer Buchbesitz als Raubgut* (Zweites Hannoversches Symposium), Frankfurt a/M 2006, pp. 243–252.

Rome, Museo Borgiano di Propaganda Fide
See *Borgiana.

Rome, Palatina
See *Heidelberg, Biblioteca Palatina.

Rome, Pia Casa dei Neofiti
The library of the Pia Casa dei Neofiti, an institution that housed Jewish apostates, was moved to the *Vatican library in the nineteenth century. Thirty-nine Hebrew MSS were described by G. Sacerdote in *I Codici Ebraici della Pia Casa dei Neofiti in Roma*, Rome 1893. These MSS and an additional 12, in all 51 MSS, were listed in *Cat. Allony–Loewinger*, III, nos. 673–723. Five Neofiti MSS in Latin were transferred to the Vatican's Latin collection in 1976. See Ruysschaert, 'Les manuscrits Vaticans', pp. 358–359. The remaining MSS were catalogued again in *Cat. Richler*, Vatican. MS Neofiti 1 is a MS of the Palestinian translation (Targum) of the Pentateuch (facsimile edition: Jerusalem 1970; critical edition by A. Diez-Macho, Vols. I–VI, Madrid 1968–1979).

Rome, Propaganda Fide
See *Borgiana.

Romm (publishers in Vilna)
About thirty MSS, mostly recent copies of older MSS presented by the Romm publishing house to *Jerusalem, JNUL (now NLI), in 1934, were described by B. I. Joel (י׳ יואל, 'אוסף כתבי־יד מבית־דפוס ראם', ק״ס, יג [תרצ״ז], עמ' 513–523). Other MSS owned by the firm were destroyed in a fire.

י' מונדשיין, 'כתבי־יד והכנות לדפוס בבית האלמנה והאחים ראם', עלי ספר, ו–ז (תשל״ט), עמ' 187–197.

Ros., HS.
Rosenthaliana. See *Amsterdam, Universiteitsbibliotheek.

Rösel Bible
Name given to a Bible MS, *Berlin, SB, Cod. Or. 2° 1–4, presented in 1692 to the Library of the Prince-Elector (Kurfürst) in Berlin by Rösel, wife of Benjamin [Neumark?].

Rosenbaum, J.
Bookseller in Frankfurt
The illuminated haggada belonging to Rosenbaum that was described by D. Kaufmann, 'Les cycles d'image du type allemande dans l'illustration ancienne de la Haggada', *REJ*, XXXVIII (1899), pp. 74–102, was eventually purchased by Abraham *Yahuda and is now *Jerusalem, Israel Museum, MS 180/50.

Jerusalem Collections, no. 12.

Rosenberg, Hayyim
Lipany, Slovakia, 1876–193?; rabbi in Ancona
Some of the MSS in Rosenberg's collection came from the library of Hayyim *Azulai, which had passed into the possession of David Abraham *Vivanti and were acquired after his death by Isaac Raphael *Tedeschi, from whom Rosenberg acquired them. Rosenberg sold some MSS to the British Museum (now *London, British Library). Rosenberg described 40 MSS of Azulai's works in his possession (ח' רוזנברג, 'חבורי רב חיד״א וכתביו שלא ראו עדיין אור הדפוס', ק״ס, ה [תרפ״ט], עמ' 142–162, 255–262, 388–395). These MSS were later acquired by *New York, JTSA (מ' בניהו, רבי חיים יוסף דוד אזולאי, ירושלים [תשי״ט], עמ' פד–פה). The remainder of the Rosenberg collection was purchased by Rabbi Daniel Lewin in Cornwall, Canada; and in 1962, *Los Angeles, University of California Library acquired the collection from him. There are about 150 MSS from the Rosenberg collection in Los Angeles, and they all bear call-numbers with the prefix 779.

Rosenthal, Leser
1794–1868
See *Amsterdam, Universiteitsbibliotheek.

Rosenthaliana
See *Amsterdam, Universiteitsbibliotheek.

Ross.

(1) de *Rossi; (2) *Rossiana.

Rossi, Giovanni Bernardo de

Castelnuovo, Italy, 1742 – Parma, Italy, 1831

A professor of Oriental languages at the University of Parma, de Rossi owned a collection of close to 1,450 Hebrew MSS. This collection was purchased by Princess Maria Luisa of Austria in 1816 and presented to *Parma, Biblioteca Palatina. In *Cat. de Rossi* (1803), de Rossi himself described 1,377 of his MSS. The de Rossi MSS that were acquired after the publication of the catalogue, nos. 1378–1432 were described elsewhere. For further details on the catalogues of the de Rossi collection, see *Parma, Biblioteca Palatina. Two MSS belonging to de Rossi were purchased by Ferdinando *Landi and are now in *Piacenza, Biblioteca Comunale (Tamani, *Piacenza*, p. 137). In his *Variae Lectiones Veteris Testamenti*, Parma 1784, de Rossi described in brief the MSS used by *Kennicott in his *Vetus Testamentum Hebraicum* (I, pp. lix–xcvi); his own biblical MSS (*ibid.*, I, pp. xcvii–cxxv; II, pp. vii–ix; III, pp. iii–vi; and IV, pp. xxii–xxviii); and 'MSS. codices exteri' (sometimes referred to as 'de Rossi ext.') – other biblical MSS not used by Kennicott (*ibid.*, I, pp. cxxvi–cxxxv; II, pp. x–xi; III, pp. v–vi; and IV, p. xxviii).

de Rossi ext.

Sometimes used to describe the MSS listed in de *Rossi's 'Ms. codices exteri' (= de Rossi, *ext.*).

Rossiana

Name of a collection of MSS brought together by Giovanni Gherardo de Rossi (1754–1825) and his son Giovanni Francesco de Rossi, who died in Naples in 1854. The collection was deposited in the Jesuit library in Lainz near Vienna (Vienna-Lainz) until 1921, when it was returned to Rome and became part of the *Vatican library. The collection includes 38 Hebrew MSS, which were described in *Cat. Allony–Loewinger*, III, pp. 87–89, and in *Cat. Richler*, Vatican, pp. 566–598. The call-numbers in *Cat. Allony–Loewinger* are incorrect. The correct numbers are listed in Ruysschaert, 'Les manuscrits Vaticans', pp. 359–360. The illuminated MSS were described by H. Tietze, *Die illuminierten Handschriften der Rossiana in Wien-Lainz*, Leipzig 1911, nos. 97, 98, 100, 160.

Cat. Allony–Loewinger, III, p. 12; C. M. Grafinger, *Beiträge zur Geschichte der Biblioteca Vaticana*, Vatican City 1997.

Rostock (Germany), Universitätsbibliothek

Fifty-five MSS, scrolls and fragments acquired from the Orientalist Oluf Gerhard *Tychsen in 1815, described in A. T. Hartmann, *Catalogus Bibliothecae Olai Gerhardi Tychsen*, Rostock 1817[?], are described in greater detail in *Cat. Striedl–Róth*, pp. 334–362. L. Donath described a few MSS in 'Ueber die hebräischen Manuscripten in der Universitätsbibliothek zu Rostock', *Magazin für jüdische Geschichte und Literatur*, I (1874), pp. 22–23, 34–35, 86–87, 89–93, 101–103.

H. Tröger, 'Judaica und Hebraica der Universitätsbibliothek Rostock', *Zeitschrift für Bibliothekswesen und Bibliographie*, LIII (2006), pp. 169–172.

Roth, Cecil

London, 1899 – Jerusalem, 1970; historian

Roth's MSS, described in his 'Catalogue of Manuscripts in the Roth Collection', in the *Alexander Marx Jubilee Volume*, New York 1950, English section, pp. 503–535, were bequeathed to the Brotherton Library, Leeds University. Earlier, Roth had sold a number of MSS to George Alexander *Kohut. Roth's collection of 50 marriage contracts (*ketubot*), described in his catalogue (*The Ketubah: The Jewish Marriage Contract: Exhibition,*

Produced by Glenda Milrod, Toronto 1980), as well as 13 decorated and illuminated *megilot*, were bequeathed to the Beth Tzedec Synagogue Museum in Toronto.

E. Fromovič and F. Felsenstein, *Hebraica and Judaica from the Cecil Roth Collection*, Leeds 1997.

Rothschild family

Edmond de Rothschild's MSS were left to his three children. James de Rothschild inherited over 80 MSS from his father and brought most of them to England. Nine Hebrew MSS left in France were looted by the Nazis. Several MSS belonging to different members of the Rothschild family are known as 'Rothschild MSS'. The 'Rothschild Miscellany', an illuminated MS including an Italian rite maḥzor, over 50 other works (some written in the margins), and over 300 illuminations, is now *Jerusalem, Israel Museum, MS 180/51. Formerly known as MS Rothschild 24, the MS was stolen by the Nazis during the occupation of France in World War II and was offered for sale by a Berlin bookdealer to *New York, JTSA, in 1950. After Alexander *Marx, the librarian of JTSA, identified the MS and its provenance, it was returned in 1951 to James de Rothschild, and in 1957 it was presented to the Bezalel Museum, now part of the Israel Museum. I. Levi published a detailed description of the MS and its contents, 'Le Manuscrit hébreu no. 24 de la bibliothèque du Baron Edmond de Rothschild à Paris', *REJ*, LXXXIX (1930), pp. 281–292 (see also *Jerusalem Collections*, no. 18; Narkiss, p. 152). A facsimile edition, including an introductory volume with essays on the contents, illuminations and palaeography of the MS, was published in 1989. The 'Rothschild Maḥzor' (also called the 'Rothschild Siddur'), an illuminated siddur written in Florence in 1492, was presented to JTSA by the grandson of its former owner, Edmond de Rothschild. Its present call-number is MS 8892 (for a description of the MS see Evelyn M. Cohen, *The Rothschild Mahzor*, New York 1983). Emil Sarnow, *Katalog der ständigen Ausstellung: Handschriften, Einbände, Formschnitte und Kupferstiche des 15. Jahrhunderts, Druckwerke und Einblattdrucke des 15. bis 20. Jahrhunderts, ...*, Frankfurt a/M 1920, lists several MSS presented to the *Frankfurt a/M, Stadtbibliothek (now Goethe Universität, Universitätsbibliothek), by members of the Rothschild family. Two of them, Cods. Ausst. 5 and 9, were presented after World War II to a private collector in New York in lieu of compensation for property expropriated during the war. Cods. Ausst. 8 and 10 were presented to the Frankfurt library by Freifrau (Baroness) Wilhelm von Rothschild. An illuminated haggada, also from the Edmond de Rothschild collection, was lost during the war, rediscovered, and for a time was in the Yale University library, where it was known as the *Murphy Haggada. It was presented to *Jerusalem, JNUL (now NLI), in 1981 by Mrs. James de Rothschild, and its present call-number is Heb. 4° 6130. Part of an illuminated maḥzor from the collection of James de Rothschild is now NLI, Heb. 8° 4450 (another part belonged to Georges *Weill of Jerusalem and was sold to David Jeselsohn of Zurich). Baron Nathaniel de Rothschild purchased the *Strauss collection and presented it to the *Paris, Musée de Cluny. One MS, a decorated copy of Hagiographa probably copied in Lisbon, was presented to Nathaniel in Baghdad in 1893 by the sons of the printer Bekhor Ḥutzin and was acquired by W. J. Myers (d. 1899) and sold by Maggs Bros. in 1925 (Cat. 467: *Judaica and Hebraica*). It was *Jerusalem, Schocken Institute, MS 12827, until it was sold at Christie's in New York, 2005. A few *Geniza fragments acquired by Edmond de Rothschild and published by M. Lambert, 'Nouveaux fragments du commentaire de Saadia sur Isaïe', in M. Brann and F. Rosenthal (eds.), *Gedenkbuch zur Erinnerung an David Kaufmann*,

Breslau 1900, pp. 138–143, are now *Paris, AIU, H 54 A. A maḥzor purchased in 1842 by Salomon Mayer of the Viennese branch of the Rothschild family in Nuremberg as a gift to his son Anselm Salomon (1803–1874) was *Jerusalem, Schocken Institute, MS 15435, and was sold by the Schocken family in the 1990s to *Vienna, Österreichische Nationalbibliothek (Cod. Hebr. 242).

C. De Hamel, *The Rothschilds and Their Collections of Illuminated Manuscripts*, London 2005.

Rothschild Miscellany
See *Rothschild.

Rothschild Siddur
See *Rothschild.

Rotterdam (Netherlands), Meerman
See *Meerman.

Rouen (France), Bibliothèque municipale
Six Hebrew MSS were described in *Catalogue général*, I (1886), nos. 1478–1480, 1485, 1487, 1490; II (1888), p. 71.

Rovigo (Italy), Biblioteca dell'Accademia dei Concordi
There are Hebrew MSS in two collections in the library, the Silvestriana (nine MSS) and the Concordiana (four MSS). Tamani, *Rovigo* (1973), describes eight MSS in the Silvestriana collection.

Royal MSS
There are seven Hebrew MSS among the Royal MSS presented by King George III to the British Museum (now *London, British Library) in 1757. A list of the MSS is found in *Cat. Margoliouth–Leveen*, IV, p. 162.

Royal Society
See *London, Royal Society.

R. Sh. b. A. Bible
See *Rashba Bible.

RSMA
*Moscow, Rossiiskii Gosudarstvennyi Voennyi Arkhiv (Russian State Military Archives).

Rubashow, S. Z.
See *Shazar.

Rubens, Meijer Barend
Amsterdam, Netherlands, 1797–1863
Seventeen MSS were listed on pp. 34–35 in the sales catalogue of his library, which forms Part II of the catalogue *Me'ir 'enayim* (מאיר עינים הוא רשימת ספרים ... רובם מעזבון ... מאיר בפו"מ כ"ה יודא יששכר בער זצ"ל לבית רובענס), with the added title: *Catalogus II van eene ... boekverzameling ... door ... Meijer Barend Rubens*, Amsterdam 1864 (Part I lists the MSS of Meijer Levien *Jacobson). For the present locations of some of the MSS see Appendix I, no. 34.

Ruzyhin, Israel
See *Friedmann, Israel.

Rylands Spanish Haggada
A name given to *Manchester, John Rylands University Library, MS 6, an illuminated fourteenth-century Spanish haggada. 'Brother of the Rylands Spanish Haggada' is the name given to a similar MS, *London, BL, MS Or. 1404 (*Cat. Margoliouth*, no. 606).

Narkiss, pp. 66–68; Narkiss, *Span. & Port.*, nos. 15–16; facsimile edition with an introduction by Raphael Loewe, *The Rylands Haggadah*, London 1988.

S

S
Strasbourg; also Saint, San or Santa.

Sachs, Senior
Kaidany, Lithuania, 1816 – Paris, 1892; scholar
While librarian of the *Günzburg library (now in *Moscow, RSL), Sachs compiled a short catalogue of the Hebrew MSS in the collection and began to publish lengthy descriptions of the MSS (for details see Moscow, RSL). A MS of *Sefer 'alilot devarim* (ספר עלילות דברים) belonging to Sachs which was mentioned in *HB*, VII (1864), p. 27, is now Moscow, RSL, Günzburg collection MS 180. The copy Sachs made of *London, BL, MS Add. 15978, which served as the basis for the 1866 edition of Jacob Anatoli's *Malmad hatalmidim* (מלמד התלמידים), is now *New York, JTSA, MS R85. Another MS belonging to Sachs is now *Paris, AIU, MS H 230 A.

Sächsische Landesbibliothek
See *Dresden, Sächsische Landesbibliothek – Staats- und Universitätsbibliothek.

Saibante, Giovanni
Verona, Italy, early eighteenth century; bibliophile and collector
Seventy Hebrew MSS are listed in S. Maffei, *Indice delli Libri che si ritrovano nella Raccolta del Nobile Signor Giulio Saibante Patrizio Veronese*, Verona 1734, pp. 220–221. According to Tamani, *Verona*, pp. 4–5, part of the collection may have come into the possession of Paolino *Gianfilippi, a portion of whose library was acquired by *Verona, Biblioteca Civica. According to Fumagalli, p. 127, eight of Saibante's MSS were in the Gianfilippi collection now in the Verona library.

St. Florian (Austria), Augustiner-Chorherren Stiftsbibliothek
Fragments from 13 MSS are listed in *Cat. Schwarz–Loewinger–Róth*, pp. 98–101. Call-numbers are listed at the end of each entry.

Ste. Geneviève
See *Paris, Bibliothèque Ste. Geneviève.

St. Germain-des-Prés
See *Paris, Bibliothèque St. Germain-des-Prés.

St. John's College
See *(1) Cambridge, College Libraries; (2) Oxford, College Libraries.

St. Marcus
See *Venice, Biblioteca Marciana.

St. Paul im Lavanttal (Austria), Stiftsbibliothek
Three MSS and fragments from two other MSS are listed in *Cat. Schwarz–Loewinger–Róth*, pp. 101–102. The old and new call-numbers are listed at the end of each entry. One of the MSS had already been described in *Cat. Schwarz*, Austria, no. 1. Two MSS and the fragments were listed in *Cat. Allony–Loewinger*, I, p. 20. Fragments removed from 47 MSS and printed books are described and displayed on the website http://www.ksbm.oeaw.ac.at/hebraica.

St. Petersburg (Russia), Asiatic Museum
See *St. Petersburg, Institute of Oriental Manuscripts.

St. Petersburg (Russia), Institut Vostochnik Rukopisi (Institute of Oriental Manuscripts of the Russian Academy of Sciences)

Formerly the Institut Vostokovedenia Rossiiskoi Akademii Nauk (Institute of Oriental Studies of the Russian Academy of Sciences, St. Petersburg branch). Founded in 1818 as the Asiatic Museum, the Institute became part of the Institute of Oriental Studies of the Academy of Sciences of the USSR in 1930, when the city was known as Leningrad. In 1951, the Academy established an Institute of Oriental Studies in Moscow, and the Institute in Leningrad, with its collection of Oriental MSS, subsequently became a branch of that institution. From 1960 to 1969 it was called the 'Institute of the Peoples of Asia' (Institut Narodov Azii, INA). In 2008, the Institute changed its status and was assigned a new name: the 'Institute of Oriental Manuscripts'. The library possesses about 1,100 Hebrew MSS, including 300 from the *Friedland collection and some from the David Maggid collection. The collection also includes Karaite MSS from the Karaite National Library in *Eupatoria and from *Karassou-Bazar. The MSS are arranged in the library according to size, in four groups, A, B, C, and D. The *Catalog of Jewish Manuscripts in the Institute of Oriental Studies*, first prepared by Yonah (I. I.) Gintsburg (1871–1942) in 1936–1941 and revised by K. B. Starkova and A. M. Gazov-Ginzberg, was printed in New York in 2003. The catalogue is in Russian, with Hebrew titles supplied. There is an English introduction by Norman Ross, the publisher, and a Russian one by Starkova and Gazov-Ginzberg, with an English translation. The catalogue is arranged by subject. It describes 464 MSS in 964 entries, with an entry for each individual text. Thus, the descriptions of MSS including several works on different subjects are dispersed throughout the catalogue, each title in its respective place. There are no indexes and no concordance of MS numbers and catalogue entry numbers.

Starkova, 'Les plus anciens MSS'; eadem, in *Vostokovednye Fondy Krupneishikh Bibliotek Sovetskogo Souiza: Stat'i i Soobshcheniia*, Moscow 1963, pp. 45–49; P. B. Kondratjev, *Palestinskiy Sbornik*, XXVIII (1986), pp. 74–88.

St. Petersburg (Russia), Jewish Historical Ethnographic Society

The MSS formerly in the library of the Society, which was closed in 1929, are now in *Kiev, Vernadsky National Library; see its entry for details of the movements of this collection.

Z. M. Baker, 'History of the Jewish Collections at the Vernadsky Library in Kiev', *Shofar*, X, no. 4 (1992), pp. 31–48; *Soviet Jewish Affairs*, XXI, no. 2 (1991).

St. Petersburg (Russia), Rossiyskaia Natsionalnaya Biblioteka (National Library of Russia, NLR)

Formerly the Imperial Public Library and, after the Revolution, the Publichnaia Biblioteka imeni M. E. Saltykova-Shchedrina (the Saltykov-Shchedrin Public Library). The Oriental MSS of the Public Library acquired until 1850 were described in B. Dorn (ed.), *Catalogue des manuscrits et xylographes orientaux de la Bibliothèque Impériale Publique de St. Petersbourg*, St. Petersburg 1852. Now they form the so-called Basic Collection of the Oriental Manuscripts (Ф 923 or Coll. 923), and the call-numbers bear the preface 'Dorn'. The Oriental MSS acquired after publication of the Catalogue were distributed at the beginning of the twentieth century into separate collections by language, forming the so called 'new series'. The collection or 'fond' (Ф) numbers were given after World War II.

When the Library opened in 1805 the only Hebrew MS in its possession was an eighteenth-century Esther Scroll from the collection of P. P. Dubrovsky (MS Dorn 604). By 1852 there were six Hebrew MSS in the library: three biblical scrolls, a *mezuza* and two manuscripts (MSS Dorn 603–608, described in the 1852 catalogue). No other Hebrew MSS entered the library until 1858, when it acquired a small number of MSS, mostly Karaite, from K. *Tischendorf, which are now included in the Hebrew new series (Coll. 913). Some of these were described by Steinschneider in the first issues of *HB* (see *Tischendorf). The expansion of the library's collection began with the purchase in 1862 of about 800 non-biblical MSS, a large number of biblical MSS, scrolls and fragments from the Karaite Abraham *Firkovich. This collection is known as the First Firkovich Collection. In 1863 the library acquired the 'Odessa Collection' from *Odessa, Society for History and Antiquities, 95 MSS that had been purchased by the Society from Firkovich, partly in 1845 (the 'First Odessa Collection') and intermittently until 1852. The First Odessa Collection had been described by E. M. Pinner in *Prospectus der der Odessaer Gesellschaft für Geschichte und Alterthümer gehörenden ältesten hebräischen und rabbinischen Manuscripte*, Odessa 1845 (for details, see Odessa). The MSS purchased in 1852 form the so-called Second Odessa Collection (see O. Vasilyeva, 'The Firkovich Odessa Collection: The history of its acquisition and research, present condition and historical value', *Studia Orientalia*, XCV, 2003, pp. 45–53). The Odessa MSS now bear call-numbers with the prefixes Евр. I A, Евр. I B, Евр. I C and Евр. I Библ. (nos. 147–170). In 1876, two years after Firkovich's death, the library acquired the Second Firkovich Collection, which contains more than 15,600 MSS and fragments. 1,350 Samaritan MSS were purchased from Firkovich in 1870. The fragments seem to have come from a geniza in Cairo or, according to M. Ben Sasson, from a Karaite geniza and from similar genizas in Crimea, although there is no way of ascertaining their origin (ז' אלקין ומ' בן־ששון, 'אברהם פירקוביץ' וגניזות קהיר', פעמים, צ [תשס"ב], עמ' 51–95). The First Firkovich Collection, together with the Second Firkovich Collection, the Firkovich Collection of Samaritan MSS and the Firkovich Personal Archives, are all included in Coll. 946. Towards the end of the nineteenth century the library acquired the 1,189 Geniza fragments from the *Antonin collection, which are stored separately in Coll. 937. The library continued to add to its collections in the twentieth century. Altogether, the collections of the library include more than 18,000 items.

CALL-NUMBERS The six Hebrew MSS of the Basic (Main) Collection of Oriental Manuscripts bear the call-numbers Dorn 603–608. MSS of the Hebrew new series bear the call-numbers with the prefix Евр. н.с. (= Yevreiskaia novaia seria.) replacing the formerly used prefix Евр. IV.

The First Firkovich Collection includes MSS of general subject matter, bearing call-numbers prefixed Евр. I (1–830). Biblical scrolls are numbered Евр. I A (nos. 1–36, from the two Odessa Collections) and Евр. I Библ. (1–47). Biblical codices from the Odessa Collections are numbered Евр. I B 1–19A (nos. 9, 12, 15, 16 and 18 are not in use); MS Евр. I B 20 is a non-biblical Karaite siddur. The bulk of the biblical codices are numbered Евр. I Библ. 48–188 (nos. 147–153a, 154–157a and 158–170 are from the Second Odessa Collection; of these, nos. 147, 149, 154, 158, 159 and 161 are missing). Other non-biblical MSS bear the prefix Евр. I C (11 MSS, mostly Talmudic and biblical commentaries from the Odessa Collection). Documents in Hebrew are divided into three sections: Евр. I D I, Евр. I D II (documents from Poland) and Евр. I D III. The call-numbers Евр. I Д (Karaite documents) and Евр. I K (marriage contracts and Krymchak documents), given by V. Lebedev, a former librarian, are no longer in use. Documents in Turkish (mostly from the Karaite community of Troki, i.e., Trakai in Lithuania) bear numbers with the prefix 'Firk. Tur.'. Documents in Polish, Latin, West-Russian (Old Byelorussian or Ukrainian) and Russian are numbered Firk. Pol. 1–323, but about 120 such items are now found in the collection of the West-Russian Acts (Coll. 293, ЗРА = Zapadno Russkie Akty).

The Second Firkovich collection consists of MSS bearing call-numbers prefixed Евр. II A (2,942 MSS and fragments of general subject matter), Евр. II B (1,582 Bibles on parchment), Евр. II C (728 biblical MSS on paper), Евр. II Ba (biblical scrolls on leather, nos. 1–160), Евр. II Ba (biblical scrolls on parchment, nos. 1–34), Евр. II K (marriage contracts), Евр.-араб. I (4,933 Judaeo-Arabic MSS, mostly fragmentary), Евр.-араб. II (3,430 Judaeo-Arabic MSS, mostly fragmentary, also known as Евр.-араб. н.с. [novaia seria or New Series]), Араб.-евр. (382 MSS in Hebrew and Judaeo-Arabic in Arabic characters), Firk. Араб. (Arabic MSS), Firk. Араб. Дп (documents in Arabic on parchment), Firk. Араб. Д (documents in Arabic on paper) and Firk. Sam. (Samaritan MSS divided into fourteen sections according to subject).

The MSS of the Antonin Collection of Hebrew and Samaritan Manuscripts and Fragments (Coll. 937), bearing call-numbers with the prefix Ант. (Евр. III is no longer in use), are divided into three sections: Ант. A (1–13, Hebrew codices and scrolls), Ант. Б (1–22, Samaritan biblical fragments), and Ант. B (1–1155, including 1,139 Geniza fragments and documents). Ант. B 1156 is the handwritten catalogue of the Antonin Collection, prepared by Y. Ravrebe.

The graphic representation of the call-numbers of the main sections in the Firkovich collections shown in Table 2 may simplify comprehension of the classification system.

Since the same letters are used in different sections, it is always necessary to quote the MSS by their full call-numbers to avoid confusion.

CATALOGUES There is no complete published catalogue of either the First or the Second Firkovich Collection. According to C. B. Starkova in *Pis'mennye Pamiainiki Vostoka ... 1970* (see bibliography, below), Hermann Strack composed a short catalogue or inventory in German. In the *Steinschneider collection in *New York, JTSA, is a handwritten catalogue in Hebrew of the First Firkovich Collection, comprising 830 numbers, probably written by A. *Harkavy. Nos. 1–553 are rabbinic MSS, and nos. 554–830 are Karaite MSS. Biblical MSS are not included. Each number generally represents a single MS, but it may also refer to a single work in a MS in which several works are included, so that the total number of MSS in the catalogue is less than 830. As early as 1837, Geiger had published in his *Wissenschaftliche Zeitschrift für jüdische Theologie*, III, pp. 441–448, a list of 20 Karaite and 50 rabbinic MSS offered for sale by a Karaite from Crimea, most probably Firkovich himself. Some of the MSS that appear in Geiger's list as one unit appear in the handwritten catalogue as two or more units. In Part 1 of A. Harkavy and H. L. Strack, *Catalog der hebräischen Bibelhandschriften der Kaiserlichen öffentlichen Bibliothek in St. Petersburg*, St. Petersburg–Leipzig 1875, 146 biblical MSS (48 scrolls and 98 MSS on parchment) from the first collection were described. Part 2 of the same *Catalog* contains descriptions of 35 scrolls and 19 codices from the Odessa collection (see above). The 'Damascusrolle' described in the Appendix on pp. 275–276 of the catalogue is now MS Евр. II (biblical MSS on leather) 160. Earlier, 44 mathematical, astronomical and astrological MSS in the First Firkovich Collection were described by J. Gurland in *Kurze Beschreibung der*

Table 2
Guide to Call Numbers of MSS in the First and Second Firkovich Collections

First Firkovich Collection	*Sample Call-numbers*
Евр. I 1–830 (non-biblical MSS)	MS Евр. I 456
Евр. I Библ. (biblical scrolls and codices)	MS Евр. I Библ. 2
Documents in Hebrew (three sections)	
Евр. I D I	MS Евр. I D I 112
Евр. I D II (documents from Poland)	MS Евр. I D II 6
Евр. I D III	MS Евр. I D III 1
Odessa Collection	
Евр. I A (biblical scrolls)	MS Евр. I A 2
Евр. I B (biblical codices)	MS Евр. I B 2
Евр. I Библ 147–170 (biblical codices)	Евр. I Библ 153a
Евр. I C (non-biblical MSS)	MS Евр. I C 8
Second Firkovich Collection	
Евр. II A (non-biblical MSS)	MS Евр. II A 3
Евр. II B (biblical MSS on parchment)	MS Евр. II B 3
Евр. II C (biblical MSS on paper)	MS Евр. II C 3
Евр. II (biblical scrolls on leather)	
Евр. II (biblical scrolls on parchment)	
Евр. II K (marriage contracts)	MS Евр. II K 76
Евр.-араб. I (Jud.-Arab., 1st Series)	MS Евр.-араб. I 31
Евр.-араб. II (Jud.-Arab., 2nd or New Series)	MS Евр.-араб. II 31
Араб.-евр.	MS Араб.-евр. 21

mathematischen, astronomischen und astrologischen hebräischen Handschriften der Firkowitsch'schen Sammlung in der Kaiserlichen öffentlichen Bibliothek zu St. Petersburg, St. Petersburg 1886. Information about the Second Collection may be obtained from the works of Harkavy, Mann, and others who published material from the collection. A card catalogue of the Second Collection, compiled and updated by A. A. Harkavy, F. Kokovtsov, I. I. Ravrebe, A. Vasilev and V. Lebedev, is in the library. On the basis of this card catalogue, P. B. Fenton published *A Handlist of Judeo-Arabic Manuscripts in Leningrad*, Jerusalem 1991. It contains brief descriptions in Hebrew of MSS in the New Series of Judaeo-Arabic MSS in the Second Firkovich Collection, and a selected list of MSS in philosophy and related subjects in the First Series. A brief handwritten description of 100 MSS from the Second Collection is found among the papers of S. Assaf in *Jerusalem, NLI. According to Pearson, p. 49, there is a handwritten catalogue of 1,189 fragments from the Antonin collection in the Paul de Lagarde Library in New York. A. Katsh published a brief catalogue of the Antonin fragments, arranged according to subject, 'The Antonin Genizah in the Saltikov-Schedrin Public Library in Leningrad' in M. M. Kasher et al. (eds.), *The Leo Jung Jubilee Volume*, New York 1962, pp. 115–131. In his *Catalogue of Hebrew Manuscripts Preserved in the USSR Acquired (on Microfilm) by Abraham I. Katsh*, I–II, New York 1957/8, Katsh published facsimiles of about 70 fragments from the Antonin collection and descriptions of about 30 Antonin fragments. L. Kh. Vilsker published a catalogue in Russian of 98 Samaritan documents (mostly seventeenth- to nineteenth-century *ketubot*): *Samaritiyànskie dokumenty Gosudarstvennoy publichnoy biblioteki imeni M. E. Saltykova-Shchedrina*, St. Petersburg 1992. Almost the entire collection of Hebrew and Judaeo-Arabic MSS has been microfilmed by the *Jerusalem, IMHM, and short or detailed descriptions are available in the IMHM's online catalogue.

Steinschneider, *Vorlesungen*, pp. 82–84 (Hebrew, pp. 105–107); Pearson, pp. 49–51; P. Kahle, *The Cairo Geniza*, Oxford 1959, pp. 5–7, 131–135; A. I. Katsh, 'Hebrew and Judeo-Arabic MSS in the Collections of the USSR', *Trudy XXV: Mezhdunarodnago Kongresa Vostokovedov*, I, Moscow 1962, pp. 421–429; idem, in *EJ Year Book, 1977/8*, pp. 70–72. K. B. Starkova wrote an article on the Firkovich collection, including a history of the collection and a survey of its contents, call-numbers, etc., in *Pis'mennye Pamiainiki Vostoka ... 1970*, Moscow 1974, pp. 165–192 (= 'Les manuscrits de la collection Firkovic conservés à la Bibliothèque publique d'Etat Saltykov-Scedrin', *REJ*, CXXXIV, nos. 3–4, 1975, pp. 101–117); V. Lebedev, in *Archaeographia Orientalis*, Moscow 1990, pp. 93–119; e-communication from Boris Zaikovskii.

St. Petersburg (Russia), Society for the Promotion of Culture among the Jews of Russia (Obshchestva dlia Rasprostraneniia Prosveshcheniia Mezhdu Evreiami v Rossii, OPE)

The MSS formerly in the library of the Society, which was closed in 1929, are now in *Kiev, Vernadsky National Library; see its entry for the movements of this collection.

Z. M. Baker, 'History of the Jewish Collections at the Vernadsky Library in Kiev', *Shofar*, X, no. 4 (1992), pp. 31–48; *Soviet Jewish Affairs*, XXI, no. 2 (1991).

Salamanca (Spain), Biblioteca de la Universidad

Seven Hebrew MSS were described by J. R. Llamas, 'Los manuscritos hebreos de la Universidad de Salamanca' *Sefarad*, X (1950), pp. 263–279. MS 2170, originally from the Colegio Mayor de Cuenca in Salamanca, was not catalogued by Llamas because it was in *Madrid, Biblioteca del Palacio Real from around 1800 to 1954, when it was returned to Salamanca. Eight MSS were briefly described in *Cat. Allony–Kupfer*, II, nos. 1263–1270. The library's call-numbers are listed in parentheses. A Tora scroll (MS 2777) recently discovered in the library was not described in either catalogue. *Jerusalem, IMHM microfilm no. 7243 contains MS Salamanca 294, an Arabic dictionary in Hebrew characters (described by Llamas), and not the Latin–Hebrew grammar described in *Cat. Allony-Kupfer*, II, as bearing that number.

Salem (Germany), Zisterzienserkloster

The MS formerly in this convent is now *Heidelberg, Universitätsbibliothek, Cod. Or. 20.

Cat. Striedl–Róth, no. 212.

Saltykov-Shchedrin Public Library

See *St. Petersburg, NLR.

Salvadore, Joseph

London, eighteenth cent.

Salvadore's MS, described by *Kennicott, no. 137, was later acquired by Kennicott and is now *Oxford, Bodleian Library, MS Kennicott 8 (*Cat. Neubauer*, 2332).

Salzburg (Austria), Archiv der Erzabtei St. Peter

Fragments from 14 MSS were described by A. Altmann in *Geschichte der Juden in Stadt und Land Salzburg* ..., Berlin 1913, pp. 254–257. Contrary to what is implied in *Cat. Allony–Loewinger*, I, p. 7, the fragments are still in the monastery library. Fragments from 39 MSS and printed books are described and displayed on the website http://www.ksbm.oeaw.ac.at/hebraica.

Salzburg (Austria), Universitätsbibliothek
Fragments from 16 MSS are described in *Cat. Schwarz–Loewinger–Róth*, pp. 95–98. Call-numbers are written at the end of each entry. The fragments were also described by E. Róth, 'Hebräische Handschriften in der Salzburger Universitätsbibliothek', in M. Karin-Karger (ed.), *Salzburgs wiederaufgebaute Synagoge*, Salzburg 1968, pp. 61–71. Ten fragments were described in *Cat. Allony–Loewinger*, I, p. 19. Photocopies of several additional fragments exist in the *Jerusalem, IMHM. Fragments removed from 45 MSS and printed books are described and displayed on the website http://www.ksbm.oeaw.ac.at/hebraica.

Samuelzoon, Salomon Cohen
See *Cohen, Salomon Samuelzoon.

San Blasii, Biblioteca Monasterio San Blasii in Sylva Nigra
Latin name of *St. Paul im Lavanttal, Stiftsbibliothek.

San Francisco (Calif.), California State Library
See *Sutro, Adolph.

San Giovanni di Verdara
See *Padua, Convento ... di S. Giovanni di Verdara.

San Lorenzo del Escorial (Spain), Real Biblioteca del Monasterio de El Escorial
The Escorial library was founded by King Philip II in the late sixteenth century. In 1577 there were 47 Hebrew MSS in the library. Most of them came from the collections of Juan Páez de Castro (acquired in 1572, 7 MSS, of which four survive), Juan de Borja (1573, 4 MSS), Alfonso de Zamora (1574, 5 MSS, of which only one survives) and Diego Hurtado de Mendoza (1576, 28 MSS, of which perhaps 15 survive). In 1599 the library received 31 Hebrew MSS from the estate of the late Benito *Arias Montano (d. 1598), and, with some additional acquisitions, the total number of Hebrew MSS in the Escorial rose to 94. In 1656, the collection of Gaspar de Guzmán (Conde-Duque de Olivares), including 16 Hebrew MSS, was acquired. In 1671, a fire destroyed 40 of the 110 Hebrew MSS then in the library.

Seventy-one MSS from the Escorial collection were described in Spanish by J. Llamas, 'Los manuscritos hebreos de la Real Biblioteca de San Lorenzo de El Escorial', *Sefarad*, I (1941), pp. 7–43, 279–311, and III (1943), pp. 41–63. J. L. Lacave described four additional MSS and added notes to the descriptions of several MSS in 'Manuscritos hebreos de la Biblioteca de el Escorial no Catalogados', *ibid.*, XXXVII (1977), pp. 293–308. One of the 'manuscripts' described by Llamas (G I 13) was found to be a printed incunabulum, and a new MS was assigned its call-number and was described by Lacave. In Llamas's catalogue the MSS are listed by subject. The call-number appears at the head of each entry. Palaeographical and codicological information; writing material, type of script, number of leaves, date, description of binding and size. There are no indexes. Seventy-two MSS are described in *Cat. Allony–Kupfer*, II, pp. 89–95, where the MSS are listed in the same order as in the Llamas catalogue and include a printed Bible with marginal notes (G III 19). Call-numbers are listed in parentheses at the end of each entry. The MSS were catalogued again in del Barco, *Catálogo ... Madrid* (see *Madrid). *Jerusalem, IMHM has microfilms of two MSS in Judaeo-Arabic, MSS 834 and 913, which were not included in the printed catalogues listed above.

נ' אלוני, 'כתבי־יד העברים בספריות בספרד', אוצר יהודי ספרד, א (תשי"ט), עמ' 74; G. de Andres, 'Historia de las procedencias de los codices de la réal Biblioteca de el Escorial', *Sefarad*, XXX (1970), pp. 9–37; M. T. Ortega Monasterio, in del Barco, *Catálogo ... Madrid*, I, pp. 34–55.

Sar.
*Saraval.

Sarajevo Haggada
Name given to an illuminated haggada written and decorated in Spain, probably in or near Barcelona in the early–mid fourteenth century. Since 1894 it has been in the possession of the Sarajevo National Museum in Bosnia-Herzegovina (Zemaljski muzej Bosne i Hercegovine). During World War II, the manuscript was hidden from the Nazis by the director of the museum. During the civil war in 1992, the haggada, together with other cultural treasures, was rescued and not harmed.

Narkiss, p. 60. Facsimile editions with scholarly introductions by D. H. Müller, J. Schlosser and D. Kaufmann (Vienna 1898), C. Roth (New York 1963), and E. Werber (Belgrade 1983).

Sarajevo, National Museum in Bosnia-Herzegovina (Zemaljski muzej Bosne i Hercegovine)
In addition to the *Sarajevo Haggada, the Museum also possessed a MS of *She'erit Yisra'el* (שארית ישראל) by Israel Najara, described by M. Levi, *Jevrejski Almanah 5687*, Vršac 1926, pp. 45–53.

Sarajevo, Oriental Institute (Orijentalni institut)
The Institute was home to over 5,000 MSS, among them several in Hebrew. All were destroyed on May 17, 1992, during the civil war.

Sarav.
*Saraval.

Saraval, Leon Vita
Trieste, Italy, 1771–1851; bibliophile
Sixty-nine Hebrew MSS belonging to Saraval were described in M. Steinschneider, *Catalogue de la Bibliothèque de littérature hebraïque et orientale d'auteurs hébreux de feu ... Léon V. Saraval*, Trieste 1853 (sometimes referred to as רשימת אורי חי סארוואל or ראח"ס). Forty-nine MSS had previously been described by Solomon Gottleib *Stern for Solomon J. L. *Rapoport in a handwritten list (MS *Jerusalem, NLI, Heb. 8° 2393). The MSS were acquired by *Breslau, Jüdisch-theologisches Seminar, and described again in the Zuckermann and Loewinger–Weinryb catalogues (see *Breslau). A concordance to the numbers in all three published catalogues is found in *Cat. Loewinger–Weinryb*, pp. 302–303. For the present locations of the MSS, see Breslau.

Sasportas, Jacob
Oran, Algeria, c. 1610 – Amsterdam, Netherlands, 1698; rabbi
A MS of Maimonides' responsa, called the 'Sasportas MS', formerly in Sasportas's possession, served as the basis for Mordecai Tama's Hebrew version of the responsa (פאר הדור). The MS was eventually purchased by David *Simonsen and is now in *Copenhagen, Kongelige Bibliothek (Cod. Sim. Jud.-Arab. 1). The MS was described by J. Blau in his edition of the responsa, Jerusalem 1961, III, pp. 4–6.

Sassoon, Solomon David
London, 1915 – Jerusalem, 1985
The Sassoon collection, put together by Solomon David's father David Solomon Sassoon (1880–1942), included 1,282 MSS. In *Cat. Sassoon* (1932), 1,153 MSS were described in English. The catalogue is arranged according to subject, though this arrangement is only partly adhered to in the appendix on pp. 604–1112. The descriptions of the MSS are very detailed and include many lengthy quotations, discussions of the works copied in the MSS and bibliographical information. The opening lines of all poems and liturgical works in the MSS are quoted in the catalogue. At the head of each entry the call-number is printed

in bold type. Palaeographical and codicological information: type of script, date, number of pages, writing material and size (in inches). Colophons and owners' entries are generally transcribed. Indexes: authors, scribes, owners, witnesses, names mentioned, liturgical poets, censors and non-Jews, family surnames, titles, place names, liturgical poems and Samaritan MSS. The indexes refer to the page numbers of the catalogue and not to the MS numbers. At the end of the catalogue is a concordance to the MS numbers and the page numbers in the catalogue. G. Scholem published some corrections and notes to the entries of the Kabbala MSS in *KS*, X (1933/4), pp. 169–171. The Sassoon library was housed on the Sassoon estate at Letchworth. After Solomon David moved to Israel, most of the MSS were put into storage. In 1975, S. D. Sassoon began to sell MSS from the collection at public auctions. Thirty-eight MSS offered for sale at the first auction in the fall of 1975 at Sotheby's in Zurich were described in the auction catalogue, *Thirty-eight Highly Important Hebrew and Samaritan Manuscripts from the Collection Formed by the Late David Solomon Sassoon, Which Will Be Sold at Auction by Sotheby & Company at Baur au Lac Hotel, Zurich ... on Wednesday, 5th November, 1975* [London 1975]. Twenty-eight of the MSS were sold at the auction. At the second auction, in Zurich in 1978, 33 MSS (actually 85 items, as one of the lots consisted of 53 marriage contracts) were offered for sale. They were described in *A Further Thirty-Three Highly Important Hebrew Manuscripts from the Collection Formed by the Late David Solomon Sassoon, Which Will Be Sold at Auction by Sotheby Parke Bernet A. G. at Baur au Lac Hotel, Zurich, on Tuesday 21st November, 1978* [London 1978]. In 1981, 116 items (one of them including 52 marriage contracts, each considered a separate MS in *Cat. Sassoon*) offered for sale were described in *Important Hebrew and Samaritan Manuscripts from the Collection Formed by the Late David Solomon Sassoon* [London 1981]. In 1982, Sassoon presented several of his MSS to the British government in lieu of taxes owed, and the MSS were distributed among British libraries already owning substantial collections. In December 1984, another sale of MSS from the collection was held at Sotheby's in New York. The MSS were described in *A Further Ninety-Seven Highly Important Hebrew Manuscripts from the Collection Formed by the Late David Solomon Sassoon* [London 1984]. MS 23, offered at the 1975 sale, was later listed in Sotheby's auction catalogue *Highly Important Judaica*, Tel Aviv 1993, lot 33. Another sale included *Seventy-Six Important Hebrew and Samaritan Manuscripts from the Library of the Late David Solomon Sassoon* [London 1994]. Six Hebrew MSS were listed in Sotheby's auction catalogue *Magnificent Judaica*, Tel Aviv 1994, lots 211, 212–217. Two illuminated Esther scrolls that were not included in *Ohel Dawid* were listed in Sotheby's auction catalogue *A Collection from the Sassoon Family Estate*, Tel Aviv 2000, lots 12 and 25. Appendix I, no. 35, lists the MSS no longer in the Sassoon collection and the present locations of those that can be traced.

Sassoon Spanish Haggada

Name given to MS *Sassoon 514, an illuminated Spanish haggada. The MS is now *Jerusalem, Israel Museum, MS 181/41.

Narkiss, p. 62.

SB or SBB

Staatsbibliothek or Stadtbibliothek.

Scal.

*Scaliger.

Scaliger, Joseph Justus

Agen, France, 1540 – Leiden, Netherlands, 1609; philologist

Scaliger taught at the University in Leiden. He bequeathed 15 Hebrew MSS to *Leiden, Universiteitsbibliotheek (MSS Scal. Hebr. 1, 3–7, 9–15, 19–20). The MSS are described in *Cat. Steinschneider*, Leiden, pp. 310–379. Another MS of Scaliger's (now MS Or. 2361) is described in M. J. de Goeje, *Catalogus Codicum Orientalium Bibliothecae Academiae Lugdono-Batavae*, V, Leiden 1873, no. 2361. The MSS bearing the call-numbers Scal. Hebr. 2, 8 and 16 (Cods. Or. 4719, 4725 and 4733) belonged not to Scaliger but to Franciscus Raphelengius and were included in the Scaliger collection by mistake, as shown by Alastair Hamilton, 'Franciscus Raphelengius: The Hebraist and his manuscripts', *De Gulden Passer*, LXVIII (1990), pp. 105–117.

A. van der Heide, *Hebrew Manuscripts of Leiden University Library*, Leiden 1977, pp. 3–10.

Schbl.
*Schönblum.

Schechter, Solomon
Focsani, Romania, 1847 – New York, 1915; scholar
Schechter brought over 100,000 *Geniza fragments to *Cambridge, University Library, and thus laid the foundation for the Taylor–Schechter Geniza Collection. Thirteen MSS and a few Geniza fragments from his private collection were bequeathed to *New York, JTSA, of which he was president (Rab., *Lit. Treas.*, p. 67). The MS of Yom Tov Zahalon's *Magen avot* that Schechter used in his edition of *Avot derabbi Natan* was sold to *Oxford, Bodleian Library, and is now MS Heb. c. 24 (*Cat. Neubauer–Cowley*, II, no. 2635).

S. C. Reif, 'Jenkinson and Schechter at Cambridge', *Jewish Historical Studies; Transactions of the Jewish Historical Society of England*, XXXII (1990–1992), pp. 279–316; Reif, *Cat. Cambridge*, pp. 28–32.

Scheid, Elie
See *Strasbourg, Gesellschaft für die Geschichte der Israeliten in Elsass-Lothringen.

Schiller-Szinessy, Solomon Mayer
Budapest, Hungary, 1820 – Cambridge, England, 1890
Schiller-Szinessy compiled a catalogue (partly published) of the Hebrew MSS in *Cambridge, University Library (q.v.), and described the Hebrew MSS in *Cambridge, Trinity College.

Reif, *Cat. Cambridge*, pp. 26–28.

Schlesinger, Akiva
Pressburg (Bratislava), Slovakia, 1843 – Vienna, Austria, 1898 ; bookseller
The MS by Bezalel Ashkenazi offered for sale by Schlesinger and described by A. Jellinek (א׳ ילינק, קונטרס המזכיר, וינה תרל״ז, עמ׳ 26–16) is now *London, BL, MS Or. 5014 (*Cat. Margoliouth*, no. 421).

Schloss, Solomon
London, 1815–1911; collector
Schloss's collection was sold at auction by Hodgson's in 1917/8. A number of MSS were purchased by David Solomon Sassoon (*Cat. Sassoon*, p. xi; see *Sassoon, Solomon David), and several others are now in *New York, JTSA.

Schloss Nikolsburg
See *Nikolsburg.

Schmid, Anton von
Vienna, 1765–1855
Schmid, a non-Jewish printer of Hebrew books in Vienna, owned a number of Hebrew MSS. Four Karaite MSS were presented to *Vienna, Österreichische Nationalbibliothek (for details see *Leonowitsch, Abraham). One MS of his is now *Jerusalem, NLI, Heb. 8° 4279.

Schocken, Salman
See *Jerusalem, Schocken Institute.

Schocken Bible

Name given to *Jerusalem, Schocken Institute, MS 14840, an illuminated Bible written in Ashkenaz at the end of the thirteenth century or beginning of the fourteenth. The MS was sold to a private collector in Israel.

Narkiss, p. 102.

Schocken Italian Maḥzor

Name given to *Jerusalem, Schocken Institute, MS 13873, an illuminated Italian maḥzor written in 1441, formerly in the collection of Fernand *Lair-Dubreuil. The MS was sold in 2005 to a private collector in Israel.

Narkiss, p. 138.

Schoenberg, Lawrence J.

Sarasota, Fl., b. 1932; businessman

Schoenberg donated a collection of medieval MSS that includes about 20 Hebrew MSS to the Rare Book and Manuscript Library in *Philadelphia, University of Pennsylvania.

Scholem, Gershom

Berlin, 1897 – Jerusalem, 1982; scholar and bibliophile

The foremost authority in the fields of Kabbala and Jewish mysticism, Scholem wrote many books on these subjects, among them a catalogue of the Kabbala MSS in *Jerusalem, JNUL (now NLI). He also described and published many MSS in his works on Kabbala. In separate articles and in reviews of printed catalogues, he described or added information on the Kabbala MSS of *London, British Library, *Milan, Biblioteca Ambrosiana, *Munich, Bayerische Staatsbibliothek, *Paris, Bibliothèque nationale de France, and the *Sassoon collections. Scholem's own library, including a few MSS, is now in the NLI. A few MSS from Scholem's collection are in *Jerusalem, Schocken Institute.

Schönbaum, Meir

Jerusalem, d. 1890

Schönbaum owned many Kabbala MSS. Some are now in *New York, JTSA. Four MSS were in *Jerusalem, Mosad Harav Kook, two are in the Meir Benayahu collection in Jerusalem, and at least one MS is in *New York, Yeshiva University.

Schönberg, Dr.

Berlin, nineteenth century

A MS belonging to Schönberg is now *London, BL, MS Add. 21967 (*Cat. Margoliouth*, no. 1026).

Schönbl.

*Schönblum.

Schönblum, Samuel

Lemberg (Lviv), Ukraine, 1833–1900; bookseller

Schönblum published two catalogues of Mordecai *Ghirondi's MSS in 1870 and 1872, the latter compiled by M. *Steinschneider. In 1872 he also published a *Catalogue d'une collection anconienne* ... listing 56 MSS belonging to Hayyim *Azulai and his son Rafael. In 1885, Schönblum published *Catalogue de manuscrits hébreux collection Schoenblum*, in which he very briefly described 278 MSS he was offering for sale. Schönblum sold MSS to most of the major libraries and collectors of his time. *Cambridge, University Library, purchased a large number, among them MSS originally in the Samuel *Luzzatto collection (see the index of owners in Reif, *Cat. Cambridge*, p. 589). MSS purchased from Schönblum's catalogues by *Oxford, Bodleian Library, are listed in *Cat. Neubauer*, p. xxxii, and *Cat. Neubauer–Cowley*, II, pp. xii–xvi. Other MSS in the Bodleian purchased from him are MSS Opp. Add. 2° 30, 31, 35, 37, 38, 42, 43; Opp. Add. 4° 67, 71–74, 100–106, 179, 183; and Opp. Add. 8° 19. *Cat. Schwarz*, Vienna, lists over 20 MSS in the *Vienna, Österreichische Nationalbibliothek, purchased from Schönblum. Other libraries to which he sold MSS are the British Museum (now *London, British Library), *Berlin, Staatsbibliothek, Or. 8° 333, 539, 396 and Or. 2° 1618 (*Cat. Steinschneider*, Berlin, nos. 165, 205, 206, 219), *New York, JTSA, MS R1093 (no. 20 in the catalogue) and MS 1343 (no. 56), and *Munich, Bayerische Staatsbibliothek (Cods. hebr. 147–150, 384–386). Among private collectors to whom he sold MSS, mention may be made of Elkan *Adler, Solomon *Halberstamm and Abraham *Merzbacher. The MS from which Schönblum published texts in *Shelosha sefarim niftaḥim* (שלשה ספרים נפתחים, למברג תרל״ז) is now JTSA, MS R34. In JTSA, MS 2861, fols. 62–96, is a list of MSS that Schönblum sent to *Steinschneider.

Schönblum–Ghirondi
See *Ghirondi.

Schorr, Joshua (Osias) Heschel
Brody, Ukraine, 1814–1895; scholar

Many of Schorr's MSS were described by him in *Heḥaluts* (החלוץ), the periodical he edited. In 1847, Schorr purchased 300 MSS from Isaac *Reggio. He sold 60 of them to *Oxford, Bodleian Library (Steinschneider, *Vorlesungen*, p, 59 [Hebrew p. 78]), and four, through *Steinschneider, to *Berlin, Staatsbibliothek (three MSS listed in the index of owners in *Cat. Steinschneider*, Berlin, as well as Cod. Or. 4° 832). Twenty-four of Schorr's MSS were in *Vienna, Israelitische Kultusgemeinde, and were listed in the index of owners in Cat. *Schwarz–Loewinger–Róth*. Many of Schorr's MSS disappeared after his death and never reached the Kultusgemeinde library (Cat. *Schwarz*, Austria, foreword). Other MSS of Schorr's are now *New York, JTSA, MS 4064 (Freimann, *Scribes*, no. 288c), *Paris, AIU, MS H 124 A (*ibid.*, no. 118c), and *Cambridge (Mass.), Harvard University, MSS Heb. 61 and 64. The latter was described in *Heḥaluts*, II (1843), pp. 159–160. A MS of Isaac Albalag's version of al-Gazzali's *Kavanot hafilosofim* (כוונות הפילוסופים), described by Schorr in *Heḥaluts*, IV (1859), pp, 83–94, VI (1862), pp. 85–94, and VII (1865), pp. 157–169, is now *Jerusalem, NLI, Heb. 8° 6287. A MS described in *Heḥaluts*, XIII (1883), p. 107, is now *Frankfurt a/M, Goethe Universität, Universitätsbibliothek, MS oct. 130. Schorr's MS of astrological works by Sahl Ibn Bishr and others, described by M. Steinschneider in *HÜ*, p. 605, and in his *Die arabische Literaturgeschichte der Juden*, Frankfurt a/M 1902, p. 25, was in the Kultusgemeinde (but not listed in the catalogue) and is now NLI, Heb. 8° 5563.

Schøyen Collection

Oslo businessman Martin Schøyen assembled a collection of over 13,000 manuscripts, and writings on other materials, in dozens of different scripts. A few dozen of the items are in Hebrew, including fragments of the Dead Sea Scrolls and other ancient writings, as well as medieval MSS acquired from bookdealers, several of them from the *Sassoon library. The Schøyen Collection is located mainly in Oslo and London. In July 2012 Schøyen offered for sale at a Sotheby's auction in London 60 fragments of ancient MSS, including a few in Hebrew.

Schulting, Cornelius
Amsterdam, Netherlands, d. 1726

Schulting's collection, including over 20 Hebrew MSS, was sold at auction after his death, and the MSS were listed in *Bibliotheca Schultingiana, sive catalogus Librorum ... a ... D. Cornelio Schultingio relictorum*, Amsterdam 1726. His Bible MSS were described in Johann Christoph *Wolf's *Bibliotheca Hebraea*, IV, pp. 79–84. Wolf listed some other MSS of Schulting's elsewhere in his book. Ten Bible MSS sold at auction after Schulting's death were purchased by Johannes van der Hagen. Adam *Clarke bought them from the heirs of the van der Hagen family in Utrecht in 1823 (see *Clarke, Adam). Clarke's MSS are now in *London, British Library. One other biblical MS from the Schulting sale (no. 2) was purchased by David Mill and eventually acquired by *Kennicott. It is now *Oxford, Bodleian Library, MS Kennicott 10. For the present locations of some of the MSS see Appendix I, no. 37.

Schwab, Moise

Paris, 1839–1918; scholar

Schwab described MSS of *Paris, AIU, *Paris, Mazarine, *Paris, Oratoire, *Basel, Öffentliche Bibliothek der Universität, *Zurich, Zentralbibliothek, and some of the later acquisitions of *Paris, Bibliothèque nationale de France.

Schwager, Lippa

Husiatyn, Ukraine, 1882 – Tel Aviv, 1961; bookseller

In 1903, Schwager began to publish catalogues, which appeared about four times a year and in which many MSS offered for sale were described. In 1906, Schwager's brother-in-law David *Fränkel became his partner, and the names Schwager & Fränkel appeared on the catalogues from no. 10 on. Catalogue no. 11 (אוצר כלי חמדה), Husiatyn 1906, lists 446 MSS, most of which were acquired by *New York, JTSA. R. Shalom Dov Ber Schneerson purchased 22 of them in 1907 (see *New York, Chassidei Chabad Ohel Yosef Yitzchak Lubavitch Library). At the outbreak of World War I, the firm's warehouse in Husiatyn was destroyed in a fire, and many books and MSS were lost. A few years after the war the partnership was dissolved, and Schwager settled in Vienna, from where he set out on expeditions to the Middle East and Yemen in search of books. Schwager sold MSS to many libraries and private collectors, among them JTSA, *Jerusalem, JNUL (now NLI), Elkan *Adler, S. Schocken (see *Jerusalem, Schocken Institute), David Solomon Sassoon (see *Sassoon, Solomon David), and Moses *Gaster (nos. 1038–1058 in his collection were purchased by Gaster from Schwager & Fränkel, mostly from their catalogue no. 11).

א"מ הברמן, אנשי ספר ואנשי מעשה, ירושלים תשל"ד, עמ' 80–81.

Schwarz, Adolf

Adász-Tevel, Hungary, 1846 – Vienna, 1931; scholar

Two MSS owned by Schwarz were described in *Cat. Schwarz*, Austria, nos. 98 and 168. No. 98 was *Jerusalem, Mosad Harav Kook, MS 757. The present whereabouts of no. 168 are unknown.

Schwarz, Arthur Zacharias

Karlsruhe, Germany, 1880 – Jerusalem, 1939

Schwarz compiled catalogues of the Hebrew MSS in *Vienna, Österreichische Nationalbibliothek (= *Cat. Schwarz*, Vienna), in *Nikolsburg, and in other Austrian libraries. In *Die hebräischen Handschriften in Österreich*, I, Leipzig 1931 (= *Cat. Schwarz*, Austria), 283 MSS in Austrian libraries (excluding those in the Nationalbibliothek, described in a separate catalogue) were described. D. S. Loewinger and E. Róth published Part II of the catalogue in Jerusalem in 1973 (= *Cat. Schwarz–Loewinger–Róth*). Part IIA (nos. 284–302) had been left in manuscript by Schwarz, and Loewinger and Róth added Part IIB: descriptions of fragments found in Austrian libraries, including those of the Erzherzog *Rainer collection in the Nationalbibliothek (pp. 55–109); a list of the collections included in the catalogue (p. 110); uncatalogued MSS in Austria (p. 111); and a list of the MSS described in both volumes of the catalogue that are now in libraries outside Austria (pp. 111–112). A more complete list of the present locations of these MSS is found herein, in Appendix I, no. 38. The second volume of the catalogue also includes the following indexes to both parts of the catalogue: authors, scribes, owners, censors, place names, titles and anonymous works.

Scotus, Bibliotheca Monast. Scotus
See *Vienna, Unsere Liebe Frau zu den Schotten.

Second
References in this *Guide* are alphabetized according to the following word (e.g., for Second Kennicott Bible, see *Kennicott Bible, Second).

Segre Amar, Sion
Turin, Italy, 1910–2003; collector
Segre Amar's collection of MSS is on deposit in the Comites Latentes ('hidden friends'), a private foundation he established, which entrusted its collection for safe-keeping to the *Geneva, Bibliothèque publique et universitaire, in 1977.

Seld.
*Selden.

Selden, John
Salvington, England, 1584 – Whitefriars, England, 1654; scholar
Selden bequeathed 21 MSS to *Oxford, Bodleian Library. A list of the MSS bearing call-numbers with the prefix 'Arch. Seld.' or 'Arch. Selden' (= Archivum Seldenianum) and their numbers in *Cat. Neubauer* is found on p. xxx of the catalogue. In *Cat. Neubauer–Cowley*, II, p. xvi, an additional four MSS, mostly written by Christians and bearing call-numbers with the prefixes 'Seld. A.' and 'Seld. supra', are listed.

Seligmann, Isaac
See *Berend Salomon, Isaac Seligmann Cohn.

Selly Oak Colleges
See *Birmingham, Selly Oak Colleges.

Senae
Latin name for Siena.

Sereni Haggada
An illuminated Italian haggada now in the museum of the Italian Synagogue in Jerusalem.

Serugiel Bible
Name given to *Oxford, Bodleian Library, MS Bodl. Arch. Seld. A. 47 (*Cat. Neubauer*, no. 7), a Spanish Bible copied by Samuel b. Jacob Serugiel in Soria in 1304.
Narkiss, *Span. & Port.*, no. 7.

Servi, Flaminio
Pitigliano, Italy, 1841 – Casale Monferrato, Italy, 1904; rabbi
Three of Servi's MSS are listed in *Il Vessillo Israelitico*, XXXIX (1891), pp. 147–148. One of these MSS, a Bible, was in the possession of William Roth in New York (Freimann, *Scribes*, nos. 33w and 278b) and was sold at Sotheby's in New York on December 17, 2008 (*Property from the Delmonico Collection*, no. 203). Another MS is now *Berlin, SB, Cod. Or. 4° 823 (*Cat. Steinschneider*, Berlin, no. 169). About 50 of his MSS were acquired by *New York, JTSA. The MS listed by U. Cassuto, 'Bibliografia delle traduzioni giudeo-italiane della Bibbia', in *Festschrift Armand Kaminka*, Vienna 1937, p. 133, no. 1, is now JTSA, MS L701.

SfarData
See *Hebrew Palaeography Project (HPP).

Shapira, Moses Wilhelm
Kamenets-Podolski, Ukraine, 1830 – Rotterdam, Netherlands, 1884; apostate, missionary and bookseller
Shapira, who emigrated to Jerusalem in 1856,

sold over 300 MSS, including 145 Karaite MSS, to the British Museum (now *London, British Library, see *Cat. Margoliouth–Leveen*, IV, p. viii; Rab., *Lit. Treas.*, pp. 19–22), and 50 MSS, mostly from Yemen, to *Berlin, Staatsbibliothek (*Cat. Steinschneider*, Berlin, I, p. v). In 1884, Adolph *Sutro purchased Yemenite MSS from Shapira's widow and brought them to California (W. M. Brinner, *Sutro Library Hebraica*, [San Francisco] 1966, pp. iii–iv). The Berlin library purchased from the widow handwritten lists of MSS that Shapira had collected (Cod. Or. 2° 1342, *Cat. Steinschneider*, Berlin, no. 176) and a handwritten catalogue of MSS that he had brought over from Yemen in the year 1879 (Cod. Or. 2° 1343, *Cat. Steinschneider*, Berlin, no. 176b). *Oxford, Bodleian Library, purchased a number of MSS from Shapira (MSS Opp. Add. 2° 65–66, Opp. Add. 4° 162 and 166–167). Shapira offered for sale a number of antiquities that were believed to be forgeries, among them fragments from a supposedly ancient scroll containing part of Deuteronomy, with many variations from the accepted text (O. K. Rabinowicz, 'The Shapira Scroll: A nineteenth-century forgery', *JQR*, LVI (1965–1966), pp. 1–21; C. Sirat, 'Les fragments Shapira', *REJ*, CXLIII [1984], pp. 95–111). Since the discovery of the Dead Sea Scrolls, interest in the Shapira scroll has revived, but all efforts to locate it have been futile. Charles Nicholson purchased three Tora scrolls from Shapira and tried to buy the Deuteronomy fragments. According to a letter kept in the library of the University of *Sydney, Australia, it seems quite probable that he did buy the fragments. If so, they were probably destroyed in the fire that burned down Nicholson's home in 1899 (A. D. Crown, 'The fate of the Shapira Scroll', *Revue de Qumran*, VII [1970], pp. 421–423).

Shazar, Zalman

S. Z. Rubashow; Mir, Belarus, 1889 – Jerusalem, 1974; President of Israel

MSS owned by Shazar are now in *Jerusalem, NLI. Two MSS of writings by Ḥabad rabbis are held in the Zalman Shazar Center for Jewish History in Jerusalem.

Shelah Lekha

Name given to *Jerusalem, NLI, Heb. 8° 2238, a copy of the pericope *Shelaḥ Lekha* alone, written in the Orient in 1106/7.

Narkiss, p. 46.

Shem Tov Bible

Name given to MS *Sassoon 82, an illuminated Bible written by Shem Tov Ibn Gaon in Soria in 1312. The MS is described in *Cat. Sassoon*, pp. 2–5, and in the sales catalogue *A Further Ninety-Seven Highly Important Hebrew Manuscripts from the Collection Formed by the Late David Solomon Sassoon* [London 1984], lot 97. The MS was formerly in Tunis (see D. Cazes, 'Antiquités judaïques en Tripolitaine', *REJ*, XX [1890], pp. 80–83).

Siddur of the Rabbi of Ruzhin

See *Friedmann, Israel.

Silvera, Ezra Solomon

Aleppo, Syria, nineteenth–twentieth cent.; merchant

A MS copy of Isaac Ibn Ezra's *diwan*, formerly in the possession of Ezra Solomon Silvera, was acquired by *New York, JTSA, in 1970 (MS 8386) and was published by M. Schmelzer (New York 1981).

Silvestriana

The collection of the Silvestri family is now in *Rovigo, Biblioteca dell'Accademia dei Concordi.

Sim.

*Simonsen, David.

Simhoni, Jacob N.

Slutzk, Belarus, 1884 – Berlin, 1926

Simhoni bequeathed his collection to Israel *Davidson. Davidson's library was presented to *New York, JTSA.

Register, 5701, p. 62 (Marx, *Bibl. Studies*, p. 313).

Simonsen, David Jacob

Copenhagen, Denmark, 1853–1932; rabbi

In 1925, 134 MSS from Simonsen's collection were acquired by *Copenhagen, Kongelige Bibliothek (*Cat. Allony–Kupfer*, II, p. 18). Among these MSS are two collections of responsa by Maimonides in Judaeo-Arabic known as MS Simonsen A (MS *Sasportas, now Cod. Sim. Jud.-Arab. 1; published in Hebrew translation under the title: פאר הדור, אמסטרדם תקכ״ה) and MS Simonsen B (Cod. Sim. Jud.-Arab. 2). The MSS were described by J. Blau in his edition of the responsa, Vol. III, Jerusalem 1961, pp. 3–6. A MS of geonic responsa from which the collection *Ḥemda genuza* (חמדה גנוזה) was probably published, formerly in the possession of D. Simonsen, was acquired by B. M. *Lewin and was in *Ramat Gan, Bar-Ilan University Library, according to Y. Alfasi (י׳ אלפסי, ׳כתב־יד חדש של תשובות הגאונים׳, ארשת, ד [תשכ״ו], עמ׳ 179–175); but it has since disappeared. Transcriptions made from various MSS by S. Poznanski, acquired by Simonsen and described by him, 'Eine Sammlung polemischer und apologetischer Literatur', *Festschrift für Aron Freimann*, Berlin 1935, pp. 114–119, are now *Jerusalem, NLI, MSS Heb. 4° 176 and 8° 751–819.

Simpson (or Simson), Joseph

New York, d. 1753

Simpson lent a Bible MS to *Kennicott (no. 144 on Kennicott's list, which gives the owner as Sampson Simson, Joseph's son). The MS was purchased from M. Levy in 1901 by the British Museum (now *London, BL, MS Or. 5956, *Cat. Margoliouth*, no. 1140).

Sister to the Golden Haggada

See *Golden Haggada.

S. L.

Supplementary List of recent acquisitions and omissions in the Margoliouth–Leveen catalogue of the British Museum Hebrew MSS, Vol. IV, pp. 151–161. See *London, British Library.

Sloane, Hans

Killyleagh, Northern Ireland, 1660 – London, 1753; scientist and collector

His collection, including thirteen Hebrew MSS, was purchased after his death by the British House of Commons for the British Museum (now *London, British Library). For a list of the MSS see *Cat. Margoliouth–Leveen*, IV, p. 163.

Slouschz, Nahum

Smorgan, Lithuania, 1872 – Gedera, Israel, 1966; scholar and author

Many of Slouschz's MSS are now in *Jerusalem, Ben-Zvi Institute. One MS, a collectanea copied in Segovia in 1437, described by Dov (Bernard) Revel (*The Jewish Forum*, I [1918], pp. 74–77; ד׳ רוול, ׳אגרת רב סעדיה גאון׳, דביר, א [תרפ״ג], עמ׳ 181–180) and listed in the auction catalogue *Important Judaica* (New York, Sotheby's December 13, 2006), lot 173, was sold.

SMAF

See *Paris, Société des manuscrits des assureurs français.

Smith-Lesouëf

See *Nogent-sur-Marne, Fondation Smith-Lesouëf.

Soave, Moise

Venice, Italy, 1820–1882; scholar

Soave owned about 200 MSS. In a letter to Moritz *Steinschneider published in *Il*

Vessillo Israelitico, XXVI (1878), p. 252, Soave listed a number of his MSS. Today, they are dispersed among various libraries, including the following: *Berlin, SB, Or. 2° 1055, Or. 4° 834, Or. 4° 836; *Cambridge, UL, MS Or. 804; *London, BL, Or. 2443; *Milan, Ambrosiana, X 133 Sup.; *Moscow, RSL, Günzburg 611; *New York, Public Library, **P, MS Heb. 182 (formerly *London, Montefiore, MS 372); *New York, JTSA, MSS 2200 (Hirsch 108), 2670 (ST 31), 3551 (ENA 675), 4715 (ENA 2007), 3891 (Halb. 430); *Oxford, Bodleian Library, MS Opp. Add. 8° 48; *Paris, AIU H 43 A; *St. Petersburg, Institute of Oriental Manuscripts, B 377 and C 88; *Vienna, ÖNB, Cod. Hebr. 181; and the collection of D. H. Feinberg, New York (formerly *London, Montefiore, MS 108).

Codex Soberanas
Name given to *Barcelona, Bibliboteca de Cataluña, MS 3090, a fourteenth-century ledger in Hebrew, Arabic and Romance languages in Hebrew script, named for its discoverer, Prof. A. Soberanas Lléo. It was edited by M. Blasco Orellana (Barcelona 2003).

Society for the Promotion of Culture among the Jews of Russia
See *under St. Petersburg.

Socin, Albert
Basel, Switzerland, 1844 – Leipzig, Germany, 1899; orientalist
Socin's MSS are in *Halle, Bibliothek der DMG.

Sofia (Bulgaria), Jewish Scientific Institute
The few Hebrew MSS in the Institute were transferred to the Institute for Balkan Studies of the Bulgarian Academy of Sciences when the two institutes merged. These MSS are now in the Centralen Darzaven Istoriceski Archiv (Central Historical State Archives).

Soissons (France), Bibliothèque municipale
One Hebrew MS was described in *Catalogue général*, III (1885), p. 72, no. 1; by M. Schwab, 'Le commentaire de R. David Qamhi sur les Psaumes', *REJ*, XIII (1886), pp. 295–296; and in C. Sirat and M. Beit-Arié, *Manuscrits médiévaux en caractères hébraïques*, I, Paris–Jerusalem 1972, no. 14.

Sommerhausen, Zvi Hirsch
Amsterdam, Netherlands, 1781 – Brussels, Belgium, 1853; scholar
Sommerhausen's MS, described by himself, 'Betrachtungen und Zusätze zum Berichte über die Purim-Literatur', *Literaturblatt des Orients*, XI (1850), pp. 181–182, and by M. Steinschneider, 'Purim und Parodie', *Israelietische Letterbode*, VII (1881/2), p. 12, is now *Amsterdam, UB, HS. Ros. 236.

Sonne, Isaiah
Galicia, 1887 – Cincinnati, Ohio, 1960; scholar
Most of Sonne's MSS are in *Jerusalem, Ben-Zvi Institute. A few are in *Jerusalem, NLI, and *New York, JTSA. Sonne's Catalonian maḥzor, from which Simon *Bernstein published a number of poems in *The American-Hebrew Year Book* (ספר השנה ליהודי אמריקה, ב [תרצ״ה], עמ׳ 197–217), was sold to Bernstein, who presented it to JTSA (MS 4418). One MS in *Oxford, Bodleian (MS hebr. e. 123), was purchased from Sonne. During the years 1935–1937, Sonne made a survey of the rare books, MSS and documents in the libraries of the Jewish communities and institutions in Italy. Sonne, *Relazione*, a typewritten copy of the survey, is in the NLI (R 50 B 954).

Soranzo, Jacopo
Venice, Italy, 1686–1761; bibliophile
After Soranzo's death, his library was divided between two families, one of which was the Corner family (see *Corneliana).
Tamani, *Venezia*, p. 248.

Sorbonne
See *Paris, Sorbonne.

Spencer Collection
See *New York, Public Library.

Spitzer, Moshe
Moravia, 1900 – Jerusalem, 1983; typographer
Spitzer's MS of *Midrash raba* (מדרש רבא), mentioned by E. S. Rosenthal (א״ש רוזנטל, 'למילון התלמוד', תרביץ, מ [תשל״א], עמ' 179), was acquired by *Jerusalem, JNUL (now NLI), in 1979 and now bears the call-number Heb. 4° 5977.

Steiermärkisches Landesarchiv
See *Graz, Steiermärkisches Landesarchiv.

Steinschneider, Moritz
Prossnitz, Moravia, 1816 – Berlin, 1907; bibliographer
Known as the 'Nestor of Jewish Bibliography', Steinschneider compiled numerous catalogues of Hebrew MS collections in various libraries, the major ones being: *Leiden, Universiteitsbibliotheek (1858), *Munich, Bayerische Staatsbibliothek (1875, 2nd ed. 1895), *Hamburg, SUB (1878), and *Berlin, Staatsbibliothek (Vols. I–II, 1878–1897). He also compiled catalogues of private collections and booksellers' catalogues in which MSS were described: *Saraval (1853), *Asher & Co. (1868), *Benzian (1869) and *Ghirondi (1872). In addition, Steinschneider described many MSS in the periodical *Hebräische Bibliographie*, which he edited, and in his many scholarly books and articles. Steinschneider owned a number of MSS. A list of books and MSS from his collection is found in *New York, JTSA, MS 2814. Most of them were purchased for JTSA by Jacob Schiff. Other MSS from Steinschneider's collection are now in *Berlin, Staatsbibliothek (see the index of owners in *Cat. Steinschneider*, Berlin, and add Cod. Or. 2° 1618), including some acquired from Solomon *Halberstamm in exchange for other MSS (Cods. Or. 8° 459 and 23). For a complete list of Steinschneider's manuscripts see B. Richler, 'Steinschneider's manuscripts', in R. Leicht and G. Freudenthal (eds.), *Studies on Steinschneider: Moritz Steinschneider and the Emergence of the Science of Judaism in Nineteenth-Century Germany*, Leiden–Boston 2011, pp. 301–318.

Stern, Moritz
Steinbach, Germany, 1864 – Berlin, 1939; rabbi
Stern sold a MS of writings by Moses Hayyim Luzzatto to *Cincinnati, HUC (MS 867).

I. Sonne, 'Some Luzzatto manuscripts', *Studies in Bibliography and Booklore*, II (1956), p. 158.

Stern, Salomon Gottlieb
Rechnitz, Austria, 1807 – Vienna, 1883; scholar
In 1846, 111 MSS formerly in the possession of Moses *Foa, acquired by Stern and Mordecai *Bislisches, were purchased by Princess Maria Luisa of Austria for the *Parma, Biblioteca Palatina (see its entry for further details). Stern also sold 18 MSS to *Vienna, Österreichische Nationalbibliothek (see index of owners in *Cat. Schwarz*, Vienna). Transcriptions made by Stern of many MSS in European libraries are extant in several collections.

Stift Heiligenkreuz
See *Heiligenkreuz, Stiftsbibliothek.

Stift Schotten
See *Vienna, Unsere Liebe Frau zu den Schotten.

Stolbergische Bibliothek
See *Wernigerode, Gräfliche Stolbergische Bibliothek.

Stowe MSS
The collection of the Dukes of Buckingham

at Stowe, purchased in the nineteenth century by the British Museum from the Earl of *Ashburnham, contains one Hebrew MS, an early starr (*Cat. Margoliouth*, no. 1206).

Strasbourg (France), Bibliothèque nationale et universitaire

Fifty-two Hebrew MSS were described by S. Landauer in *Katalog der hebräischen, arabischen, persischen und türkischen Handschriften der Kaiserlichen Universitäts- und Landesbibliothek zu Strassburg*, Strasbourg 1881. Some Hebrew MSS once found in the library were probably destroyed when the library was bombed in 1870 during the Franco-Prussian War. *Kennicott listed four biblical MSS (nos. 145–148) he consulted in the library that are no longer extant. Variant readings from these MSS were recorded in *Parma, Biblioteca Palatina, MS Parm. 2292. M. Ginsburger described 185 Hebrew MSS and three Samaritan MSS in *Catalogue général*, XLVII (1923), nos. 3927–4115. Nos. 3927–3978 had previously been described by Landauer, and the Landauer catalogue numbers are added in parentheses. The catalogue numbers, 3927–4115, are also the present call-numbers of the MSS. Among the MSS described by Ginsburger are a number of volumes of fragments, probably from the Cairo *Geniza. Since the publication of the *Catalogue général* the library has acquired the following Hebrew MSS: nos. 4771, 4809 (fragments), 4845 (fragments), 5138 (fragments) and 5988 (an illuminated eighteenth-century haggada reproduced in a facsimile edition in 1998).

Strasbourg (France), Gesellschaft für die Geschichte der Israeliten in Elsass-Lothringen

The archives, including some MSS and *ketubot*, were established in 1905 and were deposited in the Archives départementales du Bas-Rhin in Strasbourg in 1936. The MS of *Sefer zikhronot* (ספר זכרונות) by Asher b. Eliezer Halevi, from which the work was published (Berlin 1913), was presented to the Gesellschaft by Elie Scheid. Today the MS is *Jerusalem, NLI, Heb. 8° 4051.

P. Honigmann, 'Die Archivaliensammlung der Gesellschaft für die Geschichte der Israeliten in Elsass-Lothringen', *Société d'Histoire des Israélites d'Alsace et de Lorraine: XXIIIe Colloque*, 2003, pp. 155–163.

Strasbourg (France), Kaiserliche Universitäts- und Landesbibliothek

See *Strasbourg, Bibliothèque nationale et universitaire.

Strashun, Mathias

Vilna, Lithuania, 1817–1885; talmudic scholar

About 150 MSS are listed, together with printed books, in the catalogue of Strashun's collection (לקוטי שושנים, ברלין 1889). After his death Strashun's library passed into the possession of the Jewish community of Vilna. The Nazis confiscated the library after they occupied Vilna in 1941. Most of the books were lost during World War II, but some were saved and eventually reached the *New York, YIVO library. Part of the collection was given to *Jerusalem, Hekhal Shelomo Museum. Some books from Strashun's library, together with parts of the *Vilna, YIVO archives that had been hidden and preserved by a group of ghetto inmates, were discovered in 1988 and 1993 in the inner recesses of the Lithuanian National Book Chamber (see New York, YIVO). One MS, a copy of *Pinkas Lita*, is now *Moscow, RSL, MS Евр. 238. Another MS, homilies by Mattathias Hayitshari, described by A. Neubauer, 'R. Mattitya haYiçhari', *REJ*, IX (1884), pp. 116–119, is now *New York, JTSA, MS 10401.

צ' הרכבי, 'רבי מתתיהו שטראשון (1818–1886)', בתוך: שמעון פדרבוש (עורך), חכמת ישראל במערב אירופה, ג,

355–345 ירושלים 1965, עמ'; D. E. Fishman, *Embers Plucked from the Fire: The Rescue of Jewish Cultural Treasures in Vilna*, New York 1996; A. Astrinsky and M. Zalkin, *Mattityahu Strashun, 1817–1885: Scholar, Leader and Book Collector*, New York [2001].

Strauss, Berthold Baruch

London, 1901–1962; collector

Strauss described his 25 MSS in *Sifre Barukh* (ספרי ברוך): *Catalogue of the Books in the B. Strauss Library*, I: *Ohel Barukh* (אהל ברוך): *The Books in Hebrew Characters*, London 1959. An index to the MSS is found on p. 392. The entire collection was purchased by *New York, Yeshiva University.

Strauss, Isaac

Strasbourg, France, 1806 – Paris, 1888; musician and collector

The items described in the privately printed catalogue by George Stenne (pseudonym of D. Schornstein), *Collection de M. Strauss: Description des objets d'art religieux hébraïques exposés dans les galeries du Trocadéro à L'exposition universelle de 1878*, Poissy 1878, were purchased by Baron Nathaniel de *Rothschild and presented to *Paris, Musée de Cluny (q.v.). The catalogue was listed and some corrections were provided in *HB*, XVIII (1878), pp. 104–105. A manuscript siddur was later described in detail by M. Schwab, 'Manuscrits hébreux du Musée de Cluny', *REJ*, L (1905), pp. 136–139.

Striedl, Hans, and Ernst Róth

In *Cat. Striedl–Róth* (= Verzeichnis der orientalischen Handschriften in Deutschland, VI, 2 [1965]), Striedl and Róth described 656 Hebrew MSS and fragments from 59 libraries and collections in Germany. Most of the MSS had not been catalogued previously or were inadequately described in other catalogues. The MSS in each library are catalogued separately, with the libraries arranged in alphabetical order according to the cities in which they are located. Each entry has the call-number of the MS printed above it, while the catalogue serial number appears to the left. Palaeographical and codicological information: number of leaves, writing material, date, physical description of the MS, size, size of written area, number of lines per page, custos, type of writing, colophons, owners' entries and provenance. Similar catalogues for the *Frankfurt a/M, Stadtbibliothek (now Goethe Universität, Universitätsbibliothek), by Róth and L. Prijs, and the Levy collection in *Hamburg, SUB, by Róth and Striedl, appeared in Parts 1 and 3, respectively, of Vol. VI of the *Verzeichnis* (*VOH*).

Stroock, Alan M.

New York, 1906–1985; lawyer

While serving as chairman of the Board of Directors of *New York, JTSA, Stroock purchased 500 MSS and 300 single leaves and fragments from the estate of E. N. *Adler after Adler's death in 1946. The collection is known as the 'Second Adler Collection', and includes *Geniza fragments (the Adler-Stroock collection)

Strozzi

Family in Florence

The MS described by *Kennicott, no. 170, is now *Florence, Biblioteca Riccardiana, MS Ricc. 1.

Stuttgart (Germany), Württembergische Landesbibliothek

Thirty-one MSS are described in *Cat. Striedl–Róth*, pp. 366–383. Twenty-one of these MSS and another ten Tora scrolls and Latin and Arabic MSS are described in *Cat. Allony–Loewinger*, I, pp. 58–59. Call-numbers are listed in parentheses in the *Allony–Loewinger* catalogue. A fragment from a Hebrew MS, formerly *Donaueschingen, Fuerstlich Fuerstenbergische Hofbibliothek, MS A11, described in *Cat. Striedl–Róth*, p. 28, is now in the Landesbibliothek, Cod. A11. The Landesbibliothek also has a few other fragments from Hebrew MSS.

Sub Fen.

MSS from the *Canonici collection that stood under the window (*sub fenestra* in Latin) in the Oriental MSS room in *Oxford, Bodleian Library, were given call-numbers with the prefix 'sub fenestra'. The MSS are listed in *Cat. Neubauer* on p. xxv. These call-numbers were later abolished and the MSS returned to their original collection and assigned call-numbers Can. Or. 136–141. This change was noted in *Cat. Neubauer–Cowley*, II, pp. 537–540.

Sulzberger, Mayer

Heidelsheim, Germany, 1843 – Philadelphia, Pa., 1923; jurist

In the catalogue of Sulzberger's library compiled by Ephraim *Deinard, *Catalogue of the Library of Hon. M. Sulzberger* (אור מאיר, נויארק תרנ"ז), 28 MSS are listed. These MSS and hundreds of others were presented by Sulzberger to *New York, JTSA. Sulzberger acquired hundreds of other MSS for JTSA, including about 200 from the *Halberstamm collection in 1903 and about 600 from Deinard (Rab., *Lit. Treas.*, pp. 64–66), among them a collection purchased in 1908 in honour of Moses A. *Dropsie. Sulzberger also presented a number of *Geniza fragments to Dropsie College (see *Philadelphia, CAJS).

S. Berkowitz, 'The Sulzberger–Deinard relationship', in R. M. Geffen and M. B. Edelman (eds.), *Freedom and Responsibility*, Hoboken 1998, pp. 229–239.

Sussex, Duke of

Prince Augustus Frederick; London, 1773–1843

Forty-four Hebrew MSS and four scrolls were described by Thomas Joseph Pettigrew in *Bibliotheca Sussexiana: A Descriptive Catalogue ... of the Manuscripts and Printed Books Contained in the Library of ... the Duke of Sussex*, I, Part 1, London 1827. Six MSS were described in the sales catalogue *Bibliotheca Sussexiana*, London 1844. The numbers of the MSS in the sales catalogue are not identical with those in Pettigrew's. A list of the MSS in the Pettigrew catalogue and their present locations is found in Appendix I, no. 39. Other MSS from the Sussex collection not listed in either catalogue are found in *Munich, Staatsbibliothek, *Cambridge, Trinity College, and other libraries. See also *Duke of Sussex.

Sutro, Adolph Heinrich Joseph

Aachen, Germany, 1830 – San Francisco, Calif., 1898

Sutro purchased MSS, most of them from Yemen, from the widow of the bookseller Moses *Shapira in 1884. A great part of his library was destroyed in the fire that ravaged San Francisco after the earthquake in 1906. The remainder of his collection, including 167 mainly Yemenite MSS, was deposited in the California State Library in San Francisco. In 2012 it was moved to the J. Paul Leonard and Sutro Library on the San Francisco State University campus. The MSS were described by W. M. Brinner in *Sutro Library Hebraica: A Handlist*, [San Francisco] 1966. Three other catalogues had previously been compiled but were never published. They were written by S. Roubin, by Ephraim *Deinard in 1897 (111 MSS, excluding scrolls, prayer-books, etc.), and collectively by J. Solomon, J. Friedman and J. J. Davidson as part of the Works Project Administration program in the 1930s. A copy of the Deinard catalogue is *New York, JTSA, MS 2847. According to Brinner there is a catalogue of the Sutro collection in *Cincinnati, HUC. The present call-numbers of the MSS are the WPA catalogue numbers. Four MSS formerly in Sutro's collection are also found in HUC, according to Oko, p. 92.

Svajer, Amedio

Venice, 1727–1791; merchant and collector

In 1794, a MS from Svajer's collection was acquired by *Venice, Biblioteca Marciana (MS Or. 215).

Tamani, *Venezia*, p. 254.

Swindon, Bible Society

Formerly the British and Foreign Bible Society in London. The society moved to its present headquarters in Swindon, Wiltshire, in 1985. About 20 fragments from Hebrew manuscripts and scrolls, mostly biblical, and some modern works on the Bible, are described in *Historical Catalogue of the Manuscripts of Bible House Library* (London 1982), in the Arabic, Hebrew, Persian, Samaritan and Yiddish sections and in the additions at the end of the catalogue. The MSS belonging to the Society are housed in *Cambridge, University Library.

Sydney (Australia), University of Sydney, Fisher Library

Ten MSS, including scrolls, mainly from the library of Sir Charles Nicholson, were described by A. D. Crown in *Hebrew Manuscripts and Rare Printed Books Held in the Fisher Library of the University of Sydney*, [Sydney] 1973 (2nd ed., 1984).

T

T

*Turin, Biblioteca Nazionale Universitaria.

Tanner, Thomas

1674 – Oxford, England, 1735; bishop and antiquarian

Tanner bequeathed his library to *Oxford, Bodleian Library, in 1735. The library included one Hebrew MS (MS Tanner 173, *Cat. Neubauer*, 172).

Tarnopol (Ukraine), Biblioteka Szkoły Żydowskiej im. J. Perla (Joseph Perl Hebrew School Library)

The library, founded by Joseph Perl, contained many MSS, especially of writings by the *maskilim* and documents relating to them. The MSS were kept in a state of neglect for years, and attempts before the outbreak of World War II to bring them to *Jerusalem, JNUL (now NLI), were only partially successful. Many of the MSS were lost or sold as wrapping paper. Some of the MSS eventually reached Jerusalem, and others went to the *Vilna, YIVO library. During the war many of the MSS in Tarnopol and Vilna were destroyed or lost, and only a few reached the YIVO library in New York. MS *New York, Yeshiva University 1254, was formerly in the Tarnopol Library.

ש׳ ורסס, ׳גנזי יוסף פרל בירושלים וגלגוליהם׳, האוניברסיטה, יט (תשל״ד), עמ׳ 38–52.

Tauber, Arye

Tarnopol, Ukraine, 1871 – Jerusalem, 1932; librarian

Tauber's MSS were deposited in *Jerusalem, JNUL (now NLI).

Taurinum

Latin name for Turin.

Tauschweig (Germany), Kreisbibliothek Regensburg

Two MSS from this library were acquired by *Munich, Bayerische Staatsbibliothek.

Striedl, *Geschichte*, p. 35.

Taylor, Charles

Westminster, England, 1840 – Cambridge, England, 1908

Taylor, master of St. John's College, Cambridge, and a Hebrew scholar, helped to arrange Solomon *Schechter's expedition to Cairo, where Schechter collected over 100,000 fragments from the *Geniza. This collection, known as the Taylor–Schechter Collection, was presented to *Cambridge, University Library, in 1898. Taylor's own collection of Hebrew MSS was presented to the Cambridge library by his widow in 1908 (MSS Or. 785–805).

Taylor–Schechter Collection

Collection of Cairo *Geniza fragments brought by Solomon *Schechter to the *Cambridge, University Library, in 1898, with the assistance of Charles *Taylor.

Tedeschi (Ashkenazi), Isaac Raphael

Ancona, Italy, 1826–1908; rabbi

Many MSS in Tedeschi's collection came from the library of David Abraham *Vivanti, which included part of the library that had belonged to Hayyim *Azulai. Most of Tedeschi's MSS were acquired by Rabbi H. *Rosenberg and are now partly in *Los Angeles, University of California Library and partly in *New York, JTSA. The MS of *Shibole haleket* (שבלי הלקט) formerly in Tedeschi's possession, which served as the basis of Buber's edition (Vilna 1886), is now *London, BL, MS Or. 9153. A collection of kabbalistic works, purchased in 1898 by Baron David *Günzburg from the Paris bookdealer M. M. Lifschitz, is now MS *Moscow, RSL, Günzburg 1471.

Teixeira, Isaac

Amsterdam, eighteenth century

The MS belonging to Texeira described by *Kennicott, no. 643, was later MS *Sassoon 506 (the De Castro Pentateuch) and is now *Jerusalem, Israel Museum, MS 180/94.

Tel Aviv, Rambam Library

The Rambam Library was founded in 1935. Dr. Azriel Hildesheimer, formerly librarian of the Rabbinical Seminary in Berlin, joined the staff of the Rambam library in 1939 and deposited in it a number of rare books and manuscripts that he had brought from the Seminary. Since 1961, the Rambam Library has been housed in the Tel Aviv Municipal Library (Beit Ariela). Its collection includes about 300 MSS, dating mostly from the eighteenth and nineteenth centuries.

Tengnagel, Sebastian

Büren, Netherlands, 1574 – Vienna, 1636; custodian of the Imperial Library in Vienna

Tengnagel's Hebrew MSS are now in *Vienna, Österreichische Nationalbibliothek. A list of the MSS is found in the index of owners in *Cat. Schwarz*, Vienna.

Thomason, George

c. 1602 – London, 1666; bookseller

Thomason published a catalogue of Hebrew books and manuscripts bought in Italy, including many acquired from Isaac Faragi, or Pragi, entitled *Catalogus librorum diversis Italiae locis emporium*, London 1647. Spurred on by John *Selden, the English Parliament purchased the collection for *Cambridge, University Library. Reif, *Cat. Cambridge*, lists over 20 MSS acquired from the Faragi–Thomason collection.

Reif, *Cat. Cambridge*, pp. 10–12; I. Abrahams and C. E. Sayle, 'The purchase of Hebrew books by the English Parliament in 1647', *Transactions of the Jewish Historical Society of England*, VIII (1918), pp. 63–77.

Thompson, Henry Yates

Liverpool, England, 1838 – London, 1929; collector

In 1897, Thompson purchased the *Ashburnham Appendix MSS, which included an illuminated Hebrew MS erroneously attributed to Giotto. The MS was described by E. N. Adler, 'Jewish Art', in B. Schindler and A.

Marmorstein (eds.), *Occident and Orient: Gaster Anniversary Volume*, London 1936, pp. 46–49; E. Panofsky, 'Giotto and Maimonides in Avignon: The Story of an Illuminated Hebrew Manuscript', *Journal of the Walters Art Gallery*, IV (1941), pp. 27–44; Joshua Bloch, *The People and the Book*, New York 1954, p. 42; and E. Horowitz, 'Giotto in Avignon …', *Jewish Art*, XIX–XX (1993–1994), pp. 98–111. Today the MS is Princeton University Library, Garrett MS 26.

Tiktin, Gedaliah

c. 1810 – Breslau, Poland, 1886; rabbi

According to Brann, *Geschichte*, p. 79, there were about 100 MSS from Tiktin's library in *Breslau, Jüdisch-theologisches Seminar. *Cat. Loewinger–Weinryb* lists about 25 MSS written or owned by Tiktin in the Breslau library.

Tischendorf, Lobegott Friedrich Konstantin von

Lengenfeld, Germany, 1815 – Leipzig, Germany, 1874; Bible critic

The 16 MSS that Tischendorf collected in Cairo and the Near East were described by A. Jellinek in *MGWJ*, II (1853), pp. 245–247, 286–288, 360. Steinschneider added corrections and notes in *HB*, I, II, IV and V. The MSS are now in *St. Petersburg, NLR (New Series), and *Leipzig, Universitätsbibliothek.

Tłom.

Tłomackie. See *Warsaw, Gmina Wyznaniowa Zydowska (Tłomackie Street Synagogue).

To'elet Society (Amsterdam, Netherlands)

Part of the Society's library is in *Amsterdam, Universiteitsbibliotheek. A number of MSS apparently purchased from the Jerusalem booksellers *Bamberger and Wahrmann are in *Los Angeles, University of California Library.

Toledano, Jacob Moses

Tiberias, 1880 – Jerusalem, 1960; scholar and rabbi

Many of Toledano's MSS are described in his works. Catalogues of his MSS are *Catalogue of Valuable Hebrew Manuscripts and Printed Books, the Property of Grand Rabbi Jacob Toledano of Tangier and from Other Sources*, London 1927, and *Reshimat kitve yad* … (רשימת כתבי־יד: נאספו ונקבצו בארצות שונות במזרח ובמערב על ידי החו"מ יעקב משה טולידאנו, טאנג'יר תרפ"ח). Toledano sold many MSS to *New York, JTSA, among them many of the MSS now in the *Enelow Memorial Collection (Marx, *Proceedings*, p. 135 [Marx, *Bibl. Studies*, p. 411]), and to *Jerusalem, JNUL (now NLI). The autograph of Maimonides' *Commentary on the Mishna* once in Toledano's possession was acquired by David Solomon Sassoon (nos. 72–73; see *Sassoon, Solomon David) and was later purchased by the JNUL.

Toledo (Spain), Archivo y Biblioteca Capitulares

In the nineteenth century this Cathedral library possessed about 45 Hebrew MSS, most of which had been donated by Cardinal *Zelada in 1801. In 1858, when the short-lived first Spanish republic nationalized cultural treasures, most of the MSS were transferred to *Madrid, Biblioteca Nacional, and only 15 MSS remained in Toledo. These 15 MSS and one medical work in Spanish were described by J. Millás Vallicrosa, 'Los manuscritos hebraicos de la Biblioteca Capitular de Toledo', *Al-Andalus*, II (1934), pp. 395–429. The 15 Hebrew MSS were also listed in *Cat. Allony–Kupfer*, II, pp. 98–100. Call-numbers with the prefix 'Z' are printed in parentheses at the end of each entry in *Cat. Allony–Kupfer*. Nine Hebrew MSS, mostly biblical or relating to the Bible, are described in K. Reinhardt and R. Gonzálvez, *Catálogo de Códices Bíblicos de la Catedral de Toledo*, Madrid 1990, nos. 12–19 and 39. Six other

MSS of similar content formerly belonging to the Cathedral and now located in the Biblioteca Nacional are described in the Addenda to the catalogue, nos. *5–*7, *17, *19 and *20. A new catalogue has recently been published in electronic format: G. Angulo, *Hebrew manuscripts in the Toledo Cathedral Library*, Madrid 2012.

Toletum
Latin name for Toledo.

Toronto (Canada), University of Toronto, Thomas Fisher Rare Book Library
The library has 51 Hebrew MSS, 44 of them, including some Geniza fragments, presented by Albert Dov *Friedberg; six Yemenite MSS; and a scroll with the *tikun* for the eve of Shavuot.

Della Torre, Lelio
Cuneo, Italy, 1805 – Padua, Italy, 1871; rabbi
Thirty of Della Torre's MSS are briefly listed together with his printed books in *Catalogue de la Bibliothèque hebraïco-judaïque de feu ... Lelio Della Torre*, [Padua 1872] (nos. 5–7, 17, 19, 20, 26, 44, 110, 146, 154–156, 166, 204, 207, 267, 268, 362, 363, 420, 475, 476, 492, 528, 562, 571, 671, 680, 708). Some of his MSS were acquired by *Budapest, Jewish Theological Seminary (L. Blau, 'Zu Samuel Romanelli's literarischer Tätigkeit', *ZfHB*, VIII [1904], pp. 16–20). One MS is in *Jerusalem, NLI, Heb. 8° 2935. Others disappeared or were stolen (ח׳ שירמן, ׳קובץ שירי שמואל רומאנילי בכתב־יד׳, תרביץ, לה [תשט״ו/תשט״ז], עמ׳ 373).

Tours (France), Bibliothèque municipale
One MS, a Bible dated 1268, was described in *Catalogue général*, XXXVII (1900–1905), p. 8, and again in *Manuscrits médiévaux en caractères hébraïques*, I, Paris–Jerusalem 1972, no. 6.

Trebitsch, Ernst
Vienna, twentieth cent.
One MS owned by Trebitsch was described in *Cat. Schwarz*, Austria, no. 182. Its present whereabouts are unknown.

Trèves
See *Trier.

Treves, Isaac and Jacob
Venice, Italy, nineteenth cent.
Twenty-two MSS belonging to the Treves brothers are listed on the flyleaves of *London, Montefiore, MS 517. Some of these MSS were given to Abraham Lattes (see *Lattes, Mose) and are now in *Milan, Biblioteca Ambrosiana (*Cat. Luzzatto*, p. 5 and nos. 30, 34, 35, 40, 47, 48, 64, 65).

Trier (Germany), Stadtbibliothek
According to J. Bassfreund, in 'Hebräische Handschriften-Fragmente in der Stadtbibliothek zu Trier', *MGWJ*, XXXIX (1895), pp. 264–265, about 300 leaves from 15 MSS were found in the bindings of 130 volumes in the library, but only about 150 were separated. Fragments from six MSS were described by Bassfreund in *ibid.*, pp. 263–271, 295–302, 343–350, 391–398, and 492–506, and in 'Ueber ein Midrasch-Fragment', *MGWJ*, XXXVIII (1894), pp. 167–176, 214–219. Five of the fragments described by Bassfreund and an additional 11 were listed in *Cat. Allony–Loewinger*, I, p. 43. The numbers printed in parentheses at the end of the first five entries in *Cat. Allony–Loewinger* are those assigned by Bassfreund. No numbers at all are given to the other 11 fragments. All the fragments in *Cat. Allony–Loewinger* plus an additional two, constituting about 150 leaves from 16 MSS, were described in *Cat. Striedl–Róth*, pp. 385–391. The fragments were rearranged before the catalogue was printed; some fragments were joined to others, and new call-

numbers were assigned (Hebr. Fragmn. Nrs. 1–17). A number of additional fragments were subsequently recovered (Hebr. Fragmn. Nrs. 18–37). All these fragments were microfilmed for the *Jerusalem, IMHM. Recently a large number of additional fragments have been found in the bindings of books in the library and in other repositories in Trier.

Trieste (Italy), Comunità ebraica

Twenty-four MSS in the library of the Jewish community were described by Sonne, *Relazione*. Nos. 2, 3, 4, 6–8, 10, 12, 19 and 24 in Sonne's list were deposited in *Jerusalem, JNUL (now NLI) in 1950, which also acquired another 16 MSS that were not described by Sonne. No. 1 on the list is now *Cincinnati, HUC, MS Acc. 191. Parts of nos. 16 and 17 were in *Sonne's own collection and are now in *Jerusalem, Ben-Zvi Institute. The JNUL acquired eleven MSS belonging to the Talmud Tora of Trieste in 1954.

Trieste brothers

Italy, nineteenth cent.

David *Kaufmann bought 27 MSS from the Trieste brothers, including the famous Kaufmann Mishna MS (*Budapest, Hungarian Academy of Sciences, MS Kaufmann A 50). A list of the MSS is found in the foreword of *Cat. Kaufmann*, and the story of its purchase is related in Hebrew on pp. 19–20 of the catalogue. Israel Mehlmann of Jerusalem owned a handwritten catalogue of printed books and nine MSS (not those purchased by Kaufmann) belonging to the Trieste brothers (MS Mehlmann 10). The MS of Judah Barceloni's commentary on *Sefer yetsira* from which Kaufmann edited the text (Berlin 1885) was MS no. 151–152 in the Nehemiah *Allony collection and is now *Jerusalem, NLI, Heb. 4° 6990. A copy of Rashi's commentary on the Pentateuch is in the private collection of Mr. F. Greenwood in Toronto (formerly of London).

Trigland, Jacobus

1583 – Leiden, Netherlands, 1654; Christian Hebraist

A few MSS belonging to Trigland are now in *Hamburg, SUB. A list of the MSS may be found in the index of owners in *Cat. Steinschneider*, Hamburg.

Trinity College

See (1) *Cambridge, Trinity College; (2) *Dublin, Trinity College.

Tripartite Maḥzor

Name given to a fourteenth-century illuminated Ashkenazic maḥzor, parts of which are found in three libraries: *London, BL, MS Add. 22413; *Budapest, Hungarian Academy of Sciences, MS Kaufmann A 384; *Oxford, Bodleian Library, MS Mich. 619.

Narkiss, pp. 106–108.

Tripoli (Libya)

G. Raccah described seven MSS found in Tripoli in his catalogue (רשימה של כתבי־יד רבני וחכמי טריפוליטניה, טריפולי 1945). The fate of these MSS is unknown. The MS from Tripoli described by D. Cazes, 'Antiquités judaïques en Tripolitaine', *REJ*, XX (1890), pp. 80–83, is MS *Sassoon 82 (the *Shem Tov Bible).

Trivulzio, Carlo

See *Jerusalem *Mishne Tora*.

T–S

*Taylor–Schechter. See also *Cambridge, University Library, 'Geniza' section.

Tübingen (Germany), Universitätsbibliothek

One MS and a small number of fragments were described in *Cat. Allony–Loewinger*, I, p. 42, and in *Cat. Striedl–Róth*, pp. 392–395. During World War II some of the Hebrew MSS in *Berlin, Staatsbibliothek, were removed to the Tübingen library for safekeeping, and they remained there for a number of years following the war. In *Cat. Allony–Loewinger*, I, these MSS are referred to as ‘MSS Berlin-Tübingen’. The MSS have since been returned to the Berlin library.

Tübingen Haggada

Name given to *Berlin, SB, Cod. Or. 2° 14, an illuminated haggada that was deposited in Tübingen for safekeeping during and after World War II.

Tunis

J. Cohen Tanuji described 21 MSS from Tunis in 23 entries (numbered 1–18, 18bis–22) in *Bet Yisra’el* (׳כתבי יד תוניס׳, בית ישראל, ב, [טבת תרמ״ט], עמ׳ 28–31). All or most of the MSS were sold to various libraries and collectors by the bookdealer Joseph Schlesinger of Vienna. Seven of the MSS were acquired by *London, British Library, in 1889. Nos. 13 and 15 were purchased by David *Kaufmann and Abraham *Epstein, respectively. For the present locations of some of these MSS see Appendix I, no. 40.

Tur.

Turin.

Turicum

Latin name for Zurich. MS Turici = MS Zurich.

Turin (Italy), Archivio delle tradizioni e del costume ebraici ‘Benvenuto e Alessandro Terracini’

The archive was founded in 1973 with a gift of books, manuscripts and documents concerning the Jews of Piedmont from the brothers Benvenuta and Alessandro Terracini. The archive includes over 250 MSS.

Turin (Italy) Biblioteca della Comunità ebraica (Talmud Tora)

Sixteen MSS were described in Sonne, *Relazione*. These MSS apparently were destroyed by bombings in World War II.

Fumagalli, p. 98.

Turin (Italy), Biblioteca Nazionale Universitaria

Formerly Biblioteca di S. M. il Re. The library was founded in 1723 by Victor Amadeus II, King of Sardinia, with the union of the library of the dukes of Savoy, the municipal library and the University library. The earliest catalogues were a handwritten list of the Hebrew and Greek MSS made by F. *Bencini in 1732 and a catalogue compiled by G. *Pasini in 1749, *Codices manuscripti Bibliothecae Regii Taurinensis Athenaei per linguas digesti, et binas in partes distributi, in quarum prima Hebraei et Graeci ...*, Turin 1749. In 1818 the library received the MSS of Tomasso *Valperga di Caluso, which were catalogued by Amedio Peyron, *Notitia librorum manu typisve descriptorum, qui donante Ab. Thoma Valperga-Calusio. illati sunt in Reg. Taurinensis Athenaei Bibliothecam*, Leipzig 1820. All the MSS in the library were catalogued in 1880 by Bernardino *Peyron, with the assistance of Samuel Ghiron, in *Codices hebraici manu exarati Regiae Bibliothecae quae in Taurinensi Athenaeo asservatur* (= *Cat. Peyron*). In *Cat. Peyron*, MSS are listed according to their shelf-marks. At the head of each entry the catalogue number is printed in Roman numerals followed by the shelf-mark, which also serves as its present call-number, consisting of the letter ‘A’, a Roman numeral and an Arabic numeral (e.g., A.II.2). Printed in small type are the prior notations (n.p.) and numbers in the Bencini and Pasini catalogues or in the Valperga di Caluso catalogue. For those MSS described in Johann Christoph *Wolf’s *Bibliotheca*

Hebraea, the page numbers in Wolf's book are also listed. Descriptions of the MSS are in Latin. Palaeographical and codicological information: writing material, date, type of script, number of leaves and size. Indexes: titles; place names; books of the Bible; anonymous works listed according to subject; and authors. On pp. xli–xlvi is a concordance to the old numbers, the numbers in the Bencini and Pasini catalogues and the present call-numbers. Corrections to *Cat. Peyron* were published by M. Steinschneider, *HB*, XX (1880), pp. 127–132; and XXI (1881–1882), pp. 26–28, and by A. Berliner in his *Gesammelte Schriften*, I, Frankfurt a/M 1913, pp. 127–144.

Cat. Peyron lists 274 MSS. In the fire that ravaged the library in June 1904, all the Hebrew MSS in the library were destroyed or damaged. One MS (A.VI.34), which was on loan at the time, was later returned undamaged. Another MS (A.VI.38), which may have been on loan at that time, somehow reached the booksellers *Schwager and Fränkel and was listed in their catalogue no. 11 (1906), no. 446 (G. Scholem, *KS*, IV [1927/8], p. 326, n. 2). Its present location is unknown. One MS (A.III.2) was partly copied by S. Schechter and was printed with some facsimiles by A. I. Schechter in his *Studies in Jewish Liturgy*, Philadelphia 1930. Parts or fragments from 109 MSS survived the fire, but most are severely damaged. Restoration of the MSS is in progress. For a list of the MSS that were not completely destroyed in the fire, see Appendix I, no. 41. On the history of the collection and the progress made in restoration of the MSS see C. Pilocane, 'I manoscritti ebraici della Biblioteca Nazionale di Torino', *Materia Giudaica*, IX (2004), pp. 183–189. In 1970, the Peyron family library was acquired by the Biblioteca Nazionale, including six MSS from the collection of Amedio Peyron, not listed in the published catalogues.

Turri, Giuseppe

Reggio Emilia, Italy, 1802–1879; bibliophile

Five Hebrew MSS from Turri's collection are now in *Reggio Emilia, Biblioteca Panizzi.

G. Tamani, 'Manoscritti ebraici nella Biblioteca Comunale di Reggio Emilia', *Annali dell'Istituto Orientale di Napoli*, XXXI (1971), p. 256.

Tychsen, Oluf Gerhard

Tondern, Denmark, 1734 – Rostock, Germany, 1815; orientalist

Tychsen's MSS, described in A. T. Hartmann, *Catalogus Bibliothecae Olai Gerhardi Tychsen*, Rostock 1817[?], are now in *Rostock, Universitätsbibliothek. One MS, a late Pentateuch with Latin translation, is now *Madrid, Biblioteca Nacional, MS 5468.

U

Udine (Italy) Biblioteca Arcivescovile

Six Hebrew MSS, formerly in the possession of Cardinal *Grimani and now found in the Udine library, were described by Tamani, *Grimani*. The *Jerusalem, IMHM has microfilms of 16 MSS from the library, including the six from the Grimani collection.

Ufb. or Uff.

*Uffenbach.

Uffenbach, Zacharias Conrad von

Frankfurt a/M, Germany, 1683–1734; collector

One hundred and forty-one Hebrew MSS were described in the catalogue of the Uffenbach collection by J. H. Mai, *Bibliotheca Uffenbachiana*, Halle 1720. Most of the collection was purchased by Johann Christoph *Wolf and was acquired in 1749 for the *Hamburg, SUB by its librarian, Johann Christian Wolf (brother of Johann Christoph). A concordance to the Uffenbach catalogue numbers and the call-numbers in the Hamburg library is found in *Cat. Steinschneider*, Hamburg, p. 200. A few of Uffenbach's MSS did not reach the Hamburg library.

Steinschneider, *Vorlesungen*, p. 84 (Hebrew, p. 108); *Cat. Steinschneider*, Hamburg, pp. v–viii.

ULC
*Cambridge, University Library.

Ulman, Low Simon
Pfersee, Germany, eighteenth cent.
A MS of Ulman's described by *Kennicott, no. 380, is now *Hamburg, SUB, Cod. Levy 19.

Ultrajectum
Latin name for Utrecht.

Unger, Christian Gottlieb (Theophilus)
1671 – Herrnlauersitz, Poland, 1719; pastor and bibliographer
Unger's MSS were purchased after his death by Johann Christoph *Wolf, and most are now in *Hamburg, SUB (*Cat. Steinschneider*, Hamburg, p. viii). The MSS are listed in the index of owners in *Cat. Steinschneider*, Hamburg. A few MSS are in the *Leipzig, Universitätsbibliothek (MSS B.H. 26, 31).

Uppsala (Sweden), Universitetsbiblioteket
Eight MSS were briefly described by A. Neubauer, 'Handschriften in kleineren Bibliotheken', *Israelietische Letterbode*, II (1876/7), pp. 92–93. Thirty-four MSS, including the eight described by Neubauer, were described by K. V. Zetterstéen in *Verzeichnis der hebräischen und aramäischen Handschriften der Kgl. Universitätsbibliothek zu Upsala*, Lund 1900. The call-numbers of the MSS consist of the catalogue number, to which the prefix 'O. Hebr.' is added. Ten additional Hebrew MSS, mostly by Swedish Christian Hebraists, were described by Zetterstéen in *Die arabischen, persischen und türkischen Handschriften der Universitätsbibliothek zu Uppsala*, I, Uppsala 1930, pp. [415]–421.

Urb. ebr.
See *Urbinati.

Urbinati
MSS acquired by the *Vatican library in 1657 from the library of the dukes of Urbino. Federico, Duke of Urbino (Federigo da Montefeltro), attacked the city of Volterra in 1472 and confiscated the rich library of Menahem da Volterra. The 59 Hebrew MSS in the Urbinati collection, most or all of which had belonged to Menahem da Volterra, are described in *Assemani's catalogue of the Vatican MSS, I, pp. 409–455, and are also listed in *Cat. Allony–Loewinger*, III, nos. 614–672. A more detailed description is found in *Cat. Richler*, Vatican, pp. 599–638. D. V. Proverbio summarized the history of the collection in his 'Historical introduction' to *Cat. Richler*, Vatican, pp. xvi–xviii.

Urbino
See *Urbinati.

Uri, Johannes
Hungary, 1724 – Oxford, England, 1796; scholar
Uri published *Bibliothecae Bodleianae codicum manuscriptorum orientalium videlicet Hebraicorum, Chaldaicorum, Syriacorum, Aethiopicorum, Arabicorum, Persicorum, Turcicorum, Copticorumque catalogus,* Oxford 1787, a catalogue of the Oriental MSS in *Oxford, Bodleian Library, in which a number of Hebrew MSS were described. A concordance of the numbers in Uri's catalogue

with the present call-numbers and the Cat. Neubauer catalogue numbers is found in *Cat. Neubauer–Cowley*, II, pp. 537–540.

Utinum
Latin name for Udine.

Utrecht (Netherlands), Rijksuniversiteit
Three Hebrew MSS were described in *Catalogus Codicum Manuscriptorum, Bibliothecae Universitatis Rheno-Trajectinae*, Utrecht 1887–1909, and again in *Cat. Allony–Kupfer*, II, nos. 880–882. The two biblical MSS were described in somewhat greater detail by P. A. H. de Boer, 'Hebrew Biblical Manuscripts in the Netherlands', in M. Black and G. Fohrer (eds.), *In Memoriam Paul Kahle*, Berlin 1968, pp. 51–52.

V

V
(1) *Vatican; (2) Vittorio Emanuele (see *Rome, Biblioteca Nazionale Centrale).

Valladolid (Spain), Biblioteca Universitaria
The Hebrew MSS in this library came from the Santa Cruz library in Valladolid. Eight Hebrew MSS were described by F. Cantera Burgos, 'Más sobre los manuscritos hebreos de la Biblioteca de Santa Cruz en la Universidad de Valladolid', *Sefarad*, XIX (1959), pp. 223–240. A. Arce, 'Códices hebreos y judaicos en la Biblioteca Universitaria de Valladolid', *Sefarad*, XVIII (1958), had described two of these MSS and another two Spanish MSS of Jewish interest. The eight MSS described by Cantera are listed in *Cat. Allony–Kupfer*, II, p. 97.

Valperga di Caluso, Tommaso
Turin, Italy, 1737–1815; orientalist
Valperga di Caluso presented his library to the Royal Library in Turin (now *Turin, Biblioteca Nazionale Universitaria) in 1818. His 71 Hebrew MSS were described by A. Peyron in *Notitia librorum manu typisve descriptorum, qui donante Ab. Thoma Valperga-Calusio, illati sunt in Reg. Taurinensis Athenaei Bibliothecam*, Leipzig 1820, pp. 3–22. The Hebrew MSS were later described in *Cat. Peyron*; in the concordance to call-numbers on pp. xlvii–xlviii, the Valperga di Caluso MSS are marked with an asterisk.

Van Geldern Haggada
Name given to the illuminated haggada written by Moses Loeb b. Wolf Trebitsch in 1723, which was in the possession of Lazarus van Geldern (d. 1769), great-grandfather of Heinrich Heine. It was later in the possession of Abraham Frank, a rabbi in Linz (1839–1917), passed on to his son Heinz Frank (1880–1943), and in 1950 was in the hands of a collector in Amsterdam. In 1953, it was returned to Frank's son John in San Francisco. In 1997 a facsimile edition with introductions and studies was published by E. G. L. Schrijver and F. Wiesemann. The 'sister of the van Geldern Haggada', written by the same scribe in 1716/7 – also called the 'second Cincinnati Haggada' – is *Cincinnati, HUC, MS 444.1 (see F. Landsberger, 'The Second Cincinnati Haggadah', *HUCA*, XXIII [1950/51], pp. 503–521).

Vat.
*Vatican.

Vat. Barb.
See *Barberini.

Vat. Borg.
See *Borgiana.

Vat. ebr.
See *Vatican.

Vatican, Biblioteca Apostolica Vaticana (BAV)

There are over 900 Hebrew and Samaritan MSS in eight collections in the Vatican library. Of these MSS, 722 are in the Vaticana ebraici collection and the others are in the *Urbinati (59 MSS), Neofiti (see *Rome, Pia Casa dei Neofiti) (46), *Rossiana (38), *Borgiana (22), *Barberini (13), *Chigiana (1) and *Ottoboniana (1) collections. In 2007 the library purchased a collection of 105 MSS, mostly Yemenite, Persian and Oriental (Cods. Vat. ebr. 618–722). Many of the MSS, especially those from the Vatican collection, are volumes consisting of several MSS or of fragments from different MSS bound together, so that the actual number of MSS in the library is far greater than the nominal number. A sizeable portion of the Vaticana ebraici collection (288 MSS) came from the *Heidelberg, Biblioteca Palatina, in 1622 (see Cassuto, below), and many of them were written by or belonged to collectors in Candia (Heraklion, Crete). Other MSS came from convents and monasteries or from the collections of such church dignitaries as Cardinal *Zelada, Joseph *Assemani, Pope Pius IV and others. Many MSS were copied in the Vatican itself by copyists (*scriptores*), usually converted Jews, employed by the Vatican.

Steinschneider, *Vorlesungen*, p. 70 (Hebrew, p. 92). U. Cassuto wrote a detailed history of the Palatine collection in Italian (= Cassuto, *Palatina*), and a brief summary in Hebrew (‘תולדותיו של אוסף כתבי־יד עבריים’, יד לקורא, א [תש״ז], עמ׳ 62–65). L. E. Boyle described ‘The Hebrew Collections of the Vatican Library’, in P. Hiat (ed.), *A Visual Testimony: Judaica from the Vatican Library*, Miami–New York 1987, pp. 11–19. D. V. Proverbio summarized the history of the collections of Hebrew MSS in his ‘Historical introduction’ to *Cat. Richler*, Vatican, pp. xiv–xxii.

CATALOGUES *Cat. Richler*, Vatican, published in 2008, includes descriptions of 803 MSS in Hebrew characters and a few, mainly in Latin, that were included in the Hebrew collections before the acquisition of new MSS in 2007. The catalogue is arranged according to the shelf-marks in the Vatican Library. MSS in the Vaticana ebraici, the largest collection, are catalogued at the beginning and are followed by the MSS in the other collections in alphabetical order. Palaeographical and codicological information: number of leaves, writing material, size, size of written area, composition of quires, place of writing, date, watermarks and type of script. Indexes: Persons, subjects, place names, illuminated and decorated MSS, Kennicott numbers, quoted MSS, Hebrew place names, titles (in Hebrew) and poems (in Hebrew).

Previous catalogues: A number of handwritten lists of Hebrew MSS were compiled in the seventeenth century by C. F. Borromeo, J. B. Jona and J. Morosini (see Cassuto, *Palatina*). The first printed catalogue of the Hebrew MSS was *Bibliothecae Apostolicae Vaticanae Codicum Manuscriptorum Catalogus, Recensuerunt Steph. Evodius Assemani et Jos. Sim. Assemani*, I: *Codices Ebraicos et Samaritanos*, Rome 1756 (facsimile reprint, Paris 1926). According to Steinschneider, *Vorlesungen*, p. 71 (Hebrew, p. 93), the true author of the catalogue was Antonio Costanzi. In the catalogue, 453 MSS in the Vatican collection, the 59 Urbinati MSS and two Samaritan MSS are described. The MSS are arranged according to their call-numbers. The catalogue number is identical with the call-number after the prefix ‘Cod. Vat. ebr.’ or ‘Urb. ebr.’ is added. The MSS are described in Latin. Palaeographical and codicological information: size (fol. 4°, 8°), writing material, number of leaves and type of script. The *incipits* of all works are copied, and the folio on which each work begins (*incip.*) is listed at the end of each description. An index lists authors and their works. Anonymous works are listed under the heading 'Anonymous'. The Arabic numerals in the index refer to the page numbers in the catalogue, and the Roman numerals to the MS numbers. Angelo Mai, in 'Appendix ad Catalogum codicum hebraicorum Bibliothecae Vaticanae', in his *Scriptorum Veterum Nova Collectio e Vaticanus Codicibus*, IV, Rome 1831, pp. 83–93, described 78 additional MSS (454–531). A supplement to these catalogues containing descriptions of MSS 532–598 was prepared by Marianus Ugolini but has never been published (Pearson, p. 74). A. Freimann prepared a series of index cards on which the MSS were briefly described (*ibid.*). U. Cassuto was commissioned by the library to compile a full descriptive catalogue of the collection, but only the first part of this catalogue, containing descriptions of Cods. Vat. ebr. 1–115 – *Bibliothecae Apostolicae Vaticanae Codices Manuscripti Recensiti, Codices Vaticani Hebraici, Codices 1–115*, Vatican 1956 – was published before his death. The MSS in this catalogue are described in greater detail than in any of the other catalogues. At the head of each entry is the MS call-number and the following palaeographical and codicological information: date, writing material, size, number of leaves and number of lines per page. At the end of each entry is additional information concerning quires, colophons, censors, owners, etc. At the end of the catalogue is a single index of names (authors, scribes, owners, etc.), titles (in Latin transliteration) and subjects. For catalogues of the MSS in the other collections of the Vatican library see the entries for the respective collections. 801 MSS were briefly described in *Cat. Allony–Loewinger*, III. The MSS are listed according to their call-numbers. MSS from different collections are listed separately. Palaeographical and codicological information is limited to the number of leaves in the entire MS (no indication is given of the folio numbers of each work in MSS containing more than one work), date, decorations or illuminations and colophons. Indexes: authors, scribes, titles, poems, place names, languages, subjects and dated MSS. J. Ruysschaert published corrections of call-numbers and additions in 'Les manuscrits Vaticans'. Talmudic MSS in the Vatican were described by S. Ochser, 'Talmud-Handschriften der Vatikanischen Bibliothek mit besonderer Berüksichtigung der Mischna', *ZDMG*, LXIII (1909), pp. 365–393, 623. Thirty-five MSS, mostly of or on Abraham Ibn Ezra's works, were described by N. Ben-Menahem (נ׳ בן־מנחם, מגנזי ישראל בוואטיקאן, ירושלים תשי״ד). Scientific MSS in Judaeo-Arabic were described by Delio V. Proverbio, 'Manoscritti scientifici giudeo-arabi ('Praeter Lexica') nella serie dei codici Vaticani ebraici: inventario analitico', *Miscellanea Bibliothecae Apostolicae Vaticanae*, VIII (2001), pp. 351–405.

Vatican, Pia Casa dei Neofiti
See *Rome, Pia Casa dei Neofiti.

Venedig
German name for Venice.

Venetiae
Latin name for Venice.

Venice (Italy), Biblioteca Nazionale Marciana
Twenty-two MSS, including Esther scrolls, a Hebrew grammar in Latin and a Samaritan Pentateuch, are described in Tamani, *Venezia* (1972). At the end of each entry the call-number is listed. These MSS, with the exception of the scrolls and the Samaritan MSS, were previously described by M. Lattes in *Cataloghi*, III (1886), pp. 243–253. Call-numbers are not listed in the Lattes catalogue. Eight

of the MSS (11 volumes) came from *Padua, Convento ... di S. Giovanni di Verdara. They had been presented to the monastery by Pietro Montagnana in 1478. An outline of the history of the collection of Hebrew MSS in the Marciana and of other Venetian collections, including those no longer extant, is given by Tamani in the introduction to his catalogue.

Venice (Italy), Canonici
See *Canonici, Matteo Luigi.

Venice (Italy), Corneliana
See *Corneliana.

Venice (Italy), Cracovia
See *Cracovia, Abraham.

Venice (Italy), Scuole Israelitiche (Talmud Tora)
The library is presently located in the Biblioteca-Archivo 'Renato Maestro' in the Museo ebraico in Venice. In an old handwritten catalogue by R. Pacifici, 12 Hebrew MSS were listed. M. Lattes described six MSS in 'Notizie e documenti di letteratura e storia giudaica, V', *Mosé: Antologia Israelitica*, II (1879), pp. 91–93, 177–180. Today there are 13 MSS in the library. One MS (ספר דבי אליהו) that was loaned to Mose *Lattes for use in his scholarly research was presented, together with the other MSS in Lattes's library, to *Milan, Biblioteca Ambrosiana (Cod. X 110 Sup., *Cat. Luzzatto*, 44). The communal account book that was in the Talmud Tora, from which I. Sonne published a document (י' זנה, 'תעודות על שדרי"ם אחדים באיטליה', קבץ על יד, טו [תשי"א], עמ' 218), is now *New York, JTSA, MS 8593.

Fumagalli, p. 115.

Vercelli (Italy), Seminario Vescovile
The single Hebrew MS in the library, an illuminated *Mordekhai*, was described by L. Mortara Ottolenghi, 'Il manoscritto ebraico del seminario vescovile di Vercelli', *Miscellanea di Studi in Memoria di Dario Disegni*, Turin 1969, pp. 153–165.

Verdara
See *Padua, Convento ... di S. Giovanni di Verdara.

Verk. Hs.
Verkäufliche Handschriften. See *Asher, Adolf & Co.

Verkäufliche Handschriften
See *Asher, Adolf & Co.

Verona (Italy), Biblioteca Capitular
See *Verona (Italy) Biblioteca Civica.

Verona (Italy), Biblioteca Civica
Twenty-four Hebrew MSS are described in Tamani, *Verona* (1970). A. Berliner described a number of the MSS, 'Hebräische Handschriften in Verona', *ZfHB*, XVII (1914), pp. 17–18, but erred in calling the library 'Capitular-Bibliothek'.

Verona (Italy), Biblioteca e Archivio della Comunità Israelitica
The documents in the library concerning the history of the Jews in Verona, published by Sonne ('אבני בנין לתולדות היהודים בוירונה', ציון, ג [תרצ"ח], עמ' 123–169), are now *Jerusalem, NLI, MSS Heb. 4° 551–553, 555, 558, 564, 567.

ש' סימונסון, 'פנקסי הקהילה בוירונה', ק"ס, לה (תש"ך), עמ' 127.

Vesontio
Latin name for Besançon.

Viasin, Joseph Massel
See *Massel.

Vida, Samuel della
Venice, Italy, nineteenth cent.
M. *Steinschneider possessed a list of della Vida's MSS compiled by M. Soave.
HB, III (1860), p. 89; Steinschneider, *Vorlesungen*, p. 60 (Hebrew, p. 80).

Vienna, Bibl. Caesar
See *Vienna, Österreichische Nationalbibliothek.

Vienna, Bibliothek des Jesuiten Kollegium
See *Rossiana.

Vienna, Erzherzog Rainer Museum
See *Rainer.

Vienna, Fürstlich Liechtenstein'sche Fideikommissbibliothek
One Hebrew MS (MS 165-6-18), described in *Cat. Schwarz*, Austria, no. 5, is now *New Haven, Yale University, MS Heb. 136.

Vienna, Israelitische Kultusgemeinde
The library of the Kultusgemeinde contained several hundred MSS before the outbreak of World War II. According to Baron, p. 27, there were 645 MSS in the collection, including a large number of works by nineteenth and twentieth-century scholars. Included in the collection were the MSS of the Israelitisch-theologische Lehranstalt (Beth Hamidrash) of Vienna, which were acquired by the Kultusgemeinde in 1926, and MSS from the collections of Abraham *Epstein and Adolf *Jellinek. One hundred ninety-two MSS were described, together with MSS from other Austrian libraries, in *Cat. Schwarz*, Austria (1931) and and its continuation, *Cat. Schwarz–Loewinger–Róth* (1973). On p. 110 of *Cat. Schwarz–Loewinger–Róth* is a list of the Kultusgemeinde MSS described in the catalogue. For further details about the catalogue see *Schwarz, Arthur Z.
In 1938 the library was requisitioned and shipped to the central library (Zentralbibliothek) of the Reichssicherheitshauptamt in Berlin. When Berlin was bombed by Allied air forces in August 1943, most of the books were removed to several locations in Silesia. In May 1944, the archives were transferred to a remote castle in Wölfelsdorf (Wilkanów), and in the summer of 1945 all the documents were discovered there by the Red Army, shipped to Moscow and assigned to the Special Archives (now *Moscow, RSMA). In 1948, about 200 MSS, including over 50 from the Kultusgemeinde (only a few of them described by Schwarz), were transferred from the Special Archives to the Lenin State Library (now *Moscow, RSL). 78 MSS from the Kultusgemeinde, 35 of them held in the RSMA, were described in *Rukopisi i arkhivnye dokumenty Evreiskoi obshchiny goroda Veny v rossiiskikh sobraniiakh: Katalog / Manuscripts and Archival Documents of the Vienna Jewish Community Held in Russian Collections: Catalogue*, compiled by K. Akinsha, K. A. Dmitrieva, M. V. Volkova, T. A. Vasil'eva et al.; preface by Ekaterina Genieva (Moscow 2006; in Russian and English). Other MSS had been stored in Glatz (now Kłodzko, Poland) and were brought to *Warsaw, ŻIH, after the war. Some MSS are now in various other collections, and the present locations of the rest remain unknown. A partial list of present locations is found in *Cat. Schwarz–Loewinger–Róth*, p. 112, and a more comprehensive one appears herein, in Appendix I, no. 38. About 20 additional MSS, mostly medieval, were recently offered for sale by bookdealers.
R. D. Hacken, 'The Jewish community library in Vienna: From dispersion and destruction to partial restoration', *Leo Baeck Institute Year Book*, XLVII (2002), pp. 151–172.

Vienna, Israelitisch-theologische Lehranstalt
In 1926, the MSS of the Lehranstalt were

transferred to the library of *Vienna, Israelitische Kultusgemeinde.

Cat. Schwarz, Austria, p. v.

Vienna, Jüdisches Museum

Forty MSS from the Museum were described in *Cat. Schwarz*, Austria. A list of the MSS is found in *Cat. Schwarz–Loewinger–Róth*, p. 110. During the war the MSS were confiscated by the Nazis. A partial list of the present locations of the MSS is found in *Cat. Schwarz–Loewinger–Róth*, p. 112; a more comprehensive list appears herein, in Appendix I, no. 38.

Vienna, k. k. Hofbibliothek

See *Vienna, Österreichische Nationalbibliothek.

Vienna, Mechitharisten-Congregation

A MS of liturgical poetry formerly in the library was offered for sale at Auction 48 (Oct. 2006) of the F. Zisska & R. Kistner auction house in Munich.

Vienna, Österreichische Nationalbibliothek (ÖNB)

Formerly the k. k. Hofbibliothek. Forty-nine MSS were listed by D. Nessel in his *Catalogus sive Recensio specialis omnium codicum Manuscriptorum Graecorum, nec non Linguarum Orientalium Augustissimae Bibliothecae Caesareae Vindobonesis*, Vienna 1690. In their catalogue *Die handschriftlichen hebräischen Werke der k. k. Hofbibliothek zu Wien*, Vienna 1847, A. *Krafft and S. *Deutsch described about 100 MSS in 195 entries. Previously, Deutsch had described MSS from the library in 'Die hebräischen Manuskripte der k.k. Hofbibliothek zu Wien', *Österreichische Blätter für Literatur und Kunst*, 19 (1846), pp. 148–152; 63 (1846), pp. 491–495; 110 (1846), pp. 859–863; 21 (1847), pp. 81–82; 22 (1847), p. 88; 23 (1847), pp. 90–91; 45 (1847), pp. 179–180; and 54 (1847), pp. 214–215. J. Goldenthal described 40 new acquisitions and added notes to the previous catalogue in his *Die neuerworbenen handschriftlichen hebräischen Werke der k. k. Hofbibliothek zu Wien*, Vienna 1851; and A. Z. Schwarz described 84 MSS, acquired during the years 1851–1913, in his first catalogue of the collection, *Die hebräischen Handschriften der k. k. Hofbibliothek zu Wien*, Vienna 1914. Twenty-two or 23 of these new acquisitions were purchased from N. N. *Coronel and 18 from S. G. *Stern (see *Cat. Schwarz*, Vienna, index of owners).

Just over ten years later, Schwarz compiled *Cat. Schwarz*, Vienna (1925), a catalogue of all the Hebrew MSS in the library (now renamed Nationalbibliothek), containing detailed bibliographical and palaeographical descriptions of 220 MSS (in 212 entries) and 80 fragments found in bindings. Entries are arranged according to subject. At the head of each entry the catalogue number is listed. Call-numbers are printed in bold type at the end of each entry. Extensive quotations are given from the beginning and end of each work described. Palaeographical and codicological information: writing material, watermarks and their Briquet numbers, number of leaves, exact size, number of lines per page, composition of quires, size of written area, date and type of script. Colophons as well as owners' and censors' entries are transcribed. Date of acquisition, provenance and price paid by the owner are listed whenever possible. Indexes: authors, scribes, owners, censors, place names, titles, anonymous works arranged according to subject. On pp. 267–271 are concordances to the old call-numbers and the new ones. On p. 272 is a concordance to the call-numbers and the catalogue numbers. Cods. Hebr. 212–213 were not described because they are in Arabic (in Hebrew script). The MSS described in entries 206–207, which bore no call-numbers, are now Cods. Hebr. 223–224. In a handwritten catalogue in

the Nationalbibliothek (ser. nov. 2163), Cods. Hebr. 127–227 are briefly described.
E. Róth described Cods. Hebr. 221–224 in 'Interessante hebräische Handschriften der Österreichische Nationalbibliothek', *Biblos*, VIII (1959), pp. 83–88. Cods. Hebr. 212, 213, 221 and 222 were described in *Cat. Allony–Loewinger*, I, p. 8. At present, the holdings of Hebrew MSS (not including fragments) number 244. The Erzherzog *Rainer collection of papyri and fragments in the Nationalbibliothek are described in *Cat. Allony–Loewinger*, I, pp. 9–16, and in *Cat. Schwarz–Loewinger–Róth*, pp. 57–79.

Vienna, Staatsarchiv
The fragments formerly belonging to the archive that were described in 'Ein archäologischer Fund', *MGWJ*, XII (1863), pp. 72–75, are now *Vienna, ÖNB, Cod. Hebr. 184 (*Cat. Schwarz*, Vienna, no. 47).

Vienna, Universitätsbibliothek
Cat. Schwarz, Austria, lists two Hebrew MSS in the Universitätsbibliothek (nos. 193–194). In a communication to the *Jerusalem, IMHM, the library reported that the MSS were missing and may have been lost in World War II.

Vienna, Unsere Liebe Frau zu den Schotten (Benedictine Abbey)
Fragments from 33 MSS are described in *Cat. Schwarz–Loewinger–Róth*, pp. 104–109. The new call-numbers and the old ones according to *Catalogus codicum manuscriptorum qui in bibliotheca Monasterii B. M. V. ad Scotos Vindobonae servantur ... Edidit Dr. P. Albertus Hübl*, Vienna–Leipzig 1899, are listed at the end of each entry. Seven fragments listed on p. 109 were not described in Hübl's catalogue, and their present call-numbers are not known either. They had been photographed for the *Jerusalem, IMHM in 1957, but they were not found when the fragments were rephotographed in 1972. Fragments from 30 of the 33 MSS were previously listed in *Cat. Allony–Loewinger*, I, pp. 16–17, but the call-numbers were not listed. Fragments removed from over 100 MSS are described on the website http://www.ksbm.oeaw.ac.at/hebraica.

Villeneuve-lès-Avignon (France)
The Hebrew MSS in this Carthusian convent are now in *Nîmes, Bibliothèque municipale.

Vilna (Lithuania), Strashun Library (Jewish Community Library)
See *Strashun.

Vilna (Lithuania), YIVO (ייִדישער וויסנשאַפטלעכער אינסטיטוט, ייװ״א / Yidisher Visnshaftlekher Institut / Institute for Jewish Research)
Most of the MSS in the YIVO library disappeared during World War II. A few were transferred to the *New York, YIVO Library before the war. The remainder may perhaps be found in public libraries in Vilna. In 1988 and 1993, a large number of documents from the YIVO archives were discovered in Vilna in the inner recesses of the Lithuanian National Book Chamber (see New York, YIVO).

Vindobona
Latin name for Vienna.

Viterbo, Vivante (Jehiel Hayyim)
Ancona, Italy, c. 1766 – c. 1842
Some of Viterbo's MSS were purchased by Ludwig *Blau and are now mostly in *Jerusalem, NLI; others are in *Budapest, Jewish Theological Seminary. Two MSS were in the *Sassoon collection (nos. 406–407) and one in the *Jerusalem, Schocken Institute (MS 11308).
ד״ש לוינגר, ׳קובץ כ״י של יהודה אריה בלוי׳, הצופה לחכמת ישראל, יג (תרפ״ט), עמ׳ 186.

Vittorio Emanuele

See *Rome, Biblioteca Nazionale Centrale.

Vivanti (Hai), David Abraham

Ancona, Italy, 1806–1876; rabbi

Many of the MSS in Vivanti's collection were previously in the library of Hayyim *Azulai. Vivanti apparently sold some MSS during his lifetime: MSS *Oxford, Bodleian Library, Mich.168 and Mich. 321 were purchased by H. J. *Michael (d. 1846); and MSS *Cambridge, UL, Add. 652 and Add. 674, were purchased from the bookdealer S. *Schönblum in 1870. After Vivanti's death his MSS were acquired by Isaac Raphael *Tedeschi (Ashkenazi) and later came into the possession of Hayyim *Rosenberg, rabbi of Ancona. Part of the Rosenberg collection, including at least 40 MSS from the Azulai–Vivanti collection that had been described by Rosenberg (ח' רוזנברג, 'חבורי רב חיד"א וכתביו שלא ראו עדיין אור הדפוס', ק"ס, ה [תרפ"ט], עמ' 142–162, 255–262, 388–395), was purchased by *New York, JTSA, and part by *Los Angeles, University of California Library. A MS of geonic responsa was given by Vivanti to Rabbi Jacob Moses Ḥazan and served as the basis for Ḥazan's edition of *Teshuvot hage'onim*, with his glosses (תשובות הגאונים עם הגהות איי הים, ליוורנו תרכ"ט). The MS, long considered lost, was rediscovered by Rabbi Yehuda Leib Avida (Zlotnick) in Egypt (hence its name 'MS Avida') and presented by him to M. Margaliot. The MS is now in the M. R. *Lehmann collection, MS NL 48. On this MS see also Y. Tabori, 'Sources of the geonic responsa collection *Sha'are teshuva*', *'Alei sefer*, III (1977), p. 12 (י' תבורי, 'מקורותיו של ספר שו"ת הגאונים "שערי תשובה"'). The MS of *Zera' anashim* (זרע אנשים) once in Vivanti's possession was later *Warsaw, ŻIH, MS 231, and is now in *New York, Chassidei Chabad Library, MS 1191. The MS of *Shibole haleket* (ספר שבלי הלקט), which served as the basis for Buber's edition (1866) and was formerly in the possession of Vivanti and Tedeschi, is now *London, BL, MS Or. 9153. The MS of commentaries on tractates Yevamot and Nazir printed in the Romm (Vilna) edition of the Talmud is now *Jerusalem, NLI, Heb. 8° 2078. A few MSS of works by Vivanti are found in various libraries.

Vjasin

See *Massel.

VOH

Verzeichnis der orientalischen Handschriften in Deutschland. See *Striedl, Hans.

Volta, Samuel Vita Dalla

See *Dalla Volta, Samuel Vita.

Von Geldern

See *Van Geldern.

Vorau (Austria), Chorherrenstiftsbibliothek

Fragments from 14 MSS are listed in *Cat. Schwarz–Loewinger–Róth*, pp. 102–104. The call-numbers are listed at the end of each entry. Fragments removed from 18 MSS are described and displayed on the website http://www.ksbm.oeaw.ac.at/hebraica.

Vyazhin

See *Massel.

W

W

(1) Wien (Vienna); (2) *Wolf, Johann Christoph.

WI

A. Z. Schwarz, *Die hebräischen Handschriften der Nationalbibliothek in Wien*, Leipzig 1925 (= *Cat. Schwarz*, Vienna).

WII

A. Z. Schwarz, *Die hebräischen Handschriften in Österreich*, I, Leipzig 1931 (= *Cat. Schwarz*, Austria).

Wagenaar, Hyman Abraham

Amsterdam, Netherlands, d. 1888; scholar and bibliophile

Thirty-eight of Wagenaar's MSS are listed in the auction catalogue רשימה של מכירת ספרים: *Versteigerungs-Catalog einer wichtigen Sammlung Hebraica, Judaica, Handschriften, u.s.w. aus dem Nachlass des Herrn H. A. Wagenaar ... Versteigerung Montag 2 Mai 1904 und folgende Tage*, Amsterdam 1904, nos. 2305–2342. For the present locations of some of the MSS see Appendix I, no. 42.

Wagenseil, Johann Christoph

Nuremberg, Germany, 1633 – Altdorf, Germany, 1705; Christian Hebraist

Wagenseil's collection of close to 600 printed titles of Hebraica and Judaica was purchased by the *Altdorf, Universitätsbibliothek, in 1780. The University closed in 1809, and its library was transferred to the *Erlangen, Universitätsbibliothek in 1818. In addition to the printed books, there are a few Yiddish MSS in the collection. Other MSS of Wagenseil's passed into the possession of *Leipzig, Stadtbibliothek.

Wagner, Jacob H.

Germany; d. 1920

Seventy-nine Hebrew MSS, mostly dating from the eighteenth and nineteenth centuries, are described in the catalogue of Wagner's library, *Bibliothek Jacob H. Wagner: Eine Übersicht*, Berlin 1926. The fate of the collection is unknown.

Wahrmann, S.

See *Bamberger and Wahrmann.

Warn.

See *Warner, Levinus.

Warner, Levinus

Lippe, Germany, 1619 – Constantinople, Turkey, 1665

Warner was the Dutch consul in Constantinople, where he purchased many Hebrew MSS, among them a large number of Karaite MSS. His library was acquired by *Leiden, Bibliotheek der Rijksuniversiteit, in 1669. Seventy-seven MSS from Warner's collection were described in *Cat. Steinschneider*, Leiden.

A. van der Heide, *Hebrew Manuscripts of Leiden University Library*, Leiden 1977, pp. 10–15.

Warsaw (Poland), Biblioteka Judaistyczna przy Wielkiej Synagodze na Tłomackiem (Library for Jewish Studies of the Great Synagogue on Tłomackie Street)

A list of nineteen MSS in the Synagogue library was printed by M. Moszkowski (הצפירה, כ [תרנ״ג–תרנ״ד], עמ׳ 997). In 1937 Moses Schorr sent Simha Assaf a typewritten list of the MSS in the library (רשימת כתבי היד הנמצאים בספרייה הראשית למדעי היהדות על יד בית הכנסת הגדול, וארשה תרצ״ז), which is now found among the printed books in *Jerusalem,

NLI (call-number: 37A 1813). Ninety-eight MSS are described in the list. The 19 MSS described by Moszkowski are nos. 31–49 in Schorr's list. The list was published by B. Richler, 'The lost manuscripts of the Library for Jewish Studies in Warsaw', in I. Zwiep et al. (eds.), *Omnia in Eo: Studies on Jewish Books and Libraries in honour of Adri Offenberg* [= *Studia Rosenthaliana* 38/39], Leuven 2006, pp. 360–387.

According to B. Temkin-Berman (אנציקלופדיה של גלויות, א, וארשה—ירושלים—תל־אביב 1953, עמ' 517–515), the library's collection included 150 MSS. In 1940 the books in the library were confiscated by the Nazis and shipped to Berlin (for an eyewitness account of the pillage, see Chaim A. Kaplan, *Scroll of Agony*, New York 1965, pp. 57–89). The library was deposited in the central library (Zentralbibliothek) of the Reichssicherheitshauptamt in Berlin and was destroyed in the fire that engulfed the building on November 22 and 23, 1943. Photostats of over 100 *Geniza fragments are preserved in *Jerusalem, Schocken Institute.

D. Schidorsky, 'Confiscation of Libraries and Assignments to Forced Labor: Two Documents of the Holocaust', *Libraries & Culture*, XXXIII/XXXIV (1998), p. 360; A. Mężyński, 'Die Judaistische Bibliothek bei der Grossen Synagoge in Warschau und das Schicksal der Bücher aus dem Warschauer Ghetto', in R. Dehnel (ed.), *Jüdischer Buchbesitz als Raubgut* (Zweites Hannoversches Symposium), Frankfurt a/M 2006, pp. 85–95.

Warsaw (Poland), Żydowski Instytut Historyczny (Jewish Historical Institute, ŻIH)

Over 1,000 MSS found in cellars belonging to the Gestapo in the Polish town of Kłodzko after World War II were deposited in the library of the Jewish Historical Institute. Many of the MSS had previously belonged to other Jewish institutions, such as *Breslau, Jüdisch-theologisches Seminar, and *Vienna, Israelitische Kultusgemeinde. S. Strelcyn and E. Kupfer prepared a catalogue in Polish of 936 MSS, which was to have been published as Vol. VI of the *Katalog rękopisów orientalnych ze zbiorów polskich*. A typewritten copy of the catalogue is in the *Jerusalem, IMHM. According to M. Garel, 'Manuscrits hébreaux en Pologne', *Revue d'Histoire des Textes*, V (1975), p. 365, there is a typewritten catalogue in the ŻIH, compiled by Alfreda Berengaut. In 1977, the Institute returned several dozen MSS, mostly of works by rabbis of the Ḥabad movement, to *New York, Chassidei Chabad Library. Over the years a significant number of MSS have disappeared from the Institute and are now in private or institutional collections. Recently, new call-numbers were assigned to the MSS.

Washington, D.C., Library of Congress

There are about 225 MSS in the Library, many of them purchased from Ephraim *Deinard in 1914. No catalogue of the collection has been published. Myron M. Weinstein described a few dozen MSS on cards. A catalogue prepared by B. Richler incorporating information from Weinstein's descriptions may be found at the Library. The Samaritan manuscripts that were catalogued by Zuhair Shunnar in *Katalog Samaritanischer Handschriften*, Berlin 1974, are not included in this catalogue.

Rab., *Lit. Treas.*, pp. 146–147; A. J. Karp, *From the Ends of the Earth; Judaic Treasures of the Library of Congress*, Washington 1991.

Washington, D.C., Smithsonian Institution, Freer Gallery

Fifty-two *Geniza fragments purchased by Charles L. Freer from a dealer in Gizeh in 1908 are described, and most of them reproduced in facsimile, by R. J. H. Gottheil and W. H. Worrell, *Fragments from the Cairo Genizah in the Freer Collection*, New York 1927. The Smithsonian also possesses about 100 documents and inscribed objects of Jewish interest, mostly of Italian origin, as well as 50 marriage contracts from Damascus acquired from Ephraim *Deinard.

G. C. Grossman and R. E. Ahlborn, *Judaica at the Smithsonian*, Washington 1997.

Washington, D.C., U.S. National Museum
See *Benguiat, Ephraim.

Washington Haggada
Name given to *Washington, D.C., Library of Congress, Hebr. Ms 181, an illuminated haggada written by *Joel b. Simeon in 1478. A facsimile edition has been published, including an introductory volume, edited by M. M. Weinstein, *The Library of Congress Haggadah (1478)*, Washington 1991.

Narkiss, p. 140.

Weill, Georges
Jerusalem, twentieth century
An illuminated maḥzor that was in Weill's possession and is now in the collection of David and Jemima Jeselsohn of Zurich is part of a MS that originally also included *Jerusalem, NLI, Heb. 8° 4450 (from the collection of James de *Rothschild).

M. Metzger, 'Un Mahzor italien enluminé du XVe siècle', *Mitteilungen des Kunsthistorischen Institutes in Florenz*, XX (1976), pp. 159–196; ב' ריצ'לר, 'כתובי־יד עבריים שנתפצלו', אסופות, א (תשמ"ז), עמ' 142–143

Weimar (Germany), Herzogin Anna Amalia Bibliothek
Formerly Thüringische Landesbibliothek. Five MSS are described in *Cat. Striedl–Róth*, pp. 396–399. A sixth MS, Q 652a, has been microfilmed for the *Jerusalem, IMHM.

Weisz, Max
1872 – Budapest, Hungary, 1931
Weisz wrote a catalogue of the David *Kaufmann collection (= *Cat. Kaufmann*, 1906). Weisz's own MSS were given to the Jewish Community library in Pest (Loewinger, *Report*, p. vii). After World War II, the Community library was integrated into the library of the *Budapest, Jewish Theological Seminary – University of Jewish Studies.

Werner, Moritz
Frankfurt, Germany, twentieth cent.; professor
The MS of the astronomical work of Moses b. Jacob Witzenhausen (Frenkel), *Gemeine Entdeckungen von denen sieben Planeten*, formerly belonging to Werner, is now in the collection of William Gross of Tel Aviv (MS no. 30).

Wernigerode (Germany), Gräfliche Stolbergische Bibliothek
The MSS from this library are now in *Halle, Universitäts- und Landesbibliothek.

Pearson, p. 26; *Cat. Striedl–Róth*, nos. 177, 178, 182.

Wertheimer, Solomon Aaron
Jerusalem, 1866–1935; rabbi, scholar and bibliophile
Wertheimer was one of the first to acquire MSS and fragments from the Cairo *Geniza, and he published many of them. He also collected, described and published MSS he found in houses of learning, synagogues and private libraries in Jerusalem. Wertheimer sold many Geniza fragments to *Oxford, Bodleian Library (*Cat. Neubauer–Cowley*, II, pp. xii–xvi), to *Cambridge, University Library (about 100 fragments, many listed in the index of owners in Reif, *Cat. Cambridge*, p. 590) and to *Jerusalem, JNUL (now NLI; א' ילין, 'אסף כתבי ה"גניזה" אשר בבית עקד הספרים הלאמי בירושלים', ק"ס, ב [תרפ"ו], עמ' 292–297), including one Kabbala collectanea, Heb. 8° 266. Other fragments acquired from Wertheimer's descendants are in *Cincinnati, HUC (MS 2065 and others?), *Toronto, University of Toronto (MSS Friedberg 3-017 and 9-004), and *London, British Library (MS Or. 13153, acquired in 1968; see D. Rowland

Smith, 'Genizah collections in the British Library', in D. Rowland Smith and S. P. Salinger [eds.], *Hebrew Studies*, London 1991, p. 23). Many of the responsa published in his collection of geonic responsa (קהלת שלמה, ירושלים תרנ"ט) and a few midrash and other fragments are now in *New York, JTSA: MSS 5350, 5501, R1887–1892, R1894[?], R1910–1912 and R2259. The laws of Tora scrolls by Rabbenu Tam and the responsa of R. Nathan Hayarḥi, published by Wertheimer in his *Ginze Yerushalem* (גנזי ירושלם, א, ירושלים תרנ"ו), are now included together with fragments from the Cairo Geniza and other sources in *Cambridge, UL, MS T–S Misc. 34.

Westminster College

See *Cambridge, Westminster College.

Widmanstetter (Widmanstad), Johann Albrecht

Nellingen, Germany, 1506 – Regensburg, Germany, 1557; jurist and diplomat

J. A. Widmanstetter was ambassador to Rome in the first half of the sixteenth century. On his sojourns to Rome, Naples and other cities in Italy he purchased Hebrew MSS and commissioned copies of others. When Karl Albrecht V founded the Munich Stadtbibliothek (see *Munich, Bayerische Staatsbibliothek) in the middle of the century, Widmanstetter's collection was acquired. His MSS are listed in the index of owners in *Steinschneider's catalogue of the Munich Hebrew MSS.

Steinschneider, *Vorlesungen*, p. 89 (Hebrew, p. 114); Striedl, *Geschichte*, pp. 2–8.

Wien

Vienna.

Wijnkoop, Joseph David

Amsterdam, Netherlands, 1842–1910; rabbi

Twelve Hebrew MSS (and 21 Tora scrolls) are listed in the auction catalogue of his collection, *Auctions-Catalog* אהל יוסף ..., Amsterdam 1911, nos. 2029–2040, 2049–2050. For the present locations of some of the MSS, see Appendix I, no. 43.

Willmet, Johannes

Amsterdam, Netherlands, 1750–1835; orientalist

Six Hebrew MSS were described in the auction catalogue *Biblioteca Willmetiana*, Amsterdam 1837. King William I of the Netherlands purchased the entire collection out of auction and donated it to the Royal Institute, the predecessor of the Royal Netherlands Academy of Arts and Sciences. The MSS are now on permanent loan at the *Leiden, Universiteitsbibliotheek.

A. van der Heide, *Hebrew Manuscripts of Leiden University Library*, Leiden 1977, p. 18.

Winterthur (Switzerland), Stadtbibliothek

The MS from the 'Musée de Winterthur' described by Schwab, 'Les manuscrits hébreux de Zurich', *REJ*, XXIV (1892), p. 159, is actually in the Stadtbibliothek. Contrary to Schwab's assertion that the MS is dated 1499, it is in fact a much later copy, probably written in the eighteenth century.

Wolf, Albert

Dresden, Germany, 1841–1907

Wolf purchased an illuminated haggada from Carlo *Morbio. The haggada, sometimes called the 'Wolf Haggada', was described by D. Kaufmann, 'Une Haggada de la France septentrionale ayant appartenu à Jacob ben Salomon à Avignon', *REJ*, XXV (1892), p. 65. In 1905, Wolf, a jeweler and collector, donated his collection of Jewish art, at that time the biggest of its kind in Germany, to the *Berlin, Jüdische Gemeinde. After the war the MS was in *Warsaw, ŻIH, MS 242 (M. Garel, 'The rediscovery of the Wolf Haggadah', *Journal of Jewish Art*, II [1975], pp. 22–27). The Wolf Haggada disappeared after it was sent to an exhibition in the United

States in 1982. It surfaced at the Habsburg, Feldman auction in Geneva in June 1989 and was withdrawn from the sale after it became known that the haggada was a stolen item. Both the Warsaw Institute and the Berlin Jewish community claimed the MS. In 1997 the Polish government presented the MS to *Jerusalem, JNUL (now NLI), where it is now preserved as Heb. 8° 7246. A *Geniza fragment from Wolf's collection is mentioned in *ZDMG*, LI (1897), p. 448.

S. Zucker, *Books and People*, XI (1997), pp. 6–7, and in greater detail in the Hebrew version (על ספרים ואנשים, יא [תשנ״ז], עמ׳ 27 ; שם, יב [תשנ״ז], עמ׳ 12–4). See also the report by S. Shunami and Y. L. Bialer, in D. Schidorsky, *Burning Scrolls and Flying Letters* (גווילים נשרפים ואותיות פורחות, ירושלים תשס״ח, עמ׳ 146–145).

Wolf, Johann Christoph

Wernigerode, Germany, 1683 – Hamburg, 1739; Christian Hebraist

The greater part of the Hebrew MSS in *Hamburg, SUB, derives from Wolf's collection. Wolf's *Bibliotheca Hebraea*, I–IV, Hamburg 1715–1733, is based to a large extent upon the collection of MSS belonging to David *Oppenheim, now in the *Oxford, Bodleian Library. In *Conspectus Codd. Ms. in Bibliotheca Bodleiana*, in M. Steinschneider, *Catalogus Librorum Hebraeorum in Bibliotheca Bodleiana*, III, Berlin 1860, Steinschneider listed all the Oppenheim MSS used by Wolf. *Cat. Peyron*, pp. xli–xlvi, has a list of the Turin MSS quoted by Wolf (according to their old numbers) in Vol. IV of his work.

Wolf, Sandor

Eisenstadt, Austria, 1871 – Haifa 1944

In 1938, when the Jewish population of the Burgenland was expelled, Wolf's collection of archaeological and Judaica artifacts was confiscated and transferred to the Burgenländischen Landesmuseum in Eisenstadt (Austria). Wolf's three Esther scrolls, listed in *Cat. Schwarz*, Austria (nos. 19, 21, 22), were sold in Zurich in 1956 (letter to the *Jerusalem, IMHM from the Museum).

Wolfenbüttel (Germany), Herzog August Bibliothek

Thirteen Hebrew MSS were described by F. A. Ebert in *Catalogus Codicum Manuscriptorum Orientalium Bibliothecae Ducalis Guelferbytanae*, Leipzig 1831, nos. 1, 4, 5, 7, 10, 17, 18, 28, 73, 78, 128, 134, 141. These MSS are also listed in *Cat. Allony–Loewinger*, I, pp. 41–42, where the call-numbers of the MSS are listed in parentheses at the end of the entries. Nine of the thirteen MSS and four volumes of fragments not listed in the earlier catalogues are described in *Cat. Striedl–Róth*, pp. 400–411.

Worcester College

See *Oxford, College Libraries.

Worms (Germany), Jüdische Gemeinde

The *Worms Maḥzor listed in *Cat. Allony–Loewinger*, I, no. 550–551, is now *Jerusalem, NLI, Heb. 4° 781. The *Jerusalem, IMHM has a microfilm of Jospa Shamash's *Minhagim* (מנהגים), formerly in the possession of the community. *Kennicott listed two Bible MSS that were in the Worms synagogue (nos. 376–377) as well as the maḥzor (no. 378).

Worms Maḥzor

Name given to *Jerusalem, NLI, Heb. 4° 781, an illuminated Ashkenazic maḥzor in two volumes, the first written in 1272. From 1578 until the Kristallnacht in 1938, the maḥzor was in the possession of the Jewish community of Worms, Germany. After the Kristallnacht the MS was taken, together with the Jewish communal archives, to the Prince's palace in Darmstadt. In 1943 it was returned to Worms and kept in the cathedral tower. In 1956, a legal decision recognized the State of Israel as the owner of the maḥzor, and in 1957 it was presented to the JNUL (now NLI). A facsimile edition of the maḥzor, with an introduction by M. Beit-Arié, was published (Vaduz–Jerusalem 1986). It is also reproduced on the website of the NLI (http://www.jnul.huji.ac.il/dl/mss/worms/).

Wright, William Aldis

Beccles, England, 1831 – Cambridge, England, 1914; librarian and editor

Wright's MSS, most of which previously belonged to Christian *Ginsburg, were bequeathed to *Cambridge, Trinity College. H. Loewe described 159 of Wright's MSS in *Catalogue of the Manuscripts in the Hebrew Character Collected and Bequeathed to Trinity College Library by the Late William Aldis Wright*, Cambridge 1926.

Wrocław

See also *Breslau.

Wrocław (Poland, formerly Breslau), Biblioteka Uniwersytecka we Wrocławiu (Wrocław University Library)

The library was founded in 1811 and from 1919 to 1945 functioned as the Staats- and Universitätsbibliothek. Until 1945 the library had in its collection only a few dozen fragments of Hebrew MSS and two Hebrew codices. One of these MSS, Cod. Or. I.1, formerly IV F 89, a maḥzor, was described by P. de Haas, 'Beschreibung der Breslauer deutschen Machsor-Handschriften', *Soncino Blätter*, II (1927), pp. 33–35 (see also *Double Maḥzor). Thirty-five fragments removed from bindings of books in the University Library were described by D. Weinryb ('קטעי כתבי יד עבריים של יהודי שלזיה בסוף ימי הבינים', ק"ס, יד [תרצ"ח], עמ' 112–117). According to Weinryb (*ibid.*, p. 112, n. 1) the library possessed only two MSS, the aforementioned maḥzor and an eighteenth-century MS. In 1945 the holdings of the *Breslau, Stadtbibliothek were presented to the University Library, together with an additional four Hebrew codices that were listed in C. Brockelmann, *Verzeichnis der arabischen, persischen, türkischen und hebräischen Handschriften der Stadtbibliothek zu Breslau*, Breslau 1903, nos. M. 1106–1109, pp. 45–48. Seventeen fragments found in bindings and two notes in Hebrew from the Stadtbibliothek were described by M. Brann, 'Handschriftliches aus der Breslauer Stadtbibliothek', in *MGWJ*, XXXI (1882), pp. 371–381. In 2004, thirty-four additional MSS and six incunabula formerly belonging to the *Breslau, Jüdisch-theologisches Seminar, and deposited in the library of the Charles (Karlova) University in the National Library of the Czech Republic in Prague were returned to the Jewish community in Wrocław, and they are now kept in the University Library (see *Breslau, Jüdisch-theologisches Seminar).

Württembergische Landesbibliothek

*Stuttgart, Württembergische Landesbibliothek.

X

Xanten Bible

Name given to MS *New York, Public Library, Spencer Collection, MS 1, an illuminated Bible copied by Joseph ben Kalonymus of Xanten in 1294.

Ximines de Cisneros, Francisco

Torrelaguna, Spain, 1436 – Roa, Spain, 1517; cardinal and statesman

His MSS, used in the edition of the *Complutensian Polyglot*, were kept in *Alcalá de Henares, Collegio de San Ildefonso, and are now in *Madrid, Biblioteca de la Universidad.

P. Kahle, *The Cairo Geniza*, Oxford 1959, p. 125.

Y

Yahuda, Abraham Shalom

Jerusalem, 1877 – New York, 1951; orientalist

Two hundred and forty-two of Yahuda's MSS were bequeathed to *Jerusalem, JNUL (now NLI), two are now in *Cambridge (Mass.), Harvard University (MSS Heb. 40–41), and a number are in *New York, JTSA. The so-called 'Yahuda Haggada' is an illuminated fifteenth-century Ashkenazic haggada formerly in Yahuda's possession. At the end of the nineteenth century, when it was in the hands of the bookseller J. Rosenbaum in Frankfurt, the haggada was described by D. Kaufmann, 'Les cycles d'image du type allemande dans l'illustration ancienne de la Haggada', *REJ*, XXXVIII (1899), pp. 74–102. Later it was acquired by H. Eisemann of London, from whom Yahuda purchased it. In 1955 it was presented to the Bezalel Museum (later incorporated into the Israel Museum) by Yahuda's widow, and it is now *Jerusalem, Israel Museum, MS 180/50 (*Jerusalem Collections*, no. 12; מ' נרקיס, זמנים, יד [ניסן תשט"ו]). According to Z. Shunnar, *Katalog samaritanischer Handschriften*, I, Berlin 1974, p. 151, Dr. [A. S.?] Yahuda presented 32 Samaritan MSS to the Oriental Institute of the St. Petersburg University in 1904.

B. Narkiss and G. Sed-Rajna, *Index of Jewish Art: Iconographical Index of Hebrew Illuminated Manuscripts*, II: *The Yahuda Haggadah*, Jerusalem–Paris 1981.

Yellin, David

Jerusalem, 1864–1941; scholar

In *Jewish Studies in Memory of George A. Kohut*, New York 1935, Hebrew section, pp. 59–88, Yellin published poems by Israel Najara from some of the nine MSS of poems he had purchased in Damascus in 1917. These volumes are now in the Central Zionist Archives in Jerusalem, MSS 153/290–298. Seven other MSS (Heb. 8° 1482–1488) and two Arabic MSS were acquired by *Jerusalem, JNUL (now NLI).

Yevpatoria

See *Eupatoria.

YIVO

See *Vilna, YIVO.

Z

Z
*Zurich, Zentralbibliothek.

Zabara Bible
Name given to MS *Sassoon 1209, the second part of a Bible copied by Moses Zabara. The first part of the Bible was purchased in 2007 by Dr. David and Jemima Jeselsohn of Zurich. The second part was sold by the Sassoons and is now held by Joseph Safra of São Paolo.

Zelada, Francesco Javier (Saverio)
Spain, 1717–1801; cardinal
MSS formerly in the possession of Cardinal Zelada, librarian of the *Vatican Library from the end of 1779 until his death, are found in *Madrid, Biblioteca Nacional (Pearson, p. 43), *Toledo, Archivo y Biblioteca Capitulares (*ibid.*), and the *Vatican (*Cat. Allony–Loewinger*, III, p. 12).

Zemaḥ, David
Plonsk, Poland, 1859 – Warsaw, Poland, 1934; writer
The *Diwan* that once belonged to Zemaḥ and was mentioned in his article in *Mizraḥ uma'arav* (מזרח ומערב, ה [תר"ץ–תרצ"ב], עמ' 130), is now *Jerusalem, Schocken Institute, MS 37. The MS had been seen in the nineteenth century by Jacob Saphir and was mentioned in his book *Even sapir* (אבן ספיר, ב, מיינץ תרל"ד, עמ' 41). The story of the rediscovery of the MS and its eventual acquisition by Schocken was related by D. Yellin in an article in *Moznaim* ('גלגולי כתב־יד', מאזנים, ג, מס' יא [תרצ"ב], עמ' 11–12). The MS was described by H. Brody in his edition of Moses Ibn Ezra's secular poems (משה אבן עזרא: שירי החול, ירושלים תש"ב, עמ' 17–19).

Żih
*Warsaw, Żydowski Instytut Historyczny (Jewish Historical Institute).

Zuck. or Zucker
*Zuckermann, Benedikt.

Zuckermann, Benedikt
Breslau, Poland, 1818–1891; librarian
Zuckermann compiled catalogues of the library of the *Breslau, Jüdisch-theologisches Seminar. According to Brann, *Geschichte*, p. 79, Zuckermann presented nine MSS from his collection to the Seminary.

Zunz, Leopold (Yom-Tov Lipmann)
Detmold, Germany, 1794 – Berlin, 1886
Moses *Gaster bought 27 MSS from Zunz's library for the *London, Montefiore library (*Cat. Montefiore*, p. v). These MSS are listed in the index of owners in *Cat. Montefiore*. According to Freimann, 'Mitteilungen', p. 84, some of Zunz's MSS were in the Zunz-Stiftung in Berlin. Zunz described the MSS listed in **Hapalit*, Berlin 1850. MSS *Oxford, Bodleian Library, Opp. Add. 4° 27 and Bodl. Or. 661, were acquired from Zunz in 1856. The latter MS had previously belonged to Nachman Krochmal.

Zurich (Switzerland), Zentralbibliothek
Until the end of the nineteenth century the library owned only ten MSS. These were described by M. Schwab, 'Les manuscrits hébreux de Zurich', *REJ*, XXIV (1892), pp. 155–159. Other MSS were later added to the library's collection, most notably those of Moritz *Heidenheim, which were purchased by the Jewish community in Switzerland and presented to the library as a gift. About 200 of the 235 MSS in the library come from the Heidenheim collection. 235 MSS are

described in *Cat. Allony–Kupfer*, II, pp. 108–125. Call-numbers are listed in parentheses at the end of each entry. In the library are two handwritten catalogues of the MSS by A. Schechter (1921) and J. Prijs (1942–1945).

HEBREW ENTRIES
Abbreviations, Names, Cognomens and Titles

אבן רשף
אברהם פירקוביץ; ע"ע Firkovich, Abraham

אוצרות חיים
ע"ע Michael, Heimann Joseph

אפ'
אופנהיים; ע"ע Oppenheim, David

בית הספר
ע"ע Roest, Meijer Marcus

גנזי יוסף
ע"ע Chazanowicz, Joseph

גנזי מיליארד
ע"ע Black, William Mead

הפליט
ע"ע Hapalit

ואט
ואטיקן; ע"ע Vatican

חב"ה
חיים בכור הלוי; ע"ע Halevy, Hayyim Bekhor

חיד"א
חיים יוסף דוד אזולאי; ע"ע Azulai, Hayyim Joseph David

ט"ש
טיילור-שכטר; ע"ע Cambridge, University Library

יב"א הלוי
יואל בן אלכסנדר הלוי; ע"ע Horowitz, Joel b. Alexander Halevi

יה"ש
יהושע השל שור; ע"ע Schorr, Joshua Heschel

יוא"ל
יוסף אלמנצי; ע"ע Almanzi, Giuseppe

יח"ו
יחיאל חיים ויטרבו; ע"ע Viterbo, Vivante

יש"ר
יצחק שמואל ריגיו; ע"ע Reggio, Isaac Samuel

כי"ח
כל ישראל חברים; ע"ע Paris, Alliance Israélite Universelle

כי"ס
כתב־יד סימונסון; ע"ע Simonsen, David Jacob

כי"ר
כתבי־יד רומי = כתב־יד ואטיקן; ע"ע Vatican

כתר ארם צובה
ע"ע Aleppo

כתר דמשק
ע"ע Damascus

כתר הרשב"א
ע"ע Rashba Bible

כתר שם טוב
ע"ע Shem Tov Bible

סמינר
ע"ע New York, Jewish Theological Seminary of America Library

פאר הדור
ע"ע Simonsen, David Jacob

ק"ד
קהלת דוד; ע"ע Oppenheim, David

קנטבריגיא
קמבריג'; ע"ע Cambridge

ראח"ס
רשימת אורי חי סארוואל; ע"ע Saraval, Leon Vita

רד"א
ר' דוד אופנהיים; ע"ע Oppenheim, David

רח"ם
ר' חיים מיכל; ע"ע Michael, Heimann Joseph

רי"א
ר' יוסף ויאזין; ע"ע Massel, Joseph, of Viasin

ר"מ ל"ב
ר' מנדל לנדסברג; ע"ע Landsberg, Mendel

רמש"ג
ר' מרדכי שמואל גירונדי; ע"ע Ghirondi, Mordecai Samuel

רמש"ש
ר' משה שטיינשניידר; ע"ע Steinschneider, Moritz

רש"ף
ר' שמחה פנסקר; ע"ע Pinsker, Simha

שד"ל
שמואל דוד לוצאטו; ע"ע Luzzatto, Samuel David

שזח"ה
שלמה זלמן חיים הלברשטם; ע"ע Halberstamm, Solomon Joachim

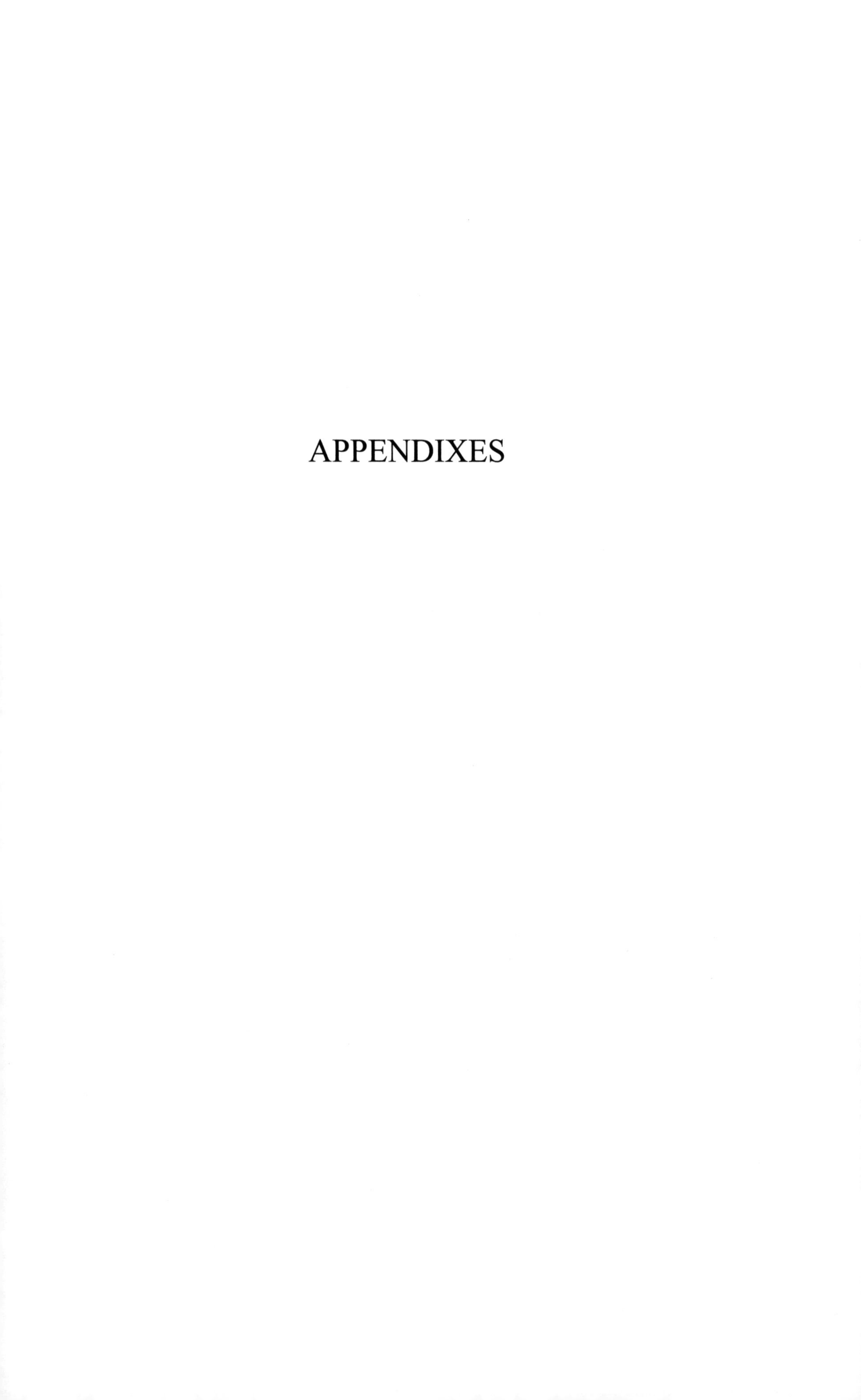

APPENDIXES

APPENDIX I

Present/Last-Known Locations or Call-Numbers of Manuscripts in Collections Treated in the *Guide*

1. MSS Asher

Present or last-known locations of MSS in Catalogue no. 86 of A. Asher & Co. (1868), and of the 'Verkäufliche Handschriften' described in *HB*, VI–X (1863–1870).

MS Asher	*Present/Last-Known Location*
1	Strasbourg, Nationale et univ., 3941 (Cat. 15)
2	Hamburg, SUB, Cod. Levy 13
3	Hamburg, SUB, Cod. Levy 14
4	Hamburg, SUB, Cod. Levy 2
6	Hamburg, SUB, Cod. Levy 10
7	Hamburg, SUB, Cod. Levy 11
8	Hamburg, SUB, Cod. Levy 106
9	Formerly London, Montefiore, 410
10	Hamburg, SUB, Cod. Levy 71
11	Munich, BSB, Cod. hebr. 308
12	Berlin, SB, Or. 8° 332 (Cat. 209)
13	Hamburg, SUB, Cod. Levy 112
14	Strasbourg, Nationale et univ., 3935 (Cat. 9)
15	Hamburg, SUB, Cod. Levy 118
16	Oxford, Bodleian, Opp. Add. 4° 114
17	Hamburg, SUB, Cod. Levy 144
18	Strasbourg, Nationale et univ., 3945 (Cat. 19)
19	Strasbourg, Nationale et univ., 3932 (Cat. 6)
20	Strasbourg, Nationale et univ., 3927 (Cat. 1)
21	Strasbourg, Nationale et univ., 3946 (Cat. 20)
22	Geneva, BPU, MS Comites Latentes 173

Verk. Hs	*Present Location*
1	Munich, BSB, Cod. hebr. 417
2	Munich, BSB, Cod. hebr. 418
3	Copenhagen, Kongelige Bibl., Cod. Hebr. Add. 6
5	Oxford, Bodleian, Opp. Add. 2° 44
9	Berlin, SB, Or. 2° 567 (Cat. 24)
10	Oxford, Bodleian, Opp. Add. 2° 36
12	Moscow, RSL, Günzburg 908
13	Oxford, Bodleian, Opp. Add. 4° 146
14	Moscow, RSL, Günzburg 433
15	Berlin, SB, Or. 4° 543
16	Berlin, SB, Or. 4° 544
17	Berlin, SB, Or. 4° 545

2. MSS Benzian

Present or last-known locations of MSS described by M. Steinschneider in *Catalogue d'une précieuse collection hébraïque ... en vente chez Julius Benzian*, Berlin 1869, and in *HB*, IX (1869), pp. 29–30, 60–62, 94, 117.

Cat. no.	*Present/Last-Known Location*
2	New York, JTSA, MS L836
3	Moscow, RSL, Günzburg 1065
4	Frankfurt, UB, Cod. hebr. 8° 161
6	Cambridge, UL, Or. 804
8	Berlin, SB, Or. 4° 521 (Cat. 69)
9	London, BL, Or. 1002
10	Frankfurt, UB, Cod. hebr. 4° 12
12	London, BL, Or. 1003
13	Frankfurt, UB, Cod. hebr. 8° 94
15	Cambridge, UL, Add. 1830
16	London, BL, Or. 1004
17	Moscow, RSL, Günzburg 1274
19	Cambridge, UL, Add. 1829
20	London, Montefiore, 35
21	Cambridge, UL, Add. 1835
23	Moscow, RSL, Günzburg 1076
27	Frankfurt, UB, Cod. hebr. 8° 152
28	Cambridge, UL, Add. 1828
29	Frankfurt, UB, Cod. hebr. 4° 10
30	Cambridge, UL, Or. 800
32	Cambridge, Trinity College, F. 12. 32
34	New York, JTSA, MS R877
35	Frankfurt, UB, Cod. hebr. 8° 130?
36	Cambridge, UL, Or. 796
37	New York, JTSA, MS 4715
40	Cambridge, UL, Or. 798
41	Cambridge, UL, Or. 797
42	Budapest, Hungarian Academy of Sciences, MS Kaufmann A 423
45	Cambridge, UL, Or. 799
46	Berlin, SB, Or. 2° 1264 (Cat. 161)
47	Moscow, RSL, Günzburg 1160
48	Moscow, RSL, Günzburg 1068
49	Formerly in *Auerbach collection, Halberstadt (see Freimann, *Union Catalog*)
50	Cambridge, UL, Add. 1833
52	Oxford, Bodleian, Opp. Add. 4° 119
53	Oxford, Bodleian, Opp. Add. 4° 118
54	Vienna, ÖNB, Hebr. 212
55	Vienna, ÖNB, Hebr. 213
59	Cambridge, UL, Add. 1831

60	Hamburg, SUB, Cod. Levy 117?
62	Moscow, RSL, Günzburg 953
65	Jerusalem, NLI, Heb. 8° 175
66	New York, JTSA, MS 1548
75	New York, JTSA, MS R1021
77	Cincinnati, HUC, MS 329
80–81	Berlin, SB, Or. 4° 694 (Cat. 166)
82	Berlin, SB, Or. 4° 691 (Cat. 145)
83	Cambridge, UL, Or. 795
84	Berlin, SB, Or. 4° 696 (Cat. 131)

MSS Benzian A–E, described in greater detail by Steinschneider in *Serapaeum*, XXX (1869), pp. 130–138, 149–150, correspond to Benzian catalogue numbers 80–84, as follows:
A = Cat. no. 84
B = Cat. no. 83
C = Cat. no. 80
D = Cat. no. 81
E = Cat. no. 82

3. MSS Berenstein

Present or last-known locations of MSS listed in the *Auctions-Catalogue* of the collection of Issachar Baer Berenstein, בינה לעתים, Amsterdam 1907, nos. 1766, 2153–2177.

Cat. no.	*Present Location*
1766	Amsterdam, UB, HS. Ros. 519
2154	Jerusalem, NLI, Yah. Ms. Heb. 216
2155	Cincinnati, HUC, Acc. 139
2159	Amsterdam, UB, HS. Ros. 116
2160	Amsterdam, UB, HS. Ros. PL-B-06
2161	Amsterdam, UB, HS. Ros. 8
2162	Amsterdam, UB, HS. Ros. 159
2166	Amsterdam, UB, HS. Ros. 12
2168	Silver Spring, Md., M. Lehmann, B70
2169	Jerusalem, NLI, Yah. Ms. Heb. 57
2170	Amsterdam, UB, HS. Ros. 421
2171	Amsterdam, UB, HS. Ros. 9
2172	Amsterdam, UB, HS. Ros. 353
2175	Amsterdam, UB, HS. Ros. 27

4. MSS Biema

Present or last-known locations of some of the MSS described in *Catalog der reichhaltigen Sammlung hebräischer u. jüdischer Bücher, Handschriften, Portraits, etc., nachgelassen von N. H. van Biema ...*, Amsterdam 1904.

Cat. no.	*Present/Last-Known Location*
2416	Amsterdam, UB, HS. Ros. 576
2495	New York, JTSA, MS R1575
3579	Copenhagen, Kongelige Bibl., Cod. Sim. Hebr. 57
3580	Jerusalem, S. Abrahams, 15
3581	Amsterdam, UB, HS. Ros. 3
3583	Jerusalem, NLI, Heb. 4° 898
3584	Jerusalem, Bookdealer
3585	Jerusalem, S. Abrahams, 20
3587	Jerusalem, S. Abrahams, 23–24
3589	Sassoon, 1271
3590	Jerusalem, S. Abrahams, 18
3591	Amsterdam, UB, HS. Ros. 28,1
3592	Jerusalem, S. Abrahams, 17
3594	Jerusalem, S. Abrahams, 14
3595	New York, JTSA, MS 2639 (ENA 1576)
3596	Amsterdam, Ets Haim, HS EH 47 C 3
3598	Jerusalem, S. Abrahams, 8
3601	Copenhagen, Kongelige Bibl., Cod. Sim. Hebr. 8
3602	Amsterdam, UB, HS. Ros. 311
3604	New York, JTSA, MS R1090
3605	Amsterdam, UB, HS. Ros. 552
3607	Jerusalem, S. Abrahams, 13
3610	Copenhagen, Kongelige Bibl., Cod. Hebr. 43
3611	Jerusalem, S. Abrahams, 21
3612	Amsterdam, UB, HS. Ros. 54
3613	Amsterdam, UB, HS. Ros. 327
3614	Amsterdam, UB, HS. Ros. 173
3615	Amsterdam, Ets Haim, HS EH 47 C 36
3616	Jerusalem, S. Abrahams, 9
3617	Manchester, John Rylands University Lib., MS Gaster 659
3619	New York, Yeshiva University, MS 1251 (formerly Berlin, Hochschule)
3620	Copenhagen, Kongelige Bibl., Cod. Sim. Hebr. 97
3621.3	Copenhagen, Kongelige Bibl., Cod. Sim. Hebr. 15
3623	Zurich, Braginsky Collection, 57
3625	Los Angeles, UCLA, MS 960 bx. 1.9 (formerly Ets Haim Library)

5. MSS Breslau

Present or last-known locations of MSS from Breslau, Jüdisch-theologisches Seminar, listed by their call-numbers, with *Cat. Loewinger–Weinryb* numbers in parentheses.

MS Breslau	*Present/Last-Known Location*
3 (291a)	Wrocław, Biblioteka Uniwersytecka
4 (52)	Warsaw, ŻIH, 10
5 (53)	Warsaw, ŻIH, 737 (part)
7 (2)	Wrocław, Biblioteka Uniwersytecka
8 (3)	Offered for sale in 1994
9 (6)	Wrocław, Biblioteka Uniwersytecka
10 (4)	Wrocław, Biblioteka Uniwersytecka
11 (7)	Wrocław, Biblioteka Uniwersytecka
13 (5)	Wrocław, Biblioteka Uniwersytecka
16 (63)	Jerusalem, NLI, Heb. 8° 2264
17 (54)	Warsaw, ŻIH, 215
21 (322)	Moscow, RSL (Trofiana)
22 (320)	Warsaw, ŻIH, 361
25(147)	Warsaw, ŻIH, 126
27 (36)	Wrocław, Biblioteka Uniwersytecka
29 (364)	Moscow, RSL (Trofiana)
30 (278)	Jerusalem, NLI, Heb. 8° 2135
31 (211)	Wrocław, Biblioteka Uniwersytecka
32 (61)	Jerusalem, NLI, Heb. 8° 2275
33 (243)	Wrocław, Biblioteka Uniwersytecka
34 (219)	Warsaw, ŻIH, 131
35 (12)	Wrocław, Biblioteka Uniwersytecka
38 (11)	Moscow, RSL (Trofiana)
40 (227)	Moscow, RSL (Trofiana)
41 (224)	Jerusalem, NLI, Heb. 8° 7031
42 (47)	Warsaw, ŻIH, 350
44,2 (58)	Warsaw, ŻIH, 265
45 (173)	Moscow, RSL (Trofiana)
47 (246)	Offered for sale by a bookdealer in 1996
48 (287)	Wrocław, Biblioteka Uniwersytecka
49 (15)	Wrocław, Biblioteka Uniwersytecka
50 (–)	Silver Spring, Md., M. Lehmann, 89
51 (–)	Silver Spring, Md., M. Lehmann, 90
52 (8)	Wrocław, Biblioteka Uniwersytecka
53 (14)	Wrocław, Biblioteka Uniwersytecka
54 (306)	Wrocław, Biblioteka Uniwersytecka
55 (–)	Silver Spring, Md., M. Lehmann, 88
57 (237)	Wrocław, Biblioteka Uniwersytecka
58 (238)	Warsaw, ŻIH, 197
59b (233)	Wrocław, Biblioteka Uniwersytecka

60 (34)	Wrocław, Biblioteka Uniwersytecka
62 (276)	Jerusalem, NLI, Heb. 8° 3100
63 (307)	Wrocław, Biblioteka Uniwersytecka
64 (23)	Wrocław, Biblioteka Uniwersytecka
65 (38)	Wrocław, Biblioteka Uniwersytecka
67 (194)	Jerusalem, NLI, Heb. 8° 4281
68 (195)	Wrocław, Biblioteka Uniwersytecka
69 (192)	Prague, Jewish Museum, 120
70 (196)	Sold in Tel Aviv, 1997
71 (205)	Moscow, RSL, fond 182, no. 456
73 (289a)	Jerusalem, NLI, Heb. 8° 4280
74 (290)	Wrocław, Biblioteka Uniwersytecka
75 (286)	London, D. Sofer, 96
76 (333)	Warsaw, ŻIH, 626
78 (345)	Warsaw, ŻIH, 366
80 (73)	Warsaw, ŻIH, 33
81,1 (323)	Offered for sale in 1994
81,2 (230)	Moscow, RSL (Trofiana)
84 (174)	Moscow, RSL (Trofiana)
85 (254)	Warsaw, ŻIH, 35
86 (251)	Warsaw, ŻIH, 25
89 (324)	Moscow, RSL (Trofiana)
91 (245)	Wrocław, Biblioteka Uniwersytecka
92 [parts]	Photostats in Jerusalem, NLI and Schocken Inst.
93 (45)	Prague, Jewish Museum, 340
95 (55)	Warsaw, ŻIH, 102
96 (24)	Wrocław, Biblioteka Uniwersytecka
98 (274)	Warsaw, ŻIH, 214
100 (240)	Wrocław, Biblioteka Uniwersytecka
101 (17)	Wrocław, Biblioteka Uniwersytecka
102 (32)	Wrocław, Biblioteka Uniwersytecka
104,2 (27)	Wrocław, Biblioteka Uniwersytecka
105 (176)	Warsaw, ŻIH, 167
107 (22)	Prague, Jewish Museum, 485
108 (51)	New York, JTSA, MS R2171
109 (39)	Warsaw, ŻIH, 440
113 (16)	Moscow, RSL (Trofiana)
115 (267)	Moscow, RSL (Trofiana)
116 (262)	Warsaw, ŻIH, 184
117,Ia (177)	Warsaw, ŻIH, 621
117,IVa–h (181)	Warsaw, ŻIH, 651
118 (282)	Offered for sale in 1999
119 (304)	Moscow, RSL (Trofiana)
120 (214)	Warsaw, ŻIH, 101
121 (148)	Moscow, RSL (Trofiana)

122 (60)	Moscow, RSL (Trofiana)
123 (346)	Silver Spring, Md., M. Lehmann, D 121
129 (229)	Warsaw, ŻIH, 181
130 (19)	Warsaw, ŻIH, 166
133 (110)	Warsaw, ŻIH, 430
134 (20)	Warsaw, ŻIH, 75
135 (228)	Warsaw, ŻIH, 135
139,1 (118)	Warsaw, ŻIH, 239
139,2 (168)	Moscow, RSL (Trofiana)
139,3 (164)	Moscow, RSL (Trofiana)
139,4 (169)	Jerusalem, NLI, Heb. 8° 2270
139,5 (165)	Warsaw, ŻIH, 239
139,6 (161)	Warsaw, ŻIH, 482
139,7 (160)	Moscow, RSL (Trofiana)
139,8 (166)	Warsaw, ŻIH, 239
139,9 (159)	Paris, Private Collection
139,10 (162)	Warsaw, ŻIH, 239
139,11 (117)	Warsaw, ŻIH, 239
139,12 (167)	Warsaw, ŻIH, 481
139,13 (158)	Warsaw, ŻIH, 239
139,14 (163)	Moscow, RSL (Trofiana)
139,15 (116)	Moscow, RSL (Trofiana)
139,16 (119)	Warsaw, ŻIH, 239
142 (21)	Moscow, RSL (Trofiana)
143 (66)	Warsaw, ŻIH, 140
144 (67)	Warsaw, ŻIH, 118
145 (72)	Warsaw, ŻIH, 82
147 (62)	Jerusalem, NLI, Heb. 8° 2284
148 (64)	Warsaw, ŻIH, 235
149 (65)	Jerusalem, NLI, Heb. 8° 2296
150 (112)	Moscow, RSL (Trofiana)
151 (68)	Moscow, RSL (Trofiana)
153 (152)	Warsaw, ŻIH, 367
154 (43)	Warsaw, ŻIH, 100
161 (273)	Warsaw, ŻIH, 63
163,2 (342)	Moscow, RSL (Trofiana)
163,4 (128)	Warsaw, ŻIH, 261
163,5 (336)	Warsaw, ŻIH, 306
166 (296)	New York, JTSA, MS 10169
167 (349)	Jerusalem, NLI, Heb. 8° 2272
168 (277)	Jerusalem, NLI, Heb. 8° 2129
171 (189)	New Haven, Yale University
173 (362)	Moscow, RSL (Trofiana)
177 (244)	Jerusalem, NLI, Heb. 4° 1201
180,1 (247)	Warsaw, ŻIH, 134

181 (200)	Warsaw, ŻIH, 69
183 (288)	Jerusalem, NLI, Heb. 8° 2132
184 (220)	Moscow, RSL (Trofiana)
185 (313)	Jerusalem, NLI, Heb. 8° 5218 (formerly Warsaw, ŻIH, 158)
186 (235)	Warsaw, ŻIH, 64
189 (308)	Warsaw, ŻIH, 288
190 (115)	Warsaw, ŻIH, 217
191 (263)	Jerusalem, NLI, Heb. 4° 652
192,1 (143)	Warsaw, ŻIH, 296
192,2 (140)	Warsaw, ŻIH, 1162 (formerly 123)
192,3 (141)	Jerusalem, NLI, Heb. 8° 2274
192,4 (142)	Warsaw, ŻIH, 70
192,5 (146)	Moscow, RSL (Trofiana)
193 (203)	Jerusalem, NLI, Heb. 8° 3718
196 (327)	Jerusalem, NLI, Heb. 8° 2271
197 (133)	Warsaw, ŻIH, 72
201 (285)	Jerusalem, NLI, Heb. 8° 2491
202 (305)	Wrocław, Biblioteka Uniwersytecka
204 (294)	Warsaw, ŻIH, 109
205 (272)	Wrocław, Biblioteka Uniwersytecka
206 (309)	Warsaw, ŻIH, 137
209 (107)	Warsaw, ŻIH, 114
213 (105)	Warsaw, ŻIH, 98
214 (265)	Wrocław, Biblioteka Uniwersytecka
216 (266)	Wrocław, Biblioteka Uniwersytecka
217 (264)	Warsaw, ŻIH, 192
218 (202)	Jerusalem, Hekhal Shelomo, Qu. 69
219 (204)	Warsaw, ŻIH, 62
222 (270)	Jerusalem, NLI, Heb. 8° 2137
225 (284)	Moscow, RSL, MS Евр. 147
230 (193)	Wrocław, Biblioteka Uniwersytecka
232 (175)	Warsaw, ŻIH, 111
234 (28)	Warsaw, ŻIH, 426
235 (279)	Warsaw, ŻIH, 259
238 (311)	Jerusalem, NLI, Heb. 8° 2989
240 (222)	Warsaw, ŻIH, 212
242 (330)	Warsaw, ŻIH, 480
243 (331)	Warsaw, ŻIH, 379
244 (95)	Warsaw, ŻIH, 143
245 (74)	Jerusalem, NLI, Heb. 8° 2322
247 (98)	Jerusalem, NLI, Heb. 8° 2283
250 (198)	Warsaw, ŻIH, 775
250 (155)	Warsaw, ŻIH, 291
251a (249)	Warsaw, ŻIH, 614
252 (241)	Warsaw, ŻIH, 352

256 (81)	Warsaw, ŻIH, 726h
258 (92)	Warsaw, ŻIH, 726g
259 (109)	Warsaw, ŻIH, 225
260 (102)	Warsaw, ŻIH, 484
262 (100)	Jerusalem, E. A. Leiner
263 (75)	Warsaw, ŻIH, 659
265 (132)	Silver Spring, Md., M. Lehmann, 231
266 (101)	Jerusalem, NLI, Heb. 8° 2299
268 (–)	Moscow, RSL (Trofiana)
271 (310)	Moscow, RSL (Trofiana)
276,2 (137)	Warsaw, ŻIH, 470
276,4 (185)	Warsaw, ŻIH, 222
277 (59)	Warsaw, ŻIH, 1195
279 (76)	Jerusalem, NLI, Heb. 4° 895
280 (88)	Warsaw, ŻIH, 1099
281 (97)	Warsaw, ŻIH, 148
287 (156)	Warsaw, ŻIH, 275
291 (89)	Warsaw, ŻIH, 81
293 (86)	Warsaw, ŻIH, 159?
294 (87)	Warsaw, ŻIH, 726c
295 (90)	Warsaw, ŻIH, 298
296 (78)	Jerusalem, NLI, Heb. 4° 878
297 (111)	Warsaw, ŻIH, 299
298 (91)	Warsaw, ŻIH, 726b
299 (153)	Warsaw, ŻIH, 227
300 (157)	Private collection
302 (184)	Warsaw, ŻIH, 1020
303 (129)	Warsaw, ŻIH, 220
305 (151)	Jerusalem, Rabbi Schochet (Karlin-Stolin), 705
309 (256)	Jerusalem, NLI, Heb. 8° 2292
311 (130)	Warsaw, ŻIH, 223
316 (232)	Warsaw, ŻIH, 796
318 (255)	Warsaw, ŻIH, 16
321 (120)	Warsaw, ŻIH, 76
327 (126)	Jerusalem, NLI, Heb. 8° 3074
335 (107a)	Warsaw, ŻIH, 201
397 (121)	Warsaw, ŻIH, 19
402 (390)	Warsaw, ŻIH, 386
404 (369)	Warsaw, ŻIH, 122
407,2 (378,2)	Warsaw, ŻIH, 879
409 (394)	Warsaw, ŻIH, 36
410 (395)	Warsaw, ŻIH, 452
418 (372)	Warsaw, ŻIH, 399
420 (393)	Warsaw, ŻIH, 209
424 (368)	Jerusalem, NLI, Heb. 8° 6397

428 (373)	Warsaw, ŻIH, 23
431 (386)	Jerusalem, NLI, Heb. 4° 667
432 (387)	Warsaw, ŻIH, 303
433 (388)	Warsaw, ŻIH,
434–5 (376)	Warsaw, ŻIH, 474
438 (377)	Warsaw, ŻIH, 151?
– (209)	Warsaw, ŻIH, 139

6. MSS Carmoly

Present or last-known locations of the MSS listed in *Catalog der reichhaltigen Sammlung hebräischer und jüdischer Bücher und Handschriften aus dem Nachlass des Seel. Herrn Dr. G. B. Carmoly*, Frankfurt a/M 1875.

Cat. no.	*Present/Last-Known Location*
1	Oxford, Bodleian, Opp. Add. 2° 51
2	London, BL, Or. 1389
3	Moscow, RSL, Günzburg 909
4	Cambridge, UL, Add. 1516
5	Cambridge, UL, Or. 790
6	Moscow, RSL, Günzburg 926
7	Frankfurt, UB, Cod. hebr. 4° 20
8	Frankfurt, UB, Cod. hebr. 4° 17
9	Cambridge, UL, Or. 787
10	Cambridge, UL, Or. 791
12	Cambridge, UL, Or. 792
13	Cambridge, UL, Or. 793
14	Moscow, RSL, Günzburg 991
15	Frankfurt, UB, Cod. hebr. 2° 14
18	New York, JTSA, MS 3704
21	Frankfurt, UB, Cod. hebr. 4° 11
22	Cambridge, UL, Add. 1746
23	Private collection in Israel (*REJ*, IV [1882], p. 5)
24	Cambridge, UL, Add. 1519
26	Frankfurt, UB, Cod. hebr. 8° 109
27	Cincinnati, HUC, MS 785?
28	Moscow, RSL, Günzburg 899
29	Moscow, RSL, Günzburg 1049
31	Moscow, RSL, Günzburg 1651?
34	Cambridge, UL, Add. 1518
35	Cambridge, UL, Add. 1502
36	Frankfurt, UB, Cod. hebr. 8° 118
37	Cambridge, UL, Add. 1512
38	Frankfurt, UB, Cod. hebr. 8° 68
39	Cambridge, UL, Add. 1527,3?

40	Oxford, Bodleian, Opp. Add. 8° 39
42	Cambridge, UL, Add. 1513
44	Moscow, RSL, Günzburg 1650
45	Cambridge, UL, Add. 1509
47	Frankfurt, UB, Cod. hebr. 8° 64
48	Frankfurt, UB, Cod. hebr. 8° 171
49	Frankfurt, UB, Cod. hebr. 8° 65
51	Frankfurt, UB, Cod. hebr. 8° 93
52	Moscow, RSL, Günzburg 1213
54	Cambridge, UL, Add. 1510?
56	Frankfurt, UB, Cod. hebr. 8° 134
60	Zurich, Zentralbibliothek, Heid. 169
61	Moscow, RSL, Günzburg 834
62	Frankfurt, UB, Cod. hebr. 8° 60
63	Frankfurt, UB, Cod. hebr. 8° 82
65	Warsaw, ŻIH, 251 (formerly Vienna, Kultusgemeinde; *Cat. Schwarz* 45)
66	Vienna, Kultusgemeinde (*Cat. Schwarz* 46)
67	Moscow, RSL, Günzburg 999
68	Frankfurt, UB, Cod. hebr. 8° 99
72	Cambridge, UL, Add. 1497
75c	Paris, AIU, MS H 96 A
76	Moscow, RSL, Günzburg 910
77	Frankfurt, UB, Cod. hebr. 8° 120
78	Frankfurt, UB, Cod. hebr. 8° 90
79	Frankfurt, UB, Cod. hebr. 8° 124
81	Cambridge, UL, Add. 1505
82	Moscow, RSL, Günzburg 976
85	Frankfurt, UB, Cod. hebr. 8° 266
86	Moscow, RSL, Günzburg 1092
87	Moscow, RSL, Günzburg 1206
89	Cambridge, UL, Add. 1870?
90	Frankfurt, UB, Cod. hebr. 8° 83
91	Moscow, RSL, Günzburg 1064
92	Moscow, RSL, Günzburg 905
94	Moscow, RSL, Günzburg 1546
95	Moscow, RSL, Günzburg 935
96	Oxford, Bodleian, Opp. Add. 8° 41
101	Moscow, RSL, Günzburg 1148
102	Moscow, RSL, Günzburg 1327
103–4	Frankfurt, UB, Cod. hebr. 8° 163
104A	Moscow, RSL, Günzburg 1008
104B	Cambridge, UL, Add. 1517
105	Cambridge, UL, Add. 1501
106	Cambridge, UL, Add. 1515
107	Moscow, RSL, Günzburg 1657

108	Frankfurt, UB, Cod. hebr. 8° 137
109	Cambridge, UL, Add. 1741
110	Frankfurt, UB, Cod. hebr. 8° 104
111	Frankfurt, UB, Cod. hebr. 8° 204
112	Moscow, RSL, Günzburg 898
113	Frankfurt, UB, Cod. hebr. 8° 76
114	New York, JTSA, MS 8244
115	Cambridge, UL, Add. 1500
116	Moscow, RSL, Günzburg 1204
117	Zurich, Zentralbibliothek, Heid. 159?
118	Paris, AIU, 197 A
119	Cambridge, UL, Add. 1514
120	Cambridge, UL, Add. 1747
121	Moscow, RSL, Günzburg 1121?
122	Frankfurt, UB, Cod. hebr. 8° 140
124	Frankfurt, UB, Cod. hebr. 8° 1
125	Frankfurt, UB, Cod. hebr. 8° 122
126	Moscow, RSL, Günzburg 1205
127	Frankfurt, UB, Cod. hebr. 8° 117
128	Moscow, RSL, Günzburg 1475?
129	Cambridge, UL, Add. 1499
130	Cambridge, UL, Add. 1520
131	Frankfurt, UB, Cod. hebr. 8° 58
132	Moscow, RSL, Günzburg 1332
133	Moscow, RSL, Günzburg 1331
134	Moscow, RSL, Günzburg 1333
135	London, Montefiore, 362
136	Moscow, RSL, Günzburg 1305
137	London, Montefiore, 368
138	Paris, AIU, MS H 83 A
139	Frankfurt, UB, Cod. hebr. 8° 148
141	Frankfurt, UB, Cod. hebr. 8° 105
142	Frankfurt, UB, Cod. hebr. 8° 137 (part)
143	Moscow, RSL, Günzburg 1185
144	Frankfurt, UB, Cod. hebr. 8° 146
145	Cambridge, UL, Add. 1511?
146	Merzbacher 54
148	Was in the Kaufmann collection in Budapest, Hungarian Academy of Sciences; now missing. See E. Róth, *KS*, XXX (1954/5), pp. 254–256.
151	Frankfurt, UB, Cod. hebr. 8° 115
152	Frankfurt, UB, Cod. hebr. 8° 175?
155	Frankfurt, UB, Cod. hebr. 8° 80
156	Moscow, RSL, Günzburg 930
158	Frankfurt, UB, Cod. hebr. 4° 14
160	Frankfurt, UB, Cod. hebr. 8° 149

161	Moscow, RSL, Günzburg 1597
163	Frankfurt, UB, Cod. hebr. 8° 96
164	Cambridge, UL, Add. 1508
165	Frankfurt, UB, Cod. hebr. 8° 110
166	Frankfurt, UB, Cod. hebr. 8° 156
168	Frankfurt, UB, Cod. hebr. 8° 144
169	Frankfurt, UB, Cod. hebr. 8° 53
170	Moscow, RSL, Günzburg 1137
172	Moscow, RSL, Günzburg 1397
173	Frankfurt, UB, Cod. hebr. 8° 57
174	Moscow, RSL, Günzburg 900
175	Cambridge, UL, Or. 802
176	Cambridge (Mass.), Harvard, Heb. 62
177	Frankfurt, UB, Cod. hebr. 8° 40
182	Amsterdam, Ets Haim, HS EH 47 A 10
183	Frankfurt, UB, Cod. hebr. 8° 47
185	Cambridge, UL, Add. 1498
187	Oxford, Bodleian, Opp. Add. 4° 135
189	Moscow, RSL, Günzburg 1739
190	New York, JTSA, MS 3194?
192	Jerusalem, NLI, Heb. 8° 5622
193	Frankfurt, UB, Cod. hebr. 8° 155
194	Frankfurt, UB, Cod. hebr. 8° 119
199	Frankfurt, UB, Cod. hebr. 8° 97
201	New York, JTSA, MS 3907–3908?
202	New York, JTSA, MS 3917–3918
204	New York, JTSA, MS 3915
205	New York, JTSA, MS 3914
206	New York, JTSA, MS 3912
207	New York, JTSA, MS 3910
208	New York, JTSA, MS 3913
210	New York, JTSA, MS 3916
211	New York, JTSA, MS 3911
214	Frankfurt, UB, Cod. hebr. 8° 98
215	Zurich, Zentralbibliothek, Heid. 161
216	Moscow, RSL, Günzburg 1264
217	Warsaw, ŻIH, 288
219	Zurich, Zentralbibliothek, Heid. 81?
221	Frankfurt, UB, Cod. hebr. 8° 85
222	Moscow, RSL, Günzburg 927
224	Frankfurt, UB, Cod. hebr. 8° 95
225	Moscow, RSL, Günzburg 1051
227	Frankfurt, UB, Cod. hebr. 8° 55
228	Frankfurt, UB, Cod. hebr. 8° 72
229	Moscow, RSL, Günzburg 1145

232	Cambridge, UL, Add. 1496
233	Moscow, RSL, Günzburg 1150
234	Frankfurt, UB, Cod. hebr. 8° 88
235	Frankfurt, UB, Cod. hebr. 8° 256
236	Frankfurt, UB, Cod. hebr. 8° 141
238	Frankfurt, UB, Cod. hebr. 8° 143
242	London, Montefiore, 494 [=New York, Public Library **P (MS Heb. 175)]
243	London, Montefiore, 492?
244	Warsaw, ŻIH, 900 (formerly Vienna Kultusgemeinde; *Cat. Schwarz* 246)
245	London, Montefiore, 306
246	Budapest, Hungarian Academy of Sciences, MS Kaufmann A 61
248	Frankfurt, UB, Cod. hebr. 8° 61?
249	Vienna Kultusgemeinde (*Cat. Schwarz* 257)
250	Frankfurt, UB, Cod. hebr. 8° 126
252	Frankfurt, UB, Cod. hebr. 8° 23
253	Frankfurt, UB, Cod. hebr. 8° 73
254	Frankfurt, UB, Cod. hebr. 8° 127
255	Frankfurt, UB, Cod. hebr. 8° 160
258	Frankfurt, UB, Cod. hebr. 8° 62
260	Frankfurt, UB, Cod. hebr. 8° 139
261	Frankfurt, UB, Cod. hebr. 8° 28
262	Jerusalem, NLI, Heb. 8° 1619
264	Moscow, RSL, Günzburg 1251
267	Moscow, RSL, Günzburg 1571
273	Frankfurt, UB, Cod. hebr. 8° 249
274	London, Montefiore, 429
277	Moscow, RSL, Günzburg 936
278	Cambridge, UL, Add. 1507?
280	Frankfurt, UB, Cod. hebr. 8° 77
281	Moscow, RSL, Günzburg 978
282	Moscow, RSL, Günzburg 1718
283	Cambridge, UL, Add. 1503
284	Cambridge, UL, Add. 1506
285	Frankfurt, UB, Cod. hebr. 8° 91

7. MSS Coronel

Present locations of the MSS listed in the catalogue published by N. N. Coronel (**רשימה מספרי כתבי־יד**), London 1871.

MS Coronel	*Present Location*
1	London, BL, Or. 1081
2	London, BL, Or. 1082
3	Moscow, RSL, Günzburg 557?

4 Moscow, RSL, Günzburg 635
5 Moscow, RSL, Günzburg 632
6 Moscow, RSL, Günzburg 558
7 Moscow, RSL, Günzburg 556
8 Moscow, RSL, Günzburg 560
9 Moscow, RSL, Günzburg 631
10 Moscow, RSL, Günzburg 559
11 Moscow, RSL, Günzburg 634
12 Moscow, RSL, Günzburg 561
13 Moscow, RSL, Günzburg 555
14 Moscow, RSL, Günzburg 554
15 New York, JTSA, MS R1116
17 Moscow, RSL, Günzburg 633
18 Moscow, RSL, Günzburg 562
19 Moscow, RSL, Günzburg 463
20 Moscow, RSL, Günzburg 387–392
21 Moscow, RSL, Günzburg 369?
22 Moscow, RSL, Günzburg 370
23 Moscow, RSL, Günzburg 371
24 Moscow, RSL, Günzburg 372
25 Moscow, RSL, Günzburg 373
26 Moscow, RSL, Günzburg 374
27 Moscow, RSL, Günzburg 375
28 Moscow, RSL, Günzburg 376
29 Moscow, RSL, Günzburg 377
30 Moscow, RSL, Günzburg 378
31 Moscow, RSL, Günzburg 379
32 Moscow, RSL, Günzburg 380
33 Moscow, RSL, Günzburg 381
34 Moscow, RSL, Günzburg 382
36 Moscow, RSL, Günzburg 383
37 Moscow, RSL, Günzburg 384–386
38 Moscow, RSL, Günzburg 393
39 Oxford, Bodleian, Opp. Add. 4° 113
40 London, BL, Or. 1083
41 Moscow, RSL, Günzburg 394
42 London, BL, Or. 1084
43 Moscow, RSL, Günzburg 395
44 Moscow, RSL, Günzburg 396
45 Moscow, RSL, Günzburg 397
46 Moscow, RSL, Günzburg 398
47 Moscow, RSL, Günzburg 399
48 Moscow, RSL, Günzburg 400
49 Moscow, RSL, Günzburg 401
50 Moscow, RSL, Günzburg 402

51	Moscow, RSL, Günzburg 403
52	Moscow, RSL, Günzburg 404
53	Moscow, RSL, Günzburg 405
54	Moscow, RSL, Günzburg 406
55	Moscow, RSL, Günzburg 407
56	Moscow, RSL, Günzburg 408
57	Moscow, RSL, Günzburg 409
58	Moscow, RSL, Günzburg 410
59	Moscow, RSL, Günzburg 411
60	Moscow, RSL, Günzburg 412
61	Moscow, RSL, Günzburg 413
62	Moscow, RSL, Günzburg 414
63	Moscow, RSL, Günzburg 415
64	Moscow, RSL, Günzburg 416
65	Moscow, RSL, Günzburg 417
66	Moscow, RSL, Günzburg 418
67	Moscow, RSL, Günzburg 419
68	Moscow, RSL, Günzburg 420
69	Oxford, Bodleian, Opp. Add. 4° 111
70	Moscow, RSL, Günzburg 495?
71	Moscow, RSL, Günzburg 421
72	Moscow, RSL, Günzburg 422
73	Moscow, RSL, Günzburg 423
74–75	Oxford, Bodleian, Opp. Add. 4° 112
76	Moscow, RSL, Günzburg 424
77	Moscow, RSL, Günzburg 425
78	Moscow, RSL, Günzburg 426
79	Moscow, RSL, Günzburg 427
80	Moscow, RSL, Günzburg 428
81	Moscow, RSL, Günzburg 429
82	Moscow, RSL, Günzburg 460
83	Moscow, RSL, Günzburg 660
84	Moscow, RSL, Günzburg 430
85	Moscow, RSL, Günzburg 431
86	Moscow, RSL, Günzburg 432
87	Moscow, RSL, Günzburg 433
88	Moscow, RSL, Günzburg 661
89–90	Moscow, RSL, Günzburg 434
91	Moscow, RSL, Günzburg 435–6
92–93	Moscow, RSL, Günzburg 437
94	Moscow, RSL, Günzburg 438
95	Moscow, RSL, Günzburg 439
96	Moscow, RSL, Günzburg 440
97	Moscow, RSL, Günzburg 441
98	Moscow, RSL, Günzburg 442

99	Moscow, RSL, Günzburg 443
100	Moscow, RSL, Günzburg 444
101	Moscow, RSL, Günzburg 445
102	Moscow, RSL, Günzburg 446
103	Moscow, RSL, Günzburg 447
104	Moscow, RSL, Günzburg 448
105	Moscow, RSL, Günzburg 449
106	Moscow, RSL, Günzburg 450
107	Moscow, RSL, Günzburg 451
108	Moscow, RSL, Günzburg 452
109	Moscow, RSL, Günzburg 453
110	Moscow, RSL, Günzburg 454
111	Moscow, RSL, Günzburg 455
112	Moscow, RSL, Günzburg 698
113	Moscow, RSL, Günzburg 456
114	Moscow, RSL, Günzburg 457
115	Moscow, RSL, Günzburg 695
117	Moscow, RSL, Günzburg 692
118	Moscow, RSL, Günzburg 694
119	Moscow, RSL, Günzburg 690
120	Moscow, RSL, Günzburg 673
121	Moscow, RSL, Günzburg 699
122	Moscow, RSL, Günzburg 696
123	Moscow, RSL, Günzburg 693
124	Moscow, RSL, Günzburg 700
125	Moscow, RSL, Günzburg 701
126	Moscow, RSL, Günzburg 702?
127	Moscow, RSL, Günzburg 458
128	Moscow, RSL, Günzburg 459
129	Moscow, RSL, Günzburg 691

8. MSS da Costa

Present or last-known locations of MSS listed in the auction-catalogue *Catalogue de la collection importante de livres et manuscrits hébreux, espagnols et portugais ... provenant de la Bibliothèque de feu Mr. Isaac da Costa à Amsterdam*, Amsterdam 1861.

Cat. no.	*Present/Last-Known Location*
2100	Oxford, Bodleian Library, Opp. Add. 4° 47
2164	Oxford, Bodleian Library, Opp. Add. 4° 51
2227	formerly Sassoon 439
2261	London, Montefiore, 308?
2266	Amsterdam, Ets Haim, HS EH 47 C 25
2270	Oxford, Bodleian Library, Opp. Add. 8° 8
2311	New York, Columbia Univ., X 893 Sa 7

2326	Oxford, Bodleian Library, Opp. Add. 4° 49
2327	Oxford, Bodleian Library, Opp. Add. 8° 7
2328	Oxford, Bodleian Library, Opp. Add. 2° 29
2329	Amsterdam, Ets Haim, HS EH 48 C 16
2463	Amsterdam, Ets Haim, HS EH 49 A 8
2464	Amsterdam, Ets Haim, HS EH 49 B 19
2468	Amsterdam, Ets Haim, HS EH 48 E 27
2476	Amsterdam, Ets Haim, HS EH 48 D 36
2521	Oxford, Bodleian Library, Opp. Add. 4° 50
2563	Jerusalem, NLI, Heb. 8° 6744?
2591	New York, JTSA, MS 3597
2595	Amsterdam, Ets Haim, HS EH 48 E 16

9. MSS Cracovia

Present locations of four MSS from the collection of Abraham Hayyim Cracovia described by Kennicott.

Kennicott no.	*Present Location*
571	New York, JTSA, MS L5
572	London, BL, Add. 15251
573	Parma, Biblioteca Palatina, MS Parm. 2338–2339 (de Rossi 11)
574	Parma, Biblioteca Palatina, MS Parm. 2151–2153 (de Rossi 3)

10. MSS in Florence (Italy), Biblioteca Medicea Laurenziana

Call-numbers of MSS described by S. E. Assemani in the appendix to A. M. Biscioni, *Bibliothecae Ebraicae Graecae Florentinae sive Bibliothecae Mediceo-Laurentianae*, II, Florence 1757.

Cat. Assemani (in Cat. Biscioni)	*Present Call-number*
528	Or. 42
529	Or. 149
530	Or. 17
531	Or. 468
532	Or. 472
533	Or. 79
534	Or. 121
535	Or. 124
536–537	Or. 451

11. MSS Gagin (Gaguine)

Present locations of MSS from the library of R. Hayyim Abraham Gagin listed in Jerusalem, NLI, 93 L 11.

No.	*Present Location*
no. 3	Sassoon 705, and part in Jerusalem, NLI, Heb. 4° 66
no. 4	Sassoon 707
no. 16	Sassoon 714
nos. 17–19	New York, JTSA, MS L1052
no. 23	Ramat Gan, Bar-Ilan Univ., MS 1041
no. 30	New York, JTSA, MS R33
no. 42	New York, JTSA, MS R832
no. 48	Jerusalem, NLI, Heb. 4° 6187
no. 51	New York, JTSA, MS 2881?

12. MSS Geiger

Present locations of MSS formerly in the Hochschule für die Wissenschaft des Judentums, Berlin.

No. in HB, XVII	*Sotheby's 1984 Cat. no.*	*Present Location*
1	37	New York, JTSA, MS 9825
2	51	New York, JTSA, MS 9829
3		Moscow, RSMA, 1325/1/98
4–6	39	New York, Yeshiva U., 1247
7	60	New York, JTSA, MS 9831
8		Private collection
9	55	New York, Yeshiva U., MS 1250
10	57	Cincinnati, HUC, MS JCF 1
11	49	Jerusalem, NLI, Heb. 8° 6426
12	43	Jerusalem, NLI, Heb. 8° 6425
13	38	New York, JTSA, MS 9826
14	44	New York, JTSA, MS 9828
15	45	
	40	New York, JTSA, MS 9827
	41	London, Leo Baeck Inst.
	46	London, Leo Baeck Inst.
	47	Jerusalem, NLI, Heb. 28° 6527
	50	Jerusalem, NLI, Arc 4° 792/A14
	53	Cincinnati, HUC, MS JCF 2
	54	New York, JTSA, MS 9830
	56	Cincinnati, HUC, MS JCF 4
	58	New York, Yeshiva U., MS 1251
	61	Cincinnati, HUC, MS JCF 5
	62	Jerusalem, NLI, Heb. 8° 6424

13. MSS Ghirondi

Present or last-known locations of MSS described in M. Steinschneider, *Catalog hebräischer Handschriften, grossten Theils aus dem Nachlass des Rabb. M. S. Ghirondi*, Berlin 1872.

Cat. no.	*Present/Last-Known Location*
1	Cambridge, UL, Add. 1051?
2	Berlin, SB, Or. 2° 1618 (Cat. 219)
4A	Warsaw, ŻIH, 174
4B–F	New York, JTSA, MS 5293
5	Frankfurt, UB, Cod. hebr. 8° 191
6B	Warsaw, ŻIH, 99
7	Frankfurt, UB, Cod. hebr. 8° 74
8	Frankfurt, UB, Cod. hebr. 8° 17
10	Oxford, Bodleian, Opp. Add. 4° 105?
11	New York, JTSA, MS 2409
12	Cambridge, UL, Add. 1052
14	London, Montefiore, 274
15	Frankfurt, UB, Cod. hebr. 8° 190
16	New York, JTSA, MS 8242
18	Edinburgh, NL, MS La III 591
20–22	Budapest, Hungarian Academy of Sciences, MS Kaufmann A 457
22D	Jerusalem, NLI, Heb. 8° 4001
23	Frankfurt, UB, Cod. hebr. 8° 15
24	Warsaw, ŻIH, 895
25	Vienna, Kultusgemeinde (*Cat. Schwarz* 284)
26	New York, JTSA, MS 1598 (ENA 885)
27	New York, JTSA, R1070 (ENA 1050)
28	Oxford, Bodleian, Heb. f. 17
29	Oxford, Bodleian, Opp. Add. 4° 181
30	Oxford, Bodleian, Opp. Add. 4° 182
31	Cambridge, UL, Add. 1051?
32	New York, JTSA, MS 1567 (ENA 792)
34	New York, JTSA, MS R1474 (ENA 797)
35	New York, JTSA, MS 2410 (ENA 829)
38	Oxford, Bodleian, Opp. Add. 4° 103?
39	New York, JTSA, MS 9150
40	New York, JTSA, MS R437 (ENA 770)
42	Paris, AIU, H 149 A
43	New York, JTSA, MS 8103 (ENA 775)
46	Frankfurt, UB, Cod. hebr. 8° 20
49	New York, JTSA, MS 5107 (ENA 899)
50	New York, JTSA, MS 1586 (ENA 843)
51	New York, JTSA, MS L462a
52	Oxford, Bodleian, Opp. Add. 4° 106
53	New York, JTSA, R1538 (ENA 795)

54	New York, JTSA, MS ENA 790?
58	Cambridge, UL, Add. 1195
59	New York, JTSA, MS R1046?
60	Oxford, Bodleian, Opp. Add. 4° 179
63	Oxford, Bodleian, Opp. Add. 4° 104
64	New York, JTSA, R1434 (ENA 1023)
65	Jerusalem, NLI, Heb. 8° 3489
66	Oxford, Bodleian, Heb. f. 16
68	New York, JTSA, MS 5069 (ENA 992)
69	New York, JTSA, MS R1022 (ENA 754)
72	Oxford, Bodleian, Heb. f. 15
73	New York, JTSA, MS 1601 (ENA 889)
74	Oxford, Bodleian, Heb. e. 19
75	Warsaw, ŻIH, 284 (formerly Vienna, Kultusgemeinde; *Cat. Schwarz* 91)
76	Cambridge, UL, Add. 1193
77	London, BL, Or. 1057
78	New York, JTSA, MS 1576 (ENA 811)
79	Ramat Gan, Bar-Ilan 275, 286, 583, 747 (formerly Vienna, Kultusgemeinde; *Cat. Schwarz* 258)
80	Berlin, SB, Or. 8° 539 (Cat. 205)
81	New York, JTSA, MS 1569 (ENA 800)
82	Paris, AIU, MS H 107 A
83	New York, JTSA, MS 1613
84–86	New York, JTSA, MS R1011–1013 (ENA 867–869)
87	New York, JTSA, MS 2412 (ENA 900)
88	New York, JTSA, MS 1604 (ENA 892)
90	Frankfurt, UB, Cod. hebr. 8° 145
92	New York, JTSA, MS 1616
93	New York, JTSA, MS 2415 (ENA 1002)
95	New York, JTSA, MS 1574 (ENA 807)
96	New York, JTSA, MS 3553 (ENA 823)
99	New York, JTSA, MS 5062 (ENA 981)
100	Frankfurt, UB, Cod. hebr. 8° 187
103	New York, JTSA, MS 3552
105	New York, JTSA, MS 1577 (ENA 813)
106	Oxford, Bodleian, Heb. e. 15
107A–G	London, Montefiore, 485
107H–L	London, Montefiore, 451
108–109	London, BL, Or. 1055
110	Berlin, SB, Or. 8° 538
112A–C	Oxford, Bodleian, Heb. e. 89
112D	Berlin, SB, Or. 8° 396 (Cat. 206)
112E–F	Oxford, Bodleian, Heb. e. 89
113	Budapest, Hungarian Academy of Sciences, MS Kaufmann A 237?
114	Cambridge, UL, Add. 1197

115	Jerusalem, NLI, Heb. 8° 2922
116	New York, JTSA, MS R445 (ENA 994)
117	Budapest, Hungarian Academy of Sciences, MS Kaufmann A 240
118	Cambridge, UL, Add. 1196
119	New York, JTSA, MS 1581 (ENA 822)
120	New York, JTSA, MS 1605 (ENA 895)
121	New York, JTSA, MS 8117 (Steinschneider 29)
123	New York, JTSA, MS 1619 (ENA 1013)
126	New York, JTSA, MS 1606 (ENA 896)
128D–F	New York, JTSA, MS 2411 (ENA 847)
129	New York, Columbia University, X 893 P 95
130	New York, JTSA, MS 1593 (ENA 860)
131	Cambridge, UL, Add. 1023
132	New York, JTSA, MS 1697 (ENA 897)
133	Vienna, Kultusgemeinde (*Cat. Schwarz* 261)
134	Vienna, Kultusgemeinde (*Cat. Schwarz* 236)
135	New York, JTSA, MS 1588 (ENA 846)
137	New York, JTSA, MS 1600 (ENA 888)
138	New York, JTSA, MS 1623 (ENA 1029)
139	New York, JTSA, MS L937 (ENA 817)
140	New York, JTSA, MS L936
141	New York, JTSA, MS 1569 (ENA 801)
142	New York, JTSA, MS 1539 (ENA 145)
143	New York, JTSA, MS 2416 (ENA 1015)
145	New York, JTSA, MS 1590 (ENA 853)

14. MSS Goldsmid

Present locations of MSS from the collection of Julian Goldsmid listed in *Catalogue of the Anglo-Jewish Historical Exhibition ... 1887*, London 1888, Nos. 775, 2070–2080.

Catalogue no.	*Present Location*
775	London School of Jewish Studies, Asher Myers 2
2070	Sydney, University, Fisher Library, MS Nicholson 33
2071	Cambridge, Trinity College, MS F. 12. 70–71
2073	Hamburg, SUB, Cod. Levy 3
2075	formerly Sassoon 512, now Geneva, N. Gaon
2077	London School of Jewish Studies, Asher Myers 6

15. MSS Listed in *Hapalit*

Present locations of MSS listed by Leopold Zunz in *Hapalit*, Berlin 1850, and not purchased by Oxford, Bodleian Library.

Hapalit no.	*Present/Last-Known Location*
4	Private dealer (in 2000)
11	Moscow, RSL, Günzburg 1141
13	Berlin, SB, Or. 4° 835
36	New York, JTSA, MS R282
50	Cluj, Romanian Academy, Ms. O. 303
52	Probably Paris, AIU, MS H 167 A
56	London, BL, Add. 18831
77	New York, JTSA, MS 2314 (= MS *Steinschneider 22)

16. MSS Heidenheim

Present or last-known locations of MSS in the catalogue of Wolf Heidenheim's estate (רשימת הספרים אשר הניח אחריו... וואלף היידנהיים), Rödelheim 1833.

MS Heidenheim	*Present/Last-Known Location*
1	Jerusalem, NLI, Heb. 8° 2132
2	Oxford, Bodleian, Mich. 416
4	New York, JTSA, MS 2287
5	Oxford, Bodleian, Mich. 497?
6	Oxford, Bodleian, Mich. 282
10	Oxford, Bodleian, Mich. 45
14	Oxford, Bodleian, Mich. 121
15	Zurich, Zentralbibliothek, Heid. 188
16	Oxford, Bodleian, Mich. 320
17	Oxford, Bodleian, Mich. 568
19	Oxford, Bodleian, Mich. 58
20	Oxford, Bodleian, Mich. 29
21	Oxford, Bodleian, Mich. 581?
22	Oxford, Bodleian, Mich. 58
23	Oxford, Bodleian, Mich. 48
24	Oxford, Bodleian, Mich. 169
25	Oxford, Bodleian, Mich. 39
30	Oxford, Bodleian, Mich. 44
32	Oxford, Bodleian, Mich. 574
33	Oxford, Bodleian, Mich. 617 and 627
34	Oxford, Bodleian, Mich. 420
35	Oxford, Bodleian, Mich. 224
37	Oxford, Bodleian, Mich. 187
38	Oxford, Bodleian, Mich. 527

40	Oxford, Bodleian, Mich. 554
41	Oxford, Bodleian, Mich. 67
42	London, Montefiore, 273
45	Oxford, Bodleian, Mich. 458
46	Oxford, Bodleian, Mich. 273
53	Oxford, Bodleian, Mich. 208
55	Oxford, Bodleian, Mich. 510
58	Oxford, Bodleian, Mich. 314
62	New York, JTSA, MS 2872
63	Oxford, Bodleian, Mich. 138
64	Oxford, Bodleian, Mich. 211
65	Oxford, Bodleian, Mich. 554
66	Oxford, Bodleian, Mich. 394
68	Oxford, Bodleian, Mich. 85
69	Oxford, Bodleian, Mich. 456
71	Oxford, Bodleian, Mich. 343

17. MSS Henriques de Castro

Present locations of MSS listed in *Catalogue de vente de la succession de feu M. D. Henriques de Castro*, Amsterdam 1899.

Cat. no.	*Present Location*
474	Jerusalem, Israel Museum, MS 180/94 (formerly MS Sassoon, 506)
475	New York, Hispanic Society of America, MS B 241
476	Amsterdam, UB, HS. Ros. PL B-73
477	New York, JTSA, MS 2400 (ENA 369)
478	Amsterdam, Ets Haim, HS EH 47 C 14
482	New York, JTSA, MS 3545 (ENA 378)
483	Amsterdam, Ets Haim, HS EH 47 A 26
484	London, BL, Or. 5600
485	Amsterdam, UB, HS. Ros. 281
486	Amsterdam, UB, HS. Ros. PL B-5 or PL A-14
487	Amsterdam, UB, HS. Ros. PL B-52
488	Amsterdam, Ets Haim, HS EH 47 D 15

18. MSS Fischl Hirsch

Present locations of MSS belonging to Fischl Hirsch described in *HB*, XI (1871) and XVII (1877).

no.	*Present Location*
1	London, BL, Or. 1098
2	Oxford, Bodleian, Opp. Add. 4° 119
3	Oxford, Bodleian, Opp. Add. 4° 122

4 London, BL, Or. 1100–1
5 Oxford, Bodleian, Opp. Add. 4° 123
6 Oxford, Bodleian, Opp. Add. 4° 120
7 Oxford, Bodleian, Opp. Add. 4° 121
8 Oxford, Bodleian, Opp. Add. 4° 117
9 Oxford, Bodleian, Opp. Add. 2° 46
10 Oxford, Bodleian, Opp. Add. 8° 25
11 Oxford, Bodleian, Opp. Add. 4° 118
12 Oxford, Bodleian, Opp. Add. 8° 24
13 London, BL, Or. 1103
14 London, BL, Or. 1104
15 Oxford, Bodleian, Opp. Add. 8° 23
16 Oxford, Bodleian, Opp. Add. 4° 116
17 Moscow, RSL, Günzburg 1652–1655
18 Oxford, Bodleian, Opp. Add. 2° 45
19 Moscow, RSL, Günzburg 1011
20 Moscow, RSL, Günzburg 1098
21 London, BL, Or. 1102
22 Moscow, RSL, Günzburg 996
23 Moscow, RSL, Günzburg 1006
25 Cambridge, UL, Add. 1527
26 Moscow, RSL, Günzburg 1174
27 Moscow, RSL, Günzburg 964
28 Moscow, RSL, Günzburg 1009
29 Oxford, Bodleian, Opp. Add. 8° 27
31 Moscow, RSL, Günzburg 1007
32 Moscow, RSL, Günzburg 914
33 Strasbourg, Nationale et univ., 3957 (Cat. 31)
34 Oxford, Bodleian, Opp. Add. 8° 26
35 Oxford, Bodleian, Opp. Add. 8° 44
36 Moscow, RSL, Günzburg 1128
37 Strasbourg, Nationale et univ., 3949 (Cat. 23)
38 Moscow, RSL, Günzburg 1073
39 Moscow, RSL, Günzburg 1209
40 Moscow, RSL, Günzburg 1113
41 Moscow, RSL, Günzburg 1024 and 1147
42 Moscow, RSL, Günzburg 1126
43 Moscow, RSL, Günzburg 1069
44 Moscow, RSL, Günzburg 1116
45 Berlin, SB, Or. 2° 1058 (Cat. 113)
46 Moscow, RSL, Günzburg 1115
47 Moscow, RSL, Günzburg 1197
51 Berlin, SB, Or. 2° 1059 (Cat. 114)
52 Moscow, RSL, Günzburg 1061
53 London, BL, Or. 1099

54	London, BL, Or. 1307
55	Moscow, RSL, Günzburg 1124
56	Cambridge, UL, Add. 2664 (part)
57	London, BL, Or. 1264–1265
58	Cambridge UL, Add. 1015,1
59	London, BL, Or. 1263

19. MSS Jacobson

Present locations of MSS from the collection of Meijer Levien Jacobson listed in *Me'ir 'enayim* (מאיר עינים הוא רשימת ספרים מאת מאיר ב׳ יאקב הלוי יאקאבסאן ...): *Catalogus I van eene boekverzameling ... door ... Meijer Levien Jacobson*, Amsterdam 1864, Part I.

Catalogue no.	*Present/Last-Known Location*
Part I, no. 1	Moscow, RSL, Günzburg 1174
no. 2	New York, Columbia University, MS X893 Ab 9
no. 4	New York, Columbia University, MS X893 G 15
no. 8	(probably) Amsterdam, UB, HS. Ros. 173
no. 11	Amsterdam, Ets Haim, HS EH 47 B 1
no. 14	Amsterdam, Ets Haim, HS EH 47 C 33
no. 17	formerly London, Montefiore, MS 145
Part II, no. 11	London, Montefiore, MS 42
No. 12	Zurich, Zentralbibliothek, MS Heid 207?

20. MSS Jessurun Cardozo

Present locations of MSS from the collection of Jacob de Raphael Jessurun Cardozo listed in *Catalog einer ... Sammlung hebräischer und jüdischer Bücher und Handschriften unter anderen sehr viele und höchst seltene Werke spanisch-jüdischer Autoren enthaltend sämmtlich nachgelassen von Jacob de Raphael Jessurun Cardozo ... Hirsch Isaacsohn und andern ...*, Amsterdam 1870, Nos. 930–950.

Cat. no.	*Present Location*
930	New York, Columbia University, X893 H 39
931	Amsterdam, UB, HS. Ros. 377
932	Paris, AIU, MS H 162 A
933	Amsterdam, UB, HS. Ros. 114
934	Amsterdam, UB, HS. Ros. 270
936	New York, JTSA, MS 5535
938	Amsterdam, Ets Haim, HS EH 47 A 26
939	Moscow, RSL, Günzburg 1554
940	Amsterdam, Ets Haim, HS EH 47 B 30
943	Amsterdam, UB, HS. Ros. 172
944	Amsterdam, UB, HS. Ros. 2
945	Amsterdam, Ets Haim, HS EH 47 B 7?

21. MSS Jacob Wolf de Jonge

Present locations of MSS listed in *Catalog einer werthvollen Sammlung hebräischer und jüdischer Bücher, Handschriften, etc., ... aus den nachgelassenen Bibliotheken des Herrn Jacob Wolf de Jonge in Amsterdam und ... Naftali H. Rubens in Haag ...* Amsterdam (J. L. Joachimsthal) 1885, nos. 1472–1483.

Cat. no.	*Present Location*
1472	Berlin, SB, Or. 4° 747
1473	Zurich, Zentralbibliothek, MS Heid 107
1474	Amsterdam, Ets Haim, HS EH 47 C 10
1479	Amsterdam, Ets Haim, HS EH 47 C 5
1483	Moscow, RSL, MS Günzburg 1554

22. MSS Kennicott and De Rossi

Present/last-known locations of MSS listed in Kennicott's *Vetus Testamentum Hebraicum* and in de Rossi, *ext.* (biblical MSS not used by Kennicott).

MSS Kennicott

Kennicott no.	*Present/Last-Known Location*
1	Oxford, Bodleian, Digby Or 32–3
2	Oxford, Bodleian, Arch. Seld. A 47
3	Oxford, Bodleian, Poc. 347–348
4	Oxford, Bodleian, Hunt. 11–12
5	Oxford, Bodleian, Opp. Add. 4° 47
6	Oxford, Bodleian, Poc. 395–396
7	Oxford, Bodleian, Hunt. 618–620
8	Oxford, Bodleian, Hunt. 69
9	Oxford, Bodleian, Marsh 635
10	Oxford, Bodleian, Rawl. Or. 48
11	Oxford, Bodleian, Bodl. Or. 164
12	Oxford, Bodleian, Poc. 7
13	Oxford, Bodleian, Marsh 10
14	Oxford, Bodleian, Hunt. 235
15	Oxford, Bodleian, Marsh Or. 51
16	Oxford, Bodleian, Hunt. 475
17	Oxford, Bodleian, Bodl. Or. 802–804
18	Oxford, Bodleian, Marshall (Or.) 1
19	Oxford, Bodleian, Poc. 30
20	Oxford, Bodleian, Hunt. 396
21	Oxford, Bodleian, Marsh 607
22	Oxford, Bodleian, Marsh 91
23	Oxford, Bodleian, Marshall (Or.) 3
24	Oxford, Bodleian, Hunt. 261

25 Oxford, Bodleian, Bodl. Or. 23
26 Oxford, Bodleian, Hunt. 234
27
28 Oxford, Bodleian, Bodl. Or. 62
29 Oxford, Bodleian, Hunt. 604
30 Oxford, Bodleian, Tanner 173
31 Oxford, Bodleian, Hunt. 591
32 Oxford, Bodleian, Laud Or. 84
33 Oxford, Bodleian, Hunt. 511
34 Oxford, Bodleian, Hunt. 72
35 Oxford, Bodleian, Laud Or. 182
36 Oxford, Bodleian, Laud Or. 118
37 Oxford, Bodleian, Laud Or. 174
38 Oxford, Bodleian, Bodl. Or. 621
39 Oxford, Bodleian, Bodl. Or. 6
40 Oxford, Bodleian, Bodl. Or. 3
41 Oxford, Bodleian, Arch. Seld. A sup. 105
42 Oxford, Bodleian, Poc. 281
43 Oxford, Bodleian, Bodl. Or. 18
44 Oxford, Bodleian, Poc. 285
45 Oxford, Bodleian, Poc. 70
46 Oxford, Bodleian, Hunt. 227
47 Oxford, Bodleian, Marsh 21
48 Oxford, Bodleian, Bodl. Or. 46
49 Oxford, Bodleian, Hunt. 367
50 Oxford, Bodleian, Laud Or. 154
51
52
53
54
55
56 Oxford, Bodleian, Arch. Seld. A sup. 106
57 Oxford, Bodleian, Poc. 274
58 Oxford, Bodleian, Hunt. 616
59 Oxford, Bodleian, Hunt. 496
60 Oxford, Bodleian, Hunt. 617
61
62 Oxford, Bodleian, Bodl. Or. 139
63
64
65
66
67 Oxford, Bodleian, Kennicott 1
68
69 Oxford, Corpus Christi College, 5–12

70	
71	
72–74	
75–76	Oxford, Jesus College, 95–97
77	Oxford, St. Johns College, 143
78	Oxford, Lincoln College (Cat. Neubauer 2544)
79	Oxford, Lincoln College (Cat. Neubauer 2545)
80	Oxford, Oriel College, 73
81	
82	Oxford, Bodleian, Kennicott 2
83	Oxford, Bodleian, Kennicott 4
84	Oxford, Bodleian, Kennicott 10
85	Oxford, Bodleian, Kennicott 5
86	Oxford, Bodleian, Kennicott 6
87	
88	
89	Cambridge, UL, Mm.5.27
90	Cambridge, UL, Ee.5.8
91	Cambridge, UL, Ee.5.10
92	Cambridge, UL, Ee.5.9
93	Cambridge, Gonville & Caius College, 404/625
94	Cambridge, Emmanuel College, I.I.5.7
95	Cambridge, St. John's College, A 1
96	Cambridge, St. John's College, A 2
97	Cambridge, Trinity College, R. 8. 6
98	Cambridge, Trinity College, R. 8. 35
99	London, BL, King's 1
100	London, BL, Harley 1528
101	London, BL, Harley 5498
102	London, BL, Harley 5710–11
103	London, BL, Harley 5586
104	London, BL, Harley 5772
105	London, BL, Harley 7619
106	London, BL, Harley 5683
107	London, BL, Harley 5706
108	London, BL, Harley 7621
109	London, BL, Harley 5709
110	London, BL, Harley 5773
111	London, BL, Harley 1861
112	London, BL, Harley 5774
113	London, BL, Harley 5722
114	London, BL, Harley 5720
115	London, BL, Harley 5721
116	London, BL, Harley 5509
117	London, BL, Harley 5506

118	London, BL, Harley 5715
119	London, BL, Harley 5775
120	London, BL, Harley 5757
121	London, BL, Harley 5686
122	London, BL, Harley 7622
123	London, BL, Harley 7620
124	London, BL, Add. 4707
125	London, BL, Add. 4709
126	London, BL, Add. 4708
127	London, BL, Cotton Claud. B VIII
128	London, BL, Loan 1
129	London, BL, Arundel Or. 2
130	London, BL, Arundel Or. 16
131	London, Lambeth Palace, 435
132	London Westminster Abbey
133	London Westminster Abbey, Ca MS 2
134	
135	Oslo, Martin Schøyen, 5070
136	Oxford, Bodleian, Kennicott 3
137	Oxford, Bodleian, Kennicott 8
138	
139	Aberdeen University, King's College, 23
140	Dublin, Trinity College, M.2.5
141	Dublin, Trinity College, M.2.6
142	Dublin, Trinity College, F.6.4
143	
144	London, BL, Or. 5956
145–8	Formerly Strasbourg, Bibliothèque Nationale et universitaire (destroyed in war)
149	Berne, Burgerbibliothek, Cod. 92
150	Berlin, SB, Or. 2° 1–4
151	St. Paul im Lavanttal, Stiftsbibliothek, MS 84.1
152	
153	Rostock, Universitätsbibliothek, MS Or. 32
154	Karlsruhe, Landesbibliothek, MS Reuchlin 3
155	Karlsruhe, Landesbibliothek, MS Reuchlin 1
156	Karlsruhe, Landesbibliothek, MS Reuchlin 10
157	Kassel, Landesbibliothek und *Murhardsche* Bibliothek, MS fol. theol. 3
158	Paris, BnF, héb. 3
159	Deventer, Athenaeum, 6144
160	Berlin, SB, Or. 2° 1210–1211
161	Florence, Biblioteca Medicea Laurenziana, Plut. I.9
162	Florence, Biblioteca Medicea Laurenziana, Plut. I.45
163	Florence, Biblioteca Medicea Laurenziana, Plut. I.52
164	Florence, Biblioteca Medicea Laurenziana, Plut. II.12
165	Florence, Biblioteca Medicea Laurenziana, Plut. I.24

166	Florence, Biblioteca Medicea Laurenziana, Plut. III.1
167	Florence, Biblioteca Medicea Laurenziana, Plut. III.4
168	Florence, Biblioteca Medicea Laurenziana, Plut. I.30
169	Florence, Biblioteca Medicea Laurenziana, Plut. III.14
170	Florence, Biblioteca Riccardiana, Cod. Ricc. 1
171	Copenhagen, Kongelige Bibl., Cods. Hebr. 7–9
172	Copenhagen, Kongelige Bibl., Cod. Hebr. 5
173	Copenhagen, Kongelige Bibl., Cod. Hebr. 1
174	Copenhagen, Kongelige Bibl., Cod. Hebr 17
175	Copenhagen, Kongelige Bibl., Cods. Hebr 3–4
176	Copenhagen, Kongelige Bibl., Cod. Hebr 6
177	Copenhagen, Kongelige Bibl., Cod. Hebr 11
178	Copenhagen, Kongelige Bibl., Cod. Hebr 2
179	
180	Hamburg, SUB, Cod. hebr. 27–28
181	Wolfenbüttel, Herzog August Bibliothek, Cod. Helmst. 3
182	Jena, Universitätsbibliothek, El. 46
183	Leiden, Universiteitsbibliotheek, Cod. Or. 6
184	Leiden, Universiteitsbibliotheek, Cod. Or. 1298
185	Milan, Biblioteca Ambrosiana, Cod. B 35 inf.
186	Milan, Biblioteca Ambrosiana, Cod. B 30 inf.
187	Milan, Biblioteca Ambrosiana, Cod. B 56 inf.
188	Milan, Biblioteca Ambrosiana, Cod. B 32 inf.
189	Milan, Biblioteca Ambrosiana, Cod. C 116 sup.
190	Milan, Biblioteca Ambrosiana, Cod. C 105 sup.
191	Milan, Biblioteca Ambrosiana, Cod. C 73 sup.
192	Milan, Biblioteca Ambrosiana, Cod. A 38 sup.
193	Milan, Biblioteca Ambrosiana, Cod. G 2 sup.
194	Milan, Biblioteca Ambrosiana, Cod. B 11 sup.
195	Milan, Biblioteca Ambrosiana, Cat. Bernheimer 13
196	Milan, Biblioteca Ambrosiana, Cod. E 52 inf.
197	Milan, Biblioteca Ambrosiana, S.P.II.248
198	Nuremberg, Stadtbibliothek, Solg. 2° 1–7
199	Nuremberg, Stadtbibliothek, Cent. V app. 1–2
200	
201	London, BL, Add. 21161
202	
203	Paris, BnF, héb. 30
204	Paris, BnF, héb. 15
205	Paris, BnF, héb. 11–12
206	Paris, BnF, héb. 5–6
207	Paris, BnF, héb. 35
208	Paris, BnF, héb. 109
209	Paris, BnF, héb. 26
210	Paris, BnF, héb. 32

211	Paris, BnF, héb. 36
212	Paris, BnF, héb. 39
213	Paris, BnF, héb. 50
214	Paris, BnF, héb. 106
215	Paris, BnF, héb. 108
216	Paris, BnF, héb. 111
217	Paris, BnF, héb. 112
218	Paris, BnF, héb. 40
219	Paris, BnF, héb. 102
220	Paris, BnF, héb. 80
221	Paris, BnF, sam. 3
222	
223	Princeton, University Library, MS Scheide M 136
224	
225	Vatican, Urb. ebr. 2
226	Vatican, ebr. 4–6
227	Vatican, ebr. 9
228	Vatican, Urb. ebr. 1
229	Vatican, ebr. 1
230	Vatican, ebr. 11
231	Vatican, ebr. 12
232	Vatican, ebr. 20
233	Vatican, ebr. 448
234	Vatican, ebr. 453
235	Vatican, ebr. 25
236	Vatican, ebr. 437
237	Vatican, ebr. 439–440
238	Vatican, ebr. 444
239	Vatican, ebr. 447
240	Rome, Bibl. Angelica, Or. 72
241	Vatican, Barb. Or. 101
242	Vatican, ebr. 482
243	Rome, Bibl. Angelica, Or. 18
244–245	Berlin, SB, Ham. 80
246	Turin, Biblioteca Nazionale Universitaria, A.I.3
247	Turin, Biblioteca Nazionale Universitaria, A.I.6
248	Turin, Biblioteca Nazionale Universitaria, A.II.8
249	Turin, Biblioteca Nazionale Universitaria, A.IV.29
250	Turin, Biblioteca Nazionale Universitaria, A.IV.3
251	Turin, Biblioteca Nazionale Universitaria, A.III.26
252	Zurich, Zentralbibliothek, Or. 152
253	Zurich, Zentralbibliothek, Or. 158
254	Vienna, ÖNB, Cod. Hebr. 35
290	Oxford, Bodleian, Kennicott 7
291	Printed

292	Printed
293–300	formerly *Pérez Bayer, Francisco
301	Paris, BnF, héb. 19
302	Paris, BnF, héb. 46
303	Paris, BnF, héb. 52
304	Paris, BnF, héb. 66?
305	Paris, BnF, héb. 65
306	Paris, BnF, héb. 73
307	Paris, BnF, héb. 87
308	Paris, BnF, héb. 84
309	Paris, BnF, héb. 16
310	Paris, BnF, héb. 89
311	Paris, BnF, héb. 107
312	Paris, BnF, héb. 114
313	Paris, BnF, héb. 99
314	Paris, BnF, héb. 58
315	Paris, BnF, héb. 59
316	Paris, BnF, héb. 60
317	Paris, BnF, héb. 26
318	Paris, BnF, héb. 25
319	Paris, BnF, héb. 28
320	Paris, BnF, héb. 29
321	Paris, BnF, héb. 31
322	Paris, BnF, héb. 34
323	Paris, BnF, héb. 72
324	Paris, BnF, héb. 70–71
325	Paris, BnF, héb. 48–49
326	Paris, BnF, héb. 105
327	Paris, BnF, héb. 95
328	Paris, BnF, héb. 113
329	Paris, BnF, héb. 103
330	Paris, BnF, héb. 33
331	Paris, BnF, héb. 119
332	Paris, BnF, héb. 20
333	Paris, BnF, sam. 5
334	Paris, BnF, sam. 1
335	Paris, BnF, héb. 41
336	Paris, BnF, héb. 81
337	Paris, BnF, héb. 83
338	Paris, BnF, héb. 43
339	Paris, BnF, héb. 51
340	Paris, BnF, héb. 47
341	Paris, BnF, héb. 68–69
342	Paris, BnF, héb. 27
343	Paris, BnF, héb. 55

344	Paris, BnF, héb. 62
345	Paris, BnF, héb. 67
346	Paris, BnF, héb. 63
347	Paris, BnF, héb. 61
348	Paris, BnF, héb. 53
349	Paris, BnF, héb. 54
350	Paris, BnF, héb. 88
351	Paris, BnF, héb. 94
352	Paris, BnF, héb. 93
353	Paris, BnF, héb. 104
354	
355	Paris, BnF, héb. 8–10
356	Paris, BnF, héb. 22
357	Paris, BnF, héb. 82
358	Paris, BnF, héb. 7
359	Paris, BnF, héb. 23
360	Paris, BnF, héb. 24
361	Paris, BnF, héb. 14
362	Paris, BnF, héb. 13
363	Paris, BnF, sam. 2
364	Paris, BnF, sam. 4
365	Paris, BnF, héb. 37
366	Paris, BnF, héb. 86
367	Paris, BnF, héb. 38
368	Paris, BnF, héb. 44
369	
370	
371	Arras, Bibliothèque municipale, 560
372	
373	
374	
375	Mainz, Wissenschaftliche Stadtbibliothek, Hs. 378
376	
377	
378	Jerusalem, NLI, Heb. 4° 781
379	
380	Hamburg, SUB, Cod. Levy 19
381	
382	
383	
384	Stuttgart, Württembergische Landesbibliothek, Cod. Bibl. fol. 1
385	Karlsruhe, Landesbibliothek, Reuchlin 5
386	Printed
387	
388	

389
390 Basel, Öffentliche Bibliothek der Universität, AN IV 25
391 Basel, Öffentliche Bibliothek der Universität, R 11
392
393 Basel, Öffentliche Bibliothek der Universität, Frey-Gryn. III 20
394 Zurich, Zentralbibliothek, Or. 157
395 Zurich, Zentralbibliothek, Or. 155?
396 Printed
397 Printed
398 Berne, Burgerbibliothek, Cod. 343
399 Geneva, BPU, m.h.1 inv. 1887
400 Geneva, BPU, m.h.2 inv. 1897
401 Geneva, BPU, m.h.3 inv. 1858
402 Geneva, BPU, m.h.6 inv. 2024
403 Turin, Biblioteca Nazionale Universitaria, A.I.1
404 Turin, Biblioteca Nazionale Universitaria, A.VI.5
405 Turin, Biblioteca Nazionale Universitaria, A.IV.20
406 Turin, Biblioteca Nazionale Universitaria, A.III.32
407 Turin, Biblioteca Nazionale Universitaria, A.VII.49?
408
409 Parma, Bibl. Palatina, Parm. 2668
410 Parma, Bibl. Palatina, Parm. 1996–97
411
412 Parma, Bibl. Palatina, Parm. 2812
413
414 Parma, Bibl. Palatina, Parm. 2698
415
416 Parma, Bibl. Palatina, Parm. 3079
417 Parma, Bibl. Palatina, Parm. 2516
418 Parma, Bibl. Palatina, Parm. 1834–35
419 Parma, Bibl. Palatina, Parm. 1998–2000
420 Milan, Biblioteca Ambrosiana, B 31 inf.
421 Milan, Biblioteca Ambrosiana, C 149 inf.
422 Milan, Biblioteca Ambrosiana, C 300 inf.
423
424
425 Cambridge, Trinity College, F. 12. 70–71
426 Parma, Bibl. Palatina, Parm. 2025
427 Parma, Bibl. Palatina, Parm. 2828
428
429
430
431 Madrid, Biblioteca Nacional, 79
432 Madrid, Biblioteca Nacional, 5464
433 Toledo, Catedral, Z–1–19

434	Rome, Casanatense, 3117
435	
436	Rome, Casanatense, 2894
437	Rome, Casanatense, 2843
438	Rome, Casanatense, 1916
439	Rome, Casanatense, 2988
440	Rome, Casanatense, 3010
441	Rome, Casanatense, 2877
442	Rome, Casanatense, 2983
443	Rome, Casanatense, 2972
444	Rome, Casanatense, 3022
445	Rome, Casanatense, 2830
446	Rome, Casanatense, 2898
447	Rome, Casanatense, 2930
448	Rome, Casanatense, 2833
449	Rome, Casanatense, 2844
450	Rome, Casanatense, 2729
451	Rome, Casanatense, 2731
452	Rome, Casanatense, 2750
453	Rome, Casanatense, 2738
454	Rome, Casanatense, 2730
455	Rome, Casanatense, 2725
456	Rome, Casanatense, 2722
457	Rome, Casanatense, 2718
458	Rome, Casanatense, 4849
459	Vatican, Rossiana 601
460	Rome, Angelica, Or. 35
461	Rome, Angelica, Or. 85
462	Rome, Angelica, Or. 39
463	Rome, Angelica, Or. 47
464	Rome, Angelica, Or. 50
465	
466	Rome, Angelica, Or. 12?
467	Rome, Angelica, Or. 36
468	Rome, Angelica, Or. 24
469	Rome, Angelica, Or. 21
470	
471	Vatican, Barb. Or. 161–164
472	
473	
474	
475	
476	Vatican, ebr. 3
477	Vatican, ebr. 8
478	Vatican, ebr. 2

479	
480	Vatican, ebr. 443
481	Vatican, ebr. 13
482	Vatican, ebr. 19
483	Vatican, ebr. 21
484	Vatican, ebr. 7
485	Vatican, Urb. ebr. 3
486	Vatican, ebr. 14
487	Vatican, ebr. 15
488	Vatican, ebr. 17
489	Vatican, ebr. 18
490	Vatican, ebr. 23–24
491	Vatican, ebr. 436
492	Vatican, Urb. ebr. 4
493	Vatican, Urb. ebr. 5
494	Vatican, ebr. 10
495	Vatican, ebr. 26
496	Vatican, ebr. 29
497	Vatican, Urb. ebr. 6
498	Vatican, ebr. 27
499	Vatican, ebr. 28
500	Vatican, Urb. ebr. 7
501	Vatican, ebr. 22
502	Vatican, Cod. Pers. 61
503	
504	
505	
506	Vatican, ebr. 468
507	
508	Vatican, ebr. 463
509	Vatican, ebr. 473
510	Vatican, ebr. 481
511	Toledo, Catedral, Z–1–18
512	Toledo, Catedral, Z–1–13
513	
514	Florence, Biblioteca Medicea Laurenziana, Plut. I.31
515	Florence, Biblioteca Medicea Laurenziana, Plut. II.1
516	Florence, Biblioteca Medicea Laurenziana, Plut. III.3
517	Florence, Biblioteca Medicea Laurenziana, Plut. III.10
518	
519	Florence, Biblioteca Nazionale, Magl. III. 44
520–521	Zurich, Braginsky Collection (formerly Warminster, Marquess of Bath)
522	
523	Parma, Bibl. Palatina, Parm. 3214
524	Parma, Bibl. Palatina, Parm. 3293

525	Bologna, Bibl. Universitaria 3570I
526	Bologna, Bibl. Universitaria 3570II
527	
528	Bologna, Bibl. Universitaria 2198
529	Bologna, Bibl. Universitaria 2201
530	Bologna, Bibl. Universitaria 2206
531	Bologna, Bibl. Universitaria 2208–9
532	
533	Bologna, Bibl. Universitaria 3571
534	Bologna, Bibl. Universitaria 2950
535	Cesena, Biblioteca Comunale Malatestiana Plut. sin XXIX.1
536	Cesena, Biblioteca Comunale Malatestiana Plut. sin XXIX.2
537	Cesena, Biblioteca Comunale Malatestiana Plut. sin XXVIII.3
538	Modena, Estense, α J. 1.22
539	
540	
541	
542	Modena, Estense, α O. 5.9
543	Modena, Estense, α W. 5.14
544	Modena, Estense, α U. 2.27
545	Printed
546	Modena, Estense, α T. 3.8
547	
548	Parma, Bibl. Palatina, Parm. 677
549	Parma, Bibl. Palatina, Parm. 250
550	Parma, Bibl. Palatina, Parm. 13
551	Parma, Bibl. Palatina, Parm. 30
552	Parma, Bibl. Palatina, Parm. 743
553	Parma, Bibl. Palatina, Parm. 300
554	Parma, Bibl. Palatina, Parm. 3288
555	Printed
556	Parma, Bibl. Palatina, Parm. 2846
557	Printed
558	
559	Paris, Paris, BnF, héb. 4
560	Paris, Paris, BnF, héb. 85
561	Formerly Padua, Comunità ebraica, IV
562	Venice, Marciana, MS Or. 207
563	Venice, Marciana, MS Or. 210
564	Oxford, Bodleian, Can. Or. 91
565	Parma, Bibl. Palatina, Parm. 2207
566	Parma, Bibl. Palatina, Parm. 2033
567	Oxford, Bodleian, Can. Or. 62
568	Uppsala, Universitetsbibliotek, Cod. O. Hebr. 3
569	Uppsala, Universitetsbibliotek, Cod. O. Hebr. 2

570	Parma, Bibl. Palatina, Parm. 1833
571	New York, JTSA, MS L5
572	London, BL, Add. 15251
573	Parma, Bibl. Palatina, Parm. 2338–39
574	Parma, Bibl. Palatina, Parm. 2151–2153
575	
576	Udine, Biblioteca Arcivescovile, MS 248 ebr. 14
577	Udine, Biblioteca Arcivescovile, MS 249 ebr. 15
578	Oxford, Bodleian, Opp. Add. 4° 26
579	Jerusalem, Israel Museum, MS 180/51
580	Parma, Bibl. Palatina, Parm. 2174
581	Parma, Bibl. Palatina, Parm. 2521
582	
583	Parma, Bibl. Palatina, Parm. 3290
584	Parma, Bibl. Palatina, Parm. 3294
585	Oxford, Bodleian, Can. Or. 138
586	Sydney, University, MS Nicholson 33
587	Vienna, ÖNB, Cod. Hebr. 4
588	Vienna, ÖNB, Cod. Hebr. 14
589	Vienna, ÖNB, Cod. Hebr. 9
590	Vienna, ÖNB, Cod. Hebr. 15
591	Vienna, ÖNB, Cod. Hebr. 5
592	Vienna, ÖNB, Cod. Hebr. 12a
593	Vienna, ÖNB, Cod. Hebr. 11
594	Vienna, ÖNB, Cod. Hebr. 28
595	Vienna, ÖNB, Cod. Hebr. 38
596	Vienna, ÖNB, Cod. Hebr. 17
597	Gottweig, Stiftsbibliothek, 10 (883)
598	Dresden, Sächsische Landesbibliothek A46 (Cat. no. 442, destroyed in World War II)
599	Leipzig, Universitätsbibliothek, B.H. 12
600	Leipzig, Universitätsbibliothek, B.H. 1
601	Berlin, SB, Or. 2° 1212
602	Berlin, SB, Or. 2° 1213
603	Berlin, SB, Or. 2° 1214
604	
605	
606	
607	Berlin, SB, Or. 2° 5–7
608	Berlin, SB, Or. 2° 8
609	Berlin, SB, Or. 2° 9
610	Berlin, SB, Or. 4° 1
611	Berlin, SB, Or. 4° 9
612	Hamburg, SUB, Cod. hebr. 4–7
613	Hamburg, SUB, Cod. hebr. 45

614	Hamburg, SUB, Cod. hebr. 9
615	Hamburg, SUB, Cod. hebr. 1
616	Hamburg, SUB, Cod. hebr. 3
617	Hamburg, SUB, Cod. hebr. 2
618	Hamburg, SUB, Cod. hebr. 25–26
619	Hamburg, SUB, Cod. hebr. 94
620	Hamburg, SUB, Cod. hebr. 179
621	Hamburg, SUB, Cod. hebr. 99
622	Hamburg, SUB, Cod. hebr. 102
623	Hamburg, SUB, Cod. hebr. 47
624	Hamburg, SUB, Cod. hebr. 46
625	Hamburg, SUB, Cod. hebr. 48
626	Hamburg, SUB, Cod. hebr. 204
627	Hamburg, SUB, Cod. hebr. 203
628	Hamburg, SUB, Cod. hebr. 202
629	Hamburg, SUB, Cod. hebr. 11
630	Hamburg, SUB, Cod. hebr. 29
631	Hamburg, SUB, Cod. hebr. 8
632	Hamburg, SUB, Cod. hebr. 22
633	Wolfenbüttel, Herzog August Bibliothek, Cod. Guelf. 659
634	
635	
636	
637	
638	
639	
640	
641	Oxford, Bodleian, Opp. Add. fol. 21
642	Lisbon, BN, 72
643	Jerusalem, Israel Museum, MS 180/94
644	Utrecht, Rijksuniversiteit, 1424
645	Utrecht, Rijksuniversiteit, 1425
646	Leiden, Universiteitsbibliotheek, Or. 1197
647	Leiden, Universiteitsbibliotheek, Or. 4737
648	Leiden, Universiteitsbibliotheek, Or. 1195
649	Leiden, Universiteitsbibliotheek, Or. 4725
650–664	Printed
665	Leipzig, Universiteitsbibliotheek, 1102
666	
667	
668	
669	
670	Printed
671	
672	

673	Oxford, Bodleian, Laud Or. 27
674	Oxford, Bodleian, Laud Or. 321
675	Oxford, Bodleian, Heb. d. 10
676	
677	
678	Oxford, Bodleian, Hunt. 484
679	Oxford, Bodleian, Hunt. 448–449
680	Oxford, Bodleian, Marshall (Or.) 42
681	Oxford, Corpus Christi College 133
683	Printed
684	
685	Oxford, Bodleian, Arch. Seld. B Sup. 101
686	Uppsala, Universitetsbiblioteket, Cod. O. Hebr. 1
687	Parma, Bibl. Palatina, Parm. 3110
688	
689	
690	
691	Parma, Bibl. Palatina, Parm. 3104
692	Parma, Bibl. Palatina, Parm. 3231?
693–694	Printed

De Rossi, *ext.*

Cod. ext.	*Present Location*
1	Paris, BnF, héb. 17–18
2	Vatican, Chigi R.IV.37
3	
4	Rome, Bibloteca Angelica, Or. 78
5	Rome, Bibloteca Angelica, Or. 70?
6	Rome, Biblioteca Nazionale Centrale, Or. 52
7	Rome, Biblioteca Nazionale Centrale, Or. 85
8	Rome, Biblioteca Nazionale Centrale, Or. 72
9	Rome, Biblioteca Nazionale Centrale, Or. 51
10	Rome, Comunità ebraica, 3
11	
12	
13	Rome, Comunità ebraica, F 287
14	
15	Sassoon, 23 (now in the possession of the Safra family, São Paolo)
16	
17	New York, Hispanic Society of America, MS HC 371/169
18	
19	
20	Jerusalem, NLI, Heb. 4° 7025
21	

22	New Haven, Yale University, Beinecke Library, MS Heb. 409
23	Genoa, Biblioteca Civica Berio
24	Turin, Biblioteca Nazionale Universitaria, A.III.7
25	Turin, Biblioteca Nazionale Universitaria, A.II. 27
26	Turin, Biblioteca Nazionale Universitaria, A.I.20
27	Turin, Biblioteca Nazionale Universitaria, A.III.8
28	
29	Piacenza, Biblioteca Comunale, MS Landi 181
30	Parma, Bibl. Palatina, Parm. 1264?
31	Parma, Bibl. Palatina, Parm. 1002
32	Parma, Bibl. Palatina, Parm. 29
33	
34	
35	
36	
37	Venezia, Biblioteca Marciana, Or. 208–209
38	Venezia, Biblioteca Marciana, Or. 211–214
39	Berlin, SB, Or. 2° 585
40	Oxford, Bodleian, Can. Or. 94
41	Oxford, Bodleian, Can. Or. 37–40
42	Oxford, Bodleian, Can. Or. 136
43	Oxford, Bodleian, Can. Or. 137
44	Oxford, Bodleian, Can. Or. 42
45	Oxford, Bodleian, Can. Or. 106?
46	Oxford, Bodleian, Can. Or. 20
47	Besançon, Bibliotheque municipal, 2
48	
49	
50	
51	New York, Yeshiva University, MS 1247
52	
53	Oxford, Bodleian, Can. Or. 49?
54	
55	Oxford, Bodleian, Can. Or. 53
56	Turin, Biblioteca Nazionale Universitaria, A.I.5
57	
58	
59	Oxford, Bodleian, Opp. 14
60	Oxford, Bodleian, Opp. 185
61	Oxford, Bodleian, Opp. 15
62	Oxford, Bodleian, Opp. 13
63	Oxford, Bodleian, Opp. 2
64	Oxford, Bodleian, Opp. 186
65	
66	Rome, Casanatense, 2836

67	Rome, Casanatense, 2831
68	
69	Rome, Casanatense, 2832
70	
71	
72	Rome, Casanatense, 2828?
73	Rome, Casanatense, 3102
74	
75	
76	
77	
78	
79	
80	Rome, Casanatense, 2763
81	Rome, Casanatense, 3147
82	Rome, Casanatense, 1938
83	Genoa, Biblioteca Universitaria, D IX 31
84	
85	
86	
87	
88	Vienna, ÖNB, Cod. Hebr. 167
89	
90	Vatican, ebr. 503
91	Copenhagen, Kongelige Bibl., Cod. Hebr. 16
92	Copenhagen, Kongelige Bibl., Cod. Hebr. 14
93	
94	
95	
96	
97	
98	
99	
100	
101	Monte Oliveto Maggiore, Biblioteca Capitolare, Cod. 37 A 2
102	
103	
104	Oxford, Bodleian, Can. Or. 62
105	Tübingen, Universitätsbibliothek, Ma IV 1?
106	
107	Vienna, ÖNB, Cod. Hebr. 16
108	Vienna, ÖNB, Cod. Hebr. 6
109	Vienna, ÖNB, Cod. Hebr. 13
110	Vienna, ÖNB, Cod. Hebr. 19
111	

112	Oxford, Bodleian, Opp. 3
113	Oxford, Bodleian, Opp. 717
114	
115	Oxford, Bodleian, Opp. 17 or 18
116	Oxford, Bodleian, Opp. 17 or 18
117	
118	
119	Oxford, Bodleian, Opp. 642
120	
121	
122	
123	Prague, Narodni Knihovna, XVIII F 6
124	
125	Vienna, ÖNB, Cod. Hebr. 25
126	
127	
128	Wrocław, Biblioteca Uniwersytecka, M 1107
129	Wrocław, Biblioteca Uniwersytecka, M 1106
130	Wrocław, Biblioteca Uniwersytecka, M 1109
131	Wrocław, Biblioteca Uniwersytecka, M 1108

23. MSS Lehren

Present or last-known locations of MSS that belonged to the brothers Jacob Meijer Lehren and Akiba Lehren, listed in *Catalog der reichhaltigen Sammlung hebräischer und jüdischer Bücher, Handschriften,* שופרות, מגילות, ספרי תורה *u.s.w. nachgelassen von den ehrw. Herren Meijer Lehren, Akiba Lehren und Moses de Lima, welche am 13 Februar bis 2. März 1899, Abends von 6 Uhr ab durch J. L. Joachimsthal im Amsterdam ... öffentlich versteigert werden sollen*, Amsterdam [1898].

Cat. no.	*Present/Last-Known Location*
3483	Amsterdam, UB, HS. Ros. 198
3484	Amsterdam, UB, HS. Ros. 125
3487	Cincinnati, HUC, MS 867
3489	Jerusalem, private collection
3490	Amsterdam, UB, HS. Ros. 5
3492	New York, JTSA, MS 2216[7]
3493	New York, Public Library, **P (MS Heb. 24)
3494	Amsterdam, Ets Haim, HS EH 47 C 30–31
3495	Zurich, Zentralbibliothek, Heid. 86
3496	Amsterdam, UB, HS. Ros. 157
3499	Haifa, J. S. Hirsch
3500	Amsterdam, UB, HS. Ros. 469
3501	Copenhagen, Kongelige Bibliothek, Cod. Sim. Hebr. 48
3502	Amsterdam, UB, HS. Ros. 213

3508	Haifa, J. S. Hirsch
4272	Jerusalem, Schocken Institute (formerly A. Epstein)
4273	Amsterdam, UB, HS. Ros. 682
4274	Amsterdam, UB, HSS. Ros. 20, Ros. 174 and Ros. 520

24. MSS de Lima

Present locations of MSS that belonged to Moses Hartog de Lima, listed in *Catalog der reichhaltigen Sammlung hebräischer und jüdischer Bücher, Handschriften ... u.s.w. nachgelassen von ... Meijer Lehren, Akiba Lehren und Moses de Lima ...*, Amsterdam [1898].

Cat. no.	*Present Location*
4184	Copenhagen, Kongelige Bibliothek, Cod. Sim. Hebr. 93
4187	Amsterdam, UB, HS. Ros. 597
4189	Amsterdam, UB, HS. Ros. 596
4191	Amsterdam, UB, HS. Ros. 173
4194	Amsterdam, UB, HS. Ros. 430
4195	Amsterdam, UB, HS. Ros. 345
4202	Amsterdam, UB, HS. PL B 75?
4272	*Jerusalem, Schocken Institute (formerly Abraham *Epstein)
4274	Amsterdam, UB, HSS. Ros. 520, Ros. 20, etc.

25. MSS Loewe

Present or last-known locations of MSS that belonged to Louis Loewe, listed in *A Descriptive Catalogue of a Portion of the Library of the Late Louis Loewe with a Portrait, a Short Biography and Some Rough Bibliographical Notices, by James H. Loewe, to Which Is Added a Reprint of the Paper Contributed to the Breslauer Monatsschrift (Vol. 38) by Hartwig Hirschfeld Describing the Manuscripts Collected by Loewe, at Present in the Possession of His Widow*, London 1895.

Cat. no.	*Present/Last-Known Location*
I	Philadelphia, Free Library, Lewis. Or. Ms. 140
II	MS Sholem Asch, 2
III	New York, Union Theological Seminary, 74
IV	New York, JTSA, MS L932
V	New York, JTSA, MS L792
VI	New York, JTSA, MS 2218
VII	New York, JTSA, MS 2318
VIII	Jerusalem, NLI, Heb. 8° 931
XII	Jerusalem, NLI, Heb. 8° 2971
XVI	Sassoon, 1240
XVIII	Jerusalem, NLI, Heb. 8° 4016

26. MSS London, Beth Din and Beth Hamidrash Library

Cat. no.	*Present Location*
9	Los Angeles, Dr. Steve Weiss, 2
14	Berlin, Jewish Museum, VII.5.262
36	Zurich, Braginsky Collection
41	Philadelphia, University of Pennsylvania, Schoenberg Collection, LJS 453
42	Berlin, Jewish Museum, VII.5.324
44	Berlin, Jewish Museum, VII.5.293
45	Berlin, Jewish Museum, VII.5.292
46	London, D. Sofer, 61
51	New York, JTSA, MS 10611
53	New York, JTSA, MS 10616
61	New York, JTSA, MS 10610
62	Jerusalem, NLI, Heb. 8° 7409
69	New York, JTSA, MS 10613
74	New York, Public Library, **P (MS Heb. 218)
87	Jerusalem, NLI, Heb. 8° 8334
90	New York, JTSA, MS 10614
99	Tel Aviv, W. Gross, 328
111	New York, Public Library, **P (MS Heb. 220)
123	New York, JTSA, MS 10615
133	Philadelphia, University of Pennsylvania, Schoenberg Collection, LJS 312
135	Madrid, Biblioteca Nacional, 23078
139	Philadelphia, University of Pennsylvania, Schoenberg Collection, LJS 311
144	New York, Public Library, **P (MS Heb. 219)

27. MSS Lotze

Present locations of MSS owned by Hermann Lotze, listed in *Verzeichniss der von ... Hermann Lotze, Privatgelehrten zu Leipzig, hinterlassen ... Bibliothek*, Leipzig 1876, Nos. 1662–1780.

Cat. no.	*Present Location*
1662	Oxford, Bodleian Library, Opp. Add. 4° 146
1664	Zurich, Zentralbibliothek, Heid. 29
1665	Moscow, RSL, Günzburg 1070
1666	New York, JTSA, MS 2079
1675	Zurich, Zentralbibliothek, Heid. 207
1679	London, BL, Or. 1425?
1684	Berlin, SB, Or. 8° 513
1687	Strasbourg, Bibliothèque nationale et univ., MS 4040
1696	Paris, AIU, MS 423
1697	Strasbourg, Bibliothèque nationale et univ., MS 3953
1698	London, BL, Or. 10845?
1706	Cambridge, UL, Add. 1735

1708 Amsterdam, Ets Haim, HS EH 47 E 24
1709 Moscow, RSL, Günzburg 892
1720 Moscow, RSL, Günzburg 975
1724 New York, JTSA, MS 2387
1738 London, Montefiore, 412?
1739 Moscow, RSL, Günzburg 1402
1741 Moscow, RSL, Günzburg 1179
1747 Zurich, Zentralbibliothek, Heid. 80
1750 Strasbourg, Bibliothèque nationale et univ., MS 4048?
1751 Amsterdam, Ets Haim, HS EH 47 E 1 or E 20
1765 Moscow, RSL, Günzburg 908
1775 Moscow, RSL, Günzburg 1389

28. MSS Luzzatto

Present or last-known locations of MSS described in *Catalogue de la Bibliothèque ... de feu Samuel David Luzzatto*, Padua 1868.

Cat. no.	*Present/Last-Known Location*
1	Berlin, SB, Or. 8° 243 (Cat. 78)
2	Paris, AIU, MS H 53 A
3	Oxford, Bodleian, Opp. Add. 8° 21
4	Cambridge, UL, Add. 633?
5	Oxford, Bodleian, Opp. Add. 8° 19
7	London, BL, Or. 1022
8	Paris, AIU, MS H 17 A
10	Paris, AIU, MS H 4 A
11	Zurich, Braginsky Collection (was London, Montefiore, 53)
13	Oxford, Bodleian, Opp. Add. 4° 80
14	Zurich, Zentralbibliothek, Heid. 53
15	Cambridge, UL, Add. 661
16	Paris, AIU, MS H 52 A
19	Paris, AIU, MS H 51 A
21	Paris, AIU, MS H 46 A
22	London, Montefiore, 269
23	New York, NYPL, MS Heb. 182 (was London, Montefiore, 372)
24	Paris, AIU, MS H 18 A
25	London, Montefiore, 255
26	Paris, AIU, MS H 48 A
27	Oxford, Bodleian, Opp. Add. 8° 20
28	Paris, AIU, MS H 9 A
30	Paris, AIU, MS H 16 A
31	Oxford, Bodleian, Opp. Add. 4° 89
32	Paris, AIU, MS H 20 A
34	Milan, Biblioteca Ambrosiana, X 161 sup.

35	Paris, AIU, MS H 14 A
36	Paris, AIU, MS H 61 A
37	Paris, AIU, MS H 21 A
38	Oxford, Bodleian, Opp. Add. 4° 89
39	Paris, AIU, MS H 3 A
41	Paris, AIU, MS H 19 A
42	Paris, AIU, MS H 31 A
44	Zurich, Braginsky Collection (was London, Montefiore, 52)
45	Paris, AIU, MS H 58 A
46	Paris, AIU, MS H 54 A
47	Cambridge, UL, Add. 640?
49	Paris, AIU, MS H 33 A
50	London, BL Or. 1024
51	Paris, AIU, MS H 8 A
52	Oxford, Bodleian, Opp. Add. 4° 83
53, I	Oxford, Bodleian, Opp. Add. 4° 88
53, II	Oxford, Bodleian, Opp. Add. 4° 86
53, III	Oxford, Bodleian, Opp. Add. 4° 87
53, IV	Oxford, Bodleian, Opp. Add. 4° 85
53, V	Oxford, Bodleian, Opp. Add. 4° 84
54	Oxford, Bodleian, Opp. Add. 4° 81
55	London, Montefiore, 15
56	Paris, AIU, MS H 10 A
57	Paris, AIU, MS H 49 A
58	Cambridge, UL, Add. 561
59	Paris, AIU, MS H 41 A
60	Paris, AIU, MS H 29 A
61	Paris, AIU, MS H 34 A
63	Paris, AIU, MS H 42 A
64	Paris, AIU, MS H 13A
65	Paris, AIU, MS H 30 A
66	New York JTSA, R1430 (Halb. 526)
67	Paris, AIU, MS H 27 A
68	Paris, AIU, MS H 2 A
71	Paris, AIU, MS H 37 A
72	New York, JTSA, MS 3720 (Halb. 527)
75	Paris, AIU, MS H 57 A
76	Paris, AIU, MS H 56 A (MS is lost)
77	Cambridge, UL, Add. 658
79	Paris, AIU, MS H 43 A
80	Paris, AIU, MS H 1 A
81	Paris, AIU, MS H 28 A
82	Paris, AIU, MS H 24 A
83	Paris, AIU, MS H 45 A
84	Cambridge, UL, Add. 664

86	London, Montefiore, 407
88	Paris, AIU, MS H 44 A
89	Oxford, Bodleian, Opp. Add. 4° 90
90	London, Montefiore, 283
91	London, Montefiore, 366
92	New York, D. H. Feinberg (was London, Montefiore, 98)
93	Oxford, Bodleian, Opp. Add. 4° 93
94	Cambridge, UL, Add. 626
95	Paris, AIU, MS H 47 A
98	Oxford, Bodleian, Opp. Add. 4° 82
99	Paris, AIU, MS H 50 A
101	Paris, AIU, MS H 11 A
102	London, Montefiore, 210
103	Paris, AIU, MS H 7 A
105	Paris, AIU, MS H 26 A
106	Paris, AIU, MS H 38 A
107	Paris, AIU, MS H 35 A
108	Paris, AIU, MS H 23 A
109	Cambridge Trinity College, F. 18. 22–4
110	Geneva, BPU, MS Comites Latentes 173
111	London, BL, Or. 832
113	Paris, AIU, MS H 55 A
114	Berlin SB, Or. 8° 244 (Cat. 79)
116	Oxford, Bodleian, Opp. Add. 4° 92
117	Paris, AIU, MS H 39 A
118	Paris, AIU, MS H 25 A
119	Paris, AIU, MS H 36 A
121	Paris, AIU, MS H 64 A

29. MSS Merzbacher

Call-numbers of MSS from the Merzbacher collection listed in the catalogue *Ohel Avraham* (אהל אברהם, Munich 1888), now in *Frankfurt am Main, Universitätsbibliothek (except for nos. 54, 134, and 156).

Cat. no.	*Present Call-number*
1	Cod. hebr. 8° 68
2	Cod. hebr. 8° 1
3	Cod. hebr. 8° 67
4	Cod. hebr. 8° 61
5	Cod. hebr. 8° 23?
6	Cod. hebr. 8° 69
7	Cod. hebr. 8° 65
8	Cod. hebr. 2° 10
9	Cod. hebr. 8° 60

10	Cod. hebr. 8° 54
11	Cod. hebr. 8° 53
12	Cod. hebr. 8° 56
13	Cod. hebr. 8° 55
14	Cod. hebr. 8° 70
15	Cod. hebr. 8° 57
16	Cod. hebr. 8° 58
17	Cod. hebr. 8° 59
18	Cod. hebr. 8° 66
19	Cod. hebr. 4° 13
20	Cod. hebr. 8° 62
21	Cod. hebr. 8° 64
22	Cod. hebr. 8° 63
23	Cod. hebr. 8° 83
25	Cod. hebr. 8° 17
26	Cod. hebr. 8° 80
27	Cod. hebr. 8° 79
28	Cod. hebr. 8° 78
29	Cod. hebr. 8° 77
30	Cod. hebr. 8° 76
31	Cod. hebr. 8° 75
32	Cod. hebr. 8° 38
33	Cod. hebr. 4° 72
34	Cod. hebr. 8° 28
35	Cod. hebr. 8° 167
36	Cod. hebr. 8° 71
37	Cod. hebr. 8° 73
38	Cod. hebr. 8° 74
39	Cod. hebr. 8° 33
40	Cod. hebr. 2° 14
41	Cod. hebr. 8° 84
42	Cod. hebr. 8° 85
43	Cod. hebr. 8° 86
44	Cod. hebr. 8° 87
45	Cod. hebr. 8° 81
46	Cod. hebr. 8° 15
47	Cod. hebr. 8° 9
48	Cod. hebr. 8° 88
49	Cod. hebr. 8° 89
50	Cod. hebr. 4° 1
51	Cod. hebr. 8° 90
52	Cod. hebr. 8° 91
53	Cod. hebr. 8° 92
55	Cod. hebr. 8° 93
56	Cod. hebr. 8° 94

57	Cod. hebr. 8° 95
58	Cod. hebr. 8° 27
59	Cod. hebr. 4° 3
60	Cod. hebr. 8° 96
61	Cod. hebr. 8° 102
62	Cod. hebr. 8° 97
63	Cod. hebr. 2° 13
64	Cod. hebr. 2° 11
65	Cod. hebr. 8° 98
66	Cod. hebr. 8° 99
67	Cod. hebr. 8° 100
68	Cod. hebr. 2° 12
69	Cod. hebr. 8° 101
70	Cod. hebr. 8° 104
71	Cod. hebr. 8° 105
72	Ausst. 7
73	Cod. hebr. 4° 12
74	Cod. hebr. 8° 103
75	Cod. hebr. 4° 10
76	Cod. hebr. 8° 106
77	Cod. hebr. 4° 11
78	Cod. hebr. 2° 15
79	Cod. hebr. 8° 114
80	Cod. hebr. 8° 107
81	Cod. hebr. 8° 116
82	Cod. hebr. 8° 131
83	Cod. hebr. 8° 119
84	Cod. hebr. 8° 130
85	Cod. hebr. 8° 129
86	Cod. hebr. 8° 18
87	Cod. hebr. 8° 134
88	Cod. hebr. 8° 127
89	Cod. hebr. 8° 123
90	Cod. hebr. 8° 12
91	Cod. hebr. 8° 2
92	Cod. hebr. 8° 120
93	Cod. hebr. 8° 117
94	Cod. hebr. 8° 132
95	Cod. hebr. 2° 16
96	Cod. hebr. 8° 111
97	Cod. hebr. 4° 2
98	Cod. hebr. 8° 3
99	Cod. hebr. 8° 133
100	Cod. hebr. 8° 112
101	Cod. hebr. 8° 113

102	Cod. hebr. 4° 15
103	Cod. hebr. 8° 126
104	Cod. hebr. 8° 122
105	Cod. hebr. 8° 121
106	Cod. hebr. 8° 118
107	Cod. hebr. 4° 14
108	Cod. hebr. 8° 115
109	Cod. hebr. 8° 124
110	Cod. hebr. 8° 125
111	Cod. hebr. 8° 109
113	Cod. hebr. 8° 110
114	Cod. hebr. 8° 128
115	Cod. hebr. 8° 108
117	Cod. hebr. 8° 162
118	Cod. hebr. 8° 157
119	Cod. hebr. 8° 156
120	Cod. hebr. 8° 163
121	Cod. hebr. 8° 153
122	Cod. hebr. 8° 154
123	Cod. hebr. 8° 160
124	Cod. hebr. 8° 155
125	Cod. hebr. 4° 21
126	Cod. hebr. 8° 150
127	Cod. hebr. 8° 161
128	Cod. hebr. 8° 151
129	Cod. hebr. 4° 20
130	Cod. hebr. 8° 152
131	Cod. hebr. 4° 19
132	Cod. hebr. 8° 158
133	Cod. hebr. 8° 159
134	Oxford, Bodleian, Opp. Add. 4° 135
135	Cod. hebr. 8° 148
136	Cod. hebr. 8° 135
137	Cod. hebr. 4° 16
138	Cod. hebr. 8° 147
139	Cod. hebr. 8° 149
140	Cod. hebr. 8° 138
142	Cod. hebr. 8° 29
143	Cod. hebr. 8° 139
144	Cod. hebr. 8° 140
145	Cod. hebr. 8° 141
146	Cod. hebr. 8° 142
147	Cod. hebr. 8° 143
148	Cod. hebr. 8° 22
149	Cod. hebr. 8° 144

150	Cod. hebr. 8° 145
151	Cod. hebr. 8° 146
152	Cod. hebr. 4° 17
153	Cod. hebr. 4° 18
154	Cod. hebr. 8° 136
155	Cod. hebr. 8° 137
156	Ausst. 4 (New York, Private collection)

30. MSS Montefiore

Present or last-known locations of MSS from the Montefiore Collection. The MSS purchased by the Les Enluminures gallery in Paris are offered for sale on the website http://www.textmanuscripts.com/ or were sold. MSS that were not sold remain in the possession of the Montefiore Endowment.

MS Montefiore	*Present/Last-Known Location*
4	Montefiore Endowment
7–8	Montefiore Endowment
11–12	Montefiore Endowment
19–20	Montefiore Endowment
22–23	Montefiore Endowment
27	Montefiore Endowment
35	Montefiore Endowment
37	Montefiore Endowment
41–43	Montefiore Endowment
52–53	Zurich, Braginsky Collection
56–57	New York, NYPL, **P (MS Heb. 177)
61	New York, JTSA, MS 10759
62	New York, D. H. Feinberg
66	New York, D. H. Feinberg
76	New York, D. H. Feinberg
98	New York, D. H. Feinberg
99	Montefiore Endowment
104	Los Angeles, Dr. Steve Weiss 1
108	New York, D. H. Feinberg
114	Montefiore Endowment
118	Montefiore Endowment
122	Montefiore Endowment
123	Paris, Les Enluminures
129–130	New York, D. H. Feinberg
134	New York, D. H. Feinberg
138	Montefiore Endowment
141	Montefiore Endowment
144	Montefiore Endowment
149	Zurich, Braginsky Collection

150	Montefiore Endowment
160–188	Montefiore Endowment
190	Montefiore Endowment
193	New York, JTSA, MS 10763
194	Paris, Les Enluminures
195–196	Montefiore Endowment
197–199	London, BL, Or. 16087
205	Montefiore Endowment
220	Montefiore Endowment
222	Montefiore Endowment
224	Montefiore Endowment
249	Zurich, Braginsky Collection
252	New York, NYPL, **P (MS Heb. 267)
276	Paris, Les Enluminures
278	Paris, Les Enluminures
280	London, BL, Or. 16082
283–286	Montefiore Endowment
287	London, BL, Or. 16088
288	Montefiore Endowment
291	New York, NYPL, **P (MS Heb. 186)
293	London, BL, Or. 16083
294	Montefiore Endowment
296	Paris, Les Enluminures
301–303	Montefiore Endowment
305	Montefiore Endowment
307	Montefiore Endowment
308	Leiden, Universiteitsbibliotheek, Or. 26.509
310	Montefiore Endowment
311	London, BL, Or. 16084
340	New York, JTSA, MS 10760
342	Jerusalem, Rabbi Schochet (Karlin-Stolin) 840
345	London, BL, Or. 16092
355	Zurich, Braginsky Collection
356	Montefiore Endowment
258	Philadelphia, University of Pennsylvania, Schoenberg Collection, LJS 470
363	New York, JTSA, MS 10762
364–366	Montefiore Endowment
368	Montefiore Endowment
374–375	Montefiore Endowment
372	New York, NYPL, **P (MS Heb. 182)
376	New York, NYPL, **P (MS Heb. 181)
379	New York, NYPL, **P (MS Heb. 176)
385	Montefiore Endowment
386	New York, NYPL, **P (MS Heb. 179)
387	New York, NYPL, **P (MS Heb. 174)

388	New York, NYPL, **P (MS Heb. 178)
390	Montefiore Endowment
392–396	Montefiore Endowment
398–399	Montefiore Endowment
401–403	Montefiore Endowment
406	London, BL, Or. 16089
414	Montefiore Endowment
419	Paris, Les Enluminures
421	Oslo, Schøyen Collection, 5412
422	Philadelphia, University of Pennsylvania, Schoenberg Collection, LJS 472
424	Philadelphia, University of Pennsylvania, Schoenberg Collection, LJS 492
435	New York, NYPL, **P (MS Heb. 183)
436	Paris, Les Enluminures
440	London, Wellcome Institute
442	London, BL, Or. 16085
443	Montefiore Endowment
444	Philadelphia, University of Pennsylvania, Schoenberg Collection, LJS 468
446–447	Montefiore Endowment
452–453	Montefiore Endowment
454	New York, NYPL, **P (MS Heb. 180)
455	New York, NYPL, **P (MS Heb. 184)
461	Montefiore Endowment
464	Montefiore Endowment
468	Philadelphia, University of Pennsylvania, Schoenberg Collection, LJS 469
471	New York, NYPL, **P (MS Heb. 185)
472	London, BL, Or. 16090
473	Montefiore Endowment
475	Montefiore Endowment
477	Montefiore Endowment
481	London, BL, Or. 16086
489	Montefiore Endowment
491	Montefiore Endowment
493	Montefiore Endowment
494	New York, NYPL, **P (MS Heb. 175)
495	Montefiore Endowment
496	Paris, Les Enluminures
499	Montefiore Endowment
500	London, BL, Or. 16091
501	Montefiore Endowment
506–591	Montefiore Endowment

31. MSS Paris, Collège de Clermont

Present locations of MSS that were in the Collège de Clermont, listed in F. Clement, *Catalogus Manuscriptorum Codicum Collegii Claromontani*, Paris 1764, and in the appended *Catalogus Manuscriptorum Codicum Bibliothecae Domus Professae Pariensis*.

Catalogus ... Claromontani

Cat. no.	*Present/Last Known Location*
I	New York, JTSA, MS 8225 (formerly Meerman 11, Duke of *Sussex 6)
II	Meerman 3
VI	Berlin, SB, Phillipps 1392 (Cat. 194, formerly Meerman 12)
VII	Meerman 4
VIII	Leiden, Universiteitsbibliotheek, Cod. Or. 2065
X	London, BL, Add. 19943 (formerly Meerman 5)
XII	Oxford, Bodleian Library, MS Mich. 207
XIII	Amsterdam, Ets Haim, HS EH 47 D 20 (formerly Meerman 23)

Catalogus ... Pariensis

I	Paris, BnF, héb. 1251
II	Paris, BnF, héb. 656
III	Paris, BnF, héb. 893

32. MSS Pinsker

Present or last-known locations of MSS that belonged to Simha Pinsker of Tarnow, described in the catalogue of his estate: מזכיר לבני רש״ף, והוא רשימה מקבוצי וכתבי יד הנשארים מעזבון ... ר׳ שמחה פינסקער, מאת יהודה ברד״ח, וינה תרכ״ט.

Pinsker no.	*Present/Last Known Location*
1	*Cat. Schwarz*, Austria, 302; now Warsaw, ŻIH, 190
2	*Cat. Schwarz*, Austria, 229; now Jerusalem, NLI, Heb. 8° 6864
3	*Cat. Schwarz*, Austria, 295
4	Jerusalem, NLI, Heb. 8° 3524
5	Cambridge (Mass.), Harvard University, Heb. 36
6	*Cat. Schwarz*, Austria, 230
7	Warsaw, ŻIH, 94
9	Warsaw, ŻIH, 112
10	Cambridge (Mass.), Harvard University, Heb. 42
11	Budapest, Hungarian Academy of Sciences, MS Kaufmann A 271
12	*Cat. Schwarz*, Austria, 301
13	*Cat. Schwarz*, Austria, 293; now Warsaw, ŻIH, 476
14	*Cat. Schwarz*, Austria, 294; now Harvard University, Heb. 40
15	Budapest, Hungarian Academy of Sciences, MS Kaufmann A 285
17	Halle, DMG B271a (8 foll. from the Koran, part of MS 17)

25	Jerusalem, NLI, Heb. 8° 5389
26	Warsaw, ŻIH, 150
27	Warsaw, ŻIH, 8

33. MSS Porges

Present locations of MSS that belonged to Nathan Porges, listed in O. Harrasowitz, *Bibliotheca Judaica–Hebraica–Rabbinica Pinczower–Porges*, Leipzig 1931/2.

Catalogue no.	*Present Location*
5233	Cincinnati, HUC, MS 847
5235	Warsaw, ŻIH, 106
5237	Jerusalem, NLI, Heb. 8° 7565 (formerly Jerusalem, Schocken Institute, MS 13847)
5239	Jerusalem, NLI, Heb. 8° 2761
5253	Los Angeles, UCLA, MS 960 bx.1.10
5254	New York, JTSA, MS 2230
5262	Jerusalem, Schocken Institute, MS 14052
5274	Jerusalem, NLI, Heb. 8° 7116 (formerly Allony 121)
5277	Jerusalem, Israel Museum 180/73
5281	New York, JTSA, MS 9487
5282	Jerusalem, Schocken Institute, MS 13992

34. MSS Barend Rubens

Present or last-known locations of MSS from the collection of Meijer Barend Rubens listed in *Me'ir 'enayim* (מאיר עינים הוא רשימת ספרים ... רובם מעזבון ... מאיר בפו״מ כ״ה יודא יששכר בער זצ״ל לבית רובענס), with the added title: *Catalogus II van eene ... boekverzameling ... door ... Meijer Barend Rubens*, Amsterdam 1864, Part II.

Cat. no.	*Present Location*
5	Hamburg, SUB, Cod. Levy 89
6	Amsterdam, Ets Haim, EH 47 E 24
9	Amsterdam, UB, HS. Ros. 173
11	Zurich, Zentralbibliothek, Heid. 207
12	London, Montefiore, MS 42

35. MSS Sassoon

MSS from the Sassoon collection sold at auction or otherwise. The present or last-known locations are indicated whenever possible. MSS for which no location is given remain in the possession of the Sassoon family.

Sassoon no.	*Present/Last-Known Location*
1	
15	

16	São Paolo, Safra family
17	
18	Oslo, Martin Schøyen, 1863
19	Oslo, Martin Schøyen, 1859
22	Jerusalem, Israel Museum
23	São Paolo, Safra family
24	Montreal, Y. Elberg (deceased) 24
27	
30	London, Valmadonna Trust Library, 6a
31 32	
33	London, Valmadonna Trust Library, 20e
37–39 41	
46	sold at Sotheby's, New York, Dec. 2, 2004, lot 8 (formerly Boesky 9)
48	
49	London, Valmadonna Trust Library, 7
50 53	
54	Sotheby's, New York, Dec. 15, 2010
55	London, Valmadonna Trust Library,16
56	New York, NYPL, **P (MS Heb. 190)
59 62–66	
67	Tel Aviv, Recanati family
69 71	
72	Jerusalem, NLI, Heb. 4° 5703,1
73	Jerusalem, NLI, Heb. 4° 5703,2
78	sold by R. D. Levy at Sotheby's auction, Tel Aviv, October 1993
79	Cleveland, Reuven Dessler
80	sold at Sotheby's, New York, Dec. 2, 2004, lot 11 (formerly Boesky)
82	
83	sold at Sotheby's, New York, Dec. 2, 2004, lot 23 (formerly Boesky)
88–101	
104 105	Cambridge, UL, Or. 2240, 2241
107	
108	London, BL, Or. 14014
109 111 112	
113	London, BL, Or. 14015
116	
119	
121	
130	
134	London, Valmadonna Trust Library, 17
138 140	
141–145	London, Valmadonna Trust Library, 20b
147	
149	London, Valmadonna Trust Library, 13
157	

158	Montreal, Y. Elberg (deceased), 10
159	London, BL, Or. 14020A
160	London, BL, Or. 14020B
161	Cleveland, Reuven Dessler
162	London, BL, Or. 14058
164	Montreal, Y. Elberg (deceased), 12
170	Silver Spring, Md., M. Lehmann K56
181	sold at Sotheby's, New York, Dec. 2, 2004, lot 15 (formerly Boesky)
182	
186	London, BL, Or. 14057
192	
199	London, BL, Or. 14054
201 203–210	
217	Silver Spring, Md., M. Lehmann
218	Cambridge, UL, Or. 2245
219	
220	Oslo, Martin Schøyen, 1864
221 222	
223	Oslo, Martin Schøyen, 1865
224	Oslo, Martin Schøyen, 1861
225	Cambridge, UL, Or. 2246
226	London, BL, Or. 13871
227	Cambridge, UL, Or. 2243
242	
244	Cincinnati, HUC, MSS 248 249 259
248 249 259	
262	Sotheby's, New York, Dec. 15, 2010
263	Toronto Univ., MS Friedberg 3–002
266	
273	Montreal, Y. Elberg (deceased)
278	
280	Paris, Société des manuscrits des assureurs français
281	Silver Spring, Md., M. Lehmann
282	London, Valmadonna Trust Library, 1
283–289	
290	Geneva, BPU, MS Comites Latentes 145
332	Sotheby's, New York, Dec. 17, 2008
333	
337	London, Valmadonna Trust Library, 14
338	
341	
344	Zurich, R. Bollag
345 363 369	
402	Jerusalem, NLI, Sam. 2° 6
403	

404	Manchester, John Rylands, Sam. 376
405 407	
408	London, BL, Or. 14055
409	Paris, V. Klagsbald
410	Oslo, Martin Schøyen, 2195
411	Jerusalem, NLI, Heb. 8° 6235
412	Jerusalem, NLI, Heb. 8° 5701
413	
414	sold at Bloomsbury Book Auction, Sept. 1992
415	sold at Sotheby's, New York, Dec. 2, 2004, lot 6 (formerly Boesky)
416	
417	Geneva, N. Gaon
422 425 428 431 432	
438	London, Valmadonna Trust Library, 12
439	
440	Zurich, J. Bollag
441 442 443 444 447	
453	London, Valmadonna Trust Library, 20c
455	Cambridge, UL, Or. 2242
457 467–8	
476	Philadelphia, University of Pennsylvania, Schoenberg Collection, LJS 204
477	Montreal, Y. Elberg (deceased)
487	Tel Aviv, W. Gross, 179 (now in the Van Kampen collection in the Scriptorium, Holy Land Experience, Orlando, FL)
491	
492	Sotheby's, New York, Dec. 15, 2010, lot 91
493	Jerusalem, M. Benayahu
494	
495	Paris, Société des manuscrits des assureurs français
499	Oxford, Bodleian, Heb. e. 183
501 502 503 504	
506	Jerusalem, Israel Museum, MS 180/94
507	Jerusalem, NLI, Heb. 24° 5702
508	Toronto Univ., MS Friedberg 5–001
511	Floersheim family, Zurich–Herzliyya
512	Geneva, N. Gaon
514	Jerusalem, Israel Museum, 181/41
516	Oxford, Bodleian, Heb. d. 102
517 518	
521	New York, D. H. Feinberg (acquired at Sotheby's, New York, Dec. 2, 2004, lot 3, formerly Boesky 3)
522	New York, D. H. Feinberg (acquired at Sotheby's, New York, Dec. 2, 2004, lot 7, formerly Boesky)
523	Jerusalem, NLI, Heb. 8° 5699
524	

525	Oslo, Martin Schøyen, 1860
526	Jerusalem, NLI, Heb. 8° 5700
527 528	
529	Paris, BnF, héb. 1463
530	Oslo, Martin Schøyen, 1862
531	sold at Sotheby's, New York, Dec. 2, 2004, lot 1 (formerly Boesky 2)
532	Oslo, Martin Schøyen, 1866
534	Toronto Univ., MS Friedberg 5-011
535	Paris, V. Klagsbald
536 537	
539	London, BL, Or. 13705
543	
557	Jerusalem, NLI, Heb. 4° 5704
559–562	
566	was Oslo, Martin Schøyen, 1858; sold at Sotheby's, London, July 10, 2012, lot 11
572	Montreal, Elberg (deceased) 13
573	Sotheby's, New York, Dec. 15, 2010
583–586	
589	New York, JTSA, MS 10882 (acquired at Sotheby's, New York, Dec. 2, 2004, lot 37, formerly Boesky)
590	Oxford, Bodleian, Heb. e. 184
591	Zurich, Braginsky Collection
592	
593	Toronto Univ., MS Friedberg 3–011
594	London, Valmadonna Trust Library, 9
595	
596	London, BL, Or. 14056
597	Geneva, BPU, MS Comites Latentes 146
598	sold at Sotheby's, New York, Dec. 2, 2004, lot 12 (formerly Boesky 5)
600	
601	Paris, BnF, héb. 1468
607	Zurich, Braginsky Collection (formerly Boesky)
608	Cambridge, UL, Or. 2244
609	
613	sold at Sotheby's, New York, Dec. 2, 2004, lot 21 (formerly Boesky 7)
614	London, BL, Or. 13704
616	London, BL, Or. 14059
618	London, BL, Or. 14017
621	
622	Leeds, Brotherton Library, Dep. 1982/1
634	London, Valmadonna Trust Library, 15
638	
640	
641	sold at Sotheby's, New York, Dec. 2, 2004, lot 10 (formerly Boesky 48)

650	purchased by Y. Elberg and later sold to a dealer who split the MS into two parts.
653 654 660	
663	Miami, R. D. Levy
683	Paris, Société des manuscrits des assureurs français
690 691 693 699	
700	Manchester, John Rylands, MS 50
701	London, BL, Or. 14060
702	sold at Sotheby's, New York, Dec. 2, 2004, lot 16 (formerly Boesky)
704	sold at Sotheby's, New York, Dec. 2, 2004, lot 27 (formerly Boesky 6)
705	
706	Paris, Société des manuscrits des assureurs français
707–709	
710	London, BL, Or. 13872
715	Brussels, Paul Dahan, 15
716	Manchester, John Rylands, Sam. 377
717	
724–726	
728	Oslo, Martin Schøyen, 1999
734 735	New York, B. Spiro
755	sold at Sotheby's, New York, Dec. 2, 2004, lot 29 (formerly Boesky 8)
756	Jerusalem, NLI, Heb. 8° 6234
761	
774	Cincinnati, HUC
783	sold at Sotheby's, New York, Dec. 2, 2004, lot 9 (formerly Boesky)
801	
803	Sotheby's, New York, Dec. 17, 2008, lot 197
804	Geneva, Jack Safra
808	London, Valmadonna Trust Library, 13a
813 822	
823	Philadelphia, University of Pennsylvania, Schoenberg Collection, LJS 57
828	London, BL, Or. 14018
829 837 850	
856	Offered for sale, Kestenbaum auction, Jan. 31, 2013, lot 272
862 869 903 904 915	
916	sold at Sotheby's, London, Dec. 7, 1999 (formerly New York, S. Glick)
918	New York, D. H. Feinberg (acquired at Sotheby's, New York, Dec. 2, 2004, lot 2; formerly Boesky 4)
919	New York, Public Library **P (MS Heb. 191)
920	Jerusalem, M. Benayahu
922	
923	London, Valmadonna Trust Library, 8
924	Silver Spring, Md., M. Lehmann, D 107
928 930 931 933	
939	Toronto Univ., MS Friedberg

942 Montreal, Y. Elberg (deceased)
943 Montreal, Y. Elberg (deceased) 15
958
959 Cincinnati, HUC
964 London, Valmadonna Trust Library, 11
969 Oxford, Bodleian, Heb. d. 103
971 972 977 978 979
983 Silver Spring, Md., M. Lehmann, M 10
984 995 1012
1016 London, D. Sofer
1017 1021 1025
1026 Toronto Univ., MS Friedberg 5-006
1027
1028 sold by R. D. Levy at Sotheby's, Tel Aviv, October 1993
1029
1041 London, BL, Or. 14019
1043 1045
1047 London, BL, Or. 14061
1049 1050 1052
1053 Geneva, Jack Safra
1058 1061
1062 Sotheby's, New York, Dec. 17, 2008
1064 London, D. Sofer, 60
1065 1066 1075 1124 1125 1136 1144 1149 1151 1203 1207–1210
1231 1235 1239 lost
1274
1287 1289 1290 lost

36. MSS Schocken

Includes, inter alia, MSS sold at the following auctions: *Important Judaica* (Sotheby's, Tel Aviv, December 9, 1999); *Magnificent Judaica* (Sotheby's, Tel Aviv, April 17, 2001); *Important Judaica* (Sotheby's, New York, March 18, 2004); *Important Hebrew Manuscripts from the Salman Schocken Collection* (Christie's, New York, November 15, 2005). MSS not listed here remain in the Schocken Library.

MS Schocken	*Present Location*
11215	Zurich, Braginsky Collection
12141	London, D. Sofer
12294	sold at Christie's, 2005, no. 7
12473	Zurich, Braginsky Collection
12474	Jerusalem, NLI, Heb. 4° 7566
12495	Sotheby's, 2001, no. 48
12827	Zurich, D. Jeselsohn (acquired at Christie's, 2005, no. 3)
13124	London, D. Sofer (acquired at Christie's, 2005, no. 1)

13131	
13160	Zurich, D. Jeselsohn (acquired at Christie's, 2005, no.9)
13207	Zurich, D. Jeselsohn (acquired at Christie's, 2005, no.15)
13208	Sotheby's, 2001, no. 54
13375	Zurich, Braginsky Collection (acquired at Christie's, 2005, no. 12)
13439	Sotheby's, 2001, no. 49
13487 [35]	Zurich, Braginsky Collection (acquired at Christie's, 2005, no. 6)
13488 [22]	London, D. Sofer
13489 [34]	Zurich, Braginsky Collection (acquired at Christie's, 2005, no. 5)
13554	Christie's, 2005, no.11
13847	Jerusalem, NLI, Heb. 8° 7565
13864	Cleveland, R. Dessler (acquired at Christie's, 2005, no. 4)
13866	
13869	Zurich, Braginsky Collection (acquired at Sotheby's, 1999, no. 45)
13873	Israel, Private collection
13926	Sotheby's, 2001, no. 50
13970	Zurich, D. Jeselsohn (acquired at Sotheby's, 2001, no. 53)
14840	Israel, Private collection
15435	Vienna, ÖNB, Cod. Hebr. 242
15878	Sotheby's, 2001, no. 45
15943	sold at Christie's, 2005, no. 2
16660	Sotheby's, 1999, no. 66
19522	Zurich, D. Jeselsohn (acquired at Christie's, 2005, no.10)
19523 [74]	Los Angeles, Private collection (acquired at Sotheby's, 1999, no. 65)
19526	Los Angeles, Private collection (acquired at Christie's, 2005, no. 8)
19999	Zurich, Braginsky Collection (acquired at Christie's, 2005, no. 8)
24086	Jerusalem, Israel Museum (acquired at Sotheby's, 2001, no. 52)
24087	Private collection (deposited in Jerusalem, NLI)
24100	Zurich, D. Jeselsohn (deposited in Jerusalem, Israel Museum)
24360	Zurich, D. Jeselsohn (acquired at Christie's, 2005, no.13)
24749	Zurich, Braginsky Collection
24750	Chicago, Sheldon Stern (acquired at Sotheby's, 1999, no. 67)

37. MSS Schulting

Present locations of MSS that belonged to Cornelius Schulting, listed in *Bibliotheca Schultingiana, sive catalogus Librorum ... a ... D. Cornelio Schultingio relictorum*, Amsterdam 1726.

Cat. no.	*Present Location*
2	Oxford, Bodleian Library, MS Kennicott 10
3	London, BL, Add. 9398
4	London, BL, Add. 9399
5	London, BL, Add. 9400
6	London, BL, Add. 9404

7	London, BL, Add. 9403
10	London, BL, Add. 9407
17	Private collection
20	Hamburg, SUB, Cod. hebr. 266
21–22	Hamburg, SUB, Cod. hebr. 70

38. MSS Listed in *Cat. Schwarz*, Austria, and *Cat. Schwarz–Loewinger–Róth*

Includes references to MSS in Moscow described in K. Akinsha et al., *Manuscripts and Archival Documents of the Vienna Jewish Community held in Russian Collections: Catalogue*, Moscow 2006.

Cat. no.	*Present/Last-Known Location*
1	St. Paul im Lavanttal, Benediktinerinnenstift, 84.1
2	Gottweig, Stiftsbibliothek, 10–11
3	Copenhagen, Kongelige Bibl., Cod. Hebr. 12
25	Warsaw, ŻIH, 736
26	Parts are in New York, JTSA, MS 10485, and in Warsaw, ŻIH, 257.
27	Warsaw, ŻIH, 119
29	Moscow, RSL, Acc. 136 (Cat. 40)
30 (ff. 1–45)	Warsaw, ŻIH, 435
31	Offered for sale in Jerusalem, 1995. Part is in New York, JTSA, MS 10484.
32	Jerusalem, NLI, Heb. 8° 5226
33	Warsaw, ŻIH, 888
34	Paris, BN, Héb. 1467 (only ff. 19–93) (formerly Warsaw, ŻIH, 260)
35	Warsaw, ŻIH, 30
36	Jerusalem, NLI, Yah. MS Heb. 228
37	Private collection
38	Private collection
40	Offered for sale in 1998
43	Silver Spring, Md., M. Lehmann, D 56
44	Moscow, RSMA, 707/3/6 (Cat. 73)
45	Warsaw, ŻIH, 251 and 907
46	Moscow, RSMA, 707/1/176 (Cat. 44)
47	Jerusalem, NLI, Heb. 8° 3427
48	Private collection
49	Warsaw, ŻIH, 89
50	Moscow, RSL, Acc. 138 (Cat. 8)
51	Warsaw, ŻIH, 4
52	Offered for sale in Jerusalem
54	Warsaw, ŻIH, 891
55	Warsaw, ŻIH, 37
56	Moscow, RSL, Acc. 31 (Cat. 31)
57	Warsaw, ŻIH, 130
59	Warsaw, ŻIH, 205

60	Jerusalem, NLI, Heb. 8° 6479
61	Jerusalem, NLI, Heb. 8° 2802
62	Jerusalem, NLI, Heb. 8° 2311
65	Warsaw, ŻIH, 346
66	Jerusalem, NLI, Heb. 8° 3045
68	Jerusalem, NLI, Yah. MS Heb. 1
69	Vienna, Jüdische Gemeinde
75	Innsbruck, Universitätsbibliothek, Cod. 291
76	Private collection
79	Private collection
80	Jerusalem, NLI, Heb. 8° 7235
83	Warsaw, ŻIH, 38
84	Private collection
85	Offered for sale in Jerusalem
86	Jerusalem, NLI, Heb. 8° 2131
87	Moscow, RSMA, 707/3/19 (Cat. 10)
88	Warsaw, ŻIH, 179
89	Warsaw, ŻIH, 133
90	Warsaw, ŻIH, 113
91	Warsaw, ŻIH, 284
92	New York, JTSA (bought in 1996)
95	Warsaw, ŻIH, 497
96	Jerusalem, NLI, Heb. 8° 5221
97	Moscow, RSMA, 707/3/14 (Cat. 26)
98	Jerusalem, Mosad Harav Kook, 757
100	Warsaw, ŻIH, 180
101	Jerusalem, NLI, Heb. 8° 2298
102	Jerusalem, NLI, Heb. 4° 896
104	Offered for sale in Jerusalem, 1995
105	Jerusalem, NLI, Heb. 4° 877
106	Warsaw, ŻIH, 77
107	Warsaw, ŻIH, 228
109	Moscow, RSL, Acc. 37/1 (Cat. 43)
110	Warsaw, ŻIH, 40
112	Warsaw, ŻIH, 154
113	Jerusalem, NLI, Heb. 8° 6857 (formerly N. Allony 137)
117	Warsaw, ŻIH, 65
118	Warsaw, ŻIH, 54
119	Warsaw, ŻIH, 213
120	Moscow, RSL, Acc. 6 (Cat. 75)
122	Jerusalem, NLI, Heb. 8° 2268
123	Moscow, RSL, Acc. 22 (Cat. 62)
124	Warsaw, ŻIH, 107
125	Warsaw, ŻIH, 368
128	Warsaw, ŻIH, 45; 71; 493

130	Warsaw, ŻIH, 1022
131	Offered for sale in New York, 1983
132 (vol. 1)	Moscow, RSL, Acc. 4 (Cat. 74)
132 (vol. 2)	Warsaw, ŻIH (without call-number, IMHM mic. 31047)
133	Warsaw, ŻIH, 73 (part i) and Jerusalem, NLI, Heb. 8° 2263 (part ii)
134	Moscow, RSL, Acc. 9 (Cat. 27)
136	Jerusalem, NLI, Heb. 8° 2647
140	New York, JTSA, MS 9685
141	Warsaw, ŻIH?
143	New York, JTSA, MS 9019
144	Warsaw, ŻIH, 1159
146	Moscow RSMA, 707/1/146 (Cat. 77)
147	Jerusalem, NLI, Heb. 8° 6282
149	Warsaw, ŻIH (without call-number, IMHM mic. 30989)
154	Warsaw, ŻIH, 254
155	Moscow, RSL, Günzburg 739 (in place of MS formerly bearing this number)
162	Johannesburg, S. Rappaport
164	Jerusalem, Private collection, IMHM mic. 70555
184	Jerusalem, NLI, Heb. 8° 2237
199	Warsaw, ŻIH, 168
201	London, D. Sofer 5
203	Jerusalem, NLI, Heb. 8° 2235
204	Warsaw, ŻIH, 221
205	Warsaw, ŻIH, 59
209	Moscow, RSL, Acc. 117 (Cat. 36)
210	Warsaw, ŻIH, 211
211–212	Warsaw, ŻIH, 668
214	Warsaw, ŻIH, 178
217	Warsaw, ŻIH, 394
218	Warsaw, ŻIH, 49
219	Jerusalem, NLI, Heb. 8° 2256
223	Jerusalem, NLI, Heb. 8° 7224
225	Warsaw, ŻIH, 110
226	Jerusalem, NLI, Heb. 8° 5336
227	Offered for sale in Jerusalem
228	Warsaw, ŻIH, 218
229	Jerusalem, NLI, Heb. 8° 6864 (formerly Warsaw, ŻIH, 247 and Jerusalem, N. Allony, 192)
231–232	Johannesburg, S. Rappaport
233	Warsaw, ŻIH, 244
234	Jerusalem, NLI, Heb. 8° 7234
235	Warsaw, ŻIH, 85
236	Offered for sale in Jerusalem, 1995
237	Jerusalem, NLI, Heb. 8° 2492

238	Jerusalem, NLI, Heb. 8° 2128
239	Offered for sale in Jerusalem, 1999
240 (ff. 1–113)	Vienna, Jewish Community
240 (ff. 114–160)	London, Private collection
242	Warsaw, ŻIH, 155
244	Offered for sale in Jerusalem, 1999
246	Warsaw, ŻIH, 900
247	New York, JTSA, MS 10636
248	Warsaw, ŻIH, 230
250	Jerusalem, Private collection, IMHM mic. 70556
251	Private collection
252	New York, Chassidei Chabad Library 1193 (formerly Warsaw, ŻIH, 1193[7])
253	Private collection
255	Jerusalem, NLI, Heb. 4° 651
256	Jerusalem, NLI, Heb. 8° 2255
257	Jerusalem, NLI, Heb. 8° 7709
258	Ramat Gan, Bar-Ilan Univ. 275, 286, 583, 747
259	Warsaw, ŻIH, 152
260	Warsaw, ŻIH, 229
261	Cat. Sotheby 1984, no. 35
262	Warsaw, ŻIH, 285
264	Warsaw, ŻIH, 164
265	Moscow, RSL, Acc. 218/1 (Cat. 25)
268	Jerusalem, NLI, Heb. 8° 2281
270	Warsaw, ŻIH, 249
271	Warsaw, ŻIH, 293
272	Warsaw, ŻIH, 193
274	Warsaw, ŻIH, 48
275	Offered for sale in Jerusalem, 1995
276	Jerusalem, Hekhal Shelomo, Qu. 49
278	Part 2 offered for sale in 2000
280	Offered for sale in 1996
282	Offered for sale in 1996
283	Offered for sale in 1996
285	Warsaw, ŻIH, 282
287	Warsaw, ŻIH, 374
288	Jerusalem, NLI, Heb. 4° 666
289	Moscow, RSL, Acc. 125 (Cat. 2)
290	Moscow, RSMA, 707/3/17 (Cat. 64)
291	Private collection
293	Warsaw, ŻIH, 476
294	Cambridge (Mass.), Harvard, Heb. 40
295	Warsaw, ŻIH, 31
296	Moscow RSMA, 707/1/209 (Cat. 33)
297	Jerusalem, NLI, Heb. 8° 2331

299	Warsaw, ŻIH, 255
300 (ff. 1–10)	Moscow, RSL, Acc. 219/2 (Cat. 23)
300 (ff. 11–133)	Warsaw, ŻIH, 189
301	Warsaw, ŻIH, 245
302	Warsaw, ŻIH, 190

Vienna, Jewish Community, VI 156, is Warsaw, ŻIH, 252.

39. MSS Sussex

Present locations of MSS described in Thomas Pettigrew, *Bibliotheca Sussexiana – A Descriptive Catalogue ... of the Manuscripts and Printed Books Contained in the Library of ... the Duke of Sussex*, London 1827.

Cat. no.	*Present Location*
1	Berlin, SB, MS Ham. 80
2	London, BL, Add. 15250
3	London, BL, Add. 15282
4	London, BL, Add. 15306
5	New York, JTSA, MS 8238
6	New York, JTSA, MS 8225
8	Cambridge, Trinity College, F. 18. 44 (Cat. 105)
9	Cincinnati, HUC, MS 653
10	Cambridge, Trinity College, F. 18. 37 (Cat. 34)
12	Hamburg, SUB, Cod. Levy 3
13	Cambridge, Trinity College, F. 12. 2 (Cat. 43)?
14	Munich, BSB, Cod. hebr. 365
15	Munich, BSB, Cod. hebr. 366
16	Cambridge, Trinity College, F. 18. 47 (Cat. 127)
17	Cambridge, Trinity College, F. 12. 153 (Cat. 120)
19	Cambridge, Trinity College, F. 12. 17 (Cat. 61)
27	Sassoon 493
30	Cambridge, UL, Add. 1565
32–41	Manchester, John Rylands, MS Rylands 5
42	London School of Jewish Studies, MS Asher Myers 2
43	London School of Jewish Studies, MS Asher Myers 7
44	London School of Jewish Studies, MS Asher Myers 6

40. MSS from Tunis

Present locations of MSS from Tunis listed by J. Cohen Tanuji in 'כתבי יד תוניס', בית ישראל, ב [טבת תרמ"ט], עמ' 28–31.

Cat. no.	*Present/Last-Known Location*
3–4	London, BL, Or. 3660
6	London, BL, Or. 3658
8–9	London, BL, Or. 3661

11	Moscow, RSL, Günzburg 1595
12	Moscow, RSL, Günzburg 1619
13	Budapest, Hungarian Academy of Sciences, MS Kaufmann A 520
14	London, BL, Or. 3656
15	Vienna, Israelitische Kultusgemeinde (*Cat. Schwarz*, Austria, 298)
16	London, BL, Or. 3659
18	London, BL, Or. 3657
18bis	Moscow, RSL, Günzburg 1835
19	Warsaw, ŻIH, 281
20	Jerusalem, NLI, Yah. Ms. Heb. 1
21	London, BL, Or. 3655

41. MSS in Turin, Biblioteca Nazionale Universitaria

Only MSS of which parts survived the fire of 1904 are listed. In many cases the surviving folios are damaged or incomplete.

* = MSS of which 90–100% of the folios survive
# = MSS of which 30–60% of the folios survive
^ = MSS of which less than 30% of the folios survive
° = MSS of which less than 20 folios survive
MSS of which 60–90% of the folios survive bear no sign.

A.I.1^
A.I.2°
A.I.3
A.I.4
A.I.5*
A.I.6*
A.I.7*
A.I.8*
A.I.9
A.I.10*
A.I.11*
A.I.12–13*
A.I.14* (complete)
A.I.15
A.I.16
A.I.17?; A.II.4?
A.I.18*
A.I.19*
A.I.20*
A.II.4?
A.II.5
A.II.6*
A.II.7
A.II.8
A.II.9*
A.II.10*
A.II.11*
A.II.12
A.II.13
A.II.14*
A.II.15* (complete)
A.II.16
A.II.17
A.II.18
A.II.20* (complete)
A.II.21*
A.II.22
A.II.24
A.II.25*
A.II.26*
A.II.27*
A.II.28*
A.II.29* (complete)
A.III.3^

A.III.4°
A.III.5^
A.III.6#
A.III.7
A.III.8
A.III.9#
A.III.10
A.III.11
A.III.12* (complete)
A.III.13#
A.III.14#
A.III.16
A.III.17#
A.III.18* (complete)
A.III.19*
A.III.20
A.III.21
A.III.22
A.III.23#
A.III.25^
A.III.26
A.III.30#
A.IV.1
A.IV.3°
A.IV.12*
A.IV.13
A.IV.15
A.IV.19#
A.IV.20
A.IV.21^
A.IV.22
A.IV.23* (complete)
A.IV.25°
A.IV.26°
A.IV.27#
A.IV.29#
A.IV.30
A.IV.34#
A.IV.38^
A.V.2
A.V.3
A.V.4#
A.V.6* (complete)
A.V.9#
A.V.10
A.V.11
A.V.12*
A.V.13*
A.V.14
A.V.15
A.V.17
A.V.18#
A.V.19^
A.V.21^
A.V.22#
A.V.24
A.V.29#
A.V.31#
A.V.32°
A.V.33
A.V.35°
A.V.43° (only 1 folio)
A.VI.7^
A.VI.11^?
A.VI.20
A.VI.23#
A.VI.24^
A.VI.25
A.VI.26#
A.VI.27*
A.VI.28#
A.VI.29°
A.VI.30^
A.VI.34* (complete)
A.VII.8^
A.VII.24°
A.VII.32°?
A.VII.34#
A.VII.36^
A.VII.38#
A.VII.42°
A.VII.53*(complete)

42. MSS Wagenaar

Present locations of MSS that belonged to Hyman Abraham Wagenaar, listed in רשימה של מכירת ספרים: *Versteigerungs-Catalog einer wichtigen Sammlung Hebraica, Judaica, Handschriften, u.s.w. aus dem Nachlass des Herrn H. A. Wagenaar ... Versteigerung Montag 2 Mai 1904 und folgende Tage*, Amsterdam 1904.

Cat. no.	*Present Location*
2309	Amsterdam, UB, HS. Ros. 214
2310	Amsterdam, UB, HS. Ros. 432
2314	New York, JTSA, MS 3601
2315	Amsterdam, UB, HS. Ros. 205
2316	New York, JTSA, MS R 1414
2317	Amsterdam, UB, HS. Ros. 40
2319	Amsterdam, UB, HS. Ros. 424
2320	Amsterdam, UB, HS. Ros. 108
2321	Amsterdam, UB, HS. Ros. 453
2322	New York, JTSA, MS 1661
2323	London, Valmadonna Trust Library, 307
2324	Amsterdam, UB, HS. Ros. 321
2325	New York, JTSA, MS L782
2329	Amsterdam, UB, HS. Ros. 263
2331	Amsterdam, UB, HS. Ros. 181
2332	Amsterdam, UB, HS. Ros. 182
2334	Amsterdam, UB, HS. Ros. 172
2335	Amsterdam, UB, HS. Ros. 42
2336	Amsterdam, Gans
2338	formerly Amsterdam, J. R. Ritman Library, BPH 406
2340	Amsterdam, UB, HS. Ros. 216
2342	Amsterdam, UB, HS. Ros. 592

43. MSS Wijnkoop

Present locations of MSS that belonged to Joseph David Wijnkoop, listed in *Auctions-Catalog* אהל יוסף ... , Amsterdam 1911.

Cat. no.	*Present Location*
2029	Amsterdam, UB, HS. Ros. 175
2030	New York, JTSA, MS 2220
2031	Amsterdam, UB, HS. Ros. 129
2033	Amsterdam, UB, HS. Ros. 120
2036	Jerusalem, NLI, Yah. Ms. Heb. 57
2037	Amsterdam, UB, HS. Ros. PL B-35?
2039	Amsterdam, UB, HS. Ros. 14
2040	Jerusalem, NLI, Yah. Ms. Heb. 216

APPENDIX II

List of Collections Microfilmed for the Institute of Microfilmed Hebrew Manuscripts (IMHM)

Collections bearing no sign are very small, containing only a few manuscripts or fragments. Many of the private collections have been dispersed or sold since they were microfilmed.

[s] Small collection containing 10–99 MSS
[m] Medium collection containing 100–499 MSS
[1] Large collection containing 500–999 MSS
[v] Very large collection containing more than 1,000 MSS
[f] Collection has been partially microfilmed
(doc.) documents
(fr.) fragments
(pr.) private collection

ARGENTINA
Buenos Aires
Jose Aljaral (pr.)
Mordechai Bornstein (pr.)
J. Moscowitz (pr. doc.)

ARMENIA
Erevan
Mastotz Institute of Ancient Manuscripts

AUSTRALIA
Melbourne
State Library of Victoria
New Norcia
Benedictine Abbey
North Ryde
Macquarie University
Sydney
University of Sydney

AUSTRIA
Admont
Benediktinerstift (fr.)
Altenburg
Benediktinerstift (fr.)
Bregenz
Voralberger Landesarchiv (fr.)
Gottweig
Stiftsbibliothek (1 MS and fr.)

Graz
    Minoriten Klosterarchiv (fr.) [now held by the Minoritenkonvent in Vienna]
    Steiermärkisches Landesarchiv (fr.)
    Universitätsbibliothek (fr.)
    Zentralbibliothek der Wiener Franziskanerprovinz (fr.)
Heiligenkreuz b. Baden
    Stiftsbibliothek (fr.)
Herzogenburg
    Augustiner-Chorherrenstift (fr.)
Innsbruck
    Prämonstratenser Chorherrenstift Wilten
    Tiroler Landesmuseum Ferdinandeum (fr.)
    Universitätsbibliothek
Klagenfurt
    Archiv der Diözese Gurk (Bischöfliche Bibliothek) (fr.)
    Kaerntner Landesarchiv (fr.)
    Bibliothek der Alpen-Adria-Universität (formerly Bundesstaatliche Studienbibliothek) (fr.)
Klosterneuburg
    Bibliothek des Augustiner-Chorherrenstifts (fr.)
Krems
    Stadtarchiv (fr.)
Kremsmünster
    Stiftsbibliothek (fr.)
Kreuzenstein bei Leobendorf
    Graf. J. Wilczek (fr.)
Lambach
    Benediktinerstift (fr.)
Linz a.d. Donau
    Oberösterreichische Landesbibliothek (fr.)
    Oberösterreichisches Landesarchiv (fr.)
Maria Saal
    Archiv des Collegiatstiftes (fr.)
Melk
    Stiftsbibliothek (fr.)
Poertschach am Wörthersee
    Dr. Karl August Neuscheller (pr.)
St. Florian
    Bibliothek des Augustiner Chorherrenstifts (fr.)
St. Paul im Lavanttal
    Stiftsbibliothek der Benediktiner (fr.)
Salzburg
    Erzabtei St. Peter (fr.)
    Universitätsbibliothek (fr.)
Schlägl
    Prämonstratenserstift (fr.)

Schlierbach
    Bibliothek des Zisterzienserstifts (fr.)
Vienna
    Erzbischöfliches Priesterseminar (fr.)
    Jüdische Gemeinde
    Magistrat der Stadt (fr.)
    Mechitharisten-Congregation (formerly)
    Österreichische Nationalbibliothek [m]
    Unserer Lieben Frau zu den Schotten (Benedictine Abbey) (fr.)
    Wiener Stadt- und Landesarchiv (fr.)
Vorau
    Chorherrenstiftsbibliothek (fr.)
Wiener Neustadt
    Stadtarchiv
Zwettl
    Bibliothek des Zisterzienserstifts (fr.)

AZERBAIJAN
Baku
    Central Scientific Library of Azerbaijan National Academy of Sciences

BELGIUM
Brussels
    Bibliothèque royale de Belgique
    Paul Dahan (pr.) [s]
    Chaim Spiegel (pr.)
Louvain
    Katholieke Universiteit
    Université Catholique

BULGARIA
Sofia
    Centralen Darzaven Istoriceski archiv (fr.)

CANADA
Edmonton
    University of Alberta Library
Montreal
    Y. Elberg (deceased) (pr.) [m]
    McGill University
    D. Rome (deceased) (pr.)
Ottawa
    Andre Elbaz (pr.) [s] (now Montreal)
    Library and Archives Canada [m]

Toronto

Beth Tzedec Congregation
Eleazar Birnbaum (pr.)
F. Greenwood (pr.)
Ilan Madina (pr.)
Royal Ontario Museum
University of Toronto [s]

Czech Republic

Brno

Archiv mesta (fr.)
Statni okresni archiv

Ceske Budejovice

Jihoceska vedecka knihovna (formerly Krajska Knihovna)

Humpolec

Muzeum Aleše Hrdličky

Olomouc

Vědecká Knihovna
Zemský Archiv (fr.)

Prague

Archiv Prazskeho Hradu (fr.)
Narodni Knihovna České Republiky (National Library of the Czech Republic) [s]
Židovské Muzeum v Praze (Jewish Museum of Prague) [m]

Rajhrad

Benediktinské opatství (Benedictine Abbey) (fr.)

Denmark

Copenhagen

J. Keiser (pr.)
Det Kongelige Bibliothek [m]
J. Margolinsky (pr.)
Mosaiske Troessamfund (Jewish Community Library)
Moshe Levy's Synagogue

Egypt

Cairo

Ben-Ezra Synagogue
Karaite Synagogue [m]

Estonia

Tartu

University Library

FRANCE

Aix-en-Provence
    Bibliothèque Méjanes
Amiens
    Bibliothèque municipale
Arras
    Bibliothèque municipale
Avignon
    Archives départementales du Vaucluse
    Bibliothèque municipale
Besançon
    Bibliothèque municipale
Caen
    Bibliothèque municipale
Cambrai
    Bibliothèque municipale
Carcassonne
    Archives départementales de l'Aude
Carpentras
    Bibliothèque Inguimbertine
Cavaillon
    Musée Judeo-Comtadin
Chantilly
    Musée Condé
Colmar
    Archives départementales du Haut-Rhin
    Consistoire Israélite
Digne-les-Bains
    Archives départementales des Alpes de Haute Provence
Dijon
    Archives départementales de la Côte-d'Or
Draguignan
    Médiathèque communautaire (formerly Bibliothèque municipale)
Grenoble
    Bibliothèque municipale
Haguenau
    Joseph Bloch (pr.)
    Médiathèque
Laon
    Bibliothèque municipale (doc.)
Le Havre
    Bibliothèque municipale Armand Salacrou [s]
Le Mans
    Bibliothèque municipale

Lyon
  Bibliothèque municipale
  Musée Historique
Marseille
  Archives Communales
  Bibliothèque municipale
  Johann Hassoun (pr.)
  Odette Valabregue Wurzburger (deceased, pr.)
Melun
  Bibliothèque municipale
Metz
  Communauté Israelite
Montbeliard
  Bibliothèque municipale
Montbrison
  J. Bruel (pr.)
  La Diana, Societé historique et archéologique du Forez
Montigny-le-Bretonneux
  Archives départementales des Yvelines et de l'ancienne Seine-et-Oise
Montpellier
  Bibliothèque interuniversitaire
Nantes
  Archives départementales de Loire Atlantique
  Bibliothèque municipale
Nîmes
  Bibliothèque municipale [s]
Orléans
  Médiathèque
Paris
  Alliance Israélite Universelle [1]
  Archives nationales
  Dr. Bernheim (pr.)
  Bibliothèque de l'Arsenal
  Bibliothèque de la Compagnie des Prêtres de Saint Sulpice
  Bibliothèque Mazarine
  Bibliothèque nationale de France [v]
  Bibliothèque Sainte Geneviève
  Bibliothèque de la Sorbonne
  G. Epstein (pr.) [s]
  Paul Fenton (pr.)
  I. Goldstein (pr.)
  Institut de France
  Institut national des langues et civilisations orientales [s]
  V. Klagsbald (pr.) [m, f]
  Mr. Kugel (pr.)

E. M. Levi (pr.)
L. Loeb (pr.)
Jean Lubetzki (pr.)
E. Malet (Elmaliah) (pr.)
Avraham Malthete (pr.)
Z. Merenlander (pr.)
S. Metal (pr.)
J. N. Mosseri (pr., fr.) (see *Mosseri)
Musée Cluny
Eliane Roos (pr.)
A. Rudi (pr.)
Séminaire israélite de France [s]
Société des manuscrits des assureurs français
Michel Zarfati (pr.)

Perpignan
Bibliothèque municipale

Poitiers
Bibliothèque municipale

Reims
Bibliothèque de Reims – Bibliothèque Carnegie

Roanne
Médiathèque

Rouen
Bibliothèque municipale

Saint-Dié-des-Vosges
Bibliothèque municipale

Soissons
Bibliothèque municipale

Strasbourg
Bibliothèque nationale et universitaire [m]
M. A. Deutsch (pr.)

Toulouse
Bibliothèque interuniversitaire
Bibliothèque municipale

Tours
Bibliothèque municipale

GEORGIA

Tbilisi
Kekelidze Institute of the Manuscripts of the Georgian Academy of Sciences

GERMANY

Ahlen
Rosenberg family (pr.)

Amberg
Staatsarchiv (fr.)
Ansbach
Staatliche Bibliothek
Aschaffenburg
Hof- und Stiftsbibliothek(fr.)
Augsburg
Staats- und Stadtbibliothek (fr.)
Bad Homburg
Stadtarchiv (fr.)
Bamberg
Staatsarchiv (fr.)
Staatsbibliothek
Stadtarchiv (fr.)
Beckum
Stadtarchiv (fr.)
Berlin
Jüdische Gemeinde
Jüdisches Museum Berlin
Menk, Lars (pr., fr.)
Ethnologisches Museum (until 1999: Museum für Völkerkunde) (fr.)
Staatsbibliothek zu Berlin – Preussischer Kulturbesitz [1]
Bernkastel-Kues
St. Nikolaus Hospital
Bonn
Universitäts- und Landesbibliothek
Braunschweig
Landeskirchliches Archiv (fr.)
Landesmusuem für Geschichte und Volkstum
Stadtbibliothek
Butzbach
Stadtarchiv (fr.)
Coblenz
Landeshauptarchiv (fr.)
Coburg
Staatsarchiv (fr.)
Cologne
Historisches Archiv der Stadt (fr.)
Crailsheim
Jüdisches Museum (fr.)
Darmstadt
Universitäts- und Landesbibliothek [s]
Hessisches Staatsarchiv (fr.)
Dessau
Anhaltische Landesbucherei

Detmold
Nordrhein – Westfälisch Staatsarchiv (fr.)
Dillingen a. d. Donau
Fürstlich und gräflich Fugger'sches Familien- und Stiftungs-Archiv (fr.)
Studienbibiothek (fr.)
Donaueschingen
Fürstlich Fürstenbergische Hofbibliothek (fr.)
Dortmund
Stadtarchiv (fr.)
Museum für Kunst und Kulturgeschichte
Dresden
Bistum Dresden-Meissen (fr.)
Sächsische Landesbibliothek – Staats- und Universitätsbibliothek
Düsseldorf
Universitäts- und Landesbibliothek
Eichstätt
Universitätsbibliothek Eichstätt-Ingolstadt (fr., in the former Staats- und Bischöfliche Seminarbibliothek)
Erlangen
Universitätsbibliothek Erlangen-Nürnberg [s]
Erfurt
Evangelisches Ministerium
Frankfurt am Main
Institut für Stadtgeschichte (fr.)
Goethe Universität, Universitätsbibliothek Johann Christian Senckenberg [m]
Freiburg im Breisgau
Universitätsbibliothek
Friedberg
Stadtarchiv (fr.)
Fulda
Hochschul- und Landesbibliothek [m]
Gelnhausen
Stadtarchiv (fr.)
Giessen
Universitätsbibliothek (Bibliothek der Justus-Liebeg Hochschule)
Gotha
Universitäts- und Forschungsbibliothek Erfurt/Gotha
Göttingen
Niedersächsische Staats- und Universitätsbibliothek [s]
Halberstadt
Gleimhaus (fr.)
Halle
Bibliothek der Deutschen Morgenländischen Gesellschaft (fr.)
Universitäts- und Landesbibliothek

Hamburg
  Museum für Völkerkunde
  Staats- und Universitätsbibliothek [v]
Hanau
  Stadtarchiv (fr.)
Hannover
  Museum August Kestner
  Niedersächsisches Landesarchiv-Hauptstaatsarchiv
Harburg
  Fürstlich Oettingen- Wallerstein'sche Bibliothek [s]
Heidelberg
  Universitätsbibliothek
Hildesheim
  Dombibliothek (fr.)
  Stadtarchiv
  Städtisches Museum
Jena
  Thüringer Universitäts- und Landesbibliothek (s)
Karlsruhe
  Badische Landesbibliothek [s]
  Generallandesarchiv (fr.)
Kassel
  Landesbibliothek und Murhardsche Bibliothek
Kiel
  Universitätsbibliothek (fr.)
Kirchheim unter Teck
  Stadtarchiv (fr.)
Klausen
  Augustiner Chorherren (fr.)
Konstanz
  Stadtarchiv (fr.)
Krefeld
  Stadtarchiv
Landshut
  Staatsarchiv (fr.)
Leipzig
  Universitätsbibliothek [s, f]
Lübeck
  Bibliothek der Hansestadt
Mainz
  Bischöfliches Priesterseminars
  Gutenberg Museum (fr.)
  Israelitische Religionsgesellschaft

Jüdische Gemeinde
Universitätsbibliothek (fr.)
Wissenschaftliche Stadtbibliothek

Marburg
Hessisches Staatsarchiv (fr.)
Universitätsbibliothek (fr.)

Meiningen
Thüringisches Staatsarchiv (fr.)

Memmingen
Stadtbibliothek (fr.)

Metten
Benediktiner-Abtei Metten (fr.)

Munich
Bayerische Staatsbibliothek [m]
Bayerisches Hauptstaatsarchiv (fr.)
Staatsarchiv (fr.)
Universitätsbibliothek (fr.)

Münster
Westfälisches Landesmuseum für Kunst und Kulturgeschichte

Neuberg a.d. Donau
Staatsarchiv (fr.)
Stadtarchiv (fr.)

Neuss
Stadtarchiv (fr.)

Nuremberg
Germanisches Nationalmuseum
Landeskirchliches Archiv der Evangelisch-Lutherischen Kirche in Bayern
Staatsarchiv (fr.)
Stadtarchiv (fr.)
Stadtbibliothek [s]

Oldenburg
Landesbibliothek (fr.)

Paderborn
Erzbischöfliche Akademische Bibliothek

Pappenheim
Gräflich Pappenheim'sche Bibliothek

Petershausen
Benediktiner-Abtei (fr.)

Pommersfelden
Graf von Schönbornsche Schloßbibliothek (fr.)

Ravensburg
Stadtarchiv (fr.)

Regensburg
  Bischöfliches Zentralarchiv (fr.)
  Fürst Thurn und Taxis Hofbibliothek und Zentralarchiv (fr.)
Rostock
  Universitätsbibliothek [s]
Rottweil
  Stadtarchiv (fr.)
Schleswig
  Schleswig-Holsteinisches Landesarchiv (fr.)
Schwäbisch Hall
  Stadt- und Hospitalarchiv (fr.)
Schweinfurt
  Städtbücherei (fr.)
Siegen
  Stadtarchiv (fr.)
Speyer
  Landesarchiv (fr.)
Stuttgart
  Hauptstaatsarchiv (fr.)
  Württembergische Landesbibliothek [s]
  Württembergische Landesmuseum (fr.)
Trier
  Bischöfliches Priesterseminar (fr.)
  Stadtbibliothek (fr.)
Tübingen
  Universitätsbibliothek (fr.)
Wangen im Allgäu
  Stadtarchiv (fr.)
Warendorf
  Kreisarchiv (fr.)
Weimar
  Herzogin Anna Amalia Bibliothek
Wertheim
  Staatsarchiv (fr.)
Wetter
  Pfarrarchiv (fr.)
Wiesbaden
  Hessisches Hauptstaatsarchiv (fr.)
Wittenberg
  Stiftung Luthergedenkstätten in Sachsen-Anhalt
Wolfenbüttel
  Herzog August Bibliothek [s]
  Niedersächsisches Staatsarchiv (fr.)
Worms
  Jüdisches Museum 'Raschi Haus'

Würzburg
  Universitätsbibliothek (fr.)

GREECE
Athens
  Jewish Museum [s]
Patmos
  Monastery St. John Theologos

HUNGARY
Budapest
  Magyar Tudományos Akadémia (Hungarian Academy of Sciences) [v]
  Országos Rabbiképző – Zsidó Egyetem Könyvtár (Jewish Theological Seminary) [m]
  Orsźagos Széchényi Könyvtár (National Szechenyi Library)
Pésci
  Tudományegyetem Egyetemi Könyvtár (fr.)
Sopron
  Győr-Moson-Sopron Megye Soproni Levéltára (National Archives) (fr.)

INDIA
Cochin
  I. S. Hallegua (pr.)
  S. S. Koder (pr.)

IRELAND
Dublin
  Marsh's Library
  Chester Beatty Library
  Trinity College Library [s]

ITALY
Agrigento
  Archivio di Stato Sezione di Sciacca (fr.)
Alessandria
  Archivio di Stato (fr.)
  Biblioteca Civica (fr.)
  Comunità ebraica
Ancona
  Luca Ancarani (pr.)
  Biblioteca Comunale Luciano Benincasa
  Comunità ebraica [s]
Anzola dell'Emilia
  Archivio Parrocchiale
Arezzo
  Biblioteca del Seminario Vescovile (fr.)

Ascoli Piceno
  Archivio di Stato (fr.)
Badia di Cava
  Biblioteca Statale del Monumento Nazionale
Bagnara di Romagna
  Archivio Storico Comunale (fr.)
Bazzano
  Archivio Storico Comunale (fr.)
Bergamo
  Civica Biblioteca 'Angelo Mai'
Bobbio
  Archivi Storici Bobiensi (fr.)
Bologna
  Archivio del Dipartimento di Astronomia dell'Università (fr.)
  Archivio Generale Arcivescovile (fr.)
  Archivio di Stato (fr.)
  Archivio Parrocchiale di Colunga (fr.)
  Biblioteca della Camera di Commercio (fr.)
  Biblioteca Comunale dell'Archiginnasio
  Biblioteca del Pontificio Seminario Regionale (fr.)
  Biblioteca Universitaria [s]
  Chiesa di San Martino, Archivio Parrocchiale (fr.)
  Conservatorio 'G. B. Martini' (fr.)
  Emilio Ottolenghi (pr.)
Brindisi
  Biblioteca Arcivescovile 'Annibale de Leo'
Cadecoppi
  Archivio Parrocchiale (fr.)
Cagli
  Biblioteca Comunale (fr.)
Calvi dell'Umbria
  Archivio Storico Comunale (fr.)
Camerano
  Archivio Storico Comunale (fr.)
Campi Salentina
  Alfredo Calabrese (pr.)
Carpi
  Museo Civico (fr.)
Casale di Mezzano
  Archivio Parrocchiale (fr.)
Castel San Pietro
  Archivio Parrocchiale (fr.)
Catania
  Biblioteche riunite Civica e A. Ursino Recupero

Cento
Archivio Notarile (fr.)
Cesena
Archivio della Curia Vescovile (fr.)
Archivio di Stato (fr.)
Biblioteca Comunale Malatestiana
Chiari
Biblioteca Comunale (fr.)
Cittá di Castello
Archivio Notarile (fr.)
Corinaldo
Archivio Storico Comunale (fr.)
Correggio
Archivio Storico Comunale (fr.)
Cremona
Archivio della Curia Vescovile (fr.)
Archivio di Stato (fr.)
Archivio Parrocchiale di S. Agata (fr.)
Biblioteca Statale e Libreria Civica (fr.)
Ugo Gualazzini (fr.)
Crevalcore
Archivio Comunale (fr.)
Faenza
Archivio di Stato (fr.)
Fano
Archivio di Stato (fr.)
Archivio Storico Diocesano (fr.)
Chiesa di S. Giovanni Bosco – Archivio Parrocchiale (fr.)
Ferentino
Archivio Storico Comunale e Notarile (fr.)
Fermo
Archivio di Stato (fr.)
Archivio Storico Arcivescovile (fr.)
Ferrara
Archivio della Curia Arcivescovile (fr.)
Biblioteca Comunale Ariostea
Comunità ebraica [s]
Fiorano
Archivio Parrocchiale (fr.)
Archivio Storico Comunale (fr.)
Florence
Archivio di Stato (fr.)
Comunità ebraica
Biblioteca Marucelliana
Biblioteca Medicea Laurenziana [m]

Biblioteca Nazionale Centrale [s]
Biblioteca Riccardiana
Università degli Studi di Firenze
Ida Zatelli (pr., fr.)

Forlì
Archivio di Stato

Fossano
Biblioteca Civica

Fossombrone
Biblioteca Civica 'Benedetto Passionei' (fr.)

Frosinone
Archivio di Stato (fr.)

Genoa
Biblioteca Civica Berio
Biblioteca Franzoniana
Biblioteca Universitaria

Grizzana Morandi
Archivio Parrocchiale (fr.)

Grotta Ferrata
J. Corello (pr.)

Guastalla
Biblioteca Maldotti

Imola
Archivio della Curia Vescovile (fr.)
Archivio di Stato (fr.)
Archivio Parrocchiale di S. Prospero (fr.)
Archivio Storico Comunale (fr.)
Bibloteca Comunale

Jesi
Biblioteca Comunale Planettiana (fr.)

Latina
Archivio di Stato (fr.)

Livorno (Leghorn)
Talmud Tora [s]

Lodi
Archivio Storico Comunale (fr.)

Lucca
Archivio di Stato (fr.)

Lugo
Biblioteca Comunale (fr.)

Macerata
Archivio di Stato (fr.)
Biblioteca Comunale 'Mozzi-Borgetti'

Mantua
Archivio Storico Diocesano (fr.)

Biblioteca Teresiana (formerly Biblioteca Comunale)
Comunità ebraica [m]
Annibale Gallico (pr.)
Norsa family (formerly, pr.)
Messina
Federico Martino (pr., fr.)
Milan
Archivio di Stato (fr.)
Biblioteca Ambrosiana [m]
Biblioteca Nazionale Braidense [s]
Elia Boccara (pr.)
Modena
Archivio Capitolare di Modena (fr.)
Archivio della Curia Arcivescovile di Modena (fr.)
Archivio di Stato (fr.)
Archivio Storico Comunale (fr.)
Biblioteca Estense Universitaria
Comunità ebraica
Fondazione Collegio San Carlo
Monchio
Archivio Parrocchiale (fr.)
Mondolfo
Archivio Storico Comunale (fr.)
Montecassino
Archivio di Stato (fr.)
Montepulciano
Archivio Storico Comunale (fr.)
Monticelli
Archivio Parrocchiale (fr.)
Naples
Biblioteca Nazionale Vittorio Emanuele III [s]
Nonantola
Archivio Abbaziale (fr.)
Archivio Storico Comunale (fr.)
Norcia
Archivio Storico Comunale (fr.)
Novara
Archivio Storico Diocesano (fr.)
Padua
Biblioteca Capitolare (fr.)
Biblioteca Civica
Pontificia Biblioteca Antoniana (fr.)
Seminario Vescovile
Palermo
Archivio di Stato (fr.)

Biblioteca Centrale della Regione Siciliana
Biblioteca Comunale (fr.)
Parma
Archivio Storico Comunale (fr.)
Biblioteca Palatina [v]
Pavia
Archivio di Stato (fr.)
Biblioteca Universitaria
Collegio Ghislieri
Pavullo nel Frignano
Biblioteca Comunale (fr.)
Pergola
Archivio Storico Comunale (fr.)
Perugia
Archivio di Stato (fr.)
Biblioteca Universitaria (fr.)
Pesaro
Archivio della Curia Vescovile (fr.)
Archivio di Stato (fr.)
Piacenza
Biblioteca Comunale Passerini Landi
Piediluco
Archivio della Delegazione (fr.)
Pieve di Cento
Archivio Parrocchiale (fr.)
Archivio Storico Comunale (fr.)
Pisa
Biblioteca Universitaria
Comunità ebraica
Pitigliano
Archivio Comunale (fr.)
Comunità ebraica [s]
Pontremo
Archivio Notarile (fr.)
Ravenna
Archivio Arcivescovile (fr.)
Biblioteca Comunale Classense
Reggio Emilia
Archivio Capitolare (fr.)
Biblioteca Panizzi (formerly Biblioteca Comunale)
Rieti
Archivio di Stato (fr.)
Rimini
Archivio di Stato (fr.)

Biblioteca Civica Gambalunga (fr.)
Seminario Vescovile (fr.)
Rome
Accademia Nazionale dei Lincei e Corsiniana
Biblioteca Angelica [s]
Biblioteca Casanatense [m]
Biblioteca Nazionale Centrale di Roma [m]
Biblioteca Universitaria Alessandrina (fr.)
Collegio Rabbinico Italiano (Centro Bibliografico dell'Ebraismo Italiano) [m]
Comunità ebraica [s]
Giuseppe Pontecovo (pr., fr.)
Pontificio Istituto Biblico [s]
Giacomo Saban (pr.)
Abraham Sermoneta (pr.)
A. Tagliacozzo (pr., fr.)
V. Vivanti (pr., fr.)
Roncofreddo
Archivio Parrocchiale
Rovigo
Accademia dei Concordi [s]
Sabbioneta
Archivio Parrocchiale (fr.)
Maurizio Germingnasi (pr., fr.)
San Lorenzo in Campo
Archivio Storico Comunale (fr.)
San Rufino
Archivio Capitolare (fr.)
San Severino
Archivio Comunale (fr.)
Sant'Agata Bolognese
Archivio storico della Partecipanza Agraria (fr.)
Sant'Angelo in Vado
Archivio Storico Comunale (fr.)
Sant'Arcangelo di Romagna
Biblioteca Comunale (fr.)
Sant'Ippolito
Archivio Storico Comunale (fr.)
Sassari
Biblioteca Universitaria
Savona
Biblioteca Civica 'A. G. Barrili'
Biblioteca del Seminario Vescovile (fr.)
Siena
Biblioteca Comunale degli Intronati

Spilamberto
- Archivio Storico Comunale (fr.)

Spoleto
- Archivio di Stato (fr.)

Stroncone
- Archivio Storico Comunale (fr.)

Terni
- Archivio di Stato (fr.)
- Archivio della Cassa di Risparmio (fr.)
- Biblioteca Comunale

Trapani
- Biblioteca Comunale

Trieste
- Biblioteca Civica (fr.)

Turin
- Archivio delle tradizioni e del costume ebraici 'Benvenuto e Alessandro Terracini' [m]
- Biblioteca Nazionale Universitaria [s]
- Biblioteca Reale
- Comunità ebraica [s]

Udine
- Biblioteca Arcivescovile [s]

Urbania
- Archivio Storico Comunale (fr.)
- Biblioteca Comunale (fr.)

Urbino
- Biblioteca Universitaria (fr.)

Venice
- Biblioteca Nazionale Marciana
- Biblioteca del Seminario Patriarcale
- Comunità ebraica [s]
- Fondazione Scientifica Querini Stampalia

Vercelli
- Biblioteca del Seminario Vescovile

Verona
- Archivio di Stato
- Biblioteca Capitolare
- Biblioteca Civica [s]
- Biblioteca e Archivio della Comunità Israelitica
- Seminario Maggiore [s]

Viterbo
- Archivio di Stato (fr.)

Jordan

Amman
- Franciscan Monastery

Luxembourg

Luxembourg

Bibliothèque nationale

Morocco

Rabat

Institut des Hautes Etudes

Netherlands

Amsterdam

M. H. Gans (pr.) [s]

Joods Historisch Museum

S. Mayer (pr.)

Nederlands Israelietische Hoofdsynagoge

Portugees Israëlitisch Seminarium Ets Haim – Livraria Montezinos [m]

J. R. Ritman Library – Bibliotheca Philosophica Hermetica (defunct)

Universiteitsbibliotheek, Bibliotheca Rosenthaliana [1]

Deventer

Athenaeumbibliotheek

Ghent

Rijksuniversiteit

Groningen

Rijksuniversiteit

The Hague

Gemeentearchief van 's-Gravenhage (doc.)

G. W. A. Juynboll (pr.)

Koninklijkc Bibliotheek

Leeuwarden

N. Beem (pr.)

TRESOAR, the Friesland Historical and Literary Centre (formerly the Provinciale Bibliotheek van Friesland)

Leiden

W. Baars (pr.)

Universiteitsbibliotheek [m]

Maastricht

Rijksarchief in Limburg (fr.)

Utrecht

Bibliotheek der Rijksuniversiteit

New Zealand

Wellington

Victor Yehudah Gradowski (pr.)

Norway
Oslo
Martin Schøyen (pr.) [s]

Poland
Cracow
Biblioteka Czartoryskich
Uniwersytet Jagielloński (fr.)
Warsaw
Biblioteka Narodowa
Polska Akademia Nauk (fr.)
Uniwersytet Warszawski
Żydowski Instytut Historyczny [ŻIH] [v]
Wrocław
Biblioteka Uniwersytecka
Polska Akademia Nauk. Zakład Narodowy im. Ossolińskich

Portugal
Coimbra
Biblioteca Geral da Universidade
Évora
Biblioteca Pública
Lisbon
Arquivo Nacional da Torre do Tombo (fr.)
R. Bachmann (pr.)
Biblioteca Nacional de Portugal
Porto
Biblioteca Pública Municipal
Vila Viçosa
Biblioteca e Arquivo do Paço Ducal (fr.)

Romania
Cluj
Romanian Academy
Biblioteca Centrala Universitara

Russia
Moscow
Rossiiskaia Gosudarstvennaia Biblioteka (Russian State Library) [v]
Rossiiskii Gosudarstvennyi Voennyi Arkhiv (Russian State Military Archives) [m, f]
Rossiiskii Gosudarstvennyi Arkhiv Drevnikh Aktov (Russian State Archive of Early Acts)
Nizhni Novgorod
State Regional Universal Scientific Library (fr.)
Petrozavodsk
Prof. Zalman Kaufman (pr.)

St. Petersburg
Institut Vostochnik Rukopisi (Institute of Oriental Manuscripts of the Russian Academy of Sciences) [v]
St. Petersburg, Rossiyskaia Natsionalnaya Biblioteka (Russian National Library) [v]
Repin State Academic Institute of Fine Arts

Serbia
Belgrade
Jevrejski Istorijski Muzej

Slovenia
Ljubljana
Narodna in Univerzitetna Knjižnica (fr.)
Semeniska Knjižnica (fr.)
Maribor
Semeniska Knjižnica (fr.)
Novo Mesto
Franciscan Monastery (fr.)

South Africa
Cape Town
Jewish Museum
L. Mallnick (pr.)
National Library of South Africa

Spain
Barcelona
Archivo Capitular de la S. I. Catedral Basilica (doc.)
Archivo de la Corona de Aragón (doc.)
Archivo de la Iglesia de Santa Maria del Mar (doc.)
Biblioteca de Catalunya
Museo Federico Mares (fr.)
Burgos
Museo de Burgos
Cervera
Arxiu Històric Comarcal (fr.)
F. Dalmasis (pr.)
Cordova
Archivo Capitular de la Catedral (fr.)
Cuenca
Archivo de la Catedral (fr.)
Gerona
Arxiu Capitular de la Catedral (fr.)
Arxiu Diocesà (fr.)
Arxiu Històric (fr.)

Huesca
- Catedral (fr. and doc.)

Madrid
- Archivo Histórico Nacional
- Consejo Superior de Investigaciones Científicas, Instituto de Filología (formerly: Instituto Arias Montano)
- Biblioteca de la Fundacion 'Lazaro Galdiano'
- Biblioteca Nacional de España [s]
- Biblioteca del Palacio Real de Madrid
- Biblioteca de la Real Academia de la Historia
- Biblioteca de la Universidad Complutense [s]

Montserrat
- Abadia de Santa Maria [s]

Palma de Mallorca
- Archivo del Reino (doc.)

Pamplona
- Archivo Real y General de Navarra (fr., doc.)
- Catedral

Ripoll
- Monasterio de Santa Maria (fr.)

Salamanca
- Biblioteca de la Universidad

San Lorenzo del Escorial
- Real Biblioteca del Monasterio de El Escorial [m]

Sant Cugat del Valles
- Biblioteca San Francisco de Borja [s]
- Catedral (fr.)

Saragossa
- Archivo Histórico de Protocolos de Zaragoza (doc.)
- Teofilio Ayuso (pr., fr.)
- Cabildo Metropolitano

Seo de Urgel
- Arxiu Capitular (fr.)

Seville
- Biblioteca Capitular y Colombina

Tarragona
- Archivo Histórico de la Diputación Provincial de Tarragona (fr. doc.)
- Archivo y Biblioteca Capitulares [fr.]

Toledo
- Archivo y Biblioteca Capitulares (s)

Tudela
- Catedral (fr.)

Valencia
- Archivo del Reino (doc.)
- Casa Professa de la Compañía de Jesús

Valladolid
  Biblioteca Universitaria
Vic
  Museu Episcopal (fr.)

Sweden
Lund
  Universitetsbiblioteket
Stockholm
  Kungliga Biblioteket
Uppsala
  Universitetsbiblioteket [s]

Switzerland
Basel
  Jüdische Gemeinde
  Öffentliche Bibliothek der Universität
Bern
  Bürgerbibliothek [s]
  Lauer Family (pr.)
  K. Marti (pr.)
  Schweizerische Landesbibliothek
Burgdorf
  Kirche (fr.)
Geneva
  Bibliothèque centrale Juive
  Bibliothèque publique et universitaire [s]
Graubünden
  Staatsarchiv (fr.)
Hergiswil
  L. Altmann (pr.)
Lausanne
  I. Elisha (Lichaa) (pr.)
Lucerne
  Staatsarchiv (fr.)
Montana
  S. Segre Amar (pr.) [s] (now in the Bibl. Publique in Geneva)
Porrentruy
  Archives de la Bourgeoisie (fr.)
St. Gallen
  Stadtbibliothek (fr.)
  Stiftsarchiv (fr.)
Schaffhausen
  Staatsarchiv des Kantons (fr.)
  Stadtbibliothek

Solothurn
  Staatsarchiv des Kantons Solothurn (fr.)
  Zentralbibliothek (fr.)
Winterthur
  Stadtbibliothek
Zurich
  Braginsky Collection (pr. [m])
  D. Jeselsohn (pr.)
  Staatsarchiv des Kantons Zürich (fr.)
  H. Wohlmann (pr.)
  Zentralbibliothek [m]

Tunisia
Djerba
  Rabbi B. Saadon (pr.)

Turkey
Istanbul
  Jewish Community
  Topkapi Sarayi Müzesi

Ukraine
Kiev
  Vernadsky National Library [m, f]
Simferopol
  Ethnographic Museum

United Kingdom
Aberdeen
  University of Aberdeen, King's College Library and Historic Collections
Birmingham
  University of Birmingham (fr.)
Bristol
  City Museum and Art Gallery (fr.)
Cambridge
  Cambridge University Library [v]
  Cambridge University Faculty of Oriental Studies
  Christ's College Library
  Clare College
  Emmanuel College Library
  Fitzwilliam Museum
  Girton College Library [s]
  Gonville & Caius College Library
  Pembroke College Library

St. John's College Library
J. Teicher (pr.)
Trinity College Library [m, f]
Westminster College Library (formerly) [s and fr.]
Edinburgh
National Library of Scotland
University of Edinburgh
Glasgow
Glasgow University Library
Holkham
Earl of Leicester (formerly) (pr.)
Leeds
University of Leeds [m]
Letchworth (formerly)
D. S. Sassoon (pr.) [v]
Liverpool
Athenaeum Library
Merseyside County Museum
University of Liverpool
London
C. Abramski (deceased, pr.)
Sholem Asch (deceased, pr.)
Beth Din & Beth Hamidrash Library [s]
A. Bornstein (pr.)
British Library [v]
Meir Brown (pr.)
S. Dzialowski (pr.)
J. Fraenkel (pr.)
Yehudah Goldenberg (pr.)
C. Gradenwitz (pr.)
S. A. Halpern (pr.)
Hirschler-Dzialowski (bookdealers)
Jewish Museum
Jews' College (School of Jewish Studies) [s]
Lambeth Palace Library
Leo Baeck College
Montefiore Library [1]
Joshua Podro (pr.)
Sonia Rosenberg (deceased, pr.)
D. Sofer (pr.) [m]
E. Stern (pr.)
University College [s]
Valmadonna Trust Library [m]
Victoria and Albert Museum
D. Weinmann (pr.)

Wellcome Institute for the History of Medicine [s]
Westminster Abbey

Manchester
Chetham's Library
John Rylands University Library [v]

Oxford
Balliol College
Bodleian Library [v]
Christ Church College Library [s]
Corpus Christi College Library
Jesus College Library
Keble College Library
Magdalen College Library (doc.)
Merton College Library
Oriel College Library
Pusey House Library
St. John's College Library
Worcester College Library

Rochdale
Alan Padwell (pr.)

Salford
R. Shasha (pr.)

Warminster
Marquess of Bath (formerly) (pr.)

Westcliff-on-Sea
Asher Azulay (pr.)

United States of America

Albany, N.Y.
State University of New York

Ann Arbor, Mich.
University of Michigan

Atlanta, Ga.
Emory University

Baltimore, Md.
Johns Hopkins University
Walters Art Museum

Berkeley, Calif.
Walter Fischl (pr.)
University of California (including former Magnes Museum) [s]

Bethlehem, Pa.
R. S. Rivlin (pr.)

Bethesda, Md.
National Library of Medicine

Birmingham, Ala.
University of Alabama, Reynolds Historical Library
Boca Raton, Fla.
Richard D. Levy (pr.)
Boston, Mass.
Boston Medical Library [s]
Buffalo, N.Y.
Shay Mintz (pr.)
Cambridge, Mass.
Harvard University [m]
Charlottesville, Va.
M. Colker (pr.)
Chicago, Ill.
Robert Hartman (pr.)
B. Kopstein (pr.)
M. Kopstein (pr.)
Newberry Library
Spertus College [s]
University of Chicago Library
University of Chicago Oriental Institute Museum
Morton B. Weiss Museum of Judaica
Cincinnati, Ohio
Hebrew Union College Library [1]
Cleveland, Ohio
Reuven Dessler (pr.)
Costa Mesa, Calif.
E. Wright (pr.)
Dallas, Texas
Southern Methodist University
Detroit, Mich.
Charles E. Feinberg (deceased, pr.)
East Lansing, Mich.
Michigan State University
Elizabeth, N.J.
Neil Rosenstein (pr.)
Haverford, Pa.
Haverford College [s]
Ithaca, N.Y.
Cornell University [s]
Lakewood, N.J.
Zev Ausch (pr.)
Los Angeles, Calif.
Jay Bisno (pr., fr.)
Lorenzo Tedesco (pr.)

Steve Weiss (pr.)
University of California [m]

Madison, Wis.
University of Wisconsin

Milwaukee, Wis.
Concordia University Library

Monsey, N.Y.
W. Loewy (pr.)

New Haven, Conn.
Yale University Library [m]

New York, N.Y.
American Bible Society Library
Biderman (pr.)
Chassidei Chabad Ohel Yosef Yitzchak Lubavitch Library [m, f]
Columbia University, Butler Library [v]
B. Goodwin (pr.)
W. Gross (pr.)
Hebrew Union College – Jewish Institute of Religion [m]
Hispanic Society of America
L. Jeselsohn (deceased, pr.)
Jewish Theological Seminary of America [v]
Simcha Leibovitz (pr.)
Leo Baeck Institute [s]
Dr. Alfred Moldovan (pr.) [s]
Benjamin Nathan (pr.)
New York Public Library [m]
New York University [m]
Pierpont Morgan Library
Union Theological Seminary
Yeshiva University [m]
YIVO Institute for Jewish Research [m]
B. Zucker (pr.)

Newton Center, Mass.
Hebrew College [s]

Orlando, Fla.
Van Kampen Collection

Palo Alto, Calif.
L. V. Berman (deceased, pr.)

Philadelphia, Pa.
Free Library of Philadelphia
Library Company of Philadelphia
S. A. Marks (pr.)
University of Pennsylvania Library (fr.)
University of Pennsylvania, Center for Advanced Judaic Studies [m]

Princeton, N.J.
Princeton University, Scheide Library
Reno, Nev.
Nevada Museum of Art
Richmond, Va.
B. A. Golden (pr.)
Rochester, N.Y.
A. J. Karp (deceased, pr.) [s]
St. Louis, Mo.
Washington University Libraries
San Francisco, Calif.
California State Library, Sutro Branch [m]
San Marino, Calif.
Henry E. Huntington Library
Silver Spring, Md.
Manfred and Anne Lehmann Foundation [l]
Skokie, Ill.
Hebrew Theological College [s]
Waltham, Mass.
American Jewish Historical Society
Brandeis University Library
Washington, D.C.
Library of Congress [m, f]
Smithsonian Institute, Freer Gallery (fr.)

VATICAN
Vatican City
Biblioteca Apostolica Vaticana [l]

ISRAEL
Most of the following are private collections.

אלעד
אבישי נקש
אמונים
יעקב בוארון
אפרת
דוד כנפו
אשדוד
אליעזר ויספיש
יואב פנחס הלוי
באר־שבע
קייס אברהם
נסים ויצמן
בית־נקופה
אתי קפלן
בית־שאן
יהושע חי שמעון
בית־שמש
י׳ שור
בני־ברק
נחום ברנהולץ
אהרן ג׳ימאני
גלוסקינוס
יוסף וולרשטיינר [s]
הרב מזוז
צמח מזוז
מכון תשא
ישראל מרגלית
אברהם עדס

מנחם פרידמן
פרייס
שמעון צאלח
ישראל קלפהולץ
שלמה עמרם קרח
ברקת (מושב)
משה מעטוף
גבעת־יערים
משה עוזרי
גבעת־שמואל
דוד בן נעים
עמוס רובין
רפאל שטרן
גבעתיים
א׳ שיל״ת
הזורע
אסתר לביד
הרצלייה
מנחם צוברי
משה רוזנברג
חולון
אלי זיתוני [s]
יהודה יצחק הלוי
יהודה לוי נחום (מפעל חשיפת גנזי תימן) [m]
יפת בן אברהם צדקה
חולתה
ידידיה פלס
חיפה
אוניברסיטה [s]
קייס ברוך אליאס
אליהו בן אליהו
נפתלי ליפשיץ
רפי סיאנו
ז׳ רבינוביץ
חיים רוזנפלד
ד״ר יוסף שיטרית
חשמונאים
מנצור צאלח חבאני
עזריאל צדוק
טבריה
בית כנסת סניור
יבנה
לאה כהן
יסוד המעלה
אליהו צפורה

יפעת
מאיר איילי
ירושלים
שלמה אברהמס [s]
אגף העתיקות
שלמה זלמן אוירבך
בנימין אונגר
יהודה אזולאי
הינדה איגר
איילון
נחמיה אלוני (נרכש על־ידי בית הספרים) [m]
לוי אלשיך
אליהו אריאלי
יוסי אסודרי
שלמה ארגוב
נפתלי באר
הרב יוסף בוקסבוים [f]
נחמן בורנשטיין
ישעיה ביק
בית כנסת אגודה (רחוב השל״ה)
בית כנסת אחוה (זיכרון משה)
בית כנסת בית אברהם (שכונת משכנות)
בית כנסת הגר״א (שכונת קטמון)
בית כנסת הגר״א (שערי חסד)
יוסף בלום
גרשון בן־אורן
זאב בן חיים
משה חיים בן מלכא
ויקטור בן נעים
רפאל בן סמחון
מאיר בניהו [v]
אורית ברזילאי
דניאל גוטליב
זאב גוטליב
מרדכי צבי גויטיין
עזרא פ׳ גורדסקי
גליק
גרייבסקי
אברהם דוד
דינוביץ
האקדמיה ללשון העברית
הארכיון העירוני
הארכיון הציוני
עזרא הדאיה
הוצאת תפארת מאיר

יהודה הורוביץ
החברה ההיסטורית הישראלית
היכל שלמה [m] (נמכר)
דב הכהן [s]
יחיאל הלוי
יעקב הלל [f]
מזל הללי
מלילה הלנר
מנחם ע׳ הרטום [s]
ישראל הרצברג
מרדכי גימפל וואלאך
גורג׳ ווייל
משה ויטל
שמואל וינגרטן
שמעון ויס
בנימין וכסלר
אליעזר ולדמן
שאול זיו
צפורה חוברה
חביב חמווי
א׳ חן [s]
יוסף טובי [m]
אסתר טיכו
יד הרב הרצוג
יד ל׳ א׳ מאיר
בית יורה
יהושע יעקבוביץ
שמחה יעקוביאן (אהרן)
ישיבת מסילת תורה
ישיבת פורת יוסף
חיים כהן
עזרא כהן
כולל חב״ד
מ׳ לבנטל
יוסף לוי
אברהם לורברבוים
יהושע ליבוביץ
בצלאל לנדאו
ליאדו
איון מאיר
ישראל מהלמן [m]
מוזיאון ישראל [m]
מוסאיוף [m] (נרכש על־ידי אוניברסיטת בר־אילן)
מוסד הרב קוק [l]
יוסף מוסקוביץ
עיזבון ד״ר א״מ מזיא [s] (נמכר)
שמעון מזרחי
יוסף מיוחס
פנינה מייזליש
משפחת מינא
ברי מינדל
מכון בן־צבי [l]
מכון ירושלים [f]
המכון לחקר יהדות איטליה [s]
מכון שוקן [m]
צבי מלאכי
מרדכי מלכה
רחמים מלמד־כהן
יוסף מלקמן
ראובן מס
מרגליות
מרכז זלמן שז״ר
ש׳ מרצבך
הרב אליהו מרציאנו, מכון הרש״ם [s]
אנדרה נהר
פנינה נוה־לויזון
מנשה ניסן
אורי סאם
גיורא סולר
יוסף סוקר (סקורצקי)
הרב סטבסקי
חוה סלומון
יצחק ורחל סער
שמואל ספראי
מאיר עבוד
משה עוזירי
יחיא עומיסי
חביב עלון
עיזבון זוסיא עפרון
יוסף פאור [s]
יעקב פולק
מנחם פלדמן [m]
חיים י׳ פלס
יצחק פלר
שאול פנט
נורית פסטרנק (נחמיאס)
פקטר
מדלין פרי
ש׳ צוברי
הרב יוסף קאפח [m] (נמכר)

שמעון קאפח
יחיאל קארה
דניאל קארפי
יהודה אריה קלוזנר
משה קליינרמן
מנשה חי קפלן
מיכאל קרופ [v]
משה גדליה ראטה
חיים רבינוביץ
י״ל רבינוביץ
ש׳ רוזנטל
עזרא רחמני
משפחת ריבלין (לשעבר)
ברכה ריבלין
יצחק רייך
רפאל רייכמן
שמעון ריינר
ב׳ ריצ׳לר
רפאלזון
רקח
שמעון שוורצפוקס
ספריית האדמו״ר מסטולין קרלין,
הרב שוחט [m]
דוד שונאק [s]
דוד ומרים שטיינר
שמעון שטמפפר
רוני שטרקשל [s]
חיים שיבי
יעקב שיבי
יוסף שיינברגר
תמר שיק
ציון שמואלי
שמעון שרוני
דוד תורג׳מן
יוסף תורג׳מן
ישעיה תשבי
כוכב יעקב
ניקול רוסמן
כפר אתא
אלדו אוטולנגי
כפר יונה
רחמים גרידיש
משה חג׳ג׳
כפר סבא
יוסף וורמסר ואחיו
יעיש כ׳ברה
לוד
שלמה כנפו
מבשרת ציון
מגנזי יהודה בן שלמה (סלימן) בדיחי [s]
אליהו הוניג
טלי דוידוף וינר
יואב חובב
מעלה אדומים
דוד בוניס [s]
ירון בן נאה [s]
נבטים
א׳ דוד
א״מ דוד
מ׳ נחמיה
נהרייה
אוסף מנחם וסעידה יעקב [m]
נתיבות
הרב יחזקאל מזוז
רפאל כציר צבאן
עומר
יוסף גז
עין הנציב
שלום איילי
עין חרוד
ישראל כהן
עפרה
יעקב פריד
ערד
רבקה דניאל
פתח־תקווה
גרדה הירש
אסתר מצגר
י״ש שפיגל
צפת
נ׳ אלבז
ארכיון ברשד–צביאלי
דוד וידובסקי
רפאל זילברמן
רוך רקובסקי
קיראון
יוסף הירש
קריית־אונו
פרטי

קריית־ארבע
ישׂשכר יעקבסון
קריית־אתא
עיזבון דוד בנימין
רפאל כהן
קריית־חיים
אורי זהבי
ראש העין
עזרא עטרי
שלום צוברי
שלמה צדוק צפר
ראשון לציון
יהודה ויס
נחום קוזי
רחובות
מנחם צברי
רמלה
הרב יחיאל אבוחצירא
הרב יוסף אלגמיל [s]
הקהילה הקראית בישראל [m]
רמת־גן
אוניברסיטת בר־אילן [m]
ידין דוויק
ישראל מרגלית
ישראל פלס
רעננה
יגאל אלמגור
יחיאל בוסי
שדה־אליהו
ש׳ אבריאל
שדה־בוקר
הצריף של בן־גוריון

שוקדה
א׳ יפרח
שכם
בית הכנסת של עדת השומרונים [s]
הכהן הגדול [s]
צדוק בן אבישע הכהן
תל־אביב
עובדיה אבוהב
יצחק אבוחצירא
בלה ומשה אביר
אגודת הסופרים העברים במדינת ישראל
אויערבך
באומינגר
בית הכנסת יבנה
דוד בן עמי
יעקב בסן
חיים גמליאל
ביל גרוס [m]
רצון הלוי [m]
ש׳ וסרצוג
א׳ חן
חפץ
גבריאל כהן
דוד מויאל
צפורה נהוראי [m]
ספרייה עירונית [m]
אברהם מרדכי פירון
אסתר רובין
יהודה רצהבי
שוואגר
יצחק שטיגליץ [m]
צבי שלזינגר

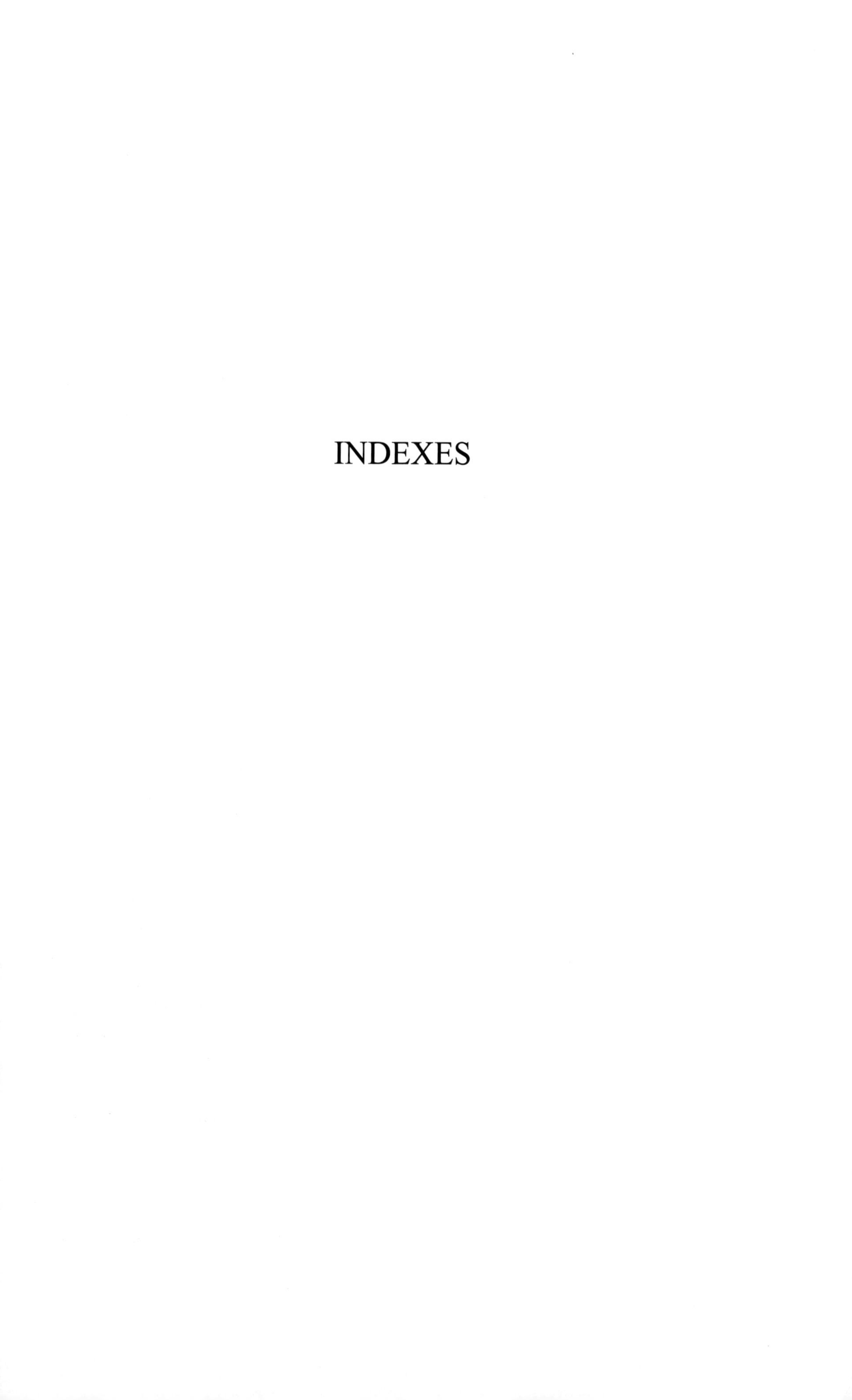

INDEXES

INDEX OF INDIVIDUAL MANUSCRIPTS MENTIONED IN THE GUIDE

The manuscript are listed by their present call-numbers. Page numbers are printed in italics.

Aberdeen, University of Aberdeen, King's College Library and Historic Collections
MS 23 *13 268*

Amsterdam, M. H. Gans Collection
unnumbered *310*

Amsterdam, Nederlands-Israelietische Hoofdsynagoge
Inv. no. 126 *86*

Amsterdam, Portugees Israelietisch Seminarium Ets Haim – Livraria Montezinos
HS EH 47 A 10 *251*
HS EH 47 A 19 *20*
HS EH 47 A 26 *262 264*
HS EH 47 B 1 *264*
HS EH 47 B 4 *108*
HS EH 47 B 7 *264*
HS EH 47 B 30 *264*
HS EH 47 C 3 *246*
HS EH 47 C 5 *265*
HS EH 47 C 10 *265*
HS EH 47 C 14 *262*
HS EH 47 C 25 *255*
HS EH 47 C 30–31 *282*
HS EH 47 C 33 *264*
HS EH 47 C 36 *242*
HS EH 47 C 44 *108 182*
HS EH 47 C 48 *116*
HS EH 47 D 15 *262*
HS EH 47 D 20 *138 294*
HS EH 47 D 38 *182*
HS EH 47 E 1 or E 20 *285*
HS EH 47 E 24 *285 295*
HS EH 48 C 16 *256*
HS EH 48 D 36 *256*
HS EH 48 E 16 *256*
HS EH 48 E 27 *256*
HS EH 49 A 8 *256*
HS EH 49 B 19 *256*

Amsterdam, J. R. Ritman Library (formerly)
BPH 406 *310*

Amsterdam, Universiteitsbibliotheek, Bibliotheca Rosenthaliana
Ros. 2 *264*
Ros. 3 *242*
Ros. 5 *282*
Ros. 8 *241*
Ros. 9 *241*
Ros. 12 *241*
Ros. 14 *310*
Ros. 20 *283*
Ros. 27 *241*
Ros. 28,1 *242*
Ros. 40 *310*
Ros. 42 *310*
Ros. 54 *242*
Ros. 72 *176*
Ros. 82 *108*
Ros. 108 *310*
Ros. 114 *264*
Ros. 116 *241*
Ros. 120 *310*
Ros. 125 *282*
Ros. 129 *310*
Ros. 157 *282*
Ros. 159 *241*
Ros. 172 *264 310*
Ros. 173 *242 264 283 295*
Ros. 175 *310*
Ros. 181 *310*
Ros. 182 *310*
Ros. 198 *282*
Ros. 205 *310*
Ros. 213 *282*
Ros. 214 *310*
Ros. 216 *310*
Ros. 226 *112*
Ros. 236 *205*
Ros. 263 *310*
Ros. 270 *264*
Ros. 281 *262*

Ros. 282 *283*
Ros. 311 *242*
Ros. 312 *98*
Ros. 321 *310*
Ros. 327 *242*
Ros. 345 *283*
Ros. 353 *241*
Ros. 377 *264*
Ros. 421 *241*
Ros. 424 *310*
Ros. 430 *283*
Ros. 432 *310*
Ros. 453 *310*
Ros. 465 *112*
Ros. 469 *63 282*
Ros. 519 *241*
Ros. 520 *283*
Ros. 552 *242*
Ros. 576 *242*
Ros. 592 *310*
Ros. 596 *283*
Ros. 597 *283*
Ros. 609 *67*
Ros. 682 *76*
Ros. PL A–14 *262*
Ros. PL B–5 *262*
Ros. PL B–6 *241*
Ros. PL B–15 *255*
Ros. PL B–35 *310*
Ros. PL B–52 *262*
Ros. PL B–73 *262*
Ros. PL B–75? *283*
Ros. PL C–20 *112*
Ros. PL. C–22 *112*

Arras, Bibliothèque municipale
560 *21 272*
969 *21*

Augsburg, Staats- und Stadtbibliothek
4° Ink. 256 *23*
Cod. fol. 68 *23*

Avignon, Bibliothèque municipale
5 *23*
7 *23*
8 *23*
1928 *23*
2336 *23*
3856 *23*

Barcelona, Biblioteca de Cataluña
MS 2595 *26*
MS 3090 *205*

Basel, Öffentliche Bibliothek der Universität
AN IV 25 *273*
Frey-Gryn. III 20 *273*
R 11 *273*

Berlin, Jewish Museum
VII.5.262 *284*
VII.5.292 *284*
VII.5.293 *284*
VII.5.324 *284*

Berlin, Staatsbibliothek zu Berlin – Preussischer Kulturbesitz
Ham. 80 *90 138 270 307*
Ham. 81 *90*
Ham. 235 *90*
Ham. 288 *90*
Ham. 547 *90*
Ham. 687 *90*
Or. 2° 1–4 *185 268*
Or. 2° 5–7 *277*
Or. 2° 8 *277*
Or. 2° 9 *277*
Or. 2° 14 *215*
Or. 2° 133 *31*
Or. 2° 134 *31*
Or. 2° 380 *31*
Or. 2° 381 *31*
Or. 2° 383 *122*
Or. 2° 567 *239*
Or. 2° 585 *280*
Or. 2° 702 *38*
Or. 2° 1055 *205*
Or. 2° 1056 *103*
Or. 2° 1058 *263*
Or. 2° 1059 *263*
Or. 2° 1210 *31 66 268*
Or. 2° 1210–1224 *66 175*
Or. 2° 1211 *31 268*
Or. 2° 1212 *277*
Or. 2° 1213 *277*

Or. 2° 1214 *277*
Or. 2° 1215 *31*
Or. 2° 1216 *31*
Or. 2° 1217 *31*
Or. 2° 1218 *31*
Or. 2° 1220 *66*
Or. 2° 1264 *240 251*
Or. 2° 1267 *175*
Or. 2° 1342 *203*
Or. 2° 1343 *203*
Or. 2° 1387 *34 114*
Or. 2° 1388 *34 114*
Or. 2° 1618 *145 200 206 258*
Or. 2° 2193 *94*
Or. 2° 3360 *31*
Or. 4°1 *277*
Or. 4° 9 *277*
Or. 4° 290 *102*
Or. 4° 291 *102*
Or. 4° 292 *102*
Or. 4° 308 *122*
Or. 4° 353–357 *175*
Or. 4° 521 *240*
Or. 4° 543 *239*
Or. 4° 544 *239*
Or. 4° 545 *239*
Or. 4° 553 *115*
Or. 4° 678–700 *175*
Or. 4° 685 *66*
Or. 4° 691 *241*
Or. 4° 694 *241*
Or. 4° 696 *241*
Or. 4° 747 *265*
Or. 4° 823 *95 202*
Or. 4° 825 *95*
Or. 4° 828 *31*
Or. 4° 830 *31*
Or. 4° 834 *205*
Or. 4° 835 *261*
Or. 4° 836 *205*
Or. 8° 23 *206*
Or. 8° 147 *66*
Or. 8° 148 *66*
Or. 8° 243 *285*
Or. 8° 244 *287*
Or. 8° 257 *31*
Or. 8° 332 *239*
Or. 8° 333 *200*
Or. 8° 353–357 *175*
Or. 8° 396 *200 259*
Or. 8° 459 *206*
Or. 8° 513 *284*
Or. 8° 518 *31*
Or. 8° 538 *259*
Or. 8° 539 *200 259*
Or. 8° 1387 *34*
Or. 8° 1388 *34*
Or. 8° 1558 *75*
Or. 8° 2409 *75*
Or. 8° 2414 *75*
Phillipps 1392 *138 174 294*

Berne, Burgerbibliothek
Cod. 92 *268*
Cod. 343 *273*

Besançon, Bibliothèque municipale
2 *280*

Bologna, Biblioteca Universitaria
2198 *276*
2201 *276*
2206 *276*
2208–9 *276*
2559 *37*
2950 *276*
3570I *276*
3570II *276*
3571 *276*
3574H *137*
3574L *139*
4100 *139*

Bonn, Universitäts- und Landesbibliothek
So 34–42 *37*
So 120 *37*
So 183 *37*
So 243 *37*
So 284 *37*

Breslau, Jüdisch-theologisches Seminar
178 *111*

Brussels, Paul Dahan
15 *300*

Budapest, Hungarian Academy of Sciences
A 18 *130*
A 50 *110 214*
A 61 *252*
A 77 *110*
A 140 *59*
A 237 *259*
A 240 *260*
A 271 *294*
A 285 *294*
A 332 *166*
A 369 *130*
A 379 *130*
A 384 *214*
A 422 *110*
A 423 *240*
A 457 *258*
A 520 *308*
A 523 *31*
A 586 *96*

Budapest, Jewish Theological Seminary
MS K 40 *181*
MS K 52 *77*
MS K 117 *77*
MS K 253 *129*

Budapest, Országos Széchényi Könyvtár
Fol. Hebr. 1 *43*
Fol. Hebr. 4 *43*
Fol. Hebr. 5 *43*
Fol. Hebr. 6 *43*
Qu. Hebr. 3 *43*
Qu. Hebr. 4 *43*

Cambridge, Emmanuel College
I.I.5.7 *34 267*

Cambridge, Gonville and Caius College
404/625 *267*

Cambridge, St. John's College
A 1 *267*
A 2 *267*

Cambridge, Trinity College
F. 12. 2 *307*
F. 12. 17 *307*
F. 12. 32 *240*
F. 12. 33 *115*
F. 12. 70–71 *37 260 273*
F. 12. 153 *307*
F. 18. 22–24 *287*
F. 18. 37 *307*
F. 18. 44 *307*
F. 18. 47 *307*
R. 8. 6 *267*
R. 8. 35 *267*

Cambridge, University Library
Add. 383 *59*
Add. 383,3 *59*
Add. 397 *59*
Add. 403 *59*
Add. 404 *59*
Add. 445–450 *122*
Add. 464–560 *122*
Add. 468 *59*
Add. 470.1 *129*
Add. 561 *286*
Add. 626 *287*
Add. 633 *285*
Add. 636 *59*
Add. 640 *286*
Add. 652 *225*
Add. 658 *286*
Add. 661 *285*
Add. 664 *286*
Add. 674 *225*
Add. 1015,1 *264*
Add. 1019 *35*
Add. 1020 *35*
Add. 1021 *35*
Add. 1023 *260*
Add. 1051 *258*
Add. 1052 *258*
Add. 1169 *24*
Add. 1170 *24*
Add. 1178 *24*
Add. 1179 *24*
Add. 1180 *24*
Add. 1180.1 *24*
Add. 1181 *24*
Add. 1183 *24*
Add. 1185.1 *24*

Add. 1186 *24*
Add. 1187 *24*
Add. 1189 *24*
Add. 1191 *24*
Add. 1193 *259*
Add. 1195 *259*
Add. 1196 *260*
Add. 1197 *259*
Add. 1494 *35*
Add. 1496 *108 252*
Add. 1497 *249*
Add. 1498 *251*
Add. 1499 *250*
Add. 1500 *250*
Add. 1501 *249*
Add. 1502 *248*
Add. 1503 *252*
Add. 1505 *249*
Add. 1506 *252*
Add. 1507 *252*
Add. 1508 *251*
Add. 1509 *249*
Add. 1510 *249*
Add. 1511 *250*
Add. 1512 *248*
Add. 1513 *249*
Add. 1514 *250*
Add. 1515 *249*
Add. 1516 *248*
Add. 1517 *249*
Add. 1518 *248*
Add. 1519 *248*
Add. 1520 *250*
Add. 1527 *263*
Add. 1527,3 *248*
Add. 1562 *35*
Add. 1563 *35*
Add. 1564 *35*
Add. 1565 *35 307*
Add. 1566 *35*
Add. 1567 *35*
Add. 1568 *35*
Add. 1735 *284*
Add. 1741 *250*
Add. 1746 *248*
Add. 1747 *250*
Add. 1751 *95*
Add. 1828 *240*
Add. 1829 *240*
Add. 1830 *240*
Add. 1831 *240*
Add. 1833 *240*
Add. 1835 *240*
Add. 1870 *249*
Add. 2664 *264*
Add. 3404–3407 *150*
Dd.10.68 *44*
Doc. 3780–3792 *176*
Ee.5.8 *267*
Ee.5.9 *267*
Ee.5.10 *267*
Mm.5.27 *267*
Or. 233 *150*
Or. 549–558 *179*
Or. 785 *211*
Or. 786 *88 211*
Or. 787 *211 248*
Or. 788 *211*
Or. 789 *211*
Or. 790 *211 248*
Or. 791 *211 248*
Or. 792 *211 248*
Or. 793 *211 248*
Or. 794 *211*
Or. 795 *211 241*
Or. 796 *211 240*
Or. 797 *211 240*
Or. 798 *211 240*
Or. 799 *211 240*
Or. 800 *211 240*
Or. 801 *211*
Or. 802 *211 251*
Or. 803 *20*
Or. 804 *205 211 240*
Or. 805 *211*
Or. 1080 *179*
Or. 1099 *263*
Or. 1102 *121 263*
Or. 2116 *13*
Or. 2240–2241 *296*
Or. 2242 *298*
Or. 2243 *297*
Or. 2244 *299*
Or. 2245 *297*
Or. 2246 *297*
T–S Arabic 51–54 *96*

T–S Misc. 34 *229*
T–S Misc. 35 *124*
T–S Misc. 36 *124*
T–S NS 172 *94*

Cambridge (Mass.), Harvard University
Heb. 20 *75*
Heb. 35 *75*
Heb. 36 *75 294*
Heb. 37 *75*
Heb. 38 *75*
Heb. 39 *75*
Heb. 40 *232 294*
Heb. 41 *232*
Heb. 42 *75 294*
Heb. 43 *75*
Heb. 44 *75*
Heb. 45 *75*
Heb. 46 *75*
Heb. 47 *75*
Heb. 48 *75*
Heb. 49 *75*
Heb. 50 *75*
Heb. 51 *75*
Heb. 52 *75 175*
Heb. 53 *75*
Heb. 54 *75*
Heb. 55 *75 119*
Heb. 57 *75*
Heb. 58 *75 103*
Heb. 59 *75*
Heb. 60 *75*
Heb. 61 *75 200*
Heb. 62 *75 103 145 251*
Heb. 63 *75*
Heb. 64 *75 200*
Heb. 65 *75*
Heb. 66 *75*

Cape Town, National Library of South Africa
6.b.i *50*
48.b.2 *50*

Cesena, Biblioteca Comunale Malatestiana
Plut. sin XXVIII.3 *276*
Plut. sin XXIX.1 *276*
Plut. sin XXIX.2 *276*

Chantilly, Musée Condé
MS 732 *52*

Chicago, Sheldon Stern
unnumbered *302*

Cincinnati, Hebrew Union College
unnumbered *300 301*
13 *59*
136 *66*
248 *297*
249 *297*
259 *297*
279 *81*
329 *241*
403 *13*
444 *54*
444.1 *218*
480 *34*
601 *59*
653 *307*
696 *62*
785 *248*
847 *295*
867 *206 282*
1085 *35*
1086 *35*
1087 *35*
1088 *35*
2001 *136*
2032 *120*
2065 *228*
Acc. 83 *18*
Acc. 139 *112 241*
Acc. 191 *118 214*
Acc. 1982–1985 *121*
JCF 1 *35 257*
JCF 2 *257*
JCF 4 *257*
JCF 5 *257*

Cleveland, R. Dessler
unnumbered *296 297 302*

Cluj, Romanian Academy
MS O. 303 *261*

Cologny-Genève, Bibliotheca Bodmeriana
81 *172*

Copenhagen, Kongelige Bibliothek
Hebr. 1 *269*
Hebr. 2 *269*
Hebr. 3–4 *269*
Hebr. 5 *269*
Hebr. 6 *269*
Hebr. 7–9 *269*
Hebr. 11 *269*
Hebr. 12 *94 303*
Hebr. 14 *281*
Hebr. 16 *281*
Hebr. 17 *269*
Hebr. 43 *242*
Hebr. Add. 6 *239*
Sim. Hebr. 8 *242*
Sim. Hebr. 15 *242*
Sim. Hebr. 48 *282*
Sim. Hebr. 57 *242*
Sim. Hebr. 93 *283*
Sim. Hebr. 97 *242*
Sim. Jud.-Arab. 1 *29 196 204*
Sim. Jud.-Arab. 2 *204*

Darmstadt, Universitäts- und Landesbibliothek Darmstadt
Or. 7 *60*
Or. 8 *60 98*
Or. 28 *60*

Deventer, Athenaeum
6144 *268*

Donaueschingen, Fuerstlich Fuerstenbergische Hofbibliothek
MS A11 *208*

Dresden, Sächsische Landesbibliothek
Cod. A 46a *62 277*
Cod. D. 22 *60*

Dublin, Trinity College Library
F.6.4 *268*
M.2.5 *268*
M.2.6 *108 268*

Edinburgh, National Library of Scotland
La. III 591 *258*
MS 18.7.23 *64*

Erlangen, Universitätsbibliothek Erlangen-Nürnberg
1262 *67*
2601 *66*

Florence, Biblioteca Medicea Laurenziana
Or. 17 *256*
Or. 42 *256*
Or. 79 *256*
Or. 121 *256*
Or. 124 *256*
Or. 149 *256*
Or. 451 *256*
Or. 468 *256*
Or. 472 *256*
Plut. I.9 *268*
Plut. I.24 *268*
Plut. I.30 *269*
Plut. I.31 *275*
Plut. I.45 *268*
Plut. I.52 *268*
Plut. II.1 *275*
Plut. II.12 *268*
Plut. III.1 *269*
Plut. III.3 *275*
Plut. III.4 *269*
Plut. III.10 *275*
Plut. III.14 *269*

Florence, Biblioteca Nazionale
Magl. III. 44 *275*
Nuovi Acq. 209 *70*

Florence, Biblioteca Riccardiana
Ricc. 1 *208 269*
Ricc. 26 *71*
Ricc. 98 *71*

Frankfurt, Goethe Universität, Universitätsbibliothek Johann Christian Senckenberg
Ausst. 4 *291*
Ausst. 5 *187*
Ausst. 6 *72*

Ausst. 7 *289*
Ausst. 8 *187*
Ausst. 9 *187*
Ausst. 10 *187*
hebr. 2° 10 *287*
hebr. 2° 11 *289*
hebr. 2° 12 *289*
hebr. 2° 13 *289*
hebr. 2° 14 *248 288*
hebr. 2° 15 *289*
hebr. 2° 16 *289*
hebr. 4° 1 *288*
hebr. 4° 2 *24 289*
hebr. 4° 3 *289*
hebr. 4° 10 *240 289*
hebr. 4° 11 *248 289*
hebr. 4° 12 *240 289*
hebr. 4° 13 *288*
hebr. 4° 14 *250 290*
hebr. 4° 15 *290*
hebr. 4° 16 *290*
hebr. 4° 17 *248 291*
hebr. 4° 18 *291*
hebr. 4° 19 *290*
hebr. 4° 20 *248 290*
hebr. 4° 21 *290*
hebr. 8° 1 *250 287*
hebr. 8° 3 *24 289*
hebr. 8° 9 *288*
hebr. 8° 12 *289*
hebr. 8° 15 *258 288*
hebr. 8° 17 *258 288*
hebr. 8° 18 *289*
hebr. 8° 20 *258*
hebr. 8° 22 *290*
hebr. 8° 23 *252 287*
hebr. 8° 27 *289*
hebr. 8° 28 *252 288*
hebr. 8° 29 *290*
hebr. 8° 33 *288*
hebr. 8° 38 *288*
hebr. 8° 40 *251*
hebr. 8° 47 *251*
hebr. 8° 53 *251 288*
hebr. 8° 54 *288*
hebr. 8° 55 *251 288*
hebr. 8° 56 *288*
hebr. 8° 57 *251 288*
hebr. 8° 58 *250 288*
hebr. 8° 59 *288*
hebr. 8° 60 *249 287*
hebr. 8° 61 *252 287*
hebr. 8° 62 *252 288*
hebr. 8° 63 *288*
hebr. 8° 64 *249 288*
hebr. 8° 65 *249 287*
hebr. 8° 66 *288*
hebr. 8° 67 *287*
hebr. 8° 68 *248 287*
hebr. 8° 69 *24 287*
hebr. 8° 70 *288*
hebr. 8° 71 *288*
hebr. 8° 72 *251 288*
hebr. 8° 73 *252 288*
hebr. 8° 74 *258 288*
hebr. 8° 75 *288*
hebr. 8° 76 *250 287*
hebr. 8° 77 *252 287*
hebr. 8° 78 *288*
hebr. 8° 79 *288*
hebr. 8° 80 *250 288*
hebr. 8° 81 *288*
hebr. 8° 82 *249*
hebr. 8° 83 *249 288*
hebr. 8° 84 *288*
hebr. 8° 85 *251 288*
hebr. 8° 86 *288*
hebr. 8° 87 *288*
hebr. 8° 88 *252 28*
hebr. 8° 89 *288*
hebr. 8° 90 *249 288*
hebr. 8° 91 *252 288*
hebr. 8° 92 *288*
hebr. 8° 93 *249 288*
hebr. 8° 94 *240 288*
hebr. 8° 95 *251 289*
hebr. 8° 96 *251 289*
hebr. 8° 97 *251 289*
hebr. 8° 98 *251 289*
hebr. 8° 99 *249 289*
hebr. 8° 100 *289*
hebr. 8° 101 *289*
hebr. 8° 102 *289*
hebr. 8° 103 *289*
hebr. 8° 104 *250 289*
hebr. 8° 105 *250 289*

hebr. 8° 106 *289*
hebr. 8° 107 *289*
hebr. 8° 108 *290*
hebr. 8° 109 *248 290*
hebr. 8° 110 *251 290*
hebr. 8° 111 *289*
hebr. 8° 112 *289*
hebr. 8° 113 *289*
hebr. 8° 114 *289*
hebr. 8° 115 *250 290*
hebr. 8° 116 *289*
hebr. 8° 117 *250 289*
hebr. 8° 118 *248 290*
hebr. 8° 119 *251 289*
hebr. 8° 120 *249 289*
hebr. 8° 121 *290*
hebr. 8° 122 *250 290*
hebr. 8° 123 *289*
hebr. 8° 124 *249 290*
hebr. 8° 125 *290*
hebr. 8° 126 *252 290*
hebr. 8° 127 *252 289*
hebr. 8° 128 *290*
hebr. 8° 129 *289*
hebr. 8° 130 *200 240 289*
hebr. 8° 131 *289*
hebr. 8° 132 *289*
hebr. 8° 133 *289*
hebr. 8° 134 *249 289*
hebr. 8° 135 *290*
hebr. 8° 136 *291*
hebr. 8° 137 *250 291*
hebr. 8° 138 *290*
hebr. 8° 139 *252 290*
hebr. 8° 140 *250 290*
hebr. 8° 141 *252 290*
hebr. 8° 142 *290*
hebr. 8° 143 *252 290*
hebr. 8° 144 *251 290*
hebr. 8° 145 *291*
hebr. 8° 146 *250 291*
hebr. 8° 148 *250 290*
hebr. 8° 149 *250 290*
hebr. 8° 150 *290*
hebr. 8° 151 *290*
hebr. 8° 152 *240 290*
hebr. 8° 153 *290*
hebr. 8° 154 *290*
hebr. 8° 155 *290*
hebr. 8° 156 *251 290*
hebr. 8° 157 *290*
hebr. 8° 158 *290*
hebr. 8° 159 *290*
hebr. 8° 160 *252 290*
hebr. 8° 161 *240 290*
hebr. 8° 162 *290*
hebr. 8° 163 *249 290*
hebr. 8° 167 *288*
hebr. 8° 171 *249*
hebr. 8° 175 *250*
hebr. 8° 187 *259*
hebr. 8° 190 *258*
hebr. 8° 191 *258*
hebr. 8° 204 *250*
hebr. 8° 249 *252*
hebr. 8° 256 *252*
hebr. 8° 266 *228 249*

Fürth, Jüdisches Museum Franken
Inv. Nr. 2–98 *76*

Geneva, Bibliothèque publique et universitaire
m.h.1 inv. 1887 *273*
m.h.2 inv. 1897 *273*
m.h.3 inv. 1858 *273*
m.h.6 inv. 2024 *273*
MS Comites Latentes 145 *297*
MS Comites Latentes 146 *299*
MS Comites Latentes 173 *239 287*

Geneva, N. Gaon
unnumbered *298*

Geneva, Jack Safra
unnumbered *300 301*

Genoa, Biblioteca Civica Berio
unnumbered *280*

Genoa, Biblioteca Universitaria
MS D IX 31 *52 81*

Gottweig, Stiftsbibliothek
10 (883) *277 303*

11 *303*
1010 *85*
1011 *85*

Groningen, Rijksuniversiteit
MS 455 *86*
MS 456 *86*
MS 457 *86*
MS 459 *86*
MS 466 *86*
MS 467 *86*

Haifa, J. S. Hirsch
unnumbered *282 283*

Halle, Bibliothek der Deutschen Morgenländischen Gesellschaft
B271a *294*

Halle, Universitäts- und Landesbibliothek
Yb.2° 7 *89*

Hamburg, Staats- und Universitätsbibliothek
Cod. hebr. 1 *278*
Cod. hebr. 2 *278*
Cod. hebr. 3 *278*
Cod. hebr. 4–7 *277*
Cod. hebr. 8 *278*
Cod. hebr. 9 *278*
Cod. hebr. 11 *278*
Cod. hebr. 22 *278*
Cod. hebr. 25–26 *278*
Cod. hebr. 27–28 *269*
Cod. hebr. 29 *278*
Cod. hebr. 45 *277*
Cod. hebr. 46 *278*
Cod. hebr. 47 *278*
Cod. hebr. 48 *278*
Cod. hebr. 70 *303*
Cod. hebr. 94 *278*
Cod. hebr. 99 *278*
Cod. hebr. 102 *278*
Cod. hebr. 155 *62*
Cod. hebr. 179 *278*
Cod. hebr. 202 *278*
Cod. hebr. 203 *278*
Cod. hebr. 204 *278*
Cod. hebr. 266 *303*
Cod. hebr. 306 *118*
Cod. hebr. 337 *90*
Cod. Levy 2 *239*
Cod. Levy 3 *260 307*
Cod. Levy 10 *239*
Cod. Levy 11 *239*
Cod. Levy 13 *239*
Cod. Levy 14 *239*
Cod. Levy 19 *217 272*
Cod. Levy 66 *39*
Cod. Levy 68 *39*
Cod. Levy 71 *239*
Cod. Levy 89 *295*
Cod. Levy 106 *239*
Cod. Levy 112 *239*
Cod. Levy 117 *241*
Cod. Levy 118 *239*
Cod. Levy 144 *145 239*

Heidelberg, Universitätsbibliothek
Cod. Or. 20 *194*

Innsbruck, Universitätsbibliothek
Cod. 291 *98 304*
Cod. 506 *98*
Cod. 1155 *98*

Jena, Universitätsbibliothek
El. 46 *269*

Jerusalem, S. Abrahams
8 *242*
9 *242*
13 *242*
14 *242*
15 *242*
17 *242*
18 *242*
20 *242*
21 *242*
23 *242*
24 *242*
28 *108*

Jerusalem, N. Allony (now in Jerusalem, NLI)
121 *259*
137 *304*
192 *305*

Jerusalem, M. Benayahu
unnumbered *298 300*

Jerusalem, Ben-Zvi Institute
MS 1 *15*
MS 2 *15*
MS 1805 *24*

Jerusalem, Central Zionist Archives
MSS 153/290–298 *232*

Jerusalem, Hekhal Shelomo Library (formerly)
Qu. 49 *306*
Qu. 69 *246*

Jerusalem, Israel Museum
unnumbered *296 302*
180/6 *77*
180/50 *185 232*
180/51 *187 277*
180/52 *58*
180/53 *75*
180/57 *33*
180/58 *67*
180/73 *295*
180/94 *94 211 262 278 298*
181/41 *197 298*

Jerusalem, Israel Mehlmann (formerly)
10 *214*

Jerusalem, Mosad Harav Kook
6 *75*
7 *75*
13 *75*
14 *75*
15 *75*
16 *75*
18 *75*
19 *75*
22 *75*
23 *75*
30 *75*
31 *75*
35–46 *75*
48–51 *75*
53 *75*
55–59 *75*
61–66 *75*
70 *75*
77–79 *75*
83 *75*
85 *75*
757 *201 304*

Jerusalem, National Library of Israel
Arc 4° 792/A14 *257*
Heb. 4° 66 *257*
Heb. 4° 176 *204*
Heb. 4° 197/20 *150*
Heb. 4° 370 *66 88*
Heb. 4° 551–553 *221*
Heb. 4° 555 *221*
Heb. 4° 558 *221*
Heb. 4° 564 *221*
Heb. 4° 567 *221*
Heb. 4° 577.5 *14 53*
Heb. 4° 577.7/8 *14*
Heb. 4° 651 *306*
Heb. 4° 652 *246*
Heb. 4° 666 *306*
Heb. 4° 667 *248*
Heb. 8° 751–819 *204*
Heb. 4° 781 *230 272*
Heb. 4° 790 *59*
Heb. 4° 877 *304*
Heb. 4° 878 *247*
Heb. 4° 895 *247*
Heb. 4° 896 *304*
Heb. 4° 898 *242*
Heb. 4° 934–941 *52*
Heb. 4° 962 *92*
Heb. 4° 1038 *28*
Heb. 4° 1096–1109 *89*
Heb. 4° 1112 *44*
Heb. 4° 1159 *23*
Heb. 4° 1192 *137*
Heb. 4° 1193 *90 96 103*
Heb. 4° 1201 *245*
Heb. 4° 1384 *146*
Heb. 4° 1404 *111*
Heb. 4° 5702 *59 298*
Heb. 4° 5703,1 *296*
Heb. 4° 5703,2 *296*
Heb. 4° 5704 *299*

Heb. 4° 5977 *206*
Heb. 4° 6130 *149*
Heb. 4° 6187 *257*
Heb. 4° 6898 *75*
Heb. 4° 6990 *214*
Heb. 4° 7025 *279*
Heb. 4° 7205 *59*
Heb. 4° 7538 *152*
Heb. 4° 7566 *301*
Heb. 8° 175 *241*
Heb. 8° 266 *228*
Heb. 8° 382 *32*
Heb. 8° 751–819 *204*
Heb. 8° 931 *283*
Heb. 8° 959 *129*
Heb. 8° 1482–1488 *232*
Heb. 8° 1619 *252*
Heb. 8° 1785 *92*
Heb. 8° 2001 *13*
Heb. 8° 2078 *20 225*
Heb. 8° 2128 *306*
Heb. 8° 2129 *245*
Heb. 8° 2131 *304*
Heb. 8° 2132 *246 261*
Heb. 8° 2135 *243*
Heb. 8° 2137 *246*
Heb. 8° 2235 *305*
Heb. 8° 2237 *305*
Heb. 8° 2238 *203*
Heb. 8° 2255 *306*
Heb. 8° 2256 *305*
Heb. 8° 2263 *305*
Heb. 8° 2264 *243*
Heb. 8° 2268 *304*
Heb. 8° 2270 *245*
Heb. 8° 2271 *246*
Heb. 8° 2272 *245*
Heb. 8° 2274 *246*
Heb. 8° 2275 *243*
Heb. 8° 2281 *306*
Heb. 8° 2283 *246*
Heb. 8° 2284 *245*
Heb. 8° 2292 *247*
Heb. 8° 2296 *245*
Heb. 8° 2298 *304*
Heb. 8° 2299 *247*
Heb. 8° 2311 *304*
Heb. 8° 2322 *246*
Heb. 8° 2331 *306*
Heb. 8° 2393 *196*
Heb. 8° 2401 *157*
Heb. 8° 2429 *30*
Heb. 8° 2491 *246*
Heb. 8° 2492 *181 305*
Heb. 8° 2647 *305*
Heb. 8° 2761 *295*
Heb. 8° 2802 *304*
Heb. 8° 2921 *103*
Heb. 8° 2922 *260*
Heb. 8° 2935 *213*
Heb. 8° 2971 *283*
Heb. 8° 2989 *246*
Heb. 8° 3045 *304*
Heb. 8° 3074 *247*
Heb. 8° 3100 *244*
Heb. 8° 3141 *129*
Heb. 8° 3167 *137*
Heb. 8° 3182 *95*
Heb. 8° 3302–3330 *52*
Heb. 8° 3427 *303*
Heb. 8° 3489 *259*
Heb. 8° 3524 *294*
Heb. 8° 3718 *246*
Heb. 8° 3791 *35*
Heb. 8° 3795 *108*
Heb. 8° 3901–4000 *89*
Heb. 8° 4001 *258*
Heb. 8° 4002 *110*
Heb. 8° 4016 *283*
Heb. 8° 4051 *207*
Heb. 8° 4279 *198*
Heb. 8° 4280 *244*
Heb. 8° 4281 *244*
Heb. 8° 4294 *130*
Heb. 8° 4450 *228*
Heb. 8° 5204 *108*
Heb. 8° 5218 *246*
Heb. 8° 5221 *304*
Heb. 8° 5226 *303*
Heb. 8° 5336 *305*
Heb. 8° 5354 *35*
Heb. 8° 5389 *295*
Heb. 8° 5492 *73 87*
Heb. 8° 5563 *103 200*
Heb. 8° 5622 *251*
Heb. 8° 5699 *298*

Heb. 8° 5700 *299*
Heb. 8° 5701 *298*
Heb. 8° 5728 *39*
Heb. 8° 6234 *300*
Heb. 8° 6235 *298*
Heb. 8° 6282 *305*
Heb. 8° 6287 *200*
Heb. 8° 6397 *247*
Heb. 8° 6424 *129 257*
Heb. 8° 6425 *257*
Heb. 8° 6426 *257*
Heb. 8° 6479 *304*
Heb. 8° 6527 *52 257*
Heb. 8° 6857 *304*
Heb. 8° 6864 *294 305*
Heb. 8° 7031 *243*
Heb. 8° 7039 *120*
Heb. 8° 7116 *295*
Heb. 8° 7224 *305*
Heb. 8° 7234 *305*
Heb. 8° 7235 *304*
Heb. 8° 7246 *230*
Heb. 8° 7409 *284*
Heb. 8° 7565 *295 302*
Heb. 8° 7709 *306*
Heb. 8° 8334 *284*
Sam. 2° 6 *297*
Yah. Ms. Heb. 1 *304 308*
Yah. Ms. Heb. 3 *122*
Yah. Ms. Heb. 57 *241 310*
Yah. Ms. Heb. 216 *241 310*
Yah. Ms. Heb. 228 *303*
93 L 11 *76*

Jerusalem, Research Center for Italian Jewish Studies
30 *16 23*
43 *16 23*

Jerusalem, Rabbi Schochet (Karlin-Stolin)
705 *247*
840 *292*

Jerusalem, Schocken Institute
unnumbered *283*
37 *233*
2041 *111*
11308 *224*
12827 *187*
13160 *64 157*
13847 *295*
13873 *114 199*
13992 *295*
14052 *295*
14840 *199*
15435 *188*
15926 *179*
15987 *121*
19520 *26*
19522 *84*
24086 *158*
24087 *158*
24100 *158*
70057 *35*
Kab. 101 *179*

Johannesburg, S. Rappaport
unnumbered *305*

Karlsruhe, Badische Landesbibliothek
Cod. Reuchlin 1 *182 268*
Cod. Reuchlin 3 *109 182 268*
Cod. Reuchlin 5 *272*
Cod. Reuchlin 6 *109*
Cod. Reuchlin 10 *268*

Kassel, Landesbibliothek und Murhardsche Bibliothek
MS fol. theol. 3 *268*

Kennicott (MSS listed in his Vetus Testamentum Hebraicum)
See also Appendix I, no. 22.
25 *37*
124–126 *58*
128 *58*
135 *116*
136 *143*
137 *194*
144 *204*
145–148 *207*
158 *56*
170 *208*
201 *257*
223 *112*

242 *183*
290 *15*
293–298 *177*
375 *134*
376–378 *230*
380 *217*
417–419 *69*
472–474 *38*
520–521 *69*
559–560 *164*
564 *57*
565 *57*
566 *57*
567 *57*
571–575 *58*
578 *119*
585 *84*
586 *144*
642 *138*
643 *211*

Königsberg, Stadtbibliothek
S 44 8° *173*

Leeds, University, Brotherton Library
Dep. 1982/1 *299*

Leeuwarden, TRESOAR, the Friesland Historical and Literary Centre
MS B. A. Fr. 23 *15*

Leiden, Universiteitsbibliotheek
Cod. Or. 6 *269*
Cod. Or. 1195 *278*
Cod. Or. 1197 *278*
Cod. Or. 1298 *269*
Cod. Or. 2065 *294*
Cod. Or. 2066 *20*
Cod. Or. 2361 *198*
Cod. Or. 4719 *198*
Cod. Or. 4720 *118*
Cod. Or. 4725 *198 278*
Cod. Or. 4733 *198*
Cod. Or. 4737 *278*
Cod. Or. 14396–14403 *108*
Cod. Or. 14655 *108*
Cod. Or. 14656 *108*
Cod. Or. 22306 *108*
Cod. Or. 22581 *108*
Cod. Or. 26509 *292*

Leipzig, Universitätsbibliothek
Cod. 1102 *118 278*
Cod. B.H. 1 *277*
Cod. B.H. 12 *277*
Cod. B.H. 17 *102*
Cod. B.H. 26 *217*
Cod. B.H. 31 *217*

Le Mans, Bibliothèque municipale
MS 191 A *135*

Lisbon, Biblioteca Nacional
MS 72 *52 138 278*

London, Sholem Asch (formerly)
2 *283*

London, Leo Baeck Institute
unnumbered *257*

London, British Library
Add. 4707 *58 268*
Add. 4708 *58 268*
Add. 4709 *58 268*
Add. 9398 *302*
Add. 9399 *302*
Add. 9400 *302*
Add. 9403 *303*
Add. 9404 *302*
Add. 9407 *303*
Add. 11416 *182*
Add. 11639 *40 141*
Add. 14761 *26*
Add. 14762 *107 28*
Add. 15250 *63 307*
Add. 15251 *256 277*
Add. 15282 *64 307*
Add. 15283 *64*
Add. 15306 *307*
Add. 15978 *189*
Add. 18831 *261*
Add. 19776 *55*
Add. 19943 *138 294*
Add. 21161 *157 269*
Add. 21967 *199*

Add. 22413 *214*
Add. 26883 *93*
Add. 26957 *113*
Add. 27120 *83*
Add. 27199 *65*
Add. 27214 *59*
Arundel Or. 2 *268*
Arundel Or. 16 *268*
Cotton Claud. B VIII *268*
Harley 1528 *267*
Harley 1861 *267*
Harley 5498 *267*
Harley 5506 *267*
Harley 5509 *267*
Harley 5586 *267*
Harley 5683 *267*
Harley 5686 *268*
Harley 5704 *65*
Harley 5706 *267*
Harley 5707 *65*
Harley 5709 *267*
Harley 5710–11 *267*
Harley 5715 *268*
Harley 5720 *267*
Harley 5721 *267*
Harley 5722 *267*
Harley 5757 *268*
Harley 5772 *267*
Harley 5773 *267*
Harley 5774 *267*
Harley 5775 *268*
Harley 7619 *267*
Harley 7620 *268*
Harley 7621 *267*
Harley 7622 *268*
King's 1 *111 267*
Loan 1 *58 268*
Or. 832 *287*
Or. 1002 *240*
Or. 1003 *240*
Or. 1004 *240*
Or. 1022 *285*
Or. 1024 *286*
Or. 1041 *151 257*
Or. 1055 *259*
Or. 1057 *259*
Or. 1081 *252*
Or. 1082 *252*
Or. 1083 *253*
Or. 1084 *253*
Or. 1098 *262*
Or. 1099 *263*
Or. 1100–1104 *263*
Or. 1263 *264*
Or. 1264–1265 *264*
Or. 1307 *264*
Or. 1389 *51 248*
Or. 1404 *111 188*
Or. 1425 *284*
Or. 2201 *98*
Or. 2443 *205*
Or. 2451–2453 *151*
Or. 2626–2628 *122*
Or. 2737 *96*
Or. 2822 *24*
Or. 2823 *24*
Or. 2884 *83*
Or. 3655 *308*
Or. 3656 *308*
Or. 3657 *308*
Or. 3658 *307*
Or. 3659 *308*
Or. 3660 *307*
Or. 3661 *307*
Or. 4220–4224 *83*
Or. 4598 *35*
Or. 5014 *177 198*
Or. 5024 *130*
Or. 5429 *179*
Or. 5435 *179*
Or. 5469 *179*
Or. 5470 *179*
Or. 5556–5566 *81*
Or. 5600 *262*
Or. 5956 *268*
Or. 6357–6359 *179*
Or. 9153 *211 225*
Or. 9180 *173*
Or. 9879 *78*
Or. 9880 *78*
Or. 9960 *137*
Or. 10012 *30*
Or. 10197 *35*
Or. 10387 *165*
Or. 10845 *284*
Or. 12186 *14 89*

Or. 12254 *175*
Or. 13153 *228*
Or. 13704 *248 299*
Or. 13705 *299*
Or. 13871 *297*
Or. 13872 *300*
Or. 13887 *140*
Or. 13888 *140*
Or. 13889 *140*
Or. 14014 *296*
Or. 14015 *296*
Or. 14017 *299*
Or. 14018 *300*
Or. 14019 *301*
Or. 14020A *297*
Or. 14020B *297*
Or. 14054 *297*
Or. 14055 *298*
Or. 14056 *299*
Or. 14057 *297*
Or. 14058 *297*
Or. 14059 *299*
Or. 14060 *300*
Or. 14061 *301*
Or. 16082 *292*
Or. 16083 *292*
Or. 16084 *292*
Or. 16085 *293*
Or. 16086 *293*
Or. 16087 *292*
Or. 16088 *292*
Or. 16089 *293*
Or. 16090 *293*
Or. 16091 *293*
Or. 16092 *292*
Stowe Ch. 297 *207*

London, Lambeth Palace
435 *268*

London, Montefiore Collection
(Most MSS were sold.)
15 *286*
20 *182*
35 *240*
42 *108 264 295*
52 *286*
53 *285*
98 *287*
108 *205*
145 *264*
210 *287*
255 *285*
269 *285*
273 *262*
274 *258*
283 *287*
296 *64*
297 *161*
306 *252*
308 *255*
362 *250*
366 *287*
368 *250*
372 *205*
407 *287*
410 *239*
412 *285*
429 *252*
451 *259*
484 *34*
485 *259*
492 *252*
494 *252*
516 *160*
517 *213*

London School of Jewish Studies (formerly Jews' College)
7 *128*
14 *128*
32 *128*
MS Asher Myers 2 *260 307*
MS Asher Myers 6 *260 307*
MS Asher Myers 7 *307*
MS Asher Myers 9 *128*
MS Asher Myers 10 *128*

London, David Sofer
unnumbered *301 302*
1 *153*
5 *305*
60 *301*
61 *284*
96 *244*
102 *69*

London, University College, Mocatta Library
MS 1 *142*

London, Valmadonna Trust Library
1 *25 297*
4 *138*
6a *296*
7 *296*
8 *300*
9 *299*
11 *59 301*
12 *298*
13 *296*
13a *300*
14 *297*
15 *299*
16 *296*
17 *296*
20b *296*
20c *298*
20e *296*
307 *310*

London, Wellcome Institute
unnumbered *293*

London, Westminster Abbey
unnumbered *268*
Ca MS 2 *268*

Los Angeles, University of California Library
960 bx. 1.9 *242*
960 bx. 1.10 *295*

Los Angeles, Dr. Steve Weiss
1 *291*
2 *284*

Madrid, Biblioteca Nacional
79 *273*
4188 *131*
5464 *273*
5468 *131 172 216*
5474 *131*
7542 *131*
23078 *284*

Madrid, Biblioteca del Palacio Real
II/3231–3246 *132*

Madrid, Consejo Superior de Investigaciones Científicas, Instituto de Filología
MS CVI–M/106 *23*

Mainz, Wissenschaftliche Stadtbibliothek
Hs. 378 *134 272*

Manchester, John Rylands University Library
MS Gaster 59 *175*
MS Gaster 659 *242*
MS Rylands 5 *307*
MS Rylands 6 *58 188*
MS Rylands 7 *58*
MS Rylands 29 *35*
MS Rylands 30 *35*
MS Rylands 32 *35*
MS Rylands 50 *300*
MS Sam. 376 *298*
MS Sam. 377 *300*

Miami, R. D. Levy
unnumbered *300 301*

Milan, Biblioteca Ambrosiana
Cod. A 38 sup. *269*
Cod. B 11 sup. *269*
Cod. B 30 inf. *269*
Cod. B 31 inf. *273*
Cod. B 32 inf. *17 269*
Cod. B 35 inf. *269*
Cod. B 56 inf. *269*
Cod. C 73 sup. *269*
Cod. C 105 sup. *269*
Cod. C 116 sup. *269*
Cod. C 149 inf. *273*
Cod. C 300 inf. *273*
Cod. E 52 inf. *269*
Cod. G 2 sup. *269*
S.P.II.248 *269*
X 110 sup. *221*
X 133 sup. *205*
X 161 sup. *285*
Cat. Bernheimer, 13 *269*

Modena, Biblioteca Estense
α J. 1.22 *37 276*
α K. 1.22 *37*
α O. 5.9 *276*
α T. 3.8 *276*
α U. 2.27 *276*
α W. 5.14 *276*

Monte Oliveto Maggiore, Biblioteca Capitolare
Cod. 37 A 2 *37 281*

Montreal, Y. Elberg
unnumbered *297 298 300 301*
10 *297*
12 *297*
13 *299*
15 *301*
24 *296*

Montserrat, Abadia de Santa María
Or. 45 *144*
Or. 51 *144*
Or. 56 *144*
Or. 59 *144*
Or. 60 *144*

Moscow, Russian State Library, Günzburg Collection
180 *189*
233 *34*
369 *253*
370 *253*
371 *253*
372 *253*
373 *253*
374 *253*
375 *253*
376 *253*
377 *253*
378 *253*
379 *253*
380 *253*
381 *253*
382 *253*
383 *253*
384–386 *253*
387–392 *253*
393 *253*
394 *253*
395 *253*
396 *253*
397 *253*
398 *253*
399 *253*
400 *253*
401 *253*
402 *253*
403 *254*
404 *254*
405 *254*
406 *254*
407 *254*
408 *254*
409 *254*
410 *254*
411 *254*
412 *254*
413 *254*
414 *254*
415 *254*
416 *254*
417 *254*
418 *254*
419 *254*
420 *254*
421 *254*
422 *254*
423 *254*
424 *254*
425 *254*
426 *254*
427 *254*
428 *254*
429 *254*
430 *254*
431 *254*
432 *254*
433 *239 254*
434 *254*
435–436 *254*
437 *254*
438 *254*
439 *254*
440 *254*
441 *254*

442 *254*
443 *255*
444 *255*
445 *255*
446 *255*
447 *255*
448 *255*
449 *255*
450 *255*
451 *255*
452 *255*
453 *255*
454 *255*
455 *255*
456 *32 255*
457 *255*
458 *255*
459 *255*
460 *254*
463 *253*
495 *254*
554 *253*
555 *253*
556 *253*
557 *252*
558 *253*
559 *253*
560 *253*
561 *253*
562 *253*
611 *205*
631 *253*
632 *253*
633 *253*
634 *253*
635 *253*
636 *96*
660 *254*
661 *254*
673 *255*
690 *255*
691 *255*
692 *255*
693 *255*
694 *255*
695 *255*
696 *255*
698 *255*
699 *255*
700 *255*
701 *255*
702 *255*
739 *305*
834 *249*
848 *59*
892 *285*
898 *250*
899 *248*
900 *251*
905 *249*
908 *239 285*
909 *248*
910 *249*
914 *263*
921 *95*
926 *248*
927 *251*
930 *250*
935 *249*
936 *252*
946 *175*
949 *24*
953 *241*
964 *263*
975 *285*
976 *249*
978 *252*
991 *248*
996 *263*
999 *249*
1006 *263*
1007 *263*
1008 *249*
1009 *263*
1011 *263*
1024 *263*
1049 *248*
1051 *251*
1061 *263*
1063 *110*
1064 *249*
1065 *240*
1068 *240*
1069 *263*
1070 *284*
1073 *263*

1076 *240*
1092 *249*
1098 *263*
1113 *263*
1115 *263*
1116 *263*
1121 *250*
1122 *95*
1124 *264*
1126 *263*
1128 *263*
1133? *24*
1137 *251*
1141 *261*
1145 *251*
1147 *263*
1148 *249*
1150 *252*
1160 *240*
1174 *263 264*
1179 *285*
1185 *250*
1197 *263*
1204 *250*
1205 *250*
1206 *249*
1209 *233 263*
1213 *249*
1251 *252 257*
1264 *251*
1274 *240*
1305 *250*
1327 *249*
1331 *250*
1332 *250*
1333 *250*
1389 *285*
1397 *251*
1402 *285*
1421 *110*
1471 *211*
1475 *250*
1481 *31*
1546 *249*
1554 *264 265*
1571 251
1595 *308*
1597 *251*
1619 *308*
1650 *249*
1651 *248*
1652–1655 *263*
1657 *249*
1658 *95*
1718 *252*
1739 *251*
1749 *95*
1835 *308*
Acc. 4 *305*
Acc. 6 *304*
Acc. 9 *305*
Acc. 22 *304*
Acc. 31 *303*
Acc. 37/1 *304*
Acc. 117 *305*
Acc. 125 *306*
Acc. 136 *303*
Acc. 138 *303*
Acc. 218/1 *306*
Acc. 219/2 *307*
Евр. 16 *39*
Евр. 147 *246*
Евр. 238 *207*
fond 182 *67 145*
fond 182, no. 456 *244*
MS Or. F. 173.II *146*
MS Or. F. 118.1–11 *146*
Trofiana *243 244 245 246 247*

Moscow, Russian State Military Archives
707/1/146 *305*
707/1/176 *303*
707/1/209 *306*
707/3/6 *303*
707/3/14 *304*
707/3/17 *306*
707/3/19 *304*
1325/1/98 *257*

Munich, Bayerische Staatsbibliothek
Cods. arab. 816a–816f *148*
Cod. hebr. 74 *65*
Cod. hebr. 81 *65*
Cod. hebr. 95 *148 179*
Cod. hebr. 96 *65*
Cod. hebr. 103 *65*

Cod. hebr. 147–150 *200*
Cod. hebr. 153 *148*
Cod. hebr. 217–219 *65*
Cod. hebr. 285 *65*
Cod. hebr. 308 *239*
Cod. hebr. 365 *307*
Cod. hebr. 366 *307*
Cod. hebr. 384–386 *200*
Cod. hebr. 390–391 *180*
Cod. hebr. 393–395 *148*
Cod. hebr. 417 *239*
Cod. hebr. 418 *239*
Cods. hebr. 421–428 *148*
Cod. hebr. 425 *182*
Cod. hebr. 436 *175*
Cod. hebr. 452–465 *134 149*

New Haven, Yale University
unnumbered *245*
MS Heb. 46–78 *112*
MS Heb. 54 *72*
MS Heb. 136 *222*
MS Heb. 409 *15 280*
MS 1824 *151*
MS 1825 *151*

New York, Chassidei Chabad Library
231 *225*
1193 *306*

New York, Columbia University
Gen. MS 153 *102*
X893 Ab 9 *264*
X893 Ez 7 *114*
X893 G 15 *264*
X893 H 13 *57*
X893 H 39 *264*
X893 K 82 *85*
X893 L 97 *114*
X893 P 95 *260*
X893 Sa 7 *255*

New York, D. H. Feinberg
unnumbered *287 291 298 300*

New York, Hispanic Society of America
B 241 *262*
HC 371/169 *66 279*

New York, Jewish Museum
F3799 *164*
JM 68–60 *164*

New York, Jewish Theological Seminary
unnumbered *304*
Acc. 01260–01270 *97*
Acc. 01272 *97*
ENA 790 *259*
ENA 1595 *14*
Ket. 49 *164*
L5 *256 277*
L44a *95*
L263 *31*
L315 *87*
L462a *258*
L510 *83*
L701 *202*
L782 *98 310*
L792 *283*
L825 *34*
L836 *240*
L883 *35 83*
L932 *283*
L936 *260*
L937 *260*
L959 *16*
L1052 *257*
MS 1343 *200*
MS 1539 *260*
MS 1548 *241*
MS 1567 *258*
MS 1569 *259 260*
MS 1574 *259*
MS 1576 *259*
MS 1577 *259*
MS 1581 *260*
MS 1586 *258*
MS 1588 *260*
MS 1590 *260*
MS 1593 *260*
MS 1598 *258*
MS 1600 *260*
MS 1601 *259*
MS 1604 *259*
MS 1605 *260*
MS 1606 *260*
MS 1613 *259*

MS 1616 *259*
MS 1618 *118*
MS 1619 *260*
MS 1623 *260*
MS 1646 *35*
MS 1661 *310*
MS 1697 *260*
MS 1730 *35*
MS 1887 *182*
MS 1966 *35*
MS 2079 *284*
MS 2098 *59*
MS 2187 *130*
MS 2194 *17*
MS 2200 *205*
MS 2216 *282*
MS 2218 *283*
MS 2220 *310*
MS 2230 *295*
MS 2240 *121*
MS 2269 *16*
MS 2287 *93 261*
MS 2314 *261*
MS 2318 *283*
MS 2321 *184*
MS 2325 *184*
MS 2341 *165*
MS 2383 *35*
MS 2387 *285*
MS 2400 *262*
MS 2409 *258*
MS 2410 *258*
MS 2411 *260*
MS 2412 *259*
MS 2415 *259*
MS 2416 *260*
MS 2604 *35*
MS 2612 *39*
MS 2639 *242*
MS 2661 *84 97*
MS 2670 *205*
MS 2806 *181*
MS 2809 *170*
MS 2810 *181*
MS 2814 *206*
MS 2816 *88*
MS 2823 *88*
MS 2833 *84*
MS 2837 *95*
MS 2846 *88*
MS 2847 *209*
MS 2858 *114*
MS 2861 *200*
MS 2863 *57 61 151*
MS 2872 *84 262*
MS 2881? *257*
MS 2891 *130*
MS 2926 *119*
MS 2945 *16*
MS 2977 *157*
MS 3194 *251*
MS 3545 *262*
MS 3551 *205*
MS 3552 *259*
MS 3553 *259*
MS 3597 *256*
MS 3601 *310*
MS 3704 *248*
MS 3720 *286*
MS 3830 *136*
MS 3881 *130*
MS 3891 *205*
MSS 3907–3908? *251*
MSS 3910 *251*
MSS 3911 *251*
MSS 3912 *251*
MSS 3913 *251*
MSS 3914 *251*
MSS 3915 *251*
MSS 3916 *251*
MSS 3917–3918 *251*
MS 4064 *200*
MS 4328 *182*
MS 4418 *32 205*
MS 4432 *139*
MS 4452a *21*
MS 4481 *156*
MS 4529 *181*
MS 4715 *240*
MS 5062 *259*
MS 5069 *259*
MS 5107 *258*
MS 5293 *258*
MS 5350 *229*
MS 5501 *229*
MS 5535 *264*

MS 8103 *258*
MS 8117 *260*
MS 8225 *138 294 307*
MS 8238 *307*
MS 8242 *258*
MS 8244 *250*
MS 8249 *119*
MS 8252 *139*
MS 8279 *156*
MS 8313 *16*
MS 8334 *181*
MS 8386 *203*
MS 8558 *75*
MS 8593 *221*
MS 8641 *84*
MS 8892 *187*
MS 9019 *305*
MS 9150 *258*
MS 9344 *67*
MS 9478 *178*
MS 9487 *295*
MS 9632 *75*
MS 9685 *305*
MS 9825 *257*
MS 9826 *257*
MS 9827 *257*
MS 9828 *257*
MS 9829 *257*
MS 9830 *257*
MS 9831 *257*
MS 10169 *245*
MS 10401 *207*
MS 10484 *303*
MS 10485 *303*
MS 10610 *284*
MS 10611 *284*
MS 10613 *284*
MS 10614 *284*
MS 10615 *284*
MS 10616 *284*
Ms 10636 *306*
MS 10713 *88*
MS 10759 *291*
MS 10760 *292*
MS 10762 *292*
MS 10763 *292*
MS 10882 *299*
R33 *257*
R34 *200*
R85 *189*
R192 *137*
R222 *25*
R282 *35 261*
R437 *258*
R445 *260*
R520 *35*
R657 *30*
R671 *130*
R673 *15 84*
R718 *59*
R736 *17*
R832 *257*
R840 *52*
R866 *97*
R877 *240*
R1011–1013 *259*
R1021 *241*
R1022 *259*
R1046 *259*
R1070 *258*
R1090 *242*
R1093 *200 260*
R1116 *253*
R1224 *33*
R1355 *108*
R1414 *310*
R1430 *286*
R1434 *259*
R1474 *258*
R1492 *43*
R1515 *121*
R1521 *35*
R1538 *258*
R1567 *258*
R1575 *242*
R1621 *139*
R1687 *109*
R1887–1892 *229*
R1894 *229*
R1910–1912 *229*
R1917 *64*
R2142 *66*
R2170 *21 66*
R2171 *244*
R2259 *229*
R2410 *258*

New York Public Library
**P (MS Heb. 24) *282*
**P (MS Heb. 100) *114*
**P (MS Heb. 124) *114*
**P (MS Heb. 174) *292*
**P (MS Heb. 175) *252 293*
**P (MS Heb. 176) *292*
**P (MS Heb. 177) *291*
**P (MS Heb. 178) *293*
**P (MS Heb. 179) *292*
**P (MS Heb. 180) *293*
**P (MS Heb. 181) *292*
**P (MS Heb. 182) *205 292*
**P (MS Heb. 183) *293*
**P (MS Heb. 184) *293*
**P (MS Heb. 185) *293*
**P (MS Heb. 186) *292*
**P (MS Heb. 190) *296*
**P (MS Heb. 191) *300*
**P (MS Heb. 218) *284*
**P (MS Heb. 219) *284*
**P (MS Heb. 220) *284*
**P (MS Heb. 224) *164*
**P (MS Heb. 225) *164*
**P (MS Heb. 236) *109*
**P (MS Heb. 238) *109*
**P (MS Heb. 246) *109*
**P (MS Heb. 267) *291*
Spencer Collection 1 *84 94 232*

New York, B. Spiro
unnumbered *300*

New York, Union Theological Seminary
74 *283*

New York, Yeshiva University
MS 1247 *63 178 257 280*
MS 1250 *257*
MS 1251 *242 257*
MS 1254 *210*
MS Lewin 76 *14*

Newton Center, Hebrew College
27 *152 173*
29 *152 173*
34 *152 173*
35 *152 173*
39 *152 173*
41 *152 173*
42 *152 173*
44 *152 173*
45 *152 173*
49 *152 173*

Nuremberg, Germanisches Nationalmuseum
2121 *158*
2107b *158*

Nuremberg, Stadtbibliothek
Cent. IV 100 *158*
Cent. V app. 1–2 269
Solg. 2° 1–7 269

Olomouc, Vědecká Knihova
Cod. 364 *160*
Cod. 484 *160*
Cod. 485 *160*

Orlando, Van Kampen
unnumbered *298*

Oslo, Martin Schøyen
1858 *299*
1859 *296*
1860 *299*
1861 *297*
1862 *299*
1863 *296*
1864 *297*
1865 *297*
1866 *299*
1999 *300*
2195 *298*
5070 *117 268*
5412 *293*

Oxford, Bodleian Library
Arch. Seld. A 47 *265*
Arch. Seld. A sup. 105 *266*
Arch. Seld. A sup. 106 *266*
Arch. Seld. B sup. 101 *279*
Bodl. Or. 3 *266*
Bodl. Or. 6 *266*

Bodl. Or. 18 *266*
Bodl. Or. 23 *266*
Bodl. Or. 46 *266*
Bodl. Or. 62 *266*
Bodl. Or. 139 *266*
Bodl. Or. 155 *92*
Bodl. Or. 164 *265*
Bodl. Or. 621 *266*
Bodl. Or. 661 *233*
Bodl. Or. 802–804 *265*
Can. Or. 20 *150 280*
Can. Or. 37–40 *280*
Can. Or. 42 *280*
Can. Or. 49 *150 280*
Can. Or. 53 *150 280*
Can. Or. 62 *57 276 281*
Can. Or. 91 *57 276*
Can. Or. 94 *280*
Can. Or. 106 *280*
Can. Or. 136 *209 280*
Can. Or. 137 *209 280*
Can. Or. 138 *84 209 277*
Can. Or. 139 *209*
Can. Or. 140 *209*
Can. Or. 141 *209*
Digby Or. 32–33 *265*
Digby Or. 32–36 *62*
Hatton Or. 34 *92*
Hatton Or. 35 *92*
Heb. c. 6 *60*
Heb. c. 22 *33 41*
Heb. c. 24 *198*
Heb. d. 10 *279*
Heb. d. 17 *33*
Heb. d. 40 *151*
Heb. d. 53 *41*
Heb. d. 102 *298*
Heb. d. 103 *301*
Heb. e. 8 *91*
Heb. e. 9 *91*
Heb. e. 15 *259*
Heb. e. 19 *259*
Heb. e. 64 *26*
Heb. e. 65 *26*
Heb. e. 68 *114*
Heb. e. 89 *259*
Heb. e. 123 *205*
Heb. e. 183 *298*
Heb. e. 184 *299*
Heb. f. 15 *259*
Heb. f. 16 *259*
Heb. f. 17 *258*
Heb. f. 55 *26*
Hunt. 11–12 *265*
Hunt. 69 *265*
Hunt. 72 *266*
Hunt. 227 *266*
Hunt. 234 *266*
Hunt. 235 *265*
Hunt. 261 *265*
Hunt. 367 *266*
Hunt. 396 *265*
Hunt. 448–449 *279*
Hunt. 475 *265*
Hunt. 484 *279*
Hunt. 496 *266*
Hunt. 511 *266*
Hunt. 591 *266*
Hunt. 616 *266*
Hunt. 617 *266*
Hunt. 618– 620 *265*
Kennicott 1 *110 266*
Kennicott 2 *110 267*
Kennicott 3 *143 268*
Kennicott 4 *267*
Kennicott 5 *267*
Kennicott 6 *267*
Kennicott 7 *15 270*
Kennicott 8 *194 268*
Kennicott 10 *201 267 302*
Laud Or. 27 *279*
Laud Or. 84 *266*
Laud Or. 118 *266*
Laud Or. 154 *266*
Laud Or. 174 *266*
Laud Or. 182 *266*
Laud Or. 321 *114 279*
Lyell 97 *131*
Lyell Empt. 62 *157*
Marsh 10 *265*
Marsh 21 *266*
Marsh 91 *265*
Marsh 607 *265*
Marsh 635 *265*
Marshall (Or.) 1 *265 265*
Marshall (Or.) 3 *265*

Marshall (Or.) 42 *279*
Marshall (Or.) 51 *265*
Mich. 29 *261*
Mich. 39 *261*
Mich. 44 *261*
Mich. 45 *261*
Mich. 48 *261*
Mich. 58 *261*
Mich. 67 *262*
Mich. 85 *262*
Mich. 121 *261*
Mich. 138 *262*
Mich. 168 *225*
Mich. 187 *261*
Mich. 207 *294*
Mich. 208 *262*
Mich. 211 *262*
Mich. 224 *261*
Mich. 273 *262*
Mich. 282 *261*
Mich. 314 *262*
Mich. 320 *261*
Mich. 321 *225*
Mich. 343 *262*
Mich. 363 *69*
Mich. 394 *262*
Mich. 416 *261*
Mich. 420 *261*
Mich. 456 *262*
Mich. 458 *262*
Mich. 497 *261*
Mich. 510 *262*
Mich. 527 *261*
Mich. 554 *262*
Mich. 568 *261*
Mich. 574 *261*
Mich. 581 *261*
Mich. 617 *261*
Mich. 619 *214*
Mich. 627 *261*
Opp. 2 *280*
Opp. 3 *282*
Opp. 13 *280*
Opp. 14 *280*
Opp. 15 *280*
Opp. 17 *282*
Opp. 18 *282*
Opp. 185 *280*
Opp. 186 *280*
Opp. 642 *282*
Opp. 717 *282*
Opp. Add. 2° 5 *22*
Opp. Add. 2° 13 *64*
Opp. Add. 2° 14 *22*
Opp. Add. 2° 17 *151*
Opp. Add. 2° 18 *22*
Opp. Add. 2° 19 *151*
Opp. Add. 2° 20 *151*
Opp. Add. 2° 21 *22 278*
Opp. Add. 2° 23 *22*
Opp. Add. 2° 29 *256*
Opp. Add. 2° 30 *199*
Opp. Add. 2° 31 *199*
Opp. Add. 2° 33 *93*
Opp. Add. 2° 34 *93*
Opp. Add. 2° 35 *199*
Opp. Add. 2° 36 *239*
Opp. Add. 2° 37 *199*
Opp. Add. 2° 38 *199*
Opp. Add. 2° 41 *122*
Opp. Add. 2° 42 *199*
Opp. Add. 2° 43 *199*
Opp. Add. 2° 44 *122 239*
Opp. Add. 2° 45 *95 263*
Opp. Add. 2° 46 *95 263*
Opp. Add. 2° 48 *24*
Opp. Add. 2° 49 *24*
Opp. Add. 2° 50 *24*
Opp. Add. 2° 51 *95 248*
Opp. Add. 2° 52 *95*
Opp. Add. 2° 53 *24 95*
Opp. Add. 2° 57 *95*
Opp. Add. 2° 64 *95*
Opp. Add. 2° 65 *203*
Opp. Add. 2° 66 *203*
Opp. Add. 4° 3 *64*
Opp. Add. 4° 4 *64*
Opp. Add. 4° 8 *64*
Opp. Add. 4° 13 *22*
Opp. Add. 4° 21 *151*
Opp. Add. 4° 22 *151*
Opp. Add. 4° 23 *151*
Opp. Add. 4° 24 *151*
Opp. Add. 4° 26 *119 277*
Opp. Add. 4° 27 *233*
Opp. Add. 4° 28 *22*

Opp. Add. 4° 29 *22*
Opp. Add. 4° 30 *22*
Opp. Add. 4° 31 *22*
Opp. Add. 4° 32 *22*
Opp. Add. 4° 33 *22 95*
Opp. Add. 4° 34 *22 95*
Opp. Add. 4° 35 *22 95*
Opp. Add. 4° 36 *22 95*
Opp. Add. 4° 38 *22*
Opp. Add. 4° 39 *22 95*
Opp. Add. 4° 40 *95*
Opp. Add. 4° 41 *95*
Opp. Add. 4° 42 *22 95*
Opp. Add. 4° 44 *22*
Opp. Add. 4° 45 *64*
Opp. Add. 4° 47 *255 265*
Opp. Add. 4° 49 *256*
Opp. Add. 4° 50 *256*
Opp. Add. 4° 51 *255*
Opp. Add. 4° 54 *93*
Opp. Add. 4° 59 *93*
Opp. Add. 4° 60 *93*
Opp. Add. 4° 67 *199*
Opp. Add. 4° 69 *122*
Opp. Add. 4° 70 *122*
Opp. Add. 4° 71 *199*
Opp. Add. 4° 72 *199*
Opp. Add. 4° 73 *199*
Opp. Add. 4° 74 *199*
Opp. Add. 4° 75 *122*
Opp. Add. 4° 78 *122*
Opp. Add. 4° 80 *285*
Opp. Add. 4° 81 *286*
Opp. Add. 4° 82 *287*
Opp. Add. 4° 83 *286*
Opp. Add. 4° 84 *286*
Opp. Add. 4° 85 *286*
Opp. Add. 4° 86 *286*
Opp. Add. 4° 87 *286*
Opp. Add. 4° 88 *286*
Opp. Add. 4° 89 *285 286*
Opp. Add. 4° 90 *287*
Opp. Add. 4° 92 *287*
Opp. Add. 4° 93 *287*
Opp. Add. 4° 97 *95*
Opp. Add. 4° 100 *199*
Opp. Add. 4° 101 *199*
Opp. Add. 4° 102 *199*
Opp. Add. 4° 103 *199 258*
Opp. Add. 4° 104 *199 259*
Opp. Add. 4° 105 *199 258*
Opp. Add. 4° 106 *199 258*
Opp. Add. 4° 107 *57*
Opp. Add. 4° 108 *57*
Opp. Add. 4° 109 *57*
Opp. Add. 4° 110 *57*
Opp. Add. 4° 111 *57 254*
Opp. Add. 4° 112 *57 254*
Opp. Add. 4° 113 *57 253*
Opp. Add. 4° 114 *22 145 239*
Opp. Add. 4° 115 *22*
Opp. Add. 4° 116 *95 263*
Opp. Add. 4° 117 *95 263*
Opp. Add. 4° 118 *95 240 263*
Opp. Add. 4° 119 *95 240 262*
Opp. Add. 4° 120 *95 263*
Opp. Add. 4° 121 *95 263*
Opp. Add. 4° 122 *95 262*
Opp. Add. 4° 123 *95 263*
Opp. Add. 4° 125 *95*
Opp. Add. 4° 126 *95*
Opp. Add. 4° 127 *95*
Opp. Add. 4° 128 *95*
Opp. Add. 4° 129 *24*
Opp. Add. 4° 130 *24*
Opp. Add. 4° 132 *24*
Opp. Add. 4° 133 *24*
Opp. Add. 4° 134 *24*
Opp. Add. 4° 135 *160 251 290*
Opp. Add. 4° 137 *95*
Opp. Add. 4° 138 *95*
Opp. Add. 4° 139 *95*
Opp. Add. 4° 140 *95*
Opp. Add. 4° 146 *95 284*
Opp. Add. 4° 151 *15*
Opp. Add. 4° 160 *95*
Opp. Add. 4° 162 *203*
Opp. Add. 4° 163 *95*
Opp. Add. 4° 164 *95*
Opp. Add. 4° 165 *95*
Opp. Add. 4° 166 *95 203*
Opp. Add. 4° 167 *95*
Opp. Add. 4° 179 *199 259*
Opp. Add. 4° 181 *258*
Opp. Add. 4° 182 *258*
Opp. Add. 4° 183 *199*

Opp. Add. 4° 194 *34*
Opp. Add. 8° 7 *256*
Opp. Add. 8° 8 *255*
Opp. Add. 8° 9 *93*
Opp. Add. 8° 10 *93*
Opp. Add. 8° 11 *93*
Opp. Add. 8° 12 *93*
Opp. Add. 8° 13 *93*
Opp. Add. 8° 19 *199 285*
Opp. Add. 8° 20 *285*
Opp. Add. 8° 21 *285*
Opp. Add. 8° 23 *263*
Opp. Add. 8° 24 *263*
Opp. Add. 8° 25 *263*
Opp. Add. 8° 26 *263*
Opp. Add. 8° 27 *263*
Opp. Add. 8° 39 *249*
Opp. Add. 8° 41 *249*
Opp. Add. 8° 44 *263*
Opp. Add. 8° 48 *205*
Opp. Add. 8° 59 (Cat. 2589) *97*
Pers. e. 27 *151*
Poc. 7 *265*
Poc. 30 *265*
Poc. 70 *266*
Poc. 274 *266*
Poc. 281 *266*
Poc. 285 *266*
Poc. 347 *265*
Poc. 348 *265*
Poc. 395 *265*
Poc. 396 *265*
Rawl. Or. 48 *265*
Tanner 173 *210 266*

Oxford, Corpus Christi College
5–12 *266*
133 *279*

Oxford, Jesus College
95–97 *267*

Oxford, Lincoln College
unnumbered *267*

Oxford, Oriel College
73 *267*

Oxford, St. John's College
143 *267*

Padua, Comunità ebraica
MS IV (formerly) *276*

Paris, Alliance Israélite Universelle
H 1 A *286*
H 2 A *286*
H 3 A *286*
H 4 A *285*
H 7 A *287*
H 8 A *286*
H 9 A *285*
H 10 A *286*
H 11 A *287*
H 13 A *286*
H 14 A *286*
H 16 A *285*
H 17 A *285*
H 18 A *285*
H 19 A *286*
H 20 A *285*
H 21 A *286*
H 23 A *161 287*
H 24 A *286*
H 25 A *287*
H 26 A *287*
H 27 A *286*
H 28 A *286*
H 29 A *286*
H 30 A *286*
H 31 A *286*
H 33 A *286*
H 34 A *286*
H 35 A *287*
H 36 A *287*
H 37 A *286*
H 38 A *287*
H 39 A *287*
H 41 A *286*
H 42 A *286*
H 43 A *205 286*
H 44 A *287*
H 45 A *286*
H 46 A *285*
H 47 A *59 287*
H 48 A *285*

H 49 A *286*
H 50 A *287*
H 51 A *285*
H 52 A *285*
H 53 A *285*
H 54 A *286*
H 55 A *287*
H 56 A *286*
H 57 A *286*
H 58 A *286*
H 61 A *286*
H 64 A *287*
H 71 A *165*
H 72 A *165*
H 80 A *145*
H 83 A *250*
H 89 A *165*
H 90 A *165*
H 96 A *249*
H 98 A *63*
H 101 A *165*
H 107 A *259*
H 124 A *200*
H 149 A *258*
H 162 A *264*
H 167 A *261*
H 197 A *250*
H 230 A *189*
H 246 *130*
H 250–257 *157*
H 332 *166*
H 370 *165*
H 423 *284*
H 428 *165*
Nahmias H 001 *84*

Paris, Bibliothèque de l'Arsenal
449 *166*
8863 *166*
8864 *166*

Paris, Bibliothèque de la Compagnie des Prêtres de Saint-Sulpice
MS 1933 *71*

Paris, Bibliothèque Mazarine
4472–4478 *166*

Paris, Bibliothèque nationale de France
héb. 1–3 *56 268*
héb. 4 *164 276*
héb. 5–6 269
héb. 7 *172 272*
héb. 8–10 *272*
héb. 11–12 269
héb. 13 *272*
héb. 14 *272*
héb. 15 *65 177 269*
héb. 16 *271*
héb. 17–18 *176 279*
héb. 19 *271*
héb. 20 *108 271*
héb. 22 *272*
héb. 23 *272*
héb. 24 *272*
héb. 25 *271*
héb. 26 *269*
héb. 27 *271*
héb. 28 *271*
héb. 29 *271*
héb. 30 *269*
héb. 31 *271*
héb. 32 *269*
héb. 33 *271*
héb. 34 *271*
héb. 35 *269*
héb. 36 *270*
héb. 37 *272*
héb. 38 *272*
héb. 39 *270*
héb. 40 *270*
héb. 41 *271*
héb. 43 *271*
héb. 44 *272*
héb. 46 *271*
héb. 47 *271*
héb. 48–49 *271*
héb. 50 *270*
héb. 51 *271*
héb. 52 *271*
héb. 53 *272*
héb. 54 *272*
héb. 55 *271*
héb. 58 *271*
héb. 59 *271*
héb. 60 *271*

héb. 61 *272*
héb. 62 *272*
héb. 63 *272*
héb. 65 *271*
héb. 66 *271*
héb. 67 *272*
héb. 68–69 *271*
héb. 70–71 *271*
héb. 72 *271*
héb. 73 *271*
héb. 80 *270*
héb. 81 *271*
héb. 82 *272*
héb. 83 *271*
héb. 84 *271*
héb. 85 *164 276*
héb. 86 *272*
héb. 87 *271*
héb. 88 *272*
héb. 89 *271*
héb. 93 *272*
héb. 94 *272*
héb. 95 *271*
héb. 98 *65*
héb. 99 *271*
héb. 102 *270*
héb. 103 *271*
héb. 104 *272*
héb. 105 *271*
héb. 106 *270*
héb. 107 *271*
héb. 108 *270*
héb. 109 *269*
héb. 111 *270*
héb. 112 *270*
héb. 113 *271*
héb. 114 *271*
héb. 119 *271*
héb. 656 *294*
héb. 670 *44*
héb. 768 *65*
héb. 893 *294*
héb. 927 *65*
héb. 981 *65*
héb. 1251 *294*
héb. 1388 *86*
héb. 1463 *299*
héb. 1467 *303*
héb. 1468 *122 299*
sam. 1 *172 271*
sam. 2 *272*
sam. 3 *270*
sam. 4 *272*
sam. 5 *172 271*
sam. 8 *172*
sam. 9 *172*
sam. 10 *172*
sam. 11 *172*

Paris, Institut de France
3371–3405 *61*

Paris, V. Klagsbald
unnumbered *298 299*

Paris, Les Enluminures
unnumbered *292 293*

Paris, Musée Cluny
Cl. 12263 *169*
Cl. 12290 *169*
Cl. 12294–95 *169*
Cl. 12296a–e *169*
Cl. 12311 *169*
Cl. 13995 *169*

Paris, Societé des manuscrits des assureurs français
unnumbered *297 298 300*

Parma, Biblioteca Palatina
13 *276*
29 *280*
30 *276*
250 *276*
300 *276*
677 *276*
743 *276*
1002 *280*
1264 *280*
1833 *277*
1834–35 *69 273*
1996–97 *273*
1998–2000 *69 273*
2025 *273*

2033 *276*
2151–2153 *256 277*
2174 *277*
2207 *57 276*
2292 *207*
2338–2339 *256 277*
2411 *171*
2516 *69 273*
2521 *277*
2596 *171*
2668 *273*
2698 *273*
2812 *273*
2828 *273*
2846 *57 276*
2948 *27*
2998 *171*
3079 *273*
3104 *279*
3110 *279 280*
3173 *171*
3174 *171*
3214 *275*
3231 *279*
3286–3287 *171*
3288 *276*
3290 *277*
3293 *275*
3294 *277*
3558 *170*

Philadelphia, Free Library
Lewis. Or. Ms. 140 *283*

Philadelphia, University of Pennsylvania, CAJS
RAR MS 26 *55*
RAR MS 47 *174*
RAR MS 73 *174*
Schoenberg Collection LJS 57 *300*
Schoenberg Collection LJS 204 *298*
Schoenberg Collection LJS 311 *284*
Schoenberg Collection LJS 312 *284*
Schoenberg Collection LJS 453 *284*
Schoenberg Collection LJS 468 *293*
Schoenberg Collection LJS 469 *293*
Schoenberg Collection LJS 470 *292*
Schoenberg Collection LJS 472 *293*
Schoenberg Collection LJS 492 *293*

Piacenza, Biblioteca Comunale
MS Landi 181 *174 280*

Prague, Jewish Museum
MS 1 *142*
MS 98 *113*
MS 120 *244*
MS 229 *181*
MS 340 *244*
MS 485 *244*

Prague, National Library
MS XVIII F 6 *64 282*

Princeton University Library
MS Garrett 26 *22 77 212*
MS Scheide M 136 *112* 223

Ramat Gan, Bar-Ilan University
181 *27*
275 *259 306*
286 *259 306*
583 *259 306*
626 *120*
747 *259 306*
1007 (= Musayof 58) *130*
1041 *257*

Ravenna, Biblioteca Comunale Classense
Cod. 27 *180*
Cod. 69 *180*

Reggio Emilia, Biblioteca Panizzi
MS Vari. D. 118 *181*

Rome, Biblioteca Angelica
Or. 12 *274*
Or. 18 *270*
Or. 21 *274*
Or. 24 *274*
Or. 35 *274*
Or. 36 *274*
Or. 39 *274*
Or. 45 *65*
Or. 47 *274*

Or. 50 *274*
Or. 70 *279*
Or. 72 *65 270*
Or. 78 *279*
Or. 85 *274*

Rome, Biblioteca Casanatense
1916 *274*
1938 *281*
2718 *274*
2722 *274*
2725 *274*
2729 *274*
2730 *274*
2731 *274*
2738 *274*
2750 *274*
2761 *51*
2763 *281*
2828 *281*
2830 *274*
2831 *281*
2832 *281*
2833 *274*
2836 *280*
2843 *274*
2844 *274*
2877 *274*
2894 *274*
2898 *274*
2930 *274*
2971 *65*
2972 *274*
2983 *274*
2988 *274*
3010 *274*
3022 *274*
3102 *281*
3117 *274*
3147 *281*
4849 *274*

Rome, Biblioteca Nazionale Centrale di Roma
Or. 51 *279*
Or. 52 *279*
Or. 72 *279*
Or. 85 *279*

Rome, Collegio Rabbinico Italiano
MS 135

Rome, Comunità ebraica
3 *279*
F 287 *279*

de Rossi, *ext.*
See also Appendix I, no. 22.
15 *144*
17 *66*
28 *174*
83 *52*
586 *144*

Rostock, Universitätsbibliothek
Or. 32 *268*
Or. 38 *102*

St. Paul im Lavanttal, Stiftsbibliothek
MS 84.1 *268 303*

St. Petersburg, Institute of Oriental Manuscripts
B 168 *110*
B 184 *102*
B 244 *67*
B 291 *69*
B 314 *67*
B 377 *205*
B 381 *145*
B 416 *67*
B 457 *110*
B 512 *75*
C 88 *205*
C 134 *67*
D 29 *67*
D 62 *109*

St. Petersburg, Russian National Library
Dorn 603–608 *191*
Евр. I A *61*
Евр. I B 19A *118*
Евр. I Bibl. 3 *173*
Евр. I C 10 *131*
Евр. II A 32 *91*

Евр. II B 17 *118*
Евр. II biblical MSS on leather 160 *60 192*

Salamanca, Biblioteca de la Universidad
MS 2170 *194*

San Lorenzo del Escorial, Real Biblioteca
G I 13 *195*
G III 19 *195*

São Paulo, Safra Family
MS Sassoon 16 *180 296*
MS Sassoon 23 *144 279*
MS Sassoon 24 *180 296*
MS Sassoon 1209 *233*

Sassoon Family Collection
See also Appendix I, no. 35.
16 *180*
17–19 *81*
23 *144 172 279*
72–73 *212*
82 *203 214*
187 *81*
217–227 *81*
280 *169*
282 *25*
368 *68*
406 *224*
407 *224*
439 *255*
493 *35 307*
495 *169*
506 *94 211 262*
507 *59*
511 *69*
512 *260*
514 *197*
521–532 *81*
537 *81*
566 *81*
601 *122*
683 *169*
705 *257*
706 *169*
707 *257*
713 *81*
714 *257*
964 *59*
1209 *233*
1240 *283*
1271 *242*
1281–1282 *137*

Silver Spring, Md., M. Lehmann
unnumbered *297*
87 *39*
88 *39 243*
89 *39 243*
90 *243*
91 *39*
231 *247*
B 70 *241*
D 56 *303*
D 107 *300*
D 121 *245*
K 56 *297*
M 10 *301*
NL 48 *225*

Strasbourg, Bibliothèque nationale et universitaire
unnumbered *268*
3927 *239*
3932 *239*
3935 *239*
3941 *239*
3945 *239*
3946 *239*
3949 *263*
3953 *284*
3957 *263*
3981 *51*
3982 *51*
4040 *284*
4048 *285*
4771 *207*
4809 *207*
4845 *207*
5138 *207*
5988 *207*

Stuttgart, Württembergische Landesbibliothek
Cod. A 11 *209*
Cod. Or. 2° 1 *272*
Cod. Or. 2° 2 *182*
Cod. Or. 4° 1 *64 107*

Sydney, University of Sydney
MS Nicholson 33 *144 260 277*

Tel Aviv, William Gross
30 *228*
179 *298*
194 *153*
272 *75*
273 *75*
328 *284*

Tel Aviv, Nehorai
5 *39*

Tel Aviv, Rambam Library
1 *30*
27 *97*

Toledo, Catedral
Z–1–13 *275*
Z–1–18 *275*
Z–1–19 *273*

Toronto, University of Toronto
Friedberg MSS
3–002 *297*
3–011 *299*
3–012 *143*
3–017 *228*
5–001 *298*
5–006 *301*
5–011 *299*
5–021 *300*
9–004 *228*

Tübingen, Universitätsbibliothek
Ma IV 1 *281*

Turin, Biblioteca Nazionale Universitaria
See also Appendix I, no. 41.
A.I.1 *273*
A.I.3 *270*
A.I.5 *280*
A.I.6 *270*
A.I.20 *280*
A.II.8 *270*
A.II.27 *280*
A.III.2 *216*
A.III.7 *280*
A.III.8 *280*
A.III.14 *59*
A.III.26 *270*
A.III.32 *273*
A.IV.3 *270*
A.IV.20 *273*
A.IV.29 *270*
A.VI.5 *273*
A.VI.34 *216*
A.VI.38 *216*
A.VII.49 *273*

Udine, Biblioteca Arcivescovile
MS 248 ebr. 14 *277*
MS 249 ebr. 15 *277*

Uppsala, Universitetsbibliotek
Cod. O. Hebr. 1 *279*
Cod. O. Hebr. 2 *276*
Cod. O. Hebr. 3 *276*

Utrecht, Rijksuniversiteit
1424 *278*
1425 *278*

Vatican, Biblioteca Apostolica Vaticana
Cod. Barb. Or. 1 *26*
Cod. Barb. Or. 101 *270*
Cod. Barb. Or. 161–164 *274*
Cod. Chigi R.IV.37 *53 279*
Cod. ebr. 1 *270*
Cod. ebr. 2 *274*
Cod. ebr. 3 *274*
Cod. ebr. 4–6 *270 275*

Cod. ebr. 7 *275*
Cod. ebr. 8 *274*
Cod. ebr. 9 *270*
Cod. ebr. 10 *275*
Cod. ebr. 11 *270*
Cod. ebr. 12 *270*
Cod. ebr. 13 *275*
Cod. ebr. 14 *275*
Cod. ebr. 15 *275*
Cod. ebr. 17 *275*
Cod. ebr. 18 *275*
Cod. ebr. 19 *275*
Cod. ebr. 20 *270*
Cod. ebr. 21 *275*
Cod. ebr. 22 *275*
Cod. ebr. 23–24 *275*
Cod. ebr. 25 *270*
Cod. ebr. 26 *275*
Cod. ebr. 27 *275*
Cod. ebr. 28 *275*
Cod. ebr. 29 *275*
Cod. ebr. 288 *140*
Cod. ebr. 436 *275*
Cod. ebr. 437 *270*
Cod. ebr. 439–440 *270*
Cod. ebr. 443 *275*
Cod. ebr. 444 *270*
Cod. ebr. 447 *270*
Cod. ebr. 448 *270*
Cod. ebr. 453 *270*
Cod. ebr. 463 *275*
Cod. ebr. 468 *275*
Cod. ebr. 473 *275*
Cod. ebr. 481 *275*
Cod. ebr. 482 *183 270*
Cod. ebr. 503 *281*
Cod. ebr. 618–722 *219*
Od. Lat. 2911 *161*
Cod. Neofiti 1 *65 185*
Cod. Pers. 61 *275*
Cod. Rossiana 601 *274*
Cod. Urb. ebr. 1 *270*
Cod. Urb. ebr. 2 *270*
Cod. Urb. ebr. 3 *275*
Cod. Urb. ebr. 4 *275*
Cod. Urb. ebr. 5 *275*
Cod. Urb. ebr. 6 *275*
Cod. Urb. ebr. 7 *275*

Venice, Biblioteca Marciana
MS Or. 207 *276*
MS Or. 208–209 *280*
MS Or. 210 *276*
MS Or. 211–214 *280*
MS Or. 215 *210*

Vienna, Jüdische Gemeinde
unnumbered *304 306 308*

Vienna, Österreichische Nationalbibliothek
Cod. Hebr. 4 *277*
Cod. Hebr. 5 *277*
Cod. Hebr. 6 *281*
Cod. Hebr. 9 *277*
Cod. Hebr. 11 *277*
Cod. Hebr. 12a *277*
Cod. Hebr. 13 *281*
Cod. Hebr. 14 *277*
Cod. Hebr. 15 *277*
Cod. Hebr. 16 *281*
Cod. Hebr. 17 *277*
Cod. Hebr. 19 *281*
Cod. Hebr. 25 *282*
Cod. Hebr. 28 *277*
Cod. Hebr. 35 *270*
Cod. Hebr. 38 *277*
Cod. Hebr. 106 *34*
Cod. Hebr. 157 *124*
Cod. Hebr. 167 *27 281*
Cod. Hebr. 181 *205*
Cod. Hebr. 184 *224*
Cod. Hebr. 212 *223 240*
Cod. Hebr. 213 *223 240*
Cod. Hebr. 218 *113*
Cod. Hebr. 223 *223*
Cod. Hebr. 224 *223*
Cod. Hebr. 242 *188 302*

Warminster, Marquess of Bath (formerly)
unnumbered *69*

Warsaw, Jewish Historical Institute (old call-numbers)
4 *303*
8 *295*
10 *243*

16 *247*
19 *247*
23 *248*
25 *244*
30 *303*
31 *306*
33 *244*
35 *244*
36 *247*
37 *303*
38 *304*
40 *304*
45 *304*
48 *306*
49 *305*
54 *304*
59 *181 305*
62 *246*
63 *245*
64 *246*
65 *304*
69 *246*
70 *246*
71 *304*
72 *246*
73 *305*
75 *245*
76 *247*
77 *304*
81 *247*
82 *245*
85 *305*
89 *303*
94 *294*
98 *246*
99 *258*
100 *245*
101 *244*
102 *244*
106 *295*
107 *304*
109 *246*
110 *305*
111 *246*
112 *294*
113 *304*
114 *246*
118 *245*
119 *303*
122 *247*
123 *246*
126 *243*
130 *303*
131 *243*
133 *304*
134 *245*
135 *245*
137 *246*
139 *248*
140 *245*
143 *246*
148 *247*
150 *295*
151 *248*
152 *306*
154 *304*
155 *306*
158 *246*
159 *247*
164 *306*
166 *245*
167 *244*
168 *305*
174 *258*
178 *305*
179 *304*
180 *304*
181 *245*
184 *244*
189 *307*
190 *294 307*
192 *246*
193 *306*
197 *243*
201 *247*
205 *303*
209 *247*
211 *305*
212 *246*
213 *304*
214 *244*
215 *243*
217 *246*
218 *305*
220 *247*
221 *305*

222 *247*
223 *247*
225 *247*
227 *247*
228 *304*
229 *306*
230 *306*
231 *225*
235 *245*
239 *245*
242 *144 229*
244 *305*
245 *307*
247 *305*
249 *306*
251 *249 303*
252 *307*
254 *305*
255 *307*
257 *303*
259 *246*
260 *303*
261 *245*
265 *243*
275 *247*
281 *308*
282 *306*
284 *259 304*
285 *306*
288 *246 251*
291 *246*
293 *306*
296 *246*
298 *247*
299 *247*
303 *248*
306 *245*
311 *170*
346 *304*
350 *243*
352 *246*
361 *243*
366 *244*
367 *245*
368 *304*
374 *306*
379 *246*
386 *247*
394 *305*
399 *247*
426 *246*
430 *245*
435 *303*
440 *244*
452 *247*
470 *247*
474 *248*
476 *294 306*
480 *246*
481 *245*
482 *245*
484 *247*
493 *304*
497 *304*
614 *246*
621 *244*
626 *244*
651 *244*
659 *247*
668 *305*
726b *247*
726c *247*
726g *247*
726h *247*
736 *303*
737 *243*
775 *246*
796 *247*
879 *247*
888 *303*
891 *303*
895 *258*
900 *252 306*
907 *303*
1020 *247*
1022 *305*
1099 *247*
1159 *305*
1162 *246*
1193 *306*
1195 *247*

Washington, D.C., Library of Congress
MS Heb. 18 *33 87*
MS Heb. 181 *228*

Weimar, Herzogin Anna Amalia Bibliothek
Q 652a *228*

Wolfenbüttel, Herzog August Bibliothek
Cod. Guelf. 659 *278*
Cod. Helmst. 3 *269*

Wrocław, Biblioteka Uniwersytecka
Cod. Or. I.1 *62 231*
M 1106 *282*
M 1107 *282*
M 1108 *282*
M 1109 *282*

Zurich, R. Bollag
unnumbered *297 298*

Zurich, Braginsky Collection
unnumbered *275 284 285 286 291 292 299 301 302*
57 *242*
67 *91*
243 *69*

Zurich, Floersheim family
unnumbered *298*

Zurich, D. Jeselsohn
unnumbered *301 302*

Zurich, Zentralbibliothek
Heid. 29 *284*
Heid. 53 *285*
Heid. 80 *285*
Heid. 81 *251*
Heid. 86 *282*
Heid. 107 *265*
Heid. 159 *250*
Heid. 161 *251*
Heid. 169 *249*
Heid. 188 *261*
Heid. 207 *264 284 295*
Or. 152 *270*
Or. 155 *273*
Or. 157 *273*
Or. 158 *270*

INDEX OF NAMES OF LIBRARIES, PERSONS AND PLACES

Abbreviations and alternative spellings of library, personal and place names appear as separate entries in the text and are not included in the Index.
Libraries are listed by the names of the cities in which they are located.
For more libraries, see the Index of Manuscripts.

Abel, W. *109 182*
Abensour *112*
Aberdeen, Christ's College *13*
Aberdeen, Free Church College *13*
Aberdeen, University of Aberdeen, King's College Library and Historic Collections ***13***
Aberdeen Bible ***13***
Aberdonia ***13***
Aboab, Samuel ***13***
Abrahams, Israel ***13*** *47*
Abulafia, Yedidya *130*
Acqui, Biblioteca del Seminario Vescovile *99*
Adler, Cyrus ***13*** *28 174*
Adler, Elkan Nathan ***13–14*** *15 52 71 79 80 84 145 153 200 201 208 211*
Adler, Israel *147*
Adler, Marcus Nathan *14 89*
Adler, Nathan b. Simeon ***15***
Adler Collection, Second *13 208*
Adler-Stroock Collection *13 208*
Advielle, Victor *21*
Afendopolo, Caleb *169*
Aghib ***15***
Agnon, Samuel Joseph ***15***
Albeck, H. *23*
Albeck, S. *23*
Alcalá de Henares, Collegio de San Ildefonso ***15*** *132 232*
Aleppo *14* ***15–16*** *55 97 176*
Aleppo Codex *15 103*
Alessandria, Biblioteca Civica e Archivio di Stato *99*
Alessandria, Comunità ebraica ***16*** *23*
Alfasi, Y. *120*
Allan, N. *128*
Allen, Thomas *62*
Allony, Nehemia ***16*** *75 104 130 140 214*
Almanzi, Giuseppe ***16*** *22 24 119 125 126*
Altdorf, Universitätsbibliothek ***17*** *226*
Alter, Abraham Mordecai ***17***
Altmann, A. *194*
Amarillo, Abraham *17*
Amarillo, Saul ***17***
Ambrosian Bible ***17***
Ameisenowa, Z. *58*
Amram, David Werner ***17–18*** *174*
Amsterdam, Ashkenazic Rabbinical Seminary ***18***
Amsterdam, Joods Historisch Museum *86*
Amsterdam, Koninklijke Nederlandse Akademie van Wetenschappen ***18*** *117 229*
Amsterdam, Nederlands-Israelietische Hoofdsynagoge *86*
Amsterdam, Portugees Israëlitisch Seminarium Ets Haim – Livraria Montezinos ***18–19*** *76 143*
Amsterdam, Universiteitsbibliotheek, Bibliotheca Rosenthaliana ***19*** *51 76 182 212*
Ancona ***20***
Ancona, Comunità ebraica ***20*** *24*
Ancona, Yeshivat Shenot Eliyahu ***20***
Angulo, G. *213*
Ansbach, Regierungsbibliothek ***20***
Anslo, Gerbrandt ***20*** *44 77*
Antonin ***20–21*** *191 192 194*
Aptowitzer, Victor ***21***
Arce, A. *218*
Arias Montano, Benito ***21*** *195*
Arras, Bibliothèque municipale ***21***
Arundel, Thomas Howard ***1*** *128*
Asch, Sholem ***21*** *138 151*
Ashburnham, Bertram ***22*** *207 211*
Asher, Adolf *16* ***22*** *140 145 206*
Asher, Asher ***22***
Asher b. Eliezer Halevi *207*
Ashkenazi, Bezalel *198*
Ashkenazi, Eliezer ***22***
Ashkenazi Haggada *107*
Ashtor, E. *106*

Assaf, Simha *22 79 91 122 193 226*
Assemani, Joseph Simon ***23*** *219*
Assemani, Stephanus Evodius ***23*** *70 219*
Asti, Comunità ebraica *16* ***23***
Atlanta, Emory University *34*
Auerbach, Benjamin Hirsch ***23***
Augsburg, Staats- und Stadtbibliothek ***23***
Aumer, J. *148*
Avida (Zlotnick), Yehuda Leib ***23*** *225*
Avignon, Bibliothèque municipale ***23***
Avivi, Joseph *103 120 149 156*
Ayuso Marazuela, Teófilo ***23***
Azubi, Solomon *63*
Azulai, Hayyim Joseph David *16 20* ***23–24*** *125 185 199 211 225*
Azulai, Judah Zerahiah *24*
Azulai, Nissim Zerahiah *24*
Azulai, Rafael *24 199*
Azulai-Mandelbaum, Abraham *24*

Bacher, Wilhelm ***25***
Badhab, Isaac Michael ***25*** *92 105 106*
Baer, Seligmann Isaac ***25*** *66 93 145 157 165 182*
Baker, Colin F. *48*
Ballard, J. F. *38 157*
Baltimore, Chizuk Amuno Congregation, Goldsmith Museum *119*
Bamberg, Staatsbibliothek ***25***
Bamberger, L. *87*
Bamberger, Moses Loeb ***25–26***
Bamberger, Samuel b. Naphtali *84*
Bamberger and Wahrmann ***25*** *29 52 77 128 212*
Baraldi, L. *100*
Barberini, Biblioteca ***26*** *219*
Barberini, Francesco *26*
Barberini Triglot ***26***
Barcelona, Biblioteca Central de la Diputación Provincial de Barcelona *26*
Barcelona, Biblioteca de Cataluña ***26***
Barcelona Haggada ***26***
Barco, Javiar del *132 133 144 167*
Bargès, Jean-Joseph-Léandre ***26***
Bar-Ilan, Meir *30*
Baron, Salo *153*
Barrois, Jacques-Marie *22*
Bartolocci, Giulio ***26–27***
Basatin cemetery *79 147*
Basel, Öffentliche Bibliothek der Universität Basel ***27*** *201*
Bashuysen, Heinrich Jacob van ***27***
Bassfreund, J. *213*
Bazzano, Archivio Storico Comunale *99*
Beatty, Alfred Chester *63*
Bedell, William *34*
Beer, Bernhard ***27*** *39 40*
Beit-Arié, Malachi *59 92 93 162*
Belgrado, Yom Tov ***27***
Bellermann, J. J. *66*
Benaim, Joseph ***27*** *153 154*
Benamozegh, Elijah ***27–28*** *95*
Ben Asher Codex ***28***
Benayahu, Meir *25* ***28*** *103 136 199*
Ben-Menahem, Naphtali *75 105 220*
Ben Sasson, M. *191*
Ben Sira *121*
Bencini, Francesco Domenico ***28*** *215*
Benguiat, Ephraim ***28***
Bennett, Solomon Yom Tov ***28***
Bension, Ariel ***28***
Benzian, Julius ***28*** *206*
Berend Salomon, Isaac Seligmann Cohn ***29*** *160*
Berengaut, Alfreda *227*
Berenstein, Issachar Baer ***29***
Berkeley, Magnes Collection ***29***
Berlin, Akademie für die Wissenschaft des Judentums *26* ***29***
Berlin, Hochschule für die Wissenschaft des Judentums ***29–30*** *35 52 78 178*
Berlin, Jüdische Gemeinde ***30*** *54 81 144 146 229*
Berlin, M. ***30***
Berlin, Naphtali Zevi Judah ***30***
Berlin, Reichssicherheitshauptamt *222 227*
Berlin, Staatsbibliothek zu Berlin – Preussischer Kulturbesitz ***30–31*** *66 173 174 206 214*
Berlin, Veitel-Heine'schen Stiftung *73*
Berlin, Zunz-Stiftung *233*
Berlin-Marburg *30*
Berlin-Tübingen *30 215*
Berliner, Abraham *25* ***31*** *150 181 216 221*
Bern, Burgerbibliothek ***32***
Bernays, Jacob ***32***
Bernheimer, Carlo ***32*** *123 140*
Bernkastel-Kues, St. Nikolaus Hospital ***32*** *59*
Bernstein, M. J. *152*
Bernstein, Simon ***32***

Besançon, Bibliothèque municipale ***32***
Besançon, St. Vincent Abbey *32*
Besson, Joseph *56*
Betesh-Levi, Salomone *171*
Bibas, Judah ***32–33***
Bicart-Sée, Edmond M. ***33***
Bick, Abraham ***33***
Biema, Naphtali Hirz van ***33*** *116*
Biesenthal, J. H. *13*
Bird's Head Haggada ***33***
Birmingham, University of Birmingham ***33–34*** *81 87 91 141 142*
Birnbaum, Eduard ***34***
Biscioni, Antonio Maria ***34*** *70*
Bishop Bedell Bible ***34***
Bislisches, Mordecai and Ephraim ***34*** *91 139 161 170 206*
Black, William Mead ***34–35*** *45*
Blau, Joshua *196 204*
Blau, Ludwig Lajos ***35*** *54 124 213 224*
Bloch, Moses ***35*** *143*
Bloch, Philipp ***35***
Bobichon, Philippe *167*
Bodenheimer, Ernst *84 159*
Bodl. Or. ***35***
Boer, P. A. H. de *86 218*
Boesky, Ivan and Selma ***36***
Bologna, Archivio di Dipartimento di Astronomia dell'Universitaria *36*
Bologna, Archivio di Stato ***36*** *99*
Bologna, Archivio Generale Arcivescovile di Bologna *36*
Bologna, Archivio Parrocchiale di S. Martino in Bologna *36*
Bologna, Archivio Provincale dei Padri Cappuccini *36*
Bologna, Biblioteca del Seminario Arcivescovile *36*
Bologna, Biblioteca Universitaria ***36–37*** *137 139*
Bologna, Camera di Commercio di Bologna *36*
Bologna, Civico Museo Bibliografico Musicale di Bologna *36*
Bologna, Monast. S. Michele in Bosco ***37***
Bologna Haggada ***37***
Bonfil, Jacob ***37***
Bonn, Universitäts- und Landesbibliothek ***37***
Borgia, Stefano *38*
Borgiana ***38*** *219*
Borja, Juan de *195*
Borromeo, Federico *140 219*
Boston, Boston Medical Library ***38*** *157*
Boston, Francis A. Countway Library of Medicine *38 157*
Boutelje, Israel Eliazer ***38***
Braginsky, René ***38*** *92*
Brann, M. *14 15 32 66 88 102 187 212 231 233*
Braunschweig, Landesmuseum für Geschichte und Volkstum ***38***
Brecher, Gideon ***38***
Breit, Chaim ***38–39***
Breslau, Gymnasialische Bibliothek zu Maria Magdalena ***39***
Breslau, Israel *29 160*
Breslau, Jüdisch-theologisches Seminar *27 32* ***39–40*** *54 111 124 146 177 196 212 227 231 233*
Breslau, Stadtbibliothek ***40*** *231*
Brinner, W. M. *209*
British Museum Miscellany *31* ***40***
Brody, Heinrich *31 119 177 233*
Brody, Robert *48*
Brookline, Hebrew College *152*
Brother to the Rylands Spanish Haggada *188*
Brugmans, H. *86*
Brüll, N. *95*
Brumer, Judah *14 154*
Bruns, Paulus Jacobus *23*
Brussels ***41***
Brussels, Bibliothèque royale (Koninklijke Bibliotheek van België) ***41*** *129*
Bry, Michel de ***41***
Buber, Solomon *33* ***41*** *111 137*
Buchanan, Claudius ***41*** *45*
Budapest, Magyar Nemzeti Múzeum (Hungarian National Museum) *43 102*
Budapest, Magyar Tudományos Akadémia, Könyvtár (Hungarian Academy of Sciences) ***42*** *81 96 110 166 214*
Budapest, Országos Magyar Zsidó Múzeum (Jewish Museum) ***42–43***
Budapest, Országos Rabbiképző – Zsidó Egyetem Könyvtár (Jewish Theological Seminary) *33 35* ***43*** *124 212 224 228*
Budapest, Orsźagos Széchényi Könyvtár (National Szechenyi Library) ***43***

Burnett, S. G. *27*
Busani, Shelomo ***43***
Busi, G. *135 175*
Buxtorf family *27*

Caen, Bibliothèque municipale ***43***
Cagliari, Biblioteca Universitaria ***43–44***
Cahen, Samuel ***44***
Cairo, Ben Ezra Synagogue *79*
Cairo, Ismalia Synagogue *147*
Cairo, Karaite Synagogue *28*
Cairo, Museum of Islamic Art *81*
Cairo, RaDBaZ Synagogue ***44***
Cambrai, Bibliothèque municipale ***44***
Cambridge, Christ College *44 102*
Cambridge, Emmanuel College *44 102*
Cambridge, Faculty of Oriental Studies *13*
Cambridge, Girton College ***44*** *73 124*
Cambridge, Gonville and Caius College *44*
Cambridge, Pembroke College *44*
Cambridge, St. John's College ***44*** *102*
Cambridge, Trinity College *20 35* ***44–45*** *77 83 124 198 208 231*
Cambridge, University Library *13 20 24 41 44* ***45–49*** *51 59 67 79 80 81 94 95 96 119 121 123 124 144 147 150 161 176 179 198 199 210 211 228*
Cambridge, Westminster College *44 47* ***49*** *81 121 161*
Cambridge (Mass.), Harvard University ***49–50*** *61 74 232*
Cambridge Medical Miscellany ***44***
Camillo Massimo, Carlo *176*
Camillo Massimo, Francesco *176*
Camondo, Isaac *169*
Campanini, S. *36 37 99 100*
Campori, Giuseppe ***50*** *142–143* ***144***
Candia *75 86*
Canonici, Giuseppe *50*
Canonici, Matteo Luigi ***50*** *57 150 161 209*
Cantera Burgos, F. *132 133 218*
Cape Town, National Library of South Africa ***50–51***
Caprotti, Giuseppe *141*
Capsali, Elia *75*
Cardina, Girolamo *50*
Carmoly, Eliakim *41 50* ***51*** *160*
Carpentras, Bibliothèque Inguimbertine ***51***
Carpi, Alberto Pio di *142*
Casanate, Girolamo *183*
Casanatense Haggada ***51***
Casanowicz, I. M. *28*
Cassuto, Alfonso ***51***
Cassuto, Jehuda de Mordechai *51*
Cassuto, Umberto ***51–52*** *70 100 202 220*
Castelbolognesi, Gustavo ***52***
Castell, Edmund *20*
Castelli, D. *70*
Castelnuovo *123*
De Castro Pentateuch *94*
Catalan Maḥzor *29* ***52***
Cazes, D. *214*
Cento ***52***
Cento, Archivio Notarile e Archivio Comunale *99*
Cervera Bible ***52***
Cesena, Archivio di Stato e Archivio della Curia Vescovile *99*
Cesena, Biblioteca Malatestiana ***52***
Chajes, H. P. *70*
Chamizer, Moritz *25* ***52***
Chantilly, Musée Condé ***52***
Chantilly Haggada ***52***
Chapira, Bernard ***52–53*** *147 165*
Chazanovich, Joseph ***53***
Cheltenham *174*
Chester, G. *47 79 162*
Codex Chethamensis ***53***
Chicago, Spertus College, Asher Library ***53***
Chigi, Fabio *53*
Chigiana, Biblioteca ***53*** *219*
Chufut-Kale ***53***
Churchill, Sidney John Alexander ***54***
Chwat, Ezra *100 143*
Chwolson, Daniel ***54***
Cincinnati *99* ***54***
Cincinnati, Hebrew Union College *30 34* ***54*** *73 81 86 111 116 209 228*
Cincinnati, Historical Society *92*
Cincinnati, Museum Center *92*
Cincinnati Haggada, First ***54***
Cincinnati Haggada, Second *218*
Città di Castello *99*
Ciucu, Cristina *167*

Clarke, Adam ***54*** *88 201*
Clement, F. *168*
Cobern, Camden McCormack ***55***
Coblenz, Landeshauptarchiv ***55***
Coburg Pentateuch ***55***
Cochran, John ***55***
Cohen, Abraham ***55***
Cohen, Evelyn M. *38 187*
Cohen, Lipmann ***55*** *160*
Cohen, Salomon Samuelzoon ***55***
Cohen Tanuji, J. *215*
Cohn, Abraham ***55***
Coimbra, Biblioteca Geral de Universidade de Coimbra *55*
Coimbra, Santa Cruz Monastery *55*
Coimbra Bible ***55***
Colbert, Jean Baptiste ***55–56*** *166*
Cologne, Collegii Societatis Jesu Colonia ***56***
Cologne, Historisches Archiv der Stadt ***56***
Comites Latentes *79 202*
Concordiana *188*
Constantinople *13 55 169 226*
Copenhagen, Danish State Archives *57*
Copenhagen, Kongelige Bibliothek ***56*** *57 83 177 196 204*
Copenhagen, Mosaiske Troessamfund ***57***
Corinaldi, Archivio Storico Comunale *99*
Corneliana, Biblioteca ***57*** *205*
Corner family *57 205*
Cornwall (Canada) *185*
Coronel, Nahman Nathan ***57*** *223*
Correggio, Archivio Storico Comunale *99*
Corsiniana, Biblioteca ***57***
Costa, Isaac da ***57***–*58*
Costa Athias, Solomon da ***58*** *125 128*
Costanzi, Giovanni Antonio *23 83 219*
Cotton, John *58*
Cotton, Robert Bruce ***58*** *125*
Cowie, M. *44*
Cowley, Arthur Ernest ***58*** *81 162*
Cracovia, Abraham Hayyim ***58***
Cracow, Jewish Community *58*
Cracow Bible (Regensburg Pentateuch) ***58***
Cramer, Hermann *106*
Crawford, Alexander William ***58*** *134 135*
Crawley, George A. ***59***
Cremona, Archivio di Stato *100*
Cremona Maḥzor ***59*** *107*
Crown, A. D. *210*
Cummings, Theodore E. *29 129*
Codex Curtisianus ***59***
Curtiss, John C. *59*
Cusa, Nicolaus von *32* ***59***

Damascus ***59–60*** *68 228 232*
Damascus, Hushbasba Al'anabi Synagogue *59*
Damascus Keter *59 60*
Damascusrolle *60 192*
Danon, Abraham ***60*** *168*
Danzig, Jewish Community *82*
Danzig, Neil *14 153*
Darmstadt, Hessische Landes- und Hochschulbibliothek *60*
Darmstadt, Universitäts- und Landesbibliothek ***60*** *74*
Darmstadt Haggada ***60*** *98*
David, Abraham *166*
Davidson, Israel ***60*** *203 209*
Davis, M. C. *48 49*
Deinard, Ephraim *13 50* ***60–61*** *97 114 153 208 209 227 228*
Delitzsch, Franz ***61*** *138*
Della Torre, Lelio ***213***
Derbent Tora ***61*** *131*
Derenbourg, Hartwig ***61*** *96 125 168*
Derenbourg, Joseph Naphtali ***61*** *168*
Deutsch, Simon ***61***
Di Capua, Angelo *183 184*
Di Donato, Silvia *167*
Di Segni, Riccardo *184*
Dietrichstein, Prince *61*
Digby, Kenelm ***61–62*** *114*
Dijon, Archives générales du Département de la Côte-d'Or ***62***
Donath, L. *186*
Donaueschingen, Fürstlich Fürstenbergische Hofbibliothek ***62***
Dönmeh *17*
Dorn, B. A. *190*
Double Maḥzor ***62*** *231*
Douglas, Alexander *90*
Dragon Haggada ***62***
Draguignan, Médiathèque Communautaire (formerly Bibliothèque municipale) ***62***
Dresden, Bücherei der Israelitischen Religionsgemeinde, Wünsche Bibliothek ***62*** *146*

Dresden, Sächsischse Landesbibliothek – Staats- und Universitätsbibliothek ***62*** *69*
Dresden Maḥzor ***62***
Dropsie, Moses A. ***63*** *208*
Dublin, Chester Beatty Library *53*
Dublin, Marsh's Library ***63*** *136*
Dublin, Trinity College Library ***63***
Dubno, Solomon ***63*** *178*
Dubrovsky, P. P. *191*
Dubsewitz, Abraham Baer *155*
Duenner, L. *56*
Dukan, Michele *166*
Dukas, Jules ***63*** *125*
Duke of Sussex Catalan Bible ***63–64***
Dukes, Leopold *22 89 125*
Dusnus, Baruch Bendit ***64***
Dyson Perrins Haggada *107*

Ebert, A. *230*
Eck, Oswald von ***64***
Edelmann, Zvi Hirsch *35* ***64*** *78*
Codex Edinburgensis ***64***
Edinburgh, National Library of Scotland ***64***
Edmonton, University of Alberta *28*
Eger ***64***
Egerton, Francis Henry ***65***
Egidio da Viterbo ***65*** *166*
Eilat MSS ***65***
Eisemann, H. *73 232*
Eisenstadt, Burgenländischen Landesmuseum *230*
Elbaz, André *27*
Elberg, Yehuda ***65***
Elboim, A. *30*
Enelow, Hyman George ***65*** *153*
Enelow Memorial Collection *65 75 88 89 137 141 153 154 178 212*
Engel, Edna *46 93*
Epstein, Abraham *31* ***66*** *88 145 215 222*
Epstein, Gershon ***66*** *156*
Erfurt, Evangelisches Ministerium *30* ***66***
Erfurt, Universitätsbibliothek *85*
Ergas, Emanuel ***66***
Erlangen, Jüdische Gemeinde ***66***
Erlangen, Universitätsbibliothek Erlangen-Nürnberg *17* ***67*** *94 158 226*
Erlangen Haggada ***67***
Erna Michael Haggada ***67***
Erpe, Thomas van *45* ***67***
Esslingen Maḥzor ***67***
Ettinghausen, M. *78*
Eupatoria ***67*** *190*
Eupatoria, Semita Isaakovna Kushul Museum *67*
European Geniza ***67–68***
Ezra, Isaac ibn *203*

Faenza, Archivio di Stato *100*
Faenza, Biblioteca Comunale *100*
Faiyum *179*
Fales Collection *109*
Faragi, Isaac *211*
Farhi Bible *60* ***68***
Federigo da Montefeltro, Duke of Urbino *217*
Feinberg, D. H. *205*
Feldman, N. *129*
Fenton, P. B. *193*
Ferrara, Comunità ebraica ***68*** *102 128 151*
Fidalgo, Benjamin Musaphia ***68***
Firkovich, Abraham *53 60 61* ***68–69*** *80 87 131 159 191*
Firkovich Collection, First *191*
Firkovich Collection, Second *191*
Firmian, Carlo Giuseppe di ***69***
Fleischer, Ezra *146*
Fleischer, Heinrich Lebrecht *62* ***69***
Flesch, H. *112 141*
Floersheim, Alexander *69*
Floersheim, Michael J. *41 69*
Floersheim, S. *106*
Floersheim Haggada ***69***
Floersheim Mishne Tora *71*
Florence *177 187*
Florence, Archivio di Stato *100*
Florence, Bibliotheca Carmelitarum S. Pauli ***69***
Florence, Biblioteca Medicea Laurenziana *23 34* ***69–70***
Florence, Biblioteca Nazionale Centrale *52* ***70*** *133*
Florence, Biblioteca Riccardiana ***70–71***
Florence, Collegio Rabbinico Italiano *71 143*
Florence, Ohave Tora Brotherhood ***71*** *184*
Florence, Università *100*
Florence, Università, Biblioteca della Facoltà di Lettere e Filosofia ***71***
Foa, Moses Benjamin *34* ***71*** *142 170 206*
Foa Bible ***71***

Forlì, Archivio di Stato *100*
Fraenkel, S. *14*
Franck, A. *167*
Franeker (Netherlands), Akademie ***71*** *115*
Frank, Abraham *218*
Frank, Heinz *218*
Frank, John *218*
Fränkel, David *13 54* ***71–72*** *98 153 154 201 216*
Frankfurt Mishne Tora ***72***
Frankfurt a/M, Gesellschaft zur Erforschung jüdischer Kunstdenkmaler *73*
Frankfurt a/M, Goethe Universitäts, Universitätsbibliothek Johann Christian Senckenberg *24 51* ***72–73*** *76 81 108 139 187 208*
Frankfurt a/M, Museum jüdischer Altertumer ***73***
Franklin, Arthur Ellis ***73***
Franz-Klauser, O. *32*
Frauberger, Heinrich ***73*** *87 111*
Freer, Charles L. *227*
Freiburg im Breisgau, Universitätsbibliothek ***73***
Freimann, Aron *31 145 155 220*
Freimann, Jacob ***73***
Frenkel, V. *100*
Frennsdorff, Solomon ***73***
Frere, Mary Eliza Isabella *44* ***73***
Friedberg, Albert Dov ***73–74*** *80 153 212*
Friedberg, Stadtarchiv ***74***
Friedberg, Theologisches Seminar *74*
Friedberg Genizah Project *49 74 80*
Friedenwald, Harry ***74***
Friedenwald, Herbert ***74***
Friedland, Moses Arye Leib ***74*** *75 137 179 190*
Friedman, Harry G. ***74***
Friedman, J. *209*
Friedman, Lee Max ***74*** *75*
Friedmann, Felix ***50*** *74–75*
Friedmann, Israel ***75***
Friedmann, Kalman *71 100*
Friedmann, Nahum Dov of Sadagora ***75*** *105*
Fuenn, Samuel Joseph *63* ***75***
Fugger, G. G. *86*
Fugger, Ulrich ***75*** *93 135*
Fuks, Leo (Lajb) *18 19* ***76*** *115*
Fuld, Aaron ***76***
Fuld, Salomon *76*
Fulda, Hessische Landesbibliothek *76*
Fulda, Hochschul- und Landesbibliothek ***76***
Fumagalli, Pier Francesco *100 101*
Fürth, Jüdisches Museum Franken *76*
Fürth, Klaus ***76***

Gaddi family *70*
Gaffarel, J. *175*
Gagin, Hayyim Abraham ***76–77***
Gagin, Isaac *76 130*
Gagin, Shalom *76*
Gale, Thomas *20 44 77*
Gans, Mozes Heiman *77 164*
Gaon, Shem Tov ibn *203*
Garel, Michel *39 169 227*
Garrett, Robert *77*
Gaspar Remiro, M. *132*
Gaster, Moses *26 77–***78*** *81 88 125 127 129 135 165 201 233*
Gaster, V. I. *78*
Gaster Bible ***78***
Gaster Bible, First *78*
Gaster Bible, Second *78*
Gaulmin, Gilbert *166*
Gayangos, Pascual y Arce de ***78***
Gazov-Ginzberg, A. M. *190*
Geiger, Abraham *29 35* ***78*** *129 178 192*
Geneva, Bibliothèque centrale juive ***78***
Geneva, Bibliothèque publique et universitaire ***78–79*** *81 202*
Geniza *13 14 17 18 20 30 33 34 35 42 43 44 45 46 47–49 52 54 55 58 61 72 73 74 77* ***79–81*** *83 89 91 94 96 104 105 106 110 111 113 119 121 123 124 126 134 135 138 140 141 142 143 146 147 153 154 155 161 162 163 165 166 168 174 179 187 191 192 193 198 207 208 209 211 213 214 227 228 229 230*
Genoa, Biblioteca Civica Berio ***81***
Genoa, Biblioteca della Comunità ebraica ***81–82***
George III, King *188*
George IV, King *111*
Gerona, Arxiu Históric ***82***
Gesellschaft zur Erforschung jüdischer Kunstdenkmäler *73*
Gheyn, J. van den *41*
Ghiron, Samuel *215*
Ghirondi, Mordecai Samuel ***82*** *136 199 206*
Gianfilippi, Paolini ***82*** *189*

Gibson, Margaret Dunlop ***121***
Gieldzinski, Lesser ***82***
Giessen, Universitätsbibliothek ***82***
Gillespie, C. G. K. *13 53*
Ginsburg, Christian David *44 81* ***82–83*** *116 231*
Ginsburger, M. *207*
Gintsburg, Yonah *190*
Ginzberg, Louis *80*
Ginze milyard *34*
Giotto *212*
Gizeh *227*
Glaser, Eduard ***83***
Glasgow, University Library ***83***
Glatz *39*
Glatzer, Mordecai *28 50 93*
Glick, S. *147*
Goeje, M. J. De *115*
Goitein, S. D. *174*
Golb, Norman *53*
Golden Haggada ***83***
Goldenberg, Samuel Lob *119*
Goldenthal, J. *223*
Goldschmidt, Lazarus *56* ***83***
Goldschmidt, Mayer Selig *15* ***83–84*** *94 103 155 158*
Goldschmidt, S. *90*
Goldsmid, Julian ***84*** *144*
Goldstein, David *126*
Goldziher, Ignaz *42*
Gollancz, Hermann ***84***
Golnitzki, Heshil ***84***
Gonzálvez, R. *212*
Gorizia, Biblioteca della Comunità ebraica ***84***
Gorizia, Biblioteca Statale Isontina *100*
Gotha, Forschungsbibliothek und Landesbibliothek *85*
Gotha, Universitäts- und Forschungsbibliothek Erfurt / Gotha ***84–85*** *138*
Gottheil, Richard James Horatio *44 70 184 227*
Göttingen, Niedersächsisiche Staats- und Universitätsbibliothek ***85***
Gottstein, M. H. *33 141 142*
Gottweig, Stiftsbibliothek ***85***
Gozlow *67*
Graz, Steiermärkisches Landesarchiv ***85***
Graz, Universitätsbibliothek ***85***
Graziano, Abraham Solomon Joseph ***85–86***
Great Maḥzor of Amsterdam ***86***
Greek Haggada ***86***
Greenwood, F. *143 214*
Gregory XV, Pope *93*
Grey, George *50*
Grimani, Domenico ***86*** *175 216*
Groningen, Rijksuniversiteit ***86***
Gross, Bery *151*
Gross, William L. ***86*** *153*
Grossman, Louis ***86***
Grünhut, Lazarus (Eleazar) *34* ***86–87***
Guesnon, A. *21*
Guggenheim, Felix *73* ***87*** *112*
Güldenstein (rabbi in Buchau) *35*
Gunther, Charles F. ***87***
Günzburg, Baron David *25 51 57* ***87*** *129 145 151 179 189 211*
Günzburg, Horace ***87***
Günzburg, Joseph ***87*** *95*
Gurland, Jonas ***87–88*** *192*
Guttmann, Alexander *29 78 178*

Haas, Philipp de *231*
Hagen, Johannes van der *54* ***88*** *201*
Hague, Museum Meerman-Westreenianum *138*
Halberstamm, Solomon Joachim *31 33 57 77* ***88*** *97 115 122 124 127 153 154 171 179 200 206 208*
Halevy, Hayyim Bekhor ***89*** *105*
Halevy, Joseph *83*
Halevy, Meyer Abraham *169*
Hallamish, Moshe *115*
Halle, Bibliothek der Deutschen Morgenlandischen Gesellschaft ***89*** *175 205*
Halle, Universitäts- und Landesbibliothek ***89*** *228*
Halper, Benzion ***89*** *174*
Halpern, Jacob *65 75* ***89*** *141*
Halpern, Joseph *14* ***89***
Hamburg, Museum für Völkerkunde ***89***
Hamburg, Staats- und Universitätsbibliothek *68 73* ***89–90*** *95 120 206 208 214 217 230*
Hamburg, Stadtbibliothek *89*
Hamburg Halakha Miscellany ***90***
Hamburger, Julius ***90*** *106*
Hamilton, William, Duke of ***90***
Hamilton Siddur *90*

Hammond, P. C. *18*
Hamway (Beyda), Shabbetai *16*
Hanau, Historisches Museum *58*
Hannover, I. *85*
Hapalit ***90–91*** *163*
Harburg, Fürstliche Oettingen-Wallerstein'sche Bibliothek ***91***
Harkavy, Abraham Elijah *16 53 60* ***91*** *111 192 193*
Harlay de Sancy, Achille de *169*
Harley, Robert ***91*** *125*
Harrasowitz, O. *177*
Harris, James Rendel *34 87* ***91*** *92*
Harrison, Sigmund ***91–92***
Harrison Miscellany *91*
Hartmann, A. T. *186 216*
Hassidah, Menahem Zev ***92***
Hatton, Christopher ***92***
Hauck, Cornelius J. ***92***
Haverford, Haverford College *91* ***92***
Hawary, H. M. El- *81*
Hayyun, Gedaliah *77*
Ḥazan, Jacob Moses *225*
Hebrew Palaeography Project ***92–93***
Hebron *32*
Heide, Albert van der *18 117*
Heidelberg, Biblioteca Palatina *75 135*
Heidelberg, Universitätsbibliothek ***93*** *138 219*
Heidenheim, Moritz ***93*** *233*
Heidenheim, Wolf *25* ***93–94***
Heiligenkreuz, Stiftsbibliothek ***94***
Heilsbronn, Zisterzienserkloster ***94***
Heine, Heinrich *218*
Held, Hans Ludwig ***94***
Hemmarxerijck, P. A. *177*
Henriques, Reginald Quixano ***94***
Henriques de Castro, David ***94***
Herlingen, Aaron Wolf *77*
Heschel, Jacob ***94***
Hess, J. ***94***
Hildesheimer, Azriel *211*
Hillel b. Moses b. Hillel *95*
Hilleli Codex ***95***
Hillesum, J. *75*
Hinckelmann, Abraham ***95***
Hirsch, Harry *27* ***95*** *153*
Hirsch, Jerocham Fischl *13* ***95*** *129*
Hirschell, Solomon ***95–96***
Hirschenson, Hayyim *20* ***96***
Hirschenson, Isaac ***96***
Hirschfeld, Hartwig ***96*** *124 128*
Hispano-Moresque Haggada ***96***
Hoepli ***96***
Hoerning, Reinhardt ***96*** *125 126*
Holkham *116*
Holon, Levi Nahum, Yehuda ***120***
Holub, David ***96***
Hönisch, Rudolf *177*
Hopkins, Simon *48*
Horovitz, Markus *72*
Horowitz, Hayyim M. ***97***
Horowitz, Joel b. Alexander Halevi ***97***
Hottinger, Johann Heinrich ***97***
Howitt, Arthur ***97***
Hübl, P. A. *224*
Hübsch, A. *64*
d'Hulst, Riamo *79 162*
Hunt. *97*
Hunt. Don. *97*
Hunter, Erica C. *48*
Hunter, William *83*
Huntington, Robert ***97*** *136 161*
Hüpsch-Lontzen, Johann Wilhelm Carl Adolph von Honvlez-Ardenn ***98***
Hurtado de Mendoza, Diego *195*
Hurvitz, Elazar *49 80 115*
Hurwitz, M. Chaim ***98***
Huschens, F.-J. *37*
Husiatyn *71* ***98*** *201*
Ḥutzin, Bekhor *187*
Hyams, Solomon M. *38*
Hyde, Thomas *44*
Hyman G. Enelow Collection *65*

Iakerson, S. M. *116*
Ibn Gaon Bible *203*
Ibn Merwas, Joseph b. Judah *98*
Ibn Merwas Bible *27* ***98***
Imbonati, Carlo G. *27*
Imola, Archivio della Curia Vescovile *100*
Imola, Archivio di Stato *100*
Imola, Archivio Storico Comunale *100*
Imola, Sezione di Archivio di Stato *100*
Innsbruck, Universitätsbibliothek ***98***
Isaacs, Haskell D. *48*
Istanbul, Topkapu Serai ***99***

Italian Geniza *68* ***99–101***
Ithaca, Cornell University Library ***101*** *179*

Jabetz, Abraham ***102***
Jabetz, Sussmann ***102***
Jablonski, Daniel Ernst ***102***
Jacob b. Meir (Rabbenu Tam) *229*
Jacobsohn, Wilhelm & Co. ***102***
Jacobson, Meijer Levien ***102*** *188*
Jaffe family *155*
James, Montague Rhodes *44* ***102***
Jankovich, Miklós *43* ***102***
Jaré, Giuseppe *42* ***102*** *110*
Jefferson, Rebecca J. E. *48*
Jellinek, Adolf *50* ***103*** *145 198 222*
Jena, Thüringer Universitäts- und Landesbibliothek ***103***
Jerusalem ***103***
Jerusalem, Beit Midrash Mizrachi for Teachers *95*
Jerusalem, Ben-Zvi Institute *17* ***103*** *204 205 214*
Jerusalem, Bezalel National Art Museum *104 187 232*
Jerusalem, Central Zionist Archives *232*
Jerusalem, Hekhal Shelomo Museum *15 83 84* ***103*** *207*
Jerusalem, Institute of Microfilmed Hebrew Manuscripts ***103–104*** *108 123 124 126 141 145 147 149 161 162 167 171 183 184 194 195 214 216 224 227 228 230*
Jerusalem, Israel Museum *15 72 84* ***104–105*** *158 159 187 232*
Jerusalem, Jewish National and University Library ***105***
Jerusalem, Ministry of Education *105*
Jerusalem, Mosad Harav Kook *75* ***105*** *134 149 199*
Jerusalem, National Library of Israel *15 16 17 18 22 25 30 35 39 52 53 65 66 73 74 75 81 84 87 91 92 96 103 104* ***105–106*** *108 120 123 142 146 147 149 150 152 158 176 177 179 181 185 187 193 199 201 203 205 210 212 214 224 226 228 231 232*
Jerusalem, Research Center for Italian Jewish Studies *16 202*
Jerusalem, Schocken Institute *22 29 30 66 72 81 84* ***106*** *157 158 187 188 199 227*
Jerusalem, Yad Harav Herzog *134*
Jerusalem, Yeshivat Shem *149*
Jerusalem, Zalman Shazar Center for Jewish History *203*
Jerusalem Mishne Tora ***106***
Jeselsohn, David *33 84 159 187 228 233*
Jesselsohn, Erica *158*
Jessurun Cardozo, Jacob de Raphael ***106–107***
JMC ***107***
Joel, B. I. *105 185*
Joel b. Simeon ***107*** *113 146 156 158 171 172 228*
Joel b. Simeon Haggada ***107***
Joffe, Judah Achilles ***107*** *153*
Jona, J. B. *219*
Jong, P. de *18 117*
Jonge, Jacob Wolf de ***107***
Jonge, Wolfe de ***107–108***
Joseph b. Joshua Hakohen *85* ***165***
Joseph b. Kalonymus *232*
Joshua Ibn Gaon Bible ***108*** *111*
Jost, Isaac Marcus ***108***
Judaeo-Arabic *27 42 47 48 49 53 106 116 117 121 126 148 161 165 192 193 194 195 205 210 220 223 232*
Judaeo-Persian *54 103 117 126 219*
Judaica Conservancy Foundation *29 78*

Kaczerginski, Szmerke *156*
Kafiḥ, Yosef ***108***
Kahana, Abraham ***108***
Kahn, Zadoc ***108***
Kaliningrad *112*
Kann, Rodolphe *169*
Kaplan, Mitchell ***108–109***
Kapon, Judah ***109***
Kara, Joseph *111*
Karassou-Bazar, Synagogue ***109*** *190*
Karassou-Bazar Codex *109*
Karl Albrecht V *229*
Karlsruhe, Badische Landesbibliothek ***109*** *114 182*
Karp, Abraham ***109***
Kasher, Menahem ***109***
Kassel, Landesbibliothek und Murhardsche Bibliothek ***109***
Katsh, A. I. *20 145 193*
Katznellenbogen, Zevi Hirsch ***110***
Kauffmann, J. ***110*** *114 129*

Kaufmann, Aaron ***110***
Kaufmann, David *42 59 84 102* ***110*** *130 144 165 179 185 214 215 228 229 232*
Kaufmann Haggada *110*
Kaufmann Mishna *110*
Kaufmann Mishne Tora *110*
Kennicott, Benjamin *58* ***110*** *126 161 163 164 172 186 201 204 207*
Kennicott Bible, First *110*
Kennicott Bible, Second *108 110*
Kerner, S. *60 168*
Khan, G. *48*
Kiev, Institute for Jewish Proletarian Culture *111*
Kiev, National Academy of Sciences *111*
Kiev, Vernadsky National Library *81 91* ***111*** *179 190 194*
Kimhi, David *109*
Kimhi, Moses *109*
King's MS or King's Bible ***111***
Kirchheim, Raphael *39 51* ***111***
Kirchheim MS *111*
Kirschstein, Salli *73 87* ***111–112***
Klagsbald, Victor *16* ***112*** *169*
Kleerekoper, Joseph ***112***
Klein, Michael L. *48*
Kłodzko *39 222 227*
Klosterneuburg, Bibliothek des Augustiner-Chorherrenstifts ***112***
Kohn, S. *43*
Kohut, George Alexander ***112*** *186*
Kokovtsov, F. *109 193*
Komlós, O. *42*
Königsberg Stadtbibliothek ***112***
Kounice, Hevra Kadisha ***112–113***
Krackovslcij, I. J. *67*
Krafft, Albrecht *61* ***113*** *223*
Kramer, Hermann ***113***
Krems Kettuba ***113***
Kremsmünster, Stiftsbibliothek ***113***
Krengel, Johann *73* ***113***
Krochmal, Nachman *233*
Krupp, Michael *14*
Künstlinger, David *95*
Kupfer, Ephraim ***113*** *140 227*
Kurrein, V. *122 124*

Lacave, J. L. *195*
Laceranza, G. *182*
Lady's Maḥzor *107* ***113***
Lainz *186*
Lair-Dubreuil, Fernand ***113–114*** *199*
Lambert, M. *187*
Landau, Emil Elias ***114***
Landauer, Samuel *109* ***114*** *182 207*
Landi, Ferdinando ***114*** *174 186*
Landsberg, Mendel *30* ***114***
Lattes, Abraham *114 212*
Lattes, Alessandro *141*
Lattes, Elia *141*
Lattes, Mosé ***114*** *141 220 221*
Laubach, Graf zu Solms-Laubach'sches Archiv *74*
Laud, William ***114*** *161*
Laud Maḥzor ***114***
Lebedev, V. *193*
Lebrecht, Fürchtegott ***115***
Lederer, Ephraim *17*
Lee, John ***115***
Leeds University, Brotherton Library *186*
Leeuwarden, Provinciale Bibliotheek van Friesland *115*
Leeuwarden, TRESOAR, the Friesland Historical and Literary Centre *71 75* ***115***
Le Havre, Bibliothèque municipale Armand Salacrou ***115***
Lehmann, Manfred R. *31* ***115–116*** *136*
Lehnardt, A. *68 74*
Lehren, Akiba ***116***
Lehren, Hirschl *33* ***116***
Lehren, Jacob Meijer ***116***
Leicester, Earl of ***115–116*** *117*
Leicht, R. *109 182*
Leiden, Bibliotheek der Rijksuniversiteit *117*
Leiden, Universiteitsbibliotheek *18 86* ***117–118*** *198 206 226 229*
Leiden MS *118*
Leiding, Gilbert ***118***
Leipnik, David *21*
Leipzig, Pauliner Bibliothek ***118***
Leipzig, Stadtbibliothek *61 118 226*
Leipzig, Universitätsbibliothek ***118*** *212*
Leipzig Maḥzor ***118***
Le Mans, Bibliothèque municipale ***135***
Leningrad Bible, First ***118*** *159*
Leningrad Bible, Second ***118***
Leonowitsch, Abraham ***119***
Lesouëf, August *157*

Letchworth *197*
Letteris, Meir ***119***
Levant Company *97*
Leveen, Jacob *46* ***119*** *126*
Levertoff, Paul P. ***119***
Levi, Abraham Zevi ***119***
Levi, Israel ***119*** *187*
Levi, M. *196*
Levi Nahum, Yehuda ***120***
Levin, Zevi Hirsch *63*
Levisson, G. and D. Proops ***120***
Levy, Heimann Baruch *90* ***120*** *208*
Levy, Joseph *106*
Levy, M. *204*
Lewenstein, Moses J. ***120***
Lewin, Benjamin Manasseh ***120*** *204*
Lewin, Daniel *185*
Lewin, Louis ***120–121*** *156*
Lewinson, Jehiel Judah ***121***
Lewis, Agnes Smith ***121***
Lewis, John Frederick ***121***
Lewis–Gibson *49* ***121***
Lewisohn, Adolph ***121***
Libowitz, Nehemiah Samuel *155*
Libri, Guglielmo *22 51*
Lieberman, Saul *26 30* ***121***
Lifschitz, M. M. *211*
Lilienthal, Max ***121–122*** *148*
Lima, Moses Hartog de ***122***
Lincoln College *163*
Lindsay, James Ludovic *58*
Linz, Bundesstaatliche Studienbibliothek *122*
Linz, Oberösterreichische Landesbibliothek ***122***
Lippert, J. F. ***122***
Lipschütz, Hirsch *45* ***122*** *144*
Lipschütz, Jacob *13* ***122***
Lisbon *177 187*
Lisbon Bible ***122–123***
Livorno (Leghorn) *132*
Livorno, Talmud Tora *13 32 105* ***123***
Llamas, J. R. *133 194 195*
Loan ***123–124***
Lodi, Archivio Storico *100*
Lodi, L. *142*
Loeb, I. *62 165*
Loewe, Herbert Martin James *44 45 46 83* ***124*** *231*
Loewe, Louis *96* ***124*** *127*
Loewe, Raphael *46*
Loewinger, David Samuel *35 40 43* ***124*** *201*
Loewy, Ernst *72*
London, Beth Din and Beth Hamidrash Library *22 96* ***124–125*** *128 151*
London, British Library *14 16 21 22 54 58 64 77 81 83 91 95 96 111 119* ***125–127*** *130 136 140 151 173 179 185 188 199 200 201 203 204 207 215*
London, British Museum Library *125* ***127***
London, House of Commons *91*
London, India Office *58*
London, Jewish Historical Society *142*
London, Jewish Museum *73 97* ***127***
London, Jews' College *96 124* ***127*** *128*
London, Lambeth Palace ***127***
London, Montefiore Collection *77 78 88 96 124* ***127*** *128 130 155 233*
London, Royal Society *58* ***128***
London, University College *142*
London, Valmadonna Trust Library *21 68* ***128*** *138*
London, Wellcome Institute ***128***
London Haggada *107*
London School of Jewish Studies *28 124 127* ***128*** *150*
Longleat *69*
Los Angeles, University of California Library *24 26 29 77* ***128–129*** *185 211 212 225*
Lotze, Hermann ***129***
Louvain, Jesuiten Collegium ***129***
Louvain, Katholieke Universiteit *129*
Louvain, Université Catholique ***129***
Löw, Immanuel ***129***
Löw, Leopold *129*
Lowe, W. H. *129*
Lowe MS ***129***
Lublin, Solomon Luria Synagogue ***130***
Luncz, Abraham Moses ***130*** *179*
Lund, Universitetsbibliothek ***130***
Lutzki, M. *154*
Luzzatto, Aldo *52 81*
Luzzatto, Joseph *130*
Luzzatto, Moses Hayyim *116 119 206*
Luzzatto, Samuel David *16 45 59* ***130–131*** *165 199*
Lvov, Jewish Community Library *180*
Lyell, James P. R. ***131***
Lyon, Bibliothèque Municipale ***131***

Madan, F. *163*
Madjalis Scroll ***131***
Madrid, Archivo Histórico Nacional and Museo Lázaro Galdiano *131*
Madrid, Biblioteca Histórica Marqués de Valdecilla *132*
Madrid, Biblioteca Nacional de España *78* ***131–132*** *212 233*
Madrid, Biblioteca del Palacio Real de Madrid *131* ***132*** *194*
Madrid, Biblioteca de la Universidad Complutense *15 131* ***132–133*** *232*
Madrid, Consejo Superior de Investigaciones Científicas, Instituto de Filología *131* ***133***
Madrid, Instituto Arias Montana *133*
Madrid, Monasterio de San Martin *132*
Madrid, Real Academia de la Historia *131* ***133***
Maggid, David *91 190*
Magliabechi, Antonio *70 133*
Magliabechiana *70* ***133***
Magnes, Judah L. *29*
Maḥzor Vitry *181*
Mai, Angelo ***134*** *220*
Mai, Johann Heinrich, the younger *89* ***134***
Maimon (Fishman), Judah Loeb *105* ***134***
Mainz, Akademie der Wissenschaften und der Literatur ***134*** *149*
Mainz, Jesuitenkolleg ***134***
Mainz, Johannes Gutenberg-Universität *134*
Mainz , Jüdische Gemeinde ***134***
Mainz, Wissenschaftliche Stadtbibliothek ***134***
Makor *97*
Maman, A. *154*
Manchester, Chetham's Library *53* ***134***
Manchester, John Rylands University Library *58 77 80* ***134–135***
Mandelstamm, Leon *26*
Manetti, Giannozzo *75* ***135***
Mann, Jacob *54 80 108*
Mantua, Biblioteca Teresiana (formerly Biblioteca Comunale) ***135***
Mantua, Comunità ebraica *135 145 184*
Maraviglia daughter of Menahem *113*
Marburg, Hessisches Staatsarchiv ***135***
Marburg, Westdeutsche Bibliothek *31*
Margaliot, Mordecai ***136*** *180*
Margolinsky, Julius ***136***
Margoliouth, George *96 125* ***136***
Margulies, Samuel Hirsch *54* ***136***
Maria Luisa of Austria *34 71 170 186 206*
Marmorstein, Arthur *14*
Marseilles, Bibliothèque diocésaine *26*
Marseilles, Bibliothèque municipale ***136***
Marseilles Bible *136*
Marsh, Narcissus *63* ***136***
Marshall (Mareschall), Thomas ***136–137*** *161*
Marsili, Luigi Ferdinando *36* ***137***
Marti, Karl ***137***
Marx, Alexander *17 31 63 88 136* ***137*** *145 154 178 181 187*
Marx Cahen ***115***
Massa Carrara, Archivio di Stato *100*
Massel, Joseph of Viasin *74* ***137***
Matera, Biblioteca Provincale *100*
Matera, Seminario Arcivescovile *100*
Mattathias Hayitshari *207*
Mazarin, Jules *166*
Medici, Catherine de *166*
Medici, Cosimo the Elder *69*
Medici, Lorenzo *69*
Medina, Henrique ***138***
Meerman, Gerard ***138*** *168 174*
Meerman, Johan M. *138 168*
Mehlmann, Israel *214*
Meiningen, Landesbibliothek ***138***
Meir b. Barukh of Rothenburg *143 179*
Meir b. Israel Yaffe *54 107*
Melbourne, State Library of Victoria ***138***
Meldola, Raphael Emmanuel *135*
Melk, Stiftsbibliothek ***138***
Melun, Bibliothèque municipale ***138***
Memmingen, Stadtbibliothek ***138***
Mendelsohn, Isaac *153*
Mendelssohn, Moses *63*
Merx, Adalbert *25 85 93* ***139***
Merzbacher, Abraham *51 72* ***139*** *148 179 200*
Merzbacher, Eugen *72 139*
Metz, Isaac *160*
Mezzofanti, Giuseppe Caspar *36* ***139***
Mich. Add. ***139***
Michael, Erna *67*
Michael, Heimann Joseph *45 93 139 161* ***140*** *225*
Michael, Jacob *41 67*
Michaelides, George ***140***
Michaelis, J. H. *66*

Milan, Biblioteca Ambrosiana *32 114* ***140–141*** *199 213 221*
Milan, Biblioteca Nazionale Braidense ***141***
Milan, Biblioteca Reina ***141***
Mill, David *201*
Mill Yard (*milyard*) *34*
Millás Vallicrosa, J. *132 212*
Miller, Linda R. (Mrs. Nathan J.) *65* ***141***
Mingana, Alphonse *33 34 81* ***141***
Mintz, Sharon L. *38*
Mirande-de Boer, M. H. *19 51*
Miroslav, Jewish Community ***141–142***
Mittwoch, Eugen *33 34 81* ***142***
Mitzri (Mitschri), Abraham ***142***
Mocatta, Frederic David *142*
Mocatta Haggada *142*
Mocatta Library ***142***
Modena, Archivio Capitolare *100*
Modena, Archivio della Curia *100*
Modena, Archivio di Stato *100*
Modena, Archivio Storico Comunale *100*
Modena, Biblioteca Comunale *50*
Modena, Biblioteca Estense *32 50 71 100* ***142–143***
Modona, L. *36*
Monaco, A. *150*
Mondolfi, Ismael Eliezer *123* ***143***
Mondolfi, Rodolfo *143*
Mongardi, E. *100 143*
Monselles, R. H. *123*
Montagnana, Pietro *221*
Montague, Ed. ***143***
Montefiore, Elia ***143*** *184*
Montefiore, M. G. *108*
Montefiore, Moses *127*
Montefiore Endowment Committee *127*
Montepulciano, Archivio Storico Comunale *100*
Montezinos, David *18* ***143***
Montfaucon, Bernard de *70*
Montpellier, Bibliothèque universitaire ***143***
Montserrat, Abadia de Santa Mariá ***143–144***
Morag, Shelomo *48*
Morbio, Carlo ***144*** *229*
Morgenweg, Joachim *95*
Morosini, J. *219*
Morpurgo, Abraham ***144***
Mortara, Marco *45 59 110 122* ***144–145***
Mortara Ottolenghi, Luisa *81 221*
Moscati Steindler, G. *150*
Moscow, Imperial Theological Academy *146*
Moscow, Lenin State Library *145*
Moscow, Rossiiskaia Gosudarstvennaia Biblioteka (Russian State Library) *25 30 39 40 87 94* ***145–146*** *152 189 222*
Moscow, Rossiiskii Gosudarstvennyi Voennyi Arkhiv (Russian State Military Archives) *39 40 57* ***146*** *222*
Moses ben Asher *28*
Moses b. Maimon (Maimonides) *157 204*
Moskowitz, Henry *146*
Moskowitz Maḥzor *107* ***146***
Mosseri, Jacques Nissim *52 80 81 137* ***147***
Moszkowski, M. *226*
Moussaieff, Rehavia *149*
Moussaieff, Shelomo *149*
Muller, Frederick ***147*** *152 155*
Munich, Bayerisches Reichsarchiv ***148***
Munich, Bayerische Staatsbibliothek *86 121 134* ***148–149*** *178 199 206 208 210 229*
Munich, Cossmann Werner Bibliothek der Isr. Kultusgemeinde *149*
Munich, Jüdische Gemeinde ***149***
Munich, Königliche Hof- und Staatsbibliothek *148*
Munk, S. *44 165 167 169*
Münster, Sebastien *160*
Murphy, Fred Towsley *149*
Murphy Haggada ***149*** *187*
Musayof ***149*** *180*
Myers, Asher Isaac *128* ***150***
Myers, W. J. *187*

Nadav, Mordecai, *87*
Najara, Israel *196 232*
Nani, Bernardo *150*
Nani, Jacopo ***150***
Naples, Biblioteca Nazionale ***150*** *183*
Naples, Collegio del Gesuiti ***150***
Napoleon *71 115 129 140*
Narboni, Moses *135*
Nash, W. L. *150*
Nash Papyrus ***150***
Natanson, Joseph Saul *102*
Nathan Hayarhi *229*
Nauheim, Sigmund ***150***
Ne'eman, Samuel *67*

Nemoy, Leon *21 112 151*
Neppi, Graziado ***151***
Nessel, Daniel ***151***
Netter, Solomon ***151***
Netzer, Amnon *103*
Neubauer, Adolf *35 82 115 124 125 128 136 137 140 150* ***151*** *162 163 217*
Neuburg an der Donau, Provenzialbibliothek *148*
New Haven, Yale University Libraries *21 112 149* ***151*** *187*
New Norcia, Benedictine Abbey ***151–152***
Newport *30*
Newton Center, Hebrew College ***152*** *174*
New York, Chassidei Chabad Ohel Yosef Yitzchak Lubavitch Library ***152*** *201 227*
New York, Columbia University *60 71 120 147* ***152–153*** *155 182*
New York, General Theological Seminary ***153***
New York, Jewish Institute of Religion *112*
New York, Jewish Theological Seminary *13 17 24 27 28 32 36 39 43 51 54 60 62 65 71 74 75 80 82 83 87 89 95 96 97 106 107 109 110 119 121 123 124 137 141* ***153–155*** *165 173 177 178 181 185 187 198 199 201 202 204 205 206 208 211 212 225 232*
New York, Metropolitan Museum of Art *72*
New York, New York University, Bobst Library *109*
New York, Public Library *26 60 119* ***155***
New York, Temple Emanu-El *120 147 152* ***155***
New York, Yeshiva University *120* ***156*** *199 208*
New York, YIVO *66* ***156*** *207 224*
New York Haggada, First *107* ***156***
New York Haggada, Second *107* ***156***
Nice ***157***
Nicholson, Charles *203 210*
Nicole, Jules *79*
Nicoll, A. *161*
Niederhoffen, Benjamin ***157***
Niessen, Friedrich *48*
Nikolsburg (Mikulov), Fürstlich Dietrichsteinsche Bibliothek ***157*** *201*
Nîmes, Bibliothèque municipale ***157*** *224*
Nissenbaum, S. B. *130*
Nogent-sur-Marne, Fondation Smith-Lesouëf ***157***
Nonantola, Archivio Storico Comunale *100–101*
Norcia, Archivio Storico Comunale *101*
Norsa Manuscript ***157***
Nuremberg ***157***
Nuremberg, Germanisches Nationalmuseum ***158***
Nuremberg, Israelitische Kultusgemeinde ***158***
Nuremberg, Landeskirchliches Archiv der Evangelisch-Lutherischen Kirche in Bayern ***158***
Nuremberg, Staatsarchiv ***158*** *165*
Nuremberg, Stadtbibliothek ***158***
Nuremberg Haggada, First *106 107* ***158***
Nuremberg Haggada, Second *106 107* ***158***
Nuremberg Maḥzor *106* ***158–159***
Nuremberg Memorbuch *134*

Ochser, S. *220*
Odessa, Odesskoe Obshchestvo lstorii i Drevnostei *61 68 69 118 131* ***159–160*** *175 191*
Odessa Collections *49 57 106 118 119 131 147 189 190 191 192*
Offord, Joseph *81*
Olivares, Gaspar de Guzmán *195*
Olomouc, Státní Vědecká Knihova ***160***
Olomouc, Zemský Archiv *160*
Omar b. Muhammad *137*
Oppenheim, David *29 45 55* ***160–161*** *230*
Oppenheim, Joseph *160*
Orléans, Médiathèque ***161***
Osimo, Leon (Judah Arye) ***161***
Oslo *200*
Ottheinrich *148*
Ottoboniana ***161*** *219*
Outhwaite, Ben *48*
Oxford, Balliol College *163*
Oxford, Bodleian Library *14 22 24 35 44 45 49 50 57 58 60 62 64 71 79 80 81 83 86 88 91 92 93 95 97 110 114 121 130 131 136 139 140 151 160* ***161–163*** *176 180 181 199 200 202 208 210 217 228 230*
Oxford, Christ Church College *163*
Oxford, College Libraries ***163–164***
Oxford, Corpus Christie College *163*
Oxford, Jesus College *163*
Oxford, Keble College *163*
Oxford, Lincoln College *163*
Oxford, Merton College *163*
Oxford, Oriel College *163*
Oxford, Pusey House *163*
Oxford, Radcliffe College *110 163*

Oxford, St. John's College *164*
Oxford, Worcester College *164*

Pacifici, R. *221*
Padua, Biblioteca della Comunità ebraica ***164***
Padua, Biblioteca di Storia della Medicina *144*
Padua, Convento dei Canonici Regolari Lateranensi di S. Giovanni di ***164*** *221*
Padua, Convento di S. Giustina ***164***
Padua, Istituto Convitto Rabbinico *184*
Padua, Seminario Vescovile ***164***
Páez de Castro, Juan *195*
Pamplona, Archivo Real y General de Navarra *165*
Pamplona, Biblioteca de la Catedral ***165***
Panofsky, E. *77 212*
Pappenheim, Gräflich Pappenheim'sche Bibliothek *158* ***165***
Paris, Alliance Israélite Universelle *53 81 130 145* ***165–166*** *168 169 201*
Paris, Bibliothecae Regiae ***168*** *182*
Paris, Bibliothèque de l'Arsenal ***166***
Paris, Bibliothèque Mazarine *56* ***166*** *201*
Paris, Bibliothèque nationale de France *20 56 129 157* ***166–168*** *169 170 172 176 182 199 201*
Paris, Bibliothèque Ste. Geneviève *166* ***168***
Paris, Bibliothèque St. Germain-des-Prés ***168***
Paris, Collège de Clermont *138* ***168***
Paris, Consistoire israélite *165* ***168***
Paris, École rabbinique ***169***
Paris, Institut de France *61* ***168***
Paris, Institut national des langues et civilisations orientales *60* ***168***
Paris, Musée de Cluny ***168–169*** *187 208*
Paris, Oratoire *166* ***169*** *201*
Paris, Séminaire Israélite de France ***169***
Paris, Société des manuscrits des assureurs français ***169–170***
Paris, Sorbonne *166* ***170*** *182*
Parma, Archivio Storico Comunale *101*
Parma, Biblioteca Palatina *34 57 71 86* ***170–171*** *172 186 206*
Parma A ***171***
Parma B ***171***
Parma Bible ***171***
Parma Haggada *107* ***171***
Pasini, Giuseppe ***172*** *215*
Pavoncello, Nello *101*
Pearson, James *46*
Peiresc, Nicolas-Claude Fabri de ***172***
Perani, Mauro *36 37 68 99–101 123*
Perera *123*
Pérez Bayer, Francisco ***172*** *271*
Pergola, Archivio Storico Comunale *101*
Peringer, Gustaf ***172***
Perissinotti, Giovanni *50*
Perl, Joseph ***172*** *210*
Perpignan Bible ***172***
Perr. Stern ***172***
Perreau, Pietro *170 171* ***172***
Perrins, Charles William Dyson ***172***
Perth *151*
Perugia, Università degli Studi, Biblioteca del Dottorato *101*
Pesaro, Archivio di Stato *101*
Pesaro Maḥzor *144* ***172***
Pescocostanzo *101*
Pest, Jewish Community Library *228*
Petermann, Julius Heinrich ***173***
Petrie, William Matthew Flinders ***173***
Petropolitanus Codex ***173***
Pettigrew, Thomas Joseph ***173*** *209*
Petty-Fitzmaurice, Sir William ***173***
Peyron, Amedio *216 218*
Peyron, Bernardino ***173*** *215*
Peyron family *216*
Pfeiffer, Augustus *112* ***173***
Pfersee MS ***173***
Pforzheimer, Carl H. ***173***
Philadelphia, Dropsie College *13 17 55 62 74 81 83 92 174 208*
Philadelphia, Free Library *121* ***173***
Philadelphia, University of Pennsylvania, Herbert D. Katz Center for Advanced Judaic Studies; and University Museum *13 17 55 62 74 81 83 89 92 109 152* ***174*** *199 208*
Philadelphia, Young Men's Hebrew Association *17* ***174***
Phillipps, Thomas *55 138 168* ***174***
Piacenza, Biblioteca Comunale Passarini Landi *114* ***174*** *186*
Piacenza, Bibliothecae Patrum Praedicatorum ***174***
Piatelli, Angelo *84*
Pico della Mirandola, Giovanni Frederico *86 142* ***175***
Pieve di Cento, Archivio Storico Comunale *101*

Pinner, Ephraim Moses *61 63 159* ***175*** *191*
Pinsker, Simha ***175***
Pisa, Biblioteca Universitaria ***175–176***
Pisa, Comunità ebraica *184*
Pitigliano, Biblioteca Comunale *176*
Pitigliano, Comunità ebraica *105* ***176*** *184*
Pius IV *219*
Pius VI ***176***
Pius XI *139*
Pococke, Edward *161* ***176***
Polak, Felix ***176***
Polak, G. I. *18 63*
Poliakov Collection *145*
Pollak, Ludwig *178*
Pollard, John E. T. ***176***
Polliacj, Meira R. P. *48*
Pontremoli, Archivio di Stato *101*
Porges, Nathan *118* ***176–177***
Pormann, P. E. *164*
Porto, Biblioteca Pública Municipal ***177***
Portuguese Bible ***177***
Poznanski, Adolph ***177***
Poznanski, Samuel Abraham ***177*** *203*
Prag, Isaac ***177***
Pragi, Isaac *211*
Prague, Jüdische Gemeinde ***177***
Prague, Narodni Knihovna České Republiky *39* ***177*** *231*
Prague, Židovské Muzeum v Praze ***177–178*** *180*
Prague Bible *29 63* ***178***
Prato, David *178*
Prato, Jonathan *178*
Prato Haggada ***178***
Preisendanz, K. *109*
Pre-Masoretic Bible *182*
Prijs, J. *27 234*
Prijs, L. *72*
Princeton Theological Seminary *17*
Princeton University Library *77*
Prins, L. P. *95*
Proceedings ***178***
Proops, D. ***120***
Proverbio, D. V. *217*

Quatremère, Etienne Marc *148* ***178***

Rabbinovicz, Raphael Nathan *72 74 139* ***179***
Rabinowitz, Isaac *101* ***179***
Rabinowitz, Louis M. *21* ***179***
Rabinowitz, Mikhel *96* ***179***
Raccah, G. *214*
Raffalovich, Samuel *47 130* ***179***
Rainer, Ferdinand Maria Johann Evangelist Franz Ignaz ***179–180*** *201 224*
Ramat Gan, Bar-Ilan University *23 120 136 149* ***180*** *204*
Ramsgate, Judith Montefiore College *127*
Raphelengius, Franciscus *198*
Rapoport, Salomon Judah Leib *177* ***180*** *196*
Rappaport, Samuel ***180***
Rashba Bible ***180***
Ravenna, Archivio Arcivescovile *101*
Ravenna, Archivio di Stato *101*
Ravenna, Biblioteca Comunale Classense *101* ***180***
Ravenna, Camaldolese Monastery *180*
Ravrebe, Y. *192 193*
Rawlinson, Richard ***180***
Regensburg, Dominican Monastery ***180***
Regensburg, Stadtarchiv ***180***
Regensburg Pentateuch ***58***
Reggio, Isaac Samuel *161* ***181*** *200*
Reggio Emilia, Biblioteca Panizzi ***181*** *216*
Reggio Emilia, Talmud Tora Library ***181***
Register ***181***
Reider, J. *174*
Reif, Stefan C. *36 46 48 68 80*
Reifmann, Jacob ***181***
Reinach, Théodore ***181***
Reinhardt, K. *212*
Reuchlin, Johann von *109* ***181–182***
Reuchlin Bible *182*
Codex Reuchlinianus *109 182*
Reutlinger, Judah Mehler *35*
Revel, Dov (Bernard) *204*
Riccardi *70*
Riccardiana *70*
Richelieu, Armand du Plessis *166 170* ***182***
Richler, Benjamin *100 206 227*
Rieti, Archivio Notarile *101*
Rimini, Archivio di Stato *101*
Robertson, Edward *77 135*
Rochester, Public Library ***182***
Roe, Thomas *21*
Roest, Meijer Marcus *19 152* ***182***
Rogers, R. W. *92*

Romano, D. *26*
Rome, Accademia Nazionale dei Lincei e Corsiniana *57* ***182***
Rome, Archivio di Stato *101*
Rome, Biblioteca Angelica ***183***
Rome, Biblioteca di Casa Farnese ***183***
Rome, Biblioteca Casanatense ***183***
Rome, Biblioteca Maronitarum ***183***
Rome, Biblioteca Nazionale Centrale ***183–184***
Rome, Casa Professa della Compagna di Gesù *183*
Rome, Centro Bibliografico dell'Ebraismo Italiano *71 143 184*
Rome, Collegio Rabbinico Italiano *71 143* ***184***
Rome, Collegio Romano *183* ***184***
Rome, Comunità ebraica ***184***
Rome, Museo Ebraico *184*
Rome, Pia Casa dei Neofiti ***185*** *219*
Rome, Sant Maria sopra Minerva *183*
Rome, Tempio Maggiore *184*
Romm (publishers in Vilna) *105* ***185***
Rösel Bible ***185***
Rosenbaum, J. ***185*** *232*
Rosenberg, Hayyim *20 24 129* ***185*** *211 225*
Rosenfeld, Moshe *151*
Rosenthal, David *79*
Rosenthal, E. S. *206*
Rosenthal, George *19*
Rosenthal, Leser *19 182*
Rosenwasser, J. *126*
Rossi, Giovanni Bernardo de *114 170* ***186***
Rossi, Giovanni Francesco de *186*
Rossi, Giovanni Gherardo de *186*
de Rossi ext. ***186***
Rossiana ***186*** *219*
Rostock, Universitätsbibliothek ***186*** *216*
Roth, Cecil *131* ***186–187***
Róth, Ernst *43 72 90 120 124 195 200* ***208*** *224*
Roth, William *202*
Rothschild, Anselm Salomon *188*
Rothschild, Edmond de *149 187*
Rothschild, James de *149 187 228*
Rothschild, J.-P. *167 168*
Rothschild, Nathaniel *169 187 208*
Rothschild, Salomon Mayer *188*
Rothschild, Freifrau Wilhelm von *187*
Rothschild family ***187–188***
Rothschild Maḥzor *187*
Rothschild Miscellany *187*
Rothschild Siddur *187*
Roubin, S. *209*
Rouen, Bibliothèque municipale ***188***
Rovigo, Biblioteca dell'Accademia del Concordi ***188*** *203*
Rovner, J. E. *153*
Royal MSS *125* ***188***
Royal Society *21*
Rubens, Meijer Barend *102* ***188***
Rubens, Naftali H. *107*
Ruysschaert, J. *220*
Ruzhin *75*
Rylands, Mrs John *58*
Rylands Spanish Haggada ***188***
Rylands Spanish Haggada, Brother to *188*

Sacerdote, G. *183 185*
Sachs, Senior *145* ***189***
Sadek, V. *113*
Safra family *144 233*
Sagradini, E. *99*
Sahl ibn Bishr *200*
Saibante, Giovanni ***189***
St. Florian, Augustiner-Chorherren Stiftsbibliothek ***189***
St. Paul im Lavanttal, Stiftsbibliothek ***189***
St. Petersburg, Asiatic Museum ***189*** *190*
St. Petersburg, Institut Narodov Azii, INA *190*
St. Petersburg, Institut Vostochnik Rukopisi (Institute of Oriental Manuscripts) *54 67 74 109 137 142* ***190*** *232*
St. Petersburg, Institut Vostokovedenia Rossiiskoi Akademii Nauk *190*
St. Petersburg, Jewish Historical Ethnographic Society *111* ***190***
St. Petersburg, Publichnaia Biblioteka imeni M. E. Saltykova-Shchedrina *190*
St. Petersburg, Rossiyskaia Natsionalnaya Biblioteka (Russian National Library) *20 60 61 67 69 80 87 91 118 159* ***190–194*** *212*
St. Petersburg, Society for the Promotion of Culture among the Jews of Russia *91 110 111* ***194***
St. Vaast, Abbey of *21*
Salamanca (Spain), Biblioteca de la Universidad ***194***
Salem, Zisterzienserkloster ***194***

Salonika *17*
Saltykov-Shchedrin Public Library *190*
Salvadore, Joseph ***194***
Salzburg, Archiv der Erzabtei St. Peter ***194***
Salzburg, Universitätsbibliothek ***195***
Samaritan *45 46 49 54 58 63 73 77 78 85 101 105 118 126 135 161 162 163 167 172 173 174 191 192 194 197 207 210 219 220 227 232*
Samson, Herman R. *57*
Samuel Hanagid *36*
San Francisco, California State Library *209*
San Francisco, San Francisco State Library *209*
San Lorenzo del Escorial, Real Biblioteca del Monasterio de El Escorial *21 131* ***195***
Sant'Agata Bolognese, Archivio della Partecipanza Agraria *101*
São Paulo, Safra family *144 172 180*
Saphir, Jacob *24 233*
Sarajevo, National Museum in Bosnia-Herzegovina ***196***
Sarajevo, Oriental Institute ***196***
Sarajevo Haggada ***196***
Saraval, Leon Vita *39 40* ***196*** *206*
Sarnow, Emil *187*
Sasportas, Jacob ***196***
Sassoon, David Solomon *81 128* ***196–197*** *198 199 200 201 212*
Sassoon, Solomon David ***196–197***
Sassoon Spanish Haggada ***197***
Sayce, A. H. *79 162*
Scaliger, Joseph Justus *117* ***197–198***
Schechter, A. *234*
Schechter, Solomon *41 47 79 123 145* ***198*** *211*
Scheiber, Sandor *42*
Scheid, Elie ***198*** *207*
Schiff, Jacob *206*
Schiller-Szinessy, Solomon Mayer *45 59 77* ***198***
Schilling, R. *72 84 150 158*
Schirmann, Jefim *30 54*
Schischa, A. *127*
Schlesinger, Akiva ***198***
Schlesinger, Joseph *215*
Schloss, Solomon ***198***
Schmelzer, Menahem *63*
Schmid, Anton von *119* ***198***
Schneerson, Joseph Isaac *145*
Schneerson, Shalom Dov Ber *152 201*
Schneerson Collection *145*
Schocken, Salman *106 158 159 198 201 233*
Schocken Bible ***199***
Schocken Italian Maḥzor ***199***
Schoenberg, Lawrence J. *174* ***199***
Scholem, Gershom *17 76 105 126 140 148 167 197* ***199***
Schönbaum, Meir ***199***
Schönberg, Dr. ***199***
Schönblum, Samuel *20 24 45 82* ***199–200*** *225*
Schornstein, D. *168*
Schorr, Joshua (Osias) Heschel *50 130 181* ***200***
Schorr, Moses *226*
Schøyen Collection *117* ***200***
Schrijver, Emile G. L. *19 218*
Schulting, Cornelius *54 88* ***200–201***
Schwab, Moise *43 138 157 165 166 167 169 181* ***201*** *205 229 233*
Schwager, Lippa *71 98 154* ***201*** *215*
Schwarz, Adolf ***201***
Schwarz, Arthur Zacharias *157 160* ***201–202*** *222 223*
Seeligmann, Sigmund *33*
Segovia *204*
Segre Amar, Sion *79* ***202***
Selden, John *58 161* ***202*** *211*
Selly Oak Colleges *34 81 141 142*
Sereni Haggada ***202***
Sermoneta, Giuseppe B. *99*
Sermoneta, Hillel M. *100 101*
Serugiel Bible ***202***
Servi, Flaminio ***202***
SfarData *92*
Shaked, Saul *80 119*
Shamama, Nissim *27*
Shapira, Moses Wilhelm *125* ***202–203*** *208*
Sharabi, Abraham Shalom Mizrahi *76*
Sharabi, Isaac *76*
Sharabi, Sar Shalom *76*
Sharabi, Shalom Mizrahi *76*
Shazar, Zalman ***203***
Shelah Lekha ***203***
Shem Tov Bible ***203*** *214*
Shivtiel, Avihai *48*
Shneur Zalman of Lyady *152*
Shunnar, Zuhair *227*
Siena, Comunità ebraica *184*
Silver Spring *116*
Silvera, Ezra Solomon ***203***

Silvestri family *203*
Silvestriana *188* ***203***
Simhoni, Jacob N. ***203–204***
Simon, J. *157*
Simonsen, David Jacob *56 120 196* ***204***
MS Simonsen A *204*
MS Simonsen B *204*
Simpson (or Simson), Joseph ***204***
Simpson (or Simson), Sampson *204*
Simsar, M. A. *121 173*
Sirat, Colette *92 93 167*
Sister to the Golden Haggada *83*
Sloane, Hans *125* ***204***
Slouschz, Nahum ***204***
Smith, William Robertson *13*
Soave, Moise ***204–205*** *222*
Codex Soberanas ***205***
Soberanas Lléo, A. *205*
Socin, Albert *89* ***205***
Sofer, David *15 84 153 158 159*
Sofia, Bulgarian Academy of Sciences *205*
Sofia, Centralen Darzaven Istoriceski Archiv (Central Historical State Archives) *205*
Sofia, Jewish Scientific Institute ***205***
Soissons, Bibliothèque municipale ***205***
Sommerhausen, Zvi Hirsch ***205***
Sonne, Isaiah *32 135 164* ***205*** *222*
Soranzo, Jacopo *57* ***205***
Soria *111*
Sosnitz, Joseph *155*
Spanier, Artur *319*
Spano, Giovanni *43*
Spertus, Maurice *53*
Spicehandler, E. *54*
Spiegelmann, J. *63*
Spitzer, Moshe ***206***
Spoleto, Archivio di Stato *101*
Stanford, University Library *57*
Starkova, K. B. *190*
Stasow, Loeb *129*
Steinhardt, Michael *72*
Steinschneider, Moritz *16 20 22 23 28 31 38 57 59 61 82 86 103 117 122 129 130 139 144 148 151 153 161 167 169 170 171 181 191 192 196 199 200 204 205* ***206*** *212 216 222 230*
Stenne, George *168 208*
Stern, Moritz *116* ***206***
Stern, Salomon Gottlieb *34 71 170 172 196* ***206*** *223*
Stowe MSS *22* ***206***
Strack, Hermann *53 60 173 192*
Strasbourg, Archives départementales du Bas-Rhin *207*
Strasbourg, Bibliothèque nationale et universitaire *81 114* ***207***
Strasbourg, Gesellschaft für die Geschichte der Israeliten in Elsass-Lothringen ***207***
Strashun, Mathias ***207–208***
Strauss, Berthold Baruch *156 187* ***208***
Strauss, Isaac *168* ***208***
Strelcyn, S. *227*
Striedl, Hans *120* ***208***
Stroock, Alan M. *13* ***208***
Strozzi (family in Florence) ***208***
Stuttgart, Württembergische Landesbibliothek *62* ***208–209***
Sub Fen. ***209***
Sulzberger, Mayer *60 62 88 95 153 174* ***209***
Sussex, Duke of *63 64 84 138 144 173* ***209***
Sutro, Adolph Heinrich Joseph *203* ***209***
Sutzkever, Abraham *156*
Svajer, Amedio ***210***
Swarzenski, G. *72 84 150 158*
Swindon, Bible Society ***210***
Sydney, University of Sydney *203* ***210***

Tamani, G. *100 135 164 171 216*
Tanner, Thomas ***210***
Tarnopol, Biblioteka Szkoły Żydowskiej im. J. Perla *172* ***210***
Tauber, Arye ***10***
Tauschweig, Kreisbibliothek Regensburg ***210***
Taylor, Charles *47* ***210–211***
Taylor–Schechter Collection *47* ***211***
Tedeschi (Ashkenazi), Isaac Raphael *185* ***211*** *225*
Teixeira, Isaac ***211***
Tel Aviv, Rambam Library *30* ***211***
Tel Aviv University Library *30*
Tengnagel, Sebastian ***211***
Terracini, Benvenuto e Alessandro *215*
Thomason, George ***211***
Thompson, Henry Yates *22* ***211–212***
Tietze, H. *186*
Tiktin, Gedaliah ***212***

Tischendorf, Lobegott Friedrich Konstantin von *191* ***212***
Toaff, Ariel *27*
Toaff, E. *27*
Toaff, Shabbetai *27*
Tobi, Yosef *103 120*
To'elet Society ***212***
Toledano, Jacob Moses *65* ***212***
Toledo *132*
Toledo, Archivo y Biblioteca Capitulares *132* ***212–213*** *233*
Toledo, Museo Sefardi *60*
Tornberg, C. J. *130*
Toronto, Beth Tzedec Synagogue Museum *186*
Toronto, University of Toronto *74 81* ***213***
Tours, Bibliothèque municipale ***213***
Trebitsch, Ernst ***213***
Trebitsch, Moses Loeb *218*
Treves, Isaac and Jacob ***213***
Trier, Stadtbibliothek ***213–214***
Trieste, Comunità ebraica *105 106* ***214***
Trieste, Talmud Tora *214*
Trieste brothers *110* ***214***
Trigland, Jacobus ***214***
Tripartite Maḥzor ***214***
Tripoli (Libya) ***214***
Trivulzio, Carlo *39 90 106*
Tsedaka, Binyamim *54*
Tsoref, Jacob b. Solomon *150*
Tübingen, Universitätsbibliothek *30* ***214–215***
Tübingen Haggada ***215***
Tunis *203* ***215***
Turin, Archivio delle tradizioni e del costume ebraici 'Benvenuto e Alessandro Terracini' ***215***
Turin, Biblioteca della Comunità ebraica ***215***
Turin, Biblioteca di S. M. il Re *215*
Turin, Biblioteca Nazionale Universitaria *28 171 173* ***215–216*** *218*
Turri, Giuseppe ***216***
Tychsen, Oluf Gerhard *172 186* ***216***

Ubach, Bonaventura *143*
Udine, Biblioteca Arcivescovile *86* ***216***
Uffenbach, Zacharias Conrad von *89 134* ***216–217***
Ugolini, Marianus *220*
Ulma-Günzburg *173*
Ulman, Low Simon *173* ***217***
Unger, Christian Gottlieb *89* ***217***
Uppsala, Universitetsbiblioteket ***217***
Urbinati ***217*** *219*
Urbino *217*
Uri, Johannes *161* ***217***
Utrecht, Rijksuniversiteit *20* ***218***

Vajda, Georges *167*
Valladolid, Biblioteca de Santa Cruz *218*
Valladolid, Biblioteca Universitaria ***218***
Valperga di Caluso, Tommaso *215* ***218***
Van Geldern, Lazarus *218*
Van Geldern, Simon *79*
Van Geldern Haggada ***218***
Vandini, R. *50 142*
Vansleb, Jean Michel *55*
Vasilev, A. *193*
Vatican, Biblioteca Apostolica *26 38 51 53 65 75 93 104 124 134 135 161 185 186 217* ***219–220*** *233*
Venice, Biblioteca Marciana *150 164* ***220–221***
Venice, Biblioteca-Archivo 'Renato Maestro' *221*
Venice, Scuole Israelitiche (Talmud Tora) ***221***
Vercelli, Seminario Vescovile ***221***
Verona, Biblioteca Capitular *221*
Verona, Biblioteca Civica *82 189* ***221***
Verona, Biblioteca e Archivio della Comunità Israelitica ***221***
Victor Amadeus II *215*
Vida, Samuel della ***222***
Vienna, Erzherzog Rainer Museum *179 224*
Vienna, Fürstlich Liechtenstein'sche Fideikommissbibliothek ***222***
Vienna, Israelitische Kultusgemeinde *66 88 103 145 146 175 200* ***222*** *223 227*
Vienna, Israelitisch-theologische Lehranstalt *50 66 103 175* ***222–223***
Vienna, Jüdisches Museum *129* ***223***
Vienna, k. k. Hofbibliothek *119 151 223*
Vienna, Mechitharisten-Congregation ***223***
Vienna, Österreichsche Akademie der Wissenschaften *83*
Vienna, Österreichische Nationalbibliothek *57 61 81 119 122 151 180 188 198 199 201 206 211* ***223–224***
Vienna, Staatsarchiv ***224***
Vienna, Universitätsbibliothek ***224***
Vienna, Unsere Liebe Frau zu den Schotten ***224***

Vienna-Lainz *186*
Vilsker, L. Kh. *146 194*
Villa-Amil y Castro, J. *132*
Villeneuve-lès-Avignon *157* ***224***
Villiers, George *67*
Vilna, Strashun Library *207*
Vilna, YIVO *156 207 210* ***224***
Vinograd, Yeshayahu *151*
Vitali, Pietro *171*
Viterbo, Vivante *34* ***224***
Vivanti (Hai), David Abraham *24 185 211* ***225***
Vivian, A. *176*
Vollers, K. *118*
Volta, Samuel Vita dalla ***59***
Volterra, Menahem da *217*
Vorau, Stiftsbibliothek ***225***

Wagenaar, Hyman Abraham ***226***
Wagenseil, Johann Christoph *67* ***226***
Wagner, Jacob H. ***226***
Wahrmann, Samuel *29*
Wallenstein, M. *134*
Warminster, Marquess of Bath *69*
Warner, Levinus *117* ***226***
Warsaw, Biblioteka Judaistyczna przy Wielkiej Synagodze na Tłomackiem (Library for Jewish Studies of the Great Synagogue on Tłomackie Street) *81 102* ***226–227***
Warsaw, Żydowski Instytut Historyczny (Jewish Historical Institute) *30 39 152 222* ***227***
Washington, Library of Congress *60 97* ***227***
Washington, Smithsonian Institution, Freer Gallery *81 85* ***227***
Washington, U.S. National Museum *28*
Washington Haggada *73 107* ***228***
Weijers, H. E. *18 117*
Weill, Georges *187* ***228***
Weill, Gerard *39*
Weill, Raymond *147*
Weimar, Herzogin Anna Amalia Bibliothek ***228***
Weimar, Thüringische Landesbibliothek ***228***
Weinberg, M. *76*
Weinryb, B. D. *40 231*
Weinstein, Myron M. *227*
Weisz, Max *110* ***228***
Wellcome, Henry *128*
Werner, Moritz ***228***
Wernigerode, Gräfliche Stolbergische Bibliothek ***228***
Wertheimer, Solomon Aaron *47 79 130 162* ***228–229***
Westminster College *49*
Westreen van Tielland *138*
Widder, S. *42*
Widmanstetter (Widmanstad), Johann Albrecht *148* ***229***
Wiener, Samuel *62 74 125 133 137*
Wiesemann, F. *218*
Wiesenberg, Ernest J. *48*
Wijnkoop, Joseph David ***229***
William I, King of Netherlands *229*
Willmet, Johannes *18* ***229***
Winterthur, Stadtbibliothek ***229***
Witkam, Jan Just *18 117*
Witzenhausen, Jacob (Frenkel) *228*
Wolf, Albert *30 144* ***229–230***
Wolf, G. *27*
Wolf, Johann Christian *89 160 217*
Wolf, Johann Christoph *15 27 89 102 118 200 217* ***230***
Wolf, Sandor ***230***
Wolf Haggada *229*
Wölfelsdorf (Wilkanów) *39 146 222*
Wolfenbüttel, Herzog August Bibliothek *940* ***230***
Wolfson, Isaac *83 103*
Worcester College *164*
Wormann, Ernest J. *49*
Worms, Jüdische Gemeinde ***230***
Worms Maḥzor ***230–231***
Worrell, W. H. *79 227*
Wright, William Aldis *45 77 83* ***231***
Wrocław, Biblioteka Uniwersytecka we Wrocławiu *39 40 177* ***231***
Württembergische Landesbibliothek *208–209*

Xanten Bible *155* ***232***
Ximenes de Cisneros, Francisco ***232***

Yafet, Abraham *67*
Yahalom, Joseph *48*
Yahuda, Abraham S. *105 122 185* ***232***
Yahuda Haggada *232*
Yahya, David ibn *130*
Yardeni, Ada *93*

Yehudayof, David *149*
Yeivin, Israel *116*
Yellin, A. *106*
Yellin, David *60* ***232*** *233*
YIVO *156 224*

Zabara, Moses ibn *110 233*
Zabara Bible ***233***
Zacuto, Abraham *129*
Zamora, Alfonso de *132 195*
Zelada, Francesco Javier *132 212 219* ***233***
Zemaḥ, David ***233***
Zetterstéen, K. V. *217*
Zotenberg, H. *167*
Zucker, Shlomo *146*
Zuckermandel, M. *111*
Zuckermann, Benedikt ***233***
Zunz, Leopold *34 41 64 77 78 90 124 127 170* ***233***
Zurich, Zentralbibliothek *93 201* ***233–234***

כתבי האקדמיה הלאומית הישראלית למדעים

החטיבה למדעי הרוח

מורה דרך לאוספי כתבי־היד העבריים

מהדורה שנייה מתוקנת

מאת

בנימין ריצ׳לר

ירושלים תשע״ד
האקדמיה הלאומית הישראלית למדעים